EUROPE
TRAVELBOOK™

THE GUIDE TO
PREMIER DESTINATIONS

2000 EDITION

AAA

President and CEO: Robert Darbelnet
*Executive Vice President, Publishing and
   Administration:* Rick Rinner
Managing Director, Publishing: Alan Borne
*Managing Director, GIS/Cartography and
   Administration:* Bob Hopkins

Director, Business Development: Gary Sisco
Director, Product Development: Bill Wood
Director, Publishing Operations: Susan Sears

AAA Development Editor: Greg Weekes
Cover Design: Mike McCrary
AAA Cover Photo Research: Diane Norden,
   Patricia Nasser

Manager, Marketing: Patty Wight
Manager, Design: Mike McCrary
Manager, Pre-Press: Tim Johnson
Manager, Product Support: Linda Indolfi
Manager, Publishing Communications:
   Josette Constantino
Manager, Retail Sales – Travel Store:
   Sharon Edwards

Published by AAA Publishing, 1000 AAA
Drive, Heathrow, Florida 32746

The *AAA Europe TravelBook – The Guide to
Premier Destinations* was created and
produced for AAA Publishing by AA
Publishing, Basingstoke, England.

Written by Des Hannigan, Sally Roy and
Nia Williams
Page make-up by Anton Graphics Ltd.

Cover photos
Main photo: Building detail along Corso del
Rinascimento, Rome, Italy
© Stephen Simpson/FPG
Cover insert: Flamenco dancer, Granada,
Andalucia, Spain
© Jean Kugler/FPG
Spine: Stonehenge, Salisbury Plain, England
© Tom Till / Tony Stone Images

ISBN 1-56251-315-X

Cataloging-in-Publication Data is on file
with the Library of Congress.

Color separations by Leo Reprographic
Ltd., Hong Kong

Printed and bound in Italy by Rotolito
Lombarda SpA

View from beneath the Eiffel Tower in Paris, France

FOREWORD

Welcome to the 2000 edition of the AAA Europe TravelBook!

If you are thinking about going to Europe, this book will help make your trip truly memorable and enjoyable. We've selected places that are among the Continent's premier destinations. Experience world capitals that have delighted visitors for centuries: Paris's broad 18th-century boulevards, wonderful museums and superb food; London, where tradition and royal pageantry are juxtaposed with a lively arts scene; Prague's medieval grandeur, now vibrantly emerging from decades of suppression; Rome, cradle of one of the world's great civilizations; and Vienna, with a magnificent opera house that is still a focus for world-renowned music.

But not all of Europe resides in its big cities. Odense, in Denmark, welcomes visitors to the charming museum that was the birthplace of famed storyteller Hans Christian Andersen. York, in England, has an atmospheric old center, the "Shambles," with ancient cobbled streets, leaning half-timbered shops and pubs, and the mighty towers of the grand York Minster cathedral. And for centuries the city of Santiago de Compostela, in Spain, has welcomed Christian pilgrims from the far corners of Europe to its monumental cathedral built around the reputed grave of St. James; pilgrims still come, drawn by the myth and beauty of this holy place.

This book will not only whet your travel appetite with lively text and striking photographs; it also provides a wealth of practical information that will enable you to get the most out of your trip, especially if you're a first- or second-time visitor. Included are tips about what you will need to bring and about getting around once you're there, maps to help you find your way, detailed descriptions of what to see, suggestions for where to stay and eat, and insider advice from specialist authors to increase your enjoyment of the fascinating cultures that make up Europe.

EUROPE TRAVELBOOK™
THE GUIDE TO PREMIER DESTINATIONS

CONTENTS

For conversion charts, see
the inside back cover

Map of Europe

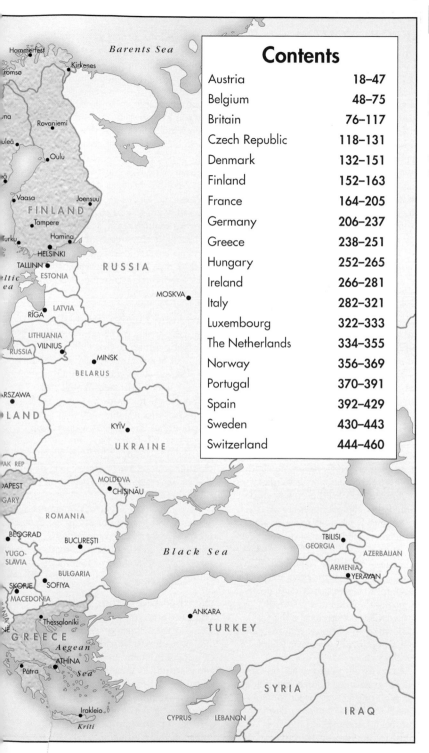

Contents

Map of Europe

Introduction to Europe

BEFORE YOU GO

Passports and Visas

The most important document you'll need to arrange before you travel is a passport. Passport application forms can be obtained by contacting any federal or state court or post office authorized to accept passport applications. U.S. passport agencies have offices in major cities; check the Yellow Pages (U.S. Government, State Department) for the one nearest you. You can also request an application form by calling the National Passport Information Center at (888) 362-8668. (Note: There is a $4.95 credit card charge to contact the center by phone.) Comprehensive passport information and application forms are available on the U.S. State Department Internet site at http://travel.state.gov. Travel warnings, consular information sheets, public announcements and publications information also can be accessed.

Each person traveling must have a passport; apply early, since processing can take several months from the time of application until it arrives. Rush service is available for an extra charge. Demand for new passports is highest between January and July, which could mean further delays. Before departure, make sure your passport is valid at least six months prior to the expiration date; some European countries require this.

Keep your passport in a safe place, since you'll need it whenever you board an international flight. In some countries, you will be required to leave your passport with the hotel when you check in; this is to satisfy regulations requiring the hotel to register all foreign visitors with local police authorities. In addition, you must show your passport whenever you cash a traveler's check.

Passports also need to be shown whenever national borders are crossed, although in practice border controls have been relaxed between many European Union (E.U.) member countries. In Geneva, the city transportation system crosses national borders and the airport also straddles the border, so you'll need a passport simply to get around.

Photocopy the identification page; leave one copy with a relative or friend in case of emergency, and carry one with you in case your passport is lost or stolen while traveling. If this occurs, inform local police immediately and contact the nearest U.S. embassy or consulate. The U.S. State Department has a 24-hour traveler's hotline; phone (202) 647-5225.

In addition to a passport, some countries require a visa. Travel visas are not necessary to visit any of the countries covered in this book, but if you'll be traveling to other nations, check their entry requirements before you leave home.

Travel and Health Insurance

Before departing, make sure you are covered by insurance that will reimburse travel expenses if you need to cancel or cut short your trip due to unforeseen circumstances. You'll also need coverage for property loss or theft, emergency medical and dental treatment, and emergency evacuation if necessary. Before taking out additional insurance, check to see whether your current homeowners or medical coverage already covers you for travel abroad.

If you make a claim, your insurance company will need proof of the incident or expenditure. Keep copies of any police report and related documents, or doctor or hospital bills or statements, to submit with your insurance claim.

Weather and When To Go

The European continent occupies a far more northerly location than its overall moderate climate would suggest. Lisbon and Athens are at about the same latitude as Washington, D.C., and Helsinki, Oslo and Stockholm lie as far north as Anchorage, Alaska. Different factors affect the weather at any given destination. One of the most prominent is the warming influence of the Gulf Stream, which affects all countries with

Introduction to Europe

an Atlantic coastline, from Spain and Portugal north through the British Isles into Scandinavia. The North and Baltic seas also affect temperatures and precipitation of the coastal areas they border, causing unpredictable weather.

Another definer is altitude, and Europe's great mountain ranges affect local temperatures and rainfall as well. The Pyrenees divide the Iberian Peninsula and France, while the Alps form an immense natural barrier across Austria, Switzerland and northern Italy south into France, where they descend to the Mediterranean Sea at Monaco. This entire region is popular with winter skiers, while summer visitors can expect clouds, mist and cool temperatures. The Apennines cut down the boot of Italy, also creating somewhat changeable conditions. But settled weather in the mountainous areas is grand indeed, with fresh air and crisp blue skies accentuating the views of craggy peaks and villages nestled in deep valleys.

Destinations bordering the Mediterranean are ideal for summer vacations, with mostly sunny skies, warm temperatures and little rain. The flip side can be the heat – especially in southern Spain and Greece – so protect yourself from overexposure to the sun and carry drinking water for any extended outdoor excursions. The combination of heat, humidity and big-city traffic also can generate an unpleasant amount of pollution, notably in Athens. Winters in the Mediterranean region are cool and rainy, although temperatures are not usually severe and snow is rare in coastal areas.

Summer also is the main vacation season in central Europe. This inland region has a typical continental climate, with warm, generally dry summers and cold winters with plenty of snow at higher elevations. The weather in spring is generally more unpredictable than in the fall.

The British Isles – infamous for damp, dreary weather – can actually have weeks of dry conditions in summer, although that is the exception rather than the rule. It's best to come prepared for rain; a collapsible umbrella should be an essential traveling companion. British winters are indeed rainy, although temperatures are rarely extremely cold. Snow is uncommon except in the higher elevations of northern England and Scotland.

Scandinavia also has widely varying weather, as well as overall lower temperatures. Daytime highs in the summer months rarely exceed 75 degrees Farenheit, and the coastal locations of Copenhagen, Oslo, Stockholm and Helsinki increases the probability of unsettled conditions. Winters are uniformly severe, with significant snowfall the rule.

European school vacations are another factor in planning when to schedule your trip. Schools in most countries are in session from September until early July. This makes May and June good months to visit, both from a weather standpoint and the fact that there are likely to be fewer crowds at major attractions.

What To Pack

Your main objective should be to travel as lightly as possible. Layers of clothing can be peeled off as the day warms up, with something waterproof to wear on top if necessary. Pack an umbrella, and a hat or other headgear to protect against the cold in winter or the sun in summer. Casual dress is acceptable in European cities, with the exception of churches – visitors will not be welcome wearing shorts or a scanty top.

Break in your shoes before you leave home. Shoes with soft, substantial soles are not only ideal for walking but can ease the difficulty of maneuvering the cobbled streets that characterize many old city centers.

Electrical appliances will require an adapter that changes the shape of the plug prongs, as well as an electrical voltage converter that will allow a normal 110-volt American appliance to take 220- to 240-volt European current. Two-in-one adapter/converters are available at some hardware stores.

Introduction to Europe

Bring a first-aid kit with plenty of bandages, sunblock, insect repellent and over-the-counter remedies for minor ailments. Include written prescriptions for prescription medicines in case you need more or need to show the prescription to customs officials. Tissues will come in handy, as local restrooms in some areas will likely be below U.S. standards. European hotel rooms provide the usual array of towels but often no washcloth, so pack one just in case.

The offerings at open-air markets, bakeries and delicatessens are great for an impromptu picnic to go. Bring a knife for cutting bread and a spoon for small cartons of salad or other edibles (utensils aren't provided). Always pack the knife in your stowed luggage for plane trips so that airport security officials don't construe it as a weapon.

Finally, pack the maps and guidebooks you'll find useful, but keep in mind that they can add weight to your luggage very quickly.

WHILE YOU ARE THERE

Emergencies
For emergency information pertaining to each of the countries covered in this book, refer to the Essential Information section, pages 462.

Health
Take sensible precautions during hot weather. Wear a hat, sunglasses and sunblock, especially if you are on or near the water. Drink plenty of fluids, and remember that alcoholic beverages and the caffeine in coffee, tea and some sodas have a dehydrating effect. Slow down or take a break in the shade if you suddenly feel tired or ill.

The tap water in northern Europe is generally safe to drink, although its high mineral content can cause minor upsets if you're not used to it. Bottled water is an inexpensive and widely available alternative. If you're in an area where the tap water is unsafe, it's best to avoid ice cubes and salads with ingredients that are likely to have been washed in water.

Pharmacists are a good first source for dealing with minor health problems; a pharmacist will be able to direct you to a doctor if necessary. For advice pertaining to specific topics, see the "Health" subheading under individual countries in Essential Information.

Language
Traveling is always more enjoyable if you can converse a bit in the local language. "Yes," "no," "please" and "thank you," accompanied by a pleasant smile and polite manner, will go far toward oiling social wheels. Refer to the "Useful Words and Phrases" subheading under individual countries in Essential Information for a helpful list.

The areas where English is most likely to be spoken are Scandinavia, the "Benelux" countries of Belgium, the Netherlands and Luxembourg, and Austria and Switzerland. In Britain and Ireland you may encounter strong regional accents, as well as unfamiliar words and expressions.

To some Europeans – particularly the French and the British – good manners are a social necessity. "Please" and "thank you" should be part of every request in Britain; in France, anyone you don't know personally (including the staff in stores and restaurants) should be addressed as "monsieur" ("sir"), "madame" ("madam") or "mademoiselle" ("miss").

If you're really stuck with communications, remember that hotel receptionists usually speak English, and are invariably helpful and friendly; you can ask them to phone for taxis and arrange for cleaning and similar personal services.

Media
Room televisions in the larger hotels have satellite or cable connections broadcast BBC channels, the British Sky network or CNN. On the radio you may be able to pick up Voice of America, Radio Canada or BBC broadcasts.

In larger cities, American newspapers (usually previous-day

editions) and magazines are widely available; the most common are *USA Today*, the international edition of the *New York Herald Tribune* and *Time* magazine. They can be purchased at airports and central train stations, as well as at newsstands, tobacconists and "stationers," shops that also sell books and stationery.

Money and Valuables

Having some of your funds in local currency is a necessity, but only carry what you'll need for a day or two. If it's lost or stolen you almost certainly won't get it back, and if you have to convert a large amount back to dollars or to another foreign currency you'll pay again for exchange charges. Customs restrictions may apply if you need to carry large amounts of currency. For additional information see the "Money" subheading under individual countries in Essential Information.

Currency exchange facilities are widely available in Europe. There are exchange offices at airports and central train stations, in the central business districts in cities, and at seaports and other international border crossing points. They are often open extended hours in summer and during vacations. Most hotel reception desks also will exchange currency. Exchange rates are normally displayed; local newspapers and the international editions of U. S. newspapers also provide the current rate of exchange. A commission is charged for each transaction. Although it is likely to be a little higher at hotels, it may be worth paying extra for the convenience.

Traveler's checks are reliable and safe. Keep a record of the check numbers you redeem, and carry numbers and receipts in a separate place in case you need to produce them in the event of loss. Be prepared to show your passport each time you cash in a check or offer one in payment. If you're going to be spending time in just one or two countries you may want to obtain traveler's checks in the local currency. You can use them for purchases in stores, although you'll still need to show your passport.

Credit cards, increasingly accepted in Europe, are an easy and trouble-free method of payment. American Express, MasterCard and VISA are the most widely accepted; check with your credit card company before departure if you have any doubt about its validity abroad. Keep a record of your card number in a separate place, and note the international phone number to report card losses in case yours is misplaced or stolen. You also can get cash advances with your credit card from an ATM, usually at favorable exchange rates.

Leave valuable jewelry at home; small items are easily lost or mislaid, and ostentatious displays mark you as a prospective target for theft. Make sure your luggage is lockable and labeled both outside and inside. Never leave your bags unattended. Train stations normally provide lockers or check desks where you can leave a heavy bag while sightseeing. If you're traveling by car, keep your doors locked in slow-moving traffic or when driving through busy urban areas, and put everything in the trunk while the car is parked.

If the worst happens and you do have belongings stolen, report the incident to the police immediately and get a written police report or statement to provide to your insurance company as evidence for your claim.

Personal Safety

Most of the rules for personal safety constitute common sense. Keep valuables (passport, money, checks, credit cards) hidden when you're on the move; a money belt or neck purse worn inside clothing is the safest option. Put money in different places so that if one bag is lost you have another source of funds. Fanny packs and pockets are not safe places to carry valuables. Any bag you'll be carrying with you during the day should have a secure fastener, with a sturdy strap that goes over your neck and crosses your body – not simply over the shoulder. This helps ensure that

Introduction to Europe

Introduction to Europe

bulkier items (cameras, binoculars, etc.) will be safe from pickpockets and petty thieves in crowded urban areas or on buses or trains.

The big tourist attractions are prime territory for pickpockets, as are buses, trains, subways, markets and airports. Be on guard for people who "accidentally" bump into you, or watch while you use an ATM. In large cities, be on the lookout for gangs of youngsters who create a commotion and then steal bags from tourists while their attention is distracted.

People begging in the street can be quite persistent; walk quickly away without responding or making eye contact. Contact a police officer if anyone becomes particularly aggressive; police on city streets throughout Europe are usually very approachable and often speak a little English. In general, avoid walking alone after dark. In southern European city centers during the summer, however, you'll almost certainly encounter throngs of locals out walking and shopping late into the evening, refreshed by a few hours of afternoon siesta.

Phone Service

You can make international calls from most European telephones; for specific information see "Telephones" under individual countries in the Essential Information section. To place a call to another country, first dial the international code, then the country code, then the area code and the local number. Sometimes you'll need to wait for another dial tone after dialing the international code. In some countries the telecommunications infrastructure is fairly fragile, and it may take two or three tries before you get through.

The easiest and least expensive way to make an international call is to use a calling card. Dialing the appropriate access number (numbers differ according to country) will connect you with an English-speaking operator who can place a collect call or a call credited to your card. To obtain a card and a list of country access numbers, contact your telephone service provider. If you use a pay phone, you may need to insert a coin in the local currency to get an outside line to make the call.

The convenience of making a phone call from your hotel room will be offset by the hefty surcharges tacked onto the bill. It's always less expensive to use the pay phone in the lobby; ask the hotel staff for assistance if you can't figure out how the phone works.

Some cell phones may be adaptable for use in Europe, but the operating frequencies are different; check with your service provider. Fax machines are available in the central business centers of cities and at some hotels. If you can't do without e-mail, cybercafes are popping up in major cities throughout Europe – handy places to stop for coffee and a bite to eat, as well as using the computers to send e-mail and check your favorite websites.

If you're staying in one country for a few days, it may be worthwhile to obtain a local prepaid telephone card, which can be used with phones that accept them. They can normally be purchased at small stores called "tobacconists" that also sell cigarettes, candy, snacks, magazines and sometimes postage stamps.

Travelers with Disabilities

Facilities for disabled visitors in northern and central European countries are generally very good, but old castles, palaces and cathedrals may not be adapted for special access. The Mediterranean countries, Czech Republic and Hungary are improving, but if you need help it is advisable to check in advance with local tourist offices. The old central cores of European cities are often difficult to change or adapt to make them suitable for those with special needs. Expect steps and stairways in city centers (some stairways have no handrails), in addition to cobbled and uneven street and sidewalk surfaces.

Almost all of the old buildings in Europe – including those that house hotels and such attractions as museums and castles – are likely to contain stairways, narrow halls and doorways, and other access irregularities. Make certain that accessibility standards meet your requirements when reserving accommodations.

Often hotels will be able to provide a room with adequate access if they know your needs in advance. Call ahead to attractions and restaurants as well to ascertain the nature of their facilities. Motorized carts at airports will whisk you to and from arrival and departure gates.

GETTING AROUND

City Transportation

A good first stop when you arrive at your destination is either a central public transportation information center or the tourist information office (see the Essential Information boxes in the introduction to each featured city). Spend time here and obtain information on how to get around the city, including transportation maps and detailed city maps. You also may be able to purchase travel tickets for public transportation, including those valid for multiple rides or more than one day; they will save you money and the inconvenience of having to buy a new ticket for every journey.

There are a variety of public transportation options in Europe:

- Subways are underground trains that tunnel beneath city centers, occasionally emerging to ground level in less congested suburban areas, or to cross rivers.
- Buses operate along designated routes in city centers; double-decked buses are common for carrying larger numbers of passengers. Some cities have special sightseeing buses in summer, with an open-topped deck for better views. Long-distance buses are commonly known as "coaches."
- Trams are vehicles that travel on rails set into the street surface. They are often powered by overhead electric cables that run along the route. If you are walking or in a car, be especially careful of trams; they always have the right of way, and because they run quietly can appear with little warning.
- Trolley buses run on tires, but are powered by overhead electric cables running above the route. Like trams, they have right of way in traffic and run quietly.
- Funiculars are passenger cars that ascend and descend steep hills or cliffs on a track set into the ground, typically on slopes leading down to a beach but also in some cities, such as Lisbon or Barcelona, where there are steep inclines.
- Cable cars are suspended from cables attached to the top of the cars. They are common at ski resorts, and also in some cities.
- Rack railways are a feature in Switzerland, where trains that need to negotiate steep mountains connect with a cog system between the rails that provides extra power up the slopes.

In many European countries, the procedure is to buy a travel ticket at a ticket office or booth and then validate it by pushing it into a special machine, either at the stop or on the vehicle, which will give the ticket a date and time stamp validating it for the appropriate journey or time period. If you buy a tourist ticket that is valid for a number of days, you will usually need to validate it only once before you first use it.

Between Cities

Trains Most countries in Europe have a national train system, with trains operating across national borders. Service is generally efficient, although local routes with frequent stops can be slow. If your entire trip is going to be by train it may be well worth obtaining a Eurail pass from your travel agent before you go (available throughout the world except in Europe). Passes are valid for periods from a few days to three months. In addition, many

Introduction to Europe

Introduction to Europe

national rail systems have their own passes for travel within a country; these are also available from travel agents in the United States and Canada, and also in Europe.

Tickets for most trains are available either in advance or just before travel, though for some special trains (some express overnight sleeper trains, the Orient Express, or the Eurostar trains between Britain and France that travel through the tunnel beneath the English Channel) you may need to buy tickets a few days in advance to be sure of getting a seat – especially during busy vacation times.

Information about main city train stations is in the Essential Information box for each city.

Airlines Most countries have a national airline as well as independent operators that operate internationally, based on hub cities within the country. Additionally, smaller airlines serve smaller destinations, usually functioning within the country. Schedules, fares and availability are subject to frequent change. If you have a specific itinerary in mind, your travel agent is the best place to start for flight information.

You are most likely to have the best choice of flights and better prices if you reserve your tickets well in advance. Big airports in major cities – in Paris, London and Rome, for example – will have the largest choice of flights, but also are the busiest. It can be a good idea to begin your trip at a smaller destination, where the number of travelers will be fewer and the pace less frantic.

Ferries Services transport individual passengers as well as cars, and in some cases trains (the cars of the train actually travel on the boat). Ferry companies offering longer-distance journeys of two or three days have very comfortable ships, and they promote these services as "mini-cruises" that can make a relaxing interlude between busy city sightseeing sessions.

Ferries operate regularly in the Scandinavian archipelago and along the Norwegian fjords; among the Scottish islands; between Britain and Ireland, Scandinavia, Germany, France and Spain; and throughout the islands and coastal ports of the Mediterranean countries and islands.

Generally speaking, transfers from ports to city centers are less straightforward than from airports and train stations. If you intend to carry a lot of luggage, it may be advisable to ask tourist information offices about this when planning your trip.

European Customs and Immigration

Each country has its own customs import regulations; see the Essential Information section (page 461). For the purposes of customs and duty-free allowances, the countries of the European Union are considered as one customs area, and there are no limits on goods for personal use when traveling between member countries. However, customs restrictions do apply when traveling between E.U. countries and non-E.U. countries. The E.U. member countries include all the countries in this book, with the exception of Norway, Switzerland, the Czech Republic and Hungary.

At the immigration barrier in E.U. countries, travelers are separated into

AAA Travel Agencies

AAA travel agencies offer various services to help simplify the logistics of international travel planning, especially for the first-time visitor. They can make airline reservations, book accommodations, set up escorted tours and independent travel packages, offer passport and visa assistance, arrange for car rentals and an official International Driving Permit, and provide fee-free American Express traveler's checks. AAA members are eligible for discounts on selected hotels and motels and receive exclusive savings on cruising vacations.

two lanes – one for E.U. citizens and one for non-E.U. citizens. Border controls between E.U. countries are gradually being relaxed. You will probably pass through an immigration desk when arriving at a new country by plane or train, but road barrier checkpoints within the E.U. have largely disappeared in recent years. Border controls remain between the E.U. and the rest of Europe, however.

DRIVING IN EUROPE

European Automobile Clubs

For the benefit of its members traveling abroad, the American Automobile Association maintains reciprocal agreements with motoring clubs in Europe. Presentation of your valid AAA membership card at participating clubs allows you to receive services they give to their own members. This does not necessarily mean that you will receive the same services as those provided by AAA at home, as operating philosophies and facilities differ from country to country. The *Offices to Serve You Abroad* leaflet, available from your local AAA club, explains in detail the services you can expect from each foreign club.

Refer to the Essential Information pages for each country for club contact details, documentation requirements and driving regulations.

Car Rental

If you intend to drive across national borders tell the rental company, as this will affect both the rate and the type of insurance documentation required. British and Irish rental agencies may require several days' notice to supply a car available for travel to continental Europe. Most car rental companies in Europe will not rent to an individual under 21.

To rent a car you will need a valid U.S. driver's license and preferably an International Driving Permit, and you will probably be asked to show your passport. Depending on which rental company you use, you may be required to produce an additional credit card or further proof of identity for renting premium or luxury cars.

European cars are generally small and have manual transmissions. Local rental companies rarely offer vehicles equipped with air conditioning. Rates vary, but a AAA travel agent should be able to give you an accurate estimate. Reciprocal arrangements with European motoring clubs may not apply if you are driving a rental car (see the Driving section under Essential Information for each country). Be sure to inquire about local taxes; in France, taxes increase rental rates by up to one-third. Find out exactly what insurance coverage is included, and check whether you need a collision damage waiver (CDW) – you might already be covered through your personal car insurance policy or credit card company. A CDW may not cover certain types of damage; for example, in Greece damage to the underside of a car caused by a rough road may not be covered.

AAA travel agencies can reserve a car for you before you leave, provide prepayment arrangements, or reserve a car for you for specified dates and destinations. Rates are lower if reservations are made in the United States prior to your departure, and guaranteed in U.S. dollars if you prepay; reserve well in advance. If you plan to travel through several countries, make certain that the rental company has been informed, and that you have the necessary documents.

Hertz Affordable Europe offers discounts to AAA members guaranteed in U.S. dollars, with 24-hour emergency roadside assistance, free unlimited mileage, computerized driving directions and English-speaking staff at 2,500 locations throughout Europe. For reservations contact Hertz, (800) 654-3080, or a AAA travel agency.

Green Card

If you drive a car in Europe you will need a Green Card (sometimes called an International Insurance Certificate) to prove that you have liability

Introduction to Europe

insurance. Car rental agencies will provide this with the vehicle; most companies include it in the rental price.

A Green Card is advised for motorists taking their own vehicle overseas; a AAA travel agency can arrange this. Coverage available to those using their own vehicles includes liability, medical payments, comprehensive and collision loss, and a Green Card. For additional information contact your local AAA club.

International Driving Permit (IDP)

An International Driving Permit is a document containing your photograph and confirming that you hold a valid driver's license in your own country. It has a standard translation in several languages and is a useful document to carry if you plan to drive in Europe, even if it is not specifically required by the country. The permit is available from AAA travel agencies.

Driving Regulations

Driving in busy European cities can be a daunting prospect if you're not used to the signs, driving habits and local regulations. If you are renting a car, be sure to get as much information from the rental company as possible. They will usually be able to provide a chart of common road signs and an area road map.If you are visiting a city by car, park outside the city center, preferably close to a public transportation link, and proceed to the center by public transportation.

Check parking signs where you leave your car: insure there are no restrictions, that you pay for and display a parking sticker if necessary, and check closing times if you use a multistory parking garage. Because of congestion in city centers, parking regulations are strictly enforced.

Specific driving regulations for each country are provided in the Essential Information section. In some countries, police can levy on-the-spot fines for serious offenses – including speeding and driving while drunk.

RETURNING TO THE UNITED STATES

Confirming Return Travel

If you are flying, it is advisable to contact the airport the day before leaving to be sure flight details are unchanged. Some carriers require you to reconfirm flights after an extended stopover of more than a few days; check the information that was supplied with your ticket. Allow plenty of time to get to the airport for check-in and clearing security.

Tax-free Shopping

Some major stores offer "tax-free shopping" to tourists. Although specific procedures differ slightly between countries, this enables you to make purchases and have them either sent to the airport of your departing flight, or directly to your home address. Such shopping saves the (often substantial) sales tax, but these items are still subject to any applicable U.S. import duty, plus postage and handling charges.

U.S. Customs

During your flight or voyage returning to the United States, you will be required to complete a customs declaration. You are allowed $400 worth of personal goods and gifts (including items purchased in duty-free shops); keep sales slips and have them ready for inspection. The duty-free exemption can include 100 cigars and 200 cigarettes, as well as one liter of wine, beer or liquor if you are 21 or over. Any purchases in excess of the $400 exemption will be subject to duty. There is no restriction on the importing or exporting of currency.

For more information contact your local customs office, listed under the U.S. Government section (Treasury Department) in the telephone directory. You can contact U.S. Customs in Washington, D.C., phone (202) 927-6724, and request a copy of their brochure *Know Before You Go*, which gives detailed information about customs requirements.

PREMIER DESTINATIONS

"IN whichever country of Europe one dwells, one feels that the other countries are near..."

From *The American Commonwealth*
by British politician and writer James Bryce

AUSTRIA

"THE country is wonderful. Mountains holding up cups of snow to the fiery sun..."

English novelist George Meredith, praising the Alps in a letter to Frederick A. Maxe, July 1861

Opposite: Snow-capped mountains dwarf a village and pastureland in the Leogang area of Austria

Austria

AUSTRIA

Small yet beautiful, Austria has unrivaled Alpine scenery, some of Europe's finest baroque architecture, a long tradition of music and culture, and a reputation for the warmth and hospitality of its people. Straddling the center of Europe, the country has exerted a critical influence on the region's history through the centuries, becoming a major player in world politics. Today, despite loss of territory and power after two world wars, Austria retains its status as the crossroads of modern Europe. The year-round grandeur of the mountains draws visitors from all over the world, while the combination of efficiency and charm makes Austria one of Europe's easiest and most beguiling tourist destinations.

The Land

Austria is the most mountainous country in Europe, with more than 70 percent of the land occupied by the Alps and Alpine valleys. This section of the eastern Alps is characterized by massive mountain chains with sheer rock faces and jagged ridges broken by deep valleys. The Tyrol region, bordering the Swiss and Italian Alps in western Austria, is renowned for its stunning scenery and is a popular skiing and hiking area. Below the tree line the mountains are heavily forested, giving way to lush Alpine meadows, grazed in summer by gentle-faced cattle and carpeted with vivid wildflowers.

Picturesque villages sit amid the pastures and along the valley bottoms, each with distinctive churches, clusters of traditional shuttered houses and wooden farm buildings. The Danube (Donau) river dominates northeastern

MORE TOP DESTINATIONS IN AUSTRIA
● Baden E2 ● Bad Ischl C2
● Eisenstadt E2 ● Eisriesenwelt C2
● Graz D2 ● Grossglockner Hochalpenstrasse C1 ● Hallstatt C2
● Kitzbühel B2 ● Maria Saal D1
● Melk D3 ● Mondsee C2
● Ötztal A2 ● Riegersburg E2
● Salzkammergut C2
● St. Anton A2 ● Stein D3
● Wachau D3 ● Zillertal B2

AUSTRIA

0   50   100 km
0   50 miles

3

N

GERMANY

Bodensee

2 **Bregenz**

Dornbirn   Bezau   Reutte   Lermods   Pertisau   Achensee   Schwaz

A14   Feldkirch   Bad   Mittelberg   **INNSBRUCK**

Bludenz   Bad   Ötztal   Igls   Zell am

LIECHTEN-   Zurs   Lech   Oetz   Ziller

STEIN   Brand   St Anton   Landeck   Steinach   Mayrho

3312m   Galtür   Sölden   A13

Piz Buin

SWITZERLAND   3774m   Obergurgl

Wildspitze

1

ITALY

A   B

Austria, and most of the country's people inhabit the rolling terrain around the river. The flat fields of the Vienna basin are intensely cultivated, producing grain, fruit and vines.

The Habsburg Legacy

Throughout six centuries of Habsburg rule, Austria dominated the politics of much of Europe. The Habsburg Empire spread from Spain to Hungary, with sons and daughters of the ruling families marrying into other European ruling houses and thus furthering its influence. Vienna, with its grandiose architecture, splendidly illustrates Austrian prestige, and the entire country is rich in buildings from the days of the empire.

The Viennese Court sent administrators and army officials into the provinces; they brought along Viennese customs, attitudes and manners, as did the nobility who spent time both in the capital and on their country estates. The high-handed approach of these outsiders throughout the provinces has left a legacy of mistrust of the Viennese still discernible today. Historically, too, because of the terrain, the different areas of Austria were immensely varied, each valley having its own dialect, dress, habits and way of life.

Crossroads of Europe

At the end of World War II, Austria was divided into four zones of occupation, with the Allied powers occupying most of the western half. With the help of the Marshall Aid after

Austria

The architecture and setting of the Old Town makes Innsbruck a popular holiday destination

large subsidies, and now employs less than 10 percent of the workforce. The vast majority of Austrians speak German or a German dialect. Austria was unaffected by the Protestant Reformation and is still a deeply Catholic country. Its glorious baroque churches are packed for Sunday Mass.

Proud Traditions

Despite sharing a common language, Austrians are very different from their German neighbors – more lighthearted, less prone to take themselves seriously and generally more relaxed in their approach to life. They see themselves, correctly, as hospitable and cordial, thus defining the term *Gemütlichkeit*. This manifests itself in an easy friendliness to everyone, and it's one of the first things visitors notice. Every region sees itself as the best, and people proudly wear regional dress and enjoy traditional music and festivals. So when you encounter people wearing *Lederhosen* (leather pants) and *Dirndl* (bodiced dresses), it's for their benefit, not yours.

There's an elegance and ease to much Austrian life; cafés buzz with the chatter of people, *Bierkellern* (taverns) are packed with young and old, and streets are full of strolling crowds. Manners are conservative, even old-fashioned; this is a country where children open doors and give up seats for adults, and every stranger is greeted with an amicable "*Grüss Gott.*"

Environmental Issues

It's not only the tree-clad mountain slopes and verdant valleys that make Austria green; this is one of the most environmentally aware countries in Europe. Austria banned all nuclear power in the 1970s, and since then its green policy has made giant strides.

Heavy investment in public transportation has dramatically lessened

World War II, this area was able to industrialize more efficiently than the Soviet-occupied zone, and the east-west divide continued even after the Second Republic was founded in 1955 and independence was regained.

Present-day Austria shares a boundary with eight other European countries: Germany, Italy, the Czech Republic, Hungary, Slovak Republic, Slovenia, Switzerland and Lichtenstein. Its 8 million inhabitants live in nine provinces, each with its own very distinctive characteristics.

More than half the working population is employed in the service sector: education, tourism, administration and health. Traditional agriculture only continues thanks to

Austria

the use of cars. This is a huge benefit to visitors, making travel in Austria, with its seamless connections between different forms of public transportation, very easy. Despite the Alpine terrain, Austrians cycle a lot, and every town has bike routes and parks. Recycling is a way of life; there are many different types of garbage cans, each clearly labeled for the appropriate trash.

There are many different types of beer, and some excellent wines. You should also try *Schnapps*, a strong fruit or herb-based liqueur, drunk as a digestive aid. Coffee is the national drink, with cafés often serving as many as 20 or more different variations; hot chocolate is good, too. And on the healthy side, there are outstanding fruit and vegetable juices.

Sauerkraut and Strudel

Austrians take food seriously and waiters are genuinely interested to know whether you've enjoyed a meal and alarmingly downcast if you can't cope with the vast portions served. Mealtimes are closer to American schedules than elsewhere, with lunch around noon and dinner any time after 6.

Each region has its own specialties, but the emphasis everywhere is on heavy soups, plenty of meat, *Knödel* (dumplings) and noodles, and cream, cream, cream. The latter appears in sauces, soups, coffee and whipped mounds decorating just about every dessert. Sauerkraut (pickled cabbage) frequently accompanies main courses, along with piles of potatoes, and salads are drenched in creamy dressings.

Austrians indulge their passion for coffee and cakes between meals, and you should certainly sample *Apfelstrudel* (apple strudel) and *Sachertorte*, a wickedly rich frosted chocolate cake oozing apricot jam.

Summer and Winter

Austria offers visitors as much in the winter as in the summer. For Europeans, the Austrian Alps have been a favorite skiing destination for many years, with impeccably organized facilities, trails ranging from gentle slopes to world-class black runs, and wonderful après-ski dining and nightlife.

Summer sees the Alpine pastures at their best, and the whole country is crisscrossed with hiking trails through glorious mountain scenery. It's in summer, too, that the cities come alive, with strolling crowds, colorful flowers and a plethora of music and folk festivals. Spring starts late, so it's best to plan a visit in June or later. In early spring and again in autumn, you may experience the dreaded *Föhn* wind in western Austria; this is a fierce, warm, dry wind from the south that is notorious for making people generally tired and grumpy, so be prepared.

The traditional *Loden* jacket and *Dirndl* skirt, worn at festival time

Austria

TIMELINE

15 BC to AD 50   Romans establish frontier provinces along the Danube and found legionary fortress of Carnuntum.

500–700   After final withdrawal of Romans, Alamanni and Bavarian tribes settle lower Alpine regions.

966   Austmark, established as a bulwark against attacks from the east, is first referred to as Ostarrichi.

1278   Founding of Habsburg Dynasty, beginning 640 years of power.

1493–1519   Foundations of the Habsburg world empire laid by marriage contracts of Maximilian I.

1699   Conquest of Hungary; Habsburgs gain hereditary right to the Hungarian throne in the male line.

1805   Napoleon defeats the Austrians at Battle of Austerlitz; end of Holy Roman Empire.

1814–15   Congress of Vienna restructures the political map of Europe.

1914   Assassination of heir to Austrian throne at Sarejevo leads to outbreak of World War I; Austria fights on losing side.

1919   Dissolution of Austro-Hungarian monarchy; loss of territories.

1938   Hitler incorporates Austria into the German Reich.

1939–45   World War II; Austrians fight in German army; following defeat, Austria is divided into four zones of occupation.

1955   Full sovereignty and founding of Second Republic; Austria is admitted to the United Nations.

1986   Kurt Waldheim is elected president.

1995   Austria joins European Community.

1999   Austria enters European Monetary Union.

THE LAST OF THE KNIGHTS

Maximilian I ruled from 1493 until 1519; these years saw the establishment of his family, the Habsburgs, as hereditary emperors of the Holy Roman Empire and rulers of Austria and far beyond, a dynasty that continued until 1918. Maximilian, through two strategic marriages, gained control over Burgundy (a region in northern France) and the Low Countries. He married his son into the Spanish royal family, giving the Habsburgs rights over Spain, Naples and Spanish America and thus laying the foundations for the vast empire that was to come. Maximilian reformed the governmental administration, patronized the arts, loved hunting and jousting, and was known as "the last of the knights" who led Austria from the Middle Ages to the bright light of the Renaissance and the empire.

Stop at a sidewalk café on the Graben to absorb the atmosphere of Vienna

SURVIVAL GUIDE

- Always return greetings; hospitality is Austria's most important national characteristic, and people expect a reply to their welcoming *"Grüss Gott,"* meaning "God's greeting."
- For the opera men should wear a jacket and tie; women, a dress, suit or smart pants.
- When going into churches, remember that it's disrespectful to show bare shoulders or upper arms.
- Take an umbrella; it can rain heavily, anywhere, at any time of year.
- For a day in the mountains, remember that the temperature drops as you gain altitude. Take warm clothes so you can layer, and if you're hiking, wear suitable footwear, and bring water and food.
- Austrians are very litter-conscious and streets are immaculately clean; do your part to leave them that way.
- It's considered polite to stand in line when waiting for a bus or at an attraction, and to defer to the elderly.
- Bedding in Austria consists of a large, puffy feather quilt in a cotton cover. This will be folded on your bed, waiting to be opened up at bedtime.
- Austrians eat and drink with gusto, and spirits as well as the noise level rise during the evening. Drunkeness, however, is considered uncouth.
- All cafés, bars and restaurants have coat hooks and umbrella stands, and it's considered more respectful to leave coats and umbrellas there rather than on your chair.
- It's acceptable to spend up to an hour lingering over one or two drinks in a café.
- Public restrooms are free, numerous and spotless; you'll find them in virtually all public buildings, and you can also use bathrooms in cafés and restaurants.
- Always cross the street at official crossings and wait for the green man signal. It's illegal, though seldom prosecuted, to cross anywhere else.

Vienna

VIENNA

For much of the 20th century, Vienna (Wien) had an air of fading grandeur, a city whose days of imperial glory had truly passed. But in the 1980s Vienna began to redefine itself, and continues to do so. The population has since increased for the first time since 1919; a vibrant youth culture has emerged; and the imperial architecture of the 18th and 19th centuries has been joined by exciting modern designs, such as the huge museum quarter being built on the site of the emperor's former stables. At the beginning of the 21st century Vienna seems to be shaking off its torpor and styling itself, once again, as a dynamic European cultural center.

Finding Your Way

Between 1857 and 1865 Emperor Franz Josef I had the bastions surrounding Vienna's Old Town (Innere Stadt) demolished, and laid out a vast boulevard known as the Ring. Within the Old Town and the Ring are Vienna's most important sights, including St. Stephen's Cathedral (Stephansdom, see page 32) and the Imperial Palace (Hofburg, see page 29).

It's possible to take in the main sights on foot, but the "Hopper" buses

The Third Man

One of Vienna's favorite parks is the Prater, situated on the former imperial hunting grounds. It was opened to the public in 1766, and its attractions now include racing tracks, a fairground and a Ferris wheel built in 1896. This is where Joseph Cotten and Orson Welles had their confrontation high over the city in the 1949 film *The Third Man*.

are a flexible alternative, allowing you to hop on or off anywhere along their route. There are also trams and underground (U-Bahn) trains running through and around the area. A more expensive option is to hire a horse-drawn carriage (*Fiaker*) at Stephansplatz, Heldenplatz or Albertinaplatz. Be sure to agree on the price and length of trip before you begin your journey.

Vienna

An outer ring road, the Gürtel (belt),
links the city with major freeways. East
of Vienna, the Danube river and the
Danube canal cut through some 23
districts, and on the southern outskirts
are the Vienna Woods (Wienerwald).
Maps showing walking routes through
the woods are available from the
efficient information center in the City
Hall (Rathaus).

Architecture

Wandering Vienna's streets is a treat
for lovers of architecture. Styles range
from the Gothic pointed arches of
St. Stephen's Cathedral and the neo-
Gothic arcades of the New City Hall
(Neues Rathaus) to the baroque of the
17th and 18th centuries.

Imperial 19th-century majesty is
typified in buildings lining the Ring

Vienna

and also in the art nouveau edifices, known here as the "Secession" style because its practitioners seceded from the staid Association of Fine Artists in 1897. They went on to set up their own exhibitions in the Secession Building on Friedrichstrasse.

There are also modern styles, such as the shining glass curves of the 1900 Haas-Haus by Hans Hollein, opposite St. Stephen's; and a postmodern housing block by Friedensreich Hundertwasser, a Hansel-and-Gretel building of colored mosaics, in Kegelgasse.

Viennese Music

Vienna is proud of its long history as a center of classical music, and celebrates with a busy schedule of concerts, balls and café concerts. On the grand end of the scale is a series of annual balls, reaching its peak with February's Opera Ball at the State Opera (Staatsoper).

The city's classical music venues are worth seeing just for their extravagant decoration. The main sights are the State Opera (on Opernring); the Konzerthaus (on Lothringerstrasse); the Musikverein (at Karlsplatz); and the Imperial Palace's Royal Chapel (Burgkapelle) where the Vienna Boys' Choir still sings at Sunday Mass.

Viennese Shopping

Expect high prices; you can get items of similar quality for up to a third less just over the border in Germany. Clothes are especially expensive – the best options are chain stores such as Humanic, in the mall at Vösendorf on the southern edge of the city (to get there, take the bus from the Oper/Karlsplatz station).

Porcelain and glassware have been produced in Vienna for more than 200 years. Several outlets on Kärntnerstrasse (near the central Stephansplatz) sell good examples, including J & L Lobmeyr, which has an exhibition of its early work on the top floor. The Old Town has plenty of window-shopping potential, and stores usually stay open until 8 one evening a week (either Thursday or Friday).

ESSENTIAL INFORMATION

TOURIST INFORMATION
• Obere Angartenstrasse 40, A-1025, Vienna ☎ 01 2111 4222

Transportation maps are available at the Opern Passage/Karlsplatz U-Bahn information counter (☎ 01 79 09 10-5). Taxis can be ordered by calling ☎ 01 31 30-0, 01 40 10-0 or 01 60 16-0.

URBAN TRANSPORTATION
Vienna has a network of subway (U-Bahn) lines, trams (Strassenbahn) and buses. U-Bahn lines U1, U2 and U4 meet at the central Oper/Karlsplatz.Subways are marked with a U on the city map. A rapid transit railroad, the S-Bahn (Schnellbahn), travels into the city center from the suburbs. Hopper buses 1A, 2A and 3A stop near major Old Town sights.

AIRPORT INFORMATION
Schwechat International Airport (☎ 01 7007 2333) is a 20-minute bus ride east of the City Air Terminal, in the city center. Shuttle buses run regularly between the two sights 24 hours a day (☎ 01 580 03 54 04); they also run from the airport to Westbahnhof railroad station via Südbahnhof railroad station.

CLIMATE – average highs and lows for the month

JAN.	FEB.	MAR.	APR.	MAY	JUN.	JUL.	AUG.	SEP.	OCT.	NOV.	DEC.
2°C	3°C	9°C	14°C	19°C	22°C	25°C	24°C	20°C	14°C	7°C	4°C
36°F	37°F	48°F	57°F	66°F	72°F	77°F	75°F	68°F	57°F	45°F	39°F
-3°C	-2°C	2°C	5°C	9°C	13°C	15°C	15°C	12°C	6°C	2°C	-1°C
27°F	28°F	36°F	41°F	48°F	55°F	59°F	59°F	54°F	43°F	36°F	30°F

CITY SIGHTS

Key to symbols

🔟 map coordinates refer to the Vienna map on page 26–27; sights below are highlighted in yellow on the map.

✉ address or location 🕿 telephone number

🕐 opening times 🚌 nearest bus or tram route

🚇 nearest subway 🍴 restaurant on site or nearby

💲 admission charge: $$$ more than $70, $$ $30 to $70, $ less than $30

HOFBURG

Kaiserappartements 🔟 C2 ✉ Michaelerplatz; Heldenplatz; Kaistertor, Innere Burghof 🕿 01 53 21 68-0 🕐 Daily 9–5 🍴 Augustinerkeller Restaurant, see page 540 🚇 Herrengasse 🚌 Hopper 3A to Habsburgergasse 💲 $$$

Hofbibliothek ✉ Josefsplatz 1 🕿 01 53 21 68-0 🕐 Mon.–Sat. 10–4, Sun. and holidays 10–1, Jun.–Oct.; Mon.–Sat. 10–noon, rest of year. Closed first 3 weeks of Sep. Schatzkammer: Wed.–Mon. 10–6 (also Thu. 6–9) 🍴 Augustinerkeller Restaurant, see page 540 🚇 Herrengasse 🚌 Hopper 3A to Habsburgergasse 💲 $$$

Blue and gold domes top the magnificent Hofburg (Imperial Palace), which took more than six centuries to build. The original fortress, built in 1275, made way for the Schweizerhof (Swiss Courtyard), whose Schweizertor (Swiss Gate) went up in the 16th century. Other sections were added in rich baroque style during the 17th and 18th centuries, including the gorgeously decorated Hofbibliothek (Library) and the Reitschule (Riding School), where white Lipizzaner horses are put through their paces for visitors (see page 32). The Kaiserappartements (State Apartments) were built in the 19th century, and new sections were added on as recently as 1913 to create today's enormous complex of 18 wings, 2,600 rooms and 19 courtyards. Tours take you through the State Apartments where Habsburg trappings are on display, including the imperial crowns in the Schatzkammer (Treasuries) and gleaming silver tableware in the Hofsilber-und-Tafelkammer (Court Silver Depot).

KIRCHE AM STEINHOF

🔟 Off the map ✉ Baumgartner Höhe 1, Penzing 🕿 01 910 60 200 31 🕐 Sat. 3–5 🚌 47A, 48A 💲 $$ ℹ Entrance only by guided tour Sat. at 3

Huge copper angels guard the portico of the eccentric, domed Kirche am Steinhof (Steinhof Church), built in 1907 for people suffering from mental illness. Its white interior is full of light; colored glass, and windows by Secessionist artist Kolo Moser brighten the vault and side altars. Short benches have plenty of space in between so that patients taken ill could be helped out. Running water was provided in the stoop (entranceway) to lessen the risk of infection. A ceiling under the cupola gives the effect of a starry sky.

Spanning 600 years of architectural history, the Imperial Palace stands in its own lovely gardens

Vienna

Neptune's Fountain stands proudly in the formal gardens of the impressive Schönbrunn Palace

SCHLOSS BELVEDERE

🕂 D1 ✉ Rennweg 6A (Unteres Belvedere), Prinz-Eugen-Strasse 27 (Oberes Belvedere) ☎ 01 79 80 70-0 or 01 79 80 70-1 🕔 Palace: Tue.–Sun. 10–5. Gardens: 6 a.m.–dusk 🍴 Im Palais Schwarzenberg, see page 540 🚋 Tram 71 (Lower), D (Upper) 💲 $$

The spectacularly baroque Schloss Belvedere (Belvedere Palace) was built for Austrian general and prince Eugene of Savoy, who led his army to many victories over the French. Building began in 1714 and was in two phases: the Unteres Belvedere (Lower Belvedere), where Eugene's military triumphs are celebrated in a ceiling fresco; and the Oberes Belvedere (Upper Belvedere), which housed his collection of paintings and later became the Imperial Picture Gallery. Archduke Franz Ferdinand, whose assassination sparked the events culminating in World War I, lived at the palace for 20 years until his death, but all of the Belvedere is now devoted to art. Austrian baroque paintings are on view in the lower palace, with medieval works in the nearby Orangerie (Orangery); the Upper Belvedere has superb 19th- and 20th-century paintings and sculptures. Look for *The Kiss* by Gustav Klimt and *Death and the Maiden* by Egon Schiele.

SCHLOSS SCHÖNBRUNN

🕂 A1 ✉ Schönbrunner Schlossstrasse 47 ☎ 01 81 11 30 🕔 Palace: Daily 8:30–5, Apr.–Oct.; 8:30–4:30, rest of year. Coach museum: Daily 9–6:30. Zoo: Daily 9–6:30, May–Sep.; 9–dusk, rest of year. Park: Daily 6 a.m.–dusk 🍴 Tyrolean Restaurant in grounds 🚇 Schönbrunn 🚌 15A; tram 10, 58 ℹ Guided tours given hourly (obligatory) 💲 $$$

The imposing size and symmetry of the Schloss Schönbrunn (Schönbrunn Palace), the imperial summer getaway, successfully made the point that the Habsburgs were very wealthy and very powerful. There are no fewer than 1,400 rooms: the original, 1695 plan was to show that the Austrians would not be outdone by the French monarchs' glorious palace of Versailles. But the first design was not finished, and between 1744 and 1749 court architect Nikolaus Pacassi came up with a new version. He was responsible for the geometric splendor of the long building that overlooks a former hunting park, now laid out with ornamental gardens and fountains. In the park beyond there's a zoo and a glass-and-iron palm house. Inside, the palace has a coach museum (to the right of the entrance) and dazzling displays of Indian and Persian miniatures, Japanese and Italian art, 18th-century porcelain and furnishings, and frescoes and painted landscapes. The palace can be seen by guided tour only.

SIGMUND FREUD MUSEUM

🕂 C3 ✉ Berggasse 19 ☎ 01 31 91 59-6 🕔 Daily 9–6, Jul.–Sep.; 9–4, rest of year 🚇 Schottentor 🚋 Tram D 💲 $$

He has many critics and his methods have been denounced by some as bogus, but there's no denying that Sigmund Freud had a profound effect on American and European psyches in the 20th century. He is widely credited with inventing psychoanalysis – pioneering theories of free association, dream interpretation, the Oedipus complex, and the influence of infant sexuality on adult development. His ideas have filtered through art, literature, film, education, social policy and even everyday conversation ("the ego," a

Beethoven's house on Probusgasse — he was drawn to the musical city of Vienna when he was only 20

CITY OF COMPOSERS

Many 17th- and 18th-century Habsburg rulers were music lovers and musicians: Leopold I was a composer, Charles VI was a violinist, and Maria Theresa played the double bass. Royal patronage drew some of the world's greatest composers to Vienna, including Beethoven and Brahms; Mozart gave his first public concert at age six in Schönbrunn's Hall of Mirrors.

The waltz is inextricably linked to Vienna thanks to Johann Strauss, the "Waltz King," and every New Year's Day the Vienna Philharmonic Orchestra plays his waltzes to a billion television viewers around the world. A gilded statue of Strauss, affectionately known as "Schoni," with jaunty moustache and playing his violin, stands in City Park (Stadtpark).

In 1498 Emperor Maximilian I engaged 12 young male choristers to sing with the court orchestra. Over the following centuries some of Austria's greatest composers served their apprenticeships with the choir, including Franz Schubert and Joseph Haydn. Schubert and Haydn would have been dressed in full imperial military uniforms, like the rest of the choir. The current naval-style dress wasn't implemented until 1919.

The elaborate and gilded Musikverein was built in the 19th century as a concert venue for the city's Society of the Friends of Music. (It's here that the Vienna Philharmonic performs its New Year concert.) In 1913 the hall was the scene of a brawl between conservatives and radicals of musical taste, at a concert performed by Arnold Schönberg.

Schönberg changed the face of modern musical composition by abandoning the standard eight-tone scale familiar to the Western ear and devising a complex 12-tone system. Together with his former pupils Alban Berg and Anton von Webern, he formed the Second Viennese School of Music and continued to compose according to his new scale, despite the hostile response of the Vienna audience.

Vienna

"Freudian slip"). Freud grew up in Vienna's Jewish community, and enjoyed the city's social life, playing cards at the Café Landtmann on the Ringstrasse (which is still in business), and taking his daily walk along the boulevard. He rented an apartment on Berggasse street, and here you can see some of his original writings, photographs, books and furniture, as well as oddities that he gathered on his travels, and personal effects such as his hat and walking stick.

SPANISCHE REITSCHULE

✚ D2 ✉ Josefsplatz ☎ 01 5339 0310 or 01 5339 0320 🕐 Performances: Sun. at 10:45 a.m. and some evenings, Feb.–Jun. and Sep.–Oct. Training: Mon.–Fri. 10–noon; closed holidays 🚇 Herrengasse 🚌 Hopper 3A to Habsburgergasse 💲 $$$

In a glittering white arena of the Imperial Palace is the Spanische Reitschule

St. Stephen's Cathedral towers above shoppers and sightseers in Stephansplatz

(Spanish Riding School), where elegant white Lipizzaner horses strut to the gavotte, the quadrille and the waltz and show off the leaping, rearing and trotting of the high school (*haut école*) of dressage. Originally the horses were brought from Spain and bred at a 16th-century stud farm at Lipica, Slovenia (hence their name) – not to go into show business, but to fight to the death. Those high-kicked hooves would be lethal at close range.

Full performances, complete with music and uniformed riders, are booked well in advance, but tickets for the less glamorous morning training sessions can be purchased at Josefsplatz 2, Gate 2.

STEPHANSDOM

✚ D3 ✉ Stephansplatz 3 ☎ 01 51 55 20 🕐 Daily 6 a.m.–10 p.m. 🍴 Do & Co Im Haas-Haus, see page 540 🚇 Stephansplatz 🚌 Hopper 1A

Stephansdom (St. Stephen's Cathedral) is an unmistakable landmark, with its black, yellow and green tiled roof and the 446-foot Gothic South Tower, known to locals as "Steffle," or "Little Steve." Relics of earlier churches are incorporated into the building, including the Giant's Door and the Tower of Heathens, supposedly the site of a pagan shrine. Inside, St. Stephen the Martyr is represented on a baroque 17th-century altar painting by Tobias Pock. The catacombs house an ossuary – a storage place for bones – where the remains of plague victims were kept.

UHRENMUSEUM

✚ D3 ✉ Schulhof 2 ☎ 01 53 32 26-5 🕐 Tue.–Sun. 9–4:30 🚇 Stephansplatz 🚌 Hopper 2A 💲 $$

In 1917 Vienna's city councillors set up a museum devoted to timepieces through the ages in Obizzi Palace. The little palace was once the home of Count Ernst Rüdiger von Starhemberg, who defended Vienna against the 1683 Turkish siege; it is tucked into a side street by the Am Hof Church. The Uhrenmuseum (Clock Museum) has more than 3,000 fascinating items on display, including an onion clock, a sand clock and an astronomical clock whose hand takes 20,904 years to complete one circuit.

VIENNESE FLAVORS

Coffeehouses and pastry shops (*Konditoreien*) are two pretty good reasons for visiting Vienna. At the turn of the 20th century, artists, musicians and writers gathered in cafés to swap ideas, work, read or just sit, and some of their old haunts are still going strong. Stop by Bräuerhof (Stallburggasse 2, ☎01 51 23 89-3); Central (Herrengasse 14, ☎01 553 37 63 26); or the grand old Schwarzenberg (Kärnter Ring 17, ☎01 51 27 39-3), which first opened its doors in 1861. Customers are generally left alone to linger in the grandiose surroundings, sipping one of the many coffee drinks.

A quiet corner to pause and sample Vienna's culinary delights

On average, Austrians drink about 423 pints of coffee a year, and the menu usually offers dozens of varieties. *Mocca* is black coffee; a *Kleiner* or *Grosser Brauner* has a little milk, a *Melange* has more; a *Fiaker* is mocca with rum or brandy; and an *Einspänner* is a mocca with whipped cream. The *café-Konditerei*, or pastry-shop-cum-café, is a showcase for Vienna's pastry-makers. Here you'll find irresistible cakes and pastries, and often a light lunch menu.

Wine made from the most recent grape harvest is known here as *Heuriger*, and this is also the name for the Viennese taverns that serve it. These *Heurigen* stand in their own vineyards in the Vienna Woods, and serve food – usually roast meat, cheese and salad – to soak up the wine. A small band is likely to be playing rousing folk music, and in summer there are often long tables and benches set outside. A bunch of fir twigs is traditionally hung outside the tavern door to show that it's open.

Viennese cooking is plain, simple and filling. It's collectively known as *Beisl* – a Yiddish word introduced by traditionally Jewish tavern owners. Dishes might include boiled beef (*Tafelspitz*), steak with crispy onions (*Zwiebelrostbraten*), chopped calves' heart and lungs in sauce (*Beuschel*) and – perhaps the best-known export – *Wiener Schnitzel*, a fried veal cutlet coated with egg and breadcrumbs. For dessert the popular choice is *Strudel*, fruit-filled baked dough with raisins and cinnamon (a perfect choice with a Viennese coffee).

Innsbruck

INNSBRUCK

Strategically and beautifully situated on the Inn river, in the heart of the Alps, Innsbruck stands at a great European crossroads. The 19th-century construction of the east-west railroad through the Arlberg valley, in combination with the city's historic control of the north-south trade route through the Brenner Pass, placed it firmly on the trans-European map. Today, travelers from across Europe pass this way, and Innsbruck, with its excellent tourist facilities, is well worth more than a brief stop en route.

Innsbruck Through Time

Innsbruck has had a checkered past. By the 12th century a fortified town was growing up beside the bridge over the Inn river, near the site of an old Roman garrison. By the 1360s, when the Habsburgs had acquired the Tyrol region, the settlement had outgrown its original fortifying walls. Under Maximilian I, Emperor of the Germans from 1507 to 1519, Innsbruck was the Habsburg empire's administrative and cultural center.

The next 100 years encompassed a golden age that continued through the reign of Empress Maria Theresa from 1717 to 1780. When Napoleon conquered the Tyrol in the 1790s Innsbruck became part of Bavaria, but was handed back to Austria in 1814. The city became part of Italy following World War I and suffered much damage during World War II. But since then Innsbruck has prospered, and today it is a university city as well as a popular tourist destination.

Exploring Innsbruck

The center of Innsbruck is small, and it's likely your hotel will be within easy walking distance of the historic Old Town (Altstadt), a pedestrianized maze of picturesque streets. Attractions outside the city are served both by regular local buses and

A spectacular view across Innsbruck from the Stadtturm, the 187-foot high Town Tower

Innsbruck

special tourist shuttles that take you right to where the action is. It's worth buying the Innsbruck Card, which gives you free entry to many museums, free use of public transportation and three mountain cable car systems, the latter otherwise very expensive. It's valid for one, two, or three days and obtainable at the tourist office.

A Rich Culture

Because of its long history, Innsbruck is richly endowed with some marvelous buildings, churches and museums. The Old Town is a tiny area packed with handsome houses and narrow arcaded streets. Outside this ancient core you'll find splendid Renaissance, baroque and rococo architecture. Many of these fine buildings house Innsbruck's museums, some devoted to history and the arts, others offering insights into such subjects as Tyrolean railroads, bells and hunting. The cathedral and churches are packed with artistic treasures.

Landmarks along the 17th- and 18th-century street, Maria-Theresien-Strasse, include a column topped by a statue of the Virgin (the Annasäule), and a resplendent arch, the Triumphforte, built in 1765. Nowadays, six bridges span the Inn river – originally called the Innbrücke – from which the city gets its name, leading to the riverfront houses of the Mariahilf neighborhood. This area is also home to a botanic garden.

You can stroll beside the river, with mountains towering in the background, to the Hofgarten – a colorful garden first laid out by Archduke Ferdinand II in the 16th century. To the east of the city center, overlooking the Inn valley, is Ferdinand's palace, Schloss Ambras.

Mountain Scenery

Dramatic mountains encircle Innsbruck, their lower slopes scattered with picturesque villages. The surrounding countryside offers year-round opportunities for fresh air and exercise against a backdrop of some of Europe's loveliest upland scenery. The best way to experience this landscape is on foot, and the tourist office arranges free guided walks outside the city; they'll even provide you with free use of boots and a backpack. You can swim, ride, play golf, go rafting or summer skiing, or just enjoy the Alps from the comfort of

INNSBRUCK

Innsbruck

a sightseeing airplane flight. Winter brings the skiing season, when sports fans flock to Innsbruck from all over the world and the city's architecture is particularly beautiful under a fresh blanket of snow.

Tyrolean Tastes

You can sample a wide range of Austrian and Tyrolean specialties at Innsbruck's restaurants, taverns and cafés (see page 540). The food is good and portions are generous, and you'll find the warm welcome that is so common all over Austria. In the summer, follow dinner with a cable car ride up the Seegrube mountain to enjoy a drink while watching the sparkling lights of the city far below, or take a lantern-lit hike to a party held in a hillside hut.

Year round you can take in a Tyrolean folklore evening, which includes traditional dances, yodeling and a performance on the alphorn; during the summer, *Schuhplatter* dancers and brass bands perform in the center

of town. Innsbruck's casino offers a more sophisticated evening, and there's always a choice of classical music, and often opera.

Woodcarvings and *Christkindl*

Some of Innsbruck's most appealing stores are tucked away in the narrow streets of the Old Town, where you'll find ethnic Austrian souvenirs, clothes, knitwear, antiques and interior design pieces. Woodcarvings make ideal presents, as do dried-flower garlands and baskets – charming decorations for Christmas and Easter – and intricately made national costumes.

Maria-Theresien-Strasse has a range of department, home furnishing and linen stores. Excellent bookstores offer English-language illustrated books about Austria, as well as beautiful calendars that make good gifts. The atmospheric Christmas market *(Christkindl)* sets up in the Old Town, its stalls brimming with gifts, traditional decorations, cookies and tempting sweetmeats.

ESSENTIAL INFORMATION

TOURIST INFORMATION
• Burggraben 3 ☎ 05 12 59 85-0

URBAN TRANSPORTATION
Many of Innsbruck's main sights are grouped together within walking distance in and around the Old Town (Altstadt); use the excellent tram and bus service for venturing farther afield. You can buy a day-use ticket, book of tickets or weekly transportation card from the tourist information office and some tobacconists. Validate your ticket when boarding,

and press the illuminated button near the door to open the doors when you want to get off. Local bus drivers are particularly helpful. There are taxi stands throughout the city center, or you can call a taxi (☎ 05 12 17 18, 05 12 53 11, 05 1220 2070 or 05 12 24 41-1).

AIRPORT INFORMATION
Innsbruck Airport (☎ 05 12 22 52-5), with domestic and some European flights, is 2 miles west of the city center. Bus F runs throughout the day to the central railroad station and the city center, or you can pick up a taxi outside the terminal.

CLIMATE – average highs and lows for the month

	JAN.	FEB.	MAR.	APR.	MAY	JUN.	JUL.	AUG.	SEP.	OCT.	NOV.	DEC.
	1°C	4°C	10°C	15°C	20°C	23°C	25°C	24°C	20°C	14°C	8°C	2°C
	34°F	39°F	50°F	59°F	68°F	73°F	77°F	75°F	68°F	57°F	46°F	36°F
	-7°C	-4°C	0°C	4°C	8°C	11°C	13°C	12°C	9°C	4°C	0°C	-4°C
	19°F	25°F	32°F	39°F	46°F	52°F	55°F	54°F	48°F	39°F	32°F	25°F

CITY SIGHTS

Key to symbols

➕ map coordinates refer to the Innsbruck map on page 35; sights below are highlighted in yellow on the map.

✉ address or location ☎ telephone number

🕐 opening times 🚍 nearest bus or tram route

Ⓢ nearest subway 🍴 restaurant on site or nearby

💶 admission charge: $$$ more than S70, $$ S30 to S70, $ less than S30

GOLDENES DACHL

➕ A2 ✉ Herzog-Friedrich-Strasse 15 ☎ 05 1258 1111 🕐 Daily 10–6, May–Sep.; Tue.–Sun. 10–12:30 and 2–5, rest of year 🚍 O, K, L, M; tram 136; 💶 $$

Innsbruck's Goldenes Dachl (Golden Roof) is, in fact, an oriel (bay) window, added onto the front of the previous ducal palace to commemorate Emperor Maximilian I's marriage to Bianca Maria Sforza of Milan in 1494. Beautifully decorated with reliefs of the Emperor, it is roofed with more than 2,000 gilt copper tiles – hence its name. From here, Maximilian watched festivities in the square below. An informative audiovisual show and small museum will fill you in on Maximilian's life and times.

HOFKIRCHE

➕ A2 ✉ Universitätstrasse 2 ☎ 05 1258 4302 🕐 Mon.–Sat. 9–5 🚍 O, K, L, M; tram 136 💶 $

The Hofkirche (Court Church) of Innsbruck is one of Europe's least known but most impressive monuments. Built in the late Gothic style between 1553 and 1563, this three-aisled structure houses the tomb (now empty) of Maximilian I, among the finest existing works of German Renaissance sculpture. Twenty-eight larger-than-life-size bronze statues surround Maximilian's black marble sarcophagus, decorated with 24 reliefs showing scenes from the Emperor's life. These represent Maximilian's ancestors and contemporaries, and were created by the best artists of the time. Albrecht Dürer was responsible for several, including the figure of the legendary King Arthur of England, considered the finest statue anywhere of a Renaissance knight.

The Golden Roof recalls 15th-century Innsbruck

Elsewhere in the church you can see bronze saints and busts of Roman emperors, all figures destined for Maximilian's unfinished sarcophagus.

HUNGERBURGBAHN AND NORDKETTENBAHN

Hungerburgbahn ➕ Off the map ✉ Rennweg 41 ☎ 05 1229 2250 🕐 Daily 8:10–6:10, Jul.–Sep.; 8:25–5:40, Apr.–Jun. and in Oct.; 8:25–5:10, rest of year. 🍴 Cafés and restaurants at top and bottom of car 🚍 C, D, E; tram 1 💶 $$$

Nordkettenbahn ➕ Off the map ✉ Höhenstrasse 145 ☎ 05 1229 3344 🕐 Daily 8:25–5:30, Jul.–Sep.; 8:40–5, Apr.–Jun. and in Oct.; 8:40–4:30, rest of year 🍴 Cafés and restaurants at top and bottom of car 🚍 Tram 1; bus C, D, E 💶 $$$

These two connecting mountain transportation systems will take you effortlessly up the Nordkette to 6,250-foot Seegrube; from here you can go even higher, to 7,674-foot Hafelekar. The Hungerburgbahn is a steep funicular, built around 1900 to link lower and upper Innsbruck; it's a fun ride to a pretty area with pleasant woodland walks and

Ride the funicular for dramatic views of Innsbruck and the surrounding mountains

attractive outdoor cafés. From here, the Nordkettenbahn cable car runs up Hungerburg mountain to the Seegrube station, with ever-widening views over Innsbruck, the valley and the high Alpine peaks. A wonderful panorama of mountains awaits you at the top. Note: Cable cars rise steeply for about 10 minutes over precipitous slopes suspended from a steel cable.

SCHLOSS AMBRAS

✚ Off the map ✉ Schloss-Strasse 20 ☎ 05 1234 8446 🕔 Wed.–Mon. 10–5, Apr.–Oct.; open Dec.–Mar. only as part of a guided city tour 🍴 Restaurant and café 🚌 Bus and special shuttle from Maria-Theresia-Strasse Altes Landhaus 🖐 $$

Schloss Ambras (Ambras Castle) lies outside Innsbruck, a beautiful 16th-century conversion of a medieval castle standing in a landscaped garden above the Inn valley. It was the home of Archduke Ferdinand from 1563 to 1595; an avid collector and patron of the arts, he built the superb Spanish Hall, with its colorful frescoes and beautiful ceiling, and amassed a collection of curiosities. They are displayed in the Wunderkammer (Wonder-room), a sort of early museum that offers great insight into the Renaissance mind. The castle also contains a fine armory and large portrait gallery, dedicated to the imperial Habsburg family, although most visitors find Ferdinand's wife's bathroom far more interesting. It is a perfect and rare example of a 16th-century bathroom, complete with sunken copper bath.

STADTTURM

✚ A2 ✉ Herzog-Friedrich-Strasse 21 ☎ 05 1257 5962 🕔 Daily 10–5, Mar.–Jun. and Sep.–Oct.; 10–6, Jul.–Aug.; 10–4, Nov.–Feb. 🚌 O, L, K, M; tram 136 🖐 $

For a bird's-eye view of Innsbruck, climb (there's no elevator) the 187-foot-high Stadtturm (Town Tower), built in the 14th century as a watchtower. The bulbous cupola was added 200 years later.

SWAROVSKI KRISTALLWELTEN

✚ Off the map ✉ Kristallweltenstrasse 1, Watten ☎ 05 224 51 08 00 🕔 Daily 9–6 🍴 Restaurant and café 🚌 Bus transfer every half hour from the Innsbruck railroad station 🖐 $$

One of the Innsbruck area's most visited attractions, Swarovski Kristallwelten (Swarovski Crystal Worlds) has to be experienced to be believed. This multi-media theme park centers around the magic of crystal and features moving walls, sculptures and sparkling crystals in underground caverns. You enter through the Giant, a leafy face on the side of a hill with glowing eyes and a water-filled mouth, to experience truly imaginative sights, sounds and smells.

TIROLER VOLKSKUNST-MUSEUM

✚ B2 ✉ Universitätstrasse 2 ☎ 05 1258 4302 🕔 Mon.–Sat. 9–5, Sun. 9–noon 🚌 O, L, K, M; tram 136 🖐 $$

The appealing Tiroler Volkskunst-museum (Museum of Tyrolean Folk Art) is a great introduction to the traditional way of life in the Tyrol. This large museum, with exhibits excellently labeled in English, has fascinating displays on every aspect of rural life, as well as complete Gothic and Renaissance house interiors. Don't miss the models of farmhouses or the charming Christmas nativity scenes, where Jesus' birth is depicted in busy Alpine villages.

Spectacular descent in the Tyrol – snowboarding is gaining in popularity

WINTER SPORTS IN INNSBRUCK

Innsbruck and its surrounding villages offer superb skiing amid beautiful Alpine landscapes. Winter sports enthusiasts will find something for every taste, and some excellent all-inclusive deals can be arranged through the Innsbruck tourist office.

Skiing

You can ski at spots throughout the Innsbruck area as well as at surrounding resorts such as Kitzbühel and Arlberg-St. Anton. There are some 322 miles of well-maintained downhill runs served by 210 lifts. Every skill level is catered to, from gentle runs of hard-packed snow for families and beginners to extreme slopes and off-run skiing for experts. Special areas are designated for snowboarding and carving, and for the truly tough and experienced back-country skier there are superb high-altitude itineraries.

Cross-country skiing on the downhill runs is very popular in Europe, and 12 different cross-country areas are accessible, offering 310 miles of tracks. Ski schools operate daily, and ski guides can be hired on a daily basis.

Several areas have snowmaking equipment to supplement early winter snow. Access to the slopes is by a combination of bus, funicular, cable car, chairlifts and surface lifts, which operate daily 8:30–4. Free buses take skiers from the city center to their chosen ski area and collect them at the end of the day; these buses also run to Kitzbühel and St. Anton. Innsbruck's season runs from early December through March.

Winter Fun

There are plenty of other activities besides hitting the slopes. With its Olympic facilities, Innsbruck offers skating and curling, or you can take a piloted bobsled ride down the Olympic run. Dog- and horse-drawn sleigh rides give you a chance to appreciate the winter beauty of the mountains, and tobogganing and winter walking provide a gentler pace. Various events are organized throughout the season, culminating on New Year's Day with torchlit celebrations in the Old Town and on the mountains.

ℹ️ Information on ski packages is available from the tourist information office (✉ A-6021 Austria Innsbruck, Burggraben 3, ☎ 05 12 53 56; fax 05 12 53 56 43)

SALZBURG

The little city of Salzburg, stretching along the Salzach river and tucked beneath Mönchsberg hill, is a delightful combination of medieval, Renaissance and baroque architecture, the birthplace of Wolfgang Amadeus Mozart and the gateway to some of Austria's most

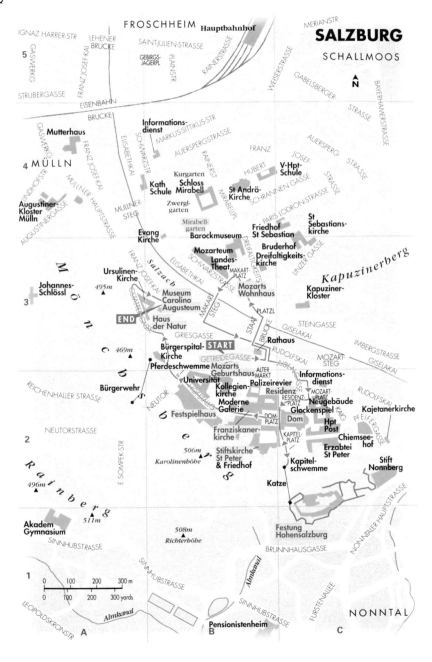

Salzburg

splendid landscapes. Add to this friendly people, a relaxed way of life and one of the world's greatest music festivals, and it's easy to see why Salzburg is popular year-round with tourists. For fans of the movie *The Sound of Music*, there's the added bonus that the city was home to the von Trapp family; movie locations are scattered around the city and are easy to visit.

Mozart's Footsteps

Many visitors simply enjoy Salzburg's beauty, atmosphere and charm although others come for specific reasons – to study the superb baroque architecture, listen to music or tread in Mozart's footsteps. Others flock here to follow *The Sound of Music* trail, and various tour companies run trips with English guides that take you to sites associated with the film.

For classical music lovers, festivals are the main draw (see page 42); the city is packed during festival season and it's hard to find accommodations. Salzburg's charming cityscape, however, can be enjoyed any time of year; late spring and autumn are good times to visit, but whenever you come it will probably rain: Salzburg has a reputation for being the country's wettest city.

Getting Your Bearings

Salzburg is an easy city to negotiate. The historic center on the left bank of the Salzach river is pedestrianized; you can walk from end to end in roughly half an hour, though you'll want to spend longer enjoying the medieval streets and spacious baroque squares. Most of what you'll want to see is concentrated here, with a few sights across the river.

The tourist offices sell Salzburg Plus cards, which give free admission to many of the museums, offer discounts in many stores and restaurants and provide free access to public transportation. They are valid for 24, 48 or 72 hours, and one type includes excellent accommodations deals, particularly useful if you're traveling with children.

Various companies will take you on city tours or farther afield to see the landscape of the Salzkammergut, one of the loveliest parts of Austria. There are fascinating walking tours around Salzburg, concentrating on different aspects of the city; or if you just want to sit back and relax, you can take a trip in a horse-drawn carriage (*Fiaker*); pick one up on the Residenzplatz.

Cosmopolitan Cuisine

You'll eat extremely well in Salzburg, which has dozens of restaurants, inns, taverns and cafés where you can enjoy anything from local and regional specialties to Japanese sushi. Traditional cooking is hearty and filling; plates of meat with solid dumplings, soups and spicy *Gulasch* (meat stew).The local specialty is *Salzburger Nockerl* (a raspberry dessert), and a variety of drinks and open wines (available by the glass) are offered.

Make a point of lingering an hour or so in one of Salzburg's traditional cafés, which specialize in coffee and cream cakes served in elegant surroundings. Many cafés and restaurants have summertime beer gardens, some beautifully situated.

Salzburg Souvenirs

Salzburg is filled with tempting stores, many of them lining the Getreidegasse (see page 44) and its surrounding streets, although there's a good cluster on the left bank of the river. The exquisite traditional women's clothes are appealing buys, but keep in mind that what looks lovely here might not look so good back home. Also look for

Salzburg

attractive wooden carvings, delicate porcelain and crystal, and bright china and linens, all with an Austrian theme, as well as big European designer names. Don't forget the well-organized tax-free shopping service offered in Austria.

Music and Marionettes

Although classical music is the heart of Salzburg's entertainment scene, it's not the only attraction. Year-round, there are concerts at citywide venues; enjoy a traditional dinner in the Fortress (Festung), followed by a Mozart serenade from musicians in period dress. The main festival season runs from late July through August, but there's something happening almost every month, including an autumn jazz festival and fairs in September and the weeks before Christmas. Experience a visit to the city's casino, and children aren't the only ones who will love a performance at the Marionette Theater.

Austrian Cafés

There's no better way to get the feel of the country than by spending an hour or so in a café, a quintessential Austrian experience. Café decor ranges from chandelier-hung baroque splendor to wood-paneled coziness, but the basic elements are always similar: excellent service, a vast range of coffees, and a wide choice of feather-light cream cakes and pastries, all indulged in by well-dressed locals chatting or reading the newspapers. Reading materials are provided by the establishment and hung on wooden poles. Cafés often serve beer and wine, and some offer savory snacks. Many have summertime terraces, the perfect place to write your postcards and rest your feet.

ESSENTIAL INFORMATION

TOURIST INFORMATION
• Information Mozartplatz, Mozartplatz 5 ☎ 06 628 89 873 30
• Information Hauptbahnhof, Bahnsteig 2a ☎ 06 628 89 873 40
• Information Salzburg-Mitte, Müncher Bundesstrasse 1 ☎ 06 628 89 873 50
• Information Flughafen, Ankunftshalle ☎ 06 6285 1211

URBAN TRANSPORTATION
Salzburg's small central core makes it possible to walk to everything you'll want to see. There are, however, good bus and trolley bus services covering the whole city. Buy your ticket before boarding, either at the machines at the main bus stops or from any tobacconist, and remember to validate it as soon as you board the bus. Validation machines are marked "Entwerter." There is no need to punch them again if you change buses. To open the doors from either outside or inside the bus you must press the illuminated button beside the door. There are several taxi stands outside the historic center, or you can call Funktaxi (☎ 06 62 17 15) or Salzburger-Funktaxi (☎ 06 6287 4400). If you are driving to Salzburg, do not try to bring your car into the city center, where parking is an enormous problem. There are large, supervised parking lots outside the city where cars can safely be left.

AIRPORT INFORMATION
Salzburg's W. A. Mozart Airport (☎ 06 628 58 02 51), with domestic and some European flights, is about 3 miles west of the city center. Bus 77 runs every 15 minutes throughout the day to the railroad station, and there is a taxi stand outside the terminal.

CLIMATE – average highs and lows for the month

JAN.	FEB.	MAR.	APR.	MAY	JUN.	JUL.	AUG.	SEP.	OCT.	NOV.	DEC.
2°C	4°C	10°C	14°C	19°C	22°C	24°C	24°C	20°C	14°C	7°C	2°C
36°F	39°F	50°F	57°F	66°F	72°F	75°F	75°F	68°F	57°F	45°F	36°F
-5°C	-4°C	-2°C	2°C	8°C	12°C	13°C	13°C	9°C	4°C	-2°C	-3°C
23°F	25°F	28°F	36°F	46°F	54°F	55°F	55°F	48°F	39°F	28°F	27°F

CITY SIGHTS

Key to symbols

➕ map coordinates refer to the Salzburg map on page 40; sights below are highlighted in yellow on the map.

✉ address or location ☎ telephone number
🕐 opening times 🚏 nearest bus or tram route
🍴 restaurant on site or nearby 💷 admission charge: $$$ more than S70, $$ S30 to S70, $ less than S30

DOM

➕ C2 ✉ Domplatz ☎ Museum 06 6284 4189
🕐 Museum: Mon.–Sat. 10–5, Sun. 1–5, mid-May to mid-Oct. 🚏 5, 6, 51, 55 💷 Dom $; Museum $$

The ornate facade of the Dom (Cathedral), the first truly Italian-style church to be built north of the Alps, dominates the Domplatz, its four huge marble statues giving an indication of the interior splendors. There's been a cathedral here since the eighth century; today's structure is the third to occupy the site. It was built between 1614 and 1628, badly damaged during World War II, and completely restored by 1959. The huge interior, accommodating 10,000 people, is a riot of stucco, marble and gilding, the simple 14th-century font providing a serene contrast. You can visit the crypt to see the foundations of the medieval cathedral, while the museum has superb treasures such as an eighth-century cross.

FESTSPIELHAUS

➕ B2 ✉ Hofstallgasse ☎ 06 6284 9097
🕐 Guided tours daily at 9, 2 and 3:30, Jul.–Aug.; at 2 and 3:30, Jun. and Sep.; at 2, Jan.–May and Oct. 1–Dec. 20 🚏 5, 51, 55 💷 $$$ ➕ Guided tours do not run if reheasals are in progress. Check before you visit

Even if you're not musically inclined, Salzburg's Festspielhäuser (Festival Theaters), used during the Salzburg Festival, are well worth visiting. They stand on the site of the old court stables, the winter riding school that was converted to form the Kleines Festspielhaus (Little Theater). The Grosses Festspielhaus (Large Theater), built in the 1950s, runs right into

An architectural delight, the domes of Salzburg nestle beneath a grand mountain backdrop

Mönchsberg hill; vast amounts of rock were removed during its construction. The only way to see the theaters, unless you attend a performance, is to take a guided tour; this will give you a chance to experience the superb acoustics of the 2,000-seat Large Theater, said to be among the best in the world.

FESTUNG HOHENSALZBURG

➕ C1 ✉ Mönchsberg 34 ☎ 06 628 42 430 11
🕐 Daily 9–5 🍴 Café and restaurant in fortress
🚠 Festungbahn funicular daily 9–9, May–Sep.; 9–5, rest of year 💷 $

The massive Festung Hohensalzburg (Hohensalzburg Fortress) dominates Salzburg from the summit of Mönschberg hill. This rambling fortress was built, altered and extended between 1077 and 1681 by Salzburg's ruling archbishops. Walk up or take the funicular to wander through the courtyards and admire the views before joining one of the guided tours, which is the only way to visit the interior. You'll be shown winding passages and ornate state rooms, the finest being the Golden Room, glittering with gilded tracery, and the Golden Hall, with its superb gold and blue coffered ceiling. The Rainer Museum, also housed in the castle complex, is a must if you're interested in instruments of medieval torture, although it also displays weapons and coats of arms.

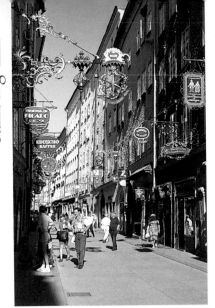

Salzburg

Medieval Getreidegasse with its attractive buildings and enticing stores

FRANZISKANERKIRCHE

⊕ B2 ✉ Sigmund-Haffner Gasse 🕐 Daily 8–7
🚌 5, 51, 55

A few steps from the Cathedral stands the Franziskanerkirche (Franciscan Church), a peaceful and lofty building dedicated to the Virgin that was Salzburg's parish church until 1635. The nave, with its Romanesque details, is the oldest part, its dimness set off by the airy Gothic choir, built in the 1400s. Be sure to go behind the altar to admire the ring of baroque chapels that encircle it.

GETREIDEGASSE

⊕ B3 ✉ Getreidegasse 🚌 5, 51, 55

The medieval street known as the Getreidegasse runs through the center of old Salzburg and is lined with stores, each with a distinctive wrought-iron sign hanging above. Most of the houses date from the 15th through the 18th centuries and were built by prosperous burghers for their businesses and families. Passages run through the buildings to connect with picturesque courtyards and squares; these are called *Durchhäuser*, meaning "through the houses." Crowds throng the street and its continuation, the Judengasse, and there's no better place to soak up Salzburg's unique atmosphere.

HAUS DER NATUR

⊕ B3 ✉ Museumsplatz 5 ☎ 06 6284 2653
🕐 Daily 9–5 🍴 Café in museum 🚌 60, 80, 81
💵 $$

A few hours in Salzburg's Haus der Natur (Natural History Museum) provides a splendid antidote to an excess of fine architecture and Mozart. Popular with families, the museum's 80 rooms house a wide range of scientific and nature displays, including a reptile zoo, European animal exhibits and an excellent aquarium complete with great white sharks. Children of all ages will enjoy the space discovery hall, with its dioramas, models and mock-up of a future space city.

MIRABELLGARTEN

⊕ B4 ✉ Rainerstrasse 🕐 Daily 7 a.m.–10 p.m., in summer; 8–5, rest of year 🚌 1, 6, 51, 55

The beautiful Mirabellgarten (Mirabell Garden) spreads around the Schloss Mirabell (Mirabell Castle), built in 1606 by Archbishop Wolf Dietrich as a home for his mistress, Salome Alt. The terraces, gardens, lawns and flower beds around the house are a splendid example of baroque garden design, where trees, shrubs and flowers contrast with statues and fountains to create a truly civilized landscape. Concerts are sometimes held in the castle's Marble Hall, one of the loveliest places to hear Mozart's music.

MOZARTS GEBURTSHAUS

⊕ B2 ✉ Getreidegasse 9 ☎ 06 6284 4313
🕐 Daily 9–5:30 🍴 Café on ground floor of museum
🚌 5, 51, 55 💵 $$

Wolfgang Amadeus Mozart was born in a modest middle-class apartment in the heart of Salzburg on January 27, 1756. These rooms are among Salzburg's most visited sights, a place of pilgrimage for music lovers from all over the world. Climb the stairs to enter the Mozarts Geburtshaus (Mozart's Birthplace), today a simple museum containing family portraits and mementos of the composer, including his first violin. The next-door flat has been filled with period furniture to give an idea of the appearance of 18th-

MOZART AND THE SALZBURG FESTIVAL

Although Mozart spent much of his adult life in Vienna, his name is inextricably linked with his birthplace, Salzburg. Considered by many to be the world's greatest composer, Mozart's spiritual legacy to his native city is one of the world's greatest music festivals, the Salzburg Festival, and a year-round program of musical events.

Austrian musicians, this music festival attracts audiences and renowned performers from all over the world. Its main venues are the Festival Theaters complex (see page 43), but performances are held in buildings all over the city. The program always includes Mozart operas and orchestral works, but many other composers are featured, as well as plays – in particular *Everyman*, which is traditionally performed outside in the Domplatz.

Mozart

Wolfgang Amadeus Mozart was born in Salzburg in 1756, the son of a respected court musician, himself a fine violinist whose treatise on violin technique is still respected. The boy soon showed signs of genius, playing a variety of instruments by sight and ear and starting to compose at an early age. Mozart's father touted his talented son all around the European courts, keeping a stern eye on his behavior, spending and morals, and thus storing up trouble for the pair's future relationship.

Eventually, the small-town atmosphere of Salzburg, with its reliance on the bishops for employment, proved too stifling, and Mozart moved to Vienna, where he married Constanze. He composed prodigiously and was capable of writing scores as if by divine dictation, while chatting to his friends. Unfortunately, Mozart's genius did not extend to managing his finances; weighed down by money worries and stress, he died in 1791 and was buried in a pauper's grave.

The Salzburg Festival

The Salzburg Festival is held annually during the last week of July and most of August. Established in 1920 by Max Reinhardt, Richard Strauss and other

If you want to attend the festival it is essential to book far ahead; the deadline is in January, when you should also have your accommodations reserved as well.

Salzburg Ticket Service ✉ Theatergasse 2, A-5024 Salzburg, Austria ☎ 06 6287 6585; fax 06 6287 6586; e-mail: ticket.service@salzburg.co.at

Mozart's birthplace, on the third floor apartment in Getreidegasse

century living quarters, where each room opens from its adjoining room and communal wooden balconies overlook a courtyard. One floor down, you can study stage sets and costumes from festival productions of Mozart's works while listening to his sublime music.

MOZARTS WOHNHAUS

➕ B3 ✉ Makartplatz 8 ☎ 06 628 83 454 40
🅖 Daily 10–5:30 🚌 15, 27, 51 💷 $$

In 1773 the Mozart family left their modest flat in Getreidegasse and moved across the river to Makartplatz to occupy a far more spacious and elegant apartment, now the Mozarts Wohnhaus museum (Mozart's House). The building was badly damaged in World War II and was finally renovated and reopened for the 240th anniversary of Mozart's birth in 1996. The result is a superb state-of-the-art museum with evocative displays of Mozart memorabilia.

A true picture of the composer emerges – a man who loved games and jokes, who had an earthy sense of humor and a difficult relationship with his father. Here are scribbled letters, musical manuscripts, instruments and books, all brought to life through an English-language commentary. Two rooms are devoted to audiovisual programs about Mozart's early life and his travels through Europe, which, given 18th-century roads, were impressive.

MUSEUM CAROLINO AUGUSTEUM

➕ B3 ✉ Haupthaus, Museumsplatz 1; Bürgerspital, Bürgerspitalplatz 2 ☎ 06 628 41 13 4 0
🅖 Haupthaus: Tue.–Sun. 9–5 (also Wed. 5–8). Bürgerspital: Tue.–Sun. 9–5 🚌 60, 80, 81 💷 $
Reduced combination ticket available for both buildings

Salzburg's primary museum has collections housed in two buildings – the Haupthaus (Head House) covers classical antiquities, art and musical instruments; the Bürgerspital is devoted to objets d'art and a charming selection of toys and dolls. You can trace Salzburg's history from Roman times and admire some

lovely 17th-century paneled rooms. Look for Herbert Sattler's 1854 painting of New York. Other highlights include a beautiful Celtic ewer and some fascinating musical instruments, accompanied by recordings of their sound. The toys and dolls, some 300 years old, include splendid train sets and puppet theaters.

RESIDENZ

➕ B2–C2 ✉ Residenzplatz 1 ☎ 06 628 04 226 90
🅖 Daily 10–4:30, May–Oct. and Dec.; Mon.–Fri. 10–4:30, Jan.–Apr. and Nov. 🚌 5, 49, 51, 55 💷 $$$

The Residenzplatz is the triumphant architectural landmark of the inner city, splendidly adorned with an ebullient baroque fountain (the largest in northern Europe) complete with horses and dolphins and topped by a conch-blowing triton. Opposite rises the Residenz (Archbishop's Palace), built in the early 1600s around three courtyards. To see the impressive baroque interiors, take the guided tour that leads through rooms of sugary magnificence, decorated with stucco, gilding, marble and astonishing painted ceilings. Nothing gives a better sense of the scale of grandeur and luxury enjoyed by Salzburg's prince bishops. The palace also contains an art gallery. Concerts are held in the state rooms.

STIFTSKIRCHE ST. PETER

➕ B2 ✉ St. Peter-Bezirk ☎ 06 628 44 57 80
🅖 Church: Daily 8–7. Catacombs: Tue.–Sun. 10:30–4, May–Sep.; Wed.–Sun. 10:30–3:30, rest of year
🍴 Stiftskeller St.Peter, see page 542 🚌 5, 51 ,55
💷 Catacombs $

The lovely Stiftskirche St. Peter (St. Peter's Church) was built between 1130 and 1143 but altered to its present rococo appearance in the 17th and 18th centuries. A simple Romanesque west door leads into a sumptuous interior, resplendent with 16 marble altars in its side chapels and decorated with green and pink molding and golden cherubs. See the monument to Mozart's beloved sister Nannerl before leaving the church to explore the charming old Friedhof (cemetery), with its flower-bedecked graves and monuments.

A DAY IN SALZBURG

Although several companies offer a variety of tours in and around Salzburg, the city is small enough to find your way around easily, so it makes sense to plan your own day's sightseeing.

A Mozart Morning

After a hearty Austrian breakfast, spend the morning concentrating on Wolfang Amadeus Mozart, Salzburg's most famous son. His father, employed as a musician in the city, lived in a house on Getreidegasse, where Mozart was born in 1756. After visiting the house and its museum you may be ready for a cup of coffee; head for the Café Tomaselli in the Alter Markt. It was here that Mozart's widow came with her second husband to write the composer's biography in 1820.

Next, cross the Staatsbrücke and walk along the river to Mozart's House (Mozarts Wohnhaus) on Makartplatz, a far grander house where Mozart's family lived between 1773 and 1780 in a spacious apartment. Nearby you'll find the Mozarteum, the music conservatory that holds the Mozart archives. The hut on the grounds is the Little Magic Flute House (Zauberflötenhäuschen) which once stood in Vienna. Here, Mozart dashed off the opera in less than five months.

An Afternoon in the Altstadt

Back across the river, have lunch and then spend the afternoon exploring the Old Town (Altstadt). Most sights are clustered around the trio of lovely squares known as the Residenzplatz, the Domplatz and the Mozartplatz. Behind the cathedral (Dom, see page 43), take the funicular up to the fortress of Hohensalzburg (see page 43).

After this, visit the fine Museum Carolino Augusteum. En route, stop at the Pferdeschwemme (literally, "horse-swim"), a frescoed fountain-cum-pool where horses once were led down sloping ramps to be washed. Leave time to enjoy the stores along Getreidegasse and in the alleys leading off it, where you'll find every imaginable Austrian souvenir.

A Salzburg Evening

No Salzburg visit would be complete without some music; many visitors enjoy special Mozart evenings, with dinner followed by a performance of the composer's works played by costumed musicians. Then wander back through the atmospheric streets to your hotel with music ringing in your ears. For the walk route, see the city map on page 40.

Take a *Fiaker* (horse-drawn carriage) for a leisurely view of old Salzburg

Breathtaking in evening light, Salzburg's medieval fortress towers over the city

BELGIUM

"THE buildings, streets, squares, all are picturesque; the houses, green, blue, pink, yellow, with richest ornaments..."

From English poet Dorothy Wordsworth's *Journal*, July 14, 1820

Belgium

Opposite: The Carpet of Flowers festival takes place biennially in Brussels' Grand-Place

Belgium

BELGIUM

Belgium is a young country in terms of "old" Europe. Its name derives from a prehistoric tribe, the Belgae, but there is no racial or cultural link with such a distant past. The country has been in the melting pot of European history for centuries and only achieved true national identity in 1839. Yet nowhere else on the Continent will you be so close to such a powerful sense of European history.

Norway is defined by its fjords, Greece by its islands, Switzerland by its Alps or Britain by its surrounding seas. Yet Belgium has a very special, very powerful identity expressed through historic cities and a peerless artistic legacy. You will be seduced by medieval Bruges and old Brussels, and by the palpable sense of history in Ghent and Antwerp and such regional cities as Louvain and Mechelen. The dazzling works of art of early Flemish Masters

Influential Neighbors

The Belgium of today is a nation born out of a divided Europe, a remarkable survivor in spite of the differences in politics, territory and language that remain within its own borders. Too often it is seen as the administrative focus of the European Union, a country preoccupied with international politics and commerce. Geographically, it is tiny relative to the size of Europe's larger nations. The Netherlands lies to its north, Germany to its east, France to its south and Luxembourg, an independent Grand Duchy linked historically to Belgium, adjoins it on the southeast.

The northwestern coastline of Belgium faces Britain across the narrow neck of the English Channel. The influences and interests of all of these countries have impacted on Belgium and, in the case of France and the Netherlands, have radically shaped the country's north-south linguistic and cultural divide.

Landscape of History

Belgium has no outstanding landscape features that define it in the way that

MORE TOP DESTINATIONS IN BELGIUM

- Alden Biesen D3
- Antwerpen C4
- Damme A4 • Ieper A3
- Kastel Ooidonk B3
- Knokke-Heist A4 • Kortrijk A3
- Leuven C3 • Mechelen C3
- Oudenaarde B3
- La Roche-en-Ardenne D2
- Villers-La-Ville C3

⊗

Belgium

and medieval painters will fascinate you: prepare yourself for Jan van Eyck, Hans Memling and Hieronymous Bosch, as well as Brueghels, Anthony van Dyck and Jacob Jordaens.

Belgium is about the landscape of history rather than of scenery. Yet outside the cities and towns, beyond the busy network of main roads, lies a quietly charming countryside of fruitful farms, serene waterways and flower-filled meadows. On the immediate

outskirts of Brussels is the Forêt de Soignes, a superb beech forest that is an oasis of peace and reflection. In the Haspengouw region to the west of Brussels are several historic castles, such as the stately Gaasbeek with its formal gardens and the 13th-century, moated Alden-Biesen. A more somber yet compelling aspect of Belgium is enshrined in the poem *In Flanders Fields*. Throughout Europe's turbulent history this northwestern corner of the

Dominating the surrounding park, the Atomium has become a symbol of Brussels

Continent has seen bitter conflict, but none so bitter as World War I. Towns such as Mons and Ieper still resonate with memories and you will find many memorials and graves in the now-healed landscape.

Beaches, Woodlands and Parks

Even along Belgium's relatively short coastline there are attractive sand dunes, beaches and resorts, and lively towns such as Oostende or the more exclusive and stylish De Haan. And though there may be no dramatic mountains, the southern provinces of Namur and Liège embrace the hill country of the Ardennes, a varied and pleasant landscape of woods, river valleys and soft moorland where you can walk or enjoy bicycle rides around Dinant and Rochefort.

For gardens and floral displays, try the National Botanical Gardens at Meise, near Brussels. If theme parks appeal to you, Belgium has a variety of exciting venues that will fascinate children and adults alike. At Bellewaerde, near Ieper, is a large safari park and a vivid flower garden; just outside Bruges, at Boudewijnpark, there is a Dolphinarium.

Exploring Belgium

Public transportation in Belgium is universally efficient, but the railroad network is by far the best way to travel. It is well integrated with systems in neighboring countries, and trains are frequent. Inter-city trains are fast and comfortable; local trains tend to be slower, and you may feel that some of the older equipment seems a little spartan and drab. Overall, however, the high standards that distinguish rail travel throughout northern Europe prevail. City transportation systems are also well run. Trams are a northern European institution, and the larger cities in Belgium have good tram and bus services. Brussels has a well organized subway system that visitors will find useful.

Renting a car will give you independence, but driving in Belgium is a challenge due mainly to the small size of the country and, in part, to its congested urban nature. The road system is excellent, but because distances between built-up areas can be short, you are frequently faced with busy intersections. Traffic in Brussels and in the larger cities is hectic, and navigation can be complicated for visitors because road signs are in French and Flemish. Out on the road, along the east-west dividing line between French-speaking and Flemish-speaking Belgium, destination names on road signs change suddenly between French and Flemish.

Diverse Foods

Food in Belgium is often characterized as being French in quality and German in quantity. The reality is more subtle. Wallonian cuisine shares the French

Scene of one of the most famous battles in history, Waterloo lies 12 miles south of Brussels

penchant for wine-based sauces, but traditional Belgian cuisine focuses particularly on beef and pork, and specializes in seafood in the west and game in the Ardennes.

In most good hotels you will find the generous buffet breakfasts that are an international staple, comprising a variety of cereals, cheeses and hams, along with fish and smoked meats. For lunch and dinner, be adventurous. Try *maatjes*, raw herring swallowed whole, but not quite the raw experience it seems. Or settle for *mosselen*, Belgian mussels in a variety of tangy sauces. For a truly filling meal, try *waterzooi*, a traditional Flemish stew of fresh vegetables with rabbit or fish, or *paling in 't groen*, freshwater eels in a green herb sauce. And do not miss Ardennes pâté or the region's excellent specialty smoked ham.

In early summer look for asparagus with a butter-based sauce, chopped boiled egg and chopped ham. This goes nicely with one of Belgium's many excellent beers, which tend to be rich, mellow and smooth. In Flemish Belgium the specialty is *jenever*, a grain spirit.

For those with a sweet tooth, Belgium's famous *chocolatiers* will be irresistible. The specialties are individually made pralines with liqueur or cream fillings, and truffles with the utterly indulgent ingredients of butter, cream and sugar. *Gaufres*, tasty waffles, are a Belgian treat that you can buy from street vendors.

Traditional Courtesy

Throughout Belgium, visitors will find the local people unfailingly helpful. This is a conservative country with a strongly Roman Catholic religious tradition, aspects that make people courteous yet reserved. The language divide (see page 54) lends a certain rivalry to relations between Flemings and Walloons, yet such cultural diversity seems to make most Belgians amenable to and interested in visitors. The people may seem busy and preoccupied, but they will respond politely and matter-of-factly if you ask for advice or information about their country, which is, after all, a distillation of the most significant aspects of old and new Europe.

Belgium

TIMELINE

57 BC   Romans in northern Europe conquer Iron Age Belgae tribe
             territory, part of land now occupied by present-day Belgium.

AD 751   Carolingian Dynasty is formed; during reign of Charlemagne,
             Holy Roman Emperor, the Low Countries prosper.

1419   Central government established at Bruges; the city becomes a
             center of the cloth trade and a focus of early Flemish painters.

1519   Charles V of Spain is crowned Holy Roman Emperor; the
             Netherlands comes under Spanish control.

1581   The Netherlands divides into United Provinces of the
             Netherlands and Spanish Netherlands (Belgium).

1713   War of Spanish Succession ends; Austria controls Belgium.

1815   Congress of Vienna; Belgium and the United Provinces of the
             Netherlands form the Kingdom of the Netherlands, ruled
             from the Hague by the Dutch William of Orange.

1839   Belgian independence recognized by the (Dutch) Netherlands.

1914–18   Most of Belgium is occupied by Germany.

1940–44   Belgium again occupied by Germany.

1957   European Economic Community (now the European Union)
             establishes its headquarters in Brussels.

1967   NATO sets up headquarters in Brussels.

1992   Belgium becomes a federal state with Flanders, Wallonia and
             Brussels made into semi-autonomous regions.

1993   Belgium signs the Maastricht Treaty, establishing the
             European Union.

2000   Brussels designated a European City of Culture.

LANGUAGE DIVIDE

There is a dramatic linguistic divide between north and south Belgium, a legacy of the country's formation from a southern French-influenced area and a northern Flemish-influenced area. In northern Belgium the dominant language is Flemish, a German-based language similar to Dutch. In southern Belgium, in the area known as Wallonia, the prevailing language is a French dialect. Brussels lies within the Flemish half of Belgium and is officially bilingual, but within the city French is the dominant language.

Be careful in comparing Flemish too closely with Dutch. Brugeans (residents of Bruges) will tell you that theirs is a far subtler language, with more lyrical twists and turns. And Ghentenaars (residents of Ghent) will tell you that they speak better Flemish than Brugeans; if you visit more remote rural districts you will find even more robust regional differences.

SURVIVAL GUIDE

- Flemish and French are both spoken in Brussels, where even street signs are in both languages. You can try out your French in Brussels and Wallonia and your Flemish in Ghent, Bruges and in the north; but to use either language in the wrong area may elicit a frosty reaction. Many Belgians speak English to a greater or lesser degree, and this is often the wisest option, wherever you are.

- You will usually find that the Flemish and French proper names have similarities; for example, Bruges is Bruges (French) and Brugge (Flemish), Louvain is Louvain (French) and Leuven (Flemish). But there are problematic differences. For example, Ghent is Gand (French) but Gent (Flemish), and Mechelen is Malines (French) but Mechelen (Flemish). If in doubt, especially when checking train or bus destinations, confirm the destination with an English-speaking official.

- There are a few public restrooms in Belgian cities, but they are often not clean. Railroad and bus stations, restaurants and the bigger cafés have public bathrooms with attendants. You are expected to pay about 10 francs to use restrooms.

- In restaurants, the *menu* usually signifies the dish of the day. If you want to choose from a selection of dishes, ask for the *kaart* (Flemish) or the *carte* (French).

- In the rue des Bouchers area of Brussels, you may find that prominently displayed *menus* at reasonable prices become suddenly replaced as soon as you are seated. You may be repeatedly offered house specialties at inflated prices. If this is

Sample one of the 400 Belgian beers at a sidewalk cafe in the historic Grand-Place

not what you want, move on to another restaurant.

- For a quick snack, there are numerous fast food outlets, stalls and, in large shopping precincts, café counter service. Apart from the universal hamburgers and french fries, there is usually a big selection of *broodjes*, baguettes crammed with mouth-watering fillings. Seasoned and smoked sausages are sold from street vendors in the northern areas of Belgium. *Gaufres*, tasty, vanilla-flavored waffles, are another treat, bought fresh from street stalls and spread with jam.

- Beer brewing is a Belgian specialty, and there are hundreds of different Belgian brews. Try a *bière* with your meal at a restaurant. It is perfectly in keeping with the cuisine, which incorporates beer in many dishes. The best Belgian beers can be as fine as wine.

BRUSSELS

Brussels (Bruxelles) takes most people by surprise. The city's name is so closely associated with the modern trappings of the European Union (E.U.) that for many it is synonymous with modern high-rise buildings and the world of suited bureaucrats. The real Brussels has a far more colorful and resonant life. It is an exciting, modern city, yet rich in beautiful medieval and art nouveau buildings, outstanding museums and galleries, and a cultural life vibrantly international in character.

Life in the City

You may feel intimidated at first by the hectic pace of the busy streets, but Brussels is genuine "old Europe" at heart – open, friendly and welcoming. Life between the busy boulevards is engagingly relaxed. There is a

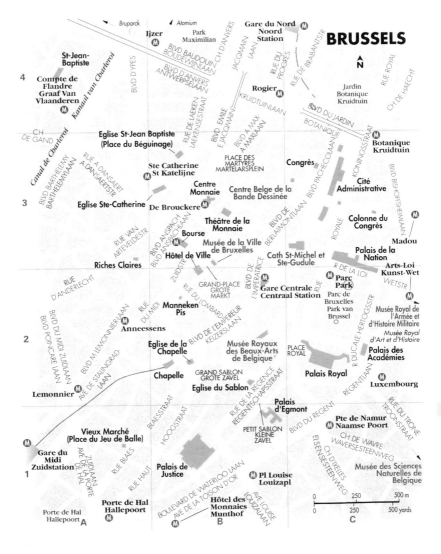

Brussels

wonderful variety about Brussels, a real sense of its being several urban "villages" within a whole.

The heart of the city lies within a barrier of encircling main roads known as the *petit ring*. You should be able to reach the inner city's finest features easily, and you should have no difficulty finding your way around; another option is to join one of the many guided tours. For areas outside the *petit ring* use the city's subway system, one of the easiest ways of getting around the larger area of Brussels.

Medieval Townscape

Historic Brussels is celebrated by the breathtaking Grand-Place (Grote Markt, see pages 59 and 61), the best-preserved medieval townscape in Europe. North of here you will find the rue des Bouchers area, where narrow cobbled streets are lined with competing restaurants more reminiscent of Mediterranean cities. Nearby are the elegant, glass-roofed shopping malls of the 19th-century Galeries St Hubert.

A short distance west of Grand-Place, along rue au Beurre, is the massive neoclassical Bourse, the city's stock exchange, its front facing busy Boulevard Anspach. Nearby is rue Neuve, a lively shopping street. Head west from

Boulevard Anspach and discover Brussels' very old heartland of place St.-Géry, with its covered market, and place Ste.-Cathérine and place du Béguinage, old cobbled squares with slightly worn but still splendid baroque churches. Between St.-Géry and Ste.-Cathérine lies rue Antoine Dansaert, a street featuring chic clothing stores.

Sightseeing and Shopping

Outside the center there are other atmospheric and stylish areas: Le Sablon, near the southern edge of the *petit ring*, is convenient to the Royal Museums of Fine Arts of Belgium (Musées Royaux des Beaux Arts de Belgique, see page 60) or a passing glance at the Royal Palace and the Palace of Justice. The place de Grand Sablon, a pleasant leafy square, is the center of Brussels' antique trade, and there are also some fine restaurants, cafés and stores here. Just south of Le Sablon is the busy and fashionable shopping street of Avenue Louise.

There is so much to see in Brussels that you'll need to use your time efficiently to visit as many of the superb attractions as possible. Branch out beyond the *petit ring* to places like Heysel, four miles north of Grand-Place. Here stands the Atomium, a vast model of a metal crystal, its steel spheres gleaming in the sun. Visit the Parc du Cinquantenaire, Leopold II's 1880 celebration of the Golden Jubilee of the Belgian State. The park has a

Petit Julien

South of Grand-Place on rue du Chène (reached via rue Charles-Buls and Stoofstraat) stands the famous *Manneken Pis*, a bronze fountain statuette of a naked little boy happily urinating. *Petit Julien*, as he is properly called, dates from 1619 and has long been an irreverent and endearing symbol of "carefree" Brussels.

Banners fly at a colorful Belgian pageant

Cuisine and Culture

Make sure you enjoy classic Brussels cuisine at superb gourmet restaurants such as Comme Chez Soi (see page 543); or try a less pricey Brussels' *geuze* or *kriek* beer in any one of the café bars in and around Grand-Place and rue Marché aux Herbes. Sample Brussels' mussels, of course, but also enjoy *anguilles au vert*, freshwater eels in sauce, or *waterzooi*, fish or chicken stew with vegetables and creamy sauce, and spoil yourself with Belgian chocolate.

Enjoy great music in the superb national opera house, Théâtre de la Monnaie, or in one of the lively rock and jazz venues. There are also colorful street theaters, annual festivals and puppet theater events for kids.

central avenue, named after John F. Kennedy, that leads to a triumphal arch linking monumental halls. Several major museums are located here.

ESSENTIAL INFORMATION

TOURIST INFORMATION
• Hotel de Ville, Grand-Place ☎ 02 513 8940
• Destination Belgium Tourist Information Centre, Brussels International Airport ☎ 02 720 5161
• Office for Promotion of Tourism for French-speaking Belgium, 61 rue du Marché aux Herbes ☎ 02 504 0200

URBAN TRANSPORTATION
Brussels has three railroad stations: the Gare du Nord/Noordstation (Brussels North), Gare Centrale/Centraal Station (Brussels Central) and Gare du Midi/Zuidstation (Brussels South). Eurostar service from London's Waterloo train station arrives at Brussels South, as does the TGV (Train à Grande Vitesse) from Paris. There are subway (metro) stops at all three stations. Subway stations are marked on the map as "M." For rail information call ☎ 02 203 2880 or 02 203 3640. Brussels has several public transportation options, including subways, buses and an underground tram, as well as a decent taxi

service. For bus information call ☎ 02 515 3064. The three subway lines with several stations are conveniently placed near major attractions. Underground trams run between Gare du Nord and Gare du Midi. For general information on city transportation call ☎ 02 515 2000.
Licensed taxis have a light on their roofs and can be hailed in the street or from a taxi stand. They are metered; rates double when traveling outside the city. There are taxi stands at Grand-Place (☎ 02 234 444) and at Brussels Gare Centrale.

AIRPORT INFORMATION
Brussels International Airport is located at Zaventem, 8 miles northeast of the city. There is an Airport City Express train that runs to all of Brussels' main stations at 20-minute intervals, from 5:25 a.m.–11:46 p.m. There is a Destination Belgium Tourist Information service in the arrival hall. Accommodations can be reserved here, and you can obtain information about Brussels and northern Belgium. For general flight information call ☎ 02 753 3913.

CLIMATE – average highs and lows for the month

JAN.	FEB.	MAR.	APR.	MAY	JUN.	JUL.	AUG.	SEP.	OCT.	NOV.	DEC.
4°C	6°C	10°C	13°C	18°C	22°C	22°C	22°C	20°C	15°C	9°C	5°C
39°F	43°F	50°F	55°F	64°F	72°F	72°F	72°F	68°F	59°F	48°F	41°F
-1°C	0°C	2°C	5°C	8°C	11°C	12°C	12°C	10°C	7°C	3°C	0°C
30°F	32°F	36°°F	41°F	46°F	52°F	54°F	54°F	50°F	45°F	37°F	32°F

Guild House, Grand-Place

CITY SIGHTS

Key to symbols

⊞ map coordinates refer to the Brussels map on page 56; sights below are highlighted in yellow on the map.

✉ address or location ☎ telephone number
🕐 opening times 🚌 nearest bus or tram route
🍴 restaurant on site or nearby
🎫 admission charge: $$$ more than 150BF, $$ 80BF–150BF, $ less than 80BF

CATHÉDRALE ST.-MICHEL ET STE.-GUDULE

⊞ C3 ✉ Place Ste.-Gudule ☎ 02 217 8345
🕐 Mon.–Fri. 7–7, Sat. 7:30–7, Sun. 8–7, Apr.–Oct.;
Mon.–Fri. 7–6, Sat. 7:30–6, Sun. 8–6, rest of year
🚌 Gare Centrale 🎫 Free; entrance to crypt $

The Cathédrale St.-Michel et Ste.-Gudule (Cathedral of St. Michael and St. Gudule) occupies an elevated site above bland modern buildings and passing traffic. Work on the cathedral began in the 13th century. Architecturally, the building is a lesson in the various forms of Brabantine Gothic that evolved over the 300 years it took to complete the work. Inside the church, baroque style is lavishly celebrated by giant figures of the apostles, while Renaissance influence shines from the exceptional stained glass of the 16th-century west window. The Romanesque remains of an 11th-century church can be seen down in the crypt.

CENTRE BELGE DE LA BANDE DESSINÉE

⊞ C3 ✉ 20 rue des Sables ☎ 02 219 1980
🕐 Tue.–Sun. 10–6 🍴 Museum restaurant
🚌 Gare Centrale 🚌 29, 38, 63, 71; tram 23, 55, 81, 92; 🎫 $$$

The rather plainly named Centre Belge de la Bande Dessinée (Belgian Center for Comic Strip Art) encompasses a dazzling celebration of the strip cartoon, the *bande dessinée*. The strip cartoon is closely associated with Belgium, not least in the shape of Hergé's (Georges Rémi's) famous character Tin Tin, created in 1929. The form has strong design links to art nouveau and it is an added delight that the museum building was designed in 1906 as a fabric shop by Victor Horta, the most distinguished of art nouveau architects.

GRAND-PLACE

⊞ B2–B3 ✉ Grand-Place 🍴 La Rose Blanche, see page 543 🚌 Bourse 🚌 Tram 23, 52, 56, 81
ℹ️ Location of numerous events throughout the year. Daily flower market, songbird market on Sundays, summer concerts, biennial Carpet of Flowers. Annual medieval festival, the *Ommegang*, in early July. Lively Planting of the Maytree procession on Aug. 9

Brussels' Grand-Place is an extravaganza of medieval architecture, as displayed in the numerous guild houses that complement the Place's monumental Hôtel de Ville (Town Hall, see page 61). Opposite stands the splendid La Maison du Roi (The King's House), which is the location of the City of Brussels Museum. There is an information center on the first floor of the Town Hall. Many events and festivals are held in the square. The spectacular *Ommegang* is an annual costume parade during the first week of July in which the Grand-Place is transformed into a stunning medieval stage.

Tin Tin's space rocket from "Destination Moon"

Brussels

Brussels

MUSÉE ROYAL DE L'ARMÉE ET D'HISTOIRE MILITAIRE

✚ Off the map ✉ 3 Parc du Cinquantenaire
☎ Museum 02 737 7811; Autoworld 02 736 4165
🕐 Museum: Tue.–Sun. 9–noon and 1–4:45, Apr.–Sep.
Autoworld: Daily 10–6, Apr.–Sep.; 10–5, rest of year
🚇 Merode 🚌 20, 28, 36, 61, 80; tram 81, 82;
💷 Museum free; Autoworld $$

The entire gamut of military artifacts is displayed at the Musée Royal de l'Armée et d'Histoire Militaire (Royal Museum of the Army and Military History), and a visit is a campaign in its own right. The main museum features display after display of military uniforms, artifacts and weaponry. The adjoining glass-roofed Hall of the Air has dozens of aircraft, including an 80-seater Caravelle frozen in mid-flight above your head.

Just across the courtyard from the museum is Autoworld, with a remarkable collection of more than 300 vehicles, including elegant landaus, broughams and calèches of past centuries to the opulence of the 20th-century Lincoln and the Hispano Suiza.

MUSÉE DES SCIENCES NATURELLES DE BELGIQUE

✚ Off the map ✉ 29 rue Vautier ☎ 02 627 4211
🕐 Tue.–Sat. 9:30–4:45, Sun. 9:30–6 🍴 Museum café 🚌 34, 80 💷 $$

The delightful Musée des Sciences Naturelles de Belgique (Museum of Natural Sciences in Belgium) is a refreshing haven of individuality at the heart of the modern European Union district. The main hall is a happy riot of dinosaur skeletons and excellent reconstructions of Tyrannosaurus Rex and other prehistoric playmates that roar and sway convincingly.

Several floors hold general biological exhibitions, including an impressive Antarctica tunnel with icy sound effects to go with its polar bears, walruses and penguins. There are no English-language labels except for part of the Antarctica section, but the exhibits speak volumes in themselves, not least to the wide-eyed youngsters who trot happily around, totally enthralled.

MUSÉE DE LA VILLE DE BRUXELLES

✚ B3 ✉ 1 rue du Poivre (entrance from Grand-Place) ☎ 02 279 4355 🕐 Mon.–Thu. 10–12:30 and 1:30–5, Sat.–Sun. 10–1, Apr.–Sep; Mon.–Thu. 10–12:30 and 1:30–4, Sat.–Sun. 10–1, Oct.–Feb. 🚇 Bourse
🚋 Tram 23, 52, 56, 81 💷 $$

The Musée de la Ville de Bruxelles (City of Brussels Museum) is a local celebration of Brussels and has very little information in English. It deserves a visit, however, because of its porcelain, pottery and Brussels' tapestries' collections, as well as its paintings, including Breughel's splendid *The Marriage Procession*. The museum is located on Grand-Place in the handsome building known as the King's House (La Maison du Roi). On the top floor there is an entertaining display of some of the 600 costumes in the "wardrobe" of the Manneken Pis (see page 57) that have been donated by heads of state and others since 1698.

MUSÉES ROYAUX DES BEAUX-ARTS DE BELGIQUE

✚ B2 ✉ 3 rue de la Regence ☎ 02 508 3211
🕐 Musée d'Art Ancien: Tue.–Sun. 10–noon and 1–5. Musée d'Art Moderne: Tue.–Sun. 10–1 and 2–5
🍴 Museum café 🚌 0, 38, 60, 95; tram 92, 93, 94
💷 $$

The Musées Royaux des Beaux-Arts de Belgique (Royal Museums of Fine Arts of Belgium) are housed in the former court of Charles Lorraine. The entrance fee includes both the Musée d'Art Ancien (Museum of Ancient Art) and the Musée d'Art Moderne (Museum of Modern Art); the two are linked by an underground passage. The complex contains one of the most comprehensive and exciting collections of paintings in Europe, covering the 14th century to the present day. Pieter Breughel, Pablo Picasso and Auguste Rodin are only a few of the leading names of Flemish and Western art represented here. You'll enjoy this stunning feast of art even more if you rent the audio program (available in many languages) for the Ancient Art section. It's not available for the superb Modern Art section.

GRAND-PLACE

The late medieval Grand-Place, or Grote Markt in Flemish, is one of the most glorious sights of urban Europe. A first glimpse of Grand-Place, whether by day or floodlit at night, should stop even the most jaded in their tracks. These are buildings that seem wrought from nature, yet their symmetry and elegance is ravishing. Any debate about the competing merits of traditional or Modernist architecture melts away in the face of such adventurous style. Even the fast-food stores, bars and cafés that have taken over the ground-floor premises shrink into insignificance.

What you see in Grand-Place today are some of the finest examples of Dutch Renaissance and Gothic architecture, most of which are 17th-century replacements of

Grandiose gables on the guild houses in Grand-Place recall the wealth of their creators

older wooden-framed guild houses. The originals were destroyed in 1695 during a devastating bombardment of Brussels by the troops of a spiteful Louis XIV. The citizens rebuilt the heart of their city in a bold act of defiance. The Town Hall (Hôtel de Ville) is the focus of Grand-Place. Its soaring tower dominates the Brussels skyline; its carved facade is crammed with dukes, duchesses, monks, saints and sinners.

The guild houses, which make up the other sides of the square, are named and represented by gilded statues, bas-reliefs, motifs and classical orders. They are a riot of exquisite forms and symbols. Look for No. 7, Le Renard (The Fox), the Drapers' guild house; and No. 6, Cornet (Horn), the guild house of the Boatmen.

Opposite the Town Hall is The King's House (La Maison du Roi), known also as the Bread House (Broodhuis) and home to the City of Brussels Museum (Musée de la Ville de Bruxelles). On the east side of Grand-Place is the restored facade of the house of the Dukes of Brabant, six individual houses united by the cool elegance of a single Renaissance facade.

Finally, in the southeast corner to the left of the Town Hall, is No. 10, L'Arbre d'Or (The Golden Tree). This is the headquarters of the Brewers' Guild, the Knights of the Mash Staff, and also houses a small museum. Next door is Le Cygne (The Swan), complete with a graceful swan motif and rounding off the magnificent Grand-Place with a flourish.

Bruges

BRUGES

In Bruges (Brugge), the survival of exquisite medieval buildings provides a vivid architectural record of 16th-century Europe. Yet that survival is the result of a commercial decline that lasted for nearly 400 years. By the early 16th century, the Zwin river, which linked Bruges and its elegant canals to the North Sea, could not be navigated because of silting; the successful cloth trade had declined, and local and foreign traders moved their businesses to the flourishing port of Antwerp. There was no wealth with which to modernize the venerable townscape. We can thank the rough handling of history for a city that now delights with the completeness of its medieval street plan and its ornate buildings.

Finding Your Way

If you arrive at Bruges railroad station you will find a small tourist information office on Stationsplein, outside the station to the right. It is only a short bus

"The Venice of the north" – take a leisurely boat trip on one of Bruges' canals

ride from Stationsplein to Bruges' grand central square, the Markt (see page 66), where the city begins. A short walk along Breidelstraat, the street that begins at the southeast corner of the Markt, is the Burg (see pages 68–69), the historic heart of Bruges.

You can enjoy Bruges through guided tours, on foot, by bus or by canal boat. Trips on the famous horse-drawn carriages and trams of Bruges are enjoyable, but expensive. The city is an easy and rewarding place to explore on your own, however.

A City of Canals

A few steps south of the Burg, along the narrow alley known as Blind Donkey Street (Blinde Ezelstraat) will bring you to the colonnaded fish market, a lively scene Tuesday to Saturday mornings. From here proceed right, to Huidenvettersplein square and then along Rosary Quay (Rozenhoed-kaai) to the canalside Dijver. Dijver has splendid museums and an exquisite complex of buildings, made up of the Municipal Museum of Antiquities and Applied Arts (Gruuthusemuseum) and the Church of Our Lady (Onze Lieve Vrouwekerk, see page 67), which are centered around St. Boniface Bridge, an enduring image of medieval Bruges.

Explore the city's ancient walls and surviving gates, and take an early morning stroll along the old central canals from Jan Van Eyckplein just north of the Markt. Even more than the canals of Amsterdam, the canals of Bruges have a style that is truly reminiscent of Venice.

Cosmopolitan Tastes

Amid this historical splendor, modern Bruges has its own delights. The city's social life is centered on a huge open area known as 't Zand. The inner side of 't Zand is lined with sidewalk cafés and bars, and there is a market on Saturday mornings. Between 't Zand

Lace

Bruges has long been famous for its lace. Lace making in Flanders originated in the 16th century, when lace makers specialized in bobbin lace, a method that used weaving and plaiting with thread-loaded bobbins, with the threads pinned to the pattern. The other great lace-making center was Italy, where needlepoint lace originated, a method of embroidering with buttonhole and other stitches.

Bruges

Intricate work of the lace maker on Wollestraat

find every type of international restaurant, but try Belgian specialties such as *kalfsblanket*, veal ragout, or *lapin à la gueuze*, rabbit cooked in *gueuze* beer.

Lace, Chocolate and Music

Between Noordzandstraat and Zuidzandstraat lies Zilverpand, a complex of 50 stores, many of them stylish fashion boutiques. If you like lace, do not miss the Gruuthuse lace shop on the Dijver for authentic work, or the many lace shops on Wollestraat, the street running south from the Markt. For antiques and craft shops, Mariastraat running south from Simon Stevinplein on Steenstraat is the place to look; and for mouth-watering *chocolatiers*, try van Oost at Wollestraat 9, or Godiva at Zuidzandstraat 36.

and the Markt lie Bruges' busiest streets, Noordzandstraat and Zuidzandstraat, the latter leading into the shopping area of Steenstraat, with connecting squares and narrow streets harboring cafés and bistros. Eating out in Bruges is a diner's delight. You will

At night, Bruges lights up spectacularly. The buildings in the Markt and elsewhere are illuminated, and there is plenty to do. Find out what's happening at Cultuurcentrum in St. Jakobsstraat, a venue for theater and music, or catch one of the summer concerts in the Town Hall.

ESSENTIAL INFORMATION

TOURIST INFORMATION
• Toerisme Brugge, Burg 11 ☎ 050 448 666
• Toerisme Brugge, Stationsplein, Bruges railroad station

URBAN TRANSPORTATION
Bruges railroad station lies just over a mile southwest of the Markt. The station is small, well kept and has standard facilities. For information call ☎ 050 382 382. There is also an efficient bus service that

caters to the city and its environs. Call ☎ 059 565 353 for information. If you'd prefer to take a taxi, cab stands are at the Markt (☎ 050 334 444) and at Stationsplein (☎ 050 384 660).

AIRPORT INFORMATION
Bruges does not have an airport; the nearest one is Brussels International Airport at Zaventem (see page 58). For flight information call ☎ 02 753 3913, daily 7a.m.–10p.m. Train connections for Bruges are made at Brussels Centraal Station and take about 90 minutes.

CLIMATE – average highs and lows for the month

JAN.	FEB.	MAR.	APR.	MAY	JUN.	JUL.	AUG.	SEP.	OCT.	NOV.	DEC.
5°C	6°C	8°C	11°C	15°C	18°C	19°C	20°C	18°C	15°C	10°C	6°C
41°F	43°F	46°F	52°F	59°F	64°F	66°F	68°F	64°F	59°F	50°F	43°F
1°C	2°C	3°C	5°C	9°C	11°C	12°C	12°C	11°C	8°C	4°C	2°C
34°F	36°F	37°F	41°F	48°F	52°F	54°F	54°F	52°F	46°F	39°F	36°F

CITY SIGHTS

Key to symbols

✚ map coordinates refer to the Bruges map on page 62; sights below are highlighted in yellow on the map.
⊠ address or location ☎ telephone number
◉ opening times 🚌 nearest bus or tram route
🍴 restaurant on site or nearby
🎫 admission charge: $$$ more than 150BF, $$ 80BF–150BF, $ less than 80BF

BASILIEK VAN HET HEILIG BLOED

✚ B2 ⊠ Burg 10 ◉ Daily 9:30–noon and 2–6, Apr.–Sep.; 10–noon and 2–4, rest of year. Closed during services 🍴 Café Tom Pouce, see page 543 🚌 1 🎫 Churches free; Treasury $

The Basiliek van het Heilig Bloed (Basilican Church of the Holy Blood, see page 68–69) has been a place of pilgrimage for many centuries, and is one of the major sights of Bruges. The basilica consists of two chapels, one above the other, and the Treasury is a small museum displaying religious objects.

BEGIJNHOF

✚ B1 ⊠ Wingaardplein ☎ 050 330 011
◉ Begijnhof: Daily 9–2 and 2:30–6. Beguine house and church: Mon.–Sat. 10–noon and 1:45–6. Closed Friday morning, Apr.–Sep.; Wed.–Thu. 11–noon and 2–4, rest of year 🚌 1 🎫 Begijnhof free; Beguine house $

The Begijnhof complex, a wonderful testimony to a more sedate spiritual age, has retained its tranquil atmosphere even though huge numbers of people visit it. It was founded in 1245 to accommodate pious single women, many of them lace makers, who lived reclusive lives. These inhabitants, known as Beguines, abandoned the complex in the 1920s, but Benedictine nuns later settled in the Begijnhof and still live here today. The 17th-century cottages surround a peaceful square. You can visit a Begijnhof museum house that has old-style furnishings and a delightful little cloister. The Begijnhof Church of St. Elizabeth has a simple grace.

BELFORT

✚ B2 ⊠ Markt ☎ 050 448 711 ◉ Daily 9:30–5, Apr.–Sep.; 9:30–12:30 and 1:30–5, rest of year 🚌 1–10, 13, 15, 16 🎫 $$ 🍴 Carillon recitals in summer

Bruges' famous Belfort (Belfry) dominates the Markt. You can reach the top of the 300-foot tower by climbing the 366 steep and narrow steps. Ascending it is a challenge but is worthwhile for those who feel fit enough, since every step will be memorable. You may marvel at the vast number of tiny bricks and the tons of mortar holding everything together high in the air, including the 27 tons that the 47-bell carillon weighs. Just below the belfry is the chamber containing the clock mechanism and copper carillon drum. The bells ring out at each quarter hour. You have time to watch the ingenious system whir and click into life, like some great mechanical beast, before you make the final short climb to the belfry to enjoy the melodic, and surprisingly muted, peals and to take in the stunning view.

Springtime at the Begijnhof – a haven of peace and serenity

Bruges

A detail from *The King Drinks* by Jacob Jordaens (1593–1678) on display in the Groeningemuseum

GROENINGEMUSEUM

B2 Dijver 12 050 448 750 Wed.–Mon. 9:30–5, Apr.–Sep.; 9:30–12:30 and 2–5, rest of year Marieke van Brugghe, see page 543 1 $$$

The Groeningemuseum, housed in a former Augustinian monastery on the Dijver, contains Bruges' superb civic collection of 15th to 20th century Belgian and Dutch paintings. There are exceptional works here, including Jan Van Eyck's *The Madonna with the Canon Georges van der Paele,* as vivid in its deployment of blue, red, white and gold as is Van Eyck's Ghent altarpiece. Other delights include the works of Pieter Pourbus and Hans Memling and the *Last Judgement* by Hieronymus Bosch, a painting that demands close attention for an appreciation of its startling details.

HUISBROUWERIJ STRAFFE HENDRIK

B1 Walplein 26 050 332 697 Daily 10–5, Apr.–Sep.; 11–5, rest of year 1 $$

For relief from Bruges' cultural and artistic delights, step into the Huisbrouwerij Straffe Hendrik (Strong Henry Brewery), where the local Strong Henry beer has been brewed since 1546. Even the air of the brewery is so aromatic that it might make your head spin, although a visit to the roof will clear it. There is a guided tour of the brewery

museum and a drink of beer at the attractive bar to finish. Tours begin when there are a minimum of 15 visitors.

KATHEDRAAL ST.-SALVATOR

B2 Zuidzanstraat Mon.–Fri. 2–5, Sun. 3–5 1–5, 89, 13 Cathedral free; museum $ Major concerts held in cathedral

Bruges' great churches reflect sober Flemish Protestantism rather than Latin exuberance, not least in their rather stark interiors. But the Kathedraal St.-Salvator (St. Saviour's Cathedral) has many enriching features to counteract its Gothic vastness. The high altar and the 15th-century choir stalls add a richly decorative note; the rood loft, beneath the organ case, contains a superb baroque sculpture of God the Father in white marble by Arthur Quellin the Younger. The great door beneath the rood loft is decorated in copper and has lively instruments in the spandrels. Visit the church museum; among its crowning glories is the vivid realism of Dirk Bouts' 15th-century triptych *The Torture of St. Hippolytus.*

MARKT

B2 Markt Most buses Horse-drawn carriage trips and mini-bus tours start from the Markt

The Markt is the bustling heart of Bruges. The majestic Gothic buildings of the Provinciaal Hof, seat of the government of West Flanders, and the adjoining Central Post Office dominate the east side of the square, where the covered Waterhalles dock once stood. The Belfry stands on the south side. The crow-stepped gables of a row of old guild houses, now painted in bright colors, catch the sun on the north side of the square. They stand behind a vigorous statue of Jan Breydel and Pieter de Coninck, Flemish heroes who led a 1302 uprising against French overlordship. The east side of the Markt has a fascinating mix of handsome buildings, including the 15th-century Maison Bouchoute and the Craenenburg House flanking the entrance to Sint Amandstraat. Look for the bear, the angry cat and a pair of snails on the roof of the east side.

The opulent mausoleum of Charles the Bold in the Church of Our Lady

MUSEUM ARENTSHUIS

✠ B2 ✉ Dijver 16 ☎ 050 448 763 🕐 Wed.–Mon. 9:30–5, Apr.–Sep.; 9:30–12:30 and 2–5, rest of year 🍽 Marieke van Brugghe, see page 543 🚌 1 💲

The genteel and charming Museum Arentshuis (Arents Museum) is housed in an 18th-century town house on the Dijver. It contains collections of impressive lace work, and has a fascinating exhibit on its upper floor of paintings by Sir Frank Brangwyn, the Bruges-born son of Welsh parents and a great painter and designer.

All labeling is in Flemish, but an excellent English-language booklet explaining the lace exhibits is on sale at the entrance. The needlepoint and bobbin work displayed includes exquisite examples of Binche, Valenciennes, Chantilly and Bruges lace. The lace maker's life is portrayed through paintings and work tools.

OUZE-LEIVE-VROUWEKERK

✠ B2 ✉ Mariastraat 🕐 Mon.–Sat. 10–11:30 and 2:30–5, Sun. 2:30–5, Apr.–Sep.; Mon.–Sat. 10–11:30 and 2:30–4, rest of year 🍽 Marieke van Brugghe, see page 543 🚌 1 💲 Church free; choir $

The exquisite Gothic gloom of the Ouze-Leive-Vrouwekerk (Church of Our Lady) is emphasized by mournful piped music. Prepare to repent. Notices everywhere exhorting *stilte* (silence) will keep you suitably hushed. Even Michelangelo's masterful sculpture the *Madonna and Child* seems constrained within the cold prison of its marble altar. Yet the church's powerful sense of sanctity and its outstanding works of sacred art overpower the initial feeling of gloominess. The pulpit, designed by Bruges artist Jan Antoon Garemijn, is a marvelous rococo extravaganza that will cheer you on your way to the choir and the magnificent, gilded Renaissance mausoleums of Mary of Burgundy and Charles the Bold.

PALEIS VAN DE BRUGSE VRIJE

✠ B2 ✉ Burg 🕐 Tue.–Sun. 10–noon and 1:30–5 🍽 Café Tom Pouce, see page 543 🚌 1 💲

The Paleis van de Brugse Vrije (Palace of the Liberty of Bruges) is an 18th-century building in the neo-classical style. One wing houses Old Recorders' House, a 16th-century building once used to hold public records.

STADHUIS

✠ B2 ✉ Burg 🕐 Daily 9:30–5, Apr.–Sep.; 9:30–12:30 and 2–5, rest of year 🍽 Café Tom Pouce, see page 543 🚌 All buses to the Markt 💲 Gothic Hall $

The Stadhuis (Town Hall) of Bruges stands in The Burg (see pages 68–69) and dates from the late 13th century. It has been rebuilt over the years and has a superb carved facade. Inside is the splendid Council Chamber, also known as the Gothic Hall.

Bruges

A MEDIEVAL EXPERIENCE: THE BURG

The Burg is medieval Bruges at its
most tangible. Once it was a jealously
guarded enclave, walled and with
locked gates. The northern side of this
outstanding architectural complex once
contained the 10th-century
Romanesque Church of St. Donation,
demolished in 1799. A scale model of
the church under the trees on the
square, the Burgplein, is a reminder of a
lost final flourish to the Burg. Also on
the northern side, on Breydelstraat, is
the handsome baroque facade of the
Provost's House of St. Donation.

On the east side of the Burg is the
Palace of the Liberty of Bruges (Paleis
van de Brugse Vrije). This was once the
ruling seat of the Bruges Vrije, a
territorial precinct of Flanders. The
building now houses the Bruges tourist
information center in one wing. The
other wing harbors a magnificent
Renaissance chimney piece created in
honor of Charles V, Count of Flanders
and Holy Roman Emperor. The lower
section is in black marble with an
alabaster frieze depicting the biblical
story of Suzanna and the Elders. The
main section is in exquisitely carved
wood and depicts the Emperor and
fellow members of the Habsburg
family, the male contingent endowed
with startling Habsburgian codpieces.

To the right of the palace across
narrow Blind Donkey Street (Blinde
Ezelstraat) is the Town Hall of Bruges
(Stadhuis). This exquisite building
dates from the late 13th century but has
been rebuilt and renovated over the
centuries. The turreted, Gothic facade
is a lyrical evocation of the mason's
craft. Inside is the Council Chamber,
the Gothic Hall (Gotische Zaal), with

Procession of the Holy Blood

historical wall paintings and a
handsome chimney piece. Its glorious
vaulted ceiling is all gilded wooden
arches with slender ribs and hanging
keystones. Fortunate couples are
married here.

To the right of the Town Hall in
the southwest corner of the Burg is the
most medieval building of all, the
Chapel of the Holy Blood (Basiliek
van het Heilig Bloed). In the building
is a sacred vial said to contain drops of
Christ's blood, brought to Bruges in
1149 from the Holy Land by the
Flemish crusader Thierry of Alsace.
The Holy Blood is still deeply
venerated. Each Ascension Day, in
May, the relic is the focus of the most
important event in West Flanders, the
Procession of the Holy Blood (Heilig
Bloedprocessie), a theatrical costume
pageant depicting religious events.

There is something strangely
compelling about the Chapel of the
Holy Blood. It has a medieval

Medieval elegance in lights – an evening meal in the atmospheric Burg, after a long day of sightseeing

authenticity that is irresistible, even to the ungodly. The building contains an upper and lower chapel. You enter the lower chapel through a modest doorway and it is as if you are stepping straight into the Middle Ages.

The chapel dates from the 12th century and was built to house the relics of St. Basil. It has been partly restored, but is still one of the finest surviving examples of Romanesque architecture in Flanders. Squat pillars support the vaulted roof of the nave. Wall carvings are simple, almost primitive. The air is dense and exterior sounds are muffled and resonant; there are worn statues, slightly garish yet of great religious significance, in gloomy side chambers.

Gothic Mood

You re-emerge into the daylight, pass through an enchanting Gothic doorway in the ornate facade of the main chapel and then mount a wide staircase beneath shallow vaults. Here, the sweet odor of incense hangs in the air. The upper chapel is a breathtaking contrast to the somber Romanesque below the stairs. It is lavishly decorated in a late Gothic style that overlays original Romanesque themes. A rococo white marble altar, barrel roof, luminous stained glass, carved wood, and gold and silver artifacts all create a mood that is reminiscent of the heavy decoration of Orthodox churches.

There is a delightful spherical oak pulpit with disk canopy but without any visible access. The secret is a small door to the side of the Holy Blood altar, which opens on hidden stairs to the pulpit. The Holy Blood is contained within a crystal sheath with gold crown stoppers and is supported by gilded copper and silver angels.

Adjoining the upper church is a small museum with a few religious artifacts on display, including the gold and silver reliquary in which the Holy Blood is carried during processions.

Ghent

GHENT

At first glance Ghent (Gent) seems slightly rough around the edges, a city lacking the sparkle of Luxembourg or the carefully preserved splendor of Bruges. Ghent has been an industrial and commercial center throughout its long history, and the fabric of the city

has suffered because of this. But behind the urban realities of Ghent lies Belgium's "City of Flowers," along with some of the finest historical and cultural artifacts in Europe and architecture that blends soaring towers with exquisitely decorative domestic buildings. Its citizens, the friendly Gentenaars, are shrewd, down to earth and personable. Many speak some

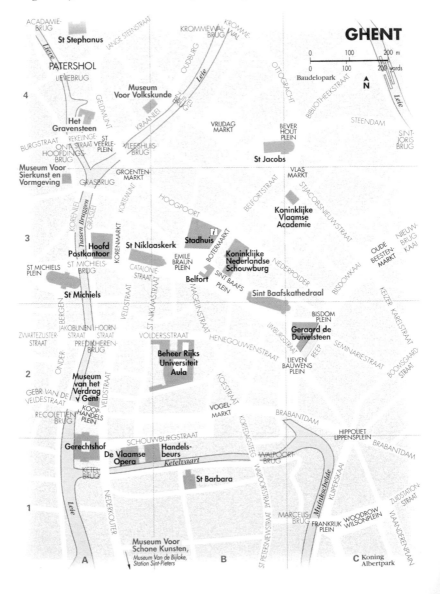

GHENT

0   100   200 m
0   100   200 yards

Baudelopark

N

ACADAMIE-BRUG
St Stephanus
LANGE STEENSTRAAT
KROMMEWAL-BRUG
KROMME WAL
OTTOGRACHT
BIBLIOTHEEKSTRAAT
STEENDAM
Leie

PATERSHOL
LIEVEBRUG
OUDBURG
Leie
SINT-JORIS BRUG

Museum Voor Volkskunde
KRAANLEI
VRIJDAG MARKT
BEVER HOUT PLEIN

Het Gravensteen
GELDMUNT
REKELINGE-ST STRAAT
ONT VEERLE-PLEIN
VLEESHUIS-BRUG
St Jacobs
VLAS MARKT

BURGSTRAAT
HOOFDINGS-BRUG

Museum Voor Sierkunst en Vormgeving
GROENTEN-MARKT
GRASBRUG
HOOGPOORT
BELFORTSTRAAT
STJACOBSNIEUWSTRAAT
Koninklijke Vlaamse Academie
NIEUW-BRUG KAAI

KORENLEI
Tussen Bruggen
GRASLEI
KORENMARKT
St Niklaaskerk
Stadhuis
i
BOTERMARKT
Koninklijke Nederlandse Schouwburg
NEDERPOLDER
OUDE BEESTEN-MARKT
BISDOMKAAI
KELZER KARELSTRAAT

Hoofd Postkantoor
EMILE BRAUN PLEIN
Belfort
SINT BAAFS PLEIN
Sint Baafskathedraal

ST MICHIELS PLEIN
ST MICHIELS-BRUG
CATALONIE STRAAT
VELDSTRAAT
BISDOM PLEIN

St Michiels
JAKOBIJNEN HOORN-STRAAT STRAAT
ST NIKLAASTRAAT
VOLDERSSTRAAT
MAGELEINSTRAAT
HENEGOUWENSTRAAT
IJZERBURGSTRAAT
Geraard de Duivelsteen
REEP
LIEVEN BAUWENS PLEIN
SEMINARIESTRAAT
BOOMSGAARD STRAAT

ZWARTEZUSTER STRAAT
PREDIKHEREN-BRUG
ONDER BERGEN

Beheer Rijks Universiteit Aula

Museum van het Verdrag v Gent
VELDSTRAAT
VOGEL-MARKT
KOESTRAAT
BRABANTDAM
HIPPOLIET LIPPENSPLEIN
BRABANTDAM

GEBR VAN DE VELDESTRAAT
RECOLETTEN BRUG
KOOP HANDELS PLEIN

Gerechtshof
SCHOUWBURGSTRAAT
De Vlaamse Opera
Handels-beurs
Ketelvaart
KORTEDAGSTEEG
WALPOORT-BRUG
Muinkschelde
KUIPERSKAAI
ZUIDSTATION-STRAAT

KETEL BRUG
St Barbara
WALPOORTSTRAAT
MARCELIS BRUG
FRANKRIJK PLEIN
WOODROW WILSONPLEIN
VLAANDERENPLEIN

NEDERKOUTER
Leie
ST PETERSNIEUWSTRAAT

Museum Voor Schone Kunsten,
Museum Van de Bijloke,
Station Sint-Pieters
Koning Albertpark

A   B   C

4

3

2

1

The towers of Ghent reflect the wealth of the city created during the 14th- and 15th-century cloth trade

English and are always ready to oblige the visitor with guidance and advice.

First Impressions

Ghent's main railroad station, St. Pieter's, lies just over a mile south of the city center. The station can be a sobering experience for the first-time visitor. It is a busy place and has reasonable facilities, but there is not much information for new arrivals. Head to the heart of the city and the helpful tourist information center in the town hall in Botermarkt, next to the central Korenmarkt.

Trams leave regularly for Korenmarkt from a covered terminal on the east side of St. Pieter's station. Ghent's trams run along extremely narrow streets, a mildly alarming experience at first; but they do so with great efficiency. Do not be surprised to see the driver stop, get out and adjust the wing mirror of a parked car so that the tram may squeeze past.

The great central squares are the best places to get a handle on Ghent. Here are the powerful Gothic churches of St. Baafskathedraal (see page 75) and St. Niklaaskerk. Civic buildings between them include the Belfry (Belfort), the Cloth Hall (Lakenhalle) and the Town Hall (Stadhuis), with their distinctive mix of architectural styles. Take the glass elevator to the top of the Belfort for superb views of this remarkable city of towers and steeples.

Old Ghent

For a taste of old Ghent, go west from St. Niklaaskerk, past the neo-Gothic, neo-Renaissance flamboyance of the 1910 post office, to the bridge of St. Michielsbrug that spans the Leie river. Look back from the bridge for a breathtaking view of the skyline. North of the bridge is Tussen Bruggen, once a busy harbor and still lined by the gabled buildings of Graslei and Korenlei.

North of Graslei is Groentenmarkt, a tree-shaded square flanked by the sturdy 15th-century Meat Hall, which has little jewelry shops between deep bays where tripe stalls once stood. Today the Groentenmarkt is the scene of a daily fruit and vegetable market except on Sundays, when there's an open-air art forum. A few steps farther

Ghent

is the Sint Veerleplein, with a monumental baroque archway to the old fish market and handsome gabled houses. These are all overshadowed by the brooding mass of Gravensteen, the Castle of the Counts.

Across the street, to the east of Gravensteen, is the side street of Kraanlei, a row of late medieval buildings lining a stretch of the Leie river. This is one of Ghent's finest streetscapes. From Kraanlei's far end, the Zuivelbrug bridge crosses the canal into the square of Vrijdagmart; the surrounding streets are crammed with stores to explore.

Shopping in Ghent

Ghent's main commercial and shopping area lies to the south of Korenmarkt and Botermarkt. The busy Veldstraat has stores of all types, but if you walk through the network of little streets just east of here, including Magelinstraat, St. Niklaasstraat, Kortedagsteeg and Koestraat, you'll find numerous specialty shops. These include chic fashion salons, delicatessens, *chocolateries*, antiques and crafts shops, and a cheese shop and coffee shop that are second to none. At the heart of the area are Kouter and the Vogle Markt, famous flower markets at their colorful best on Sundays, a vivid indication of Ghent's fame as the "City of Flowers."

Night Lights

Eating out in Ghent is an essential experience. Try such local specialties as *Gentse hazenpeper* (jugged hare) or *Gentse waterzooi van riviervis* (freshwater fish stew). There are intimate little restaurants in the Patershol area north of Kraanlei. Enjoy Ghent by night, when the main buildings are lit up and the shopping streets hum with life. Spend an evening at the Royal Dutch Theater on St. Baafsplein; at De Vlaamse Opera, at Schouwburgstraat; or at the classical music venue Biijloke Festivalhal, on Jozef Kluyskensstraat.

ESSENTIAL INFORMATION

TOURIST INFORMATION
• Ghent Information Office, Belfry, Botermarkt ☎ 09 266 5232

There are taxi stands at the Korenmarkt and outside St Pietersstation. To call a taxi, phone ☎ 09 222 2222, 09 223 2323 or 09 225 2525.

URBAN TRANSPORTATION
Ghent railroad station is 1 mile south of the city center. For information on train services phone ☎ 09 222 4444/ 09 241 2210. Ghent's main bus and tram stations adjoin the railroad station. Most buses and trams also converge from the Korenmarkt, in front of the main post office. For information, call ☎ 09 210 9491.

AIRPORT INFORMATION
Ghent does not have an airport. The nearest airport is Brussels International Airport at Zaventem (see page 58). For flight information, call ☎ 02 753 3913 daily 7 a.m.–10 p.m. Train connections to Ghent can be made at Brussels Centraal Station. The trip from Brussels airport to Ghent takes about 70 minutes.

CLIMATE – average highs and lows for the month

JAN.	FEB.	MAR.	APR.	MAY	JUN.	JUL.	AUG.	SEP.	OCT.	NOV.	DEC.
5°C	6°C	9°C	11°C	17°C	21°C	22°C	22°C	20°C	15°C	9°C	5°C
41°F	43°F	48°F	52°F	63°F	70°F	72°F	72°F	68°F	59°F	48°F	41°F
0°C	1°C	2°C	5°C	8°C	11°C	12°C	12°C	11°C	7°C	4°C	2°C
32°F	34°F	36°F	41°F	46°F	52°F	54°F	54°F	52°F	45°F	39°F	36°F

CITY SIGHTS

Key to symbols

➕ map coordinates refer to the Ghent map on page 70; sights below are highlighted in yellow on the map.

✉ address or location ☎ telephone number

🕐 opening times 🚌 nearest bus or tram route

🍴 restaurant on site or nearby

🎟 admission charge: $$$ more than 150BF, $$ 80BF–150BF, $ less than 80BF

GRASLEI AND KORENLEI

➕ A3 ✉ Graslei and Korenlei 🚌 16, 18, 38; trolley bus 3

Medieval guild houses line the Leie

Graslei and Korenlei are the two wharves flanking the medieval harbor Tussen Bruggen (meaning "between the bridges") that lies to the north of the bridge of St. Michielsbrug. Their names relate to their role in the early grain trade; their flanking buildings were the trade and guild houses of the medieval period, carefully restored for the World Exhibition of 1913. The facades of these magnificent buildings offer an impression of Ghent in the days when the wharves were alive with the raucous, colorful world of medieval trade.

HET GRAVENSTEEN

➕ A4 ✉ Sint Veerleplein ☎ 09 225 9306 🕐 Daily 9–6, Apr.–Sep.; 9–5 rest of year 🚌 Tram 1, 10, 11, 13 🎟 $$$

The magnificent Het Gravensteen (Castle of the Counts) has all the authentic menace of 12th-century feudalism. A visit to this well-restored building is irresistible, and merely passing through the shadowy, arched entrance feels like a commitment. The main castle is a series of intriguing rooms, including the impressive Great Hall, which is linked by winding staircases. In the upper rooms there are historical exhibitions, one of which dwells on the tools of torture and execution.

KRAANLEI

➕ A4 ✉ Kraanlei 🍴 De Hel, see page 542 🚌 Tram 1, 10, 11, 13

Kraanlei is one of Ghent's finest surviving canal-side streets. Its name derives from a wooden crane that was used to unload cargo. Today the baroque facades of Kraanlei's buildings, with touches of Gothic, are splendid survivors of an exuberant age of prosperity and Flemish culture. The houses have stepped gables and pediments. Look for Ghent's version of Brussels' *Manneken Pis* (see page 57), perched above the door of a restaurant a few buildings from the beginning of the street. Halfway along is the Museum Voor Volkskunde (Museum of Folklore, see page 74). Three of the finest facades are at the far end of Kraanlei and include the exquisite 17th-century house known as "The Flying Deer." A few steps north of Kraanlei takes you into the Patershol area, a warren of narrow cobbled streets lined with tall buildings. Once the factory workers' district, Patershol is being rejuvenated, with restaurants, art galleries and refurbished apartments.

MUSEUM VOOR SCHONE KUNSTEN

➕ Off the map ✉ Nicolaas de Liemaeckereplein 3, Citadelpark ☎ 09 222 1703 🕐 Tue.–Sun. 9:30–5 🚌 5, 50, 70, 71, 90, 91 🎟 $$

The Museum Voor Schone Kunsten (Museum of Fine Arts) is located in Ghent's attractive Citadelpark. The collection is exceptional and includes works by Flemish and other European masters, including Rogier van der Weyden, Frans Hals and Gustave Courbet. Of special note are works by Hiëronymus Bosch, including the compelling *The Bearing of the Cross*. Other

Magnificent St. Bavo's Cathedral and Belfry

superb works include Pieter Breughel the Younger's *Wedding Feast*. Jef Lambeaux's monumental relief panel, *Human Passions*, will keep you occupied and amazed. The Museum van Hedendaagse Kunst (Museum of Contemporary Art) was once part of the Museum of Fine Arts. A new location for the museum is scheduled to open in 2000 in the one-time casino building directly opposite the Museum of Fine Arts.

MUSEUM VOOR SIERKUNST EN VORMGEVING

A3 ⊠ Jan Breydelstraat 5 ☎ 09 225 6676 🕐 Tue.–Sun. 9:30–5 🚊 Tram 1, 11, 12 💰 $$

The Museum Voor Sierkunst en Vormgeving (Museum of Decorative Arts and Design) is a Ghent experience not to be missed. Housed in the handsome old Hotel de Coninck, and with a stunning contemporary extension, the museum exhibits Belgian decorative and applied art, crafts and design from the Renaissance to 20th-century art nouveau and contemporary work. The older part of the museum displays superb period interiors and has lucid explanations of baroque, rococo and classical styles in several languages helpfully related to individual exhibits. In the modern section there is no labeling in English, but the fascinating furniture and design artifacts

speak for themselves in the most vivid terms. Look for the amazing "banana skin" armchair.

MUSEUM VOOR VOLKSKUNDE

A4–B4 ⊠ Kraanlei 65 ☎ 09 223 1336 🕐 Tue.–Sun. 9–12:30 and 1:30–5:30, Apr.–Oct.; Tue.–Sun. 10–noon and 1:30–5, rest of year 🍴 De Hel, see page 544 🚊 Tram 1, 11, 12 💰 $
ℹ️ Puppet shows are held regularly. Check with museum for details

The intriguing Museum Voor Volkskunde (Museum of Folklore) owes much of its charm to its location among the old buildings of the 14th-century Kindrenhalyns Hospice, on the canal-side street of Kraanlei. Children will be thrilled with the museum's marionette theater and other delights. The collections are spread throughout a number of quaint little houses surrounding a central square. The domestic and commercial life of Ghent through the ages is exhaustively represented in excellent set-piece tableaux and displays. The museum's puppet theater company *Spelleke Van de Folklore* is based here, and performances are staged regularly.

SINT BAAFSKATHEDRAAL

B3 ⊠ Sint Baafsplein 🕐 Cathedral: daily 8:30–6. Ghent Altar and Crypt: Mon.–Sat. 9:30–noon and 2–6, Sun. 1–6, Apr.–Oct.; Mon.–Sat. 10:30–noon and 2:30–4, Sun. 2–5, rest of year 🍴 St. Jorishof, see page 544 🚊 16, 17, 18, 19, 38; tram 12, 41
💰 Cathedral free; altar and crypt $

The tall four-stage tower of Sint Baafskathedraal (St. Bavo's Cathedral) dominates the east end of Botermarkt. Externally, the cathedral is a stern mix of Gothic styles beneath a patina of city grime. Inside is one of the great art treasures of the world, the multi-paneled *Het Lam Gods* (*The Mystic Lamb*) known as the Ghent Altar. Other treasures include the rococo pulpit in Carrara marble and Danish oak, its staircases like twisted tree roots and the canopy a mass of writhing branches. The 12th-century Romanesque crypt of St. Baffs is full of religious artifacts and works of art.

HET LAM GODS – THE ADORATION OF THE MYSTIC LAMB

The famous Ghent Altar, *Het Lam Gods* (*The Mystic Lamb*), lives up to your highest expectations. Whatever else you do in Ghent, a visit to Sint Baafskathedraal and a view of the altar should not be missed. This luminous, enthralling work has the kind of impact that can change lives and attitudes.

The Ghent Altar is a polyptych, a painting made up of many panels. It is allegedly the work of two 15th-century Flemish painters, the brothers Hubert and Jan van Eyck. There are doubts over whether or not Hubert van Eyck even existed, however. In any case, Jan van Eyck was unquestionably the most famous painter of his generation. He was a technical master who is credited with developing oil painting to such an extent that the paint he used has retained its vivid colors to this day, with a little help from restoration and refurbishment through the ages.

The Ghent Altar is composed of two rows of paintings, one above the other. The centerpiece in the upper row is of Christ the King, who is flanked by the Virgin Mary, St. John the Baptist, singing angels, a musician, and nude portraits of Adam and a pregnant Eve within the wing panels. The focus of the lower row is the Adoration of the Lamb of God. The flanking panels depict processions of the faithful, judges, knights, hermits and pilgrims. The painted wing panels fold over to enclose the central panels. All of this is presented in breathtaking color and luminosity against superbly detailed Flanders landscapes.

The altar has survived the dangerous meddling of history. Iconoclasts sought to destroy it. In the 1780s, Emperor Joseph II prudishly replaced the sensual nude figures of Adam and Eve with clothed versions. During World War II, German soldiers stole the work and hid it in a mine, from which it was liberated by American troops. Two panels were stolen in 1934; the thief demanded a ransom, but was refused. The panel depicting John the Baptist was later found wrapped in a blanket in Brussels Centraal railroad station. The panel of the Righteous Judges has never been traced and was replaced by a copy, painted by a Belgian artist, who incorporated his own likeness into one of the figures, a forgivable indulgence for any painter dreaming of immortality.

BRITAIN

"*A LITTLE foggy island in the north-west corner of Europe...*"

From *The Australians*, 1893, by Australian poet and essayist Francis Adams

Opposite: Colorful tudor pond garden at London's Hampton Court Palace

Britain

Shetland Islands

Lerwick

Kirkwall

Orkney Islands

Thurso

NORTH

SEA

Orkney Islands

Wick

Thurso

A882

A9

Inverness

North West Highlands

Ullapool

A835

A832

A82

A87

A9

Isle of Lewis

Isle of Skye

N Uist

S Uist

Rum

Mull

Islay

Outer Hebrides

SCOTLAND

Grampian Mountains

Fort William

Glen Coe

Oban

A82

A9

A93

Dee

Deeside

Pitlochry

Perth

A90

Aberdeen

A96

Dundee

St Andrews

The Trossachs

Stirling

M90

M9

M9

EDINBURGH

Berwick-upon-Tweed

A1

Tweed

Selkirk

Southern Uplands

Moffat

A74

A702

M74

A74(M)

A74(M)

Dumfries

Stranraer

A75

A77

Ayr

Arran

A83

Glasgow

M8

GLASGOW

A77

Cheviot Hills

Newcastle-Upon-Tyne

A69

A68

Durham

A1(M)

Sunderland

Middlesbrough

A66

Penrith

Lake District

M6

Carlisle

A596

A66

Workington

NORTHERN

BRITAIN

N

100 km

50 miles

50

25

0

0

Britain

Britain

BRITAIN

Within this remarkable nation, an island barely 700 miles from north to south and less than 350 miles at its widest point, live nearly 60 million people. From this small island, a large percentage of the world's population inherited many of the linguistic and cultural influences that shaped their lives.

A Diverse Unity

England, Scotland and Wales – collectively known as Britain – each retain individual cultural characteristics. To complicate matters further for the visitor, there are distinct regions within regions, all reflecting the resilient and determined individuality that is typically British. If you spend any time traveling through Britain, you will find that the landscape and the customs of the people change dramatically, sometimes within only a few miles.

People have been arriving at all points around Britain's corrugated coastline for centuries, but London is the focus of the country as a whole. Here history, politics and culture meet in one of the most invigorating cities in the world. Beyond London lies provincial and rural England. You'll find a landscape of meadows, hedgerows and woods, its earth relentlessly farmed for centuries. The countryside has retained, in between the maze of roads and highways, a semblance of Old England, and in treasured corners the beauty of the past is preserved.

At Canterbury, in Kent, is the great cathedral that drew tens of thousands of medieval pilgrims to the relics of the revered Thomas à Becket, the great English churchman. These pilgrims inspired the country's first great poet, Geoffrey Chaucer, to write his *Canterbury Tales*, as vivid a picture of the medieval world as you will find.

Yet before Chaucer and before Canterbury, the earliest Britons had raised their own pagan equivalents to the Christian cathedrals. At Stonehenge, and perhaps more hauntingly at Avebury in Wiltshire, at the heart of southern England, are the standing stones and burial chambers of Britons who commanded England centuries before Romans, Danes, Anglo Saxons and Normans ever did.

Britain Explained

The name "Britain" (or "Great Britain") refers to the countries of England, Scotland and Wales located on the main island of Britain. To include Northern Ireland, the correct name is the "United Kingdom." The United Kingdom is the official unified entity, governed by the central parliament in London and (nominally) by Queen Elizabeth II.

However, political boundaries are becoming increasingly blurred by the European Union. Member countries are subject to E.U. rules and regulations, and regions are now being encouraged in their efforts at self-determination, with the result that Scotland and Wales – historically uneasy with what they saw as an English parliament (and Queen) in London – now have their own national assemblies and a degree of autonomy. However the legacy of London remains, and when the British talk about "this country," they usually mean Britain.

Sunrise over ancient Britain – Stonehenge is a reminder of the achievements of early inhabitants

Village Greens and Seaside

Throughout scores of picturesque villages in southern and western England, you will find the essence of the country where people still play cricket on village greens, dance around maypoles on May Day and sell jars of local honey at village festivals – weather permitting, of course.

Yet England also boasts great cities and historic towns that bustle with life. The great seaport of Bristol is one. The Georgian city of Bath, where golden Cotswold stone and the classical elegance of 18th-century fashion conspired to create one of the world's most astounding cityscapes, seems consumed with golden light in the summer sun.

Miles of coastline fringe the English Channel. On the southern coast are the cliffs of Beachy Head, famous resorts like Brighton and Bournemouth, as well as long stretches of green and peaceful coast that run westward past Dorset's limestone cliffs and the red cliffs of Devon to the golden beaches of Cornwall.

From Oxford to the Lakes

North and west of London, in the counties of Oxfordshire and Warwickshire, are such cities as Oxford, university town par excellence, matched only by its rival Cambridge in the fen country of eastern England. Here, too, you will find the Cotswold Hills and the historic town of Stratford-upon-Avon.

Progress through the cultural heart of England is not an idyllic rural journey by any means. Yet the cities of

MORE TOP DESTINATIONS IN BRITAIN

- Avebury D2 • Bath D1
- Caernarfon Castle C3
- Canterbury E1 • Chester D3
- Cotswolds D2 • Dartmoor C1
- Deeside D5 • Glen Coe C5
- Isle of Skye B6 • Lake District D4
- Snowdonia C3 • St. Andrews D5
- St. Michael's Mount B1
- Stratford-upon-Avon D2
- Stonehenge D1 • The Trossachs C5 • Windsor Castle E2
- Yorkshire Dales D3

Scottish piper in full regalia

Manchester, Leeds, Birmingham and Liverpool are vibrant and exciting places, while historic cities such as Chester, on the Welsh borders, and York in the east have managed to preserve their medieval townscapes. Beyond this great sprawl an unspoiled England survives. Derbyshire's Peak District, the Yorkshire dales, the exquisite Lake District of Cumbria and the lonely heights of Northumbria seem to appear like magic in the landscape.

Wild Wales

Wales is renowned as a land of poetry and song and as a part of Britain that seems older than time. In these green borderlands, the ruined castles of Norman Britain survive, relics of a time when England failed to entirely subdue the "wild Welsh." Strongholds of the Anglo Norman conquerors, such as Caernarfon Castle, are reminders of a later age of determined feudalism. But in the beautiful countryside of central Wales, on the rugged west coast and in the great mountains of Snowdonia, the spirit of the ancient Welsh lives on, the powerful identity of modern Wales a token of that endurance.

North to the Highlands

North of Cumbria and Northumberland, the Southern Uplands guard Scotland's borderland, once infamous for its violent robber clans. It was this raw border country that gave courage to heroic Scottish patriots like Robert Bruce and William Wallace as they pitted themselves against England's might. And across these hills in 1745 marched Charles Edward Stuart – Bonnie Prince Charlie, the last of a moribund royal line – supported by the cream of the Highland clans in a doomed final gesture of defiance by Scotland against English domination.

North of the Southern Uplands are the Central Lowlands of Scotland, with the capital city of Edinburgh to the east and Glasgow, the great powerhouse of old industrial Scotland, to the west. Edinburgh is the historic distillation of all things Scottish, the political and cultural focus of the nation from a time when poet Robert Burns and novelist Walter Scott graced fashionable 18th-century salons, to the vigorous and progressive Edinburgh Festival of today.

Across the Forth river (Firth of Forth) from Edinburgh lies the county of Fife, home to the university town and golfing mecca of St. Andrews. To the north and west are the Scottish Highlands, Britain's most dramatic landscape, consisting of rugged mountain plateaus, deep glens and deeper lochs, and some of the last great wilderness areas of Europe.

At the edge of the Highlands are the Trossachs, Scotland's equivalent to England's Lake District, steeped in the history of real-life characters like Rob Roy Macgregor, inspiration for the classic novels of Sir Walter Scott. Farther north are the mountains of Aberdeenshire. Here, on Royal Deeside, sits Balmoral Castle, traditional retreat of the Queen and her family. Scotland's most spectacular mountain country lies to the far west and north, at the Pass of Glen Coe, and then for more than 100 miles northward along the west coast to Kintail and Wester Ross. Out to sea is the Isle of Skye and the misty Hebrides, romantic islands at Britain's far western edge.

Seeing the Country

Britain's essence lies in its diversity and in the hidden corners between the most popular places. Traveling independently by train or bus is one way to explore off the beaten track, but you will need to plan carefully. Britain's long-distance bus network is generally good, but away from major cities and main roads service can vary greatly. Organized bus tours, on the other hand, will whisk you efficiently to all the major tourist sights. Traveling by car is another option; Britain is so diverse that you can drive for a few hours on a main highway and then veer off onto quieter byways.

London is a year-round destination, but outside the main summer season and major vacation periods, Britain's hidden corners are extremely quiet. May and June are good months to visit – the freshness of early June is invigorating in England's upland areas, northern Wales and the Scottish Highlands. Winter is another story, of course, but even in December and January Britain's larger cities are vibrant; London, Manchester, Liverpool, Edinburgh and Glasgow all pulse with British fashion and style.

Great classical music can be savored year-round in London, Manchester and Edinburgh. Attend world-class theater in Cardiff and Glasgow. Outstanding choirs fill England's cathedrals with truly heavenly music, and the open-air performances by Welsh and Cornish choirs are enchanting. Join the singing customers or listen to folk music at a neighborhood pub, or discover a colorful local festival or time-honored custom in a Devonshire hamlet or Yorkshire town.

The Taste of Britain

The same variety applies to shopping. The British were dismissed by Napoleon as a "nation of shopkeepers," but the intended slight is actually a compliment. The British engaged in trade the world over, and today that spirit of enterprise, curiosity, good business sense and eclectic style is maintained. Fashion salons rival those in France and Italy. Britain has some of the finest antique shops, art galleries and auction houses in Europe. Traditional and modern styles are blended to produce some colorful and out-of-the-ordinary clothing and craft items, and it is often in the provinces that the best examples are found.

Not so long ago, British food was seen as typically uninspired and overcooked. But British nouvelle cuisine is exciting yet still essentially British, the ingredients fresh and flavorful. British beer has rediscovered great traditions, too; every English county has a lively range of local ales to back up the standard brews. In Scotland, sample the best from the country's range of whiskies and superb single malts.

Cornish pasties – with tasty, savory fillings

Britain

TIMELINE

8000 BC	Mesolithic hunter-gatherers journey into southern Britain.
4000 BC	Neolithic "Stone Age" people settle in southern Britain.
circa 500 BC	Iron age culture develops in Britain.
55–54 BC	Julius Caesar makes expeditions to Britain.
AD 43	Roman conquest of Britain begins; first settlement of London by Romans.
circa 400	Roman army and administration withdraws from Britain.
1066	Battle of Hastings; Norman Conquest of Britain.
1314	Battle of Bannockburn, in which England suffers disastrous defeat at the hands of Scotland's Robert Bruce.
1534	Henry VIII appoints himself head of the Church in England; beginning of English Reformation.
1649	King Charles I executed; British Commonwealth established.
1707	Scotland and England unite by Act of Union.
1776	American colonies declare independence from Britain.
1815	Battle of Waterloo; Napoleon defeated by combined European force led by Duke of Wellington.
1914–18	Britain plays major part in World War I.
1939–44	World War II begins; Winston Churchill becomes Prime Minister of Britain; D-Day, Allied forces invade Normandy.
1945	War ends; Churchill loses in national elections.
1973	Britain joins European Community.
1999	Britain part of NATO alliance in bombing campaign over Serbian ethnic cleansing in Kosovo.

PROTECTED BY SEA

Britain's island location has protected it from invasion over the centuries. The country has experienced two definitive "invasions," by the Romans in the first century and by the Normans in 1066. Others tried their best. The Danes, or Vikings, steadily occupied eastern England during the ninth century but were later repulsed. The Anglo Saxons did not invade in the sense of armed occupation, but rather by a slow and steady immigration and integration after Roman withdrawal left chaos and uncertainty within the country. In later centuries Britain developed a powerful military and naval force, and although almost constantly at war with various European powers during the medieval period was itself never invaded. In more recent times both Napoleon and Hitler tried and failed to conquer. The English Channel and the surrounding seas have been Britain's greatest strategic blessing.

Royal pageantry at the annual Trooping of the Colour, a celebration of the Queen's "official" birthday, held in June at the Horse Guards Parade in central London

SURVIVAL GUIDE

- If visiting London, try to see one of the city's pageants, such as Trooping the Colour on Queen Elizabeth's birthday, or the Lord Mayor of London's Procession in September. For something altogether informal, join the fun at the fantastic Notting Hill Carnival at the end of August.
- In York, be careful where pedestrian zones end and traffic begins. Also watch out for pickpockets on crowded streets.
- Try Britain's various regional foods. The national dish – fish and chips – can be found almost anywhere. In London, seek out genuine East End whelks. In Cornwall, look for Cornish pasties, a true hand-held meal. In Wales, sample Caerphilly cheese; in Yorkshire, try beef and Yorkshire pudding; and don't miss steak-and-kidney pie in any English country pub. In Scotland, tackle haggis, tatties (potatoes) and neeps (turnips), or kippers (smoked herring) – all accompanied by a thick and creamy regional beer or a good strong cup of tea.
- Be prepared for dramatic changes in the weather. They say that Britain has no climate, it just has weather. The truth is that the country is caught between the extremes of northern and southern Europe, while its island nature allows vast amounts of condensed Atlantic sea water to be deposited as wind-blown rain at regular intervals. Expect rain, and if it comes, enjoy it; or, like the British do, blame the government.
- Make sure you always know what county of England you are in, and try not to confuse counties, especially not Yorkshire and Lancashire. Never refer to Welsh or Scottish people as English.
- In southwest England especially, enjoy a cream tea. This grand traditional indulgence is fresh, fluffy scones (biscuits) spread with jam and clotted cream – a delicious thick cream. The cream – lots of it – is slathered on top of the jam.
- The strength of the summer sun can deceive in Britain, often because a wind may be blowing or there are passing clouds. Guard against sunburn even if there is a cool breeze.

London

LONDON

London is one of the world's great experiences, a city that is always exhilarating, sometimes bewildering, sometimes exhausting, but never

disappointing. This financial, commercial and political center is also a year-round tourist city. The excitement is palpable. There is a feeling that something is always happening, that you are in the middle of one of a handful of truly great cities.

London

London needs to be taken very much on its terms; if you do so, you will enjoy it thoroughly. It is an expensive and a sometimes stressful place; admission prices to major attractions are steep and the crowds of fellow visitors can be huge.

There are excellent guided tours, and bus tours are an easy way to sample all London (and beyond) has to offer. Exploring independently can be hugely rewarding, however, provided you plan well. Many of London's attractions are some distance apart, and if you set out blindly determined to see everything you may end up frustrated and exhausted. Orient yourself by establishing two or three familiar focal points from which you can connect to other parts of the city.

Trafalgar Square to Big Ben

Trafalgar Square should be one of these focal points. It is the symbolic center of London; the towering pillar of Lord Nelson's column rises 172 feet into the London sky. At the base of the column are fountains and monumental guardian lions. All around the central square a constant throng of people is besieged by fluttering pigeons. Trafalgar Square is overlooked from the north by the National Gallery. At the southwest corner of the square is Admiralty Arch, through which you reach The Mall and progress toward Buckingham Palace.

Whitehall, London's "political" street, runs due south from Trafalgar Square. You'll see such landmarks as Big Ben, the clock tower of Westminster, as you walk past the Old Admiralty Building and the Horse Guards, where helmeted troopers in scarlet or blue sit immobile on their sleek, black, patient horses. Soon you pass the gates of Downing Street, where Britain's Prime Minister and Chancellor of the Exchequer have their homes. In the middle of the street is the Cenotaph, a stark and simple memorial to the dead of two world wars. Beyond the Cenotaph, Whitehall merges with Parliament Street and then meets Parliament Bridge Street. To the left is Westminster Bridge and the River Thames. To the right are the Houses of Parliament and Westminster Abbey.

Piccadilly Circus to Covent Garden

Another prime focus of central London is busy Piccadilly Circus, with the elegantly poised statue of Eros at its center. You can reach Piccadilly from Trafalgar Square by walking along Pall Mall East from in front of the National Gallery and then turning right up Haymarket. From Piccadilly you can plunge into London's world of great shopping. To the north lies Soho, the long-established heart of late-night London, slightly risqué but full of character. Here are some of the capital's best theaters, cafés and restaurants, a multitude of offbeat and specialty stores, and a resident population that maintains the area's tradition of eccentricity, style and eclectic fashion.

Soho spills eastward through the rather small Chinatown area around Gerrard Street to reach another of London's focal points, Leicester Square, lined with movie theaters and restaurants. To the east, along Cranbourne and Garrick streets, is Covent Garden, one of London's liveliest and most entertaining venues, featuring stores, cafés, restaurants and a nonstop show of street entertainers.

Beyond the Center

Once familiar with central London, you can start to venture beyond the focal points. This is where the city's excellent subway network, the Tube (London Underground), comes in handy. London buses also supply excellent service, but if you can master the subway system you can reach just about everything worth seeing. Use of the subway does mean you lose some grip of how London lies above ground; sometimes it is more rewarding if you walk to your destination, provided it isn't too far.

Head east from Trafalgar Square, by subway or on foot, along the Strand, Fleet Street and Ludgate Hill, to St. Paul's Cathedral. Then proceed east to the Tower of London and Tower Bridge.

London

Or go west from Trafalgar Square, beyond Buckingham Palace, to the great green space of Hyde Park and fashionable Knightsbridge, where you will find Harrods department store. Here, too, are three great London museums: the Victoria and Albert, the Science Museum and the Natural History Museum.

Something for Everyone

To get the most out of London during a short stay, pick and choose carefully. Visit museums in which you have a particular interest. Tackle shopping the same way. Attend a performance at the Royal National Theatre, at the South Bank Centre, or take in a West End show. Eat out in style if you can afford it, or enjoy the atmosphere at one of London's many traditional pubs.

You will find a fascinating mix of people; this is one of the most cosmopolitan cities in the world. There can be a sharp edge to Londoners, but you will never be short of advice or direction. And when in doubt, remember that London policemen are perhaps the most helpful and courteous citizens of all.

ESSENTIAL INFORMATION

TOURIST INFORMATION
• London Tourist Board: main tourist office, Victoria Station ☎ 020 7932 2000
• Heathrow Airport, Terminals 1, 2 and 3
• Selfridges department store, 400 Oxford Street
• Waterloo International railroad station
• British Visitor Centre, 12 Regent Street

URBAN TRANSPORTATION
For schedule and fare information, contact the National Rail Enquiry Bureau (☎ 0345 484950) 24 hours daily. The London Underground (subway) trains operate daily 5:30 a.m.–midnight and serve central London stations every 5–10 minutes. Lines are color-coded on an easy-to-follow map, posted in stations. Buy tickets from attended booths in station entrance halls or from machines. The symbol of the subway is a red circle crossed by a horizontal line – marked on the city map. London's red buses cover central London and suburbs. Tickets are bought on board from an attendant. For information about the subway and buses, contact the London Regional Transport Information Office (✉ Piccadilly Circus Underground Station ☎ 020 7222 1234). London's cabs (formerly black, now in various colors) can be expensive if you are traveling alone. They are metered and are available for hire when the yellow light is on. Taxis can be flagged

down in the street or ordered by calling ☎ 020 7272 5471 or 020 7272 0272.

AIRPORT INFORMATION
London is served by two major airports; Heathrow (☎ 020 8759 4321), 15 miles west of the city, and Gatwick (☎ 01293 535353), about 30 miles south. Services below operate during the day, daily 8–8; outside these times services will be less frequent. From Heathrow, the Heathrow Express nonstop train goes to Paddington Station every 15 minutes; journey time is 20 minutes. The subway's Piccadilly Line to central London departs every 5 minutes; journey time is 40 minutes. Buses from the Heathrow bus terminal operate to various city destinations about every half hour, with journey time of about an hour; the schedule (which varies periodically) is available from the bus terminal. Taxis (expensive) are available 24 hours from passenger arrival areas; time to central London is about an hour. From Gatwick, Gatwick Express and Connex trains go to London's Victoria Station every 15 to 30 minutes; journey time is 30 to 40 minutes. Thameslink trains go to King's Cross Station every 15 to 30 minutes; journey time is 50 minutes. Flightline buses travel to London's Victoria Coach Station hourly; journey time is 1 hour 15 minutes. Taxis operate from taxi stands at all of the London bus and railroad stations.

CLIMATE – average highs and lows for the month

JAN.	FEB.	MAR.	APR.	MAY	JUN.	JUL.	AUG.	SEP.	OCT.	NOV.	DEC.
6°C	6°C	10°C	13°C	16°C	20°C	21°C	21°C	18°C	14°C	10°C	7°C
43°F	43°F	50°F	55°F	61°F	68°F	70°F	70°F	64°F	57°F	50°F	45°F
2°C	2°C	3°C	5°C	8°C	11°C	13°C	13°C	11°C	7°C	5°C	3°C
36°F	36°F	37°F	41°F	46°F	52°F	55°F	55°F	52°F	45°F	41°F	37°F

The Houses of Parliament, a spectacular example of 19th-century Victorian Gothic Revival architecture

CITY SIGHTS

Key to symbols
✚ map coordinates refer to the London map on page 86–87; sights below are highlighted in yellow on the map.
✉ address or location ☎ telephone number
🕐 opening times 🚌 nearest bus route
Ⓜ nearest subway 🍴 restaurant on site or nearby
🎟 admission charge: $$$ more than £6, $$ £2–£6, $ less than £2

BRITISH MUSEUM

✚ D4 ✉ Great Russell Street ☎ 020 7636 1555
🕐 Mon.–Sat. 10–5, Sun. 2:30–6 🍴 Museum restaurant Ⓜ Russell Square 🚌 7, 10, 14 🎟 Free
The British Museum is a treasure house of global artifacts, many of them the riches of Britain's imperial past. There are more than 4 million exhibits, including the Elgin Marbles, magnificent fifth-century BC relief sculptures taken from the Parthenon in 1801 by Thomas Bruce, the Earl of Elgin, and still the subject of Greek demands for their return. Other highlights are the Rosetta Stone, key to the understanding of Egyptian hieroglyphics; the 2,000-year-old Lindow Man, whose preserved body was found in an English peat bog; the Mildenhall Treasure, a collection of Roman silver; and Anglo Saxon artifacts from a ship burial. A visit to the museum can be exhausting; be selective. Don't miss the Egyptian Hall, the finest collection outside Egypt itself.

HOUSES OF PARLIAMENT

✚ D2 ✉ St. Margaret Street ☎ 020 7219 4272 (House of Commons), 0207 219 3107 (House of Lords)
Ⓜ Westminster 🚌 3, 11, 12, 88, 159 🎟 Free
The Houses of Parliament, also known as the Palace of Westminster, are mainly to be admired from the outside. The present building replaced an older palace dating from the 11th century. Most of this earlier building burned down in 1834. The present structure's linear form is doubly enhanced by the vertical thrust of Victoria Tower and the clock tower known as Big Ben. Inside access is limited because of security reasons and because it is the workplace of British government. You can attend debates in the House of Lords and House of Commons on a first-come-first-served basis in a line for the "Stranger's Galleries" (public galleries) outside St. Stephen's Porch gate. Embassies can help arrange a guided tour of the Houses of Parliament, but plans should be made well in advance.

IMPERIAL WAR MUSEUM

✚ E2 ✉ Lambeth Road ☎ 020 7416 5000 🕐 Daily 10–6 🍴 Museum restaurant Ⓜ Elephant and Castle or Lambeth North 🚌 3, 15, 59 🎟 $$
Two vast guns stand in front of the handsome Ionic portico of the Imperial War Museum, where the story of 20th-century conflict is documented. There is a cruel irony in the fact that the museum

London

was formerly the infamous Bethlehem Royal Hospital, notorious asylum for the insane, and known as "Bedlam," a word well-suited to the horror of war. There are more than 50 historic aircraft tanks, and other field weapons on display, but the most fascinating exhibits involve the human element through re-creations of World War I trench warfare and the London Blitz. The cruel lessons of conflict are not shirked, especially in the section dealing with the liberation of Belsen concentration camp.

KEW GARDENS

🕂 Off the map 🖂 Kew Road, Richmond ☎ 020 8940 1171 🕓 Daily 9:30–7:30; closing time may vary seasonally 🍽 Restaurant in gardens 🚇 Kew Gardens 💷 $$$

The Royal Botanical Gardens at Kew and their location away from central London are a delightful antidote for those suffering from city fatigue. The gardens date from 1759 and represent one of the finest collections of plants in the world, all contained within a 300-acre site. Wander at will through the world's hugely varied climatic environments. The vast Temperate House contains plants from every continent, and the architectural wonders are just as fascinating. Highlights include the Palm House, a billowing pavilion in glass and wrought iron that is a classic expression of creative 19th-century design. Scattered throughout the gardens are such interesting buildings as a 10-story pagoda and Kew Palace (closed until 2001), the latter built in 1631 by a Dutch merchant and used as a nursery for George II's children, and a superb example of classical brickwork.

LONDON ZOO

🕂 Off the map 🖂 Regent's Park ☎ 020 7722 3333 🕓 Daily 10–5:30, Mar.–Oct.; 10–4, rest of year 🍽 Restaurant at zoo 🚇 Camden Town or Regent's Park 🚌 13, 274 💷 $$$

London Zoo is irresistible for children but a treat for all. In keeping with contemporary attitudes, the zoo has a strong conservation ethic and is working hard toward transforming the captive-

animal emphasis of old-fashioned zoos. There are daily events and programs, including feeding time, "Animals in Action" and the Childrens' Enclosure, where kids can handle docile animals. The spectacular Snowdon Aviary is a highlight, as is the Penguin Pool with its spiral ramp.

MADAME TUSSAUD'S AND THE PLANETARIUM

Madame Tussaud's 🕂 B4 🖂 Marylebone Road ☎ 020 7935 6861 🕓 Mon.–Fri. 10–5:30, Sat.–Sun. 9:30–5:30 🍽 Café 🚇 Baker Street 🚌 2a, 2b, 13, 74, 274 💷 $$$. Combination ticket available 🚹 Earlier opening Jul.–Aug. Book ahead by credit card for a timed entrance to avoid the sometimes hour-long line.
Planetarium 🕓 Mon.–Fri. 12:20–5, Sat.–Sun. and school vacations 10:20–5 🚇 Baker Street 🚌 Bus 2a, 2b, 13, 74, 274 💷 $$

A visit to Madame Tussaud's celebrated wax model museum could be described as blatant people-watching. The experience is expensive, but where else can you peer up the nose of a world leader or make faces at the rich and famous? Just about everyone is here: royalty, presidents, politicians, celebrities, stars, heroes and villains. You can tell those with charisma and those without, even in wax.

Exhibits such as The Garden Party and The Grand Hall cast new light on the phrase "rubbing shoulders with the rich and famous." The Chamber of Horrors has hideous charm, although perhaps not for the very young; the murderous are still menacing, even in effigy, and you'll watch them uneasily out of the corner of your eye. Other attractions include a quick trip through London history as glimpsed from a miniature city taxicab. The adjacent planetarium provides a relaxing half-hour's mocked-up stargazing and several space exhibits.

MILLENNIUM DOME

🕂 Off the map 🖂 Greenwich ☎ 0870 606 2000 🕓 Open daily. Admission pre-booked only 🍽 Several restaurants 🚇 North Greenwich 🚌 108

The construction of the huge geodesic Millennium Dome, 164 feet high and half a mile in circumference, was attended by the inevitable British mix of disapproval by many and ecstatic support by those contributing to the £758 million estimated cost. The dome is located on the south bank of the River Thames and dominates riverside Greenwich. It is supported by tall steel masts. The daring futuristic design was by the architect Richard Rogers, who designed Lloyd's Building in London and the Pompidou Centre in Paris. The interior contains themed sections filled with computerized features and exhibitions. Even the new Jubilee Line subway stop for the Millennium Dome, at North Greenwich, is an experience in its own right.

MUSEUM OF LONDON

✚ E4 ✉ London Wall ☎ 020 7600 3699
🕐 Tue.–Sat. 10–5:50, Sun. noon–5:50 🍴 Restaurant at museum 🚇 Barbican or St. Paul's 🚌 4, 6, 11
💷 $$ Entrance ticket valid for free return within three months 🎟 Free admission after 4:30; last admission at 5:30

To really get a handle on London and its utterly fascinating history, visit this rewarding and enjoyable museum. The story of the city from prehistoric times to the present is told through set piece galleries focusing on important periods. The Roman section is superb; its reconstructed rooms, one with a fabulous mosaic floor, and its sculptures are particularly special highlights. Another highlight is the Lord Mayor's State Coach from the 1750s, a glittering golden extravaganza that is still used during the Lord Mayor's Show each November. Numerous displays, special exhibitions, reconstructions and events add to this special London experience.

NATIONAL GALLERY

✚ D3 ✉ Trafalgar Square ☎ 020 7747 2885
🕐 Daily 10–6 (also Wed. 6–9) 🍴 Restaurant in gallery 🚇 Charing Cross or Leicester Square 🚌 3, 6, 9, 11, 12, 24, 53, 109, 159 💷 Free; donation requested 🎟 The National Gallery stages temporary exhibitions of major artists

London's National Gallery is astounding. It contains one of the finest collections of Western art in the world. You may find most of the world gathered here on a busy day, but "the National" seems able to absorb the crowds. The collection is displayed chronologically in four wings: the Sainsbury Wing (1260–1510), West Wing (1510–1600), North Wing (1600–1700) and East Wing (1700–1900). You will need a floor plan to navigate. Portable CD players are available; the Gallery Guide Soundtrack provides guidance and commentaries There are also regular guided tours.

There are so many dazzling highlights at the National that it is difficult to select the best. Don't miss the Leonardo da Vinci cartoon *The Virgin and Child with St. Anne and John the Baptist;* da Vinci's accompanying *Virgin of the Rocks;* Sandro Botticelli's *Venus and Mars;* Titian's vivid and agile *Bacchus and Ariadne;* Jan van Eyck's *The Arnolfini Marriage;* Diego Velazquez's sensual *The Toilet of Venus;* Rembrandt's haunting *Self Portrait;* and Vincent Van Gogh's *Sunflowers.* The list of great works is endless.

The best moments can be unexpected and breathtaking, such as when you find yourself in the North Wing's octagonal Room 15, the Pierre Bergé Room, where there are glorious works by the great landscape painters Claude Lorrain and J. M. W. Turner. And where else would you find a room such as Room 34, the Sackler Room, where you are surrounded by the works of such English masters as Thomas Gainsborough, Sir Joshua Reynolds and John Constable?

NATIONAL MARITIME MUSEUM

✚ Off the map ✉ Greenwich Park ☎ 020 8312 6565 🕐 Daily 10–5 🍴 Café in museum
🚇 Docklands Light Railway to Island Gardens; pedestrian tunnel leads to museum 🚢 River boat to Greenwich Pier from Westminster, Charing Cross or Tower Piers 💷 $$

A visit to the National Maritime Museum also gets you away from central London and offers salty insight into one reason why Britain became great, through the maritime expertise of an emphatically island nation. This is the world's largest

COVENT GARDEN THROUGH TIME

London is an ever-changing city and, over the years, has evolved from surprising origins. A classic example of London's fascinating development is Covent Garden, today a lively focus of entertainment, dining and shopping. The area gets its name from being the medieval-era "Garden of the Convent," when vegetables were grown for the kitchens at Westminster Abbey.

During the 17th century it was laid out as the finest square in London, complete with the Church of St. Paul and arcaded houses. The architect was Inigo Jones, who planned it in Italianate style, with the square known as the piazza. Then the owner of Covent Garden, the Earl of Bedford, decided to hold a market in the square. Commerce overcame culture; some of the buildings were erected – first the older fruit and vegetable market and then the floral market. The Opera House was added later.

In 1974 the market moved to new premises and the piazza market halls were renovated and filled with stores, cafés and restaurants that have transformed the old "Garden of the Convent" into a major leisure area.

Covent Garden Today

From Covent Garden subway station, turn right and walk southeast, past Evelyn and Crabtree (renowned for bath oils and soaps) on your right, into the heart of Covent Garden. This is an excellent place to browse and wander at your leisure. There are fashion stores for all tastes. These line the cobbled piazza tastefully blending in with the Italianate architecture and elegant columns. Under the glass-and-iron roof of the renovated market building set in the middle of the square, you'll find craft stalls selling arts, jewelry and clothing. There is a small branch of the much-loved London toy shop, Hamleys, on the northern side of the central market. In front of St. Paul's Church, on the western side of the market, street performers often entertain the crowds with comedy or magic tricks. It all adds to the exciting bustle of this area.

If you walk back toward the Covent Garden subway and head two blocks north, you will find yourself in the maze of small streets that intersect with Neal Street. Neal's Yard has a bohemian air, and there are some good places to buy vegetarian food and light meals. Neal's Yard Dairy sells some of the best cheese in the country – it's all British or Irish made.

Back to traditional roots – selling flowers in the "Garden of the Convent"

Classical facade of St. Paul's Cathedral

Galleries. There are a reputed 50 million objects on display, from the tiniest of preserved insects to a reconstructed blue whale. The Dinosaur Gallery features an animatronic tableau of three extremely vicious deinonychi taking noisy bites out of a floored tenontosaurus. This is not quite Disney, but the main exhibits tell the dinosaur story through a clever mix of science and entertaining effect. The museum's other section, the Earth Galleries, deals with the world's geology and is every bit as fascinating.

ST. PAUL'S CATHEDRAL

✠ E3 ✉ Ludgate Hill ☎ 020 7246 8348
🕐 Mon.–Sat. 8:30–4 🍴 Restaurant at Cathedral
🚇 St. Paul's or Mansion House 🚌 11, 15, 23
🎟 Cathedral and crypt $$, if Galleries included $$$

St. Paul's Cathedral is one of Sir Christopher Wren's greatest achievements, but its awkward site, now crowded by indifferent buildings, robs it of some grandeur. However, the stupendous facade – with twin towers and baroque elements – and the crowning glory of its magnificent dome are still breathtaking. The interior is bright and airy and full of stately monuments, memorials and statues. You can descend to the crypt or ascend heavenward up 530 steps, first to the famous Whispering Gallery, where you can whisper your thoughts for everyone else to hear, and then to the Golden Gallery, from which there are superb views over London.

maritime museum. The special Nelson Gallery celebrates the great admiral, with William Turner's painting *The Battle of Trafalgar* adding drama. In the glass-roofed Neptune Court are preserved 17th-century river barges and the gilded rococo extravaganza of a state barge, created for Frederick, Prince of Wales in 1732. Children will delight in Waterworld, where the marine environment is imaginatively explained, and they will be even more absorbed by the All Hands Gallery, where they can try their hand at things nautical.

NATURAL HISTORY MUSEUM

✠ A2 ✉ Cromwell Road (Life Galleries entrance),
Exhibition Road (Earth Galleries entrance) ☎ 020
7938 9123 🕐 Mon.–Sat. 10–5:50, Sun. 11–5:50
🍴 Café in museum 🚇 South Kensington 🚌 14, 74
🎟 $$; Mon.–Fri. free after 4:30, Sat.–Sun. free after 5

The Natural History Museum is another of London's experiences that shouldn't be missed, and is a great favorite with children. Be prepared, though, for much unrestrained excitement. It's housed in a self-consciously Gothic revival building of great style, and there may be times when you feel you have stumbled into someone's rather grand house as you roam the rooms and interconnecting halls of the Life

SCIENCE MUSEUM

✠ A2 ✉ Exhibition Road ☎ 020 7938 8008, 020
7938 8080 or 020 7938 8000 🕐 Daily 10–6 🍴 Café in
museum 🚇 South Kensington 🚌 14, 74 🎟 $$; if
Science of Sport included $$$

The vast collection of the Science Museum is of world importance. Every aspect of science and technology is covered, and you will find everything from atoms to the *Apollo 10* command module. The museum's official guidebook is a handy purchase that will help you find your way around the seven floors. On display are George Stephenson's early locomotive, the *Rocket*, and Charles

The Tower of London recalls some of the most dramatic times of British history over 900 years

Babbage's enormous prototype computer. The huge Flight Galleries contain ranks of aircraft, and the East Hall's great steam engines from the Industrial Revolution hiss and revolve like iron behemoths. Children and adults can get close to science through the hands-on element of many exhibits. Check to see if there are any special events or demonstrations on the day you visit.

TATE GALLERY

Tate Gallery of British Art ✚ D1 ✉ Millbank
☎ 020 7887 8000 🕐 Mon.–Sat. 10–5:50, Sun. 2–5:50
🍴 Café and restaurant at galleries 🚇 Pimlico
🚌 2b, 36, 53, 88 💷 Free; special exhibitions $$
Tate Gallery of Modern Art ✚ E3 ✉ Bankside
☎ 020 7401 7271 🚇 Blackfriars or Southwark
🚌 17, 149, 344 ℹ️ Gallery due to open May 2000

London's exciting Tate Gallery is due to be reincarnated in 2000 in a dual form. The original Tate Gallery, at Millbank south of Westminster Abbey, has become the Tate Gallery of British Art and exhibits major British works from the 16th through 20th centuries, including paintings by John Constable, Sir Joshua Reynolds, William Hogarth and J. M. W. Turner. The Tate's outstanding collection of modern art will be housed in the new Tate Gallery of Modern Art, in the refurbished Bankside Power Station on the south bank of the River Thames, opposite St. Paul's Cathedral. It is due to open in May 2000. The collection is international and includes works by major figures such as Salvador Dali, Pablo Picasso, Henri Matisse, Edvard Munch, Piet Mondrian, Jackson Pollock, Andy Warhol and Roy Lichtenstein. Adventurous and often controversial conceptual works and installations also feature in the Tate Gallery of Modern Art's exhibitions.

You can approach the Bankside Tate in style from north of the river. A millennium project, a pedestrian-only bridge complete with sculptures, slices straight across the Thames between Peter's Hill, below St. Paul's, and Bankside, creating a convenient link between north and south London.

TOWER OF LONDON

✚ F3 ✉ Tower Hill ☎ 020 7709 0765
🕐 Mon.–Sat. 9–5, Sun. 10–5, Mar.–Oct.; Tue.–Sat. 9–4, Sun.–Mon. 10–4, rest of year 🍴 Café at tower
🚇 Tower Hill 🚌 15, 25 💷 $$$

The Tower of London is a major national attraction, and there are crowds of visitors most of the year. You will never be alone, and you may find yourself being marched

London

The simple memorial to World War I victims lies beneath the soaring arches of Westminster Abbey

through some of the sections, especially the Crown Jewels exhibition, where moving walkways do the walking for you. The tower is an astonishing place all the same, steeped in Britain's remarkable history. It's the place where the nation's most interesting, daring, difficult and damned personalities ended up, as prisoners or as reluctant "guests"; or, like Henry VIII's wives Anne Boleyn and Catherine Howard, on a final forlorn trip to the executioner's block. Tours conducted by the famous Yeoman Warders, or "Beefeaters," give an excellent introduction, after which you can wander at will to ponder the Bloody Tower, Traitors' Gate, the Tower Ravens and the execution site at Tower Green.

VICTORIA AND ALBERT MUSEUM

✛ A2 ✉ Cromwell Road ☎ 020 7938 8500 or 0207 938 8349 (recorded information) 🕓 Tue.–Sun. 10–5:45 (also Wed. 6:30–9:30), Mon. noon–5:45 🍴 Cafés and restaurant at museum 🚇 South Kensington 🚌 14, 74 💷 $$

The "V&A," as it is affectionately known, is recognized as being the world's greatest repository of applied and decorative art, containing a ravishing collection of jewelry, silverware, ceramics, textiles, dress, furniture, sculpture, paintings and photographs from all over the world. Decide what you want to see amid the 7 miles of corridors, galleries and stairs.

This is a genuine journey of discovery; the European Galleries alone are a day's work. The Sculpture Galleries; the Asian and Near Eastern Galleries; the Ceramics, Glass and Jewellery Galleries; and the superb art collection are all worth seeing. Take a guided tour for a quick and informative overview; otherwise arm yourself with floor plans, obtainable from the information desks, and launch forth unforgettably.

WESTMINSTER ABBEY

✛ D2 ✉ Dean's Yard ☎ 020 7222 5152 🕓 Mon.–Fri. 9–4:45 (also Wed. 6–7:45), Sat. 9–2:45; last admission 1 hour before closing. Nave and cloisters: Daily 8–6. Abbey Museum: Daily 10:30–4. 🚇 Westminster or St. James' Park 🚌 3, 11, 12, 88, 159 💷 $$

Like the Tower of London, Westminster Abbey resonates with British history. It has been the ceremonial site of every British coronation, from William the Conqueror in 1066 to Queen Elizabeth II in 1953. Monarchs buried here include Henry VII, Elizabeth I and Mary, Queen of Scots. The abbey is full of monuments and memorials to famous people.

It is hugely popular with visitors, so don't expect to find solitude here. Yet there is also serenity within the venerable walls, and the architectural features are thrilling. The present abbey dates, in part, from the 13th century and is a powerful expression of English Gothic style, with distinctive French elements.

The abbey's most sublime Gothic touches are found in Henry VII's chapel; it is designed in Late Perpendicular style, a style of airy elegance that represented Gothic at its finest. Tiered sculptures line the walls, and the lofty roof is hung with exquisite fan vaulting. The abbey's monuments include the haunting Tomb of the Unknown Warrior, a commemoration of the hundreds of thousands of British servicemen killed in World War I. In the south transept is Poets' Corner, resting place of Chaucer, Robert Browning and Alfred Tennyson, among others. Also worth seeing are the abbey's Cloisters, the Chapter House and the Abbey Museum.

Looking from St. James' Park to the exuberant Victoria Monument and Buckingham Palace beyond

A ROYAL STROLL

Royal London begins at Admiralty Arch, at the southwest corner of Trafalgar Square. The arch dates from 1911 and was erected as part of a general celebration of Queen Victoria's life and reign. Beyond the arch is The Mall, a broad open avenue that runs southwest, directly toward Buckingham Palace. It was first laid out by Charles II in the 1660s as part of St. James' Park. It is open to traffic, but as soon as you pass beneath Admiralty Arch the city's character becomes less frantic.

Keep to the sidewalk on the left of the avenue and you'll soon pass a statue of the seafarer Captain James Cook. St. James' Park spreads out to the left – a great sweep of open lawns, trees and gardens with a lake at its heart. The right (north) side of The Mall is lined with stately buildings. First is Carlton House Terrace, broken halfway by the Duke of York's Steps that lead up to the Duke of York's Column. At St. James' Palace, sentries guard the Tudor Tower. Next to the palace is Clarence House, the London home of the Queen Mother.

On your way to the large open area in front of Buckingham Palace is Lancaster House (a building now used by the government). In front of the palace is the spectacular bronze and marble Victoria Monument, erected in 1911 constructed with more than 2,300 tons of marble. A marble Queen Victoria stares frostily from the east side. The exuberant bronze winged Victory crowns the monument.

Beyond the monument and behind a barricade of railings and gates stands Buckingham Palace, a heavy-handed building rather than a fairy-tale one. The "royal standard" (the Queen's flag) flies when the Queen is in residence. The Changing of the Guard takes place daily at noon from April through June, and on alternate days the rest of the year (weather permitting). The crowds pressed against the railing can be large, and the experience may well rob you of a more relaxed stroll down The Mall.

Eighteen of Buckingham Palace's state rooms are open from the second week in August until the end of September, when the royal family are not in residence. The Royal Mews are worth a visit for their state carriages and splendid horses. For the walk route, see the city map on pages 86–87.

Horse Guards ride along The Mall

Edinburgh

EDINBURGH

Edinburgh is Scotland in microcosm.
In this vibrant capital city, buildings do
not overpower the spectacular
landscape of hills and crags that march
across the southeastern horizon. Yet
Edinburgh's buildings – from the old
houses of the Royal Mile to the elegant
Georgian terraces and crescents of the
New Town – are outstanding
complements to the city's natural
setting. Few other capitals seem to
reflect the history and culture of their
country so potently.

Edinburgh's famous castle sits high
on a craggy promontory, Castle Rock,
made inaccessible on three sides by
steep cliffs and with a long descending
ridge on its fourth side. The city's
layout is linear, a pattern set by Castle
Rock and Castle Ridge, down which
the Royal Mile descends to the Palace
of Holyroodhouse. North of the Royal
Mile lies a shallow valley once covered
by swampy Nor' Loch, and now
occupied by the lovely Princes Street
Gardens, with Waverley Station, the
city's main railroad station, at their
eastern end. Above the gardens and to
the north is Edinburgh's main

thoroughfare, Princes Street, its south
side uncluttered by buildings and thus
serving as a splendid place from which
to view the castle and Old Edinburgh.

First Impressions

Most visitors arrive by train at Waverley
Station. From the station you emerge
onto Waverley Bridge and get an

Greyfriars Bobby

This sky terrier's devotion to his dead master is
enshrined in Edinburgh folklore. The famous
Greyfriars Bobby was a trained police dog who worked
with his master, Constable John Gray, guarding livestock at
Edinburgh's city market, the Grassmarket, during the
1850s. When Gray died at age 45 he was buried in
Greyfriars churchyard, and his devoted terrier took up what
became a 14-year vigil by his grave. Bobby was cared for and
beloved by everyone in the neighborhood. Just inside the
church gate is Bobby's Bothy, a gift kiosk. Nearby, a
statue of Greyfriars Bobby stands at the junction of
Candlemaker Row and the George IV Bridge.

Edinburgh

immediate first impression of the city's visual drama. The castle and the dark soaring back walls of the buildings that enclose the Royal Mile rise to the south like extensions of the cliffs of Castle Rock. To the north is Princes Street. Here, the Sir Walter Scott Monument, a towering Gothic steeple, dominates one view; the bulk of the North British Hotel, itself castle-like, dominates the other. At night all of these buildings are spectacularly illuminated.

From Waverley Bridge you can take an instant Guide Friday bus tour that will introduce you to the city. Details about city transportation are available from the Edinburgh Traveline office, which is diagonally opposite the south end of Waverley Bridge, at the corner of Cockburn and Market streets. Next door is the Edinburgh Festival Centre. You can also find out about various other guided tours from the Edinburgh tourist information center on Princes Street, only a minute or so from Waverley Station. They include historical walking tours and highly entertaining Ghost or Witchery tours that take you through the Old Town's maze of historic lanes and courtyards.

Two Edinburghs

Exploring the city on your own is straightforward. Old Edinburgh is the southern part, encompassed by the castle and the Royal Mile; beyond them are the areas of Southside, the Grassmarket and Canongate. To the south of the Royal Mile you will find the Royal Museum, the new Museum of Scotland (see page 102) and the Festival Theatre, a venue presenting fine drama and opera. Edinburgh Castle and the Royal Mile are Old Edinburgh's main attractions. You can easily spend an entire day here, and amid the souvenir shops and tourist spots there is a potent sense of history embodied by the splendid clutter of tall old sandstone buildings. Also take time

Edinburgh

for a walk in Holyrood Park, a green world of spectacular craggy hills, lochs and glens that is a genuine slice of Highland Scotland.

North of Waverley Bridge is Edinburgh's New Town, where Old Edinburgh expanded during the 18th century as part of a typically Georgian exercise in town planning. Above Princes Street is George Street, with handsome Charlotte Square and St. Andrew Square at either end. The elegance and unity of Georgian architecture – an exhilerating contrast to the equally splendid Royal Mile – can be appreciated at such locations as Queen Street Gardens, the Royal Circus (a circular residential street), Great King Street and Drummond Place – all north of George Street – as well as around Moray Place, west of Queen Street Gardens.

Life in Edinburgh

George Street and Princes Street, and the short connecting streets between them, are Edinburgh's main shopping streets. On Princes Street you will find an Edinburgh institution, Jenners, a department store that sells luxury items and has a wonderful food hall. This street also has branches of House of Fraser, Debenhams, Next and Gap.

Edinburgh is crowded during the summer, but the cultural feast of the Edinburgh Festival, in late August and early September, is well worth taking in. There are also worthy alternatives outside the festival season – modern Scottish drama at the Traverse Theatre, or musical performances at Usher Hall.

Stylish Edinburgh restaurants offer distinctive Scottish dishes like wild salmon, Aberdeen Angus beef, or game such as grouse. Local residents are friendly and down to earth, always willing to help visitors. Traditional Scottish reticence is replaced here by a style that reflects sophistication without pretension, and by pride in the city's internationalism. And with a historic return to the Royal Mile by Scotland's recently formed governing body, the Scottish Parliament, Edinburgh enters a new millennium with renewed stature and optimism.

ESSENTIAL INFORMATION

TOURIST INFORMATION
• 3 Princes Street ☎ 0131 473 3800
• Turnhouse Airport tourist office, walk-in only.

URBAN TRANSPORTATION
The main train station for visitors is Waverley Station on Princes Street, (☎ 0131 556 2451). A good bus network services Edinburgh. For information contact Traveline (✉ 2 Cockburn Street ☎ 0800 23 23 23 or 0131 225 3858). Taxis can be hailed on

the street; there are also stands at Waverley Station and on Waverley Bridge. For information call Central Radio Taxis ☎ 0131 229 2468 or City Cabs ☎ 0131 228 1211.

AIRPORT INFORMATION
Edinburgh's international airport, Turnhouse, is 7 miles west of the city center. There's a tourist office in the main concourse, and buses run regularly to and from Waverley Station. Taxis also serve the airport. For airport information call ☎ 0131 333 1000.

CLIMATE – average highs and lows for the month

JAN.	FEB.	MAR.	APR.	MAY	JUN.	JUL.	AUG.	SEP.	OCT.	NOV.	DEC.
5°C	6°C	7°C	10°C	13°C	16°C	18°C	17°C	15°C	12°C	9°C	6°C
42°F	43°F	45°F	50°F	55°F	61°F	64°F	63°F	59°F	54°F	48°F	43°F
1°C	1°C	2°C	4°C	6°C	9°C	11°C	11°C	9°C	6°C	4°C	2°C
34°F	34°F	36°F	39°F	43°F	48°F	52°F	52°F	48°F	43°F	39°F	36°F

Dramatically perched on a volcanic crag, Edinburgh Castle dates back to the 12th century

CITY SIGHTS

Key to symbols

⊞ map coordinates refer to the Edinburgh map on page 98–99; sights below are highlighted in yellow on the map.

⊠ address or location ☎ telephone number

⊙ opening times 🚌 nearest bus route

🍴 restaurant on site or nearby

🎟 admission charge: $$$ more than £6, $$ £2–£6, $ less than £2

CALTON HILL

Calton Hill ⊞ D2–D3 ⊠ Waterloo Place 🚌 26, X85, X86 🎟 Free

Nelson Monument ⊙ Mon. 1–6, Tue.–Sat. 10–6, Apr.–Sep.; Mon.–Sat. 10–3, rest of year 🎟 $

Calton Hill, at the east end of Princes Street, is crowned with neoclassical buildings that have earned Edinburgh the nickname "The Athens of the North," but their dark stonework hardly matches the bare, bright brilliance of the Parthenon or the Temple of the Winds. There are great views of Princes Street, Edinburgh Castle and Arthur's Seat from this hilltop, as well as distant panoramas of the Forth river and the hills beyond. You can also climb the 143 steps of the tall monument to Admiral Horatio Nelson for an even

better view from its top. Note: This site should be avoided at dusk and after dark.

EDINBURGH CASTLE

⊞ B1–C1 ⊠ Castlehill ☎ 0131 225 9846 ⊙ Daily 9:30–6, Apr.–Sep.; 9:30–5, rest of year 🍴 Restaurant 🚌 1, 6 🎟 $$$ 🎫 Last admission 45 minutes before closing

You can tackle Scotland's most visited attraction in several ways. There are official guided tours, which are captive experiences rather than captivating ones, but are nonetheless entertaining and informative. A self-guiding audio tour is a good option that helps focus the mind amid inevitable crowds. Brace yourself for the One O' Clock Gun, a 25-pounder that blasts off a single blank charge from the Half Moon battery at 1 p.m. daily, except Sunday. Castle highlights are the 12th-century St. Margaret's Chapel; the Stone of Scone; the Vaults, where the mighty siege gun, Mons Meg, stands in grim splendor like some huge black beast; and the Great Hall, with its glorious hammer beam roof and masses of weaponry. The Honours of Scotland exhibition is an evocative journey through history that culminates with a display of Scotland's luminous Crown Jewels.

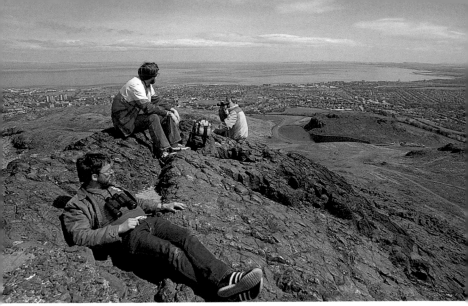

Hikers enjoy the view of Edinburgh from Arthur's Seat in Holyrood Park, 822 feet above the city

GEORGIAN HOUSE

⊞ B2   ✉ Charlotte Square   ☎ 0131 225 2160
🕐 Mon.–Sat. 10–5, Sun. 2–5, Apr.–Oct.   🚌 124
💷 $$ ℹ Last admission 30 minutes before closing

The Georgian House is the showplace of New Town's Charlotte Square and one of the most prestigious addresses in Scotland. Once home of the chief of the Lamont clan, the upper floor of the building is the present residence of the Moderator of the General Assembly, the leader of the Church of Scotland. The lower floors are open to the public and are full of delectable furnishings and fine paintings. The basement houses the original wine cellar and kitchen.

HOLYROOD PARK

⊞ E1   🚌 1, 6   💷 Free

Few cities are blessed with such a marvelous open space as Holyrood Park, or Queen's Park, as it is also known. The park is dominated by the dramatic Salisbury Crags and by Arthur's Seat, a high, rounded hill. You can enter the park from the bottom of the Royal Mile (see pages 104–105), just beyond Holyrood House. The park's high ground is encircled by a public road, the Queen's Drive, but the area is better enjoyed on foot. A broad, slanting path slices up the slopes below Salisbury Crags. It takes you high above the city, and the views are outstanding. Arthur's Seat can also be climbed, but it is a challenging hike. You can keep to the low ground of the park and still enjoy the splendid sights.

MUSEUM OF SCOTLAND AND ROYAL MUSEUM OF SCOTLAND

⊞ D1   ✉ Chambers Street   ☎ Royal Museum: 0131 225 7534; Museum of Scotland: 0131 247 4219, 0131 247 4422   🕐 Mon.–Sat. 10–5 (also Tue. 5–8), Sun. noon–5   🍴 Café and restaurant at museums   🚌 40, 41, 42, 46   💷 $$ (for access to both museums)

The story of Scotland from ancient times to the 20th century is vividly presented in these adjoining museums. The long-established Royal Museum is a splendid 19th-century building enclosing a vast space framed by elegant ironwork, with galleries rising through several floors. Here are traditional displays covering the natural world, science and industry and the decorative arts. The Royal Museum has been merged with an adventurous new building, the Museum of Scotland, a dramatic modern design in golden stone. The new complex contains several levels, each displaying a particular era of Scotland's history. Ask at the information desk for floor plans and advice on how to find your way around the galleries, or take a guided tour.

NATIONAL GALLERIES OF SCOTLAND

➕ C2 ✉ The Mound ☎ 0131 624 6200
🕐 Mon.–Sat. 10–5, Sun. 2–5 🚌 3, 4, 11, 17, 21, 26, 33
💷 Free; special exhibitions $

The National Galleries is a large, 19th-century neoclassical building with a good selection from all periods, including a splendid altarpiece, the *Trinity Panels*, by Hugo van der Goes, and the seductive *Venus Anadyomene*, by Titian. Most of the major names in 17th-century European art are represented; there are some fine landscapes by Claude Lorrain in Room 4, and Nicholas Poussin's *Seven Sacraments* is on view in the Octagon Room. In Room 11 there is a powerful work by Frederick Edwin Church, *Niagara Falls from the American Side*. Scottish painting is well represented by Gavin Hamilton and Allan Ramsay. Look for *Edinburgh Castle and the Nor' Loch,* by Alexander Nasmyth, for some idea of what Old Edinburgh looked like before the Nor' Loch was drained and supplanted by Princes Street Gardens. Sir Henry Raeburn's *The Rev. Robert Walker Skating on Duddingston Loch* and Sir George Harvey's *The Curlers* are wonderfully lively and very typical Scottish narrative works.

PALACE OF HOLYROODHOUSE

➕ E2 ✉ Canongate ☎ 0131 556 1096 🕐 Daily 9:30–5:15, Apr.–Oct.; 9:30–3:45, rest of year ℹ Closed two weeks in mid-May and first two weeks in July for state functions 💷 $$$

Ancient Holyroodhouse was part of the Abbey of Holyrood, but was built in its present form as a royal palace for King Charles II. The severe neoclassicism of the courtyard block reflects the distinctly English fashion of the time; nevertheless it exudes Scottish history. The State Apartments of Charles' palace are luxurious and grand, crammed with artifacts and paintings elegantly displayed beneath superb stucco ceilings. Deep in the Historical Apartments is the bedchamber of Mary, Queen of Scots and the adjoining closet where, in 1566, her secretary and confidante, David Rizzio, was stabbed to death by associates of the Queen's delinquent husband, Lord Darnley. You can view the palace by guided tour only, but you'll be in the hands of highly entertaining and knowledgeable staff.

ROYAL BOTANIC GARDEN

➕ Off the map ✉ Inverleith Row ☎ 0131 552 7171
🕐 Daily 10–8, May–Aug.; 10–6, Mar.–Apr. and Sep.–Oct.;10–4, rest of year 🍴 Café 🚌 23, 27
💷 Free

The Royal Botanic Garden is just north of the New Town. Its showpiece features are the rhododendrons, which are at their colorful best from late April to early June. Other attractions are the Glasshouse Experience, where orchids, palms and other exotics flourish in defiance of Scotland's less than tropical climate; a Chinese Garden; and a decidedly Scottish heather garden.

ST. GILES CATHEDRAL

➕ D2 ✉ Parliament Square ☎ 0131 225 9442 (for guided tours) 🕐 Mon.–Fri. 9–7, Sat.–Sun. 9–5, Easter–Sep. 30; Mon.–Sat. 9–5, Sun. 1–5, rest of year 🍴 Restaurant in crypt 🚌 Bus 1, 6 💷 Free; donation requested for viewing Thistle Chapel

St. Giles Cathedral (or the High Kirk of St. Giles) is the seat of Scotland's Presbyterian religion and a powerful feature of the Royal Mile (see pages 104–105). The Kirk is an uneasy mix of medieval Gothic and Georgian Gothic, the latter grafted on in the early 19th century; the interior reflects an enthusiastic Victorian restoration. There are some superb external features, including the 19th-century west door and the late medieval tower and spire, a dramatic sight on Edinburgh's skyline. Inside, St. Giles has many fine features and memorials. A 20th-century addition is the Thistle Chapel, built in 1911 as a private chapel for the Knights of the Most Holy Order of the Thistle. Richly carved stonework enlivens the interior of the chapel, and the lierne vaulting of the roof, with its carved bosses, is outstanding. Look carefully near the entrance door for the tiny bagpipe-playing angel.

Edinburgh

STROLL DOWN THE ROYAL MILE

Edinburgh's Royal Mile is the epitome
of Old Edinburgh. Made up of four
linked streets – Castlehill, Lawnmarket,
High Street and Canongate – it
descends the sloping back of a long,
steep-sided ridge from Edinburgh
Castle (see page 101) at the west end to
the Palace of Holyroodhouse (see page
103) at the east end. On either side of
the Royal Mile are tall buildings,
riddled with courtyards and
passageways known as "closes" and
separated by narrow streets known as
wynds, all of it a delight to explore. All
the way down the Royal Mile historic
buildings punctuate the general
streetscape, and there are numerous
stores, cafés, restaurants and pubs.

The start of the atmospheric Royal Mile, marked
by tall, narow sandstone buildings

You can begin a relaxed descent of
the Royal Mile from the entrance to the
Castle Esplanade, starting with Castle
Hill. Attractions beckon from either
side. On the left is the Old Town
Weaving Company, with its masses of
tartan cloth and working mill. On the
right is the Scotch Whisky Heritage
Centre. Next on the left and well worth
a visit is the fascinating Outlook Tower,
a camera obscura where moving images
of the surrounding area are projected
onto a white viewing table. The street is
narrow here but opens up just past the
powerful Tolbooth Kirk, a handsome
Gothic building with the tallest spire in
Edinburgh. It is now the headquarters
of the Edinburgh Festival Centre and
Club. At this point, the Royal Mile
becomes the much wider Lawnmarket,
once the city's linen market.

Keep to the left side of the street,
where steps rise from street level to the
pavement. There are several stores here
selling woolen and tartan goods. Soon
you come to Gladstone's Land, a 17th-

century merchant's house now restored
by the National Trust for Scotland. The
house's Painted Chamber is stunning.
Just a bit farther is the entrance to Lady
Stair's Close. A narrow alleyway leads
to an open square and to Lady Stair's
House, now the Writers' Museum, a
quiet little corner housing memorabilia
associated with Scotland's finest
writers, including Robert Burns, Robert
Louis Stevenson and Walter Scott. The
spiral stairs have an uneven step halfway
up, a common trick in medieval houses
aimed at tripping an intruder in the dark.

The Lawnmarket reaches a junction
with Bank Street and the street called
George IV Bridge, where the Royal
Mile becomes High Street. Here you
will find a remarkable concentration of
historic buildings. On the east corner
with Bank Street is the High Court,
with a bronze statue of Scottish
philosopher David Hume in front of it.
Next to the High Court is Edinburgh
City Chambers, with an arcaded
entrance screen. Opposite is St. Giles
Cathedral (see page 103). Behind St.

At the foot of the Royal Mile on the fringe of Old Edinburgh, Holyroodhouse is the official Scottish residence of Queen Elizabeth II

Giles is Parliament Square and the old Parliament House, seat of the Scottish Parliament until the union with England in 1707.

High Street then descends gently to a junction with North and South Bridge Street. Stay on the north side of High Street, past the entrances to various passageways, and look for Chalmer's Court. Go through the entrance and down the steps to the preserved apse of the 15th-century Trinity College Church, now a fascinating brass rubbing center.

On the other side of High Street opposite Chalmer's Court is the entertaining Museum of Childhood. Farther down High Street, just before the junction with Jeffrey Street and St. Mary's Street, is the John Knox Museum, a celebration of the 16th-century religious reformer who brought the Protestant Reformation to Scotland with more than a whiff of fire and brimstone. Beyond Jeffrey Street the Royal Mile becomes Canongate and narrows once more. Halfway down

Canongate is the Old Tolbooth, with its wonderful clock and conical-roofed towers. The Tolbooth was once a courtroom and jail and is now the Canongate Tolbooth Museum, the People's Story, an exhibition of Edinburgh life. Just opposite is Huntly House Museum, a late 16th-century building now beautifully restored and containing an excellent collection of Edinburgh artifacts.

Diagonally opposite Huntly House is the 17th-century Canongate Kirk and Kirkyard, which has a wonderfully bright interior. The church has close royal connections; the royal family worship here when they are in residence at nearby Holyroodhouse, and the royal coat of arms can be seen on one of the church benches, or pews. A short distance past the church the Royal Mile reaches its junction with Abbey Hill and Horse Wynd, where it becomes Abbey Street and ends its progress through Scottish history at the gates of the Palace of Holyroodhouse. For the walk route, see the city map on page 98–99.

With the spires of Christ Church and Merton College in the background, a rowing "eight" carries on Oxford student sporting traditions

OXFORD

Oxford, 56 miles northwest of London, is a typical English market town at heart. It is located within a hollow amid low hills at the gentle confluence of the Thames and Cherwell rivers. What makes Oxford exceptional is its university, the oldest in the English-speaking world, an institution that is represented not by a single campus but by 36 independent colleges that are scattered throughout the city. They represent elegant seats of learning, but are also blessed with beautiful buildings.

The history of Oxford is said to have begun with the founding of a priory by the Saxon St. Frideswide, near where the Thames and Cherwell rivers meet. Christ Church Cathedral supplanted the priory, and in time wealth from the medieval wool trade led to the founding of other religious houses, where learning was revered. Scholars were drawn to Oxford, and from these beginnings the university evolved.

Unless you're a student, Oxford is more of a journey through history and great architecture than through academia. For the visitor, the experience may seem faintly voyeuristic. You visit the colleges, picking your way through elegant quadrangles, chapels, arched passageways, gardens, and libraries, and at times you may feel you are intruding on a select world of academic privilege and of cultural paradigms.

Yet the physical integration of Oxford's colleges with the realities of Oxford as a city dispel any sense of intrusion. This is a living, vibrant place that retains its own identity and commercial life. Take a ride on a Guide Friday bus to see the principal sights, leaving the bus where and when you like, or take a guided walking tour of historic Oxford or of the colleges. Stroll by the Thames or take a river cruise.

Oxford's Colleges

This is a small city, and you can walk around central Oxford in under an hour, but it is the density and

Oxford

complexity of colleges and great buildings that is so absorbing. The heart of the university lies between High Street and Broad Street and is enclosed by the colleges of Brasenose, All Souls, Hertford and Exeter. The Church of St. Mary the Virgin (see page 110) is on High Street. Behind St. Mary's is Radcliffe Square, which has the elegant 18th-century Renaissance rotunda of the Radcliffe Camera (chamber) at its heart. On the east side of the square is All Souls College. On the west side is Brasenose College, named after a traditional brass "mask" door knocker and a treasured college possession; a replica can be seen on the great oak doors.

From Radcliffe Square you can walk into the Schools Quadrangle of the Bodleian Library, with its superb Jacobean entrance tower and decorative inner walls. Through the arch on the north side of the quadrangle is the Sheldonian Theatre, where the

Encaenia – the degree ceremony for Oxford graduates – is held.

The Radcliffe Square area is the heart of the university, but try to visit some of the colleges when their grounds are open to the public. Include Christ Church (see page 109), the largest and most famous of the colleges, and do not miss nearby Merton College, reputedly the oldest of them all and certainly one of the finest, with its delightful gardens, ancient quadrangle, medieval library and chapel. Adjoining Merton Street, cobbled and quiet, is one of the finest parts of the city. Merton counts among its alumni 14th-century religious reformer John Wycliffe, poet T. S. Eliot and actor-singer Kris Kristofferson. Then head east toward Magdalen (pronounced "Maudlin") and its superb tower, Cloister Quad, gardens and riverside walks. Magdalen alumni include playwright Oscar Wilde and actor Dudley Moore.

Oxford

The Market Town

Oxford itself is famous for automobile manufacturing, and is the home of the Morris Oxford and the T-series MG sports car. They were produced at Oxford Cowley factories, built up by William Richard Morris, later Viscount Nuffield, a self-made man who founded Oxford's Nuffield College among his numerous charitable acts. Visit the Museum of Oxford and discover the history of the city, and take in the Pitt Rivers Museum and the University Museum. Climb to the top of Carfax Tower for great views of Oxford.

The streets radiating from Carfax constitute Oxford's main shopping area. Cornmarket has a range of well-known stores. Off Cornmarket's east side is Golden Cross Walk and the Oxford Collection, a souvenir store. Just beyond is the celebrated covered market, with excellent food stalls and other outlets.

Oxford's university population and townspeople exhibit a fascinating contrast of lifestyles. In medieval times this duality led to occasional bloody

The Original Alice

The children's books *Alice in Wonderland* and *Alice Through The Looking Glass* were inspired by Oxford life. Charles Ludwidge Dodgson, a lecturer and ordained deacon at Christ Church College, wrote the books during the latter part of the 19th century. Dodgson formed an intense friendship with Alice Liddell, the young daughter of the dean of Christ Church. He entertained her and her sisters with his stories of Wonderland, and they were later published under the pseudonym Lewis Carroll, becoming two of the best-known books of all time.

battles, but although today's students are noted for their often boisterous post-exam antics, Oxford is an eminently civilized place where the traditions of "town and gown" rest easily side by side.

ESSENTIAL INFORMATION

TOURIST INFORMATION
• The Old School, Gloucester Green
☎ 01865 726871

URBAN TRANSPORTATION
Oxford railroad station (✉ Hythe Bridge Street) offers regular train connections to and from London. Central Oxford is a 10-minute walk from the station. Local bus services in and around the city are frequent. Two companies provide all local services: the Oxford Bus Company (☎ 01865 785400) and Stagecoach Oxford (☎ 01865 727000).

Taxi stands are located at the railroad station, Carfax and the Gloucester Green bus station. Call ☎ 01865 240000 for information.

AIRPORT INFORMATION
London's Heathrow and Gatwick airports (see page 89) have bus connections to and from Oxford; buses depart every half hour, daily 24 hours. For information call City Link (☎ 01865 785400). Birmingham Airport has daily rail (☎ 0345 484950)and bus (☎ 08705 808080) connections to and from Oxford.

CLIMATE – average highs and lows for the month

JAN.	FEB.	MAR.	APR.	MAY.	JUN.	JUL.	AUG.	SEP.	OCT.	NOV.	DEC.
7°C	7°C	10°C	13°C	16°C	16°C	21°C	18°C	18°C	14°C	10°C	8°C
45°F	45°F	50°F	55°F	61°F	61°F	70°F	64°F	64°F	57°F	50°F	46°F
3°C	3°C	4°C	5°C	8°C	10°C	13°C	13°C	11°C	8°C	6°C	4°C
37°F	37°F	39°F	41°F	46°F	50°F	55°F	55°F	52°F	46°F	43°F	39°F

CITY SIGHTS

Key to symbols

✚ map coordinates refer to the Oxford map on page 107; sights below are highlighted in yellow on the map.

⊠ address or location ☎ telephone number

⊙ opening times 🚌 nearest bus route

🍴 restaurant on site or nearby

🎫 admission charge: $$$ more than £6, $$ £2–£6, $ less than £2

ASHMOLEAN MUSEUM

✚ A3 ⊠ Beaumont Street ☎ 01865 278000 ⊙ Tue.–Sat. 10–5 (and Wed. 10–8), Sun. 2–5 🍴 Café 🚌 61 🎫 Free

The Ashmolean is a fascinating museum of grand oddities and elegant art, housed in an equally grand and elegant neoclassical building dating from the 1840s. The oldest museum in Britain, the Ashmolean's collection is extensive and includes much medieval material; Greek, Roman and Egyptian artifacts; and fine Asian porcelain. The upper floor contains a dazzling collection of Italian Renaissance paintings, including works by Michelangelo and Raphael.

CHRIST CHURCH COLLEGE

✚ A1–B1 ⊠ St. Aldates ☎ 01865 276150 ⊙ Mon.–Sat. 9–5, Sun. 12:45–5:30 🚌 2, 4, 13, 15, 22 🎫 $ 🍴 May close unexpectedly at any time and for several weeks at a time

Oxford's largest college, Christ Church College, is the most visited of all the university's colleges. Entry is through a turnstile by the War Memorial Gardens in the street known as St. Aldates, where college "bulldogs," immaculately dressed custodians in bowler hats, cheerfully order you around. Christ Church is unquestionably magnificent.

The present cathedral, known familiarly as "The House," dates from the late 12th century. Among its many fine features are exquisite stained-glass

Above: Porcelain figures in the Ashmolean

windows. Tom Quad is Christ Church's glorious central quadrangle; Mercury Pond, with Mercury Fountain at its center, adds an elegant accent. The figure of Mercury sports tiny patches of well-watered moss and often sprouts neckties and other "dress" donated by students. The entrance to Tom Quad and to Christ Church is the mighty gate tower, Tom Tower, that holds a massive seven-ton bell, Great Tom. Visit Christ Church's vaulted Great Hall, the Picture Gallery and the smaller Canterbury and Peckwater quadrangles.

MUSEUM OF OXFORD

✚ A1 ⊠ St. Aldates ☎ 01865 252761 ⊙ Tue.–Sat. 10–4 (also Sat. 4–5), Sun. noon–4 🚌 2, 13, 15, 22 🎫 $

The Museum of Oxford is housed in the Town Hall and gives an excellent account of Oxford's history from the earliest times. Everyone who played a part in the making of Oxford is here, from prehistory through the Roman, Saxon and Norman periods to the present day. The museum's well-arranged exhibits and organized layout make a visit here very rewarding. The realities of town life, from both sides of the track, are depicted through 19th-century house interiors from residential and working class districts.

THE OXFORD STORY

✚ A2 ⊠ 6 Broad Street ☎ 01865 728822 ⊙ Daily 9–6, Jul.–Aug.; 9:30–5, Apr.–Jun. and Sep.–Oct.; 10–4:30, rest of year 🚌 2, 60 🎫 $$

For those who have visited York's Jorvik Viking Centre, The Oxford Story's mobile "desks" will be a familiar form of transportation through the varied tableaux and sound effects of this enjoyable attraction. You enter from Broad Street, view a short video introduction and then climb into old-fashioned school desks that travel gently up a steep ramp. They glide past displays about the university, its history and many of the personalities associated with it, accompanied by persuasive commentary.

Oxford

PITT RIVERS MUSEUM

✚ Off the map ✉ Parks Road (enter from interior of the University Museum) ☎ 01865 270927
🕒 Mon.–Sat. 2–4:30 🚌 2, 60 🎫 Free ℹ Museum due to reopen Spring 2000

This fascinating museum is a marvelous example of 19th-century museum culture. It displays the often wildly eccentric collection of Lieutenant General Augustus Henry Lane Fox Pitt Rivers, who served throughout the British Empire and gathered a great many artifacts along the way. The collection reflects the general's intense interest in tribal cultures and is an invaluable comment on the human condition worldwide. Ritual masks, shrunken heads and weird magical objects are just part of the huge collection. Children will love it all.

ST. MARY THE VIRGIN

✚ B2 ✉ High Street ☎ 01865 279111
🕒 Mon.–Sat. 9–7, Sun. 11:30–7, Jul.–Sep.; Mon.–Sat. 9–5, Sun. 11:30–5, rest of year 🍴 Café in adjoining Convocation House 🚌 2, 4, 13, 15, 22 🎫 Church free; tower $

St. Mary the Virgin is both the parish church of Oxford and the university's

Dramatic wrought-iron arches over dinosaur skeletons at the University Museum

church. It is a splendid building that forms the southern side of Radcliffe Square. The early 14th-century tower rises above all of Oxford's dreaming spires, domes and cupolas. The south porch, facing High Street, is a splendid baroque extravagance, a daring 17th-century addition that trumpeted Italian influence with its twisted columns and heavily decorated segmental arch. The interior of the church is filled with monuments and wall tablets. You can plod up the tower as far as the base of the spire for fine views over Oxford, in the company of grinning gargoyles and fellow visitors. The climb is narrow and steep, and the up and down flow of people can cause traffic jams.

UNIVERSITY MUSEUM

✚ Off the map ✉ Parks Road ☎ 01865 272950
🕒 Mon.–Sat. noon–5 🚌 2, 60 🎫 Free

The University Museum is housed in an inspirational 19th-century building in Italianate Gothic style, its facade embellished with marvelous carvings. The interior is a single open space, surrounded by an ambulatory and forested with slender iron columns that support a wrought-iron vault and glass roof. The exhibits range from large dinosaur skeletons to minerals and fossils. Visitors can access the Pitt Rivers Museum from the rear of the University Museum.

UNIVERSITY OF OXFORD BOTANIC GARDEN

✚ C1 ✉ Rose Lane ☎ 01865 276920 🕒 Garden: daily 9–5, Apr.–Sep.; 9–4:30, rest of year. Glasshouses: daily 10–4 🎫 Apr.–Aug. $; rest of year, free ℹ Closed Good Friday

The University of Oxford Botanic Garden was founded as a "physic garden" in 1621. In imitation of the herbal gardens of mainland Europe, it has evolved into a delightful enclave with a collection of more than 8,000 plants. The Cherwell river and Magdalen College's handsome tower enhance the setting, and the original layout survives today. South of the main garden is the New Garden, a less geometrically designed display created in the 1940s. There are also splendid glasshouses.

Anne Hathaway's cottage, just west of Stratford, the childhood home of William Shakespeare's wife

SHAKESPEARE'S STRATFORD-UPON-AVON

Stratford-upon-Avon was the birthplace of William Shakespeare and today the town is something of a shrine to the poet-playwright, its numerous Tudor and Jacobean half-timbered houses enhancing the Shakespearean theme. Shakespeare's Birthplace on Henley Street has been restored with late 16th-century furnishings and is full of fascinating memorabilia. Another fine old building is the Elizabethan Harvard House, which, although having no connection to Shakespeare, is interesting as the birthplace of John Harvard, who founded Harvard College in Massachusets.

After an intriguing life, Shakespeare died in 1616 at the early age of 52 in a house called New Place in Stratford. The original house was demolished by the owner in 1759 because he found visitors a nuisance. The foundations remain and are adjoined by the Elizabethan Garden and Nash's House, the superbly restored 17th-century home of Thomas Nash, husband of Shakespeare's grand-daughter, Elizabeth Hall.

Another famous Stratford building is Holy Trinity Church, located on the banks of the Avon river. Here you will see the remarkable alabaster bust of Shakespeare, modeled on a wax impression of the playwright's face at his death. Nearby is Shakespeare's tomb and those of his wife, Anne Hathaway, and his daughter, Susanna. On the banks of the Avon river to the north of the church is the Shakespeare Memorial Theatre.

Arrange day trips to Stratford at the Oxford tourist office or through Cotswold Roaming.

Tourist Information Centre ✉ The Old School, Gloucester Green, Oxford ☎ 01865 726871 🕐 Mon.–Sat. 9:30–5, Sun. 10–3:30, mid-May to Oct. 31 🎟 Tours $$

Cotswold Roaming ✉ Box 784, Headington, Oxford ☎ 01865 250640 🕐 Daily 10–6:30 🎟 Tours $$

ℹ Tours run on demand for groups of five or more

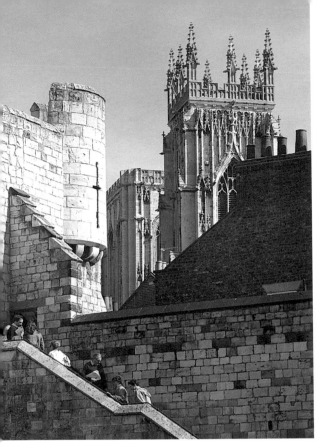

Walk along the city walls for a view of York Minster, Britain's largest medieval cathedral

YORK

Two thousand years of English history are written across the face of York. Within the old city's walls, and within sight and sound of the magnificent York Minster cathedral, narrow, cobbled streets, ancient remains, medieval buildings, historic churches and award-winning museums sit happily alongside modern stores, restaurants and hotels.

York is a small town at heart. It began life as a riverside encampment established by an ancient British tribe, the Brigantes. In turn, Brigantes were usurped in AD 71 by Roman invaders who made York their empire's northern European capital. Anglo Saxons, who established York as a center of early Christianity, followed the Romans. In AD 867, the settlement was captured by the Danes – the plundering Vikings of romantic history.

In subsequent centuries York fell under the control of the Normans, who laid the first substantial foundations of the present minster and built the original city walls. During the 16th and 17th centuries, religious and dynastic struggles kept the city in the national forefront, at a time when poverty, plague and famine often made ordinary life harsh and terrible. The more enterprising world of the 18th and 19th centuries and the emergence of York as the railroad capital of northern England made the city a fashionable commercial center, one that was only lightly touched by the more brutal aspects of the Industrial Revolution. Today visitors walk on hallowed ground that has supported more than 2,000 years of human achievement, as well as misery.

Sightseeing in York

Many parts of central York are pedestrian-only, and though crowds may throng the narrow streets, people have precedence over vehicles. In the nicest areas of old York there is no stream of roaring traffic pinning you to the sidewalk. You go with the flow, but there is no rush-hour element even during the busiest times of day.

York's flavor can be captured via open-top double-decker bus or in a horse-drawn carriage. The inner city can be explored on one of numerous city tours, led by local experts. Or you can take a "ghost walk," complete with an entertaining guide and actors making impromptu, phantom appearances in dark alleys. Leisurely daytime guided walks take in the city walls and ancient streets.

You could also explore on your own. Central York is not large, and you're never far from the next fascinating building, museum or attraction. Few houses in York rise above two or three stories, and the sun finds its way into hidden corners, lighting the upper parts of old buildings. Take time as you stroll to appreciate the colorful facades and

architectural features, like Stonegate's little red devil above the corner with Coffee Yard Lane.

The many different people who colonized York left an engaging but confusing legacy of local words. The word "bar" means gate and refers to the magnificent stone gateways, such as Bootham Bar and Monk Bar, that punctuate the city walls. On the other hand, the Viking word "gate," as in Stonegate and Petergate, means street.

Walk part of the city walls for a superb overview of York. Try the section from Monk Bar (location of the fascinating Richard III Museum), at the north end of Goodramgate, to Bootham Bar at the west end of High

York

Petergate. The views of York Minster along this stretch are outstanding.

Visit such main attractions as York Minster and the Jorvik Viking Centre, but do not neglect other sights like the hands-on Archaeological Resource Centre in St. Saviourgate and the York Dungeon on Clifford Street, both great fun for children. Enjoy the talented street entertainers, and check out the many festivals and events staged each year in and around the city.

Shopping in Old York

Shopping in York is fun. Streets such as Stonegate and the Shambles are overflowing with specialty stores, including antique shops, art and craft galleries, bookstores, jewelers, tea blenders and boutiques. Every major chain store is represented in the main shopping areas of Coney Street, St. Mary's Square and Parliament Street.

A huge variety of eateries will tempt you, from traditional English tea and coffee houses – such as Betty's in St. Helen's Square and Taylor's Tea Rooms and Coffee Shop in Stonegate – to

Minster

The word "Minster" was first used in medieval England as a version of the word "monastery." It was often applied simply to describe the church attached to a monastery, which was used for worship by the monks. Through time the word became associated with certain cathedral churches, like York Minster.

dozens of restaurants. Authentic English pubs include Stonegate's Ye Old Starre Inne and the 15th-century Black Swan, on Peasholme Green.

York is essentially English at heart, but its northern regional identity makes it very different from London and southern England. Expect friendliness and helpfulness from locals, but be prepared for that matter-of-fact approach for which Yorkshire people are famous. You will be given facts rather than fiction and guidance rather than gossip to help you get the best out of the heartland of historic England.

ESSENTIAL INFORMATION

TOURIST INFORMATION
• De Grey Rooms, Exhibition Square ☎ 01904 621756
• York railroad station, Station Road ☎ 01904 621756
• 20 George Hudson Street ☎ 01904 554488

URBAN TRANSPORTATION
York railroad station (☎ 0345 484950) is the main terminal, with frequent service to and from major cities. Local service is offered by First York (☎ 01904 435637)

and York Pullman (☎ 01904 622992). There are taxi stands at York railroad station (☎ 01904 623332) and at Duncombe Place, near York Minster.

AIRPORT INFORMATION
Leeds-Bradford Airport is an hour's drive from York; for information call ☎ 0113 250 9696. Manchester Airport, 56 miles southwest by road, has direct train service to York; for information call ☎ 0161 489 3000.

CLIMATE – average highs and lows for the month

JAN.	FEB.	MAR.	APR.	MAY	JUN.	JUL.	AUG.	SEP.	OCT.	NOV.	DEC.
6°C	7°C	9°C	13°C	16°C	19°C	21°C	20°C	18°C	14°C	9°C	7°C
43°F	45°F	48°F	55°F	61°F	66°F	70°F	68°F	64°F	57°F	48°F	45°F
0°C	1°C	2°C	4°C	7°C	10°C	12°C	11°C	10°C	7°C	4°C	2°C
32°F	34°F	36°F	39°F	45°F	50°F	54°F	52°F	50°F	45°F	39°F	36°F

CITY SIGHTS

Key to symbols

➕ map coordinates refer to the York map on page 113; sights below are highlighted in yellow on the map.

⊠ address or location ☎ telephone number
🕐 opening times 🚌 nearest bus route
🍴 restaurant on site or nearby
🖐 admission charge: $$$ more than £6, $$ £2–£6, $ less than £2

The opulent salon in Fairfax House

CASTLE MUSEUM

➕ C1 ⊠ The Eye of York, Tower Street ☎ 01904 653611 🕐 Mon.–Sat. 9:30–5:30, Sun. 10–5:30, Apr.–Oct.; Mon.–Sat. 9:30–4, Sun. 10–4, rest of year 🍴 Museum café 🖐 $$$

This museum is housed in two former prisons. Behind the handsome neoclassical facade of the building is an outstanding collection of exhibits illustrating the social history of York, and of Britain, over the past 400 years. Walkways lead past vivid reconstructions of complete Victorian and Edwardian streets, lined with old stores full of authentic contents. Allow several hours to enjoy the experience, which includes a visit to the condemned cell that once held legendary highwayman Dick Turpin.

FAIRFAX HOUSE

➕ C1 ⊠ Castlegate ☎ 01904 655543 🕐 Mon.–Thu. and Sat. 11–5, Sun. 1:30–5, early Mar.–late Dec. 🚩 Last admission at 4:30. Guided tours Fri. 11 and 2 🖐 $$

This elegant house was lavishly decorated by Viscount Fairfax in 1759, but was neglected in later years. It was bought in 1980 by the York Civic Trust, which carried out an inspired restoration. Today, Fairfax House is one of the finest examples of an 18th-century town house in England. Enjoy the sumptuous plasterwork ceilings, damask hangings, marble fireplaces, and magnificent furnishings.

JORVIK VIKING CENTRE

➕ C2 ⊠ Coppergate ☎ 01904 643211 🕐 Daily 9–5:30, Apr.–Oct.; 9–3:30, rest of year 🖐 $$$

This very popular attraction reveals the archeological remains of Viking York, or

"Jorvik." Deep underground, you're shuttled back in time 1,000 years to a reconstructed Viking street complete with thatched houses, lifelike figures and the evocative sounds and smells of everyday life. Traveling in a "time car" you pass through the actual remains of the same street as it was discovered during excavations. A final section on foot passes through a modern archeological laboratory and a fascinating exhibition of Viking artifacts. Be prepared for the time car's initial backward progress as it takes you back to the year 948. Try not to look over your shoulder.

MERCHANT ADVENTURERS' HALL

➕ C2 ⊠ Piccadilly ☎ 01904 654818 🕐 Daily 8:30–5, Apr.–Sep.; 9–3, rest of year 🍴 The Blue Bicycle, see page 547 🖐 $

This medieval Guild Hall is the finest of its kind to survive in Europe. Its brick and timber-framed exterior, the vast, open timber work of the Great Hall and the interior paneling effortlessly transport visitors from the present into a convincing medieval environment. The hall was built in 1357 by a religious fraternity that evolved into a merchants' guild, which survives today as a charitable organization and guardian of this outstanding building.

NATIONAL RAILWAY MUSEUM

➕ Off the map ⊠ Leeman Road ☎ 01904 621261 🕐 Daily 10–6 🍴 Museum café 🖐 $

For travel enthusiasts young and old, this

York

atmospheric museum – the largest of its kind in the world – offers vivid insight into 200 years of transportation history. Displays of almost 50 steam, diesel and electric locomotives include a restoration of George Stephenson's famous 1829 *Rocket* and the wonderful *Mallard*, still operating and the fastest steam engine in the world.

YORK CITY ART GALLERY

✚ B3 ✉ Exhibition Square ☎ 01904 551861 ⏰ Mon.–Sat. 10–5, Sun. 2:30–5 🎟 Free ℹ Last admission at 4:30

The excellent collection in this small, friendly and informative gallery provides an overview of European art, from the Italian Renaissance to the contemporary scene. There are a number of paintings by York artist, William Etty, who had a liking for exuberant nudes. There is also a collection by leading 20th-century potters such as Bernard Leach and Shoji Hamada.

YORK MINSTER

✚ B3 ✉ Minster Yard ☎ 01904 557216 ⏰ Daily 9–8:30, Jun.–Aug.; 9–8, in Sep.; 9–7:30, in May; 9:30–7, in Oct.; 9:30–6:30, in Apr.; 10–6, rest of year 🍴 Minster restaurant/café 🎟 Entry to main building is free, but a donation is requested. Crypt, Chapter House, Foundations Exhibition and tower $ ℹ Free tours (except Sun.) begin at 9:30 (10 in winter). Ask at the reception area or book by phone 10 days in advance.

York cathedral's present foundations were laid by the Normans in the 12th century. The Minster is a historical experience as well as a religious one; the walls are crowded with dramatic monuments and the architectural features are superb.

Past the broad introductory nave is the central crossing, where north and south transepts, nave and choir all meet below the soaring vaulted roof of the central tower, 200 feet above. The choir is full of intricate design and ornamentation. At the east end of the church you will find the Lady Chapel and the great East Window – as big as a tennis court and the largest medieval stained-glass window in the world.

Tower and spires of York Minster

Also visit the intriguing crypt and the splendid Chapter House. In the Chapter House, look for the wickedly irreverent figures scattered among the carvings above the encircling stalls. The Foundations Exhibition in the Minster's undercroft, or "basement," has displays of Roman and Norman remains.

Consider climbing the 275 spiral steps of the great 234-foot tower, but do so only if you're in good physical condition; it can prove to be a small Everest for some.

YORKSHIRE MUSEUM

✚ A3–B3 ✉ Museum Gardens ☎ 01904 629745 ⏰ Daily 10–5, Apr.–Oct.; Mon.–Sat. 10–5, Sun. 1–5, rest of year 🎟 $$ ℹ Events and changing exhibitions at various times; opening times vary

This award-winning museum includes some of the finest Roman, Viking, Anglo Saxon and medieval artifacts in Europe. The grounds feature handsome gardens that contain York's oldest ruins – the Multiangular Tower, part of fourth-century Roman fortifications. Brightly feathered peacocks strut around the approach to the building.

A major exhibit is the luminous Middleham Jewel, a beautiful 15th-century sapphire set within a gold pendant. The museum building incorporates part of the ruins of medieval St. Mary's Abbey. This section, with its haunting reconstructions and medieval music, is a delight.

York

WALK THROUGH THE PAST

York's appeal stems largely from the survival of its central streets in their original form. While many cities and towns had their centers remodeled over the years, central York was spared wholesale change. Plans to demolish the city walls during the Victorian period were resisted, and within the precise boundaries of those restored walls the narrow streets and interlocking alleys and courtyards make up one of the best preserved late medieval cities in Europe.

Many of York's old houses are not the original buildings; they have been rebuilt or restored over time. But their styles are medieval, and so venerable is the layout of central York that when you walk down Stonegate you follow the exact line of the Roman approach road to the imperial encampment of AD 71.

The most famous of York's ancient thoroughfares is the Shambles, a narrow street overhung by timber-framed houses. Its name derives from the butchers' shops and slaughterhouses once located here. Today's Shambles is a delight. It typifies York's medieval character, but in times past this would have been a filthy, raucous, rough-and-ready place that would horrify modern sensibilities. Today it can be enjoyed for its quaintness, free of medieval realities. Don't miss bustling Newgate Market behind the Shambles, where – within the rules of modern hygiene and legality – some of the liveliness of medieval times still survives.

To get the most out of old York, explore the interlocking alleys that connect the center. Wander at will with a city map, which will show you the main landmarks, but investigate the twists and turns of the numerous passages leading off Stonegate, Petergate, Davygate and Church Street. They'll land you unexpectedly in the bustle of St. Helen's Square, with its handsome Mansion House and Guildhall, or in King's Square, where old gravestones make up part of the paving. Brimming with charming little shops, cafés and restaurants, old York exudes unforgettable character.

A rainy night in the Shambles, where medieval buildings overhang cobbled lanes

CZECH REPUBLIC

"NOT all the seductions of Vienna...nor the dominion of a German bureaucracy have broken the stubborn heart of the Czech..."

From *A History of Europe*, by English historian H. A. L. Fisher

Opposite: The 15th-century Astronomical Clock dominates the front of the Old Town Hall in Prague

Czech Republic

CZECH REPUBLIC

Since 1989, the Czechs have been embracing change and finding their footing as a new republic. In that year, the Velvet Revolution saw Czechoslovakia discard 40 years of Communist rule without firing a single shot. At the dawn of the 21st century, the country is coping with the difficulties and benefits of adapting to Western capitalism and establishing a new social, and economic order.

Bohemia and Moravia

Most visitors to the Czech Republic head straight for Prague, but there is plenty to enjoy in the country's diverse landscapes. Locked between Poland, Germany, Slovakia and Austria, the republic takes in two regions: Bohemia, itself surrounded by a ring of mountains, and the lowlands of Moravia. Both have suffered adversely from the effects of heavy industrialization – acid rain and deforestation among them – but both also have areas of real beauty.

In southern Bohemia, such medieval towns as České Budějovice (home of Budweiser beer) and Česky Krumlov, with its great 13th-century castle, recall a time when kings and lords were eager to build in one of Europe's richest regions. To the west are famous spa towns best known by their German names: Carlsbad (Karlovy Vary) and Marienbad (Mariánské Lázně).

In Moravia, wedged between the western uplands and the eastern White Carpathian mountains, the 19th-century city of Brno gives access to the Punkva Caves (Punkevní jeskyně).

Czech Culture

Despite the hijacking of the term "bohemian" by the West to mean "unconventional," the Czechs are generally rather reserved. Beyond this, though, is a friendliness and genuine interest in other cultures. Young Czechs often speak English, and are tuned in to Anglo-American pop culture.

Love of arts and literature is not confined to Prague. Václav Havel, the

The face of the modern Czech Republic – President Vaclav Havel

CZECH REPUBLIC

| 0 | 20 | 40 | 60 | 80 km |
| 0 | 10 | 20 | 30 | 40 | 50 miles |

first post-Communist president, was better known among Czechs as a poet and playwright. Music has a special place in Czech life, too – from oompah-style brass bands to the classical tradition that produced such composers as Anton Dvořák.

Overall, most people who travel around the Czech Republic will be struck by the diversity of this small nation. As the republic moves away from Communism towards capitalism, there is anxiety as well as hope. A visit to this society in transition between two worlds is sure to be rewarding.

MORE TOP DESTINATIONS IN THE CZECH REPUBLIC

- České Budějovice B1
- Český Krumlov B1 • Český ráj C3
- Karlovy Vary A3 • Krkonoše C3
- Mariánské Lázně A2
- Olomouc D2
- Punkevní jeskyně D1 • Šumava A1–B1 • Telč C1 • Vranov C1

Czech Republic

TIMELINE

AD 700	The Přemyslid Dynasty begins its 500-year rule of Bohemia.
929	Good King Wenceslas (Václav I) is assassinated by his brother and made the country's patron saint.
1346	Devout Charles IV, Holy Roman Emperor, is crowned king of Bohemia and ushers in its Golden Age.
1415	Religious reformer Jan Hus is burned at the stake in Constance; in Prague his supporters throw Catholic councillors from town hall windows and start the Hussite Wars.
1583	The Habsburg court moves to Prague.
1848	The Habsburgs suppress an uprising of Czech nationalism.
1914	Czechs are forced to fight for the Austrian Habsburgs in World War I, but thousands desert to the Russians.
1918	With the defeat of Austria-Hungary, the new state of Czechoslovakia is proclaimed.
1938	Czechoslovakia is forced to hand over Sudetenland to Hitler; the following year, Nazis round up Prague's Jewish community.
1945	Slovakia and the Czech lands are liberated by the Red Army; the Communist Party seizes power in 1948.
1968	The First Secretary, Alexander Dubček, introduces "socialism with a human face" in the reforms of the "Prague Spring"; in August, Soviet troops invade Czechoslovakia.
1989	"Velvet Revolution"; Václav Havel elected president of Czechslovakia.
1993	Czechoslovakia splits into Czech and Slovak republics.
1997	Czech Republic becomes a NATO member and prepares to join the European Union.

THE VELVET REVOLUTION

On November 17, 1989, a week after the fall of the Berlin Wall, there was an officially sanctioned demonstration in Prague to mark the Nazi suppression of Czech universities. It soon turned into a protest march against the authorities, and was forcefully put down by riot police. A rumor began that the police had killed one demonstrator. In fact, it wasn't true, but the story was enough to fuel public anger. People poured into the streets night after night, watched by television viewers across the world. Alexander Dubček was brought back from obscurity in Bratislava to address the crowds. Václav Havel headed a newly established Civic Forum, and on December 10 a new government was formed, with the Communists reduced to a minority. Less than three weeks later, Havel was installed as president.

Clean, fast and cheap – Prague's excellent subway system is a good way to get around

Survival Guide

- Czech pronunciation is difficult, but worth mastering if only for place names. Some Czechs – particularly young city-dwellers – may speak a little English, but some grasp of German is more useful.
- The cuisine is heavily meat-based and dull – dumplings and pork are popular dishes. Coffee and cakes are a highlight, and the cafés (*kavárna*) are excellent. This is the home of light beer, and the products of Budějovice (Budweis) and Plzeň (Pilsen) are only the most famous among a multitude of local varieties.
- It's worth looking through bookstores, despite the language barrier, as the illustrated books are a treat. For souvenirs, take home Bohemian crystal, porcelain, lacework, ceramics and prints.
- Easter is a more important holiday in Orthodox churches than Christmas, and is marked by the bizarre ritual of boys whipping girls' legs with birch twigs.
- At Christmas, neighborhood St. Nicholas figures walk the streets with an angel, giving candy to good children and coal to bad. Christmas dinner is traditionally carp – sold live at street stalls to be eaten on Christmas Eve with potato salad and schnitzel.
- Prague is even busier than usual in May and early June, as it hosts the International Music Festival: Reserve accommodations several weeks in advance for this period.
- Public transportation is an enjoyable way of seeing the republic. Almost every town has a railroad station (*nádraží*), and side trips are cheap. The fast trains (*rychlík*) stop at major cities; local trains (*osobní vlak*) are slow, stop everywhere and usually have only second-class carriages.
- The Czech Republic has suffered from a shortage of hotels and hostels, although this is fast changing. Some of the Communist-era hotels still operate, and many have been overhauled. There's been a surge of new accommodations in converted buildings. A sign saying *Zimmer frei* ("rooms available") indicates bed and breakfast in a private home.

Prague

PRAGUE

Nothing can prepare you for the beauty of Prague. Its title of "Golden City" barely conveys the color and elegance of its historic center: painted medieval facades glinting pink and green and silver in the sun; a jumble of rust-red rooftops; mellow stone, turquoise domes, steel-gray Gothic spires. Prague's buildings and streets span 1,000 years. Wandering the cobbled passageways and alleys thus becomes the highlight of any visit.

Compass Bearings

Central Prague is made up of four towns, joined together in 1784. On the west bank of the Vltava river are Hradčany and the Lesser Quarter (Malá Strana); on the east bank are the Old Town (Staré Město) and New Town (Nové Město). In the 19th century the Jewish ghetto, Josefov, was also incorporated into the Old Town. Beyond this core is a circle of suburbs, but the main historic sights are within the substantially traffic-free center.

Nerudova

A steep street climbs from Malostranské Square, near Prague Castle, in the Lesser Quarter. This street, Nerudova, was named after journalist and writer Pavel Neruda. He wrote stories about daily life in 19th-century Prague, and was born at No. 47, near the top. Eighteenth-century houses line the street, identified by intricately crafted signs; numbers weren't introduced until the 1770s. Look for The Three Fiddles (No. 12), The Green Lobster (No. 43) and Neruda's home, The Two Suns.

Prague Castle

The two banks of the Vltava are connected by a series of 15 bridges, the oldest of which, the Charles Bridge (Karlův Most), is a magnet for tourists, performers and vendors. On the West Bank, Hradčany, the area around Prague Castle and its hill, is the major

PRAGUE
HRADČANY
Chotkovy sady
Belvedér
CHOTKOVA
Královská zahrada
Mičovna
4   Pražský hrad
Ledeburská zahrada
Bazilika sv Jiří   Ledeburský palác
Katedrála sv Víta   Starý Královský palác   Valdštejnský palác   VALDŠTEJNSKÁ
Schwarzenberský palác-Vojenské muzeum   Sternberský palác   Kostel sv Tomáš
UVOZ NERUDOVA   MALOSTRANSKÉ NAM   Vojanovy sady
Loretánská kaple,   Lichtenštejnský palác   Malostranská radnice
Strahovský Klášter   Morzinský palác   Chrám svatého Mikuláše   MOSTECKÁ
Schönbornská zahrada   Vrtbovská zahrada   MALTÉZSKÉ NAM   Kostel Panny Marie pod řetězem
3   Kostel Panny Marie Vítězná   Muzeum hudebních nástrojů
Seminářská zahrada   Státní ústřední archiv
MALÁ STRANA   Muzeum tělesné vychovy a sportu
Petřín
Lanova dráha
Petřínské sady
2   Hladová zeď   VÍTĚZNÁ
Kinského zahrada
NÁMĚSTÍ KINSKÝCH
Národopisné muzeum   VODNÍ   Dětský ostrov
ARBESOVO NAM
1   0   100   200   300 m
0   100   200   300 yards
N   Letohradek Portheimka
A   Kostel sv Václava   B

Prague

attraction. It includes (as well as the castle itself) Golden Lane (Zlatá Ulička), with tiny houses originally occupied by the Emperor's gatekeepers; the Gothic Powder Tower (Prašná věž), where alchemists once struggled to produce gold from base metals; and the palaces surrounding Hradčany Square.

Old and New Prague

Across the river in the Old Town is Old Town Square, perhaps the most popular with tourists. Here are the sprawling Old Town Hall (Staroměstské Radnice, see page 130), the white Church of St. Nicholas and the dark towers of Týn Church. This is where street artists

Prague Castle and the spires of St. Vitus' Cathedral

perform. The hub of the New Town is Wenceslas Square, a busy boulevard renowned as the focus of protests during the Velvet Revolution.

Locals love their music – as Mozart found out, when he triumphed here after only moderate success in Vienna. Classical music seems to be everywhere in Prague, advertised in listings guides and on posters across the city. Tickets are reasonably priced and the performances are invariably superb.

Czech Beer and Puppets

Restaurants and cafés fill up quickly in Prague, but Czechs tend to eat early, so your chances of getting a table will improve by about 8 p.m. There's a wide range of options, from American and Italian to Lebanese and Japanese. Don't leave the city without tasting at least one Czech beer. Prague's own brews are Staropramen and U Feků.

The best shopping is in the maze of arcades under the buildings of Wenceslas Square along the pedestrian-only street Na Příkopě and also along Narodní trída. There are interesting craft shops on Karlova, near the Charles Bridge. Puppets make ideal gifts – they're works of art, not just playthings. Try the Theater Bookstore and Marionettes (Divadelní Knihku-pectrí a Louthy) at Celetná 17.

ESSENTIAL INFORMATION

TOURIST INFORMATION
• Česká centrála cestovního ruchu (Czech tourist authority), Národní trída 37 ☎ 02 24 21 14 58
• Prague Information Service (PIS), Na příkopě 20, Nové Mesto ☎ 02 26 40 22
• Praha Llavní nádraží (Prague railroad station) ☎ 02 24 22 42 00
• Staroměstská Radnice (Old Town Hall), Staroměstské náměstí ☎ 02 24 22 42 00

URBAN TRANSPORTATION
Prague has three subway lines: A (green), B (yellow) and C (red). Stations are indicated by the letter "M" (marked in a red circle on the city map). Trains run frequently every day between 5 a.m. and midnight. Trams and buses are also frequent, but buses run mainly outside the city center. One ticket can be used for the subway, buses and trams: for information call ☎ 02 24 22 51 35. Taxis can be hailed on the street or located at taxi stands. A lit sign on the car shows that it's free. Make sure the taxi has a meter registering the fare.

AIRPORT INFORMATION
Ruzyně Airport, 10 miles west of the city, is a bus ride from the center. Airport buses run to Dejvická subway station or Náměstí Republiky, on the edge of the Old Town. There are also shuttle services to the main hotels. A Czechoslovak Airlines (ČSA) bus travels to their terminal (Revoluční 25) every half hour daily 5:30 a.m.–7 p.m. Call for flight information (☎ 02 36 78 14 or 02 36 77 60), or call Czechosolovak Airlines on ☎ 02 20 11 11 11.

CLIMATE – average highs and lows for the month

JAN.	FEB.	MAR.	APR.	MAY	JUN.	JUL.	AUG.	SEP.	OCT.	NOV.	DEC.
2°C	2°C	8°C	12°C	18°C	20°C	22°C	23°C	18°C	12°C	5°C	2°C
36°F	36°F	46°F	54°F	64°F	68°F	72°F	73°F	64°F	54°F	41°F	36°F
-4°C	-4°C	0°C	2°C	7°C	10°C	13°C	12°C	9°C	0°C	0°C	-2°C
25°F	25°F	32°F	36°F	45°F	50°F	55°F	54°F	48°F	32°F	32°F	28°F

City Sights

Key to symbols

✚ map coordinates refer to the Prague map on page 124–125; sights below are highlighted in yellow on the map.

⊠ address or location ☎ telephone number

⊙ opening times ⊟ nearest bus or tram route

❚❚ restaurant on site or nearby

◧ admission charge: $$$ more than 110Kčs, $$ 70Kčs–100Kčs, $ less than 70Kčs

Chrám svatého Mikuláše

✚ A3 ⊠ Malastranké náměsti ⊙ Daily 9–5, Apr.-Oct.; 9–4, rest of year ⊟ Malostranská ⊟ Tram 12, 22 ◧ $

Mozart played the 2,500-pipe organ here in 1787; he couldn't have chosen a more grandiose setting than the Chrám Svatého Mikuláše (Church of St. Nicholas). It was constructed in the 18th century as a fanfare of Catholic counter-Reformation propaganda. It's a frenzy of decoration: pink-and-green mock-marble pillars; a 16,146-square foot ceiling fresco; a copper statue of St. Nicholas; and huge sculptures of the four church fathers, including St. Cyric killing the devil.

Josefov

✚ C4 ⊠ Státní židnovské muzeum, Jáchymova 3, Josefov ☎ 02 24 81 00 99 ⊙ Sun.–Fri. 9–4:30; closed Jewish holidays ❚❚ Kosher Restaurace Shalom, see page 548 ⊟ Tram 17, 18 ◧ $$

Walls went up around Prague's Jewish community in 1254, in keeping with a church law that Christians and Jews should live apart. But the walls did nothing to protect the inhabitants of the ghetto from centuries of persecution and murder. In 1389, 3,000 were massacred in a pogrom, and at regular intervals, kings passed laws forcing Jews to wear particular clothes or colors to single them out.

Even in the face of such vicious discrimination, the ghetto developed as a center of learning, and some of its members were able to buy occasional privileges for the community from the imperial court. In 1784 Joseph II abolished residence restrictions (the

Inside the dome of St. Nicholas' Church

area was subsequently named after him). Over a century later, most of its slums were demolished.

In the confined space of the Old Jewish Cemetery, 100,000 people are buried. Crooked gravestones lean and overlap; pebbles and prayers are still left on them as tributes. At the entrance, the Old Gravediggers' Hall has an exhibition of drawings by children held here before being sent by the Nazis to Auschwitz concentration camp; about 15,000 children passed through. By the end of World War II, Prague's Jewish population had been virtually wiped out. A museum devoted to the Holocaust is housed in the Pinkasova Synagóga (Pinkas Synagogue).

The oldest building is the 13th-century Synagogue, where legend has it the clay man, or Golem, created by Rabbi Löw in 1580 to serve and guard the ghetto, is still kept in the attic. The Rabbi had to return his creation to lifeless clay after it ran rampant through the streets. This and other synagogues around the cemetery survived World War II because of Hitler's perverse plan to create a museum dedicated to a vanished race. The synagogues, still active places of worship, collectively form the State Jewish Museum and can all be visited on one ticket.

The 17th-century cloisters of the Loreta shrine

KARLŮV MOST

✚ B3–C3   ✉ Staroměstska/Malá Strana
🍴 Reykavík, see page 548   🚊 Tram 12, 22 to Malá Strana Square

Karlův Most (Charles Bridge) is more than just a river crossing. A walk across the 1,700-foot span takes you past more than 30 sculptures, plus countless courting couples, puppeteers, musicians, souvenirsellers and tourists, and offers a breathtaking view both of the river and of the city's domes and spires. It was the work of Petr Parléř, who also created much of St. Vitus' Cathedral, and was built in 1357 to link the Old Town with the Lesser Quarter. Known until 1870 as the Prague Bridge, it has 16 sandstone arches but was originally relatively plain. The first ornament, a bronze crucifix, was added in 1657. Over the following 60 years statues were erected, evenly spaced along the parapets; they include St. John of Nepomuk (with the spangled halo), who was thrown from the bridge in 1393 after taking the side of the church in a dispute with the king.

LORETÁNSKÁ KAPLE

✚ Off the map   ✉ Loretánské náměstí, Hradčany
☎ 02 24 51 07 80   🕐 Tue.–Sun. 9–noon and 1–4:30
🍴 U Ševce Matouše, see page 548   🚊 Tram 22 to Pohorelec   ✋ $$

As part of their campaign to win worshipers back to Catholicism after the Reformation, the church made much of the cult of the Virgin Mary, and the ornate Loretánská kaple (Loreta Chapel) is one result. It was built in 1626 around a replica of Mary's house, supposedly flown by angels from Nazareth to Loreto in Italy, and it soon became a site of pilgrimage. Don't miss the painting of St. Starosta, who grew a beard to repel her suitor and was crucified by her infuriated father.

PETŘÍN

✚ A3   ✉ Funicular railway: Újezd, Malá Strana
🕐 Lookout Tower: daily 10–7, Apr.–Aug.; daily 10–6, Sep.–Oct.; Sat.–Sun. 10–5, rest of year   🚊 Tram 22 to Strahov   ✋ Tower $$

Woods and orchards cover this hill on the city's western bank, and a funicular railway, the Lanovka, takes passengers up and down. The carriages were installed in 1891, the same year that the Rozhledna (Lookout Tower) was constructed at the top, both great Czech achievements. Steps (299 of them in all) lead to the tower's viewing platform and a panorama of the city and the mountains far beyond.

PRAŽSKÝ HRAD

✚ A4   ✉ Hradčany   ☎ 02 24 37 33 68
🕐 Tue.–Sun. 9–5, Apr.–Oct.; 9–4, rest of year   🍴 U Ševce Matouše, see page 548; U Zlaté Hrusky, see page 548   🚊 Tram 22 to Pražský hrad   ✋ $$

Looming over the city and the river, Pražský hrad (Prague Castle) has been a symbol of Czech authority since the first fortress was built on this high, rocky site in the ninth century. The name actually refers to a complex of palaces, courtyards, churches and streets, all spread across the hill known as Hradčany. A long flight of broad steps (usually lined with souvenir sellers), climbs to the castle itself, a mixture of styles spanning 450 years of restoration and guarded by a series of

KAFKA

Franz Kafka's diminutive house in Golden Lane

Franz Kafka wrote two of the 20th century's most significant novels – *The Trial* and *The Castle* – but he died practically unknown, having made his friend, Max Brod, promise to destroy all his writings. It's only because Brod broke that promise that Kafka is read throughout the world today.

His tales of helpless individuals caught in the workings of massive bureaucracy were inspired by the overgrown Habsburg administration. They came to represent the menace and detachment of authority in general, and the term "Kafkaesque" was coined to describe a seemingly ordinary but surreal and dangerous world of systems with their own life and logic.

Kafka was born in Prague, and moved with his family from house to house around Old Town Square, where his father was a haberdasher. He studied law and worked as an insurance clerk, writing his stories by night. The city appears throughout his writings. *The Castle* was inspired by Prague Castle; his story *The Great Wall of China* was based on the "Hunger Wall" on Petrín Hill, built as part of a 14th-century job creation scheme and funded by money

expropriated from Jews. Kafka rented a house on Golden Lane, but his health was always poor and he died of tuberculosis at the early age of 41. His grave can be seen at the Old Jewish Cemetery. He left a third, unfinished novel, *Amerika*, and many short stories.

The most famous, *Metamorphosis*, related the story of Gregor Samsa, who awakens to find himself transformed into a giant insect and to his family becomes an object first of horror, then of pity and eventually of contempt. The theme of a bewildered victim of inexplicable events is characteristic of Kafka's style.

The author also recorded his wanderings around Prague, his relationship with his father and with Felice Bauer (to whom he was twice engaged), and his tortured nights of writing in his diaries, which were also posthumously published.

The Communist regime subsequently suppressed Kafka's work, but he is now, finally, acknowledged and honored in the city he described as "a little old mother with sharp claws: she won't let go."

The Astronomical Clock on the Old Town Hall

courtyards. At the entrance to the outer courtyard, two soldiers stand at attention under grotesque and threatening statues of the Titans. The guard is changed every hour. In the second courtyard, entered through the 17th-century Matthias Gate, are the castle's art gallery and information center. Finally, you reach the courtyard of Katedrálá sv Vital (St. Vitus' Cathedral), which took 600 years to complete and was only consecrated in 1929. The royal palace, to the right, is a maze of rooms centered around the 15th-century Vladislav Hall, where mounted knights would trot down the Riders' Staircase to take part in indoor jousting matches. Nearby are the Chancellery of Bohemia offices, where two Catholic governors were hurled from the window in 1618.

STAROMĚSTSKÁ RADNICE

➕ D3   ✉ Staroměstská náměstí   ☎ 02 24 48 11 11
🕐 Daily 9–6, Apr.–Sep.; Tue.–Sun. 9–5, Mon. 11–5,

rest of year   🍴 Reykavík, see page 548   🚋 Tram 17 to Staroměstská námestí

Since a merchants' house was earmarked by the city council in 1338, the Staroměstská radnice (Old Town Hall) has gradually expanded and taken over a whole row of houses. A tower and chapel were added; features range from the original carved facade to the 19th-century house known as "At the Cock." Its main attraction is the intricate Astronomical Clock high on one wall, which gives the time, month, season, zodiac signs, course of the sun and Christian holidays. On the hour a skeleton appears and chimes the bell, followed by the Twelve Apostles and other assorted characters, all parading from their little doors above the clock face.

ŠTERNBERSKÝ PALÁC

➕ A4   ✉ Hradčanské náměstí 15   ☎ 02 20 51 45 95
🕐 Tue.–Sun. 10–6   🍴 Kavárna ve Šternberskén Palčí, in the palace   🚋 Tram 22 to Pražský hrad
✋ $$

Tucked into an alley off Hradčany Square is Šternberský palác (Sternberg Palace), a town house built for Count Sternberg in 1698. It has an impressive collection of old masters: Highlights include *The Feast of the Rosary*, by German Renaissance painter and engraver Albrecht Dürer, and *Adam and Eve*, by painter, etcher and woodcut-designer Lucas Cranach.

STRAHOVSKÝ KLÁŠTER

➕ Off the map   ✉ Strahovské nádvoří 1, Hradčany
☎ 02 20 51 66 71   🕐 Daily 9–noon and 1–5   🍴 Peklo ("Hell") restaurant in the cellars   🚋 Tram 22 to Pohořelec   ✋ $$

The baroque spires of Strahovský klášter (Strahov Monastery) dominate the hilltop west of Hradčany: the monastery's name means "to watch over," and it has guarded this sight since the 12th century. Elaborately decorated library halls store more than 130,000 books and manuscripts; the oldest, the *Strahov Gospels*, is displayed at the entrance. The upper floor of the cloisters is now a gallery of artworks returned to the monks by former Communist rulers.

EXCURSION TO KUTNÁ HORA

When silver and copper ore deposits were found on this hill 40 miles southeast of Prague, a town shot up virtually overnight, taking the appropriate name of Kutná Hora, or "Mining Mountain." That was in the late 13th century, and soon a royal mint was set up, hammering out the silver coin known as *Pražské grosé* in its workshops. Also constructed was a royal palace known as the Italian Court, a reference to the Florentine advisers of King Wenceslas II (1278–1305). The town flourished on its mining proceeds, and even managed to recover after being taken over by one force after another during the Hussite Wars. But by the end of the 16th century the mountain was all mined out and the town fell into decay, suffering the final blow with a disastrous fire in 1770.

The handsome Cathedral of St. Barbara was paid for by miners and dedicated to their patron saint. For its design they turned to the prestigious architect of Prague's St. Vitus' Cathedral, Petr Parléř, who rose to the occasion with distinctive tent-like spires and flying buttresses. In the side chapel, frescoes show the coin makers and the miners at work.

Sculptures line Barbarská ulice, a street leading to an impressive 15th-century house built for a profiteer who ran an illegal private mining operation. It's now the Mining Museum, and behind it is the medieval mine itself, consisting of 820 feet of tunnels; a horse-drawn winch at the entrance drew out the bags of ore. The royal mint is gone

The 14th-century Italian Court at Kutna Hora, built on the proceeds from mining

(although it is still possible to make out its outline); parts of the Italian Court – including the chapel, adorned with art nouveau frescoes – can be visited.

About two miles north of the town, in Sedlec, is an ossuary (storehouse for bones) originally owned by Cistercian monks. During the 19th century its 40,000 human bones were put to artistic use by František Rint, who made them into chandeliers, bells and other disconcerting items.

Contact a tourist information office for details of public transportation to Kutná Hora and Sedlec. Agencies organizing tours from Prague to Kutná Hora include:

Martin Tour ✉ Stepanska 61, Praha 1-110 00 ☎ 02 24 21 24 73; fax 02 24 22 54 37

Jomys ✉ Na Morani 5, Praha 2-120 00 ☎ 02 29 45 10; fax 02 29 58 67

DENMARK

"C*OPENHAGEN is the best-built city of the north."*

From *Travels into Poland, Russia, Sweden, etc.*
by English historian and travel writer William Coxe

Opposite: *The Little Mermaid*, Copenhagen's most enduring symbol

Denmark

DENMARK

Denmark was the cradle of ancient Scandinavia. Talk of the first Vikings and you talk of Danes. It was from this fragmented mosaic of peninsulas and islands between mainland Europe and the Swedish-Norwegian landmass that those consummate seamen first struck out in search of plunder and new territory. Denmark is the smallest of the four Scandinavian nations, yet the Danes have made their country one of the most advanced and progressive in the world.

Danish Archipelago

The Kingdom of Denmark is just over 200 miles long, and the Jutland peninsula (the primary landmass) is only 75 miles wide. Nowhere in Denmark is much higher than 100 feet above sea level, and the country's highest point – Yding Skovhøj in central Jutland – is only 567 feet in elevation. Jutland's narrow southern border is with Germany; its west coast adjoins the North Sea.

East of Jutland, and with barely a sliver of water in between, is Denmark's second-largest island, Funen (Fyn). East of Funen is Zealand (Sjælland), the largest island, its northeastern edge a stone's throw from the Swedish coast, and home to the capital, Copenhagen (København). Zealand and Funen lie like natural fortresses across the Kattegat, the channel separating Denmark from Sweden. This strategic position across the entrance to the Baltic Sea has always placed the country at the maritime heart of northern Europe.

The Jutland Peninsula

Copenhagen is the magnet for visitors, but the rest of this disparate and fascinating country has much to offer. Far western Jutland has an invigorating coastal landscape of long, sandy beaches backed by broad dunes and moorland. This landscape is repeated in north Jutland beyond the dividing waters of the Limfjord and all the way to the Skagen peninsula, the bird-like beak of land that thrusts into the sea at Denmark's northern edge. In north Jutland, outside the city of Aalborg, are evocative traces of Scandinavia's Viking culture at Lindholm Høje, a remarkable Viking burial ground of nearly 700 graves, many marked by stones in the shape of long ships.

The heathland of the west coast of central Jutland gives way in the east to a fertile undulating countryside of small farms and woodland, interspersed with country towns and pretty villages. On the east coast is Århus, a sophisticated and historic university city and

Attractive half-timbered houses in Ronne on the Danish island of Bornholm

Denmark's second largest. Here you will find the mighty Århus Cathedral and the intriguing Den Gamle By, the Old Town and its dozens of restored, timber-framed buildings. South of Århus is a great stretch of woodland where you can enjoy peace and quiet along walking, bicycling and horseback riding trails. Southwest of Århus is the

MORE TOP DESTINATIONS IN DENMARK

- Århus B2 • Bornholm C4
- Egeskov B1 • Frederiksborg C2
- Køge C2 • Kronborg C2
- Legoland A2 • Lindholm Høje B3
- Louisiana C2 • Møgeltønder A1 •
Møn C1 • Nyborg B1 • Ribe A1 •
Roskilde C2 • Skagen B4

Denmark

town of Billund and Denmark's famous Legoland, the country's most visited attraction outside of Copenhagen. Beyond all the plastic bricks is the farming country of south Jutland, with such fascinating towns and villages as the ancient settlement of Ribe, which has a handsome cathedral, cobbled streets and gabled houses. The little village of Møgeltønder, in the far southwest, has a superb frescoed church and charming thatched houses.

Country of Islands

Denmark is a world of islands. There are more than 400 of them scattered around the country's coasts and across the Kattegat and the Baltic Sea. About 100 islands are inhabited. Funen (Fyn) is hailed as the "Garden of Denmark" because of its rich alluvial soils, legacy of the glacial debris left by retreating ice sheets.

The capital of Funen is Odense, the birthplace of Hans Christian Andersen. Funen has a gentle rural nature overall, its lush farmland complemented by a pleasant southern coastline and by good beaches on the peaceful island of Langeland, off the southeast coast.

Funen is connected to Denmark's largest island, Zealand, by a typically Danish feat of remarkable engineering. The 11-mile-long Great Belt fixed link rail and road bridge island-hops, via the island of Sprogø, across the Great Belt (Storebælt) channel.

Prior to 1998 visitors had to make ferry connections between Funen and Zealand; it was more romantic, but Scandinavian efficiency eventually triumphed with a combination of tunnel, conventional bridge and the world's second-largest suspension bridge. All of Denmark is now physically united, with work under way on a similar bridging project between Zealand and Sweden.

Historic Zealand

Copenhagen may dominate Zealand, but the whole island is a treasure house of Danish history. North Zealand has much to offer in terms of historic buildings: the lakeside setting of magnificent Frederiksborg Castle (Frederiksborg Slot); Kronberg Castle (Kronberg Slot) at Helsingør; and Elsinore Castle (Elsinore Slot), the setting for Shakespeare's *Hamlet*, overlooking the Øresund and the Swedish coast.

Just west of Copenhagen is Roskilde, Denmark's medieval capital, with a splendid cathedral housing the decorated crypts of 37 Danish kings and queens. In southern Zealand is the city of Køge, whose medieval center survives; at Trelleborg, on the west coast where the new rail bridge slices across the Great Belt, are the remains of the finest Viking ring fort in Denmark. Finally, just off the south coast of Zealand are the islands of Møn, Falster and Lolland, all linked to the main islands by bridges. Of these, Møn is the most interesting because of its chalk cliffs, a startling contrast to Denmark's almost uniform flatness.

Exploring Denmark

Denmark is one of the most accessible European countries. Its compact size and the smooth transition from island to island that modern engineering has accomplished makes exploring various regions by car an easy option once you are clear of Copenhagen's urban center.

This compactness makes traveling by public transportation almost as convenient. Fast, comfortable trains can whisk you from Zealand to Funen, and then on to Jutland, in a few hours. The efficient and extensive rail network offers stiff competition to long-distance bus services in Denmark, although buses are less expensive than trains.

Legoland, where millions of tiny Lego bricks have been made into an amazing model world

Denmark's climate is typical of a maritime environment, and the low elevation means there are no great extremes of temperature. Summers are pleasantly mild, but there can be wet spells; in winter snow is likely at times, but much less so than in the other Scandinavian countries.

Denmark is different in other ways as well, yet in matters of food and drink it remains engagingly – and tastily – Scandinavian. Danes relish the same hearty sandwich feast, here called the *smørrebrød*, that you find in Norway and Sweden, complete with its garnished mixes of delicious meat and seafood.

Beer is a Danish specialty, and the famous Danish breweries of Carlsberg and Tuborg produce some of the most popular brews in the world.

You will find that Danes are generally helpful and friendly. In rural areas and in provincial cities such as Odense, people are unfailingly so, but in Copenhagen there may be a sharper edge to people's attitudes. At times you may detect an apparent reserve on the part of Danish people. It is not a negative sentiment; the Danes are a supremely accomplished people, and beneath the reserve is a fierce national pride in their enduring country.

Denmark

TIMELINE

4000 BC	Neolithic settlers begin developing a farming economy.
500 BC to AD 500	Iron Age people set up trading centers in Jutland and Funen.
AD 793	Danish Vikings raid England's east coast, plundering the monastery of Lindisfarne, and penetrate deep into mainland Europe along the northern rivers.
circa 925	Gorm the Old becomes first king of a united Denmark.
1167	Founding of Copenhagen by Absalon, Bishop of Roskilde.
1596	Christian IV becomes king of Denmark and promotes the construction of great Renaissance buildings, particularly in the city of Copenhagen.
1648–79	Periodic wars with Sweden.
1901	First democratically elected government takes power.
1914–18	Denmark is neutral during World War I.
1940	Denmark is invaded by the German army in spite of its declared neutrality; the Danish Resistance carries out a vigorous campaign against Germany.
1945	Denmark is liberated and begins a program of postwar reconstruction.
1949	Denmark joins NATO.
1973	Denmark joins the European Community.
1993	Danish people vote to join the European Union.
1996	Copenhagen designated as a European City of Culture.
1998	Opening of the fixed link rail and road bridge across the Storebælt (Great Belt).

A TALENTED ROYAL LADY

Denmark's current queen, Margrethe II, was born in 1940. She was the eldest daughter of King Frederik IX, who had no sons. After a favorable 1953 referendum, the Danish constitution, which allowed only for a male heir to the throne, was amended to enable female succession. Margrethe became queen at the age of 32, after Frederik's death in 1972. She is Denmark's first female monarch since the 15th century. Queen Margrethe qualified as an archeologist after studying at Copenhagen, Århus, Cambridge and Paris. She is a talented artist and illustrator, illustrating an edition of J. R. R. Tolkein's fantasy *Lord of the Rings* and designing stamps for the Danish postal service. The queen has also designed theatrical costumes and stage settings for the Danish Royal Theatre. An accomplished linguist, Queen Margrethe has translated the work of the French novelist Simone de Beauvoir, a task in which she worked with her husband, French-born Prince Henrik.

Survival Guide

- If you drive through Denmark, ask the tourist office for details about "The Marguerite Route," which is a series of linked routes along quieter roads throughout the most scenic parts of the country. Signs display a daisy motif on a brown background.
- If you are touring Denmark in late July, take in the exciting Viking Fair *(Vikingespil)* at the ancient city of Roskilde, complete with its gathering of Viking ships.
- In Denmark *frokost* means "breakfast," but is actually the common word used for lunch, while *morgenmad* is the true "morning meal." *Smørrebrød*, the tasty Scandinavian open-faced sandwich, remains a lunchtime favorite; but try *frikadeller*, delicious fried meat or fish patties with salad and potatoes; and dip into the heftier *koldt bord*, a buffet-style selection. For main meals, enjoy *kogt torsk*, poached cod in mustard sauce, or old-fashioned *Hvid labskovs*, Danish stew.
- Delicious Danish pastries are called *wienerbrød* and come in a variety of shapes and tasty flavors. In every town and large village you will find a bakery selling pastries.
- Amber is a Danish specialty. The Amber Specialist shop on Strøget is the place to look in Copenhagen, but you will find distinctive amber jewelry in stores throughout the country. If you're shopping for a colorful Scandinavian sweater go to Sweater Market, one of the biggest outlets, in Copenhagen's Frederiksberggade.
- Denmark, like Sweden, is noted for its distinctive furnishing designs. Known as "Danish Modern," there is a classic merging of the functional with the aesthetic. Visit Illums Bolighus on Strøget in Copenhagen for some of the finest examples.
- Unlike the northern Scandinavian countries, Denmark has a more relaxed approach to the sale of liquor. You can buy wines, spirits and beers in grocery stores, and you may find that prices are lower than in Norway, Sweden or Finland.
- Soft drinks in ring-pull cans are currently banned because of their damaging potential to the environment and wildlife when discarded. Bottled drinks are therefore the norm and carry a hefty deposit, which will be refunded when empty bottles are returned to the place of purchase.
- Traditionally formal, Danes have become more relaxed about what to wear when eating out. Smart, casual clothes, especially during the summer months, are fine for dining at most restaurants.

Standing guard at the Amalienborg Palace

Denmark

Copenhagen

COPENHAGEN

Copenhagen (København) is where the European experience becomes Scandinavian. This is a magnificent city, far more a "Wonderful Copenhagen" than even the Danny Kaye song implies. It is a city of towers and steeples that are elegant and sculptural, as well as monumental. It is a city that draws you in along

Universitet Bibl

Frilandsmuseet (Lyngby)

Fælled Parken

FREDERIK BAJERS PLADS

Rigshospitalet

Eksperimentarium; Tuborg Bryggerierne; Dyrehaven (Bakken)

LILLE TRIANGEL

5

De gamles By

Garnisons Kirkegård

Blegdams Hospitalet

Holmes Kirkegård

Østerpo Statio

Nørre Hospitalet

Østre Anlæg

Østre VOLDGADE

4

Mosaisk Kirkegård

SKT HANS TORV

Den Hirschsprungske Samling

Statens Museum for Kunst

Danmarks-tekniske Høskole

Assistens Kirkegård

Tinghus

Danmarks-tekniske Høskole

SOLVTORVET

SKT PAULS PLADS

Kommune Hospital

DSB

Palmehus

Geologisk Museum

Botanisk Have

Rosenborg Slot

Marmork (Frederikski

BLÅGÅRDS PLADS

Botanisk Museum

Kongens Have

C L Davids Samling

Arbejdermuseet

Musikhistorisk Museum

3

Nørreport Station

Radiohusets Konzertsaal

HERMES TRIERS PLADS

Søpavillionen

KULTORVET

Rundetårn

KONGENS

JULIUS THOMSENS PLADS

Ørsteds-parken

Telefonhus

GRÅBRØDRE TORV

Charlotter NYTORV

SKT MARKUS PLADS

Universitet

FRUE PLADS

Helligånds-kirken

Rongelige Teater

Tekn Inst

BISPE-TORVET

Nikolaj Kirke

DANASVEJ

JARMERS PLADS

Vor Frue Kirke

GAMMEL-TORV

VIMMELSK AMAGER (STRØGET)

HØJBRO PLADS

2

NYTORV

Thorvaldsens Museum

Tycho Brahe Planetarium

Domhuset

Lurblowers

CHRISTIANSBORG SLOTSPLEIN

Holmens K

Scala

RÅDHUS PLADSEN

Rådhuset

Christiansborg Slot

Børsen

SAS

National-museet

Minesterialbygn Det kongelige Bibliotek

Tivoli

DANTES PLADS

Tøjhusmuseet

Københavns Bymuseet

BANEGARDS PLADS

VESTERBRO TORV

KIRKEPLADS

Hovedbanegård

Ny Carlsberg Glyptotek

OTTO MONSTEDS PLADS

1

Central Postbygn

Postgiri Kontoret

Carlsberg Bryggerierne

A

Godsbanegården

B

C

Statens Serumims

pedestrian-only streets that lead in and out of delightful squares. It is a city with museums and attractions, restaurants, cafés and entertainment that place it among the finest of European capitals.

COPENHAGEN

N

0   250   500 m

0   250   500 yards

Den lille Havfrue

Yderhavnen

Langeliniepavillionen

ke

Kastellet

Frihedsmuseet

ESPLANADEN

Søndre Tolbod

stindustri-
eet

NYHOLM

Sankt Ansgar
Kirke

malienborg   LARSENS
PLADS

MALIENBORG
PLADS

DOKØEN

T ANNÆ
LADS

FREDERIKSHOLM

GRØNLANDSKE
HANDELS
PLADS

KRØYERS
PLADS

ISLANDS
PLADS

ARSENALØEN

BODENHOFFS
PLADS

WILDERS
PLADS

ATISK
ADS

Orlogsmuseet

CHRISTIANSHAVN

Vor Frelsers
Kirke

Stadsgraven

Kaninøen

Ravelinen

Kl Pumpest

CHRISTMAS
MØLLERS
PLADS

VERMLANDSGADE

dsgraven

ULEVARD

AMAGERBROGADE

E

Copenhagen originated, like so many other Scandinavian towns and cities, as a small fishing village, its occupants taking advantage of the sheltered waters around Slotsholmen Island, the island that is now home to the Danish National Parliament (Folketing), and the Christiansborg Palace (Christiansborg Slot). By the 12th century Slotsholmen had been fortified in keeping with the settlement's growing commercial status, a status signified by its name, Kømandshavn, the "port of the merchants," later amended to København. By the middle of the 15th century, Copenhagen was the recognized capital of Denmark.

The city's status was enhanced by the construction of many fine buildings during the reign of Christian IV of Denmark in the 17th century, and by the 19th century Copenhagen had emerged as a major European capital. Development continued during the 20th century, and at the start of a new millennium Copenhagen stands as a mature and hugely successful city.

First Impressions

The initial impression visitors have of Copenhagen is of a city overpowered by traffic. To reach the central City Hall Square (Rådhuspladsen) from Copenhagen's central railroad station (Hovedbanegården), visitors pass Tivoli and then negotiate busy downtown streets. Hans Christian Andersens Boulevard, a broad and howling stream of traffic, is as far removed from Andersen's fairy-tale world as can be imagined. Keep your eyes open for cyclists as well as cars. The broad expanse of City Hall Square, a relaxed, traffic-free environment, leads to a refreshing world of lively streets, colorful squares and hidden corners, where pedestrians are the priority.

Copenhagen

Copenhagen

There is a lot to see in Copenhagen. Some attractions, such as Rosenborg Palace and the National Museum for Fine Arts, are some distance from City Hall Square. Even the famous statue of *The Little Mermaid* is a long walk along the waterfront from the central parts of the city. Getting around is easy, however, if you take advantage of the various guided walking tours that are available. They include the service of authorized guides who attend to just about all your needs. Other sightseeing tours go by bus and by harbor or canal boats. The city's bus service is extremely efficient and comprehensive. Because of the city center's pedestrian-only status, however, exploring on your own here is a pleasure.

Strøget and Beyond

Start at City Hall Square. Look back across the rushing traffic and up at the Unibank building, where you will see a unique bronze weathervane featuring a girl who appears on her bicycle when the weather is fine, and with an umbrella when it rains.

The sequence of streets known collectively as Strøget begins at City Hall Square, at the narrow Frederiksberggade. Amid the stores and restaurants fascinating side streets lead to antique and specialty outlets; vistas suddenly reveal the city's impressively grand architecture and fashionable people.

City on the Water's Edge

At the far end of Strøget, cross the big, bustling square of New Royal Market (Kongens Nytorv) to reach New Harbor (Nyhavn), the old harbor inlet, now an area of fashionable restaurants. Visit Amalienborg Square and Amalienborg Palace, then head east to waterside Larsens Plads; from this square a pleasant walk north takes you to *The Little Mermaid*.

Nearby is the Museum of the Danish Resistance (Frihedsmuseet), an inspiring celebration of resistance against the Nazis. These attractions all spotlight Copenhagen's chief lure for visitors: its astonishing variety.

ESSENTIAL INFORMATION

TOURIST INFORMATION
• Copenhagen tourist information center, 1 Bernstorffsgade ☎ 38 38 30 25 for general information; ☎ 33 25 38 44 for hotel information
• Use It information office: 13 Råhusstræde ☎ 33 73 06 20

URBAN TRANSPORTATION
Copenhagen's main railroad station is Hovedbanegård, on Bernstorffsgade. The station has modern facilities, including many stores, and is only a few minutes from the city center.
Copenhagen has a very good network of bus routes. City buses leave from Rådhuspladsen. For information call ☎ 36 45 45 45. Taxis have fixed rates. For service, call ☎ 35 35 35 35 or 32 51 51 51.

AIRPORT INFORMATION
Modern, efficient Copenhagen Airport is located at Kastrup, about 6 miles south of the city center on the island of Amager. An Airport Express train runs from Hovedbanegård every 20 minutes, daily 5:30 a.m.–11:30 p.m. Airport buses leave every 15 minutes from outside Hovedbanegård, on Bernstorffsgade. For airport information, call ☎ 32 47 47 47.

CLIMATE – Average highs and lows for the month

JAN.	FEB.	MAR.	APR.	MAY	JUN.	JUL.	AUG.	SEP.	OCT.	NOV.	DEC.
3°C	3°C	5°C	10°C	15°C	19°C	20°C	20°C	16°C	11°C	7°C	4°C
37°F	37°F	41°F	50°F	59°F	66°F	68°F	68°F	61°F	52°F	45°F	39°F
-2°C	-2°C	0°C	2°C	7°C	11°C	13°C	12°C	10°C	7°C	3°C	0°C
28°F	28°F	32°F	36°F	45°F	52°F	55°F	54°F	50°F	45°F	37°F	32°F

CITY SIGHTS

Key to symbols

➕ map coordinates refer to the Copenhagen map on page 140–141; sights below are highlighted in yellow on the map.

✉ address or location ☎ telephone number

🕐 opening times 🚌 nearest bus route

🍴 restaurant on site or nearby

🎟 admission charge: $$$ more than DKr25, $$ DKr12–DKr25, $ less than DKr12

AMALIENBORG PLADS

➕ D3 ✉ Amalienborg Plads ☎ 33 12 21 86
🕐 Daily 10–4, May–Oct.; Tue.–Sun. 11–4, rest of year
🚌 1, 6, 9, 29 🎟 Amalienborg Slot Museum $$

The royal heart of Copenhagen is the octagonal Amalienborg Plads (Amalienborg Square), with an equestrian statue of Frederick V at its center, rococo palaces on four sides, and broad avenues leading off from the other four. The Danish royal family spends most of autumn and winter in the palaces. Royalty's very private presence gives the square a rather detached, lifeless atmosphere, except during the picturesque and colorful changing of the guard, which takes place daily at noon when the Queen is in residence.

On the northwest corner of the square is the Amalienborg Slot Museum, containing a charming collection of royal memorabilia and a sequence of reconstructed rooms that illustrate the life of the royal Glücksborg family from the mid-18th to mid-19th centuries.

CHRISTIANSBORG SLOT

Christiansborg Slot ➕ C2 ✉ Christiansborg Slotsplad ☎ 33 11 18 80 🚌 1, 2, 6, 8, 10, 37
Tøjhusmuseet 🕐 Tue.–Sun. noon–4 🎟 $$
Slotsholmen ruins ☎ 33 92 64 92 🕐 Daily 9:30–3:30, May–Sep.; Tue., Thu. and Sat.–Sun. 9:30–3:30, rest of year 🎟 $$
De Kongelige Repræsentationslokaler ☎ 33 92 64 92 🕐 Guided tours daily at 11, 1 and 4, Jun.–Aug.; daily at 11 and 3, May and Sep.; Tue., Thu. and Sat.–Sun. at 11 and 3, rest of year 🎟 $$$
Kongelige Stalde og Kareter 🕐 Fri.–Sun. 2–4, May–Sep.; Sat.–Sun. 2–4, rest of year
Teatermuseet 🕐 Sat.–Sun. noon–4, Wed. 2–4 🎟 $$

The monumental complex that makes up Christiansborg Slot (Christiansborg Palace) dominates the little island of Slottsholmen. It presents a rather stern face to the city when approached across the encircling canal from the direction of Strøget and Højbro Plads (Højbro Square). A visit here may take you all day. The vast west wing houses the Danish Parliament, the Supreme Court and the Foreign Office. It was built between 1907 and 1916 to replace a more stylish building that burned down in 1884. The west wing also contains the De Kongelige Repræsentationslokaler (Royal Reception Chambers), with lavishly decorated rooms, and grand Renaissance hall.

Below the palace, in the dense, muffled air of the basement, are the preserved ruins of Absalon's Fortress, the original Slotsholmen castle dating from 1167; and its successor, Copenhagen Slot (Copenhagen Castle). The rest of Christiansborg has a number of museums located around the central royal riding grounds, amid the healthy odor of horses. They include the Kongelige Stalde og Kareter (Royal Stables and Museum of Royal Coaches), the Teatermuseet (Theater Museum) and the Tøjhusmuseet (Museum of Danish Defense).

Den Lille Havfrue

Most visitors don't leave Copenhagen without seeing *The Little Mermaid* (*Den Lille Havfrue*), the most popular expression of Hans Christian Andersen's fairy-tale world. Some may find the experience disappointing. The mermaid, designed in 1913, languishes in rather stark isolation at the northern end of the city's waterfront. Sadly, vandals have damaged *The Little Mermaid* by sawing off her arm and her head on separate occasions. The original molds survive, however, making the Mermaid – in one sense – forever renewable.

Copenhagen

Palace, but was not completed until 1894. Modeled on St. Peter's in Rome, its dome measures 100 feet in diameter.

The nave is circular and is surrounded by a circular walkway, above which there is a whispering gallery with superb acoustics. Try whispering, and see how far the sound carries. The paneled frescoes on the inside of the dome are glowingly painted and gilded.

NATIONALMUSEET

C2 ✉ 10 Ny Vestergade ☎ 33 13 44 11
🕐 Tue.–Sun. 10–5 🍴 Museum café 🚌 1, 2, 6, 28
💰 $$$

Copenhagen's Nationalmuseet (National Museum) is one of the finest of its kind in Europe. There is a lot to see and the experience can be tiring if you try to take in everything during one visit; use the floor plan to get your bearings. The museum has outstanding exhibits on Danish history, with such superb Bronze Age artifacts as burial remains in oak coffins, a golden sun chariot and the silver Gundestrip cauldron. Among Iron Age finds are the magnificent North Slesvig Golden Horns. Other artifacts include a collection of *lur*, the wonderful horn instruments that were used for ceremony and communication. Other major collections cover the Middle Ages and the Renaissance, Egyptian and classical antiquities, and human cultures. There is also a children's museum. The museum has a film theater.

ROSENBORG SLOT

C3 ✉ 4a Øster Voldgade ☎ 33 15 32 86
🕐 Rosenborg Slot: Daily 10–4, May–Sep.; daily 11–3, in Oct. and Dec. 27–30; Tue., Fri. and Sun. 11–2, Jan.–Apr. and Nov. 1–Dec. 17 (daily 11–2, Feb. 13–21). Treasury: Daily 10–4, May–Sep.; daily 11–3, in Oct. and Dec. 27–30; Tue.–Sun. 11–3, Jan.–Apr. and Nov. 1–Dec. 17 (daily 11–3, Feb. 13–21). 🍴 Café/restaurant 🚌 14, 16 💰 $$$

The early 17th-century Rosenborg Slot (Rosenborg Palace) is an outstanding example of Renaissance architecture and style; it stands at the edge of the lovely Kongens Have, the King's Gardens. The lavishly decorated rooms reflect the regal

The great marble dome of Marmorkirken

KØBENHAVNS BYMUSEET

A1 ✉ Vesterbrogade 59 ☎ 33 21 07 72
🕐 Wed.–Mon. 10–4, May–Sep.; 1–5, rest of year
🚌 6, 16, 28 💰 $$ (free on Fri.)

The Københavns Bymuseet (Copenhagen City Museum) tells the story of Copenhagen through paintings, scale models of the city and a slide show, which has a commentary in English during the summer months. The exhibits give a vivid picture of the city from medieval times to the present, and will appeal to children as much as to adults. There is an exhibition about Søren Kierkegaard, the 19th-century Danish philosopher whose writings had a major impact on what became the 20th-century philosophy of existentialism. Alongside the museum is Absalonsgade, a cobbled "museum street" with all the trappings of an old street.

MARMORKIRKEN

D3 ✉ 4 Frederiksgade ☎ 33 15 01 44
🕐 Mon.–Fri. 11–2 (also Wed. 2–6), Sat. 11–4, Sun. noon–4 🚌 1, 6, 9, 29 💰 Free

Frederikskirken, known universally as Marmorkirken (Marble Church), seems out of place in a Copenhagen of slender, convoluted steeples and towers. The church was begun in 1749 as a final flourish to the nearby Amalienborg

Silkworms feed on mulberry leaves which are prevalent in southern France

LYON AND THE SILK TRADITION

Nearly 5,000 years ago the Chinese discovered that the cocoon of an insignificant moth could be gently unraveled in a continuous thread and woven to produce a light and luxurious fabric. This fabric is silk, still one of the softest and most desirable of all textiles.

Silk made its way overland from China to Europe by the 12th century, and by the 1600s Lyon had become the center for European silk production. (The silkworm, *bombyx mori*, also came to Europe and is now a domesticated insect with a ravenous appetite for mulberry leaves, which grow well in southern France and elsewhere.) The industry thrived, producing sophisticated weaves to supply France's rich and demanding upper classes. Sumptuous designs in dazzling colors were achieved on hand looms; silk damask, patterned silks and brocades, and figured silk velvets poured out of the workshops of Lyon.

In 1804, Joseph-Marie Jacquard invented the mechanical loom, which enabled patterns to be programed using a punch-card system. These very large looms were moved from the Old Town into special buildings in the Red Cross area (see page 189) that were designed to accommodate their size. The silkworkers (*canuts*), who also moved, were paid an abysmally low price for each pattern, with the middleman scooping the profits. Finally, in 1831 social unrest erupted, after a three-year struggle by the *canuts* to get better pay and conditions.

By 1870 the industry had recovered and Lyon silk was considered to be among the best fabrics in the world. The creation of artificial silk and other man-made fibers in the 20th century brought an end to large-scale silk production. Lyon's 30,000 weavers dwindled, and today there are only a handful of workshops where people still weave manually; hand-woven weaves are in high demand and are used to help restore the interiors of France's historic buildings.

If you're interested, you can follow the silk trail in Lyon, from the Old Town to the slopes of the Red Cross district, where you can visit silk workshops and working hand looms. Be sure not to miss the Fabric Museum (see page 190), keeping in mind that the most a skilled worker could hope to weave was three to four inches a day.

NICE

Nice, France's fifth-largest city and its biggest tourist resort, is perfectly situated on the sweeping Bay of Angels (Baie des Anges). With hills as its backdrop, it is blessed with gorgeous surroundings, a superb climate, a historic past and friendly people. Until 1860 Nice belonged to Italy, and to this day both the way of life and the inhabitants seem to combine the best of both cultures: Italian charm and flair tempered with a strong dash of Gallic sophistication.

The City

The Greeks built their settlement on the hills above the bay, and 300 years later the Romans settled here. The modern city stands on the same spot and has spread down to the flat land along the sea. Sheltered to the east and west by substantial promontories, and with the Maritime Alps to the north, Nice has its own microclimate, with mild winters and perfect summers. Over the centuries city planners and gardeners have taken advantage of these conditions, resulting in one of the most graceful and flower-filled cities in Europe – the average Frenchman's retirement-home fantasy.

In recent years, Nice has marketed itself as a convention center and vacation hot spot, attested by the variety of hotels. It has more museums than any other French city outside of Paris, and plenty of festivals and events throughout the year.

Getting Around

Nice is a big city, with several districts – each of which you'll want to experience. The best way to orient yourself is to take a bus or taxi to an area, then explore on foot. Start with the

atmospheric and picturesque Old Town (Vieille Ville, see page 198), which you'll probably want to visit more than once. Its seafront stretches nearly four miles to the west, with the famous Promenade des Anglais running along much of it. Behind the promenade and situated around the place Masséna is the commercial and business center, punctuated by peaceful gardens. The upscale residential suburb of Cimiez lies on the hill behind the old port and is home to several excellent museums. As you explore, notice how the

NICE

4 0   250   500 m
   0   250   500 yards

N

3

BLVD

ST-ÉTIENNE

Cathédrale
Orthodoxe
Russe

2

RUE F PASSY

AVENUE DES FLEURS

1   Musée des
    Beaux-Arts   Hôtel Négresco

Jardin
Botanique
Parc Floral
Phoenix

RUE DE FRANCE   PROMENADE DES ANGLAIS

A   B

BOULEVARD DE CESSOLE
BOULEVARD DE GORBELLA
SQUARE R BOYER
BOULEVARD GAMBETTA
RUE DE CHÂTEAUNEUF
BOULEVARD FRANÇOIS GROSSO
BOULEVARD DE LA MADELEINE

ambience varies, from the earthy gaiety in the streets of the Old Town to the haute couture you'll find along the Promenade des Anglais. You can see the different parts of Nice in style by hiring a *calèche* (horse-drawn carriage), or by taking the tourist train that trundles around the old quarter.

Flavors of the South

The French- and Italian-influenced cuisine of Nice is complemented by the sunny flavors of southern France. Look for an array of fish and seafood.

Vegetable dishes include *salade Niçoise* (made of lettuce, anchovies, tomatoes, hard-boiled eggs and black olives) and *ratatouille* (Mediterranean vegetable stew), which were created here. Also try *mesclun*, a bitter selection of wild leaves. Stuffed vegetables and zucchini flowers fried in batter accompany grilled fish and meat. *Estocaficada* is a Niçois dish made from dried Norwegian haddock and tomatoes. *Socca*, a type of pancake made from chickpeas, and *pissaladière*, an onion and anchovy tart, make good light lunches. The area produces several wines, de Bellet and Villars among them, and there's an international selection of wines and beer.

Local Wares and Souvenirs

Nice combines the temptations of big-city chain stores and designer outlets with local markets, antique shops and souvenir stores. Department stores and big-name labels are found around place Masséna, while local products are sold in the Old Town. Traditional brightly printed cottons, scents from the hills around Grasse, food, oils and wines make lovely gifts, but the best souvenirs from Nice are traditional carved figurines, known as *santons.*

Carnaval

Nice has a clutch of dynamic theaters, concert halls and an opera, as well as movie theaters, nightclubs, a casino and a host of cabaret restaurants, live-music bars and throbbing discos. The best place to learn about what's going on is in *7 Jours/7 Nuits,* available free from tourist offices. Enjoy the local festivals, popular no matter what time of year. The big ones are *Carnaval* and the *Batailles des Fleurs* (Battle of Flowers).

Beaches

Nice has public beaches, but to spend a day in the sun as the Niçois do, go to one of the city's 15 private beaches. Included in the fee is an outdoor lounge chair and sun-shade umbrella, changing rooms, freshwater showers, a range of activities and access to a private bar/restaurant. Topless sunbathing is the rule rather than the exception on the French Riviera, but there's no need to partake unless you're comfortable doing so.

ESSENTIAL INFORMATION

TOURIST INFORMATION
- SNCF railroad station, avenue Thiers ☎ 04 93 87 07 07
- 5 Promenade des Anglais ☎ 04 92 14 48 00
- Terminal 1, Aéroport Nice-Côte d'Azur ☎ 04 93 21 44 11
- Nice Ferber, Promenade des Anglais, west end ☎ 04 93 83 32 64

URBAN TRANSPORTATION
Since Nice is so large, you'll probably want to get to each area by bus or taxi, though the latter is more expensive. Sun Bus operates all over the city; maps are available from their headquarters (10 avenue Felix-Fauré) or from any tourist office. Buy your ticket, or *carnet* (book) of tickets at a kiosk before you board, and don't forget to validate it.

A "Nice by Bus" tourist pass is available for 1, 5 or 7 days and is a good deal. Buses run until 1 a.m. Taxis can be found at city-center cab stands (Esplanade Masséna, Promenade des Anglais and place Garibaldi are probably the most convenient locations); or call Central Taxi Riviera (☎ 04 93 13 78 78).

AIRPORT INFORMATION
Aéroport Nice-Côte d'Azur (☎ 04 93 21 30 30 or 04 93 21 30 12) is west of the city. International flights leave from terminal 1; Paris and other French destinations are served by terminal 2. Shuttle bus 23 runs every half-hour to the SNCF railroad station in town daily 6 a.m.–9 p.m. Taxis can be found near the airport exits, and take about 15 to 20 minutes to reach the city.

CLIMATE – average highs and lows for the month

JAN.	FEB.	MAR.	APR.	MAY	JUN.	JUL.	AUG.	SEP.	OCT.	NOV.	DEC.
13°C	13°C	14°C	17°C	20°C	24°C	25°C	27°C	24°C	20°C	17°C	13°C
55°F	55°F	57°F	63°F	68°F	75°F	77°F	81°F	75°F	68°F	63°F	55°F
5°C	6°C	8°C	9°C	13°C	17°C	19°C	20°C	17°C	13°C	9°C	6°C
41°F	43°F	46°F	48°F	55°F	63°F	66°F	68°F	63°F	55°F	48°F	43°F

Nice

City Sights

Key to symbols

➕ map coordinates refer to the Nice map on page 194–195; sights below are highlighted in yellow on the map.

✉ address or location ☎ telephone number
🕐 opening times 🚌 nearest bus route
🍴 restaurant on site or nearby
💰 admission charge: $$$ more than 75F, $$ 25F to 75F, $ less than 25F

Cathédrale Orthodoxe Russe

➕ B2 ✉ Boulevard du Tzarevitch 🕐 Mon.–Sat. 10–noon and 3–6, Sun. 3–6 🚌 5, 17, 24 🍴 Regular services in Russian

The Cathédrale Orthodoxe Russe (Russian Orthodox Cathedral), an exuberant pink-and-gray church with six green onion-shaped cupolas and an ornate exterior, looks out of place in southern France. Tzar Nicolas II built it in 1903 in memory of his son Nicolas, who is buried on the grounds. Inside is a dazzling collection of glittering treasures and icons.

Cimiez

Franciscan Church, Monastery and Museum ➕ D4 ✉ place du Monastère ☎ 04 93 81 00 04 🕐 Mon.–Sat. 10–noon and 3–6 🚌 15, 20, 22 💰 Free 🍴 Concerts in monastery cloisters in Aug.
Archeological Museum and Site ✉ 160 avenue des Arènes ☎ 04 93 81 59 57 🕐 Tue.–Sun. 10–noon and 2–6, Apr.–Sep.; Tue.–Sun. 10–1 and 2–5, rest of year 🚌 15, 20, 22 💰 $$
Jardin des Arènes ✉ avenue des Arènes 🕐 Gardens open dawn–dusk 🚌 15, 20, 22 💰 Free

Cimiez, set above the town center, was a smart residential area in Roman times and remains so today. It's packed with interesting attractions, including the Matisse Museum, a Franciscan church and monastery that have stood in their peaceful gardens since the 16th century, a small museum and harmonious cloister devoted to St. Francis, and the cemetery where artists Henri Matisse and Raoul Dufy are buried. The Roman site has been excavated, revealing the remains of its amphitheater and public baths. Housed in a nearby archeological museum are the

The entrance to the remarkable Museum of Modern and Contemporary Art

treasures uncovered here, and much more. The Jardin des Arènes (Arena Gardens), with its olive tree grove, makes a pleasant place for a picnic lunch.

Musée d'Art Moderne et Contemporain

➕ D2 ✉ Promenade des Arts ☎ 04 93 62 61 62 🕐 Daily 11–6 (also Fri. 6–10) 🚌 2, 5, 10, 17 💰 $$

There are sweeping views from the roof of the Musée d'Art Moderne et Contemporain (Museum of Modern and Contemporary Art), an architecturally stunning museum constructed of four gray marble towers linked by glass walkways. Nice artist Yves Klein founded the museum, whose collection covers French and American avant-garde art from the 1960s to the present. New realism, minimalism and pop art, including works by Roy Lichtenstein and Andy Warhol, are represented here. If you are visiting on Friday evening, Klein's *Mur du Feu* (Wall of Fire) is illuminated.

Musée Matisse

➕ D4 ✉ 164 avenue des Arènes de Cimiez ☎ 04 93 81 08 08 🕐 Wed.–Mon. 10–6, Apr.–Sep.; 10–5, rest of year 🍴 Café/restaurant 🚌 15, 17, 22 💰 $$

The peaceful setting of the Musée Matisse (Matisse Museum) amid olive tree groves makes a visit to this superb museum even more worthwhile. Inside are stunning drawings, paintings, hangings, paper cutouts and sculptures covering the

Nice

working life of this remarkable artist. The collection, given to Nice by Henri Matisse in 1954 and by his widow in 1960, is housed in an elegant, vibrantly red, Genoese-style 17th-century villa, fronted by terraced gardens. You can trace the evolution of the artist, whose style was influenced by late 19th- and early 20th-century art movements such as Impressionism and Fauvism.

PLACE MASSÉNA AND VICINITY

✚ C1 ✉ Promenade des Anglais 🚌 3, 7, 10, 22
🌳 Gardens free

The Niçois regard the elegant, arcaded place Masséna, situated behind the Promenade des Anglais, as the heart of their city. Around the square, with its sparkling fountain representing the planets, are broad boulevards lined with designer stores. On both sides of place Masséna run more than a mile of gardens. Take time to see the palms and roses at the Jardin Albert 1er (Albert I Garden), Nice's oldest gardens, and the Promenade du Paillon (Hanging Gardens of Paillon), a stepped garden filled with azaleas, camellias and aromatic pines.

PROMENADE DES ANGLAIS

✚ A1–B1 ✉ Promenade des Anglais 🚌 3, 7, 10 22
ℹ️ Nice *Carnaval* and *Bataille des Fleurs* (Feb.), *Jour de la Bastille* fireworks display (Jul. 14), *Bataille des Fleurs* (Jul. and Aug.), *Nuits Festivales* (Summer music evenings, Jul. and Aug.)

Early in the 19th century the English discovered that France's sheltered Mediterranean coast had mild winters, and soon they flocked here in large numbers. Afternoon strolls were fashionable, but the rocky, six-foot-wide path along the shore was hardly suitable for gentle walks. In 1820 the Reverend Lewis Way organized the construction of a sweeping promenade, planted with palm trees and decked with flowers. Not surprisingly, the locals soon called it the Promenade des Anglais (the Englishmen's Walk). Today a busy highway cuts between the sea and the ornate exteriors of the *belle époque* luxury hotels. Even amid the sprawl of ugly concrete apartment blocks, the palms, flowers, strolling crowds and views remain unchanged – a superb background for Nice's festivals.

VIEILLE VILLE

✚ D1 🍎 Fruit and vegetable markets: Tue.–Sun. morning. Antiques market: Mon. morning. Flower market: Tue.–Sat. all day, Sun. morning 🚌 6, 9, 12

Until the 1970s Nice's Vieille Ville (Old Town) was a decaying slum, with neglected buildings and narrow streets little visited by tourists. Today it's one of the liveliest, most colorful neighborhoods in the city, brimming with life, shops, bars – and noise. Interesting old houses, baroque churches, and 17th- and 18th-century civic buildings line its streets, making it an interesting place to stroll. The cours Saleya is the hub of the quarter, a spacious elongated square that is the home of Nice's famous flower, fruit and vegetable markets. Take time to enjoy the scents, and the beautiful produce and flowers on display and for sale.

Strolling along the Promenade des Anglais

PARKS, GARDENS, TREES AND FLOWERS

Many Mediterranean cities have lovely parks and *jardins* (gardens), but none more so than Nice. The green swath cutting through the city's heart is only one example, and every street is decked with tubs, planters and window boxes filled with colorful flowers.

Flowers at a colorful market stall in Old Nice

Parks

Formal parks lie within the city center, forming a green oasis for locals and visitors; the Jardin Albert 1er, Promenade du Paillon and the Espace Masséna are good examples. Also in the city center, the wooded Parc du Château features winding paths and cascading water. The wilder Jardin des Arènes de Cimiez is a beautifully tended olive grove, the wind rustling the silver-gray foliage on the shapely trees. Lovely, aromatic Aleppo pine trees, planted in 1866, abound in the Parc Forestier Mont-Boron; they line almost seven miles of trails that are edged with wild carnations and tiny orchids. Views from this park are spectacular: to the east is St.-Jean Cap Ferrat, and to the west is Nice's own Bay of Angels.

Gardens

Avid gardeners should head for Nice's Jardin Botanique (Botanic Garden), with a comprehensive and classic collection of Mediterranean flora. The Parc Floral Phoenix is another garden attraction, where you'll find tropical plants and fruit trees. A vast greenhouse – packed with numerous exotic and rare orchids, among other delights – dominates the 17-acre site.

Trees and Flowers

Most of Nice's trees and flowers are common to all Mediterranean countries, where this vegetation thrives in lime-rich, sandy or poor soil; can withstand months of summer heat and drought; and can endure an occasional wet or cold spell in winter. Olives, palms and pines are native; citrus trees, bougainvillea, mimosa, gerbera and many succulents have been introduced. Roses love Mediterranean conditions, which is why you'll see bigger and brighter ones here than anywhere else. If you're in the countryside – nature's own glorious garden – in April, May or June, you'll find spreads of wildflowers to rival any city park.

STRASBOURG

Strasbourg's tiny historic center, circled by arms of the Ill river, could easily lull a visitor into thinking that there was little more to the city than picturesque streets, a breathtakingly beautiful cathedral and a huge number of restaurants. But beyond its medieval core lie grandiose 19th-century civic buildings, an ancient university and the gleaming buildings housing European institutions, since Strasbourg is the seat of the European Parliament. It's a prosperous, cosmopolitan city, a beguiling blend of ancient and modern, Teutonic and French.

A Visitor's Strasbourg

For tourists, modern everyday Strasbourg need not intrude upon enjoyment of the old city. Aim to stay within the old, mostly pedestrian quarter; it's a delightful place to walk around, with an impressive choice of

hotels, bars and restaurants. There's a large presence of European parliamentary officials, many of whom speak English, and the range of English-language tourist literature is excellent.

Strasbourg's appeal lies in its combination of history, architecture and culture. First impressions are of a very German city, the timbered houses and cobbled streets reminiscent of villages across the Rhine river, a little to the east. But the atmosphere is definitely French, with the style and way of life that it implies. Lying so near the German border, however, Strasbourg is a favorite destination for day and weekend visits by Germans, so you'll also see and hear many Germans.

Exploring the City

Undoubtedly, it's best to explore Strasbourg on foot. Apart from visiting the wonderful cathedral, museums and fine churches, most visitors spend time simply strolling the streets. You'll find hidden corners and buildings waiting to

Strasbourg

be photographed around every corner, so take your time. Water plays a large part in the city's layout; the center is encircled by water, divided into different channels and crossed by graceful bridges. Old mills and fortifications along the river bear witness to the city's historic importance, while the mighty Rhine, the German border, lies only a stone's throw away.

If you're interested in architecture, you could follow one of several marked routes through the heart of the old city center (see Petite France, page 204). The tram can be useful for saving your legs, and taxis are easily available. There's also the peaceful boat trip around the center (see page 205).

Sample Alsace wines in the Old Town

Eat, Drink and Enjoy

Strasbourg and Alsace is one of the few areas in Europe that produces both notable wines and beers, and it is also home to some of the finest cooking in France. There are strong German influences here, giving the cuisine a different character from typical French fare. History has played a part in this, and it's a pleasure to see the past so clearly reflected at the table – the popular dish *choucroute*, for instance, is really the same thing as sauerkraut.

But don't be fooled. There's much more to the cuisine in Strasbourg than German cooking; you'll find Italian, Chinese, Lebanese, Tex-Mex, Moroccan and others. With all these options, make sure you don't overlook the opportunity to try some real Strasbourg specialties (see page 554). Stop in a *winstub*, a small family-run restaurant often housed in an historic building, where you'll be able to sample the best of local cooking and flavors.

Alsace produces some notable wines, mainly whites, which are similar in character to the best of German wines.

They are traditionally labeled with the name of the grape rather than the place of origin. Riesling, Gewurtztraminer, Pinot Blanc and Muscat are all reliable varieties to look for. Beer is also big in Alsace, the home of Heineken and Kronenbourg, two of Europe's biggest sellers. Other smaller local breweries produce excellent beer.

Evening Diversions

Strasbourg has a rich cultural life, with its own orchestra participating at the internationally renowned Festival of Music in summer; in September there's the annual *Musica*, a festival of contemporary music. Opera, theater, jazz and dance performances are held year-round and are widely advertised. In summer, most tourists are drawn to the nightly folklore displays of music and dance held in some of the old city's most picturesque squares.

Malls and Markets

Shopping in Strasbourg is a real pleasure, with an excellent choice of the world's best-known designer names,

Timber-framed buildings line cobbled streets in the old part of the city

jewelers, antique shops and international bookstores clustered around the center of the old city. Across the river, Halles is a fair-sized shopping mall housing France's familiar chain stores. The weekly market takes place on Wednesdays in the place Kléber – stalls of fresh produce, cheese and meat jostle with inexpensive and cheerful clothes and household goods. Souvenir shops sell Alsatian handicrafts; pottery, lace and carved wood are worth looking at.

ESSENTIAL INFORMATION

TOURIST INFORMATION
• 17 Place de la Cathédrale ☎ 03 88 52 28 28

Transportation maps are available at the railroad station and the tourist office. Taxis are plentiful and reasonably priced; you can pick them up at the station, place Kléber or place Gutenberg, or call for one (Taxis 13 ☎ 03 88 36 13 13 or Novo Taxi ☎ 03 88 22 19 19).

URBAN TRANSPORTATION
Walking is a delight in historic Strasbourg, although the smooth, modern trams that run across the central island are useful at the start or end of the day. Buy tickets from machines located at stops, and validate them before boarding. Outer Strasbourg is served by an efficient bus service, which you may want to use to visit the Palais de l'Europe (again, validate your ticket).

AIRPORT INFORMATION
Strasbourg-Entzheim International Airport (☎ 03 88 64 67 67), with connections to most major European cities, is about 20 minutes south of the city by car. A shuttle bus runs every 15 minutes daily 5:30 a.m.–11:30 p.m. to Baggersee, where tram A connects directly with the city center.

CLIMATE – average highs and lows for the month

	JAN.	FEB.	MAR.	APR.	MAY	JUN.	JUL.	AUG.	SEP.	OCT.	NOV.	DEC.
	4°C	5°C	10°C	15°C	19°C	22°C	24°C	24°C	20°C	14°C	8°C	4°C
	39°F	41°F	50°F	59°F	66°F	72°F	75°F	75°F	68°F	57°F	46°F	39°F
	-2°C	-2°C	1°C	5°C	9°C	12°C	14°C	13°C	10°C	6°C	2°C	0°C
	28°F	28°F	34°F	41°F	48°F	54°F	57°F	55°F	50°F	43°F	36°F	32°F

CITY SIGHTS

Key to symbols

📍 map coordinates refer to the Strasbourg map on page 200; sights below are highlighted in yellow on the map.

✉ address or location ☎ telephone number

🕐 opening times 🚌 nearest bus route

🍴 restaurant on site or nearby

💰 admission charge: $$$ more than 75F, $$ 25F to 75F, $ less than 25F

CATHÉDRALE NOTRE-DAME

📍 B2 ✉ place de la Cathédrale 🕐 Cathedral: daily 8:30–7, Jul. and Aug.; 9–6:30, Apr.–Jun. and in Sep.: 9–5:30, Mar. and Oct.; 9–4:30, rest of year 🍴 Au Bon Vivant, see page 553 🚌 A, D

A superb example of Gothic architecture, the Cathédrale Notre-Dame (Cathedral of Our Lady) dominates old Strasbourg; its single steeple soars to 466 feet over the surrounding rooftops. It was built between 1176 and 1439, and it stands in a cobbled square on the site of an earlier basilica. A team of masons from Chartres worked on it in the 13th century, creating superb statuary and a harmonious interior, subtly lit by fine stained-glass windows. The main facade, a riot of sinuous, graceful biblical figures and saints, was completed half a century later. Don't miss the astronomical clock in the south transept, a huge timepiece with a planetary dial, constructed in the 1540s. Its automated figures perform daily at 12:30, when the Apostles march before Christ, a cock crows and beats its wings, and the seven ages of man can be seen. In front of the clock is the Cathedral's loveliest sculpture, the *Pilier des Anges* (*Pillar of the Angels*), a wondrously carved pillar entwined with the four evangelists and trumpeting angels, all heralding the Last Judgment.

LES GRANDES PLACES

📍 B1–B2 ✉ place Kléber, place Gutenberg, place de la Cathédrale 🚌 A, D 🎄 Christkindelsmärik, last week in Nov. through Dec.

Strasbourg is scattered with *grandes places* (large squares). The main three – place Kléber, place Gutenberg and the place de

Top: The Cathedral of our Lady, embellished with statuary and flanked by four turrets
Above: Flying the flags – Strasbourg is the center of the European Union

la Cathédrale – are all within a 5-minute walk of each other. They make an appealing and contrasting trio. The cathedral square, with its cobblestones and timber-framed houses, is distinctly medieval; Renaissance-style Kléber square has an elegant spaciousness; and place Gutenberg nicely bridges the architectural time gap. In December, all three squares are the backdrop for Strasbourg's famous *Christkindelsmärik* (Christmas Market), a monthlong street market dating from 1570, when the whole town glitters with light and smells of tantalizing spice.

MUSÉE ALSACIEN

📍 B1 ✉ 23–25 quai St.-Nicolas ☎ 03 88 52 50 00 🕐 Wed.–Sat. and Mon. 10–noon and 1:30–6, Sun. 10–5 🍴 Au PetitTonnelier, see page 553 🚌 A, D 💰 $

If you only have time to visit one museum, it should be the Musée Alsacien (Museum of Alsace) – a charming regional venue housed in a disorderly canal-side building. Not only does it give a chance to see the interior courtyards and inside of a 15th-century house, but it's

Strasbourg

crammed with many attractive displays, all illustrating traditional Alsatian life. There are complete rooms and workshops, colorful pottery and glass, regional costumes and much more. Look for the votive pictures – naive religious paintings commissioned as prayer and thanks to God, and illustrating farm animals, children and loved ones far away.

MUSÉE ARCHÉOLOGIQUE

🚩 C1   ✉ 2 place du Château   ☎ 03 88 52 50 00
🕐 Wed.–Sat. and Mon. 10–noon and 1:30–6, Sun. 10–5   🍴 Aux Armes de Strasbourg, see page 553
🚇 A, D   💲 S

Strasbourg is proud of its Musée Archéologique (Archeological Museum), one of France's most important museums of its kind. Imaginatively laid out, it's housed in the basement of the Rohan Palace, and takes the visitor through Alsace from 600 BC to AD 800. There are interesting prehistoric sections, but more appealing are the reminders of everyday life in Roman Gaul.

MUSÉE D'ART MODERNE

🚩 Off the map   ✉ 1 place Hans-Jean-Arp   ☎ 03 88 23 31 31   🕐 Fri.–Sun. and Tue.–Wed. 11–7, Thu. noon–10   🚇 2, 3, 10, 20   💲 S

Opened in 1998, the Musée d'Art Moderne (Modern Art Museum) is an airy building across the water from the Old Town. It covers painting and sculpture from the 1860s to the 1990s. If you're a modern art enthusiast you will not be disappointed, as there is much to enjoy. The room devoted to Gustave Doré gives a fine introduction to this French artist's work.

MUSÉE DES BEAUX-ARTS

🚩 C1   ✉ 2 place du Château   ☎ 03 88 52 50 00
🕐 Wed.–Sat. and Mon. 10–noon and 1:30–6, Sun. 10–5   🍴 Aux Armes de Strasbourg, see page 553
🚇 A, D   💲 S

The elegant first-floor rooms of the Palais Rohan (Rohan Palace) house the Musée des Beaux-Arts (Fine Art Museum), a comprehensive provincial collection covering European paintings from the

Middle Ages to the late 19th century. Memling's *Polyptich of Vanity* steals the show, although the museum is justly proud of *La belle Strasbourgeoise*, by Nicolas de Largillière – a portrait of an enigmatic local lady, with more than a hint of the coquette. The ground floor of this same Renaissance building is home to Strasbourg's Musée des Arts Decoratifs (Decorative Arts Museum).

MUSÉE DE L'ŒUVRE NOTRE-DAME

🚩 B1   ✉ 3 place du Château   ☎ 03 88 52 50 00
🕐 Wed.–Sat. and Mon. 10–noon and 1:30–6, Sun. 10–5   🚇 A, D   💲 S

The Musée de l'Œuvre Notre-Dame (Museum of Cathedral Works of Art) occupies a building used from the 14th to 16th centuries for cathedral maintenance. In addition to the rambling warren of fine rooms and staircases, there are courtyards, one of which is planted as a 13th-century garden with medicinal herbs and plants. Some of the Cathedral's most precious sculptures are kept here, safely protected from pollution and the elements, and giving the public a chance to admire the elegance of 14th-century Gothic sculpture. The streamlined *Seven Wise Virgins* is a highlight, as is the nearby group of singularly unintimidating lions from the cathedral's main facade.

PETITE FRANCE

🚩 A1   ✉ place Benjamin-Zix   🍴 Winstub le Wuerthel, see page 553   ℹ The "Strolling in Strasbourg" guide – available from the tourist office – has five walking tours focusing on the architecture of five different periods

As you stroll around Strasbourg, sooner or later you'll reach the picturesque Petite France (Little France). On the banks of the Ill, at the west end of the historic center, cobbled streets are lined with some exceptionally lovely medieval timbered houses, dripping with colorful geraniums and shaded by ancient trees. Little France got its name in the 16th century, when sufferers of syphilis were isolated here, to keep them well away from "worthier" citizens.

Cruising down the Ill river – a perfect way to see the city

A DAY IN STRASBOURG

You awake early in the morning, and your time in this wonderful old city is limited. Here's what to do:

Spend an hour or so strolling around the historic center, visiting one of the daily produce markets and taking some photos in the morning light. Bakers and *patisserie* shops will be open, and you may be tempted to nibble on something as you go. Around mid-morning head for the Ill river, near the Palais Rohan, and buy your ticket for one of the 90-minute boat tours of Strasbourg. On the tour you can sit back and listen to the English commentary about the city's history and important monuments. The tour circles the central island, passing churches, fine buildings and flower-hung, timber-framed houses before heading upstream to give you a glimpse of the modernistic glass and steel palaces housing the buildings connected with the European Union.

Head next for the Cathedral, timing your visit so that you'll be there at 12:30, when the marvelous astronomical clock (see page 203) swings into action. Next, it's lunchtime, with a wide choice of pretty outdoor eating places. Try a local specialty, such as *tarte flambée* (onion tart) or a beautifully presented *salade composée* (chef's salad).

If you enjoy museums, the afternoon's the time for checking out two of the best. At the top of the list is the Museum of Alsace (Musée Alsacien), closely followed by the Gothic treasures in the Museum of Cathedral Works of Art (Museé de l'Œuvre Notre-Dame). After this, you may be ready for a drink at a sidewalk café, or a nap back at your hotel.

Evenings in Strasbourg feature a special dinner in one of the dozens of superb restaurants; be sure to eat a local dish, or follow the set menu, which is bound to be good. Afterward you can go to the movies (in English), a concert or enjoy a folklore display. For many people, a late-night stroll through the atmospheric old streets, followed by a nightcap at a music bar, will nicely round off the day. For others, there are discos and clubs that keep going until the early hours.

🔢 Boat tours leave daily on the half-hour from the landing stage near the Palais Rohan, Apr.–Nov., and four times a day Nov.–Mar. Call ☎ 03 88 32 75 25 for details. Consult the tourist office for evening events.

GERMANY

"IN Germany one breathes in love of order with the air..."

From the 1900 novel *Three Men on the Bummel* by English writer Jerome K. Jerome

Germany

Opposite: Tree-clad gorges and dramatic river views of Bad Schandau, in the Bastesti region

Germany

GERMANY

N

*NORTH
SEA*

Westerland
Nord-
friesische
Inseln
Sylt
Flensburg
Schleswig
*Kieler
Bucht* Puttgarden
DENMARK

*Deutsche
Bucht*
Heide
Itzehoe
Kiel
Neumünster
*Mecklenburger
Bucht*
Bad
Doberan
Rostoc

*Ostfriesische
Inseln*
Cuxhaven
Brunsbüttel
Stade
Lübeck
Wismar
Güstrow
A1

Wilhelmshaven
Bremerhaven
E45
Hamburg
Schwerin
Mecklenb

Emden
A24 E26
Parchir

Oldenburg
Bremen
E22
Lüneburg
A7
Ludwigslust
Elbe
Wittenberge

Soltau
Uelzen
Ha

Cloppenburg
Nienburg
E45
Salzwedel
Stenc

Lingen
E37
Celle
Wolfsburg

Osnabrück
Minden
A2
Hannover
Braunschweig
Magdebu

Gronau
Rheine
E30
A30
Hildesheim
Wolfenbüttel
Halberstad

Münster
Herford
Bielefeld
Lemgo
Hameln
Saltzgitter-Bad
Goslar
*Brocken
1142m*
Quedlinburg
Dessc

Bocholt
A31
Detmold
Harz
Hall

Wesel
A43
Gütersloh
A2
E34
Paderborn
Northeim
Saa

Oberhausen
A57
Gelsenkirchen
Bochum
Lippstadt
Scherfede
Göttingen
Nordhausen
Naumburg

Moers
Duisburg
Essen
Dortmund
Kassel
Mühlhausen
Buchenwald
Weimar

Düsseldorf
Wuppertal
Ruhr
Eder
Werra
Fulda
A4
Gotha
Erfurt
Jena

Mönchengladbach
Solingen
Leverkusen
Marburg
A7
E45
Eisenach
Arnstadt
Ger

COLOGNE
A45
Siegen
Alsfeld
Bad
Hersfeld
Thüringer Wald
Plaue

Aachen
Siegburg
E41
Giessen
Wetzlar
Rhön
Bad Neustadt
Ho

Bonn
A1
A3
Limburg
Fulda
Coburg
A9
E51

BELGIUM
Euskirchen
Remagen
Westerwald
Lahn
Bad Nauheim
Taunus
Bad Homburg

Koblenz
Rhein
Bad
Ems
Wiesbaden
Frankfurt am Main
Aschaffenburg
Bad
Kissingen
Schweinfurt
A70

Cochem
E35
A61
Offenbach
Main
Würzburg
Bamberg
Bayre

Eifel
Bitburg
A48
Rüdesheim
Mainz
E31
Darmstadt
Michelstadt
A3 E45
Erlangen
Weide

LUXEMBOURG
Bad Kreuznach
Worms
Odenwald
Wertheim
Fürth
Nürnberg
A3

Trier
A1
Idar-Oberstein
A5
Mannheim
Rothenburg ob
der Tauber
Ansbach
A9
E56

Kaiserslautern
A6
Heidelberg
Bad
Mergentheim
Bad Wimpfen
A6
Dinkelsbühl
Regensbur

Saarlouis
Homburg
Ludwigshafen
Neustadt-an-der-
Weinstrasse
Heilbronn
Öhringen
Eichstätt

Saarbrücken
Pirmasens
Landau
Maulbronn
Schwäbisch
Hall
Nördlingen
Ingolstadt

Karlsruhe
Rastatt
Pforzheim
A7
E43
Donau

Baden-Baden
Stuttgart
Tübingen
Reutlingen
A8
Dachau
Freis

FRANCE
Offenburg
A81
Freudenstadt
Schwäbische Alb
Ulm
Augsburg
Amp

Schwarzwald
Hechingen
Triberg
Sigmaringen
A96
Ottobeuren
MUNICH

Freiburg
A5
E35
Villingen
Donaueschingen
Ravensburg
Kempten
Oberammergau
Rosenh

Titisee
Überlingen
Meersburg
Friedrichshafen
Füssen
Garmisch-
Partenkirche

Lörrach
Konstanz
Bodensee
Lindau
*Allgäuer
Alpen*
*2962m
Zugspitze*
Mittenwald

SWITZERLAND
Oberstdorf

5

4

3

2

1

A

B

C

GERMANY

Germany

Germany is not easily summed up. Before 1871 there was no single, unified German state: the area was made up of several territories, loosely knit together in alliance. Their local languages and loyalties still have first claim on many Germans' hearts.

After World War II, the country was split between two opposed powers: the West, whose territory was known as the Federal Republic of Germany, and the Soviets, who created the German Democratic Republic (G.D.R.). In 1989, faced with popular protests and a retreating Soviet authority, the G.D.R.'s government opened the Berlin Wall, which had divided the city's eastern and western zones since 1961. A year later the country was reunited, and a new Germany was born. But within its unified political boundaries, this is still a nation of diversity, where the people and cultures vary as dramatically as the landscapes.

MORE TOP DESTINATIONS IN GERMANY

- Bamberg C2 • Berchtesgaden D1
- Bodensee (Lake Constance) B1
- Dresden D3 • Freiburg B1
- Goslar C4 • Hamburg C5
- Heidelberg B2 • Lübeck C5
- Mecklenburgische Seenplatte D4
- Regensburg D2 • Rheintal B2
- Sächsische Schweiz E3 • Trier A2
- Tübingen B1 • Ulm C1

Germany

Traveling in Germany

Germany's 16 administrative states (*Bundesländer*) extend from the tail of Denmark south to the Swiss and Austrian Alps; the Netherlands, Belgium, Luxembourg and France border on the west, Poland and the Czech Republic on the east. Each state has enough of interest for the visitor to occupy a whole vacation in its own right, and Germans are themselves often tourists in their own country, especially as westerners and easterners explore each other's previously unknown territories.

Traveling – by automobile or by public transportation – is not a problem, despite the country's size. The road network in western Germany is excellent, from the highways (*Autobahnen*) to minor roads. In the east, roads were in poorer condition for many years, but there have been recent improvements.

The biggest culture shock to drivers is likely to be the speed of traffic. There is no official upper limit on highways, and many drivers ignore the recommended 130 k.p.h., the equivalent of which is 80 m.p.h. Driving etiquette is taken seriously, though: you can be stopped and fined for swearing or making rude gestures.

Taking the train is a convenient way to cover large areas. The quickest and most comfortable trains are the InterCity and Eurocity trains, linking major centers – but the InterRegios, connecting smaller towns, are also fast.

The North and the Baltic

Northern Germany has a maritime character. Schleswig-Holstein, a province Germans and Danes have often fought over, is made up of two former dukedoms and shares the coastline with Lower Saxony. Together they take in a shore ranging from the fjords and hills of the Baltic coast to the wind-lashed North Sea beaches. Inland, the countryside is wide, rolling farmland and peat bogs; offshore, the North Friesian islands are favorite summer destinations, with beaches and brisk sea air. The inhabitants of coastal Friesland have maintained their own separate culture and dialect.

Northern Germany's cities were a force to be reckoned with in the Middle Ages. In the interests of trade and power, they banded together to form the Hanseatic League, a protected market that monopolized trade between the North and Baltic seas. The league's merchants made huge fortunes and had impressive houses and churches built in seaports such as Hamburg, Lübeck and Bremen.

Some of their legacies have survived – or at least have been rebuilt after the heavy bombing raids of World War II. The Gothic/Renaissance architecture of Bremen's Town Hall and Lübeck's Music Academy, both converted from merchant homes, still suggests the affluence and style of the region's medieval heyday.

Lower Saxony has many features that are quintessentially German. Its historic center, Hannover, is a thriving commercial city; towns such as Hildesheim and Wolfenbüttel, the latter with its painted, half-timbered facades, have been immaculately restored after wartime damage.

The winter sports resort of Goslar, once a silver- and lead-mining town, has picture-book streets and squares lined with Gothic, Renaissance and baroque buildings, some inscribed with gold lettering, others featuring curving, sinuous slate roofs. To the east are the Harz Mountains, on the old East/West border, where witches are said to celebrate their Sabbath on *Walpurgisnacht*, the eve of May Day.

Sumptuous Renaissance and baroque style draws the crowds to Linderhof Castle

The Rhine

The great 820-mile Rhine flows from the Swiss Alps across the western regions of Germany, through the ancient city of Koblenz and the recently deposed seat of West German government, Bonn, and through the industrial country of Ruhr toward Rotterdam. Its valleys and those of its tributaries, the Mosel, Main, Nahe and Neckar, have been producing wines (mainly white) since Roman times. Castles with fairy-tale Gothic towers loom over the river, built for their powerful princes' protection and profit, which was gleaned from tolls on passing river traffic.

On the Lorelei rock, above the twisting Rhine gorge, the beautiful siren Lorelei is said to lure sailors to their death with her enchanting song. This is a romantic, myth-laden part of the country, and a river cruise is one of the most popular ways of seeing it.

The East

After years of restricted travel, border guards and obsessive document checking, eastern Germany is now completely open to visitors. When the Berlin Wall came down, East Germans poured into the West, eager to boost incomes, and some West Germans raised their voices against the sudden influx and resulting unemployment and uneasiness. After the initial euphoria of reunification came the backlash of mutual resentment and offshoots of xenophobia. Integration has pressed on, nevertheless, and financial investment in the east (another grievance to some western taxpayers) has brought new business and better facilities, although there is still a marked difference compared to the affluent west. English is less likely to be spoken here.

One of eastern Germany's highlights is Dresden, which re-created itself after devastation by more than 2,000 Allied

Bavarian craftsmanship – the astrological clock on the Old Town Hall in Munich

bombers in 1945. Fine 18th-century buildings surround its Brühlsche Terrace, an elevated section on the bank of the Elbe river, and the nearby baroque Zwinger pavilions house a marvelous collection of museums. Leipzig, the famous medieval university town, is also worth visiting, with its pedestrian-only center and attractive gardens and squares.

Weimar, once the home of poet and dramatist Johann Wolfgang von Goethe, composers Franz Liszt and Richard Strauss, and philosopher Friedrich Nietzsche, has a core of lovely historic buildings, parks and boulevards. The gentle hills and red-roofed villages of the Thüringian Forest form a stretch of popular walking country, despite some parts suffering the effects of industrial pollution; the region has a growing industry of family-run lodgings and restaurants.

The Black Forest and Bavaria

Two states make up southern Germany: Baden-Württemberg in the southwest and Bavaria in the southeast. As the name suggests, Baden-Württemberg is itself made up of two distinct areas: mainly Catholic Baden, where the inhabitants are reputed to be amiable and easy-going, and traditionally Protestant Württemberg (Swabia), where the work ethic is strongly established and the Swabian dialect is spoken.

Lovers of the outdoors flock to the Black Forest (Schwarzwald), a swath of highlands reaching over 3,900 feet and encompassing attractive villages, lush valleys, orchards and meadows as well as woods. Clock-making has been a successful industry here since the 1660s, and cuckoo clocks are on sale at every gift shop. The other notable local product is Black Forest cake – the authentic and superior original is called *Schwarzwälder Kirschtorte.*

East of the Black Forest is a range of limestone cliffs and hills known as the Swabian Jura, where castles peer down at the Danube (Donau) river as it begins its long journey to the sea. Pleasant resorts surround the "Swabian Ocean," Lake Constance (Bodensee), which straddles the German-Austrian border. The Neckar river flows through Swabia's vineyards and past romantic Heidelberg, where students and tourists really do raise huge beer tankards over tavern tables, as they did in Sigmund Romberg's operetta *The Student Prince.*

Clichés also come true in southern Bavaria. Here the people are characterized by their detractors as loud and brash, and by their admirers as humorous, warm and fun-loving. They are often seen in traditional leather trousers (*Lederhosen*) or embroidered dresses, and are primarily Catholic and conservative: The standard daily greeting here is *"Grüss Gott,"* or "God's greeting."

Between the Bavarian capital, Munich (München), and the magnificent Alpine peaks lie the wooded hills, pretty villages, lakes and castles that attract so many visitors to this part of the country. The spectacular Alpine Road takes in the mountain scenery and passes the theatrical 19th-century castles of Linderhof, Herrenchiemsee and Neuschwanstein – all three are almost always packed to the brim with sightseers.

Northern Bavaria has its own character. In fact, not everyone here appreciates being labeled "Bavarian": this is the region known as Franconia (Franken), and its main city is Nuremberg (Nürnberg). Architecture and art come into their own here. During the late Middle Ages and early Renaissance, artists such as Lucas Cranach and Albrecht Dürer were prominent in Germany, and Nuremberg's wonderful German National Museum displays some of their best work. A more sinister aspect of the city's past is recalled in the giant stadium and Hall of Congress, built for Hitler's mass rallies, and preserved as chilling memorials to that era.

The hugely popular Romantic Road, running from ancient Würzburg and the Franconian wine country all the way to the Alps, 217 miles south, links several unspoiled medieval towns. On the way, it passes Rothenburg ob der Tauber, one of the loveliest old towns in Germany – and as a result one of the most crowded. Also on the route are the old walled, half-timbered town of Dinkelsbühl and the splendid Renaissance city of Augsburg.

Spa Towns

Health and fitness are national preoccupations, apparent in the German love of soccer, skiing and tennis, and in the spa towns that thrive all over the country. In addition to their statutory annual vacation, German employees are given six weeks a year to reap the benefits of medicinal waters and enjoy the spas' other facilities, which can include mud baths, saunas and steam treatments.

Germany's oldest casino is one of the features of Baden-Baden, a celebrated spa town with graceful 19th-century hotels. Other spas are also worth investigating. Bad Ems, in the Rhineland's picturesque Lahn valley, was 19th-century ruler Kaiser Wilhelm's personal favorite. A steam train travels from Bad Doberan, near Rostock in eastern Germany, to the country's oldest seaside resort, Ostseebad Heiligendamm, founded in 1793. Bad Kissingen, Bavaria's most popular spa, is on the banks of the Saale river.

Germany

TIMELINE

800–700 BC	Celtic tribes settle around the Rhineland.
AD 800	Franks overrun the territory; Charlemagne, the Frankish king, is crowned Holy Roman Emperor.
1273	Rudolf of Habsburg is elected emperor, founding the 600-year Habsburg dynasty.
1517	Martin Luther precipitates the Reformation.
1740	Frederick the Great is crowned king of Prussia.
1871	Franco-Prussian War ends with states united under the Prussian Kaiser Wilhelm and chancellor, Otto von Bismarck.
1914–19	Habsburg claims to the Balkans lead to World War I; the Treaty of Versailles demands huge war reparations and surrender of territories from defeated Germany.
1930	The Nazis gain power in elections.
1933	Adolf Hitler is made chancellor; under Hitler's dictatorship, millions of Jews and minorities are persecuted and killed.
1939	Hitler invades Poland; Britain and France declare war.
1945	Allied forces enter Berlin; Hitler kills himself.
1949	Western occupying powers create the Federal Republic of Germany; Russia forms the German Democratic Republic.
1961	The Berlin Wall is built.
1990	A year after the demolition of the wall, East and West Germany reunite; Germany leads support for a politically and economically integrated European Union.
1999	Newly refurbished, glass-domed Reichstag unveiled in preparation for the return of seat of government in Berlin.

MAD KING LUDWIG

Ludwig II of Bavaria lost all interest in running his kingdom after it was drawn first into war and then into the German Empire by the Prussian Chancellor, Otto von Bismarck. The late 19th-century ruler was left with nothing to do but amuse himself, which he did by having three flamboyant castles built – Herrenchiemsee, Linderhof and Neuschwanstein – and watching them take shape through his telescope. Ludwig found other ways to spend his money, too, supporting Richard Wagner while he wrote his operas, but eventually he ran out of cash altogether. This and his eccentric manner made him an increasing liability to the Bavarian government. Its ministers plotted with Ludwig's uncle Luitpold to depose him and certify him insane. Only days later, Ludwig and his doctor drowned in the Starnberger See, a boating lake near Munich – whether by accident or design, no one knows.

SURVIVAL GUIDE

Germany

- Formality plays an important part in everyday German life. Don't address people by their first names unless invited to; always use *Herr* (Sir) or *Frau* (Madam) at first.
- Job titles are used frequently in social exchange; doctors, for instance, are addressed as *Frau Doktor* or *Herr Doktor.*
- People tend to shake hands upon meeting, but women are often kissed on both cheeks, Continental-style.
- Local dishes, particularly in southern Bavaria, use the classic German ingredients of *Sauerkraut* (pickled cabbage), *Wurst* (sausage), dumplings, pork and potatoes. German cooking (*Gutbürgerliche Küche*) can be sampled at a *Gasthaus*, a restaurant serving simple meals.
- German wine is mainly white. *Tafelwein* is table wine, less expensive and harsher than the quality stuff; *Deutsches Tafelwein* is guaranteed to be wholly German, rather than a mix of different countries' grapes. *Qualitätswein* is the better product, from a specified range of vineyards. Some of the best grapes are *Riesling*, the fruity *Müller-Thurgau* and the spicy *Gewürztraminer.*
- Brewing is big business in Germany, with hundreds of local outfits all over the country. *Bock* is a strong beer, light or dark, and popular in Bavaria; *Weisse* is pale wheat beer, and *Malz,* an unfermented black malt beer.
- *Imbiss* (snack) stands are found everywhere and sell hamburgers, meatballs, sausages and other fast food.

- Stores in the main cities are usually open from 9 a.m. until 6:30 p.m. Many close on Saturday afternoons, but some stay open until 4 p.m.
- Germany has a long tradition of toy-making, particularly china dolls and the famous Steiff teddy bears. New versions make excellent souvenirs; antiques sell for enormous sums.
- Beer and wine festivals take place all over the country. Munich's September/October *Oktoberfest* is the best known; *Weinfeste,* celebrations held in the Rhine-Mosel area during the harvesting of the grapes, are also worth attending.
- Dinkelsbühl's 10-day *Kinderzeche* festival, held in July, recalls the Thirty Years' War, when local children persuaded Swedish soldiers not to ransack their town. It features plays, a pageant and the boys' band, the *Knabenkapelle*, decked out in 18th-century military garb.
- The music of Richard Wagner is performed in the summer *Bayreuth Festival*, northeast of Nuremberg near the composer's former home. Tickets are often snapped up a year in advance. Call ☎ 092 178 780 for information.

Traditionally decorated
beer mugs

BERLIN

No other city better illustrates the upheaval in late 20th-century Europe than Berlin. For nearly 30 years it was, for all intents and purposes, two cities. Tourists posed on the Western side of the Berlin Wall, and those who crossed the East-West boundary at Checkpoint Charlie did so with the trepidation of travelers to another planet.

Then, in 1989, Berlin changed virtually overnight. The wall has all but vanished; Checkpoint Charlie is a museum; the No Man's Land that lay between the two zones is now the site of a new complex of ministries, offices, stores and hotels, ready for the return of the German parliament and government. Reunified Berlin is an exciting, restless place, reinventing itself at a fast pace.

Berlin Flavors

There are many restaurants and cafés in Berlin, serving every imaginable kind of food. The most popular restaurant areas are around Savignyplatz and Hardenbergstrasse and on the Ku'damm, and all buzz late into the night. Berlin has a larger Turkish community than any other city outside Turkey, and many live in the old quarter of Kreuzberg, where inexpensive Turkish meals are served in dozens of restaurants, especially in the neighborhood of Kottbusser Tor.

Kaffee und Kuchen (coffee and cakes) is an institution, usually indulged at about 4 p.m., but it doesn't come cheap. The café that started it all – Café Kranzler, which opened in 1835 – still operates on the Ku'damm.

Heavy, hearty German food can be sampled all over the city, in restaurants or in a tavern (*Kneipe*). There are more than 4,000 taverns, many offering *Hackepeter* (meatloaf), *Aal grün* (eel in parsley sauce) and *Solei* (pickled eggs).

If you find the traditional fare daunting, try the lighter new German cuisine (*neue Deutsche Küche*) at restaurants such as Trio, on Klausenerplatz.

Beer is, of course, a favorite beverage. One custom is to have a *Korn* – a light beer with a *Schnapps* chaser; another, a summer choice, is *Berliner Weisse mit Schuss*, light beer turned pink with raspberry liqueur or green with extract of woodruff.

Music and Cabaret

In the 1920s Berlin had a reputation for "divine decadence," as portrayed in the 1972 film *Cabaret*. The cabaret tradition has been revived, albeit in a milder form, and there are clubs all over the city; there are also folk, jazz and other music venues. For the latest details consult *Berlin TutGut* (from tourist offices), which has English-language listings, or the *Berlin Das Magazin* (quarterly). The busiest district for entertainment is in Scheunenviertel.

The Berlin Philharmonic, perhaps the world's best-known orchestra, has its home at the Philharmonie, in the Kulturforum, a complex of concert halls and museums on Potsdamer Strasse. The Berlin Symphony Orchestra performs in the 19th-century National Theater, at Gendarmenmarkt. Berlin's oldest opera house is the German State

BERLIN

Berlin

Opera, a lovely baroque concert hall on Unter den Linden – its glittering list of past directors includes Franz Liszt.

Store of the West

One of Europe's biggest department stores – second only to Harrods of London – is found in Berlin: the KaDeWe (Kaufhaus des Westerns, or Store of the West), which stocks more than 250,000 items in its building on Tauentzienstrasse and stays open late on Thursdays.

A branch of the Paris flagship, Galeries Lafayette, is on Französische Strasse, near the designer shops of Friedrichstrasse. In the leisure and shopping complex EuropaCenter, not far from KaDeWe, there are more than 100 stores, cafés and bars.

Berlin porcelain makes a perfect souvenir. It's been produced here since 1763, when the Royal Porcelain Factory (K.P.M.) opened, and the factory's main store is on the Ku'damm.

Street markets flourish in this city; try Nollendorf flea market, which operates from Wednesday to Monday in the old Nollendorf S-Bahn station. The popular morning Winterfeldtmarkt, a lively affair on Winterfeldtplatz, has anything and everything for sale.

Berlin Classicism

Sculptor, painter, set-designer and architect Karl Friedrich Schinkel left his mark all over Berlin. After designing the Prussians' military medal, the Iron Cross, he was commissioned to create a series of civic buildings, including the National Theater, the museums on Museum Island and St. Nicholas' Church in Potsdam. He mixed his own Romantic tastes with the royally approved Classical style to form "Berlin Classicism," and gave his undivided attention to every detail, right down to the doorknobs.

ESSENTIAL INFORMATION

TOURIST INFORMATION
• Verkehrsamt Berlin, EuropaCenter, Budapester Strasse ☎ 030 262 6031
• Berlin Tourismus Marketing GmbH, Am Karlsbad 11 ☎ 030 230 025
• Tegel Airport ☎ 030 4101 3145
• Bahnhof Zoo ☎ 030 313 9063

URBAN TRANSPORTATION
There are two city rail networks: the subway (U-Bahn) and the city railroad (S-Bahn), and tickets are interchangeable. The S-Bahn is marked on the Berlin city map as an "S" in a red circle. Buy tickets in the station foyer and validate them in the machine on the platform. Trains run Mon.–Fri. 4 a.m.–1 a.m., Sat.–Sun. 4 a.m.–2 a.m. U-Bahn lines 1

and 9 run all night Friday and Saturday. Bus route 100 runs through the center from Bahnhof Zoo (Zoo station) in the west to Unter den Linden in the east. The main bus terminal is Funkturm (☎ 030 301 8028). Taxi stands are all over the city. Use only metered cabs (☎ 030 261 026 or 030 210 101).

AIRPORT INFORMATION
Berlin has three international airports: Tegel (north), Schönefeld (east) and Tempelhof (south). Bus 109 runs from Tegel to the Ku'damm and Bahnhof Zoo. U-Bahn line 6 runs from Tempelhof (Platz der Luftbrücke station) to Friedrichstrasse, and bus 119 runs to Ku'damm. S-Bahn lines 9 and 10 run from Schönefeld to Bahnhof Zoo. For information, call Tegel ☎ 030 410 11 or Tempelhof ☎ 030 695 036.

CLIMATE – average highs and lows for the month

JAN.	FEB.	MAR.	APR.	MAY	JUN.	JUL.	AUG.	SEP.	OCT.	NOV.	DEC.
2°C	3°C	8°C	12°C	18°C	21°C	23°C	23°C	18°C	13°C	7°C	3°C
36°F	37°F	46°F	54°F	64°F	70°F	73°F	73°F	64°F	55°F	45°F	37°F
-3°C	-3°C	0°C	2°C	7°C	11°C	13°C	13°C	10°C	5°C	2°C	-1°C
27°F	27°F	32°F	36°F	45°F	52°F	55°F	55°F	50°F	41°F	36°F	30°F

CITY SIGHTS

Key to symbols

✚ map coordinates refer to the Berlin map on page 216–217; sights below are highlighted in yellow on the map.

✉ address or location ☎ telephone number

🕐 opening times 🚌 nearest bus route

Ⓜ nearest subway 🍴 restaurant on site or nearby

🎟 admission charge: $$$ more than DM8, $$ DM3–DM8, $ less than DM3

ALEXANDERPLATZ

✚ E3 🕐 Fernsehturm: daily 9 a.m.–11:30 p.m. (second and fourth Tue. of each month 1–11:30). St. Marienkirche: Mon.–Thu. 10–noon and 1–5, Sat. noon–4:30 🍴 Zum Nussbaum, see page 554 Ⓜ U-Bahn/S-Bahn to Alexanderplatz 🚌 100, 157, 25 🎟 Fernsehturm $$

Alexanderplatz, the marketplace known to Berliners as "Alex," was the heart of the old city. After World War II it was rebuilt in a bleak style, and is now scheduled for renovations. Two old buildings have survived: the Rotes Rathaus (Red Town Hall), built in 1869 to emulate the Italian Renaissance style; and the 15th-century Marienkirche, Berlin's second-oldest parish church. At the center of the square, Fernsehturm, a 1,188-foot television tower, soars above the city; there's a revolving restaurant and a viewing platform at the top.

BAUHAUS-ARCHIV

✚ C2 ✉ Klingelhöferstrasse 14 ☎ 030 254 0020 🕐 Wed.–Mon. 10–5 🍴 Café on site Ⓜ U-Bahn to Nollendorfplatz 🚌 100, 129, 187, 341 🎟 $$

Following World War I Walter Gropius founded a new architectural movement in Weimar, stressing function above beauty and encouraging collaboration between art and industry. The Bauhaus (Building House) school had an immense influence on 20th-century design, but was condemned by the Nazis and moved first to Dessau and then to Berlin before being closed in 1933. The Gropius-designed Bauhaus-Archiv (Bauhaus Museum), built in 1964, shows examples of the style – from chairs to models of buildings – and explains the aims of the Bauhaus artists.

Symbol of reconciliation – east meets west at the Brandenburg Gate

BERLINER DOM

✚ D2 ✉ Am Lustgarten ☎ 030 202 690 🕐 Mon.–Sat. 9–7, Sun. 1–5 🍴 Lutter & Wegner, see page 554 Ⓜ U-Bahn to Hausvogteiplatz 🚌 100, 157

Berliner Dom, Berlin's Protestant Cathedral, is a monument to imperial wealth and power, containing 90 tombs of the royal Hohenzollern dynasty in its vault. Completed in 1905, its dome is intricately decorated with mosaics.

BRANDENBURGER TOR

✚ D2 ✉ Pariser Platz 🍴 Borchardt, see page 554 Ⓜ U-Bahn to Französische Strasse; S-Bahn to Unter den Linden 🚌 100

Built in 1788 as an "arch of peace," the Brandenburger Tor (Brandenburg Gate) was modeled after the entrance to the Acropolis temple in Athens. A sculpture of the goddess Viktoria and her chariot was added to the top in 1794. It was stolen by Napoleon 12 years later; on its return, Karl Friedrich Schinkel added a triumphal wreath and iron cross to the goddess' staff. Hitler was fond of torchlight processions through the arch. During the East-West split, it stood forlornly in No Man's Land. Now it is celebrated as a symbol of reconciliation and hope, and forms an occasional backdrop for pop concerts.

Modern scuplture at the Kulturforum

HAUS AM CHECKPOINT CHARLIE

✚ D2 ✉ Friedrichstrasse 43 ☎ 030 253 7250
⊕ Daily 9 a.m.–10 p.m. 🍴 Café on site 🚇 U-Bahn
to Kochstrasse 🚌 Bus 129 💰 $$$
The crossing point of the Berlin Wall,
known as Haus Am Checkpoint Charlie
(House at Checkpoint Charlie), is now a
tourist attraction. The Eastern border
guards' hut was taken down in 1990 and
moved to the Deutsches Historisches
Museum on Unter den Linden. The site
has a display of paraphernalia and
photographs illustrating the effects of the
wall and various escape attempts. A video
on the history of the wall includes a look
at the graffiti artists who decorated the
Western side.

KAISER-WILHELM-GEDÄCHTNISKIRCHE

✚ B2 ✉ Breitscheidplatz ☎ 030 218 5023
⊕ Memorial Hall Tue.–Sat. 10–4; New Chapel
Tue.–Sat. 9–7 🍴 Berliner Stube, see page 554
🚇 U-Bahn to Zoologischer Garten or
Kurfürstendamm 🚌 100, 119, 129, 146
Although it stands in poverty-ridden
Breitscheidplatz, the landmark Kaiser-
Wilhelm-Gedächtniskirche (Kaiser
William Memorial Church) is worth
visiting as a memorial to the devastation
of World War II. The 19th-century
Romanesque hall was all that remained of
Kaiser Wilhelm II's church after the 1943
air raids; it has been left as it was, and a
modern octagonal chapel and hexagonal
blue stained-glass tower has been added

to it. Inside, the church displays a cross of
nails donated by Coventry, in Britain –
another city devastated by bombs.

KULTURFORUM

✚ C2 ✉ Potsdamer Strasse 50 ☎ Museum für
Angewardte Kunst, 030 266 2911; Musikinstrumenten-
Museum, 030 254 810; Neue Nationalgalerie, 030 266
2662 ⊕ Tue.–Fri. 9–5, Sat.–Sun. 10–5 🍴 Cafés on
site 🚇 U-Bahn to Kurfürstenstrasse 🚌 129, 148,
248, 348 💰 Museum für Angewardte Kunst $, other
museums $$
This complex of galleries, halls and
museums, all angles and curves, was
designed in the 1960s and houses some
outstanding collections of art. The
Gemäldegalerie (Picture Gallery) displays
European art from the 13th to the 18th
centuries; look for works by the 16th-
century Dutch master Pieter Brueghel
and the collection of Italian Renaissance
art. In the glass-and-steel Neue
Nationalgalerie (New National Gallery)
19th- and 20th-century paintings,
drawings and sculpture include works by
Salvador Dalí, Paul Klee and others.
   One of the highlights of the
Kulturforum complex is the Museum für
Angewardte Kunst (Museum of Applied
Arts), where gold, silver, glass, porcelain
and jeweled arts and crafts are displayed.
The star item is the eighth-century Burse
Reliquary, a casket glittering with silver,
pearls, gems and gold inlay. Next door to
the Philharmonic Hall, the intriguing
Musikinstrumenten-Museum (Museum
of Musical Instruments) has everything
from ancient bagpipes to synthesizers.

MUSEUMSINSEL

✚ D3 ✉ Museumsinsel ☎ 030 2090 5555
⊕ Temporary exhibitions: Tue.–Sun. 10–6
🍴 Borchardt, see page 554 🚇 S-Bahn to
Hackescher Markt 🚌 100, 157 💰 $$
The first of a group of imposing museum
buildings was begun on an island in the
Spree river in 1830. In 1841, Frederick
William IV designated the area a "space
for art and science," and now many of
Berlin's antiquities, dispersed during
World War II, are being brought together
for display in the complex. Altes Museum

THE BERLIN WALL

On August 13, 1961, the German Democratic Republic began work on an "Anti-Fascist Protection Wall." Relations between the Eastern and Western sectors of Berlin had never been easy. The Soviets closed off their access routes in 1948, so supplies had to be flown in from the West in a year-long airlift. There had been popular protests against the Soviet authorities, and a steady exodus of East Berliners to the West. Finally the Eastern government decided to mark its boundary with bricks and barbed wire.

The border was based on a 1920 map of Berlin, and this was the course taken by the wall, without regard for any houses, or streets that might be in the way. The houses on Bernauer Street, which happened to be on the route, became part of the barrier, and their exits were bricked up. Residents tried to jump to freedom from the upper windows; 20 people were shot down. One border guard took the opportunity to leap over the partially built wall before it grew too high. Those who didn't make it across were cut off from the West and from their friends and families as the 13-foot barricade took shape.

After the escape of 30 people through a tunnel from a bakery cellar in 1964, a large part of Bernauer Street was demolished, and a No Man's Land was created, guarded by dogs and 295 watchtowers. Booby traps were sunk into the Teltow canal, at the point where the border crossed the Spree river, after Gunter Litfin was shot trying to swim his way to the West. As the restrictions increased, the escapes grew more daring. One steamship's crew got the captain drunk and shut

Ray of hope – a segment of the Berlin Wall (top) and colorful fragments after its demolition in 1989

him in his cabin before sailing to the western bank. A homemade hot-air balloon was used to float over the wall. But the risks were very high: 80 people were killed in these attempts, including 25 guards.

At 9:15 p.m. on November 9, 1989, under pressure from an increasingly impatient crowd, border guards lifted the barriers and let Easterners cross the border freely for the first time since 1961. Fittingly, the first to cross were residents of Bernauer Street.

Berlin

(Old Museum), originally designed to resemble a Greek temple, has been restored after its destruction in 1943. It is being stocked with displays of ancient sculpture and art, as is the magnificent Pergamonmuseum, whose main exhibit is the 52-foot Pergamon Altar, from a 164 BC royal temple in Bergama, Turkey. The Bode-Museum will display medieval sculpture, art and coins. The Egyptian collection is in the Neues Museum (New Museum); 19th- and 20th-century German art will be in the Alte Nationalgalerie (Old National Gallery).

SCHLOSS CHARLOTTENBURG

✚ A3   ✉ Luisenplatz   ☎ 030 320 911   ⏰ Tue.–Fri. 9–5, Sat.–Sun. 10–5   🍴 Altes Luxemburg, see page 553   🚇 U-Bahn to Richard-Wagner-Platz   🚌 109, 110, 121, 145   💲 $$

When building started on the huge rococo Schloss Charlottenburg (Charlottenburg Palace) in 1695, it was designed as an understated rural home for Sophie-Charlotte, wife of the future King Frederick I of Prussia. Over the next 100 years, with the help of a series of architects, it grew into a sprawling palace with a suite of royal apartments, dazzling rooms such as the White Hall and Golden Gallery, and gardens in formal French and landscaped English style, sloping down toward the Spree river.

The palace wings house the Great Orangery and Theater, an exhibition of German Romantic paintings and the Museum of Pre- and Early History.

Statue of Frederick the Great on Unter den Linden

TIERGARTEN

✚ C2   ⏰ Tue.–Sun. 9–6, Mon. 1–6   🚇 S-Bahn to Tiergarten   🚌 100

Once this was a hunting ground, well stocked with boar and deer, hence the name Tiergarten (Animal Garden). Now it's a 524-acre breath of fresh air in the center of the city, with woodlands, lakes and waterways, gardens and open-air concerts. Originally landscaped in the 1830s, the park is divided by the wide avenue Strasse des 17 Juni, where an 1873 Siegessäule (victory column) crowned with a golden goddess commemorates Prussian successes against Denmark, Austria and France.

TOPOGRAPHIE DES TERRORS

✚ D2   ✉ Stresemannstrasse 110   ☎ 030 2548 6703   ⏰ Daily 10–6   🚇 U-Bahn to Kochstrasse; S-Bahn to Anhalter Bahnhof   🚌 129, 341

The grim Topographie des Terrors (Topography of Terror) occupies the site of the former Nazi secret police headquarters, where prisoners were interrogated and tortured. Photographs trace the emergence of Nazism, and a nearby viewing platform overlooks the enormous Regierungsviertel (Government Quarter), where the Third Reich had its administrative offices.

UNTER DEN LINDEN

✚ D2   ✉ Unter den Linden 2   ☎ Museum 030 203 040   ⏰ Museum: Thu.–Tue. 10–6   🍴 Borchardt, see page 554   🚇 U-Bahn to Französische Strasse   🚌 100, 147, 257   💲 Museum free

The street called Unter den Linden (Under the Lime Trees) was laid out in 1648 as a route to the Tiergarten hunting grounds. It runs from the Brandenburg Gate to Museum Island and the river, and is lined with baroque and neoclassic buildings. Included in the line up is the 1695 Zeughaus (Arsenal), which houses the Deutsches Historisches Museum (German History Museum). An equestrian statue of Frederick the Great stands at the eastern end – turned by the Communist regime to ride toward the East rather than the West.

Popular day trip – the extravagant Sanssouci Palace, where Frederick the Great spent his summers

AN EXCURSION TO POTSDAM

Visits to several palaces can be combined on a trip to Potsdam, southwest of Berlin. The setting for the 1945 Potsdam Conference, at which Allied leaders redrew the European map, is Cecilienhof Palace (Schloss Cecilienhof), a mock-Tudor 1916 building now partly used as a hotel. It was built for Kaiser Wilhelm II; although his nation was two years into a war with Britain, the Kaiser chose to have it built in the style of an English country house. The royal Hohenzollern family lived here until 1945. The conference hall, delegates' studies and the reception rooms used by Churchill, Truman and Stalin are unchanged and can all be seen.

The palace that really draws crowds to Potsdam is the Sanssouci Palace (Schloss Sanssouci), on the town's western outskirts. This summer retreat was where Frederick the Great could enjoy life "without care" (*sans souci*). A green dome tops the single-story, yellow rococo facade; inside the richly furnished rooms are artworks and ornaments. Sanssouci Park has fountains, temples, gardens, an 18th-century Chinese teahouse and the third Potsdam palace: Frederick's New Palace (Neues Palais), with its vast marble hall and indoor grotto decorated with shells.

The town of Potsdam is also worth seeing. St. Nicholas' Church (Nikolaikirche) is one of Karl Friedrich Schinkel's classical monuments. In the Old Town, sculptures of rearing horses mark the site of the former royal stables, the 17th-century Marstall building, now a movie museum. The New Town was actually built in 1732, and became the focus of Potsdam's exiled French Huguenot (Protestant) community. In the Dutch Quarter, several streets of redbrick, gabled houses survive; they were built for Dutch construction workers who came to build the New Town.

🕓 Cecilienhof: Tue.–Sun. 9–5. Sanssouci: Tue.–Sun. 9–5, Apr.–Oct.; 9–3, rest of year. New Palace: Wed.–Mon. 9–5, Apr.–Oct.; 9–3, rest of year 🚌 All can be reached by bus 695 or the S-Bahn (Potsdam Stadt). Private tour operators in Berlin offer day trips by bus (inquire at the tourist office).

Surrounded by soaring spires and shaded by trees, Cologne's cafés serve a variety of delicious fare

COLOGNE

The two spires of Cologne (Köln) Cathedral soar above the Rhine, reminders of its past glory as a center of pilgrimage and the biggest city in medieval Germany. Despite the destruction of most of its central core in World War II, the city has retained and restored considerable evidence of its long and distinguished past. Today Cologne is thriving again, in business, trade, the arts and education, and its renowned sense of fun adds to the character that makes this one of Germany's most attractive cities.

Old Town

Cologone's Old Town (Altstadt) forms a vast semicircle on the west bank of the Rhine (Rhein) river, hemmed in by the Ring, a long boulevard that changes names along its route. It extends along the line of the former city fortifications and passes the old city gates of Eigelseintor, Hahnentor and St. Severinstor. Within this area, the Cathedral (Dom, see page 227) is the main attraction and, in fact, the most visited monument in Germany. The railroad station and a group of major museums are within easy reach of it.

The Gothic-Renaissance Town Hall (Rathaus, see page 228) stands at the heart of the Old Town, just south of the Old Market Square; to the east, toward the river, is the 12th-century church of Gross St. Martin (see page 227), one of 12 wonderful pre-Gothic churches still standing in the city. These sights form the old core. Head across the river via the Deutzer Brücke or Hohenzollern Brücke bridges for a look back at an unrivaled view of historic Cologne.

Cafés and Taverns

There are 24 breweries here, more than in any other German city. All produce the local beer, *Kölsch*, which is light and clear and served in tall, slim glasses. Beerhalls, known in the local dialect as *Weetschaften*, also serve food at very reasonable prices. Specialties at these establishments include rolls with cheese (*Halve Hahn*) or rye bread with black sausage (*Kölsche Kaviar*).

You will find plenty of restaurants in the historic center, ranging from the traditional *Gasthaus* (tavern) to trendy bistros, and the range of cuisines includes Japanese, French, Burmese, Chinese, Turkish and East European. Wine bars and cellars are another source of refreshment, serving wines from the Rhine valley. There are many excellent cafés serving the ubiquitous *Kaffee und Kuchen* (coffee and cakes).

Karneval and Concerts

To see Cologne at its most boisterous, come before Easter for Carnival (*Karneval*) week. Precise dates change every year, but the fun always reaches its peak before Ash Wednesday, in time for the abstinence of Lent. On

Cologne

the Thursday before the seventh Sunday prior to Easter, the festival begins in a morning ceremony at Old Market Square, and everyone gears up for the three "crazy days" (*Tolle Tage*) – Thursday, Sunday and Monday. There are costume balls at night, and more informal revelry on the streets and in the taverns. On Sunday there's a procession of floats, and on Monday a spectacular parade provides the lively and colorful climax.

For the rest of the year, there's calmer entertainment at the city's main cultural centers. Concerts are performed at the Philharmonie, in the Wallraf-Richartz/Ludwig Museums building on Bischofsgartenstrasse. Other concerts take place regularly in the city's churches, and are usually free.

Opera is staged at the Opernhaus. Cologne has a famous puppet theater – the Puppenspiele – but dialogue is in the local *Kölsch* dialect.

Listings for movies, theater and concerts are published in the magazines *Kölner Illustrierte* and *Stadt Revue*, and in the tourist office's own monthly *Köln-Monatsvorschau*. Nightclubs and discos are concentrated on the streets around Gross St. Martin; in the St. Severin quarter, Südstadt; and in the university quarter – the Quartier Lateng, in the southwest part of the city.

Eau de Cologne

Probably the most appropriate Cologne souvenir is a bottle of *eau de Cologne*, first distilled from flower blossoms in the 18th century and intended as an aphrodisiac. Known here as *Kölnisch Wasser*, it's made by about 20 businesses, including one of the originals, Farina, which has been in operation since 1709. Stores all over the city sell it, but the Old Town is the best place to browse for gifts. An all-day market takes place Friday in Old Market Square. On spring weekends (April and May) the same square is taken over by flower stalls. A wine market sets up in New Market in late May and early June. All shops close during Carnival's crazy days.

Crazy Days

On the first of the crazy days of Carnival, a procession takes place based on the local legend of Jan and Griet. Jan von Werth was a cavalry officer in the 17th century, and Griet was his sweetheart, who nobly urged him to follow his career as a soldier rather than stay with her. Jan went on to become a hero, saving Cologne from destruction during the Thirty Years War, but he and his love never crossed paths again – until he was a distinguished general, entering the city at the head of his troops, and watched by the old spinster Griet.

ESSENTIAL INFORMATION

TOURIST INFORMATION
• Unter Fettenhennen 19, in front of the Cathedral ☎ 0221 221 3345

URBAN TRANSPORTATION
Cologne has a peculiarly integrated transportation system. Trams travel through the Old Town, some above ground (east-west lines), some underground (north-south lines); they also share some lines with freight trains. Subway stations are marked on the Cologne city map as the letter "U" in a red circle. Tickets are sold individually or in strips of four; you can also buy a 24-hour or 3-day travel card. The bus and railroad stations are next to the Cathedral. For information call Cologne transportation information ☎ 0221 547 3333.

AIRPORT INFORMATION
The Cologne/Bonn airport is less than 30 minutes from the city center. Bus 170 travels to and from the airport and the main railroad station (near the Cathedral) every 20 minutes daily 5:30 a.m.–11 p.m. Taxis operate from the airport to the city center. For flight information, call ☎ 0220 340 4001 or 0220 340 4002.

CLIMATE – average highs and lows for the month											
JAN.	FEB.	MAR.	APR.	MAY	JUN.	JUL.	AUG.	SEP.	OCT.	NOV.	DEC.
3°C	4°C	10°C	14°C	19°C	22°C	24°C	24°C	20°C	14°C	8°C	3°C
37°F	39°F	50°F	57°F	66°F	72°F	75°F	75°F	68°F	57°F	46°F	37°F
-2°C	-2°C	0°C	4°C	8°C	12°C	14°C	13°C	10°C	6°C	3°C	0°C
28°F	28°F	32°F	39°F	46°F	54°F	57°F	55°F	50°F	43°F	37°F	32°F

CITY SIGHTS

Key to symbols

✚ map coordinates refer to the Cologne map on page 225; sights below are highlighted in yellow on the map.

✉ address or location ☎ telephone number
🕐 opening times 🚌 nearest bus or tram route
Ⓜ nearest subway 🍴 restaurant on site or nearby
🎟 admission charge: $$$ more than DM8, $$ DM3–DM8, $ less than DM3

DOM

✚ B3 ✉ Am Hof ☎ 0221 9258 4720 🕐 South Tower: daily 9–6 in summer; 9–4 in winter. Erzbischöfliches Diözesanmuseum: Fri.–Wed. 10–5 🍴 Brauhaus Sion, see page 554 Ⓜ Lines 5, 12, 16, 18 to Dom/Hbf 🎟 South Tower $

It took more than 600 years to complete the Dom (Cathedral), a Gothic masterpiece that incorporated the original architects' plans right to the end. The purpose of the project (begun in 1248) was to provide an appropriately grand setting for the relics of the Three Magi, which were snatched from Milan and kept here in a golden shrine. The final result is majestic, with intricately worked masonry serving to lighten the great mass of the facade and the two 515-foot spires – at the time they were built, the tallest structures in the world.

The golden shrine is, of course, the main focus of the interior, but there are many other treasures. In the south ambulatory chapel, the altarpiece of the *Adoration of the Magi* is a superb work by Stefan Lochner, one of the 15th-century artists of the Cologne School. In the north chapel is the ninth-century Gero Crucifix. One of the most inspiring features of the Cathedral is the stained glass, ranging from the 13th-century Bible Window in the ambulatory to the Bavarian windows in the nave, donated by King Ludwig I in the 19th century.

GROSS ST. MARTIN

✚ C3 ✉ Frankenwerft ☎ 0221 257 7924 🕐 Daily 🍴 Päffgen in der Altstadt, see page 555 Ⓜ Lines 5, 12, 16, 18 to Dom/Hbf 🚌 Tram 7, 9 to Heumarkt

From its completion in 1172 until the

The glorious Gero Crucifix in Cologne Cathedral

completion of the Cathedral in the 19th century, the church of Gross St. Martin was the most distinctive feature of Cologne's skyline. Its tower, with four turrets at the corners, makes an interesting contrast to the lacy stonework of the Cathedral's spires. Originally this was a monastery church, built for Benedictine monks from Ireland and Scotland.

MUSEUM FÜR ANGEWANDTE KUNST

✚ B3 ✉ An der Rechtschule ☎ 0221 2212 3860 🕐 Tue.–Sun. 11–5 (also Wed. 5–8) Ⓜ Lines 5, 12, 16, 18 to Dom/Hbf 🎟 $

Next door to the Gothic church Minoritenkirche is the Museum für Angewandte Kunst (Museum of Applied Arts), with an exquisite collection of applied arts ranging from the medieval period to contemporary times. One of the most interesting pieces is a panel of *The Nativity* by Hans Memling, a Flemish painter whose calm, precise style was very popular in his time. The museum also has a fine collection of art nouveau works.

Cologne

RATHAUS

✚ B3　✉ Rathausplatz　☎ 0221 2210　🕐 Rathaus:
Mon.–Thu. 7:30–4:45, Fri. 7:30–2. Mikwe: Sun. 11–1
🍴 Päffgen in der Altstadt, see page 555　🚇 Lines 5,
12, 16, 18 to Dom/Hbf　🚋 Tram 1, 7, 9 to Heumarkt
The Rathaus (Town Hall) is a Cologne
landmark at the heart of the Old Town. A
flamboyant, octagonal 15th-century tower
tops off the 14th-century body of the
building. The Renaissance *loggia* (porch)
was added in the 1570s. Under a glass
pyramid in front of the hall is a 12th-
century Jewish bathhouse, the *Mikwe*.
There was once a ghetto here, where the
city's Jewish community lived until they
were expelled in 1424.

RÖMISCH-GERMANISCHES MUSEUM

✚ B3　✉ Roncalliplatz 4　☎ 0221 244 38 or 0221 245
90　🕐 Tue.–Fri. 10–5 (also Thu. 5–8), Sat.–Sun. 11–5
🚇 Lines 5, 12, 16, 18 to Dom/Hbf　💵 $
For hundreds of years Cologne was under
Roman rule; city status was granted in AD
50 by Emperor Claudius. The Römisch-
Germanisches Museum (Roman
Museum) gives some idea of day-to-day
life in the Roman Empire through items
that were excavated locally. The main
exhibit is the astonishing 230-foot
Dionysus Mosaic, once part of a third-
century Roman villa: it shows Dionysus,
god of wine – also known as Bacchus –
indulging in drunken revelry. An older
exhibit is the 49-foot-high tomb of a
legionnaire called Poblicius, who died
about AD 40. Cologne's glass workshops
were busy producing their own designs in
the third and fourth centuries, and
there's a display of their work, and a
collection of jewelry found at Frankish
burial sites.

ST. URSULA

✚ B4　✉ Ursulaplatz　☎ 0221 133 400　🕐 Church:
daily. Goldene Kammer: Mon.–Tue. and Thu.–Sat.
9–noon and 1–5, Wed. 9:30–noon and 1–5
🍴 Bosporus, see page 554　🚇 Lines 5, 12, 16, 18 to
Dom/Hbf
North of the city center is the church of
St. Ursula; it was named after the

daughter of a fourth-century king of
Britain, who was said to have been killed
in the city by Huns, along with her
11,000 virgin companions. The popularity
of the cult of St. Ursula contributed to the
city's development as a center of
pilgrimage, and she appears in the Cologne
coat of arms. The church sacristan can
provide visitor access to the baroque
Goldene Kammer (Golden Room).

SCHNÜTGEN MUSEUM

✚ B2　✉ Cäcilienstrasse 29　☎ 0221 2212 3620
🕐 Tue.–Fri. 10–5 (also Wed. 5–8), Sat.–Sun. 11–5
🍴 Brauhaus Sion, see page 554　🚇 Lines 3, 4, 12,
16, 18 to Neumarkt　🚋 Tram 1, 2, 7, 9 to Neumarkt
Some of the best religious art and
furnishings in the city can be seen at the
Schnütgen Museum, which occupies the
deconsecrated church of St. Cäcilien.
Among other treasures are original
carvings from the Cathedral altar and
some beautiful ivory pieces. The carved
memento mori (reminders of mortality) are
chilling depictions of human bodies in a
state of decay.

WALLRAF-RICHARTZ/ LUDWIG MUSEUM

✚ B3　✉ Bischofsgartenstrasse 1　☎ 0221 2212
2379　🕐 Mon.–Fri. 10–6 (also Tue. 6–8), Sat.–Sun.
11–6　🚇 Lines 5, 12, 16, 18 to Dom/Hbf　💵 $$
Cologne's major collection of German
and international art is here, with works
through the 19th century shown in the
first-floor Wallraf-Richartz Museum, and
20th-century art shown in the Ludwig
Museum, which occupies the rest of the
building. At the Wallraf-Richartz you can
study the work produced in Cologne in
the 15th century, when the city was at the
forefront of artistic development. In
particular, look for the triptychs by the
artist known as the Master of St.
Bartholomew, one of the last of the
Cologne School, whose brightly colored
paintings resemble carvings.
　Many 20th-century greats are
represented in the Ludwig Museum,
including Otto Dix and Max Ernst; the
section on pop art has works by Andy
Warhol and Roy Lichtenstein.

Cologne

AN EXCURSION TO KLOSTER ALTENBERG

Kloster Altenberg, about 11 miles northeast of Cologne, is set on the Dhün river in the woods of the hilly country called Bergisches Land. This former Cistercian monastery is better known as the Bergischer Cathedral (Bergischer Dom). The original monastery church was built using stone from the manor of the Count of Berg, who left it to the monks after moving his headquarters elsewhere in 1133. It took a little more than 100 years to finish building the present monastery, which was begun in 1255 – only seven years after work had started on the Cathedral in Cologne (which took more than six centuries to complete).

The end result is one of Germany's best examples of 13th-century Gothic style: no elaborate embellishments and no tower, but a marvelous sense of space and light, enhanced by the simple, silvery stained-glass windows in the chancel. The window representing *Holy Jerusalem* is the biggest stained-glass window in the country. There are tombs of the past counts of Berg in the north transept.

During the Napoleonic Wars in the late 18th and early 19th centuries, the church fell into disuse and was in danger of crumbling. Luckily, King Frederick William IV took an interest in its restoration, and it was opened again to worshipers on the condition – laid down by the king – that both Catholics and Protestants could attend. This holds true today, and on Sundays both Catholic and Protestant congregations from the city come here for services. The outbuildings now house restaurants; at any of these

Küchenhof, you can ask for the key to the oldest standing part of the monastery, the 13th-century chapel Markuskapelle. One of the most exquisite features of the whole complex is the choir surrounded by chapels, viewed most rewardingly from the slope east of the monastery.

It takes an hour to reach Kloster Altenberg from Cologne's center: the underground trams (U-Bahn lines 4, 15 and 16) take you to Wiener Platz for a connection with bus 434.

Guided excursions from Cologne can be arranged by the convention department of the tourist information office (✉ Unter Fettenhennen 19, 50667 Köln, ☎ 0221 221 2333, 0221 2212 3325 or 0221 2212 3326; fax 0221 2212 3311).

Nestled in the woods – Bergischer Cathedral

Munich

MUNICH

The capital of Bavaria is one of Germany's most appealing and popular cities. Even though Munich is the country's third-largest city, with a cosmopolitan society and culture, it has also retained a village-like atmosphere with parks and a pedestrian-only center. It's only an hour from the Alps, and also has the easygoing feel of a Mediterranean town. Even on the briefest German tour, Munich is a city not to be missed.

Munich on Foot

Central Munich is compact and attractive, and easy to explore on foot. Long pedestrian streets (Neuhauser Strasse and Kaufingerstrasse) run from the main railroad station and from Karlstor, one of the city gates, to Marienplatz, the square at the heart of the Old Town. Here you can watch the mechanical characters of the carillon (*Glockenspiel*) at the front of the New Town Hall (Neues Rathaus, see page 234) and visit the twin-towered Cathedral. To the north of the square is the tree-lined Maximilianstrasse, which leads to the Bavarian Parliament building and the Residenz Palace. Two great art collections – the Old and New Picture Galleries – are a short distance northwest of the city center; to the south are the history museum and, on an island in the Isar river, the world's foremost museum of science and technology, the German Museum.

Bavarian Eateries

There are innumerable restaurants and cafés in Munich, and its large foreign population ensures a wide range of cuisines. At specifically Bavarian cafés, the Munich *Weisswürste* (white veal sausage with parsley) is a staple, served in hot water to be peeled and covered in mustard before eating. This particular delicacy is usually eaten at about 11 a.m. Meals are generally early in Munich, as people start work at 7 or 8 a.m. Lunch can begin at 11:30 but is often substantial, and the "lunch hour" can last until 2 p.m. Dinner is served between 6:30 and 11 p.m., but locals tend to stick to a light supper, or *Abendbrot*. The Schwabing district, north of the city center, is a busy area of sidewalk cafés and taverns. Snack bars (*Lokal* or *Schnellimbiss*) and even butchers shops (*Metzgerein*) sell snacks such as meatloaf and sausages all day. And nobody should leave Munich without visiting one of the beer gardens.

Music and Film

Munich is a major European cultural center, with thriving movie and publishing industries and a proud musical tradition. There are no fewer than three symphony orchestras based here, and the Residenz provides an impressive venue – either in the concert hall or, in summer, in the courtyard. Opera and ballet are staged at the National Theater, where the July Opera Festival is the highlight of the city's cultural calendar. The main cultural center is the modern Gasteig, home of

Munich

the Munich Philharmonic Orchestra; students from the Richard Strauss Conservatory give free lunchtime recitals in the Little Concert Hall during the week. The annual Film Festival takes place at the Gasteig in June – the high point of a series of festivals devoted to the movies.

Munich tends to shut down early, but Schwabing has many cabarets, theaters, and live music venues ranging from rock 'n' roll to folk to jazz – including the well-known jazz club Unterfahrt on Kirchenstrasse 96.

Boutiques and Markets

There's good window-shopping all over the old center of Munich, especially along the pedestrian-only Neuhauser Strasse and Kaufingerstrasse. Maximilianstrasse is a browser's paradise, lined with designer fashion boutiques, art galleries and jewelers. More stores can be found in the arcades and lanes leading off Residenzstrasse.

City of Monks

Munich's city emblem is the *Münchener Kindl*, or "little monk," recalling its origins as a monastic settlement. The first recorded mention of *Munichen*, "the home of monks," was in AD 777. The city itself was founded nearly 400 years later by Henry the Lion, Duke of Saxony.

Antiques, less expensive fashion and second-hand stores are concentrated in the student area of Schwabing, and Bavarian crafts can be found in the streets that run off Max-Joseph-Platz. Munich's famous open-air food market, Viktualienmarkt, with its formidable women vendors and fresh goods ranging from local cheese to Alpine flowers, sets up south of the Marienplatz every day except Saturday afternoon and Sunday.

ESSENTIAL INFORMATION

TOURIST INFORMATION
• Fremdenverkehrsamt München, Sendlingerstrasse; U-Bahn or S-Bahn to Marienplatz ☎ 089 233 03 00
• Hauptbahnhof; U-Bahn or S-Bahn to Hauptbahnhof ☎ 089 23 33 02 56.

URBAN TRANSPORTATION
A U-Bahn (subway) and S-Bahn (suburban) train network covers the city center and beyond. The U-Bahn is marked on the Munich city map by the letter "U" in a red circle; the S-Bahn is marked by the letter "S" in a red circle. Trains run daily from 5 a.m.–1 a.m. Tickets are bought from machines at MVV stations. Tickets can be purchased individually or in strips: multiple tickets are valid for buses and

trams, too. Validate your ticket in the automatic stamping machine as you board. One ticket is good for up to five bus/tram or three train stops; two tickets for additional stops. For MVV information call ☎ 089 23 80 30.

AIRPORT INFORMATION
The international airport, Flughafen München Franz-Josef-Strauss, is 19 miles north of the city center. S-Bahn trains run 24 hours a day to the main railroad station (Hauptbahnhof); airport buses run to the station from the North Terminal daily 7:05 a.m.–8:05 p.m. (a 45-minute journey). For flight information call ☎ 089 97 52 13 13.

CLIMATE – average highs and lows for the month

JAN.	FEB.	MAR.	APR.	MAY	JUN.	JUL.	AUG.	SEP.	OCT.	NOV.	DEC.
2°C	3°C	8°C	11°C	17°C	20°C	22°C	23°C	19°C	13°C	7°C	3°C
36°F	37°F	46°F	52°F	63°F	68°F	72°F	73°F	66°F	55°F	45°F	37°F
-4°C	-4°C	0°C	2°C	7°C	10°C	12°C	12°C	8°C	4°C	0°C	-3°C
25°F	25°F	32°F	36°F	45°F	50°F	54°F	54°F	46°F	39°F	32°F	27°F

CITY SIGHTS

Key to symbols

✚ map coordinates refer to the Munich map on page 230–231; sights below are highlighted in yellow on the map.

✉ address or location ☎ telephone number

🕐 opening times 🚌 nearest bus or tram route

Ⓜ nearest subway 🍽 restaurant on site or nearby

✋ admission charge: $$$ more than DM8, $$ DM3–DM8, $ less than DM3

ALTE PINAKOTHEK

✚ B4 ✉ Barerstrasse 27 ☎ 089 23 80 52 16 🕐 Tue.–Sun. 9:15–4:30 (also Tue. and Thu. 7–9 p.m.) Ⓜ U-Bahn to Königsplaatz 🚌 Tram 27 ✋ $$

Over 850 pre-18th-century paintings are being rehoused in the huge Alte Pinakothek (Old Picture Gallery), built in 1836 to store the expanding royal art collection. After suffering extensive war damage, the gallery was restored in the 1950s and underwent a further renovation in the 1990s, during which time its paintings were shown in the Neue Pinakothek (New Picture Gallery, see page 234). Among the treasures are works by Albrecht Dürer and the world's best collection of work by Peter Paul Rubens.

ASAMKIRCHE

✚ B2 ✉ Sendlinger Strasse 62 🕐 Daily 8–5:30 Ⓜ U-Bahn to Sendlinger Tor 🚌 31, 56; tram 17, 18, 20, 21, 27

The Asamkirche (Asam Church) is a stunning example of rococo architecture. It was built as a private chapel in 1729 for architect and sculptor Ägid Quirin Asam, and was opened to the public in 1746. Every available inch of its small interior is decorated with gold leaf, sculptures and frescoes, and one of Asam's own works is at the altar, showing the crucified Christ in God's embrace – *The Throne of Mercy*.

BMW MUSEUM

✚ Off the map ✉ Petuelring 130 ☎ 089 38 22 56 52 🕐 Daily 9–5 Ⓜ U-Bahn to Olympiazentrum or Petuelring 🚌 36, 41, 43, 81, 136; tram 27 ✋ $$

The BMW Museum occupies a half-spherical silver structure next to the Bavarian Motor Works headquarters – itself a striking building with four silver cylinders. Cars, motorcycles, videos and slides illustrate the history of the automobile and its place in our lives, and visitors can even design their own cars with the aid of computer graphics.

DEUTSCHES MUSEUM

✚ D1 ✉ Museumsinell, Ludwigsbrücke ☎ 089 217 94 33 🕐 Daily 9–5 🍽 Café on site Ⓜ S-Bahn to Isartor 🚌 Tram 18 ✋ $$

One of the biggest science and technology museums in the world has more than 17,000 items on display, and deals with everything from lightning demonstrations to space travel to hydraulics to the first German submarine. Audiovisual displays and hands-on exhibits add to the fun.

ENGLISCHER GARTEN

✚ D4–E4 🕐 Daily dawn–dusk 🍽 Beer gardens, cafés and restaurants in park Ⓜ U-Bahn to Odeonsplatz, Universität, Giselastrasse or Münchener Freiheit 🚌 44, 54, 154; tram 17

Stretching along the bank of the Isar river, the landscaped park Englischer Garten (English Garden) was created in 1789 on a former hunting ground. Today it is busy with street entertainers and people lunching, boating and taking in the fresh air. Boats can be rented at the Kleinhesseloher See, and there is a beer garden, the Seehaus, near the lake. Enjoy good city views from the circular "temple," the *monopteros*; other popular attractions are the Chinese Tower and beer garden,

Early touring car at the BMW Museum

The onion domes of Munich's Cathedral

the Japanese Tea House, the carousel and the brass band that regularly plays here.

FRAUENKIRCHE

✚ C2 ✉ Frauenplatz 1 ☎ 089 290 08 20
🕐 Towers: Mon.–Sat. 10–5, Apr.–Oct. 🚇 U-Bahn/S-Bahn to Marienplatz 🚌 52; tram 19
Munich's twin-towered Cathedral, a famous city landmark, was built between 1468 and 1488, but was left without a roof. In 1524 its green onion domes were "temporarily" added – and have been there ever since. Near the entrance is a footprint in the floor, said to be that of the devil, who stamped with glee thinking that the architect had forgotten to put in the windows. In fact, the windows can't be seen from where the devil was standing – but they are there.

HAUS DER KUNST

✚ D3 ✉ Prinzregentenstrasse 1 ☎ 089 21 12 71 37
🕐 Tue.–Sun. 10–5 (also Thu. 5–8) 🍴 Café 🚇 U-Bahn to Odeonsplatz or Lehel 🚌 53; tram 17 ✋ $$
The Haus der Kunst (House of Art) was opened by the Nazis in 1937, as a white-columned building known to its detractors as the *Weisswurst* (white sausage) gallery. It was part of Hitler's campaign against modern artists such as Paul Klee and Max Beckmann: while their work was ridiculed in an exhibition of "degenerates" in the Hofgarten, this gallery showed state-approved art. It now gives pride of place to the work denounced by the Third Reich.

LENBACHHAUS

✚ B3 ✉ Luisenstrasse 33 ☎ 089 23 33 20 00
🕐 Tue.–Sun. 10–6 🍴 Café 🚇 U-Bahn to Königsplatz ✋ $$$
A 19th-century Italianate villa, home of aristocratic painter Franz von Lenbach, the Lenbachhaus is now the city's art gallery. It shows the progression of art in Munich from the Gothic art of the 15th and 16th centuries to the 18th- and 19th-century Romantics. Highlighting the collection are works by the Munich Expressionists, the so-called *Blaue Reiter* (Blue Rider) group of the 20th century, including more than 300 abstract paintings by Wassily Kandinsky.

NEUE PINAKOTHEK

✚ C4 ✉ Barerstrasse 29 ☎ 089 23 80 51 95
🕐 Tue.–Sun. 10–5 (also Tue. and Thu. 5–8) 🍴 Café
🚇 U-Bahn to Theresienstrasse 🚌 Tram 27 ✋ $$
Across the street from the Renaissance-style Old Picture Gallery (see page 233) is Neue Pinakothek (New Picture Gallery), a modern concrete, granite and glass building featuring art from the late 18th to the 20th centuries. It covers French and German Impressionists, Romantic paintings, and the art nouveau style known in Germany as *Jugendstil*.

NEUES RATHAUS

✚ C2 ✉ Marienplatz ☎ 089 233 03 00 🕐 Tower: Mon.–Fri. 9–4, Sat.–Sun. 10–7, May–Oct. Mon.–Thu. 9–4, Fri. 9–1, Nov.–Apr. 🍴 Ratskeller, see page 555 🚇 U-Bahn/S-Bahn to Marienplatz 🚌 52 ✋ Tower $
A forest of neo-Gothic turrets, towers, spurs and gargoyles, the 19th-century Neues Rathaus (New Town Hall) sprawls around its six courtyards on the north side of Marienplatz. On its central tower is a 43-bell clock, which bursts into life at 11 every morning, as life-size figures from Munich's history come dancing out to its four melodies. One dance, the *Schäfflertanz*, which celebrates the passing of the plague in 1517, is performed by dancers in the city streets every seven years (next perfomance is due in 2005).

Wilhelm V of Bavaria founded Munich's Hofbräu brewery in 1589 to brew a dark ale more to his liking than the local beer. At this time, beer was a drink restricted to the Bavarian upper classes: They had made it their own preserve after losing their vineyards in a series of bad winters. In 1828, the brewery became an inn, and the delights of its beer were made accessible to all.

HOFBRÄUHAUS

The huge beer hall and its tree-shaded courtyard has been the scene of political upheaval and violence in recent history. The Nazi party held its early mass meetings here, and a fight broke out during one of Adolf Hitler's speeches that became known as the Battle of the Hofbräuhaus.

Nowadays, there is nothing sinister about the hall's fame: tourists flock to the long benches, listen to the Bavarian brass bands and drink beer served by traditionally dressed waitresses. They no longer practice the customary quality test for *Bock* beer, though, which is probably just as well. The test apparently consisted of drinkers sitting at one of the Hofbräuhaus' beer-soaked benches and consuming *Bock* beer for hours at a time, staying put even while nature took its course. If, at the end of the session, they stuck to the benches when they tried to get up, the beer was reckoned to be thick enough and ready to sell.

The Hofbräuhaus is the city's most popular beer hall and fills up very quickly, especially during the world-famous, 16-day *Oktoberfest*, a beer festival that

ends on the first Sunday in October. Barbecues, processions and music all play their part in this annual jamboree, but beer is the main ingredient.

If the Hofbräuhaus is too crowded, there are other options all over town: The biggest is the Mathaser Stadt in Bayer Strasse, near the railroad station. Much of the main *Oktoberfest* action takes place on the fairground at Theresienwiese, west of the city.

Whether you drink at the Hofbräuhaus or elsewhere, make sure you don't sit at the regulars' table (*Stammtisch*). You'll know you're there if the waitresses refuse to take your order!

Service with a smile at Munich's most famous beer hall

Munich

ODEONSPLATZ

➕ C3　🍴 Halali, see page 555　Ⓤ U-Bahn to Odeonsplatz　🚌 53

This regal square was laid out for Ludwig I early in the 19th century and marks the beginning of two great Munich boulevards – Ludwigstrasse and Prinzregentenstrasse. The Bavarian Ministry of Finance now has its offices in the Leuchtenberg-Palais, built in Italian Renaissance style along one side of the square. The Feldherrnhalle (Military Commanders' Hall) was added as a tribute to the Bavarian army, and is guarded by two bronze lions – one roaring, the other mute. Overlooking Odeonsplatz is the lovely baroque, golden-stone Theatinerkirche, the church where Wittelsbach family members were laid to rest. The immaculate gardens of Hofgarten are next to the square.

OLYMPIAPARK

➕ Off the map　✉ Spiridan-Louis-Ring 21　☎ 089 30 67 24 14　🕐 Olympiaturm: daily 9 a.m.–midnight. Stadium: daily 8:30–6, Apr.–Oct.; 9–4:30, rest of year 🍴 Revolving restaurant, Olympiaturm　Ⓤ U-Bahn to Olympiazentrum　🚌 36, 41, 43, 81, 136, 184; tram 20, 21, 27　✋ Olympiaturm $

North of the city center, beyond Schwabing, the park built for the 1972 Olympics has become a focus for strollers, joggers and swimmers. Its television tower, the Olympiaturm, is the highest reinforced concrete tower in Europe, and has a platform and revolving restaurant

with fantastic Alpine views. A tour train takes visitors around the Olympiasee Lake, the Olympiaberg Hill, made of wartime debris, and the Olympic Village – scene of the terrible shooting of Israeli athletes during a terrorist siege on September 5, 1972.

RESIDENZ

➕ C3　✉ Residenzstrasse/Max-Joseph-Platz ☎ 089 29 06 71　🕐 Tue.–Sun. 10–4:30 🍴 Spatenhaus, see page 555　Ⓤ U-Bahn to Odeonsplatz; U-Bahn/S-Bahn to Marienplatz　🚌 53; tram 19　✋ $

The Wittelsbach dynasty's dazzling palace has taken 40 years to restore after wartime damage. Its 112 rooms are once again a treasure-trove of artworks, ornaments, furnishings and statues – too much to take in during just one visit. Some of the highlights are the vaulted Antiquarium hall, built in 1568; the rococo Cuvilliés Theater; the crown jewels in the Treasury; and the Ahnengalerie (Ancestral Portrait Gallery) featuring 121 Wittelsbachs.

SCHLOSS NYMPHENBURG

➕ Off the map　☎ 089 17 90 80　🕐 Tue.–Sun. 9–12:30 and 1:30–5, Apr.–Sep.; 10–12:30 and 1:30–4, rest of year. Closed bank holidays. Gardens: daily 7–dusk 🍴 Schlosscafé Palmenhaus, see page 555 Ⓤ U-Bahn to Rotkreuzplatz　🚌 41; tram 17　✋ $$

For centuries the mighty Wittelsbach family ruled Bavaria, with Munich as their base. Schloss Nymphenburg (Nymphenburg Palace), on the city's western outskirts, was built as their summer villa by Agostino Barelli in 1674. Every generation of Wittelsbachs subsequently added to his creation, and the palace now measures 1,640 feet from end to end. In the central section is the Schönheitsgallerie, or Gallery of Beauties – 36 paintings of beautiful women produced between 1827 and 1850 for Ludwig I. Some are believed to have been his mistresses. The former palace stables house a museum of porcelain and a collection of state carriages and sleighs, and on the grounds a Hall of Mirrors (in the 1734 Amalienburg hunting lodge) lets you see yourself many times over.

Ceiling detail at the fabulous Residenz

A WALK ALONG PRINZREGENTEN-STRASSE

This grand old boulevard runs east from the 17th-century Court Garden (Hofgarten), with its beautiful fountains and Renaissance arcades. A startling modern addition, the steel-and-glass Staatskanzlei, houses the Bavarian State Chancellery. Prinzregentenstrasse was laid out at the end of the 19th century and named for Prince Luitpold, who ruled as regent after his nephew, Ludwig II, had been declared mad and deposed.

Today it takes visitors through one of the city's main museum and gallery quarters. Running past the southern end of the English Garden, the boulevard first reaches the House of Art, formerly a gallery of Nazi-approved art but now the home of the State Gallery of Modern Art (Staatsgalerie Moderner Kunst). It exhibits the kind of work the Nazis had condemned. Next door is the Bavarian National Museum (Bayerisches National museum), in a turn-of-the-20th-century building incorporating many different architectural styles.

The next notable monument is the former Prussian embassy, now the Schackgalerie, named for one of the 19th-century's great patrons of the arts, Count Schack. His own collection of paintings is represented by such artists as Franz von Lenbach and Arnold Böcklin, who relied on the Count for their livelihoods. The gallery is open Wed.–Mon. 10–5.

Fountain in the Hofgarten

Prinzregentenstrasse continues across the Isar river and past the *Angel of Peace (Friedensengel)*, a golden monument to peace, where citizens gather on New Year's Day to enjoy fireworks displays and the view of Munich. Farther along, past the Europaplatz, is the Villa Stuck, a 19th-century house built in a mix of styles by artist Franz von Stuck. Von Stuck was part of the 1890s *avant-garde* school known as the Munich Secession, and his own work is displayed inside; open Tue.–Sun. 10–5 (also Thu. 5–9).

The boulevard continues east to the Prinzregenten-Theater (☎ 089 29 16 14 14), which stages drama, concerts and musicals. It was designed in 1900 to emulate the Wagner Festival Theater in Bayreuth. The theater sits on Prinzregentenplatz, where there is a U-Bahn station; trains travel back to Odeonsplatz and the Hofgarten. For the walk route, see the city map on pages 230–231.

GREECE

"*IGHTY indeed are the marks and monuments of our empire we have left. Future ages will wonder at us, as the present age wonders at us now...*"

From *The Peloponnesian War*, circa 400 BC, by Athenian historian Thucydides

Opposite: Verdant olive groves on the fertile Lasithi plateau – in eastern Crete

GREECE

Somewhere, subconsciously, we all feel we have a stake in Greece. Our language, our political systems, our values and ethics are inextricably connected to this beautiful country's ancient civilization. Visitors arrive with high expectations and romantic notions, muddled snippets of myths and folklore, history and hearsay mingled in their minds. Those experiencing the country for the first time are likely to be dazzled. Greece evokes strong feelings, and months of travel would scarcely be enough to do this stunning country justice.

The Land

Islands are by definition beautiful, and there are 166 inhabited islands in Greece, scattered on three sides of the mainland. Some are studded with pine and eucalyptus, and some are arid or mountainous. Most have idyllic beaches and picturesque villages, and many have superb ancient sites, Frankish castles or Venetian fortifications.

You could spend years discovering them all, so spare at least a few days to visit one or two. Greek islands are a vital part of the country and have bedazzled travelers for centuries. Ferry

Greece

services are excellent and even in the height of summer you can find somewhere to stay, so an island-hopping trip can be a spur-of-the-moment decision.

Much of mainland Greece is very mountainous. The slopes of Olympus and Parnassus are carpeted with huge spreads of wildflowers in spring, offering superb vistas and alluring hiking. But there's more: the eerie and stony landscape of the Mani and the gentle coastal hills of the Peloponese. Traveling is easy by public transportation, and renting a car is simple to arrange. If you do decide to drive, beware of aggressive Greek motorists and be prepared for roads in poor condition.

Traditional Culture

Greece has one of Europe's most vigorous cultures, perpetuated through architecture, crafts, music and dance. Traditional ways permeate everyday life, despite the growing impact of Western consumer values. If you can, see traditional dancing and listen to the music – the real thing is often easier to find in rural areas.

As in many other Mediterranean countries, much of life is lived in the full gaze of the public eye, hence the strolling crowds and packed cafés. Tempers can quickly flare, and you'll see the ubiquitous worry beads carried by Greek men, which serve mainly as an outlet for their stress.

The Greeks and You

Tourism is not a slick operation in Greece; everything works, things eventually happen, but not necessarily with streamlined efficiency. So relax, slow down and you'll get much more out of your trip.

The Greeks have been dealing with foreign invaders for centuries, so the

20th-century tourist influx has hardly thrown them at all. The classical Greek tradition of hospitality to strangers is still strong, which makes for a matter-of-fact and laid-back attitude toward visitors, particularly when you go off the beaten track.

Hospitality often takes the form of innumerable personal questions, among which "How much do you earn?" is usually near the top of the list. Don't be offended, as this is considered an acceptable and friendly exchange. If someone offers you something – a drink, some fruit, a flower – accept it graciously, as the donor is acting out a tradition that goes back thousands of years in time.

Greeks have a strong code of honor, which helps to make Greece one of the safest countries to visit. It's highly unlikely you'll be cheated in any way, and you can safely walk mosts streets at night without worrying. Society has changed beyond recognition in the last 40 years and young Greeks – especially boys – are far more emancipated than their parents. However, especially in the country, girls are still sheltered and virginity still counts, so foreign girls are an attractive target for local youths.

There's still a large peasant class in Greece, and outside cities and tourist areas you'll see black-garbed figures laboring in tiny fields as they have for centuries, their lifestyle a million miles from that of city dwellers.

MORE TOP DESTINATIONS IN GREECE

- Ágios Efstrátios B3 - Alónnisos B2
- Kefalloniá A2 - Delfoí B2
- Ioánnina A3 - Léros C2 - Metéora A3 - Ólympos A3 - Mykonos C2
- Náfpaktos A2 - Óros Píndos A3
- Samothráki B3 - Thíra/Santorini C1
- Skópelos B2 - Máni B1

TIMELINE

776–700 BC   City-states established; first Olympic Games.

499–400 BC   Persian Wars; Golden Age of classical Greek culture; Peloponnesian Wars against Sparta.

336–323 BC   Alexander the Great conquers the known world.

146 BC   Greece becomes a Roman province.

AD 394   Christianity established throughout the Roman Empire; the Olympic Games finish and the Delphic Oracle is closed.

476–1453   Greece ruled from Constantinople; fall of Constantinople in 1453; Greece ruled by Turks for next 400 years.

1821–29   Greek War of Independence; Greece becomes an independent modern state.

1917–18   Greece sides with Allies in World War I.

1940–44   Axis occupation during World War II.

1945–60   Many Greeks emigrate to the United States and Australia; others flood into Athens from the countryside.

1974   Conflict with Turkey over Cyprus; situation remains tense into the 1990s.

1975   Tourist boom begins with foreigners visiting classical sites, islands and coastal resorts.

1981   Greece joins European Community; community funding catapults much of the country into mainstream Europe.

1996   Macedonian claims by former Yugoslavs seen as implicit threat to northern Greek region of Macedonia.

1997   Greece fails to qualify for first-wave entry to European monetary union (euro currency).

THE GOLDEN AGE OF CLASSICAL GREECE

The peace following the defeat of the Persians in the fifth century BC marked the start of a cultural, artistic and intellectual blossoming for Athens and the other city-states. Much of what truly epitomizes "the glory that was Greece" dates from this era. The great architectural triumphs, the start of drama and comedy, and the first steps in philosophical thought can all be traced to Athens at this time. The Acropolis took the form whose remains are seen today, decorated by Pheidas' sublime marbles, and subtly harmonious temples were built everywhere. The names Sophocles, Euripides, Aristophanes, Socrates and Plato are familiar worldwide; it's worth remembering that they lived and worked in this tiny state in the eastern Mediterranean more than 2,500 years ago.

Greece

SURVIVAL GUIDE

- Athens is best avoided during the sweltering summer months, when temperatures can soar, noise levels are high around the clock, and the ever-present pollution is at its worst.

- Head for restaurants and *tavernas* where locals eat; the food will be good and it's a delight to watch Greek families dining together. If you don't understand the menu in a *taverna* you'll probably be invited into the kitchen for a look – choose what you want and point! Remember, too, that Greeks firmly believe that hot food harms the stomach, so food is generally served lukewarm.

- Remember to *never* flush lavatory paper down the toilet – it goes in the basket provided. Greek plumbing is antediluvian, and you'll flood the bathroom if you put paper down the drains. This applies throughout Greece. Greek public restrooms are few and far between and leave much to be desired, so seize every opportunity you have to use them in cafés, museums and restaurants.

- Athens is a capital city, and you should dress appropriately. Greeks are generally cool and comfortable rather than stylish, but usually don't wear shorts in the city. It's respectful to cover bare shoulders and upper arms in churches. Unlike some other European countries, topless and nude sunbathing are unacceptable in this deeply religious country.

- Taxis are inexpensive, but check the meter before starting out; it's not unknown for the price to mysteriously triple for foreign visitors.

- Don't rent a scooter; more tourists have accidents on them than by any other means.

- At important sites you'll be inundated by guides wanting to be paid for their services; some are good, others barely speak English. If you want guide service, use an official one or take a tour.

- There's a plethora of attractive, handmade items to buy in Greek stores and markets. Leather goods, hand-woven rugs, sponges, olive-wood bowls, sweaters and antique reproductions are all worth looking for; just make sure the piece you choose is of good quality. Most prices are fixed, but you can try a little gentle haggling in markets, where you'll also find some of the world's best honey and olive oil.

Parliamentary guard in traditional uniform

ATHENS

Athens is one of the Mediterranean's great cities, boasting some of the world's most treasured relics; it's also noisy, crowded and polluted, with sprawling, unattractive suburbs. Summertime heat and the lack of green, shady spots can be oppressive, but the city is exhilarating, fascinating and stimulating, as much for its past as its present. Accept it and enjoy it for the colorful place it is.

Tackling Athens

You'll probably spend most of your visit in Athens' tiny historical center. Base yourself near Syntagmatos Square or Pláka, which are only a 10- to 15-minute walk from most of the main tourist sights. Try to plan your day carefully, getting an early start, so you can lay low during the heat of the afternoon. If you need information or advice, you will find that most people connected with tourism speak English, ranging from a few words to polished and idiomatic speech.

Moving around the city is easiest by taxi, although a ride on a trolley bus or the subway is a real, if not particularly enjoyable, Athenian experience. The existing subway system is being extended as Greece prepares for the 2004 Olympics Games, resulting in mounds of building debris and greater chaos than usual around the city. There's heavy traffic, and drivers often have a light-hearted disregard for other drivers and pedestrians, so take care when crossing busy roads.

AVEROF **ATHENS**

LEÓFOROS ALÉXANDRAS

IPOKRÁTOUS

Gípedo
Panathinaïkoú

Lykavittós

gios
eórgios

VASILISSIS SOFÍAS

PAPADIAMANTÓPOULOU

OLONÁKI   ILÍSIA

Mouseío Kykladikís
ai Archaías
Ilinikís Téchnis   Ethnikí
                      Pinakothíki
                Polemikó
                Mouseío   Álsos
                                                Syngroú
Vizantinó
Mouseío

KONSTANTINO

SPYROU

VAS ALÉXANDROU

ÓFOROS VAS GEORGÍOU II

ROS VAS

FORMIÓNOS

YMITTOÚ

MERKOÚRI

RATÓSTHENOU

Stádio

EFTIKHÍDOU

CHIMIDOUS

EFRANOROS

CHREMONÍDO

FILOLAOÚ

EMPEDÓKLEOUS

YMITTOÚ

Profítis
Ilías

NIKOFORÍDI NIK

D   PAGKRÁTI

E AMALIPSEOS

Athenian Flavors

Sitting at a shady café table, lingering over a gargantuan lunch, munching sunflower seeds, melon, pistachio and pine nuts, or eating ice cream as you stroll on balmy evenings are true Athenian pleasures.

In a country where hospitality to strangers is one of the bedrock rules of society, it's not surprising that eating and drinking socially play an important role. Eating establishments are known as *estiatorio* (restaurants) or *tavernas* (less expensive, simpler and often family-run).

Greek food is delicious and healthy – fresh salads with feta cheese and olives, fantastic hors d'oeuvres (*mezédhes*), grilled meats, moussakas, and tasty stews and vegetables, washed down with *retsina,* the barrel-stored, pine-resonated white wine.

Dessert is normally fresh local fruit; if you want something sweeter, head for a *zaharoplastío*, a café serving the honey-soaked pastries much loved by the Greeks. The cuisine seems at times to have more in common with the Middle East than with the rest of mainstream Europe.

Festivals and Theater

Athens has theater, movies, dance, galleries and nightlife; everything changes rapidly, so pick up a free copy of such English-language magazines as *Athens Today* or *Now in Athens* to find out schedules.

In summer, the main tourist attractions are the sound-and-light show at the Acropolis and the Athens Festival, which runs from June until early October. The festival has a wonderful spread of excellent cultural events, although it's most famous for classical Greek theater, stunningly staged in the second-century Herodes Atticus Theater.

Athens

The delicious Greek salad, topped with feta cheese and oregano

The Greek Alphabet

At first it may be daunting to see Greek script everywhere, but it won't be a major inconvenience. All street signs are in both Greek and Roman, as are signs to museums and most restaurants and shops. Public transportation is usually signed in Greek. But you'll get the hang of figuring it out and will feel a real sense of achievement when you do.

Ceramics and Honey

There's a wide range of shopping in Athens, from international labels to traditional Greek products. In Kolonáki and on and around Ermoú Street, the smartest retail areas, you'll find familiar merchandise.

Ethnic buys are another matter, with much to hunt down around Pláka and vicinity. Leather and woolen goods, traditional ceramics and tapestries, felt slippers, natural sponges, fruity olive oil, honey and pistachios are all excellent buys. For something special, check out jewelry or religious stores; Greece has a long tradition of fine gold craftsmanship, and traditional icons are still made. Watch for Athens' kiosks – much more than newsstands, they sell everything from snacks and drinks to bus tickets, simple medicines and cassette tapes. In central Athens many are open 24 hours a day.

ESSENTIAL INFORMATION

TOURIST INFORMATION
• Odós Amerikis 2 ☎ 01 322 3111

available at kiosks and are interchangeable with subway tickets, which can be bought at stations or kiosks. Remember to validate all tickets when boarding.

URBAN TRANSPORTATION
The easiest way to get around Athens is to walk or take one of the numerous, inexpensive, yellow taxis, as public transportation can be jam-packed and unbearably hot. Taxis are hailed on the street and often shared; you pay for your segment of the journey, so check the meter when you get in. Alternatively, your hotel can arrange a taxi for you. Buses, trolley buses and the limited subway system operate daily 5 a.m.–midnight; tickets are

AIRPORT INFORMATION
Athens' Ellenikou Airport has two terminals, connected by trolley bus 19; the west (☎ 01 936 3363) is used by Olympic Airways, the east (☎ 01 969 4466) by all other airlines. Ellenikou is about 10 miles south of the city and is easily accessible by taxi or by the half-hourly bus. Bus 91 runs to Syntagmatos Square and bus 19 to Piréas; buy your ticket in the terminal before boarding.

CLIMATE – average highs and lows for the month

JAN.	FEB.	MAR.	APR.	MAY	JUN.	JUL.	AUG.	SEP.	OCT.	NOV.	DEC.
13°C	13°C	15°C	19°C	24°C	30°C	31°C	32°C	28°C	23°C	17°C	14°C
55°F	55°F	59°F	66°F	75°F	86°F	88°F	90°F	82°F	73°F	63°F	57°F
6°C	6°C	7°C	11°C	15°C	20°C	22°C	22°C	19°C	15°C	11°C	8°C
43°F	43°F	45°F	52°F	59°F	68°F	72°F	72°F	66°F	59°F	52°F	46°F

Room with a view – a quiet place to stop for a picnic

Stunning under floodlights, the Acropolis rises serenely above the city

CITY SIGHTS

Key to symbols

➕ map coordinates refer to the Athens map on page 244–245; sights below are highlighted in yellow on the map. ✉ address or location ☎ telephone number ⏱ opening times 🚌 nearest bus or tram route 🚇 subway station 🍴 restaurant on site or nearby 💰 admission charge: $$$ more than Dr2000, $$Dr1000 to Dr2000, $ less than Dr1000

AGORÁ

➕ B2 ✉ Adrianou or Theorias ☎ 01 321 4825 ⏱ Tue.–Sun. 8:30–2:45 🚇 Theseion or Monastiráki 💰 $$

The stately civic center and marketplace of ancient Athens is at the foot of the Acropolis, to which it was linked by the Panathenaic Way. Today the site is a bewildering jumble of atmospheric, tree-shaded ruins, and you'll need to use your imagination to visualize its glorious heyday. Dominating one end is the virtually reconstructed, fifth-century BC Doric temple known as the Thieío. Opposite, the two-story Stoá Attálou, a second-century BC arcade, has been restored by the American School of Archeology to give an idea of the glory of these ancient public buildings. It contains a museum with finds from the site.

AKRÓPOLI

➕ B2 ✉ Acrópoli ☎ 01 323 6665 or 01 321 4172 ⏱ Mon.–Fri. 8–7, Sat.–Sun. 8:30–3, Apr. to mid-Oct.; Mon.–Fri. 8–5, Sat.–Sun. 8:30–3, rest of year. Closed holidays 🍴 Psara's, see page 556 🚇 Thission 🚌 1, 5, 9, 230, 231 💰 $$ ℹ️ Acropolis Sound and Light, in English nightly, Apr.–Oct.; tickets from Athens Festival Box Office ✉ 4 Stadiou ☎ 01 322 1459

The Akrópoli (Acropolis) should top your sightseeing list. This naturally defensible rock was the sacred focal point of ancient Athens, and what you see today dates mainly from the fifth century BC, an era of peace and prosperity. You reach the summit through the Propylaia, a magnificent stepped gateway, with the graceful little temple of Athena Nike to your right. Ahead rises the great Doric temple of the Parthenón; built using no perpendicular lines, its columns actually taper, giving the whole structure a feeling of superb lightness. It was decorated by leading Athenian sculptors and dedicated to the goddess Athena Parthenos, whose statue by the sculptor Pheidias stood inside. To the left of the Parthenón stands the Erechtheion, shrine to Athena and Poseidon, and said to be the place where the goddess created the first olive tree. The roof of the south portico is supported by six caryatids, stately maidens dressed in pleated tunics. At the Acropolis' foot you can see two Roman theaters, the Théatro Iródou Attikoú and the Théatro Dionysou.

ETHNIKÓ ARCHAIOLOGIKÓ MOUSEÍO

➕ C4 ✉ 44 Patission ☎ 01 821 7717 or 01 821 7724 ⏱ Tue.–Fri. 8–7, Sat.–Sun. 8:30–3, Mon. 12:30–7, Apr. to mid-Oct.; Tue.–Fri. 8–5, Sat.–Sun. 8:30–3, Mon. 11–5, rest of year 🍴 Café in museum 🚇 Omonia 🚌 2, 3, 11, 13, 15, 18 💰 $$

Athens

For lovers of classical art the Ethnikó Archaiologikó Mouseío (National Archeological Museum) is one of the world's top sights. This vast and varied collection covers all the finest from ancient Greece, with the bonus of an exceptional Egyptian collection. The museum needs a full day to do it justice, and some perseverance to track down the main highlights in a very poorly organized venue.

The best approach is to concentrate on only the finest examples. Head first for the treasures from the royal tombs at Mycenae, opposite the entrance, dating from 1500 BC; they include exquisite gold funerary masks, necklaces and filigree flowers. Next, take in the sixth-century BC *kouros*, vibrant statues of nude male athletes; Aristodikos' superbly tactile athlete is one of the finest ever carved. Move on to admire the huge statue of Poseidon and the little jockey urging on his horse, both found in the sea in 1927. There's also a stunning bronze by the famous sculptor Praxiteles in room 28. Upstairs you'll find frescoes from Thera, buried 3,500 years ago during a volcanic eruption, showing charming riverside scenes. Next door are the fascinating pottery collections; look for the rare *lekythoi* (white-ground clay ware), as well as the exquisite red and black Attic vases.

ETHNIKÓS KÍPOS

⊞ C2 ⊠ Amalias ⓒ Daily dawn–dusk
🚌 2,4,11,12

The green and somber Ethnikós Kípos (National Gardens) provide a wonderful oasis of cool. Laid out in the 19th century by Queen Amalia, this is a true southern Mediterranean garden – no colorful flowerbeds, but deep shade and sylvan green. With plenty of benches and cafés, the gardens are a good place for a picnic.

Greek head at the National Archeological Museum

LYKAVITTÓS AND KOLONÁKI

⊞ D3 ⊠ Kolonáki ⓒ Funicular: Fri.–Wed. 8:45 a.m.–midnight, Thu. 10:30 a.m.–midnight 🍴 Terrace café at top 🚌 3, 13 💰 $$

From Kolonáki Square, the hub of one of Athens' smartest shopping areas, the slopes of Lykavittós (Lykabettus) rise steeply to the 912-foot-high summit, one of the city's great vantage points. You can walk up or take the funicular to enjoy panoramic views over the city, from the Acropolis down to the sea at Piréas. Aim to get there for sunset, and leave time to visit the whitewashed chapel of Agios Giorgios (St. George) at the top.

MONASTIRÁKI

⊞ B2 ⊠ Monastiráki ⓒ Market open daily, but largest on Sun. 🚇 Monastiráki

This cacophonous area centers round Monastiráki square, named after a former monastery on this site. Today the square's focal point is the 18th-century Tzistarakis Mosque, a relic of Turkish rule, which houses the Keramiki Silogi (Museum of Greek Ceramics). However, most people head straight for Monastiráki's famous flea market, where you can find anything from clothes and kebabs to icons and compact discs. Sunday is the big day.

MOUSEÍO AKROPÓLEOS

⊞ B2 ⊠ Akrópoli ☎ 01 323 6665 or 01 321 4172 ⓒ Mon.–Fri. 8–7, Sat.–Sun. 8:30–3, Apr. to mid-Oct.; Mon.–Fri. 8–5, Sat.–Sun. 8:30–3, rest of year. Closed holidays 🍴 Psara's, see page 556 🚇 Thission 🚌 1, 5, 9, 230, 231 💰 $$ (included in Acropolis entrance)

Tucked behind the Parthenon is the Mouseío Akrópoleos (Acropolis Museum), housing a fine collection of sculptures found on the Acropolis. The original caryatids from the Erectheion are best known, but spend time admiring the superb fragment of a horse and rider and the splendid marble hound, straining forward in motion, in room IV.

The great Doric temple of the Parthenon, the crowning glory of the Acropolis

MOUSEÍO KYKLADIKIS KAI ARCHAÍAS ELLINIKÍS TÉCHNIS

✚ D2   ✉ 4 Neophytou Douka   ☎ 01 722 8321
🕓 Wed.–Fri. and Mon. 10–4, Sat. 10–3   ⬛ 3, 7, 13
🚪 SS

The beautifully presented Mouseío Kykladikis kai Archaías Ellinikís Téchnis (Goulandris Museum of Cycladic Art), once a shipowner's private collection, took its present form in 1986. Packed with fine antiquities, it's primarily famous for its collection of artifacts and statuettes from the Cycladic civilization, which flourished on the Greek islands from 3000 until 2000 BC. The figures, carved from local marble, could be taken for 20th-century work; elegant and minimalist, yet full of powerful feeling.

OLYMPÍEION ZEUS AND PYLI ADRIANOÚ

✚ C1   ✉ 1 Vasilissis Olgas   ☎ 01 922 6330
🕓 Daily 8:30–3   🍴 Achillion, see page 556   ⬛ 2, 4, 11   🚪 $

Along with the Tower of the Winds in the Roman Agora, Olympíeion Zeus and Pyli Adrianoú (Temple of Olympian Zeus and Hadrian's Arch) are Athens' most impressive Roman legacy. Both were completed around AD 130 by the Emperor Hadrian; the temple as a shrine to this paramount Roman god, and the arch to mark the boundary between the old Greek city and Hadrian's new one. Fifteen massive columns remain of what was once Greece's largest temple.

PIRÉAS

✚ Off the map   ☎ 01 461 2457   🚇 Piréas
🍴 Vassilenas, see page 556

Piréas is a town in its own right, although it's only five stops on the subway from Athens' center. It's a noisy, bustling port, one of the biggest in the Mediterranean, and many of the inter-island boats leave from its harbor. It boasts a magnificent Cathedral, rebuilt after World War II; a fine archeological museum; and Greece's naval museum. Sunday is a good day to browse in the flea market, then enjoy a delicious fish dinner at one of the restaurants around Mikrolimano Harbor.

PLÁKA

✚ B2   ✉ Pláka   🚇 Thission   ⬛ 9, 11, 15, 18

Visitors return time and again to the picturesque Pláka neighborhood, at the foot of the Acropolis. The maze of colorful narrow streets, flower-bedecked squares and huge range of stores and *tavernas* may be touristy, but also radiate charm. Bustling Kidhathineon and Adrianoú, the main streets, teem with street life and are lined with mainly 19th-century, colorfully painted houses. Don't miss the dazzling white alleys that comprise Anafiotika, on the northern slopes of the Acropolis; built in the 1840s by masons from the Cycladic islands, they still retain a village atmosphere.

PLATÉIA SYNTAGMATOS

✚ C2   ✉ Syntagmatos   ⬛ 1, 2, 4, 5, 12, 15, 18
ℹ Changing of the guard at varied times Mon.–Fri., at 11:25 a.m. on Sun.

Noisy, crowded and commercial, Platéia Syntagmatos (Constitution Square) is the heart of modern Athens, where you'll find hotels, offices, banks, restaurants, cafés and myriad jostling Athenians. The vast neoclassical edifice at the top is the Voulí (Parliament Building), once the royal palace. In front of it is the Tomb of the Unknown Soldier, patrolled around the clock by the Evzones, a guard of honor whose dress uniform features a short pleated kilt and pom-poms on their shoes.

The Athenian Treasury and Sacred Way at Delphi

AN EXCURSION TO DELPHI

The sacred site of Delphi (Delfoí), 93 miles northwest of Athens, is the obvious choice for a day trip. The greatest shrine of the ancient Greek world, the center of their earth, lies in an unrivaled position below the great peaks of Mount Parnassós. Dedicated to the god Apollo, in ancient times Delphi was independent – belonging to no state – so enemies could worship there together. It was famed for its oracle, which gave enigmatic and prophetic advice through the medium of a priestess.

In return for this, petitioners brought gifts and erected treasure houses to hold them; ancient writers referred to the marble and precious stones of the sanctuary. For centuries, pilgrims trudged through the mountains to bathe in the sacred Castalian spring and worship here, but in the fourth century Christianity triumphed and the last oracle slipped away. Below the site, olive groves spread down to the sea, the ground is carpeted with flowers and the sky is full of birds.

The French excavated Delphi in the 1890s, and today it lies on a series of terraces below Parnassós. The paved Sacred Way leads past treasure houses – one sensitively reconstructed – to the

Temple of Apollo. Six columns still stand, giving an idea of its former size and grandeur. Up the hill you'll find the 5,000-seat theater, and higher still, the marvelously evocative athletic stadium, set amid pine trees. To visit the ruins of the Sanctuary of Athena, leave the main site and cross the modern road. Use the columns of the fourth-century BC Tholos, undoubtedly the most photographed of all Delphi's wonders, as your guide.

Delphi Museum

The adjacent museum contains the finds from Delphi, some of the finest in Greece. Sculptures from the Temple of Apollo, two superb examples of archaic *koroi* (statues), ivory, jewelry and pottery are all here. The highlight is the bronze *Charioteer*, dating from 478 BC, an artistic and technical masterpiece.

✚ See page 240, grid reference B2 ✉ Delphi
☎ 02 658 2313 🕒 Mon.–Fri. 7:30–6:15, Sat.–Sun.
8:30–2:45, Apr.–Oct.; Mon.–Fri. 7:30–5, Sat.–Sun.
8:30–2:45, rest of year 🚌 A guided excursion is the
easiest way to visit Delphi
Excursion Operators
Chat Tours (✉ Intermed Travel, 46 Eleftheriou
Venizelou ☎ 01 957 8441) is the best-known and
most experienced tour operator in Athens.

HUNGARY

"*B*EYOND *the river the hills…behold they lead to Heaven.*"

By early 20th-century Hungarian poet Árpád Tóth

Opposite: View across the rooftops from the Firewatch Tower in Sopron, western Hungary

Hungary

HUNGARY

Hungary is situated at the heart of Europe. Surrounded by Austria, Slovakia, the Ukraine, Romania, Serbia, Croatia and Slovenia, it has absorbed the cultures of such peoples and conquerors as the Romans, Magyars, Turks and Habsburgs. Its majestic capital, Budapest, sits on the Danube river, which has brought trade and settlers through the country on its course from Austria to Serbia. For centuries Hungary has been a nation in flux, its territories expanding or diminishing through a series of invasions, occupations and liberations. It is today undergoing yet more change after emerging from 40 years of life behind the Iron Curtain.

Landscape of History

Northern, western and southern Hungary are different worlds. In the north, beyond the urban centers of Budapest and Miskolc, are the uplands and their wide, rolling, forested hills. The vineyards here produce famous Tokay and Bull's Blood wine.

In the west there are strong links with Western European culture. The rich farmlands are punctuated with historic towns that are packed with Renaissance and baroque buildings. In the south the landscape changes completely. Vast, flat grasslands form the Great Plain (*puszta*), dotted with tiny farmsteads and presided over by the capital, Debrecen. In the far south, the medieval city of Pécs preserves many relics of its 143 years under Turkish rule.

Making Contact

The Hungarian language, related only to Finnish and Estonian, can be daunting for visitors. Some English may be spoken in the tourist areas, but German is more frequently used. When you find a common language, however, you will discover that Hungarians are courteous, generous and formal. Hungary is a proud, multiracial nation, and despite its vicinity to the Balkan region, considers itself to be European.

Hungarian Heritage

Hungarians have strong folk traditions and customs, especially music and dance. You can enjoy them at a dance house (*tánchbáz*); there are several in Budapest. Bands usually include bagpipes and a hurdy-gurdy, and the dancing is fast and furious.

In Kiskunság National Park, between the Danube and the Tisza river, a horse-drawn buggy takes visitors to see farmsteads, long-horned cattle and curly-horned Podokan sheep. There are also displays at Hortobágyi National Park – Hungary's first national park.

In the Cserhát hills of the north, the village of Hollókö sits at the foot of its 13th-century castle. The village is home to the Palóc people, who speak a distinct dialect of Hungarian and wear colorful embroidered costumes and

elaborate headdresses. For another insight into Hungary's heritage, visit the famous Király thermal baths in Budapest and enjoy the luxury of a Turkish-style bath or massage.

MORE TOP DESTINATIONS IN HUNGARY

- Balatonfüred B2
- Bugac-Puszta C1 ● Eger D3
- Fertöd A2 ● Gödöllö C3
- Hollókö C3 ● Hortobágyi Nemzeti Park D3 ● Kecskemét C2
- Mátra C3 ● Pécs B1 ● Sopron A2
- Szabadtéri Néprajzi Múzeum C3
- Szentendre C3 ● Tihany B2
- Tokaj D3 ● Visegrád C3

Hungary

Hungary

TIMELINE

13 BC   The Roman province of Pannonia is established on the west bank of the Danube; nomadic tribes occupy the east.

AD 896   Seven Magyar tribes cross the Carpathian Mountains and invade the Hungarian plains.

1000   King Stephen is crowned and makes Hungary a centralized, Christian state.

1526   Sultan Suleiman I and his Turkish army defeat the Hungarians at Mohács; most of the country is brought under his rule.

1686   Habsburg troops recapture Buda, on the west bank of the Danube (later united with Pest, on the east).

1896   The Great Exposition celebrates the 1,000th anniversary of the Magyar Conquest.

1919   Hungary briefly becomes a Bolshevik republic.

1920   Under the Treaty of Trianon, Hungary loses two-thirds of its territory to Czechoslovakia, Yugoslavia and Romania, and comes under the rule of an Austro-Hungarian regent.

1943   After regaining its lands, Hungary loses the majority of its army at Stalingrad.

1944   German occupation; most of the Jewish population is deported.

1948   Communists take power.

1956   Rebellion against Communist rule is crushed by Soviet troops.

1989   Hungary opens its borders to Austria and the Iron Curtain begins to lift.

1990   Free elections are won by a center-right coalition.

1999   Hungary officially joins NATO.

THE GOOD OLD DAYS

Hungary enjoyed two "golden ages" – one in the 15th century and another in the 19th. Under 15th-century ruler King Matthias, the son of a Transylvanian general, the nation expanded its borders and established its court in Vienna. Matthias patronized some of Europe's most brilliant scholars, and employed the best Italian artists to work on his palace in Visegrád. Ruins were unearthed here in the 1930s. His reign became a byword for good government. When he died, say Hungarians, justice died with him. The man known as "the greatest Hungarian" ushered in a second age of achievement. In the 19th century Count István Széchenyi modernized the country, laying surfaced roads, introducing steam ships and founding an academy of sciences. He also linked Buda and Pest with the Chain Bridge, and stopped the regular cycle of floods around the Tisza river by building dams that regulated its flow.

SURVIVAL GUIDE

- Hungarian cuisine's best-known export, *gulyás* (goulash), is made with beef, onions, potatoes, paprika, tomatoes and garlic. Salami is a regular item, as is *lecso*, a mix of peppers, tomatoes, onions and bacon fried in pork fat. Pastries are also specialties, sold in the *cukrászda* (pastry shop). Try *palacsinta*, thin pancakes filled with chocolate or sour cream.

- Rural Hungarians produce and sell beautifully crafted items such as embroidered blouses and carved wood furniture. You can buy these in city stores, at national parks and from street sellers like the brightly costumed Transylvanian (Romanian) Hungarians.

- Wine is another good Hungarian buy, sold by dealers in the main vineyards, such as Eger. Many give tastings in their barrel-lined cellars.

- Go to street markets in the main towns and cities, such as the popular morning flea market on the southwest outskirts of Pécs. This is one of the biggest open-air markets in the country, selling antiques, crafts and food. On Sundays it also sells livestock, and the place is packed with country people.

- Some of the most fascinating ethnic communities have inevitably become big tourist magnets. Hollókö is filled with visitors for the August Palóc Festival and for Easter – an important celebration everywhere, marked with processions, egg-painting and a ceremony involving splashing girls with water or perfume.

- Summer festivals attract the crowds to Pécs and Sopron in June, and on St. Stephen's Day on August 20. There are fireworks, fairs and processions all over Hungary.

A miscellany of merchandise on display at one of the many antique shops in Budapest

- The state railroad (MÁV) travels to most of the country; express trains link the main centers. There are special tickets offering unlimited use of the network for seven or 10 days: contact the MÁV (✉ Andrássy útca 35, Budapest ☎ 01 342 9150 or 01 322 7860).

- Accommodations are not limited to city hotels. The Danube bend, a spectacular deep gorge north of Budapest, is lined with attractive towns where many private homes offer rooms, often for negotiable rates. The resorts around Lake Balaton are another option.

- For overnight stays on the Great Plain, try the Rider Village in Hortobágyi National Park (✉ 4071 Hortobágyi-Máta, Czinege útca 1 ☎ 5236 9092) or Pongrácz Manor near Kesckemét (✉ 6041 Kunpuszta 76 ☎ 7637 1240).

Budapest

BUDAPEST

Until the 19th century, two communities faced each other across the Danube. Royal, medieval Buda, with its majestic architecture, stood on the hilly western bank; and modern Pest, a flat area of busy boulevards, was on the east bank. Then the Chain Bridge (Széchenyi Lánchíd) was built and Budapest, "Queen of the Danube," was created, linking the western and eastern landscapes of Hungary: the green uplands behind Buda, and the flat fields of the Great Plain beyond Pest.

BUDAPEST

N

Óbuda

Margit-sziget

Centenáriumi emlékmű

ÚJLIPOTVÁROS

4 RÓZSADOMB

ÁRPÁD FEJEDELEM ÚTJA

LIPTHAY U

MARGIT HÍD

ÚJPEST RAKPART

POZSONYI ÚT

RADNOTI

VICTOR HUGO U

HEGEDŰS

MIKLÓS U

VÁCI

FERDINÁND

LEHEL TÉR

LEHEL U

TERÉZVÁROS

MARGIT KÖRÚT

BEM JÓZSEF U

FŐ U

BEM RAKPART

Duna

RAKPART

SZENT ISTVÁN KÖRÚT

MARKÓ U

NYUGATI TÉR

PODMANICZKY

Nyugati pályaudvar

VÍZIVÁROS

Néprajzi Múzeum

MOSZKVA TÉR

KRISZTINA

VÉRMEZŐ ÚT

BATTHYÁNY U

VÁRFOK

BATTHYÁNY TÉR

Országház

KOSSUTH LAJOS TÉR

ALKOTMÁNY U

BÁTHORY U

LIPÓTVÁROS

SZABADSÁG TÉR

BAJCSY-ZSILINSZKY U

NAGYMEZŐ U

ANDRÁSSY ÚT

TERÉZ KÖRÚT

OKTOGON

3

KÖRÚT

ATTILA ÚT

Vérmező

SZÉCHENYI

NÁDOR U

Magyar Állami Operaház

LISZT FERENC TÉR

Zeneakadé

Hadtörténeti Múzeum

VÁRHEGY

Mátyás-templom

Halászbástya

Budai Várbarlang

ROOSEVELT TÉR

Szent István bazilika

KIRÁLY U

KAZINCZY U

Déli pályaudvar

KRISZTINA

Várszínház

CLARK ADAM TÉR

SZÉCHENYI LÁNCHÍD

JÓZSEF ATTILA U

ERZSÉBET TÉR

DEÁK FERENC TÉR

DOB U

Zsidó Múzeum

ALAGUT U

Magyar Nemzeti Galéria

Budavári Spalota

Vigadó

VÖRÖSMARTY TÉR

KÁROLY KÖRÚT

LAJOS U

KRISZTINAVÁROS

GRÓZA PÉTER RAKPART

BUDA

Budapesti Történeti Múzeum

PEST

BELVÁROS

Városháza

KOSSUTH

MÚZEUM KÖRÚT

BRO

MESZÁROS UTCA

BELGRÁD

2

ALKOTÁS U

LÁNCHÍD U

KÖRÚT

NAPHEGY

TABÁN

DÖBRENTEI TÉR

ERZSÉBET HÍD

Belvárosi Plébánia templom

FERENCIEK TERE

VÁCI U

RAKPART

Magyar Nemzeti Múzeum

KÁLVIN TÉR

VÁMHÁZ KÖRÚT

HEGYALJA ÚT

Citadella

Jubileumi Park

SZT GELLÉRT RAKPART

FÖVAM TÉR

SZABADSÁG HÍD

Központi Vásárcsarn

GELLÉRT-HEGY

SZT GELLÉRT TÉR

i

Duna

KÖZRAKTÁR U

SASHEGY

1

VILLÁNYI ÚT

BUDAÖRSI ÚT

KÁROLINA ÚT

0   200   400   600   800 m

0   200   400   600   800 yards

BARTÓK BÉLA ÚT

BUDAFOKI ÚT

MŰEGYETEM RKP

PETŐFI

A   B   C

Crossing the Divide

The best place to get a feel for the capital's character and history is at Buda. Here you will find the oldest and grandest architecture, a cluster of museums and galleries, and countless cafés and bars. You can survey the whole city from Gellért Hill (Gellért-hegy), and visit Castle Hill (Várhegy), a renovated medieval quarter reached by funicular railroad (from the Buda end of Chain Bridge). This is where you'll find the Buda Castle Palace (Budavári Palota) and the Fishermen's Fortress (Halászbástya).

Pest has a much more contemporary feel; its main landmark is the Gothic parliament building (Országház) dominating the riverbank. Also worth visiting are the State Opera House (Állami Operaház) and the Academy of Fine Arts (Kepzö Müvészeti Köiskola). Between the riverbanks is tranquil Margaret Island (Margit-sziget), providing a haven of gardens in the middle of the Danube.

Local Flavors

In the late 19th and early 20th centuries, Budapest ranked with Vienna and Paris as part of the European café society drawing artists and intellectuals to argue, work and read newspapers. After World War II, few of these hubs of creative life remained. For a terrific art nouveau interior and a hint of the former literary and theatrical clientele, try the Café New York, at Erzsébet Körüt 9–11.

Traditionally, Hungarian meals rely on the staples of spices, meat and cream and include intriguing specialties such as *túrós csúsza* (pasta with curd and sour cream). Since 1989 the range of international restaurant options has increased immeasurably.

Budapest at Night

The main home of opera and ballet is the Hungarian State Opera House (Magyar Állami Operaház, Andrassy út 22), a massive neo-Renaissance confection. Classical concerts take place in the art nouveau Franz Liszt Academy of Music (Zeneakadémia), at Liszt Ferene tér 8.

Panoramic view of Budapest from the top of Gellert Hill

There are many bars, clubs, rock venues and discos, and rock bands have emerged from their underground status of the Communist years. The English-language paper *Budapest Week* has entertainment listings.

Shopping

Pedestrian-only Váci utca, on the Pest side of the river, is the perfect place to start shopping trips, and to look for antiques and art bargains. The other main boulevards in central Pest are also lined with stores. In Buda, there's a good browsing area around Móricz Zsigmond körtér.

A well-known flea market sets up at Nagykörösi út on weekday and Saturday mornings. It's also a pleasure to wander among the heaped food stalls of the renovated Central Market Hall on Fövám tér. The market is open all day Monday to Friday and also on Saturday mornings.

ESSENTIAL INFORMATION

TOURIST INFORMATION
• Tourinform, Sütó´utca 2, Budapest V, near Deák tér subway station
☎ 01 317 9800
• Dorottya utca 4, off Vörösmarty tér, Budapest V ☎ 01 318 3968.

URBAN TRANSPORTATION
Subway lines are color coded: yellow (M1), red (M2) and blue (M3). Buy tickets from the counter (*pénztár*) until 8 p.m., then from the section called *forgalmi ugyelét*. Trains run daily 4:30 a.m.–11:10 p.m. Buses with red-and-black numbers and no letter stop all over the city; avoid the express buses, which have a letter "E." Trams and trolley buses also have an extensive network. Tickets for all three are available from subway stations or from newsstands. Subway stations are marked with an "M" on the city map. Do not take taxis that don't display a sign, and check that the meter is on and running. The biggest city company is Fötaxi (☎ 01 222 2222).

AIRPORT INFORMATION
Ferihegy Airport is 12 miles southeast of the city. An airport shuttle (☎ 01 296 8555) travels to any downtown area (daily 5 a.m.–10 p.m.), and farther for a small surcharge. Purchase tickets from the LRI counter at the airport. Centrum–Airport–Centrum minibuses run to and from Erszébet tér bus station (daily 5:30 a.m.–9 p.m.), and bus 93 runs to Kóbánya Kispest subway station. For information call ☎ 01 296 7155.

CLIMATE – average highs and lows for the month

	JAN.	FEB.	MAR.	APR.	MAY	JUN.	JUL.	AUG.	SEP.	OCT.	NOV.	DEC.
	2°C	4°C	10°C	15°C	22°C	24°C	26°C	26°C	22°C	15°C	7°C	3°C
	36°F	39°F	50°F	59°F	72°F	75°F	79°F	79°F	72°F	59°F	45°F	37°F
	-4°C	-3°C	1°C	5°C	10°C	14°C	15°C	15°C	11°C	6°C	1°C	-3°C
	25°F	27°F	34°F	41°F	50°F	57°F	59°F	59°F	52°F	43°F	34°F	27°F

CITY SIGHTS

Key to symbols

✚ map coordinates refer to the Budapest map on page 258–259; sights below are highlighted in yellow on the map.

✉ address or location ☎ telephone number
🕐 opening times 🚌 nearest bus or tram route
Ⓜ nearest subway 🍴 restaurant on site or nearby
💵 admission charge: $$$ more than 1,000Ft, $$ 600Ft–1,00Ft, $ less than 600Ft

BUDAI VÁRBARLANG

✚ B3 ✉ Uri utca 9 🕐 Tue.–Sun. 10–6 Ⓜ Hösök tere 🚌 Várbusz (Castle bus) 🍴 $$

A maze of catacombs extends for 16 miles under Várhegy (Castle Hill), made up of caverns linked by passageways originally built for use by the Turkish military. Only a tenth of the Budai Várbarlang (Castle Caverns) complex can be visited, but even this gives a vivid impression of a strange, enclosed, underground world. Waxworks illustrate the history of Hungary from the misty past to the golden Renaissance age of King Matthias. During the siege of Budapest in World War II, thousands of people took shelter down here while their city was destroyed.

BUDAVÁRI PALOTA

Történeti Múzeum ✚ B2 ✉ Várhegy ☎ 01 355 8849 🕐 Tue.–Sun. 10–6 🚌 5, 16, 78; Várbusz (Castle bus) from Moszkva tér; tram 18; funicular from west end of Chain Bridge 💵 $; free Wed.

Kortars Muveszeti Múzeum ✉ Várhegy ☎ 01 375 9175 🕐 Tue.–Sun. 10–6 🚌 5, 16, 78; Várbusz (Castle bus) from Moszkva tér; tram 18; funicular from west end of Chain Bridge 💵 $; free Wed.

Nemzeti Galéria ✉ Várhegy ☎ 01 375 7533 🕐 Tue.–Sun. 10–6 🍴 Café in Namzeti Galéria 🚌 5, 16, 78; Várbusz (Castle bus) from Moszkva tér; tram 18; funicular from west end of Chain Bridge 💵 $; free Wed.

Orszá gos Széchenyi Könyvtar ✉ Várhegy ☎ 01 324 3700 🕐 Tue.–Sat. 9–9, Mon. 1–9 🚌 5, 16, 78; Várbusz (Castle bus) from Moszkva tér; tram 18; funicular from west end of Chain Bridge 💵 $; free Wed.

Budavári Palota (Buda Castle Palace) looks down over the Danube from its clifftop setting at the southern end of

Take a back seat for a view of Buda Castle Palace

Várhegy (Castle Hill). Hardly anything is left of the earliest castle, which was built in the 13th century. What remains is in the cellars and underground passages, now part of the Budapesti Történeti Múzeum (Budapest History Museum), in Wing E. Before the building was flattened during World War II, it was an amalgam of 18th- and 19th-century Habsburg architecture. This is the version that has been carefully restored.

The Nemzeti Galéria (National Gallery) collection of Hungarian art is housed in the central wings B, C and D, under a landmark dome. A walk from here through a garden square and past the lovely Matthias Well fountain takes you to the west wing (F) and the Orszá gos Széchenyi Könyvtar (National Szecheny Library), which stores about 2 million books. Contemporary art is displayed in the Kortars Muveszeti Múzeum (Ludwig Collection), in Wing A.

Statues outside the palace represent Prince Eugene of Savoy, who routed the Turkish armies; King Matthias, in the west courtyard; and a mythical bird called the Turul.

Magyar chiefs stand guard in Heroes' Square

GELLÉRT-HEGY

✚ B1   ☒ Between Erzsébet Bridge and Szabadság Bridge   🍴 Duna, see page 557   🚇 27; tram 18, 19, 47, 49

Bishop Gellért failed to convert the pagan Magyars to Christianity; legend has it they stuck him in a barrel and threw him into the river from this 771-foot-high limestone cliff. His statue stands at the bottom of Gellért-hegy (Gellert Hill). At the top is the Citadella, a stronghold built after the 1848–49 War of Independence to keep an eye on the restive citizens. The Freedom Monument, also at the top, was erected by the Russians in 1947. Before the fall of Communism, the monument featured a Soviet soldier as well as the now lone woman brandishing a palm leaf.

HALÁSZBÁSTYA

✚ B3   ☒ Várhegy   🕐 Daily 24 hours
🍴 Alabárdos, see page 557   🚇 Várbusz (Castle Bus) from Moszkva tér

Halászbástya (Fishermen's Fortress) is one of the city's greatest tourist draws: a fairy-tale seven-towered rampart in pale stone wedged into the eastern rim of Castle Hill. The architect, Frigyes Schulek, designed the fortress as part of the city's millennial celebrations of Magyar nationhood in 1896. There are great river views, and plenty of souvenir stalls and shops.

HÖSÖK TERE

✚ D4   ☒ Városliget   🚇 Hösök tere   🚌 20, 30, 105; trolley bus 75, 79

At the end of the grand Andrássy út boulevard and on the edge of Városliget (City Park) is magnificent Hösök Tere (Heroes' Square), part of the city's 1896 celebrations. On either side are the Mücsarnok (Art Gallery) and the Museum of Fine Arts; between them is a monument to Hungarian successes. Perched on a 118-foot-high column is the Archangel Gabriel; guarding the foot of the column are statues of the seven fierce and triumphant Magyar chiefs, with Árpád, their leader, in the center. They are flanked by colonnades bearing the figures of Fame, Knowledge, Peace and War; between the columns are more Hungarian icons, including King Stephen (who would later be sainted).

MAGYAR ÁLLAMI OPERAHÁZ

✚ C3   ☒ Andrássy út 22   ☎ 01 331 2550   🕐 Tours daily at 3 and 4   🍴 Müvész, see page 557   🚇 Opera
🚌 105   🎫 Tour $

Take one of the daily guided tours of the Magyar Állami Operaház (State Opera House) building to marvel at its marble, gold leaf and frescoes. Opened in 1884, it celebrates the musical world with statues of composers Wolfgang Mozart, Guiseppe Verdi, Richard Wagner and Ludwig van Beethoven, which stand on the stone cornice of the front terrace. Pride of place goes to Hungarians Franz Liszt and opera composer Ferenc Erkel, whose statues flank the entrance. Inside the building an enormous bronze chandelier hangs over the auditorium, which is decorated with Greek gods.

MAGYAR NEMZETI MÚZEUM

✚ D2   ☒ Múzeum körút 14–16   ☎ 01 338 2122
🕐 Wed.–Sun. 10–6, May–Sep.; 10–5, rest of year
🍴 Astoria Empire, see page 557   🚇 Astoria, Kálvin tér   🚌 9; tram 47, 49   🎫 $

Five collections form the Magyar Nemzeti Múzeum (Hungarian National Museum), Hungary's largest museum, covering an area of 861,111 square feet.

The Chain Bridge crosses the Danube, linking Buda and Pest

They include archeology, medieval and modern displays, and historical portraits. The great prize among the exhibits is St. Stephen's 11th-century crown, which was stolen by Hungarian fascists after World War II and kept in the United States until President Jimmy Carter ordered its return. The upper part of the crown, a gold cap set above the jeweled headband, may date even earlier. Other curiosities are the inscribed brick from a 13th-century monk's tomb and the tent of a Turkish commander taken at the siege of Vienna in 1683.

MÁTYÁS-TEMPLOM

🕂 B3 ✉ Szentháromság tér 2 ☎ 01 355 5657
🕐 Daily 7–7 🚌 Várbusz (Castle Bus) from Moszkva tér

Fifteenth-century King Matthias was married twice in the Mátyás-templom (Matthias Church), which had already been in existence for two centuries. It later served the Turks as a mosque, and was subsequently remodeled in the 19th century in striking neo-Gothic style. Medieval touches have been reproduced in the interior, along with dramatic features such as the soaring 262-foot spire. The tombs of 12th-century monarch Béla III and his wife, Anne of Châtillon, are in the Trinity Chapel near the main door.

ORSZÁGHÁZ

🕂 B3 ✉ Kossuth Lajos tér ☎ 01 268 4904
🕐 English guided tours: Wed.–Sun. at 10 a.m. (when parliament is in session); Mon.–Fri. at 10 a.m. and 2 p.m., Sat. at 12:30 p.m., Sun. at 10 a.m. (during recess) 🍴 Astoria Empire, see page 557
🚇 Kossuth Lajos tér 🚌 15; tram 2; trolley bus 70, 78
💷 $$

Bristling with neo-Gothic spires and turrets, the Országház (Parliament) building sits on the eastern bank of the Danube, covering an area of nearly 200,000 square feet. Its magnificent red dome is 315 feet high and rises above a 16-sided hall between the upper and lower houses of parliament.

SZENT ISTVÁN BAZILIKA

🕂 C3 ✉ Svent István tér ☎ 01 317 2859 🕐 Daily 9–5, Apr.–Sep.; 10–4, in Oct. 🚇 Arany János utca

Budapest's biggest church, Szent István Bazilika (St. Stephen's Basilica), took 55 years to finish. It can house a congregation of 8,500, and its dazzling interior includes 90 pounds of 24-carat gold, as well as frescoes, paintings and tapestries by Hungarian artists. Transylvanian and Hungarian heroes are represented by 88 statues, and the most cherished item – the mummified right hand of St. Stephen – is displayed in a glass case.

Budapest

The golden dome of St. Stephen's Basilica

SZÉPMÜVÉSZETI MÚZEUM

🚩 D4 ⊠ Hösök tere ☎ 01 343 9759 🕐 Tue.–Sun. 10–6, Mar.–Dec.; 10–4, rest of year Ⓜ Hösök tere 🚌 4, 20, 30, 105; trolley bus 75, 79 🚹 $

Along the edge of Hösök tere (Heroes' Square) is the Szépmüvészeti Múzeum (Fine Arts Museum), a neoclassical temple built to celebrate the millennial anniversary of the Magyar nation and to house the nation's art. Its 120,000 exhibits are now restricted to foreign work and include ancient Egyptian mummy cases, first-century BC ceramics and a world-renowned collection of old masters. Of particular note are works by the Spanish painter El Greco and those by such 20th-century greats as Pablo Picasso.

VÁROSLIGET

Mezögazdasági Muzeum 🚩 E4 ⊠ End of Andrassy út ☎ 01 343 8573 🕐 Tue.–Sat. 10–5, Sun. 10–6 🍴 Gundel, see page 557 Ⓜ Széchenyi furdö 🚌 20, 30, 105; trolley bus 70, 72, 75, 79 🚹 $

Fövárosi Nagycirkusz ⊠ End of Andrassy út ☎ 01 142 8300 🕐 Mon., Thu., and Fri. at 3; Sat. at 10, 3, and 7; Sun. at 10 and 3 🍴 Gundel, see page 557 Ⓜ Széchenyi furdö 🚌 20, 30, 105; trolley bus 70, 72, 75, 79 🚹 $

Közlekedési Múzeum ⊠ End of Andrassy út ☎ 01 343 0565 🕐 Tue.–Fri. 10–5, Sat.–Sun. 10–6 🍴 Gundel, see page 557 Ⓜ Széchenyi furdö 🚌 20, 30, 105; trolley bus 70, 72, 75, 79 🚹 $

Állatkert 🚩 D4 ⊠ End of Andrassy út ☎ 01 268

1970 🕐 Daily 9–7, May–Aug.; 9–5 rest of year 🍴 Gundel, see page 557 Ⓜ Széchenyi furdö 🚌 20, 30, 105; trolley bus 70, 72, 75, 79 🚹 $

Vidámpark ⊠ End of Andrassy út 🕐 Daily 10–8, Apr.–Sep.; 10–6, rest of year 🍴 Gundel, see page 557 Ⓜ Széchenyi furdö 🚌 20, 30, 105; trolley bus 70, 72, 75, 79 🚹 Free

Beyond the bustling boulevards of Pest is Városliget (City Park), a great green area providing a number of facilities. It was laid out in the 18th century and has acquired several extras over the years, the oddest being the Vajdahunyad Castle, on an island in the boating lake. Put together for the 1896 exhibition, its design was based on a Transylvanian fortress and its popularity ensured permanent survival. Inside the walls is the Mezögazdasági Muzeum (Agricultural Museum). The Állatkert (zoo), with art nouveau animal houses and a special section for newly born residents, is another favorite. There's also the Fövárosi Nagycirkusz (circus) and a slightly faded Vidámpark (amusement park) with a Ferris wheel and carousel.

In the park's southeast corner are the Közlekedési Múzeum (Transportation Museum), a garden for people with sight impairment and the Petöfi Csarnok youth center, where Hungarian youth come to hear pop music and to watch open-air movies in the summertime.

The Danube Promenade

Running alongside the river on the Pest bank, between Chain Bridge (Széchenyi Lánchíd) and Elizabeth Bridge (Erzsébet Híd), is a long, paved, tree-lined promenade called the Danube Promenade (Dunakorzó). The views over Buda on the far side are wonderful. In the 19th century, this was the most fashionable place to be seen. Café tables were set out in the evening, and gypsy bands played by lamplight under the stars. The elaborate Vigado is a legacy of that era, and still a venue for classical music concerts.

Esztergom's Cathedral entrance, dominated by eight Corinthian pillars

EXCURSION TO ESZTERGOM

Hungary's largest Cathedral towers over the stunning scenery of the Danube Bend at Esztergom, former royal city and the birthplace of King Stephen I (975–1038). There has been a settlement here, guarding the western approach to the gorge, since Roman times. Medieval Esztergom was destroyed by the Turks in 1543, but the city rose again, and it now boasts a center full of baroque buildings.

The Cathedral (Basilika) is by far the most imposing: it is 328 feet from the floor to the top of its huge, glittering dome. It includes one of the world's biggest paintings – an altarpiece based on the work of 16th-century Italian artist Titian. The white marble altar itself was designed in 1519 and made by expert craftsmen from Florence, Italy.

Among other treasures are the impressive Renaissance interior of the Bakócz Chapel and a gold and enamel Gothic cross known as the Calvary of Matthias Corvinus. The dome offers a spectacular view over Esztergom and its surroundings.

The present version of the Cathedral was begun in the 1820s: Hungarian composer Franz Liszt celebrated its reconsecration in 1856 with a Mass. Long before this second lease on life, Esztergom was the seat of the Hungarian Primate – head of the nation's Catholic Church – and an important royal base. King Stephen was crowned in a church on the site in AD 1000, and the remains of a royal palace are housed in the Castle Museum (Vár Múzeum) next door.

Two other museums are worth a visit. The Museum of Christian Art (Keresztény Múzeum) has a superb collection of medieval religious paintings and works by Italian artists such as Duccio di Buoninsegna, Lorenzo di Credi and Giovanni di Paolo. The Danube Museum (Duna Múzeum) features displays that clearly illustrate (despite Hungarian-only captions) the role of the river and its effects on the life of the town.

Esztergom is 41 miles north of Budapest. Buses travel from Budapest's Árpád híd bus station and there is a regular service from Nyugati railroad station.

For tour information contact Komturist (✉ Lorincz utca 6, Esztergom ☎ 01 33 312 082) or Gran Tours (✉ Szechenyi tér 25, Esztergom ☎ 01 33 313 756).

IRELAND

"THERE lay the green shore of Ireland, like some coast of plenty. **"**

On arriving in Ireland, from *English Traits*, 1856, by essayist and philosopher Ralph Waldo Emerson

Opposite: This view of the mountains and lakes of Killarney is known as "Ladies View"

IRELAND

Ireland

People long for Ireland in a way that they pine for few other countries. Call it romantic, call it sentimental, but there is something about this remarkable country that tugs at the heart-strings of even those who have no Irish blood. The beauty of the country, its powerful Gaelic traditions and the irrepressibly romantic and creative nature of the Irish people underscore this potent appeal. This is a country that is not without problems, however, and its political and religious divide has had far-reaching, universal impact.

Mists of Time

Ireland claims with pride that it was a "land of saints and scholars" when the rest of Europe was deep in the Dark Ages. It is often described as a Celtic country, with all the myth-making that goes along with that term. The Celts are seen as being a distinctive lost race of Iron Age people who, in the face of first Roman and then Anglo Saxon aggression, retreated into Scotland, Ireland, Wales and Cornwall, from where they passed down the cultural

values of their time. They did not call themselves Celts, and the term may be only a convenient label, but what is certain is that the influence of the earliest Bronze Age and Iron Age cultures survives on the peripheries of the British Isles. This is especially true in Ireland, where the evocative Gaelic language – still heard in modern Ireland – is its greatest expression.

Today there are thousands of prehistoric sites in Ireland: on the remote western seaboard, on the Beara peninsula, in County Kerry, and at exceptional places such as the Newgrange burial complex, in County Meath north of Dublin. Even where they are ruinous and vestigial, these ancient sites are hauntingly evocative.

You will find within the same landscape the music, song, wit and drama of Ireland that have been enshrined in hundreds of films, songs, dances and stories. The sense of the past is intense here; it has shaped Ireland in a seminal way, for better or for worse.

From Dublin to Kerry

Dublin is the boisterous heart of Ireland, the "family home." It should not be missed, of course, but Dublin will only whet your appetite for the rest of the country. Save time to explore other areas for the essential Irish experience. South of the capital lie the Wicklow Mountains, with the popular Glendalough at their heart – half religious site, wholly spectacular from a scenic point of view.

Farther south lies the fascinating Viking town of Wexford, from where the long, rambling southern coast of Ireland runs through endless great bays toward the distant west (and the most spectacular scenery). The western coast stretches for nearly 180 miles north to south, but measures much more if all the sinuous indentations, bays, river

MORE TOP DESTINATIONS IN IRELAND

- Aran Islands A2
- Beara Peninsula A1
- Blarney Castle B1 • The Burren A2
- Clifden A2 • Dingle A1
- Galway A2 • Giant's Causeway C4
- Glendalough C2 • Kilkenny B2
- Killarney A1 • Newgrange C3

Ireland

mouths, peninsulas and islands are taken into account.

Try to visit the far southwest. Take in the charming historic city of Kilkenny on the way; and visit Cork, the Irish Republic's second largest city, where you can kiss the nearby Blarney Stone if you feel that you should. Beyond Cork lies the glorious Beara peninsula. The bigger Iveragh peninsula lies in exquisite County Kerry to the north, land of the great mountains of Macgillycuddy's Reeks and the delightful lakes, and town, of Killarney.

Islands and Lakes

North of County Kerry lies the lovely Dingle peninsula and County Clare. Clare's southern half is mundane, but becomes increasingly spectacular the farther north you go, past the huge, echoing Cliffs of Moher and into the limestone country of the Burren, with its natural pavements of moonscape rock, dramatic stone burial chambers and hill forts.

In the pubs of Clare you will encounter the heart-stopping, foot-tapping essence of Irish music and

The great open spaces of the peat country as seen from Sligo Bay

song, in an environment that preserves the best of the past with energy, vitality and lyricism.

Off Clare's northwestern coast are the stunning Aran Islands, the magic names of Inishmor, Inishmaan and Inisheer resonating with all things Irish. Beyond Clare is Galway Bay and Galway city, the latter a vibrant, unfailingly charming place on the threshold of the Gaeltacht, the major area of Gaelic-speaking Ireland. Here, the mountains of Connemara and the broad lakes Loughs Corrib and Mask match an astonishing coastline of raw, rocky wilderness that lies to either side of the romantic town of Clifden.

Inland, Ireland also has much to offer. The heart of the country is a green bowl of rich farmland, of lakes, rivers and isolated ranges of rounded hills. Landlocked Ireland is outshone by the stupendous coastline of the far west, but it is a charming country full of character and tradition, where you will hear talk of horses and history and where lakes and rivers throng with fish.

Traveling North

Farther north is the remote county of Mayo, where you can follow the pilgrims' route up the Holy Mountain of Croagh Patrick, if you feel fit enough for the grueling four-hour clamber over rough rocks. Beyond Mayo are Sligo and Donegal, and golden beaches and tumbling Atlantic surf. Lakes and remote peninsulas enhance north Donegal, where the coast turns east toward the beautiful yet troubled city of Londonderry, gateway to Northern Ireland and the six counties of Ulster.

This British-ruled area has been riven for decades by sectarian violence and a divisiveness that is still struggling to resolve itself. Ulster's image has suffered much from "the Troubles" (the resumption of political violence since 1969), yet the beauty of its coast and countryside is of classic Irish quality.

"Organ-pipe" cliffs of the Giant's Causeway – County Antrim

The Giant's Causeway area, on County Antrim's north coast, is an astonishing landscape of perfectly formed hexagonal rock sections. Farther east lies the seaside town of Ballycastle, beyond which are the towering cliffs of Fair Head and then the green and peaceful Antrim Glens. South of Antrim lies Belfast, Ulster's capital, a city that has shown a grim face for far too long, and one that might yet be recognized, along with all of Ulster, for its majority of law-abiding, determined and hardworking citizens and for its deeply rooted Ulster-Irish traditions.

The Gaelic Lifestyle

In Dublin you will find museums, stores, theaters and restaurants to match those anywhere else in Europe, all suffused by the richness of Irish culture and by a modern sophistication.

In parts of rural Ireland things are different. You may come across an easygoing attitude, a relaxed approach reflecting the fact that the Irish have been around for a long time and often see no reason to rush things. At the same time, you may find yourself swept off your feet in places like beautiful, bustling Galway city, where a vigorous student population adds contemporary chic to the Gaelic culture most young people continue to embrace.

If you travel through Ireland, you will find the Irish hospitable and friendly. Often, if you ask a local for directions to a nearby site or place in town, you will be taken there rather than given complicated directions.

The Irish are fired by an all-consuming curiosity and have an almost total lack of pretension. They are a people whose history has often been terrible, bleak and unforgiving. Yet they have survived as the inheritors of a bewitching country that lies off the western edge of the continent but is also an integral part of modern Europe.

TIMELINE

circa 3000 BC	Neolithic, Stone Age farmers construct sacred burial chambers at Newgrange and Knowth in the valley of the Boyne river.
AD 430	"Saint" Patrick begins the conversion of Ireland to Christianity.
circa 795	Vikings settle on the Liffey river, thereby founding Dublin.
1170	Powerful Anglo-Irish hegemony established in Ireland.
circa 1610	The six counties of Northern Ireland are confiscated by the English Crown.
1845–51	The Great Famine; a million Irish people die and a million emigrate, chiefly to America.
1921	Anglo-Irish Treaty partitions Ireland into the Irish Free State and mainly Protestant Ulster, which remains under British rule.
1948	Ireland is declared a republic.
1969	Beginning of "the Troubles" in Northern Ireland.
1972	Republic of Ireland becomes a member of the European Community.
1995	Republic of Ireland becomes a member of the European Union.
1998	"Good Friday" agreement paves the way for a Northern Ireland Assembly; intense negotiations continue.

DIVIDED IRELAND

Ireland has been a divided country for long, bitter centuries. The reasons for this are immensely complex and lie in historical developments over hundreds of years. The larger southern part of modern Ireland is the Republic of Ireland, *Poblacht na h' Eireann* – mainly Roman Catholic, with a small minority of Protestants. There is a strong Irish Gaelic culture and identity in this part of the country. After years of stagnation, the nation is now enjoying economic success and modernization, partly through its early embracing of the European Community.

The smaller northern part of Ireland is Ulster, or Northern Ireland, part of the United Kingdom of Great Britain. It is mainly Protestant, with a substantial Roman Catholic minority, and has a culture and identity that is essentially Irish, but with strong British elements. Ulster Protestants consider themselves Irish but wish to maintain a union with Britain. In Ulster, Roman Catholics, many of whom wish to be thought of as Northern Irish, are seen by many Protestants as representing a rival religion as well as representing southern Irish Republicanism. The tensions of this duality in Ulster have given rise to violent conflict that, in the past 25 years, has caused immeasurable suffering. The "Good Friday" agreement in 1998 began a process to create a multiparty governing assembly that is still under way.

SURVIVAL GUIDE

- If you visit Dublin in the early spring, try to be there on March 17, St. Patrick's Day, when the city is bursting with activity. For the literary-minded (and the lively) there is Bloomsday, held on June 16. It celebrates the great Irish novelist James Joyce, and especially his most famous work, *Ulysses* (see page 278).

- If you're interested in shopping for Celtic crafts, don't miss the Kilkenny Design Centre in Dublin. This is the city's finest showcase for stylish Irish homeware, glass, books, fashion and jewelry. The upstairs restaurant serves generous portions of delicious homestyle food.

- Ireland is rapidly modernizing its road system, but there are still some very poor public roads, especially in the rural parts of the country. Look for unexpected potholes on otherwise smooth surfaces.

- Politics in Ireland is a very serious subject. It is best not to get involved in too much political discussion, especially in Northern Ireland. The subject is hugely complex and emotive. In the Republic of Ireland you should avoid referring to the "United Kingdom" or the "British Isles." The republic is emphatically a separate country. Speak of Ulster as Ulster or as Northern Ireland.

- Visit the local pubs in rural Ireland, especially in Clare, where in towns like Ennis you will find some of the greatest Irish music of all.

- Visit popular places such as Glendalough in County Wicklow, Killarney in Kerry and the Cliffs of Moher in Clare outside the peak season of July and August. Glendalough, especially, can become jammed with traffic.

- Enjoy the beautiful and often remote beaches of Ireland's west coast, but always be careful if you go swimming. Tides are very strong and there can be unexpected currents.

- Street signs in Ireland are often confusing because just about anyone who has something to sell attaches his own sign to an already groaning signpost. You'll find this is true for location markers, hotels, guest houses and local attractions as well.

- Ireland's Roman Catholic churches are extremely important places to the communities they serve, and you'll usually find someone praying if you visit. Be as discreet as possible when walking around the interiors of churches, and especially when in front of the altar. People may not take kindly to photographs being taken inside churches.

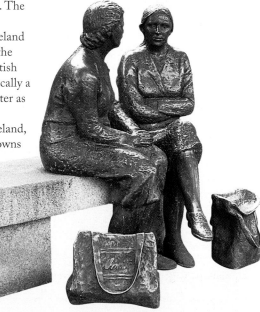

Shoppers frozen in time

Dublin

DUBLIN

All roads seem to lead to Dublin in the
end; it is a homecoming city where the
visitor will feel as welcome as the Irish
do. Dublin is celebrated today as one of
Europe's most vibrant, colorful cities,
something that Dubliners have always
known. It is a rich distillation of all
things Irish – music, conversation and
laughter amid the city's lively streets,
buzzing pubs and magnificent
Georgian buildings.

Finding Your Way

The Dublin tourist office is located
in the handsome old church of
St. Andrew's, just southwest of Trinity
College in the city center. Here you can
obtain information about guided
summer walking tours. Central Dublin
is a reasonably easy and rewarding place
to explore on foot. The main museums
and notable buildings are concentrated
in more fashionable south Dublin, but
there are not-to-be-missed attractions
across the Liffey river in north Dublin.
A good starting point is the famous

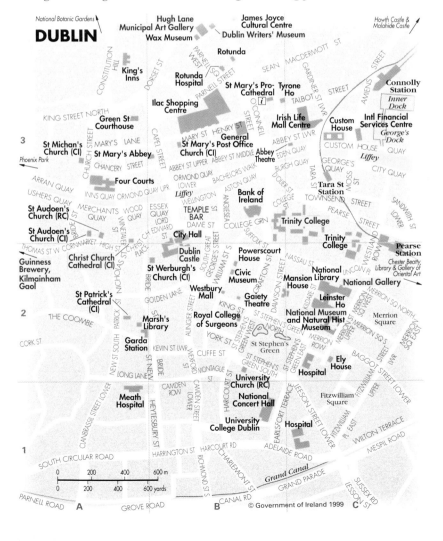

O'Connell Bridge, where Dublin begins with a rush.

Take time to adjust to the breezy pace of it all. To the north is O'Connell Street – the "broadest street in Europe." Lively shopping streets such as Abbey Street Lower and Earl Street North lead off to either side. On Earl Street you will find a genial, roguish statue of James Joyce, Ireland's most famous writer and the masterful chronicler of Dublin life. Go down Earl Street and turn left onto Marlborough Street to visit St. Mary's Pro-Cathedral, a magnificent neoclassical building that's always thronged with worshipers.

Opposite Earl Street is very busy Henry Street, with the huge ILAC Shopping Centre and the adjoining fruit and vegetable market on Moore Street. The women who work the stalls are famous for their lively Joycean banter. On O'Connell Street, just before Henry Street, is the site of the Easter Rising of 1916, when Irish nationalists staged an uprising against British rule and took over the General Post Office.

At the north end of O'Connell Street, by the Parnell Monument, is Parnell Square; on the square's north side is the Hugh Lane Municipal Art Gallery (see page 279) and the Dublin Writers' Museum (see page 277).

The Heart of Dublin

South of O'Connell Bridge is the brimming heart of Dublin. From the south side of the bridge, walk down Westmoreland Street to College Green, a frantic concentration of traffic that initially detracts from the stupendous buildings that surround it. Admire the neoclassical splendor of the Bank of Ireland and the elegant entrance to Trinity College, through which you can escape to the crowded but relaxing college campus. Otherwise, carefully

cross College Green to the south and then continue past the buxom statue of Molly Malone, heroine of the famous "Cockles and Mussels" refrain, wheeling her cart in the midst of Dublin shoppers. The statue has become cheerfully known, through irrepressible Dublin wit, as "The Tart with the Cart."

Ahead lies pedestrian-only Grafton Street, crammed with interesting stores and delightful side streets on both sides. Expect street performers of all kinds, from guitarists and mimes to harpists or half an orchestra of music students. Stop at Bewley's Coffee House, a famous Dublin institution. Head east to Leinster House, seat of Irish government, and to the National Museum and National Gallery.

Beyond these lie the 19th-century Georgian splendors of Merrion Square and Fitzwilliam Street. Alternatively, go west from Grafton Street along store-lined Wicklow Street, then on to Dublin Castle and Christ Church Cathedral; or head back north across Dame Street and into Temple Bar, the rejuvenated old riverside district that is the exciting focus of Dublin by night.

The Ha'penny Bridge

Dublin's Ha'penny Bridge, over the Liffey river, is best reached from Temple Bar by going down the narrow Merchant's Arch – look closely for the symbols of nearby stores carved into the pavement. The bridge dates from 1816 and is made of cast iron; its elegant arches are lit up at night. It was officially named the Wellington Bridge after England's Duke of Wellington, but gained its popular name from the half-penny toll once charged for crossing it.

Elegant 19th-century Georgian architecture frames Ha'penny Bridge on the Liffey

Vary your Dublin experiences. Enjoy Temple Bar's restaurants and lively streets like Crow Street and Crown Alley, or visit St. Patrick's Cathedral on Patrick Street, where Jonathan Swift, writer of *Gulliver's Travels*, was dean. Enjoy outstanding drama at Dublin's Abbey Theatre on Abbey Street, or classic Irish entertainment at the Olympia on Dame Street. Above all, visit Dublin's famous pubs (see page 281) for great music and talk. There is a quicker, sharper edge to the Irish here, as befits a busy, cosmopolitan city.

ESSENTIAL INFORMATION

TOURIST INFORMATION
• Irish Tourist Board, St. Andrew's Street ☎ 1850 230 330

URBAN TRANSPORTATION
Dublin has two main railroad stations: Heuston Station, Kingsbridge, is where most service from within Ireland terminates. Connolly Station, on Amiens Street, is where ferry connections arrive and where most north–south services, including the Belfast train, terminate. The Dublin Area Rapid Transit (DART) line runs north to Howth and south to Bray. Connolly Station and Pearse Station, on Westland Row south of the Liffey river, are convenient DART stops. For train information call ☎ 01 836 6222.
There is a good citywide bus service run by the Dublin Bus Company (✉ 59 Upper O'Connell Street, ☎ 01 873 4222). The main bus station,

Busáras, is on Amiens Street.
Dublin taxis are expensive and are often difficult to hail on the street. Stands are at O'Connell Street, St. Stephen's Green (near the Shelbourne Hotel) and College Green. Call ☎ 01 872 7272 or 01 677 2222.

AIRPORT INFORMATION
Dublin Airport is located about 6 miles north of the city. It contains a tourist office, open daily 8 a.m.–10 p.m. An Airline Express Coach runs between the airport and the central bus station. The service runs about every 30 minutes; the journey takes 30 minutes. There is also a slower, cheaper regular bus service; for more information call ☎ 01 814 1111.
Taxis also run from the airport and are less expensive than single bus fares if the ride is shared by a group. Only accept taxis with meters turned on.

CLIMATE – average highs and lows for the month

JAN.	FEB.	MAR.	APR.	MAY	JUN.	JUL.	AUG.	SEP.	OCT.	NOV.	DEC.
8°C	8°C	9°C	11°C	14°C	17°C	19°C	18°C	16°C	13°C	10°C	8°C
46°F	46°F	48°F	52°F	57°F	63°F	66°F	65°F	61°F	55°F	50°F	46°F
3°C	3°C	4°C	5°C	7°C	10°C	12°C	12°C	10°C	8°C	5°C	4°C
37°F	37°F	39°F	41°F	45°F	50°F	54°F	54°F	50°F	46°F	41°F	39°F

CITY SIGHTS

Key to symbols

Ornate interior decoration at Dublin Castle

✚ map coordinates refer to the Dublin map on page 274; sights below are highlighted in yellow on the map.

✉ address or location ☎ telephone number
🕐 opening times 🚌 nearest bus route
🍴 restaurant on site or nearby
💷 admission charge: $$$ more than £4, $$ £2 to £4, $ less than £2

CHRIST CHURCH CATHEDRAL

Christ Church Cathedral ✚ A2 ✉ Christ Church Place ☎ 01 677 8099 🕐 Daily 10–5 🚌 16, 49, 68A, 78A, 123 💷 $
Dublinia ✉ Winetavern Street ☎ 01 679 4611 🕐 Daily 10–5, Apr.–Sep.; Mon.–Sat. 11–4; Sun. 10–4, rest of year 🚌 16, 49, 68A, 78A, 123 💷 $$

Dublin's great Cathedral dates from the 12th century, but much of the surviving building is a 19th-century refurbishment in Gothic revival style. The interior has numerous fine memorials and features, but the most authentic parts of Christ Church are the late 12th-century transepts and the ancient crypt, one of the largest medieval crypts in Europe. It is 175 feet long. Thickets of rough stone pillars support the entire weight of the massive building above; the air is dense with age. Weird monuments and artifacts lurk menacingly in niches and dark corners. They include battered statues of English kings, medieval carved stones and oddities such as a mummified cat and rat, thought to have become trapped during a chase through organ pipes. Linked to the Cathedral by a covered stone bridge is Synod Hall, where the colorful exhibition "Dublinia" details Dublin's history from the medieval period.

DUBLIN CASTLE

✚ B2 ✉ Dame Street ☎ 01 677 7129 🕐 Mon.–Fri.10–12:15 and 2–5, Sun. 2–5 🍴 Castle restaurant 🚌 50, 54A, 56, 77 💷 $ ℹ️ Guided tours only. State apartments may be closed at times for official functions

Dublin Castle dates from the early 13th century but has been thoroughly rebuilt, renovated and extended. It is a powerful and at times brooding reminder of the past. Look for deep scars in the stonework of the Guardroom, at the main (north) entrance leading to the cobbled upper yard. They are the result of repeated bayonet sharpening, an eerie symbol of 950 years of British rule. The state apartments that are open to the public include St. Patrick's Hall, the Throne Room, the State Drawing Room and the Picture Gallery, all of which have sumptuous decorations and furnishings. A reconstruction during the 1980s uncovered original ninth- and 10th-century Viking defenses, a fascinating other world. The castle's Chapel Royal is a glorious neo-Gothic indulgence dating from 1814. Its exterior bristles with pointed Gothic motifs and 90 or so carved heads of historical figures. The interior has lavish plaster vaulting and superb carved oak galleries.

DUBLIN WRITERS' MUSEUM

✚ B3 ✉ 18–19 Parnell Square ☎ 01 872 2077 🕐 Mon.–Sat. 10–5, Sun. 11:30–6, Sep.–May; Mon.–Fri. 10–7, rest of year 🍴 Museum restaurant 🚌 3, 10, 11, 13, 16, 19 💷 $$

Literary Dublin in all its glory is represented by this engrossing museum's large collection of documents, artifacts, portraits and general memorabilia of famous Irish writers, including Oscar Wilde and Samuel Beckett. The combined buildings that contain the museum date from the late 18th century

JAMES JOYCE

Ireland's most controversial novelist James Joyce was one of world literature's most important figures. Joyce was an innovator of the highest order, a writer of dazzling intellect. He was born in 1882 into a Dublin Catholic family of some gentility, although poverty overtook the family while Joyce was in his teens. He was educated at Ireland's leading Jesuit school and then at the Catholic University College in Dublin.

Joyce rebelled early against the tenets of his class and religion and against Ireland's prevailing politics and culture, both of which he felt were too "nationalistic." He left Ireland in 1904 with Norah Barnacle, who became his lifelong partner. After a visit in 1912, Joyce never returned to Ireland and remained in Europe until his death in Zurich in 1941.

Joyce wrote several books of poetry and novels; his most famous novels were *Ulysses* and *Finnegan's Wake*. *Ulysses* was a monumental work, an allegorical saga describing the daylong wandering of its central character, Leopold Bloom, through the streets of Dublin. The novel developed new literary forms in its exploration and use of language and in its epic structure. It was published in Paris in 1922 but was banned for obscenity in Britain and in the United States until 1936. *Finnegan's Wake* was published in 1939 and carried the "stream of consciousness" style of writing to revolutionary limits.

Joyce is a national hero in Ireland, something that would have amused this complex and essentially solitary man. The James Joyce Cultural Centre is at No. 35 North Great George's Street in North Dublin. And each year on June 16 Dublin celebrates Bloomsday, during which there are guided walks, readings and numerous events based on Leopold Bloom's progress through the Dublin of *Ulysses*. Visits to famous Dublin pubs play a lively part in the festivities; participants dress in Edwardian clothes from the period featured in the novel and readings, and other celebrations of *Ulysses* are staged.

A portrait of the artist by Jeffrey Morgan (top) and the James Joyce Martello Tower at Sandycove in south Dublin which houses a small museuem of Joycean memorobilia and are themselves an experience. There is magnificent stucco, especially in the first-floor rooms. The colonnaded main salon, now the Gallery of Writers, has busts and paintings of famous names, a decorative ceiling and boisterous freizes.

GUINNESS BREWERY

➕ Off the map ✉ Crane Street ☎ 01 453 6700
🕐 Mon.–Sat. 10–5:30, Sun. 2:30–5:30 🚍 21A, 78a, 123 🍽 Museum café/bar 💷 $$
Dublin without Guinness is like the earth without air. You can sample Guinness in its creamy, lip-smacking originality in the city's multitude of pubs (see page 281), but to reach the heart of things visit the enlightening and entertaining Guinness Museum, located in an old hop store at the brewery. Admission includes a pint of the famous stout; visitors have been known to burst into song.

HUGH LANE MUNICIPAL ART GALLERY

➕ B3 ✉ Parnell Square North ☎ 01 874 1903
🕐 Tue.–Thu. 9:30–6, Fri.–Sat. 9:30–5, Sun. 11–5, Sep.–Apr. (also Thu. 9:30–8, rest of year) 🍽 Gallery restaurant 🚍 3, 10, 11, 13 💷 Free
The Hugh Lane Gallery is located in the delightful Charlemont House. The collection, bequeathed by Sir Hugh Lane to Dublin Corporation in 1905, comprises 19th- and 20th-century Irish and international painters, including Claude Monet, Sir John Everett Millais and Edgar Degas. There are several outstanding works, not the least of which is Renoir's *Les Parapluies*. Notable Irish artists include Jack B. Yeats, and there are contemporary Irish works and temporary exhibitions, often of daring conceptual art. The gallery also has a fine collection of stained glass and is a venue for music recitals, poetry readings and lectures.

KILMAINHAM GAOL

➕ Off the map ✉ Inchicore Road ☎ 01 453 5984
🕐 Daily 9:30–6 (last admission at 4:45), Apr.–Sep.; Mon.–Fri. 9:30–5 (last admission at 4), Sun. 10–6 (last admission at 4:45), rest of year 🚍 51, 51B, 78A, 79 💷 $$

Compelling atmosphere at Kilmainham Gaol

The notorious prison Kilmainham Gaol has been the scene of great misery. A visit to this awesome place is a sobering experience. Kilmainham opened in 1796, and just about every famous name in the struggle for Irish independence and statehood was a "guest" at one time. They included Robert Emmet, Charles Stewart Parnell and Eamon de Valera. Fourteen leaders of the Easter Rising were executed in the prison yard. Explore the warren of gloomy cells and chilly corridors. Guided tours give a graphic picture of Irish history.

NATIONAL GALLERY

➕ C2 ✉ Merrion Square West ☎ 01 661 5133
🕐 Mon.–Sat. 10–5:15 (also Thu. 5:15–8), Sun. 2–5
🍽 Gallery restaurant 🚍 5, 6, 7, 7A, 8, 10, 44, 47, 47B, 48 💷 Guided tours $, entrance free
Ireland's national art collection eschews quantity for quality, and this fine building holds a manageable and satisfying collection that represents all major schools of European art. The gallery's interiors are splendid. The Shaw Room, dedicated to early benefactor George Bernard Shaw, is an elegant statement in its own right. Painters represented include Titian, Francisco de Goya and Nicolas Poussin. Thomas Gainsborough and J. M. W. Turner are here as well, and there are strong collections of leading Irish artists such as Nathanial Hone, Jack B. Yeats and Roderic O'Conor. The gallery has excellent computer facilities for obtaining information about its paintings.

The National Gallery under the shadow of its founder, William Dargan

NATIONAL MUSEUM

➕ C2 ✉ Kildare Street ☎ 01 661 8811
🕒 Tue.–Sat. 10–5, Sun. 2–5 🍴 Museum café
🚌 10, 18, 46 ⓘ Guided tours $, entrance free

This museum is part of a splendid complex of buildings that date from 1890. Together with the matching National Library, opposite the museum, the complex forms the approach to Leinster House, the seat of Irish government. This is an excellent museum with a relaxing atmosphere that inspires curiosity instead of exhausting it. The collection of Bronze Age and Iron Age gold artifacts is dazzling. Included are the Tara Brooch, the Broighter Hoard and the Ardagh Chalice. Other exhibitions depict prehistoric and Viking Ireland and the Irish independence struggle.

ST. STEPHEN'S GREEN

➕ B2 ✉ St. Stephen's Green 🕒 Mon.–Sat. 8–dusk, Sun.10–dusk 🚌 11, 13, 44, 46, 48

The delightful St. Stephen's Green has been a public park since 1664, when Dublin Corporation set aside 27 acres of open ground, albeit for use by its more well-to-do citizens. Access was by payment only until 1880, when the park was made free to all. There are numerous statues and busts of famous Irish men and women, including James Joyce, Robert Emmet, Wolfe Tone and Sir Arthur Guinness. The park is surrounded by some of the finest buildings in Dublin. They include the fashionable Shelbourne Hotel, on the south side, and the neo-Byzantine interior of the Roman Catholic University Church, Cardinal John Henry Newman's great indulgence of 1856.

TRINITY COLLEGE

Campus ➕ C3 ✉ College Green 🕒 Daily 🚌 All city buses ⓘ Free ℹ During summer, walking tours leave regularly from main gate Mon.–Sat. 9:30–4:30, Sun. noon–4. (Price includes admission to Old Library)
Old Library ✉ College Green 🕒 Mon.–Sat. 9:30–5:30 (also Sun. 9:30–5, Jun.–Sep.) 🚌 All city buses ⓘ $$
Dublin Experience ✉ College Green 🕒 Daily 10–5, Jun.–Sep. 🚌 All city buses ⓘ $$

Dublin's Trinity College is one of the world's great college campuses, an outstanding architectural and cultural oasis at the heart of a busy city. It was founded in 1592, but all of the present buildings date from after 1700. The complex is best entered from College Green, between statues of poet Oliver Goldsmith and orator Edmund Burke, and then through the Corinthian facade of the Palladian Regent House. This leads instantly from the roaring rush of College Green into cobbled Parliament Square, often thronged with students and visitors but with a wonderfully subdued atmosphere. The square's focal point is a tall campanile, and grand buildings line its sides. Trinity's Old Library and its Long Room contain a number of outstanding artifacts, including the ninth-century *Book of Kells*, an exquisite illuminated manuscript of the four gospels of the New Testament. Another campus attraction is the Dublin Experience, an audiovisual overview of the city. It is housed in the modern Arts and Social Science Building.

DUBLIN'S PUBS

Irish pubs are fueled by good drink, but are rooted in the gregarious nature of the Irish, and in lively gossip. Many pubs are also outstanding folk music venues, inevitable in a country so well suited to such spontaneous music.

A local favorite is the Brazen Head, at 20 Lower Bridge Street, hailed as the oldest pub in Dublin. Davy Byrne's, on Duke Street just off busy Grafton Street, has an art deco lounge with lively murals that were painted by Irish playwright Brendan Behan's father-in-law. For Victorian authenticity try the Stag's Head, on Dame Court.

You can hear great Irish music with your Guinness in busy Temple Bar pubs like the Oliver St. John Gogarty, on the corner of Fleet and Anglesea streets. One of the best Dublin music pubs is O'Donoghues, on Merrion Row down from St. Stephen's Green. This was the favored haunt of the Dubliners folk group in its 1960s heyday, and the city's best folk musicians regularly raise the roof here.

Other good traditional pubs are Doheny and Nesbitt's on Lower Baggott Street; the Palace Bar on Fleet Street; O'Neill's, at the corner of Pearse and Shaw streets; and old-fashioned Mulligan's on Poolbeg Street, a last outpost of Joycean Dublin amid the chilly lifelessness of modern office blocks. South of St. Stephen's Green at the corner of Camden Street Upper and Harcourt Road is The Bleeding Horse, formerly a blacksmith's shop and a church; its warren of little rooms are called "snugs."

If you want Dublin sophistication try the Horse Shoe Bar in the Shelbourne Hotel or the Kildare Bar next to the Kildare Hotel; the latter is favored by Irish politicians from nearby Leinster House and the Irish

Guinness in lights (top), and behind the bar at one of Dublin's 800 pubs

Parliament. For a down-to-earth atmosphere visit Joxer Daly's on Dorset Street Upper in north Dublin, where Old Dublin reigns unchanged. These are just a small selection from the multitude of Dublin's pubs.

ITALY

*"**L**UMP the whole thing! Say that the Creator made Italy from designs by Michael Angelo. "*

From Mark Twain's 1869 novel *The Innocents Abroad*

Opposite: The village of Altangnana nestles on a hillside beneath Italy's magnificent Alpi Apuane

Italy

ITALY

N

SWITZERLAND

AUSTRIA

SLOVEN

Studerno-
Schluderns

Merano-
Meran

Cortina
d'Ampezzo

5

Courmayeur

Lago
Maggiore

Lago di
Como

Edolo

Adamello
3554m

A22

Bolzano-
Bozen

A23

Belluno

E55

Udine

Cividale di Friuli

Baveno

Bellagio

Molveno

Trento

Asolo

A27

Pordenone

Monfalcone

Aosta

Stresa

Como

Bergamo

Lago di
Garda

E45

Treviso

A4

Trieste

4061m
Gran
Paradiso

Ivréa

A8

E64

Bréscia

Verona

Vicenza

Novara

A4

Asola

A5

Milano

Dolomiti

Vercelli

A4

E25

Pavia

A1

Cremona

Mantova

Padova

VENICE

A32 E70

Torino

A21

Piacenza

A22

Rovigo

Golfo
di
Venézia

Pinerolo

A6

Asti

Alessandria

A35

Reggio
Nell'Emili

A13

Po

Ferrara

FRANCE

E717

Alba

A26

A7

Parma

Módena

E76

Bologna

Ravenna

Cúneo

Génova

A15

E25

Rapallo

E33

A1

Faenza

A14

Rímini

Savona

Portofino

A12

La Spézia

Massa

A35/E76

SAN MARINO

A10

Portovénere

Pistóia Prato

E45

Pésaro

4

San Remo

E80

Impéria

Viaréggio

Lucca

ADRIATIC

Bordighera

MONACO

Mare
Ligure

Pisa

FLORENCE

Urbino

Ancona

Livorno

Arezzo

Gúbbio

Loreto

San Gimignano

Siena

Cortona

Perúgia

E55

Volterra

Montepulciano

Assisi

Ascoli Piceno

Ísola
d'Elba

Grosseto

Todi

Spoleto

Teramo

Orvieto

Terni

Pescara

Piombino

Savana

E35/E45

L'Aquila

Viterbo

Rieti

A24

Chieti

3

Corse
(Corsica)

FRANCE

Civitavécchia

A12

Tívoli

A25

Avezzano

A1

Vas

Viesfe

Subiaco

Campobas

ROME

Latina

A1

Cassino

Benevel

Anzio

Terracina

E45

Caserta

1277m
Vesuvi

NAPLES

Costa
Smeralda

Olbia

Ísola d'Ischia

Pompeii

Sássari

Ísola di Capri

Amalfi

Alghero

Sorrento

Ravel

Nuoro

Paes

Oristano

Lago
Omodeo

Sardegna
(Sardinia)

T Y R R H E N I A N

2

S E A

Cágliari

San Antioco

M E D I T E R R A N E A N   S E A

Palermo

Cefalù

A2

Trápani

Erice

1

Segesta

A19

332
Mt E

A29

Enna

Selinunte

Caltanissetta

Piazza
Armerino

ALGERIA

TUNISIA

Agrigento

*Sicilia
(Sicily)*

Ragus

A

B

C

Italy

ITALY

Few countries have as much to offer as Italy (Italia), with its warm and passionate people; varied and beautiful landscape; a rich artistic, historic and cultural heritage; some of the world's best food and wine; and a stylish and relaxed philosophy on life. Italy truly has something for everyone, whether the visitor is seeking great cities, tiny villages, idyllic countryside or beautiful beaches.

Bella Italia

Of all European countries, Italy is the one to which travelers return time and again, their love affair blossoming with each trip. Whether your visit is a chance opportunity or the dream of a lifetime, Italy will fulfill and exceed your expectations, capture your heart and senses, and send you away longing to return.

From the Alps in the north, through the prosperous and fertile heartland to the stark beauty of the deep south, Italy is blessed with some of the world's most beguiling landscapes. The northern half features Tuscany's classic olive, vine and cypress-studded rolling countryside; the dramatic peaks of the Dolomites

MORE TOP DESTINATIONS IN ITALY

- Agrigento C1 • Assisi C4
- Lago di Garda B5 • Molveno B5
- Paestum D2 • Piazza Armerina D1
- Portovénere B4 • Ravello D2
- Ravenna C4 • San Gimignano B4
- Siena B4 • Savana C3 • Urbino C4
- Verona B5 • Vieste D3

Italy

(Dolomiti); pine-clad white cliffs and turquoise seas; and the eerie loveliness of mist-laden mornings in the great river valleys. The south is equally lovely, with an arid and fierce beauty during the long hot summers, when the intense color of the sea offsets the bleached ocher mountains.

Most of Italy is mountainous, the long spine of the Apennines (Appennini) running almost from top to bottom and stretching virtually from coast to coast. Some hilly areas are immensely fertile, as in Tuscany and Umbria in central Italy, while in other places, such as Basilicata and Calabria in the south, the combination of altitude and extreme climate make the land unproductive.

The largest area of flatland is the great plain of the Po river valley in the north, which extends down the eastern seaboard, an agriculturally rich and productive swath. Much of upland Italy is wooded, and there is a wide variety of indigenous plants.

Diverse Regions

Until 1870 Italy was a collection of separate and disparate states with a complex history, which does much to explain the diversity of people and attitudes. Camillo Cavour (statesman and first prime minister of a united Italy) remarked after unification in 1860, "We have made Italy, now we must make Italians." This aim still seems to await fruition, such is the gulf between the different regions. Italy has been a republic since 1946, the 21 regions (*regione*) enjoying a large degree of self-government; some, such as Sicily and Sardinia, are semi-autonomous.

Italians would be the first to agree that there is no such thing as "an Italian." Ask an Italian where he's from and the answer will be "from Tuscany, from Rome, from Naples, from Sicily,"

but never "from Italy." Primary loyalties are firmly local and regional. The Italian character, attitudes, outlook and prejudices have been formed by the native region, not by the country as a whole. So the fiery Sicilians are light years away from the Milanese and their urbane efficiency, the cool and rational Tuscans or the abrasive Romans.

Language has also played a part. Modern Italian, rich, elegant and musical, derives from Tuscan, a medieval dialect used by Dante and Petrarch and firmly based on Latin. But throughout Italy there are some 1,500 diverse dialects, which were in daily use until widespread literacy and access to television. There are still some elderly people who have difficulty speaking modern Italian, although mass media is rapidly weakening dialects.

The considerable geographic differences between the north and south have produced another element of regionalism – a very real economic and cultural divide between the halves of the country. The cooler, more fertile north is richer, more advanced and more successful than the arid and impoverished south.

The People

All Italians do seem to share the same attitude toward life, one that is instantly apparent to foreigners. Life is for living, for enjoying, for savoring. There's always time to pause to chat, time for kindness, time to laugh; passions run high but anger is quickly over and forgotten. Pause in any Italian piazza and listen to the voices; there are no strident tones or harsh and ugly notes. Watch the way Italians treat children or the elderly, without condescension but with respect for their age. Problems are solved with little fuss on a personal level, although the labyrinth of Italian bureaucracy might drive visitors crazy.

Opposite: The medieval Campo, in the heart of Siena

Italy

Despite having the world's lowest national birthrate, family ties are exceptionally close, with children often living with their parents into their 30s, and elderly people are still mainly cared for at home. The mother's role is pivotal; Italian men, it is said, spend their whole lives searching for a woman to live up to their mother – hence the constant philandering.

If you want to attract the opposite sex, you have to look good. This helps explain the importance of the *bella figura*, literally "beautiful form," but meaning infinitely more. Italians have an innate sense of style, and it matters greatly that clothes, cars and personal possessions are stylish and contemporary. *Bella figura* dictates that these must all be admired, and what better way to display them than during that great Italian tradition, the *passeggiata*? This nightly outdoor perambulation occurs in every village, town and city in the land, when citizens exit en masse from their homes, strolling through the streets, exchanging news and gossip, but above all admiring and hoping to be admired in return.

Country of Contrasts

A rich historical and cultural past has shaped the townscape in Italy. Cities, towns and villages are crammed with fine buildings, churches and works of art, a legacy of pre-Unification days. But over the past century, and notably since World War II, there has been huge development and growth in urban areas, with unattractive spreads of industrial buildings and blocks of soul-less apartments on the outskirts of countless towns. Every town still retains its central piazza, with civic buildings and a church grouped around or near it.

In many rural areas, people have traditionally lived in villages rather than on the land they work, traveling daily to the fields, so in some areas isolated country farmhouses are rare. There has always been a huge gulf between the urban and rural populations, possibly due to the very early development of Italian towns.

The middle class was a late arrival in Italy and only really emerged during the great economic boom of the '50s and '60s. Even now there are still large numbers of *contadini*, peasant farmers and small shareholders, working the land as it has been worked for centuries, while their cousins may be employed in hi-tech industries.

Exploring Italy

Prosperous Italy has one of Europe's highest standards of living, making traveling easy and pleasurable. Tourism is a major industry, so you'll find English widely spoken in city hotels and restaurants, although not away from the main tourist areas.

Italian engineering prowess has produced an excellent road network, with both toll roads and good highways. Minor roads are often unsurfaced. Italians drive fast and aggressively but mostly safely, and once you're accustomed to the style of driving you should have no problems. All major cities have an airport, with frequent internal flights. Trains are cheap and punctual, although cross-country routes can be slow and complicated; it's safer to stick to the inter-city services. Buses connect even the smallest villages.

Italian hotels are all rated and inspected by regional authorities; regardless of the price range, they are spotlessly clean. Bathtubs are rare except in deluxe establishments, and showers frequently dribble when turned on; water is precious in many parts of the country. Air-conditioning is becoming more widespread but is by no

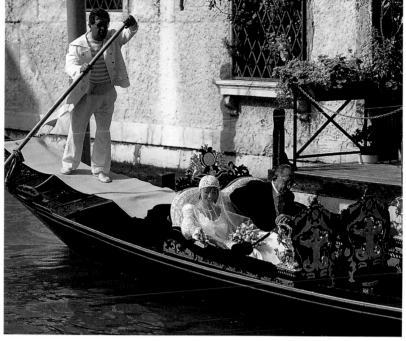

A wedding party make their way through Venice in a specially decorated gondola

means universal, and buildings can be stifling in summer. By law, heating in public places is not turned on until November 1.

Culinary Traditions

Italian cooking is regional and simple, relying on the superb quality of the ingredients, and you'll find wonderful dishes wherever you go. In a country where frozen food is practically nonexistent, menus are dictated by the seasons, with a rich variety of dishes punctuating the different months.

The different types of restaurant can be confusing. The terms *ristorante, osteria* and *trattoria* are fairly interchangeable; *tavola calda* and *pizzeria* imply something a bit more humble. Lunch has traditionally been the main meal, but there is a trend toward making dinner the extravaganza. The evening menu often consists of *antipasto* (hors d'oeuvre), the first course (*primo*) of pasta, soup or rice, the meat or fish second course (*secondo*) with its accompanying *contorni* (vegetables) or *insalata* (salad), followed by *formaggio, dolce* or *frutta* (cheese, dessert or fruit). If a meal this size seems a bit daunting, choose just a couple of courses.

Italians automatically drink wine with their meals. *Denominazione d'Origine Controllata* (DOC) is a method of classification that guarantees the origin of the wine, and that it has been made following the guidelines for a particular area. However, it is no indication of quality.

Pastimes

The favorite Italian pastimes are probably eating, drinking and talking; preferably all together. Immensely sociable people, Italians tend to relax en masse, making group activities of every type very popular. Soccer is the national sport, and almost every Italian male either attends or follows Sunday matches. Deeply traditional, Italians prefer their pleasures to be family-oriented; a Sunday drive, a day at the beach or a gentle stroll, accompanied by a non-stop stream of chatter, constitutes most people's idea of leisure.

TIMELINE

3000–1800 BC First traces of migratory peoples in peninsula.

700–300 BC Etruscan federation exists alongside Roman republic.

264–146 BC Punic Wars against Carthage.

AD 200–400 Decline of Roman Empire.

550–770 Peninsula fragmented with different areas under Byzantine, Papal, Lombard and Frankish influence.

1300–1400 Emergence of the city-states in north; Renaissance era.

1500–1848 Fragmentation of peninsula under foreign domination.

1848–61 Struggle for unification, with brief republic established in 1848; kingdom of Italy proclaimed in 1861.

1870 Rome and the Papal States become part of a unified Italy.

1915–18 Italy sides with Allies during World War I.

1940 Italy enters World War II on Axis side.

1943 Fall of Mussolini and armistice with Allies; Mussolini reinstated by Germany as head of puppet republic; Rome liberated in 1944.

1946 Italian Republic established.

1957 Treaty of Rome; Italy becomes a founding member of European Community.

1960–85 Period of political confusion, inflation and terrorism.

1985–99 Corruption is rife, but Italy flourishes as desire for political and institutional reform grows.

THE ETRUSCANS

Travelers in central Italy will frequently come across signs of the Etruscans in monuments, tombs and museums. For centuries historians have questioned exactly who they were. This enigmatic race preceded the Romans and were at the height of their power from 800 to 400 BC. They formed a confederacy of 12 cities, built towns, passed laws, traded overseas and believed firmly in an afterlife. A lively and imaginative people, they also had highly developed cultural, political and social systems. The Romans, admirers of Etruscan culture, absorbed much of it as they rose to power. By the third century BC the Romans had virtually assimilated the entire nation, along with much of its language, customs and religious beliefs. Today only the monuments remain, particularly those to the Etruscan dead. Wonderful finds have been made in these tombs – jewelry, vases, sculpture and frescoes. They are preserved in museums all over ancient Etruria, the name given to the area they inhabited. You can visit Etruscan sites at Tarquinia and Cerveteri, both a short distance north of Rome, and see the finest Etruscan collection in the world at the Villa Giulia museum in Rome.

SURVIVAL GUIDE

- The fashion-conscious Italians spend much time and thought on looking good, and appreciate it if tourists do as well. Dressing appropriately means no shorts in cities. If you do show too much leg or arm, you won't be allowed to enter churches.

- Inevitably, Italy's star attractions in Rome, Venice, Florence and other major cities become packed during the hot summer. Get out early to avoid the main rush or, better still, visit in the late fall or winter when it's quieter and cooler.

- Italy closes down from around 12:30 until 4:30 or 5 while most of the population eats a large lunch and has a siesta. Plan your day around this, remembering that museums, churches, galleries and stores will all be closed for several hours. You'll enjoy your sightseeing more if you do as the locals do and take a midday rest.

- Italians enjoy wine, which they drink at all meals, but they disapprove of people who drink to excess.

- It is unusual to eat dinner before 7:30 or 8, and lunch is served from around 12:30 to about 2:30. Some restaurants offer fixed-price set menus, but you'll get a better meal if you choose some of the local specialties. Vegetarians will find plenty of choices in most restaurants. As for children, Italians genuinely love them, and most restaurants –

even upscale ones – welcome them. Italian coffee is extremely strong, so if you want it weaker just ask for a *caffè americano.*

- Bars are much more than the name suggests. They are open from dawn until midnight or later, and offer coffee, tea, soda, snacks and pastries, as well as alcohol. All bars have restrooms and a public telephone.

- Smoking is common in public places throughout the country.

- One of the joys of Italy is shopping in little local stores and at the colorful street markets; there are very few department stores and virtually no shopping malls. Shop and market prices are fixed.

- Facilities for visitors with disabilities are improving, but are not yet as good as those back home. If you need help it's best to check ahead with local tourist offices.

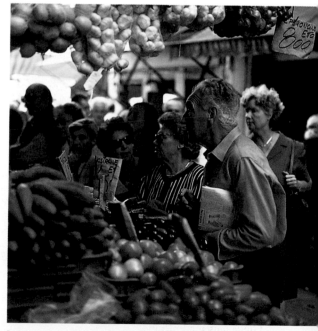

Italians make serious choices at a colorful city market

Rome

ROME

There's almost too much to Rome (Roma); too much history, too much art, too much noise, confusion, traffic. This is an overwhelming city in every way, with splendors and frustrations in equal measure. Nowhere else will your

senses be assaulted by such a glorious mélange of ancient, medieval, Renaissance, baroque and modern sights. Expectations run high, and every visitor comes with preconceptions of sun-filled days of dolce vita and romantic strolls through ancient streets. Put them aside, take it slow, accept Rome not as you think it should be, but as it is, and you'll discover a city that is virtually impossible to describe.

Mapping the City

It's a good idea to stay as centrally located as you can, but avoid the unwholesome area around the central railroad station, Stazione Termini, and keep in mind that few areas of the city offer peace and quiet. You'll quickly realize that Rome has no discernible center, although Piazza Venezia, dominated by the vast, wedding cake-like monument of Victor Emmanuel, is a good place to orient yourself. From here, the Via del Corso stretches north, and to the south lies the Forum (Foro Romano), the heart of classical Rome.

Between the Corso and the Tiber (Tevere) river lies the *centro storico*, or historic center, a maze of narrow medieval streets and Renaissance squares and one of the city's most beguiling areas. On the other side of the Corso are Rome's most elegant shopping streets, more sun-dappled piazzas, some lovely green spaces and the charms of the Via Veneto, with its luxury hotels and galaxy of smart cafés. Across the river lies Trastevere, filled with charming streets and squares and noted for its excellent restaurants. To the north is Vatican City (Città del Vaticano), home of the Pope and St. Peter's Basilica (Basilica di San Pietro).

Seeing the Sights

It would take months to see all of Rome, so before you arrive, decide where your priorities lie. It's a mistake to rush out, exhausted from travel, and see the Vatican on your first day; instead wander around the back streets or linger over a cup of coffee before you plunge into serious sightseeing. If you're not a sightseer, enjoy the street life and the stylish stores and restaurants.

It's best to tackle the highlights early in the day, before the crowds and heat intensify and while you're still fresh. Make a point of resting during the early afternoon; most stores and attractions are closed then anyway, and you can venture out again refreshed and relaxed in the late afternoon. If time is short and you want to see a lot, think about taking a tour; your hotel will be able to

Rome

Running repairs at the fountain in Piazza Navona

advise you. Other options include walking tours with local experts to explore off-the-beaten-track areas or a boat trip on the Tiber river.

Peace and Quiet

Tranquility is in short supply in Rome, but there are moments when it seems within reach. In addition to the Villa Borghese (see page 296), other green spaces exist around the city, where the roar of the traffic is at least muted. One of the best is Palatine Hill (Palatino) above the Forum, a good place to picnic after a morning's sightseeing, with scattered ruins, cypresses and wildflowers. The Botanical Gardens (Giardino Botanico) in Trastevere provide cool shade amid the 7,000 botanical species, while Colle Oppio garden, with its strolling mothers and babies, is a good bet after a morning at the Colosseum.

Roman Cuisine

Romans enjoy dining out, and there are plenty of restaurant choices. Trastevere and the streets around Piazza Navona are packed with eateries; as always in Italy, head for somewhere patronized by locals. Roman specialties center

heavily around the less attractive parts of animals, such as offal, brains and tripe, but staples like grilled meat and the delicious *saltimbocca alla Romana* (veal scaloppine cooked with prosciutto and sage) are easy to find. Pasta dishes include spicy *rigatoni all'amatriciana* (pasta with bacon, chili and tomato), the delicious and familiar *spaghetti alla carbonara* with bacon and egg, and fettuccine.

Artichokes are a great Roman specialty, eaten either deep fried or raw; look for asparagus in early summer. Desserts are simple, but Roman ice cream is mouthwatering, and it's worth forgoing restaurant desserts and opting instead for a *gelateria*. Pizzas are excellent. Local wines come from the hills outside Rome, in an area known as the Castelli Romani; Frascati is the best known. You'll also find wines from all over Italy as well as herbal aperitifs and liqueurs.

Boutiques and Markets

Shopping can be a pleasure in self-indulgent Rome, where there is a superb range of luxurious silk, linens,

Roman Fountains

Lovely fountains are scattered around Rome, and their beauty will stick in your mind when much else has faded. They provide cool places for a few minutes of rest, and the soothing sound of splashing water somehow manages to make itself heard over the noise of Rome's frenetic traffic. Be sure to pause at the Fontana delle Naiadi in Piazza della Repubblica, with its bronze nymphs; the dolphin-decorated Fontana del Tritone in Piazza Barberini; and the charming tortoise fountain, the Fontana delle Tartarughe, in Piazza Mattei.

Rome

leather and accessories. Shoes, bags, handmade evening wear, and exquisite china and porcelain are found in the smartest stores clustered around the Via Condotti and the Via Frattina, just off the Piazza di Spagna. You'll find moderately priced shops along the Via del Corso and the Via Nazionale; knitwear and sweaters are good buys. Rome also has several department stores, including the upscale La Rinascente in Piazza Colonna; Upim and Standa are inexpensive and cheerful chain stores with plenty of surprisingly stylish buys. If you enjoy markets, head for the daily food and vegetable market in the lovely Campo dei Fiori, or the main city market in Piazza Vittorio Emanuele II.

Nightlife

Romans consider a restaurant meal the pinnacle of evening entertainment, but there are other events going on as well. Pick up a copy of *Roma c'è* or *Trovaroma* for up-to-date information. There are plenty of music bars and discos. Opera is a good option, either at the Teatro dell'Opera or outdoors in summer at the Villa Borghese. Rome has a clutch of movie theaters showing films in their original language, and concerts and recitals are frequently held in the city's churches.

ESSENTIAL INFORMATION

TOURIST INFORMATION
- Largo Goldoni ☎ 06 6813 6061 Piazza S Giovanni in Laterano ☎ 06 7720 3535
- Lungotevere Castel Sant' Angelo (Piazza Pia) ☎ 06 6880 9707
- Piazza del Tempio della Pace (Fori Imperiali) ☎ 06 6992 4307
- Via Nazionale ☎ 06 4782 4525
- Stazione Termini, Galleria Gommata ☎ 06 4890 6300

subway. Taxis are yellow or white and can be picked up from one of the stands indicated by a blue-and-white sign; they do not stop on the street. You can call a taxi from Autoradio Taxi (☎ 06 3570), Capitale Taxi (☎ 06 4994) or Cosmos Radio Taxi (☎ 06 88177); the meter will start running immediately after your call. Do not trust anyone offering private taxi service, and be sure the meter is set at zero if you begin your ride at the taxi stand.

URBAN TRANSPORTATION
Public transportation in Rome can be slow, consisting of orange buses and trams and a two-line subway system. Subway stations are marked on the Rome city map by the letter "M" in a red circle. Bus tickets must be purchased from automatic machines before boarding, or from shops and newsstands displaying an ATAC sticker. They are valid for any number of bus trips plus one subway trip within a 75-minute period, and must be validated at the rear of the vehicle when boarding. The *biglietto integrato* is valid for a day's unlimited travel on buses, trams, subway and the suburban train service. A weekly pass, the *carta integrata Settimanale*, is valid only for buses and the

AIRPORT INFORMATION
Rome has two airports: Leonardo da Vinci, at Fiumicino (west of the city); and Ciampino, south of Rome, which handles charter flights. The easiest way to get to and from Leonardo da Vinci is by train from Stazione Termini (the central railroad station); trains leave every 30 to 60 minutes between 7 a.m. and 9:30 p.m. Trains also run from the airport to Ostiense and Trastevere train stations; if you use these you will have to make a connection. There is a nightly bus service between the airport and Stazione Termini. To reach Rome from Ciampino, take the subway line A to Anagnina and connect with the COTRAL bus service; both are scheduled to run daily 6:50 a.m.–11:40 p.m.

CLIMATE – average highs and lows for the month

JAN.	FEB.	MAR.	APR.	MAY	JUN.	JUL.	AUG.	SEP.	OCT.	NOV.	DEC.
13°C	13°C	15°C	17°C	21°C	25°C	28°C	28°C	26°C	21°C	17°C	14°C
55°F	55°F	59°F	63°F	70°F	77°F	82°F	82°F	79°F	70°F	63°F	57°F
4°C	4°C	5°C	8°C	12°C	16°C	19°C	19°C	17°C	13°C	8°C	5°C
39°F	39°F	41°F	46°F	54°F	61°F	66°F	66°F	63°F	55°F	46°F	41°F

The Colesseum – the world's largest surviving structure from Roman antiquity

CITY SIGHTS

BASILICA DI SAN PIETRO

➕ A3 ✉ Piazza San Pietro, Citta del Vaticano ☎ 06 698 4466 🕐 Daily 7–7, mid-Mar. to Oct. 31; 7–6, rest of year 🚌 64, 19, 81

The spiritual heart of Catholicism, the Basilica di San Pietro (St. Peter's Basilica) stands on the site of the saint's burial place. This is architectural grandeur on a triumphant scale, from the sweeping colonnades branching from the magnificent facade to the soaring dome above the twisted columns of Giovanni Bernini's High Altar *baldacchino*. There's a lot that dates from 1506 to 1626, when Donato di Angelo Bramante and Bernini were the principal architects. Near the end of his life, Michelangelo designed the dome, from which there are superb views; inside you can see the sublime *Pietà*, one of his earliest works. The right nave contains a bronze statue of St. Peter, his right foot worn away by pilgrims' caresses.

BORGHESE

➕ C4 ✉ Porta Pinciana 🕐 Daily dawn–dusk 🚇 Flaminio 🚌 52, 57, 95

The time will come when you're sated with art and architectural splendors and long for some cool green grass. This is the moment to head for the Borghese gardens, central Rome's largest park, with an oasis of verdant lawns, umbrella pines, lakes and fountains. The adjoining Pincio Gardens offer wonderful views across the rooftops to St. Peter's.

COLOSSEO

➕ D2 ✉ Piazza del Colosseo ☎ 06 700 4261 🕐 Daily 9–6, Apr.–Sep.; 9–3, rest of year 🚇 Colosseo 🚌 11, 15, 27, 81 ✋ $$

The massive Colosseo (Colosseum) dates from AD 72, and the design has never been bettered. This is a functional stadium seating 55,000, but can be cleared in less than 20 minutes; its sophisticated "backstage" facilities even allow the arena to be flooded. Most ancient entertainment featured animals, slaves and gladiators, sometimes fighting to the death, but few Christians were martyred here. During the Middle Ages the Colosseum was an excellent source of building stone, which explains the missing sections.

FONTANA DI TREVI

⊞ C3 ✉ Piazza Fontana di Trevi 🚇 Spagna or Barbarini 🚌 52, 53, 60

Among Rome's delightful fountains, none is more famous than the Fontana di Trevi (Trevi Fountain), tucked into a tiny piazza set in a maze of lanes that makes its impact all the more dramatic. There's been a fountain here since Roman times; the present exuberant example dates from 1732 and takes its name from the three roads – *tre vie* – that converged here. Throw a coin in the fountain before you leave Rome; legend claims this guarantees your return.

FORO ROMANO

⊞ C2 ✉ Via dei Fori Imperiali ☎ 06 699 0110 🕐 Mon.–Sat. 9–6, Sun. 9–1, Apr.–Sep.; Mon.–Sat. 9–3, Sun. 9–1, rest of year 🚇 Colosseo 🚌 11, 27, 85 💵 $$$

Heart of the Roman Empire, the Foro Romano (Roman Forum) contained all of the ancient city's most important political, religious and municipal buildings. Today, it's a romantic jumble of tumbled columns and walls set amid cypresses and wildflowers. It's worth spending time here, tracking down the fine second-century Arch of Septimius Severus, the Temple of Antoninus and Faustina (AD 141), the stately columns of the fourth-century Portico of the Dei Consentes, and the House of the Vestal Virgins, home of the guardians of the sacred fire.

GALLERIA E MUSEO BORGHESE

⊞ D4 ✉ Villa Borghese, Piazzale Scipione Borghese 5 ☎ 06 841 7645 🕐 Tue.–Sun. 9–7 🚇 Spagna 🚌 52, 19, 56, 910 💵 $$$

The Galleria e Museo Borghese (Borghese Museum and Gallery), housed in the 17th-century summer palace of Cardinal Scipio Borghese, is a treasure-trove of sculpture, mainly collected by the Cardinal. He admired Giovanni Bernini, whose works dominate – the *David* is said

Rome's magical Trevi fountain

to be a self-portrait. Look for Antonio Canova's *Paolina Borghese*; this little minx, with her come-hither look, was Napoleon's sister, married off to a later Borghese. The gallery has some stunning paintings, including Caravaggio's famous *Boy with a Fruit Basket*.

MUSEO CAPITOLINI

⊞ C2 ✉ Piazza del Campidoglio ☎ 06 671 02071 🕐 Tue.–Sun. 9–7 🚌 44, 46, 64, 110 💵 $$

The two palazzi housing the great classical collection of the Museo Capitolini (Capitoline Museum) are set on either side of a magnificent Michelangelo-designed square. Look out for the *Dying Gaul* and the tautly muscled *Discobolus* (Discus Thrower), while bronzes include the famous fifth-century BC *Capitoline Wolf suckling Romulus and Remus* and, finest of all, the superb equestrian statue of *Marcus Aurelius*. Paintings include some major works by Titian and Paolo Veronese.

MUSEI VATICANI

⊞ A3 ✉ Musei Vaticani, Viale Vaticano ☎ 06 698 83333 🕐 Mon.–Fri. 8:45–4, Sat. and last Sun. of month 8:45–1, Apr. to mid-Jun. and Sep.–Oct.; Mon.–Sat. and last Sun. of month 8:45–1, mid-Jun. through Aug. 31 and Nov.–Mar. 🚌 19, 23, 64 💵 $$$

Rome

The Musei Vaticani (Vatican Museums) make up the world's largest museum complex, with around a dozen self-contained museums in 1,400 rooms. It would take days to see everything, so it makes sense to follow either one of the color-coded routes or pick out the highlights that personally appeal to you. However, do not miss the Cappella Sistina (Sistine Chapel), with its frescoes by Michelangelo covering the ceiling and the altar wall, and showing scenes from the Old Testament and the extraordinarily powerful *Last Judgment*. The Stanze di Raffaello (Raphael Rooms), one of the artist's masterpieces, were executed in 1508. Classical sculpture, an Egyptian collection and modern religious art are among the many other features at this rich venue.

Detail from Bernini's *Il Moro* in Piazza Navona

PANTHEON

✚ C3 ✉ Piazza della Rotunda ☎ 06 683 00230
🕐 Mon.–Sat. 9–6:30 (9–4:30, winter months), Sun. 9–1 🚇 Spagna 🚌 119, 67, 75

The superbly engineered Pantheon, erected between AD 119 and AD 128 and still in use today, fires the imagination and gives a better idea of the splendor of ancient Rome than any other monument. Built as a temple, it became a Christian church in AD 609 and now houses Raphael's tomb and also those of two Italian kings.

PIAZZA DI SPAGNA AND SCALINATA DELLA TRINITÀ MONTI

✚ C3–C4 ✉ Piazza di Spagna ☎ Museum, 06 678 4235 🕐 Museum: Mon.–Fri. 9–1 and 3–6
🚇 Spagna 🚌 119 👜 Museum $$

The Scalinata della Trinità Monti (Spanish Steps), curving gracefully up from Piazza di Spagna to the church of Trinità dei Monti, attracts myriad visitors; this is a favorite meeting place, situated at the heart of Rome's smartest shopping area. The steps, built in 1723, get their name from the piazza, which once housed the Spanish embassy. The eccentric-looking "sunken boat" fountain dates from 1627, while on the right of the steps you'll

find the Museo Keats-Shelley (Keats-Shelley Museum) housed in the lodgings where John Keats died in 1821.

PIAZZA NAVONA

✚ B3 ✉ Piazza Navona 🚇 Spagna 🚌 70, 81, 90

Piazza Navona owes its unmistakable shape to the Roman racetrack, used well into the Middle Ages, that once stood here. Pope Innocent X, who commissioned Giovanni Bernini to design the focal point, the *Fountain of the Four Rivers*, rebuilt the piazza in 1644. The 17th-century church of Sant' Agnese is Francesco Borromini's work.

SAN CLEMENTE

✚ D2 ✉ Via di Giovanni in Laterano ☎ 06 704 51018 🕐 Daily 9–12:30 and 3:30–6 🚌 15, 85, 13
👜 $

No church in Rome gives a better idea of history than San Clemente, a multilayered structure whose newest part dates from the 12th century. In its dim interior, the apse mosaics glitter above the marble panels of the choir screen and pulpits. From here, descend to the fourth-century lower church, with its ghostly traces of 8th- to 11th-century frescoes, before plunging deeper to examine the fine altar of the Roman Mithraic temple.

SANTA MARIA IN ARACOELI

✚ C2–C3 ✉ Piazza d'Aracoeli ☎ 06 679 8155
🕐 Daily 7–noon and 4–6:30, Jun.–Sep.; 7–noon, rest of year 🚌 44, 56, 90

THE VATICAN

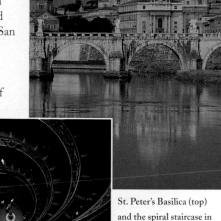

Vatican City (Città del Vaticano), an area covering about 109 acres around the Basilica of St. Peter (Basilica di San Pietro), is the world's smallest independent state. Until Italian unification in 1870, the Papacy had held territory covering a large part of central Italy, known as the Papal States. These became part of the new united Italy, and the Pope, Pius IX, retreated to the Vatican, a virtual prisoner. The supreme head of a worldwide religion clearly needed some type of sovereign territory to retain his independent spiritual authority, and in 1929 the Treaty of the Lateran was thrashed out with Mussolini, bringing the Vatican State into existence.

St. Peter's Basilica (top) and the spiral staircase in the Vatican (left)

The Vatican Today

The Pope, as well as being head of the Catholic church, is also Europe's only absolute monarch, ruling over the 200-odd inhabitants of the Vatican. The Vatican retains worldwide diplomatic relations; foreign ambassadors to the Holy See live around Rome, as do more than 800 other workers who commute across the "border" daily. The Vatican has its own judiciary, currency, bank, stores and postal system – you can send cards home from the post office outside the Basilica. It issues a daily newspaper, the *Osservatore Romano*, and broadcasts 24 hours a day from its radio station. A branch railroad line runs from the Italian State system into the Vatican. Despite the vernacular spoken at Mass, Latin is still the official language.

Defending the Pope

The Pope has been defended by the Swiss Guard since 1506. Their colorful striped red, yellow and blue dress uniform, said to have been designed by Michelangelo, is instantly recognizable to visitors. The 90 members are indeed Swiss, young men recruited between the ages of 19 and 25, from Switzerland's four Catholic cantons. They then serve tours of duty ranging from two to 20 years. The Agenti di Vigilanzi, a more drably garbed unit, augments them.

Papal Audiences

The Pope gives a weekly general audience on Wednesdays in the huge Paul VI Hall. These occasions, shared by up to 7,000 people, are open to everyone and tickets are free. The Pope also gives a blessing from the windows of his rooms overlooking the piazza on Sundays at midday.

Audience tickets are available on Mondays and Tuesdays from the Prefetura della Casa Pontifica (through the bronze doors in the right-hand colonnade of Piazza San Pietro).

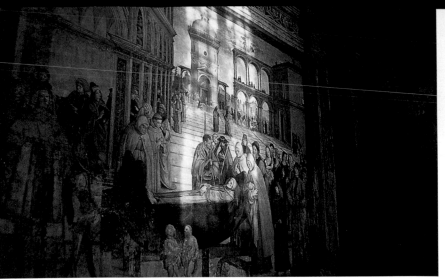

A calm retreat from the crowds – St. Mary Major houses the Pintoricchio frescoes

Santa Maria in Aracoeli (Our Lady of the Altar of Heaven) was built around 1260 to replace an older church. Approached by 124 steep steps, built in 1348 to celebrate the end of a plague epidemic, the church's plain facade hides a superb interior. The nave columns were taken from Roman buildings, while the gilded ceiling, lit by chandeliers, dates from the 1570s.

SANTA MARIA MAGGIORE

✚ D3 ✉ Piazza di Santa Maria Maggiore ☎ 06 483 195 ⏰ Daily 7 a.m.–8 p.m., Apr.–Sep.; 7–7, rest of year Ⓜ Cavour 🚌 27, 70, 93

As you enter Santa Maria Maggiore (St. Mary Major), pause to remember that Mass has been said daily in this building since the fifth century, when it was built on a site marked by an alleged miraculous summer snowfall. The mosiacs are the chief treasure: those in the nave date from the fifth century, those in the apse from the 13th century. The gilding on the coffered ceiling reputedly comes from the first gold to arrive from the New World, a gift from Spain.

SANTA MARIA IN TRASTEVERE

✚ B2 ✉ Piazza Santa Maria in Trastevere ☎ 06 581 4802 ⏰ Daily 7:30–12:30 🚌 44, 60, 170

The facade of Santa Maria in Trastevere, with its lustrous 12th-century mosaics, overlooks an atmospheric fountained piazza. The charming portico, added in

1702, leads to an interior with nave columns that once supported Roman buildings. The 12th-century, Byzantine-style mosaics of the apse represent the glorification of the Virgin.

VIA APPIA ANTICA

✚ D1 ✉ Via Appia Antica 136 ☎ 06 785 0350 Ⓜ Catacombs: Mon.–Sat. 8:30–noon and 2:30–5, Dec.–Oct. 🚌 118

A short bus ride from central Rome takes you to the Via Appia Antica (Old Appian Way), built in the fourth century BC to link Rome with Brindisi. Here, Spartacus and his slaves were executed, and St. Paul marched on his way to prison. Today this cobbled way, shaded by pine trees, is lined with monuments and tombs; you can visit the fascinating catacombs, with their mementos of early Christian life.

VILLA GIULIA

✚ C4 ✉ Piazzale di Villa Giulia 9 ☎ 06 320 1951 ⏰ Tue.–Sat. 9–7, Sun. 9–1:30 Ⓜ Flaminio 🚌 52, 95, 19 💰 $$

Visit the Villa Giulia to learn more about the enigmatic Etruscans (see page 290). The world-class collection is housed in a late Renaissance villa; its architects included Michelangelo. Highlights are the Castellani exhibits, fine Greek vases, and gold, silver and ivory artifacts. Be sure to see the *Sarcofago degli Sposi*, sixth-century BC figures of a reclining married couple, and the terracotta *Hercules* and *Apollo*.

Water is the dominant feature in the gardens of the Villa d'Este

EXCURSION TO TIVOLI

Most visitors to Rome seize the chance to escape the city's noise and heat by taking an excursion to Tivoli, a small town in a lovely wooded location some 19 miles northeast of Rome. Its main attractions are the gardens of the Villa d'Este, among the world's most beautiful, and the vast classical site of Villa Adriana (Hadrian's Villa), around 4 miles southwest of Tivoli.

It's easy to make an independent trip to Tivoli, either by train from the central railroad station, Stazione Termini, then local bus, or by bus from central Rome. There are also guided excursions from the city, which take you straight there, while an English-speaking guide tells you all you need to know.

Villa d'Este

The Villa d'Este is famous not so much for the villa itself, built by Cardinal d'Este in 1550, but for the gardens, terraces and fountains. The main attractions are two Giovanni Bernini fountains, the elegant Fontana di Biccierone and the Fontana dei Draghi, and the breathtaking Avenue of a Hundred Fountains (Viale delle Cento Fontane). Nearby lies the Villa Gregoriana, where a pair of waterfalls cascade into a gorge.

Villa Adriana

Many prosperous Romans built retirement villas at Tivoli, and in AD 125 the Emperor Hadrian embarked on the construction of his own. The villa and its gardens grew and grew, eventually covering as much ground as Imperial Rome itself. The site is vast and romantic, and you'll need a map to make sense of it all. Don't miss the Maritime Theater (Teatro Marittimo), a palace on an island in the lake.

Villa d'Este ✚ See page 284–285, grid reference C3 ✉ Piazza Trento ☎ 0774 22070 ☻ Tue.–Sun. 9 a.m.–1 hour before dusk 🍴 Refreshments available in gardens 🚉 Train to Tivoli 🚌 COTRAL bus from via Gaeta to Tivoli 🎫 $$$
Villa Adriana ✉ Via Tiburtina ☎ 0774 530203 ☻ Tue.–Sun. 9 a.m.–90 minutes before dusk 🍴 Refreshments available at villa site 🚉 Train to Tivoli 🚌 COTRAL bus from via Gaeta to Tivoli 🎫 $$$

Tour Companies
Appian Line ✉ Piazza dell'Esquilino 6/7 ☎ 06 487 861
Vastour ✉ Via Piemonte 34 ☎ 06 481 4309
American Express ✉ Piazza di Spagna 38 ☎ 06 676 42413

Florence

FLORENCE

More than 3 million tourists annually visit Florence (Firenze), the capital of Tuscany, whose resident population is under 380,000. Visitors come with high expectations of beauty, stunning art, history and stylish people. Sadly, they

are often so overwhelmed by heat, crowds, noise and cultural overload that the city fails to live up to expectations. When touring Florence, more so than most cities, planning pays off.

Choose the time you visit carefully. If art and architecture are the main purpose of your trip, try to come off-season when Florence is quieter and the

Florence

heat in this largely non-air-conditioned city won't wipe you out. If the city is one stop on a summer tour, be prepared for crowds, time museum visits for early and late in the day, and don't try to do too much. Book accommodations before you come, and don't plan to use Florence as a base for touring in the rest of Tuscany.

Florence and Florentines

Florentines are Tuscans – restrained and rational, and less given to fiery displays than other Italians. They are also more reserved, without the superficial and easy charm of people from other regions. Accustomed to huge numbers of visitors, they do not go out of their way to befriend tourists, but are courteous and professional in their everyday dealings.

Florence is not as instantly appealing as Rome or Venice – let it grow on you and experience it as a living city, not merely as a vast treasure house of art. Get away from the major sights and explore the quieter areas, with atmospheric streets and a wealth of traditional activities. Vary the artistic glories with a bit of hedonism, and give yourself time to relax. The best way to see Florence is on foot. Most of the main attractions are clustered together in the largely pedestrian central core, making walking easier (but watch out for ebullient scooter riders).

Eating in Tuscany

Florence is well endowed with restaurants of every type, from fast-food joints to world-class establishments. Many are specifically aimed at tourists and have prominently displayed fixed price (but mediocre) menus. To ensure a memorable meal, eat where the Italians eat and be prepared to pay somewhat high prices. For a simple lunch, try a slice of fresh-baked pizza to go or a quick snack in a *vinaio* or *fiaschetteria*, traditional wine bars. Food markets are particularly tempting, with the makings to put together a picnic. Tuscan food is simple and excellent, with plenty of soups, superb pork dishes, grilled meats and vegetables. Bean dishes are especially popular (Tuscans are fondly nicknamed *mangiafagioli*, or "bean-eaters"). The most famous wine is

Chianti, but look for Brunello di Montalcino, a superb red from Tuscany.

Pucci, Gucci and More

Intriguing stores, markets and boutiques are scattered throughout the center of Florence. Shoes and leather goods are famous, as are fine china, exquisite bed and table linen, and gold jewelry. Designer-label fans can visit Pucci and Gucci on their home ground; other tempting gifts include brilliantly glazed majolica pottery, marbled paper, prints and antiques.

Via Tornabuoni and the surrounding streets house the most elegant stores; less expensive fashion is found around Piazza della Repubblica and Via Calzaiuoli, while jewelers line the Ponte Vecchio. There are many factory leather outlets near Santa Croce. Be sure to spend time browsing in a market; the huge Mercato San Lorenzo is probably the most enjoyable. Most stores will ship direct to the United States.

Festivals Galore

A summer visit is likely to coincide with one of the cultural festivals, the *Estate Fiesolana* or the *Maggio Musicale Fiorentino*. Together they run from May through August, with concerts, opera and ballet, often performed outdoors in an historic setting, creating an unforgettable experience.

Excursions

Even if your time in Tuscany is limited, try to fit in an excursion outside Florence, viewing the timeless landscape en route to another of the region's superb historic towns. Possibilities include Pisa, Siena, San Gimignano and the wine country of Chianti, all easily reached by tour bus or public transportation. Nearer still lies Fiesole, a picturesque hill town just above Florence, the perfect escape from noise and heat.

ESSENTIAL INFORMATION

TOURIST INFORMATION
• Piazza della Stazione ☎ 055 212 245
• Via Cavour 1r ☎ 055 290 832 or 055 290 833
• Borgo Santa Croce ☎ 055 234 0444

URBAN TRANSPORTATION
Buses, both regular and electric, run from Sta Maria Novella station all over town. Tickets must be purchased before boarding. They are available from machines and tobacconists and are valid for an unlimited number of trips over a period of 70 or 120 minutes; 24-hour passes are also available. You can pick up a map and timetable from the ATAF office (✉ Piazza del Duomo 57r). Stamp tickets as you get on, in the orange box on the bus. Taxis can be hailed at various central locations, or by calling Radio Taxi Cotafi (☎ 055 4390) or Radio Taxi Socata (☎ 055 4242).

AIRPORT INFORMATION
Most visitors arrive and leave from Pisa's Galileo Galilei Airport (☎ 050 500 707), connected to Florence's Sta Maria Novella railroad station (where luggage can be checked) by hourly trains. Florence's own airport is at Perètola (☎ 055 306 1700), about 4 miles outside the city and easily reached by bus or taxi; if you're flying to another Italian destination, it's likely you'll leave from here.

CLIMATE – average highs and lows for the month

JAN.	FEB.	MAR.	APR.	MAY	JUN.	JUL.	AUG.	SEP.	OCT.	NOV.	DEC.
4°C	8°C	13°C	18°C	23°C	26°C	28°C	27°C	23°C	17°C	10°C	6°C
39°F	46°F	55°F	64°F	73°F	79°F	82°F	81°F	73°F	63°F	50°F	43°F
0°C	2°C	5°C	9°C	13°C	17°C	20°C	19°C	16°C	11°C	5°C	2°C
32°F	36°F	41°F	48°F	55°F	63°F	68°F	66°F	61°F	52°F	41°F	36°F

CITY SIGHTS

Key to symbols

➕ map coordinates refer to the Florence map on page 302–303; sights below are highlighted in yellow on the map.

✉ address or location ☎ telephone number

🕐 opening times 🚌 nearest bus or tram route

🍴 restaurant on site or nearby

🎟 admission charge: $$$ more than L5,000, $$ L3,000 to L5,000, $ less than L3,000

CAPPELLE MEDICEE

➕ C4 ✉ Piazza Madonna degli Aldobrandini
☎ 055 238 8602 🕐 Daily 8:30–2 (except alternating Sun. and Mon., when it's closed) 🚌 In pedestrian zone 🎟 $$$

Set behind San Lorenzo, the Cappelle Medicee (Medici Chapels) were built as the mausoleum for Florence's most powerful family. The *Sagrestia Nuova,* built by Michelangelo between 1520 and 1534, contains some of his most powerful sculpture. Reclining figures representing *Night* and *Day* and *Dawn* and *Dusk* decorate the tombs of Lorenzo the Magnificent and his son, Giuliano. The figures' fluid lines are a perfect foil for the austerity of the architecture, and are offset by the artist's lovely *Madonna.*

DUOMO, BATTISTERO AND CAMPANILE DI GIOTTO

➕ C3–D3 ✉ Piazza San Giovanni ☎ 055 271 071
🕐 Duomo: Mon.–Fri. 10–5, Sun. 1–5. Battistero: Mon.–Sat. 1:30–6:30, Sun. 9–1. Campanile: daily 8:30–7:30, Apr.–Sep.; 9–6, in Oct.; 9–5, rest of year
🚌 1, 6, 7, 11, 14 🎟 $

The richly marbled Gothic Duomo (Cathedral) of Santa Maria del Fiore, the first domed structure erected in Europe since Roman times, was built between 1296 and 1436. Pass through the Cathedral's austere interior, with its fine Paolo Uccello fresco, to climb the 463 steps to the top of Brunelleschi's dome. The chief draw of the 11th-century marble Baptistery is the three sets of bronze doors, with their Old Testament scenes. Andrea Pisano cast the south pair in 1326, and they inspired Lorenzo Ghiberti to design those at the north and east in the 1400s.

The graceful Campanile (Bell Tower) was designed by Giotto, and built by Pisano and Francesco Talenti between 1334 and 1359. Its pink, green and white marble walls are decorated with superb relief sculptures. The 280-foot, 414-step climb offers lovely, if vertiginous, views over Florence.

Scuptures by Michelangelo adorn the tombs of his patrons at the Medici Chapels

Florence

GALLERIA DELL'ACCADEMIA

⊞ D4 ✉ Via Riccasoli 60 ☎ 055 238 8609
🕐 Tue.–Sat. 8:30–7, Sun. 8:30–2 🍴 Gauguin, see
page 559 🚇 San Marco 💲 $$$

Founded as an art school in 1784, the Galleria dell'Accademia (Academy Gallery) today houses the world's most important collection of Michelangelo sculptures, as well as works by other artists. The main attraction is his *David*, a huge, anatomically precise and technically perfect nude male figure, possibly the most famous in the history of sculpture. More moving by far are the other sculptures by the artist, particularly the four *Prisoners*, the figures struggling to escape the stone.

GALLERIA DEGLI UFFIZI .

⊞ C2 ✉ Loggiato degli Uffizi 6 ☎ 055 238 8651
🕐 Tue.–Sat. 8:30–7, Sun. 8:30–2 🍴 Ponte Vecchio,
see page 559 🚇 In pedestrian zone 💲 $$$

Arguably the world's greatest collection of Renaissance paintings, the Galleria degli Uffizi (Office Gallery) is housed in an elegant arcaded building designed by Vasari as administrative offices – hence the name. Here, in chronological order, are paintings representing the greatest names in art, among them Giotto, Paolo Uccello, Botticelli, Piero della Francesca, Leonardo da Vinci, Michelangelo, Raphael and Caravaggio. Come early or late to try to avoid the lines.

MUSEO NAZIONALE DEL BARGELLO

⊞ D2 ✉ Via del Proconsolo 4 ☎ 055 238 8606
🕐 Daily 8:30–2 (except alternating Sun., when it's
closed) 🍴 Dino, see page 559 🚇 19 💲 $$

Surrounding a courtyard, in a building constructed in 1255, the Museo Nazionale del Bargello (National Bargello Museum) houses Italy's finest collection of Renaissance sculpture. The first floor has works by Michelangelo, Benvenuto Cellini and the flamboyant Giambologna, but the vaulted second-floor hall contains the museum's masterpieces. Here are Donatello's jaunty bronze of

David, his exquisite *St. George,* and the superb Baptistery door reliefs by Lorenzo Ghiberti and Brunelleschi, made for a competition in 1401. Upstairs are bright enameled terracottas by the della Robbia family.

PONTE VECCHIO

⊞ C1–C2 ✉ Ponte Vecchio 🚇 In pedestrian zone

Not the most beautiful Florentine bridge, but certainly the most photographed, the Ponte Vecchio (Old Bridge) was built in 1345 to replace an earlier one. It has been picturesquely lined with exclusive goldsmiths and jewelers' shops since 1593. Above it runs a corridor used by members of the Medici family to travel from the Pitti to the Uffizi. It was not only the sole bridge not destroyed by the Germans in World War II, but also survived the floods in 1966.

SAN MARCO

⊞ D4 ✉ Piazza San Marco ☎ 055 238 8608
🕐 Daily 8:30–2 (except alternating Sun. and Mon.,
when it's closed) 🚇 1, 6, 7, 10, 11, 17, 20, 25, 31, 32,
33 💲 $$

Rebuilt in 1437, the convent of San Marco, decorated by Fra Angelico, is one of Florence's loveliest treasures. It's a peaceful religious house, where each monk's cell is adorned with a tiny fresco to aid prayer. The pilgrim's hall contains many paintings by Angelico and his school, and additional works are on view in the cloisters and on the stairs, notably the radiant *Annunciation.*

SANTA CROCE

⊞ E1 ✉ Piazza Santa Croce ☎ 055 244 619
🕐 Daily 8–12:30 and 3–6:30 🚇 23, 13, B 💲 $

This huge, plain Franciscan church was built in 1294, but was badly damaged by the 1966 floods. Today it contains superb early frescoes telling the story of the Santa Croce (Holy Cross). Michelangelo is buried here, along with Machiavelli and Galileo Galilei. In the serene cloisters stands the Cappella dei Pazzi (Pazzi Chapel), among the most beautiful of Renaissance buildings.

A DAY IN FLORENCE

Many Florentines start working by 8 a.m., when food stores also open. Since Italian cities don't have American-style suburbs, most people live in centrally located apartments, so visitors have the chance to see the neighborhoods waking up. Housewives go to market early, children walk to school and people pause for a quick bar breakfast on their way to work.

A detail from the bronze east door at the Bapistery, by Lorenzo Ghiberti (1378-1455)

For the tourist in Florence an early start makes sense. Head straight for major sights such as the Uffizi, Accademia, Duomo or Pitti Palace while you're still fresh and before the big tour groups arrive. Most of the museums open around 9 a.m. and the churches earlier, so it's feasible to pop into a specially noted church first thing. Pause mid-morning for a drink and a rest, but bear in mind that some attractions shut for several hours in the middle of the day, as do stores. It's a good idea to follow the siesta habit – a leisurely lunch and a quiet hour or so digesting all you've seen will leave you fresh for more touring in the late afternoon. Early evening is a popular time for Florentines to shop, and a good opportunity for you to track down that must-have leather bag, beautiful fabric, silk tie or marbled paper souvenir.

Florentines are back at work and out on the streets again some time after 4:30, looking rested, relaxed and ready for the rest of the day and evening. By 6:30 the town is thronged with well-dressed crowds, strolling, meeting friends and whole-heartedly enjoying the evening *passeggiata* through the streets of their beautiful city. Crowds thin out and shops close around 8:30, when people head home or to a restaurant for dinner, and there's a break before the evening's activities. Florence has plenty of nightlife to choose from, with a wealth of cultural offerings such as theater, opera and classical music, movies and numerous live-music bars and discos. The streets are busy well into the early hours – especially in summer – with locals and foreigners alike enjoying the balmy night air.

Shopping is important to the fashionable Florentines

Naples

NAPLES

Vibrant, noisy, crumbling Naples
(Napoli), the capital of southern Italy
and one of Europe's most beautifully
located cities, is light years removed in
atmosphere from the prosperous north.
The city epitomizes southern Italy:
confusing, passionate, dirty and
charming, redolent with a rich and
complicated history that has physically
shaped it and emotionally shaped its
residents. Naples can feel alien and
intimidating, but also inspires fierce
loyalty as visitors are quickly won over
by its exuberance, way of life,
attractions and, above all, its people.

Old and new – a view of Naples

    The people of southern Italy are
charming, warm and enthusiastic and
the Neapolitans are no exception. They
live at what appears to be a fever pitch
of excitement and noise, which you'll be
very aware of on the street. You'll find
people genuinely eager to help, and
anxious for you to enjoy Naples. In
recent years authorities have
encouraged citizens to welcome
tourists, and have succeeded admirably.
The friendliness of locals to visitors
here far exceeds that of any other big
Italian city.

Getting Around

Once you get your bearings, central
Naples is best tackled on foot, as the
traffic is so horrendous that any form of
transportation can be excruciatingly
slow. Much of what you'll want to see is
walkable, and sights are grouped
together in different areas, so take a bus
or cable car to your general destination
and then walk. Wandering around is an
essential part of the Naples experience,
as the street life is lively and beguiling –
but stick to well-frequented areas.
    You'll want to travel down the coast
to Pompeii and the Sorrento peninsula;

both can be reached by train. The best
way to appreciate the beauty of Naples'
spectacular setting on the bay is from
the sea; you could combine this with a
boat trip to Sorrento or to the ravishing
islands of Capri and Ischia.

Mediterranean Flavors

Neapolitan cooking ranks among the
best in Italy, with a strong emphasis on
the freshest fish and seafood, and local
fruit and vegetables from the fertile
volcanic soil of the hinterland. Flavors
are intense, and the combination of
ingredients unusual and interesting.
There are pasta dishes with shellfish,
grilled fish of all varieties, mozzarella
cheese dripping with freshness, and
numerous salamis, as well as some
excellent local prosciutto.
    Naples is the home of thin, tasty and
crisp pizzas; they are always baked in
wood-fired ovens, and can be eaten as a
snack or light meal. Neapolitan cakes
and pastries are famous and best
enjoyed from a *pasticceria* (a specialist
pastry and cake shop). Don't miss out
on the ice cream – the flavors

Naples

encompass every imaginable type of fruit. Local wines to try are Lacryma Christi and Greco di Tufo. Be sure to sample Limoncello, a lemon-flavored liqueur made all along the coast.

Shopping and Nightlife

Naples' upscale stores are clustered along the Via Toledo and the Via Chiaia, where you'll find outlets for Italy's top designers, as well as local

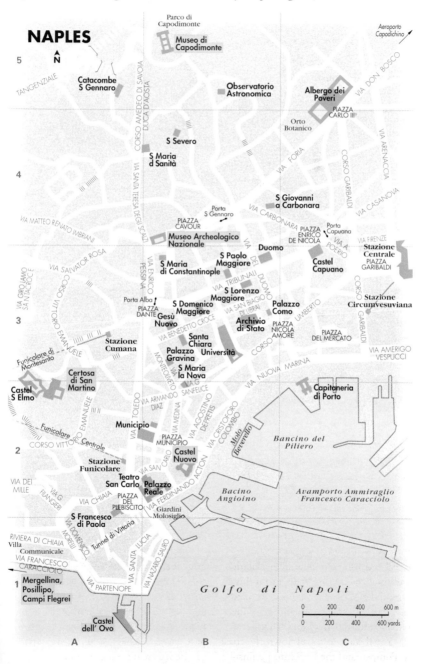

NAPLES

N

Parco di
Capodimonte

Museo di
Capodimonte

Catacombe
S Gennaro

Observatorio
Astronomica

Albergo dei
Poveri

PIAZZA
CARLO III°

Aeroporto
Capodichino

VIA DON BOSCO

Orto
Botanico

S Severo

S Maria
d Sanità

VIA FORIA

VIA ARENACCIA

CORSO AMEDEO DI SAVOIA
DUCA D'AOSTA

TANGENZIALE

VIA SANTA TERESA DEGLI SCALZI

S Giovanni
a Carbonara

CORSO GARIBALDI

VIA CASANOVA

VIA MATTEO RENATO IMBRIANI

PIAZZA
CAVOUR

Porta
S Gennaro

VIA CARBONARA

PIAZZA
ENRICO
DE NICOLA

Porta
Capuana

VIA FIRENZE

Museo Archeologico
Nazionale

Duomo

Castel
Capuano

Stazione
Centrale

PIAZZA
GARIBALDI

VIA SALVATOR ROSA

VIA GIROLAMO
SAN TACROCE

CORSO VITTORIO EMANUELE

VIA ENRICO
PESSINA

S Maria
di Constantinople

S Paolo
Maggiore

VIA DEL DUOMO

VIA A
POERIO

VIA TRIBUNALI

S Lorenzo
Maggiore

Porta Alba
PIAZZA
DANTE

S Domenico
Maggiore

Gesù
Nuovo

VIA SAN BIAGIO
DEI LIBRAI

Palazzo
Como

Stazione
Circumvesuviana

CORSO GARIBALDI

VIA BENEDETTO CROCE

Archivio
di Stato

PIAZZA
NICOLA
AMORE

PIAZZA
DEL MERCATO

VIA AMERIGO
VESPUCCI

Stazione
Cumana

Funicolare di
Montesanto

Santa
Chiara

Palazzo
Gravina

Università

S Maria
la Nova

MONTEOLIVETO

VIA G
SANFELICE

CORSO UMBERTO I

VIA NUOVA MARINA

Castel
S Elmo

Certosa
di San
Martino

Funicolare
Centrale

CORSO VITTORIO

VIA TOLEDO

VIA ARMANDO
DIAZ

VIA MEDINA

VIA AGOSTINO
DEPRETIS

VIA CRISTOFORO
COLOMBO

Molo
Beverello

Capitaneria
di Porto

Bancino del
Piliero

Municipio

PIAZZA
MUNICIPIO

Castel
Nuovo

VIA SAN

Stazione
Funicolare

Teatro
San Carlo

Palazzo
Reale

PIAZZA
DEL
PLEBISCITO

VIA FERDINANDO ACTON

Giardini
Molosiglio

Bacino
Angioino

Avamporto Ammiraglio
Francesco Caracciolo

VIA DEI
MILLE

VIA G
FLANGER

VIA CHIAIA

S Francesco
di Paola

VIA DOMENICO
MORELLI

Tunnel di Vittoria

RIVIERA DI CHIAIA
Villa
Communicale
VIA FRANCESCO
CARACCIOLO

VIA PARTENOPE

VIA SANTA
LUCIA

VIA NAZARIO SAURO

Golfo   di   Napoli

Mergellina,
Posillipo,
Campi Flegrei

Castel
dell' Ovo

0   200   400   600 m

0   200   400   600 yards

A   B   C

Naples

stores selling fine leather goods, fashion and knitwear. Jewelers abound near Via San Biagio; the traditional best buys in Naples are coral necklaces, bracelets, earrings, and cameo brooches. If you like antiques, head for Via Domenico Morelli, where stores specialize in 18th-century furniture and paintings.

Wonderful traditional nativity figurines are still made in the historic area around San Biagio, along with dolls and masks. There are shopping centers at Galleria Vanvitelli and Galleria Scartelli in the Vomero district, and you'll find a branch of the department store la Rinascente in downtown Naples.

If you like opera and classical music, a performance in the wonderful San Carlo opera house should be high on your list. Traditional Neapolitan music is easy to find, and even the least tourist-oriented restaurants have musicians serenading diners.

Safety in Naples

The city authorities have done much over the past few years to clean up Naples in every way, making it a safer and more attractive city. However, it is still wise to avoid the labyrinthine back streets, the docks and, at night, the railroad station. Do not carry much cash on your person, and be aware of pickpockets, particularly in crowded tourist areas.

Be careful when crossing the street: Neapolitan drivers often ignore pedestrian crossings, and unless you step off the pavement you could be stranded for what seems like hours. Scooters appear to come out of nowhere; they frequently use the sidewalks or go against the direction of the traffic.

ESSENTIAL INFORMATION

TOURIST INFORMATION
• Stazione Centrale ☎ 081 26 8779
• Stazione Mergellina ☎ 081 761 2102
• Capodichino Airport ☎ 081 780 5761

URBAN TRANSPORTATION
Neapolitan traffic makes any form of transportation slow, so it's best to walk if it's feasible. Longer distances can be covered by subway, bus and cable car (funiculari), all of which are slow. There are two types of Giranapoli transport tickets, valid for either 90 minutes or all day; they are interchangeable between buses, cable cars and subway, and obtainable from tobacconists or newsstands. They must be validated in the special machines on board buses; before boarding cable cars; and at the entrance to subway platforms. To travel around the bay, use the Circumvesuviana

railway, which leaves from the railroad station on Corso Garibaldi every half-hour and takes an hour to reach Sorrento, its farthest point. You can also travel to Sorrento by ferry or hydrofoil from the Mergellina or Molo Beverello docks; the same companies also serve Capri, Ischia and the other islands. There are taxi stands throughout the city, or you can call Taxi Napoli (☎ 081 556 4444), Taxi Free (☎ 081 551 5151) or Taxi Partenope (☎ 081 556 0202). Taxis will also take you sightseeing outside Naples for fixed rates.

AIRPORT INFORMATION
Naples' Capodichino Airport (☎ 081 789 6259), with internal and European flights, is northwest of the city center. Airport buses (☎ 081 531 1646) run at 50-minute intervals to Piazza Municipio via Piazza Garibaldi, daily 6 a.m.–midnight. Bus 14 runs every 15 minutes as far as Piazza Garibaldi.

CLIMATE – average highs and lows for the month

JAN.	FEB.	MAR.	APR.	MAY	JUN.	JUL.	AUG.	SEP.	OCT.	NOV.	DEC.
12°C	13°C	15°C	18°C	22°C	26°C	29°C	29°C	26°C	22°C	17°C	13°C
54°F	55°F	59°F	64°F	72°F	79°F	84°F	84°F	79°F	72°F	63°F	55°F
4°C	5°C	7°C	9°C	13°C	17°C	19°C	19°C	17°C	13°C	8°C	5°C
39°F	41°F	45°F	48°F	55°F	63°F	66°F	66°F	63°F	55°F	46°F	41°F

City Sights

Key to symbols

✚ map coordinates refer to the Naples map on page 309; sights below are highlighted in yellow on the map.

✉ address or location ☎ telephone number
🕐 opening times 🚌 nearest bus or tram route
🚇 nearest subway 🍴 restaurant on site or nearby
💰 admission charge: $$$ more than L5,000, $$ L3,000 to L5,000, $ less than L3,000

Castel Nuovo

✚ B2 ✉ Piazza Municipio ☎ 081 795 2003
🕐 Mon.–Sat. 9–7 🍴 Trattoria Medina, see page 559 🚌 R2, R3 💰 $$
The five massive towers of the 15th-century Castel Nuovo (New Castle) dominate the Naples waterfront. A magnificent Renaissance gateway accesses the central courtyard, which is surrounded by buildings housing the Museo Civico (Civic Museum), the splendid Gothic

Sala dei Baroni (Baron's Hall) and the Cappella Palatina (Palatina Chapel), the only surviving part of an earlier 13th-century building. Nearby is the huge and imposing 17th-century Palazzo Reale and San Carlo, the famous opera house.

Castel dell'Ovo

✚ A1 ✉ Borgo Marinaro 🍴 La Cantinella, see page 559 🚌 R3; tram 1
Encircled by the sea, Castel dell'Ovo (Egg Castle), Naples' oldest castle, was built between the ninth and 16th centuries. Run-down and dilapidated by the 1970s, it has been restored and is now used for cultural events.

Certosa di San Martino

✚ A2 ✉ Vomero ☎ 081 578 1769 🕐 Tue.–Sun. 9–2 🚇 Montesanto 🚌 V1 💰 $$
Visible from all over Naples is the hilltop complex of the Certosa di San Martino

Pompeii

The 20,000 inhabitants of first-century Roman Pompeii enjoyed a civilized lifestyle in their prosperous city which boasted fine civic amenities, temples, public baths, and housing suitable for every taste and pocket. The one drawback was Pompeii's location on the slopes of Vesuvius, an active volcano. In AD 79 its worst eruption occurred, engulfing the city and many of its inhabitants in a thick layer of pumice and volcanic ash.

For nearly 1,700 years Pompeii remained buried, perfectly preserved beneath a hard layer of volcanic debris. About 1750 it was rediscovered, excavations started, and gradually the city emerged. It's a complete small city that can be explored like any other, wandering the streets and visiting the sites that appeal. It has the main features of every Roman city – the forum that was the center of public life; two theaters; an amphitheater; a sports stadium; and symmetrical rows of streets laid out in a grid pattern.

Start at the forum and make your way through the paved streets, looking into houses and shops as you go. Track down the covered market, the bakery, the laundry and the numerous taverns, some advertising bargain prices on the outside walls. The House of the Vetii, with its lovely garden and frescoed dining room, is a highlight, as is the House of the Tragic Poet, whose owners had a portrait mosaic of their dog laid by the front door with "*cave canem*," "beware of the dog," carefully inscribed.

✉ Pompeii ☎ 081 850 8451 🕐 Daily 9–1 hour before dusk 🍴 Self-service restaurant and bar outside forum, many in modern Pompeii 🚌 Pompeii (Circumvesuviana) 💰 $$$

The hilltop complex of St Martin's Chaterhouse looks down on the city of Naples

(St. Martin's Charterhouse), mainly constructed between the 16th and 18th centuries. Highlights include the sumptuous baroque church, the arcaded Chiostro Grande (Main Cloister) and the lavishly decorated Quarto del Priore (Prior's Quarters). Don't miss the exhibition of *presepe* (crib figures), a charming collection of figures, animals and everyday objects fashioned for Christmas cribs in the 19th century.

MERGELLINA

✚ Off the map ✉ Mergellina 🚇 Mergellina
🚌 R3, C21
This waterfront area, traditionally the fishermen's quarter, is a delightful place to stroll and enjoy ice cream. Fishing boats and island ferries still leave from the harbor here.

MUSEO ARCHEOLOGICO NAZIONALE

✚ B4 ✉ Piazza Museo ☎ 081 440 166
🕐 Wed.–Mon. 9–2 🍴 Al 53, see page 559 🚌 1, 24, 42 💶 $$$
The Museo Archeologico (Archeological Museum) houses one of the world's most important collections of classical sculpture, mosaics, gems, glass, silver and Egyptian antiquities. Finds from Pompeii

are here; don't miss the graceful fresco portrayal of Flora. The *Farnese Hercules* and *Farnese Bull* are equally impressive; the *Bull* is the largest classical sculptural group to have survived, dating from 200 BC. Allow two or three hours for your visit to do the museum justice.

MUSEO DI CAPODIMONTE

✚ B5 ✉ Parco di Capodimonte ☎ 081 744 1307
🕐 Tue.–Sat. 10–7, Sun. 9–2 🚌 R4, 24 💶 $$
Built in the 18th century as a palace and museum, and surrounded by a wooded park, Capodimonte has been recently restored and rearranged. Be sure to see Masaccio's *Crucifixion*, the star of the Renaissance painting collection, and the majolica and porcelain collection, much of it made by the Capodimonte factory.

POSILLIPO AND THE CAMPI FLEGREI

✚ Off the map ✉ Posillipo 🚇 Mergellina, Campi Flegrei
Posillipo and the Campi Flegrei (literally "Burning Fields," named because of the area's volcanic activity) lie to the east of Naples on what is still a lovely stretch of coast. Dotted with classical ruins, fishing villages, beaches, inlets and grottos, this is an area well worth exploring.

EXCURSION TO CAPRI

A favorite with the Roman emperors, Capri has been a tourist hot spot for more than 150 years. This tiny island, with its spectacular scenery and crystal-clear waters, now welcomes more than 2 million visitors annually.

Capri's Marina Grande is the starting point for visiting this enchanting island

Getting There

You can travel from Naples' Mergellina or Molo Beverello docks by ferry or hydrofoil, a lovely trip across the Bay of Naples that takes between 50 and 90 minutes. Spectacular views open up back to the city and across to Mount Vesuvius as you approach the steep hills of the Sorrento peninsula, with Capri lying off its tip. Boats dock at Marina Grande, the island's main harbor.

What to See

The charm of Capri lies in the combination of lovely scenery, picturesque villages and a laid-back holiday atmosphere. The two main settlements are Anacapri and Capri; their whitewashed houses and narrow, winding streets are crammed with boutiques, outdoor cafés and lively fish restaurants, and many visitors do no more than enjoy these. Most, however, take a boat trip to the Grotta Azzurra (Blue Grotto), a spectacular sea cave filled with refracted turquoise light. Another highlight is the beautiful Villa San Michele in Anacapri. Built in the late 19th century by Swedish physician Axel Munthe, this dreamlike villa is filled with classical statues. There is also a peaceful green garden, and from its

shady pergola you can enjoy some of the island's loveliest views.

Walk out to the ruins of Villa Jovis, Emperor Tiberius' clifftop villa, from where he allegedly threw his enemies into the sea. Another stroll leads to a lookout above the Faraglioni, a cluster of offshore rocks rearing more than 360 feet above the water.

Capri ✚ See page 284–285, grid reference C2
☎ Tourist offices: Marina Grande ☎ 081 837 0634, Capri ☎ 081 837 0686, Anacapri ☎ 081 837 1524
🚢 From Marina Grande to Marina Piccola, Capri and Anacapri 🚢 Ferry operator: Caremar, from Molo Beverello, Naples (☎ 081 551 3882). Hydrofoil operators: Caremar, from Molo Beverello, Naples (☎ 081 551 3882); NLG, from Molo Beverello, Naples (☎ 081 552 7209); SNAV, from Mergellina, Naples (☎ 081 761 2348)
Blue Grotto 🚢 From Marina Grande 🕐 Daily 9–1 hour before dusk (weather permitting) 🎟 $$$
Villa San Michele, Anacapri ☎ 081 837 1401
🕐 Daily 9:30–6, May–Sep.; 9:30–5, Apr. and Oct.; 9:30–4:30, in Mar.; 10:30–3:30, Nov.–Feb. 🚢 From Capri 🎟 $$
Villa Jovis, Anacapri 🕐 Daily 9–1 hour before sunset 🎟 $

Venice

VENICE

No matter how many pictures or films you've seen, nothing can prepare you for the real Venice (Venezia), one of the world's most captivating cities. Whether it's sparkling in late spring

sunshine or shrouded in winter mist, it will enchant you in every way.

Tackling Venice

When you first arrive in Venice, don't head straight for the main sights (which will invariably be packed); take time to get a feel for the city, either from the

Venice

vantage point of a ferry or by strolling the streets and squares. As for accommodations, luxury hotels lining the Grand Canal (Canale Grande) are clearly the optimum choice, but there are many with great charm elsewhere. The *sestiere* (city areas) of Dorsoduro, San Marco, Castello and San Polo are among the nicest parts of the city to stay. Avoid the area around the train station, which is noisy and less attractive. Under no circumstances should you stay in Mestre, an industrial sprawl across the causeway on the mainland.

Accept that you will do a great deal of tiring walking around the city, and come prepared with comfortable shoes. Take time working out your daily itinerary; short cuts across the city save valuable time. Main routes are clearly marked along the streets by yellow signs. There are numerous tour options; if time is short these can be helpful, and you'll have the benefit of English-speaking guides.

Venetian Glass, Velvet Slippers

The city's main fashion and leather stores cluster along the Calle dei Fabbri, the Frezzeria and the so-called Mercerie, made up of the streets connecting Piazza San Marco with the Rialto. Glass is a true Venetian specialty, made for centuries on the island of Murano. Marbled paper is another good buy, and Venetian masks make wonderful souvenirs. Other typical products are velvet slippers in jewel-bright colors or a real gondolier's hat; you'll find one at Emilio Ceccato, near the Rialto.

Gondolas

The shiny black gondola – symbol of Venice – is a shallow-draft vessel propelled by a single oarsman, the gondolier, who stands at the back of the boat. A ride in a gondola is a great Venetian experience for many visitors, but they are expensive and normally follow a set route. Be sure to ascertain what you're getting before you set out.

Murano
Collona
San Michele
Cimitero San Michele
Isola di San Michele
Canale delle Fondamenta Nuove
Gesuiti (Santa Maria Assunta)
Fondamenta Nuove
FONDAMENTA NUOVE
Rio dei Gesuiti
Rio dei Mendicanti
Ospedale Civile
Santa Maria dei Miracoli
Santi Giovanni e Paolo
Colleoni
CAMPO SANTI GIOVANNI E PAOLO
Rio di San Giustina
Tana Celestia
CAMPO SANTA MARIA FORMOSA
San Francesco della Vigna
Santa Maria Formosa
Palazzo Querini-Stampalia e Pinacoteca
CASTELLO
Scuola di San Giorgio degli Schiavoni
Torre dell' Orologio
Basilica di San Marco
San Giorgio dei Greci
Rio della Pietà
PIAZZA SAN MARCO
Palazzo Ducale
CAMPO SAN ZACCARIA
San Zaccaria
CAMPO BANDIERA E MORO
Arsenale
Prigioni
Santa Maria della Pietà
Campanile
RIVA DEGLI SCHIAVONI
San Giovanni in Brágora
San Martino
Procuratie Nuove
San Zaccaria
Riva degli Schiavoni
Museo Storico Navale
Ponte dei Sospiri
Giardini ex Reali
Arsenale
San Marco
Bacino di San Marco
San Biagio
Canale di San Marco
San Pietro di Castello
San Giorgio
Isola di San Giorgio Maggiore
San Giorgio Maggiore
D
E

Venice

Festivals

Carnival lasts for 10 days before the start of Lent, when thousands of people wearing costumes parade the city streets. The summer sees several ancient festivals, notably the feast of *La Sensa*, when the mayor and his entourage sail out in the state barge and enact a symbolic marriage to the waters. This is followed in July by the *Festa del Redentore*, a thanksgiving festival for deliverence from a plague. During the *Regata Storica* in September, there are races of decorated craft manned by crews in period dress.

Getting Around

No cars, taxis, motorcycles or trucks are within the city of Venice. If you arrive in a wheeled vehicle you must leave it in a parking lot on the city outskirts and enter Venice by boat or on foot. Every single item used in Venice, from paper and pens to vegetables and vinegar, arrives at its destination by water, and so must every visitor. Take a water bus, water taxi or gondola to the landing point nearest your destination and then walk.

ESSENTIAL INFORMATION

TOURIST INFORMATION
• Palazzina dei Santi, Giardinetti Reale
☎ 041 522 6356
• Aeroporto Marco Polo
☎ 041 541 5887
• Stazione Santa Lucia ☎ 041 529 8727
• Viale Santa Maria Elisabetta, Lido di Venezia
☎ 041 526 5721

URBAN TRANSPORTATION
If you arrive by car, you must leave the vehicle in one of the parking lots on the outskirts of the city. The parking at Piazzale Roma is the nearest to the city center. Venice's public transportation system is operated by ACTV (office at Piazzale Roma, ☎ 041 522 2633) and uses two types of boats, *vaporetti* (big and slow) and *motoscafi* (small and fast). All are numbered on the front of the boat and follow set routes. Check to make sure the routes given here are still valid. *Vaporetti* boats leave from *pontile* (floating docks), which are clearly marked with service numbers and a route map. As the same numbers head in two directions, check that you are going the right way before you board; there are normally separate boarding points for each direction. Tickets can be bought at the *pontile* or at shops showing the ACTV sticker. You can save money by buying a 12-, 24- or 72-hour pass. All tickets must be validated at the machine on the dock before boarding. There is a limited night

service on most routes. *Vaporetti* stops are marked on the Venice city map with a "V." Water taxis are fast and expensive; they can be hailed on various canals, but it is easier to call (☎ 041 523 5775, 041 522 2303 or 041 522 1265). Gondolas can penetrate even the narrowest canals, but are very expensive. As there are only three bridges over the Grand Canal, the seven *traghetti* (ferries) crossing at various points are also useful. These ferries are old gondolas and are marked by yellow signs. Pay as you board and watch your balance, as it is customary to stand.

AIRPORT INFORMATION
Venice's Marco Polo airport (☎ 041 260 6111) is 5 miles from the city center on the northern edge of the lagoon, and handles both domestic and international flights. For city connections you can take a bus from outside the terminal to the Piazzale Roma at the edge of the city, where the road ends, and then connect with your hotel by *vaporetto* (water bus). The transfer takes around 20 minutes; tickets must be purchased from the office inside the airport arrivals terminal before boarding. A *vaporetto* leaves from the dock outside the terminal for San Marco and the Lido; the transfer takes around 50 minutes. The fastest way to reach the city is by water taxi; they leave from the dock outside the terminal and take only 20 minutes to reach the center, but are expensive.

CLIMATE – average highs and lows for the month

JAN.	FEB.	MAR.	APR.	MAY	JUN.	JUL.	AUG.	SEP.	OCT.	NOV.	DEC.
5°C	8°C	12°C	17°C	21°C	24°C	27°C	26°C	23°C	18°C	12°C	8°C
41°F	46°F	54°F	63°F	70°F	75°F	81°F	79°F	73°F	64°F	54°F	46°F
0°C	2°C	5°C	9°C	13°C	17°C	19°C	18°C	16°C	12°C	7°C	3°C
32°F	36°F	41°F	48°F	55°F	63°F	66°F	64°F	61°F	54°F	45°F	37°F

Crowds converge on St. Mark's Basilica – one of the world's greatest medieval buildings

CITY SIGHTS

BASILICA DI SAN MARCO

✚ D2   ✉ Piazza San Marco   ☎ 041 522 5205 or 041 522 5697   🕓 Basilica: daily 9:30–4:30. Pala d'Oro and Tesoro: Mon.–Sat. 9:30–4:30, Sun. 2–4:30   🚤 1
🎫 Tesoro $, Pala d'Oro $

The Basilica di San Marco (St. Mark's Basilica), glittering with mosaics and flickering candles, is an architectural hybrid, a fusion of western and Byzantine styles. Dating from 1094, it stands on the site of the ninth-century basilica built to house the body of St. Mark. Pause before entering to admire the Romanesque carvings, then proceed inside to take in the ornate marble pavements; the gem-encrusted altar screen, the Pala d'Oro; and the third-century bronze horses, which once adorned the facade.

CA' D'ORO

✚ C3   ✉ Calle di Ca' d'Oro, off Strada Nova   ☎ 041 523 8790   🕓 Daily 9–2   🚤 1   🎫 $$

The picture-book facade of the Ca' d'Oro (House of Gold), so called because it was once gilded, is a perfect example of the finest Venetian-Byzantine architecture. Behind the facade is a beguiling small museum with an impressive *St. Sebastian* by Andrea Mantegna and a lovely *Madonna* by Giovanni Bellini, as well as sculptural fragments, bronzes and tapestries. All pieces are arranged in rooms around the palazzo's central *portego*, or inner courtyard.

CAMPANILE

✚ D2   ✉ Piazza San Marco   ☎ 041 522 4064
🕓 Daily 9:30–3:30 (opening hours vary; check before visiting)   🚤 1   🎫 $$$

The graceful Campanile, Venice's tallest building, is less than 100 years old. The original bell tower, reputedly built in AD 912, collapsed in 1902, killing no one and leaving St. Mark's unscathed. A cry of *"Dov'era e com'era"* ("where it was and how it was") went up, and 10 years later a perfect replica was completed. Take the elevator up for superb views – on a clear day you can see as far as the Alps.

CANAL GRANDE

B2, C1, C2, C3, D2, D3 **1**

The allure of the Canal Grande (Grand Canal), Venice's magical highway, never fades. It divides Venice in two and is crossed by three bridges. The canal is lined with a wondrous procession of palaces, built over the course of 500 years and each lovelier than its neighbor. By day numerous boats chug up and down; at night it epitomizes romance, with reflected lights twinkling on the water. Take a number 1 water bus from any of the stops on the Grand Canal.

COLLEZIONE PEGGY GUGGENHEIM

C1 **Palazzo Venier dei Leoni, Calle San Cristoforo** **041 520 6288** **Wed.–Mon. 11–6** **1** **$$$**

American Peggy Guggenheim's modern art collection is installed in her 18th-century palazzo on the Grand Canal. Here you'll find works by Pablo Picasso and Salvador Dalí and fine examples of Jackson Pollock and Mark Rothko, all beautifully displayed. The garden makes a wonderful background for some Henry Moore sculptures and Marino Marini's *Angel of the Citadel*.

GALLERIE DELL'ACCADEMIA

C1 **Campo della Carità** **041 522 2247** **Tue.–Sat. 9–7, Sun.–Mon. 9–2** **Taverna San Trovaso, see page 560** **1** **$$$**

Allow plenty of time for the Gallerie dell'Accademia (Academy Gallery), the finest collection of Venetian painting in the world. Arranged chronologically, the gallery's 24 rooms contain masterpieces such as Giorgio Giorgione's enigmatic *Tempest*, Giovanni Bellini's luminous *Virgins*, and superb Mantegnas. Don't miss the dramatic *Translation of the Body of St. Mark* by Jacopo Tintoretto and Paolo Veronese's sumptuous *Feast in the House of Levi*. Among other highlights are the cycles of paintings in rooms 20 and 21; *The Miracle of the True Cross* had several contributors, while the *Life of St. Ursula* is wholly by Vittore Carpaccio.

MUSEO STORICO NAVALE

E1 **Campo San Biagio** **041 520 0276** **Mon.–Sat. 8:45–1:30, Sun. 8:45–1** **1** **$**

Venice's Museo Storico Navale (Maritime Museum) is fittingly housed near the Arsenale, the great shipyards that once manufactured the city's fleets. It tells the story of the city's sea power through displays of every type of maritime artifact; the highlight is the collection of gondolas and other historic boats, which are housed in one of the Arsenale's old sheds.

PALAZZO DUCALE

D2 **Piazzetta San Marco** **041 522 4951** **Daily 9–5 (last admission at 3:30)** **1** **$$$**

The huge Gothic complex of the Palazzo Ducale (Ducal Palace) was the seat of Venice's government, where the Council of Ten met, ambassadors were received and the Doge held councils of state. The present building dates from the 15th century, with later alterations following two fires in the 1500s. The marked route leads through a succession of sumptuous rooms to the vast Sala del Maggior Consiglio (Great Council Chamber), dominated by Jacopo Tintoretto's *Paradiso*, the world's largest oil painting. Be sure to have a look at the famous Ponte dei Sospiri (Bridge of Sighs), spanning a canal to the right of the Palazzo's waterfront facade.

PIAZZA SAN MARCO

D2 **Piazza San Marco** **1**

The only piazza in Venice (all the others are officially *campi*) was described by Napoleon as "Europe's largest drawing room," and is thronged around the clock with strolling and chattering crowds. Go early or late to avoid the worst crush, and marvel at the harmony of this wonderful open space. Highlights here are the 15th-century Torre dell'Orologio (Clock Tower) and its zodiac clock, the graceful architecture of the Libreria Sansoviniana (Sansoviniana Library), and the two columns near the waterfront topped by the lion of St. Mark and St. Theodore with his crocodile emblem.

Time to reflect on the beauty of Venice – sample the local fare in view of the Rialto Bridge

RIALTO

✚ D2 ✉ Rialto 🚤 1

Throughout the Middle Ages the Rialto was Europe's financial and banking center; the name had the same connotations as does Wall Street now. Today, you can admire the bridge and browse in Venice's food markets, one of the city's great sights. Wander through the fruit and vegetable stalls, but leave time to enjoy the scents and sights of the fish market, full of delicious delights.

SAN GIORGIO MAGGIORE

✚ E1 ✉ Campo San Giorgio, Isole San Giorgio
☎ 041 522 7827 🕐 Mon.–Sat. 9:30–1 and 2:30–5, Sun. 9:30–10:30 and 2:30–5 🚤 82 💲 $

To visit the superb Palladian church of San Giorgio Maggiore (St. George the Great), whose serene bulk dominates the view of St. Mark's Basin, you must take a waterbus across the canal of St. Mark's to St. George's island. Built to strict neoclassical standards by Andrea Palladio in 1559, the church embodies order, grace and harmony. Take the elevator up the Campanile (bell tower) to enjoy one of Venice's finest views across to the Doge's Palace and the Campanile tower.

SANTA MARIA DEI MIRACOLI

✚ D3 ✉ Campo dei Miracoli ☎ 041 528 3903
🕐 Mon.–Sat. 10–noon and 3–5 🚤 1, 82

The tiny jewel-like church of Santa Maria dei Miracoli (Our Lady of the Miracles) was built around 1480 to house a miraculous image of the Virgin. Pietro Lombardo, who faced his church with colored marble and porphyry rock, created the harmonious interior as a frame for some fine sculpture and intricate carvings.

SANTA MARIA DELLA SALUTE

✚ C1 ✉ Campo della Salute ☎ 041 522 5558
🕐 Daily 9–noon and 3–5 🍴 Taverna San Trovaso, see page 560 🚤 1

During the 1630 plague, the Senate promised to build a church in honor of the Virgin if she would save the city. The pestilence passed, an architect was commissioned, and the great dome of Santa Maria della Salute (Our Lady of Health and Salvation) rose at the entrance to the Grand Canal. One of the city's outstanding skyline features, the interior has fine sculptures and paintings.

The Annunciation by Jacopo Tintoretto in the Scoula Grande di San Rocco

SANTA MARIA GLORIOSA DEI FRARI

✚ B2 ✉ Campo dei Frari ☎ 041 522 2637
🕐 Mon.–Sat. 9:30–noon and 2:30–6, Sun. 3–6 🚌 1, 82 💲 $

Santa Maria Gloriosa dei Frari (Glorious Virgin Mary of the Brothers), a lofty Franciscan church, is the resting place of Titian and the composer Claudio Monteverdi. Built as a preaching church about 1250, it contains Titian's great *Assumption*, prominently hung over the high altar, and his *Madonna of Ca' Pesaro*. Best of all, though, is Giovanni Bellini's *Madonna and Child with Saints*, considered among the world's finest paintings. You'll find it tucked away in the right transept.

SANTI GIOVANNI E PAOLO

✚ D3 ✉ Campo SS Giovanni e Paolo ☎ 041 523 5913 🕐 Daily 7:30–12:30 and 3–7:30 🚌 12, 52

More than 20 of Venice's Doges are buried in the Gothic church of Santi Giovanni e Paolo (St. John and St. Paul), rising majestically on one side of its *campo* (square). The focal point is the great equestrian statue of Bartolomeo Colleoni, a 15th-century Venetian army officer. The 13th-century church contains many tombs, their monuments representing the best of Venetian medieval sculpture, and some lovely paintings, including Giovanni Bellini's *St. Vincent Ferrer.*

SCUOLA DI SAN GIORGIO DEGLI SCHIAVONI

✚ E2 ✉ Calle dei Furlani ☎ 041 522 8828
🕐 Tue.–Sat. 10–12:30 and 3–5, Sun. 10–12:30
🍴 Da Franz, see page 560 🚌 1, 52 💲 $$

Carpaccio painted one of the city's most delightful picture cycles between 1502 and 1508 for the headquarters of Venice's Dalmatian, or Slavic, community – the Scuola di San Giorgio degli Schiavoni (School of St. George of the Slavs). He used Dalmatia's patron saints, St. George, St. Tryphon and St. Jerome, as his inspiration, painting scenes from the lives of all three. Highlights are *St. George Slaying the Dragon* and *St. Augustine in his Study*, accompanied by his dog.

SCUOLA GRANDE DI SAN ROCCO

✚ B2 ✉ Campo San Rocco ☎ 041 523 4864
🕐 Mon.–Fri. 10–1, Sat.–Sun. 10–4 🚌 1, 82 💲 $$

In 1564, the brotherhood of St. Roche ran a competition to choose an artist to decorate the walls of their Scuola Grande di San Rocco (Grand Meeting Halls of the Confraternity of St. Roche). Tintoretto won, and spent the next 23 years working on a stupendous cycle of paintings. There are 54 paintings in all; highlights include the wonderful *Crucifixion*, in a room off the gallery upstairs. New Testament scenes line the walls of the main hall on the ground floor.

THE LAGOON ISLANDS

You can spend a delightful day exploring some of the islands in the lagoon. Most visitors opt for Murano, famous for its glass; Burano, with its lace-making; or Torcello, a virtually deserted island with an ancient cathedral and church. Guided excursions run to all three, but a more flexible option is to take boat number 12, which leaves from the Fondamenta Nuove and takes around 40 to 50 minutes to reach Burano and Torcello, the two farthest islands.

Colorful waterfront at Burano

Murano

Venetian glass has been made on Murano since 1291, when the furnaces were moved away from the city as a fire precaution. A visit to the fascinating Glass Museum (Museo Vetrario) will give you an idea of glass-blowers' skills through the ages. Murano also has two exquisite churches: San Pietro Martire, which contains a glowing altarpiece by Giovanni Bellini, and SS Maria e Donato, a 12th-century structure with mosaics on its walls and floor.

Burano

Burano's colorful canal-side houses, narrow streets and sun-splashed squares are as picturesque as anything in Venice itself. This is still a fishing community, with a robust workaday atmosphere, and you'll see moored fishing boats and nets drying in the sun. Local ladies have always been skilled lace-makers, and you can admire the fragility of their exquisite

work in the Lace-Making School (Scuola dei Merletti).

Torcello

Timeless Torcello is one of the most evocative and magical places in Venice. This sleepy island, with its overgrown canals and green fields, was the lagoon's first settled area, and once had fine buildings and palaces. Silt and malaria caused its 12th-century decline. Today the only remaining signs of its past importance are the Cathedral of Santa Maria Assunta and the adjacent church, Santa Fosca. The cathedral's main glories are two 12th-century mosaics, which completely cover the apse and the opposite rear wall. High above the seventh-century altar stands a lovely Byzantine *Madonna and Child*, their poignant beauty highlighted by the simple gold background, while the graphic *Judgment* scenes make a telling contrast. The nearby church of Santa Fosca, with its arcaded porch full of nesting swifts, is as lovely in its own way.

Elaborate glass candlestick produced on the Venetian island of Murano

LUXEMBOURG

" ***A****LL that we see is superb, the Ardennes are enchanting... "*

From a letter written by French author Victor Hugo

•

Opposite: Castle Vianden overlooks the valley of the Our, on the border with Germany

Luxembourg

LUXEMBOURG

Luxembourg lies at the heart of the European landmass. It is a minuscule country, measuring 50 miles from north to south and a mere 35 miles from east to west. Belgium lies to the north and west, France to the south and Germany to the east. Because of its attractive financial laws and constitutional stability, it has become a center of European politics and finance. And despite a turbulent history, Luxembourg retains its independence and sovereignty; it is a true survivor of the Continent's stormy past.

Luxembourg Landscapes

Luxembourg is a Grand Duchy, with the city of Luxembourg as its main focus, although its rural areas are remarkably varied for such a small country. They include part of the delightful Ardennes region, the hilly area that lies across the northern third of Luxembourg and extends into Belgium. The Ardennes have a distinctive landscape of forested plateaus sliced through by deep valleys that are drained by beautiful rivers. Fairy-tale castles crown wooded bluffs. At Vianden a medieval castle, one of the Grand Duchy's finest historic sites, dominates the landscape. The equally magnificent Bourscheid Castle stands above the Sûre and Wark rivers. At Clervaux, the castle is matched by the red-roofed Clervaux Abbey, which stands amid the wooded heights above the beautiful town.

At the southern edge of the Ardennes, where the hills meet the flatter, more fertile land known as the Bon Pays, or "Good Land," lies the picturesque town of Diekirch. Only a short distance southwest is Ettelbrück, where there is a monument to General George Patton and a Patton Museum commemorating World War II's bitter Battle of the Bulge.

Southern Luxembourg is the country's economic powerhouse. Here in the "Good Land" are farms and orchards, forests and even more castles. In fact, the lovely valley of the Eisch river is known as the Valley of the Seven Castles.

View over the Old Town, city of Luxembourg

MORE TOP DESTINATIONS IN LUXEMBOURG

- Abbaye Benédictine C3
- Abbaye St.-Maurice B4
- Château Bourscheid B3
- Diekirch B3
- Esch-sur-Sûre A3
- Grevenmacher C2 • Mondorf-les-Bains B1 • Vallée du Mullerthal C3
- Vallée du Sept Châteaux B2
- Vianden B3

Farther south and west from the city of Luxembourg is the "red earth" country around Dudelange and Pétange, where much of the country's industry is located. West of here is the delightful Mondorf-les-Bains, a fashionable spa town on the edge of the Moselle region. This area, running north to south along the border with Germany, is Luxembourg's wine-growing district.

Exploring the Country

You will find Luxembourgers are very cosmopolitan and friendly, and a large percentage of them speak English. The Duchy has an excellent road system and distances are short between the many towns and villages, making independent travel a good option. There are also numerous day trips organized from the city of Luxembourg.

Luxembourg

TIMELINE

AD 963   Count Siegfried of the Ardennes builds a castle on the Bock promontory called the Lützelburg ("Little Castle").

1354   Luxembourg becomes a duchy.

1447   The Duchy of Luxembourg comes under the rule of the Habsburgs through marriage.

1542   The city of Luxembourg is captured by the French.

1554   The Spanish capture the city of Luxembourg.

1713   Under the terms of the Treaty of Utrecht, Luxembourg comes under the control of the Kingdom of the Netherlands.

1815   Congress of Vienna establishes the Grand Duchy of Luxembourg as a sovereign, neutral state.

1839   Under the terms of the Treaty of London, the western part of the Grand Duchy is ceded to Belgium.

1867   Luxembourg becomes an independent state.

1914   Germany occupies Luxembourg in World War I.

1940   Germany invades Luxembourg again in World War II.

1944   American troops liberate Luxembourg; in December, Germany launches its "Ardennes Offensive"; the Battle of the Bulge follows as chiefly American forces repel the attack.

1945   Luxembourg becomes a member of the United Nations.

1948   Luxembourg joins Belgium and the Netherlands in forming BENELUX, a trading and economic union.

1949   Luxembourg abandons neutrality and joins NATO.

1992   Luxembourg ratifies the Maastricht Treaty, securing its place in the European Union.

LUXEMBOURG: THE GREAT SURVIVOR

Luxembourg, with its long history at the heart of Europe, has secured a major part in the working of the European Community (now the European Union). The country today is a constitutional monarchy ruled by Grand Duke Jean, who heads a cabinet of 12 ministers appointed from an elected chamber of deputies. Consensus politics is used in Luxembourg's government, and coalitions of more than one party usually hold power. So open is Luxembourg's government that the telephone numbers of ministers are often listed in public directories. On the international front, Luxembourg is home to the European Court of Justice, the European Monetary Fund and the General Secretariat of the European Parliament – all of which are based in the city of Luxembourg's European Center.

Sidewalk cafés amid the downtown bustle of the city of Luxembourg

SURVIVAL GUIDE

- If you are in Luxembourg during August, visit the city of Luxembourg during the *Schueberfouer* Festival – a fair and market.
- For lunchtime treats try Oesling ham from the Ardennes, or a selection of cold meats and sausages with salad. In rural areas look for *friture*, delicious fried river fish.
- Most shops in the city of Luxembourg are closed on Monday mornings but often stay open until 8 p.m. on Thursdays.
- There are numerous stores in the Gare district of the city of Luxembourg, especially on Avenue de la Liberté. Enjoy an evening in the Grund district. There are lovely areas, good bars and restaurants, and a different ambience to the city center, known as the Ville area.
- Both Belgian and Luxembourg francs are used in Luxembourg, but it's wise to exchange larger amounts of Luxembourg francs for Belgian francs if you are leaving Luxembourg for Belgium.
- The city of Luxembourg has many designer shops, such as Hermès, Dolce & Gabbana, Armani, Louis Vuitton and Claudia Sträter, in

Grande Rue and Neuve rue Philippe II. There are also tempting treats in Leonidas, the renowned Belgian chocolatiers. Try rue Boucherie for antique and specialty shops.

- Typical Luxembourg souvenirs include cast iron from the Mersch foundry, in the heart of the duchy. Designs incorporate castles and coats of arms. Authentic Luxembourg porcelain and earthenware are produced by Villeroy & Boch.
- If you travel in the Moselle wine-producing region, enjoy some of Luxembourg's dry white and sparkling vintages, such as the subtle Rivaner; Pinot Blanc to go with fish dishes; or the satisfyingly strong Pinot Gris to complement a meal of *judd mat gaardebounen* (roast, smoked pork).
- Children will especially love the Butterfly Garden in Grevenmacher. They will also enjoy Parc Merveilleux in Bettembourg, at the southern tip of Luxembourg, where there are attractions from fairy-tale tableaux and exotic birds to children's animal enclosures and games of all types.

CITY OF LUXEMBOURG

The city of Luxembourg is known as the landlocked "Gibraltar of the North" because of its once-fortified location. It is set above the cliffs that flank the canyon-like valleys of the Alzette and Pétrusse rivers. Today, the city of Luxembourg is more fairy tale than fortress. The old city, especially, is a pleasing mix of the past and present. Its elegant towers, spires and turrets and its attractive walls of golden sandstone helped win Luxembourg the United Nations' designation of World Heritage Site in 1995.

The steep-sided plateau on which Luxembourg stands explains its origins. The Romans first set up camp here. They had one eye on military control and the other on the advantages of a strategic trading position at the crossroads of northern Europe. In AD 963, Count Siegfried of the Ardennes built a castle on the narrow Bock promontory above the Alzette river.

Over the next 900 years Luxembourg evolved into one of the mightiest fortifications in Europe. In 1867 the terms of the 1831 Treaty of London were applied, and Luxembourg became

a neutral state. The military fortress was dismantled and the encircling walls were replaced by the present city's outer boulevards.

Ville and *Gare*

The main parts of Luxembourg are the city center, known as Ville, perched on the high plateau above the Pétrusse and Alzette river gorges; and the more modern district, known as Gare, south of the river. The two are connected by bridges across the Pétrusse gorge; the main ones are the pont Adolphe and the pont Viaduc, the latter known locally as *Passerelle*. Below the cliffs lies Grund, the main part of the city's valley settlements.

The area around the railroad station is emphatically modern and downtown. Buses leave regularly from outside the station and take you – within minutes via the pont Adolphe – to place E.-Hamilius, on the western side of Ville. This is a different world from down-to-earth Gare. From here a short walk east along rue de la Poste leads to the large central square of place d'Armes.

At the east end of place d'Armes is the handsome City Palace (Palais Municipal), where the tourist information office is located. Ask for details about guided tours and the Luxembourg Card, which is good for free entry or discounts on admission fees to numerous museums and attractions and free use of public transportation. The largely pedestrian-only city center makes Luxembourg a very walkable place. The maze-like streets of the Old Town (Vieille Ville, see page 332) and the marvelous complex of steps and terraces that connect plateau and valley floor can be easily enjoyed on foot.

Conversation and Music

The place d'Armes is a public space shaded by lime trees. In summer it is

A Lift in Luxembourg

You can reach the riverside Grund district in the Alzette valley by public elevator from place du St.-Esprit, near the intersection with boulevard Franklin-Roosevelt. Look for the glass-fronted elevator shelter in the corner of the place du St.-Esprit. The elevator takes you to a tunnel that emerges at Montée du Grund.

filled with the chairs and tables of the surrounding restaurants and cafés, where you can enjoy the hum of relaxed conversation and the music of regular concerts on the nearby bandstand.

All round the place d'Armes are the pedestrian-only shopping streets of the city. To the north is Grande Rue, known locally as *Groussgaass*, the city's main shopping street. Here, and in the adjoining streets of rue Phillipe II and rue des Capucins, are fashion boutiques, as well as good restaurants and cafés. Stop for coffee at Namur, on the corner

City of Luxembourg

City of Luxembourg

of Grande Rue and rue des Capucins. At the east end of Grande Rue look for the fountain known as Hämmelsmarsch, "The March of the Sheep."

Exploring Historic Luxembourg

To reach historic Luxembourg, leave the southeast corner of place d'Armes, where a covered passage leads between bookshops and into the large place Guillaume II. A colorful flower market is held here on Wednesdays and Saturdays. From here you can quickly reach the Grand Ducal Palace on rue du Marché aux Herbes.

Behind the palace lies the Old Town. Look for rue de l'Eau, with its cluster of restaurants known collectively as Ilot Gastronomique. Then head down rue Sigefroi to the stunning viewpoint of the Bock, above the Alzette gorge.

From here you can see the famous Grand Duchess Charlotte Bridge, known as the Red Bridge because of its color. It connects the city center plateau with the Kirchberg plateau and the ultramodern European Center (Centre Européen), home of numerous European Community institutions. Visit the famous Bock Casemates, the maze of underground tunnels in the cliffs, and then walk the Corniche, the terrace that leads south above the Alzette gorge.

Visit the valley district of Grund, a riverside haven of well-preserved old houses and attractive restaurants and taverns. From here you can turn left and wander along the paths and terraced lanes of the Alzette to reach the riverside church of St. John on the Stone, with its rich baroque altar and famous Black Madonna statue.

Luxembourg's Ville is more relaxed than the centers of other, more cosmopolitan European cities, although city life is sophisticated in its restrained way. Fine music can be enjoyed at the city's Municipal Theater, Capuchin Theater and Music Conservatory. The top fashion stores of Grande Rue speak for themselves, and Ville restaurants are second to none for international cuisine; there are some superb fish restaurants as well.

ESSENTIAL INFORMATION

TOURIST INFORMATION
• place d'Armes ☎ 352 22 28 09 and 352 22 75 65
• Findel Airport ☎ 352 82 82 21
• Luxembourg railroad station ☎ 352 82 82 20

URBAN TRANSPORTATION
Buses are the only form of public transportation in the city of Luxembourg. There is a reliable and regular bus network, mainly serving the outlying districts. Visitors will probably require service only between the railroad station and the city terminus

at place E.-Hamilius. Taxis are expensive, but can be hired by calling ☎ 352 43 43 43.

AIRPORT INFORMATION
Luxembourg's Findel Airport is located 4 miles east of the city of Luxembourg. Luxair runs a bus service between the airport and the railroad station in Gare. Public bus No. 9 runs between the airport and the city center and railroad station, and is much cheaper. Taxis between airport and city are expensive. For airport information call ☎ 352 47 981.

CLIMATE – Average highs and lows for the month

	JAN.	FEB.	MAR.	APR.	MAY	JUN.	JUL.	AUG.	SEP.	OCT.	NOV.	DEC.
	3°C	4°C	9°C	14°C	18°C	21°C	23°C	22°C	19°C	13°C	7°C	4°C
	37°F	39°F	48°F	57°F	64°F	70°F	73°F	71°F	66°F	55°F	45°F	39°F
	-2°C	0°C	2°C	4°C	8°C	11°C	13°C	12°C	10°C	6°C	3°C	0°C
	28°F	32°F	36°F	39°F	46°F	52°F	55°F	54°F	50°F	43°F	37°F	32°F

CITY SIGHTS

Key to symbols

➕ map coordinates refer to the Luxembourg map on page 329; sights below are highlighted in yellow on the map.

⊠ address or location ☎ telephone number

🕐 opening times 🚌 nearest bus route

🍴 restaurant on site or nearby

🍷 admission charge: $$$ more than 150F, $$ 100F–150F, $ less than 100F

CASEMATES

Casemates du Bock ➕ C3 ⊠ montée de Clausen ☎ 352 22 67 53; 352 47 96 27 09 or 352 22 28 09 for guided tours 🕐 Daily 10–5, Mar.–Oct. 🍷 $
Casemates de la Petrusse ➕ B3 ⊠ boulevard Franklin-Roosevelt ☎ 352 22 67 53; 352 47 96 27 09 or 352 22 28 09 for guided tours 🕐 Daily 11–4, Jul.–Sep. (also 11–4, Easter and Whitsunday) 🍷 $

The great cliffs of the Pétrusse and Alzette gorges are honeycombed with tunnels, stairways and chambers, called the Casemates, hollowed out of rock during the 17th and 18th centuries. Originally the network of Casemates measured over 14 miles and accommodated thousands of soldiers. There was room for the stabling of their horses, and for all necessary garrison services from bakeries to workshops. Today about 10 miles of the Casemates survive. Two sections, the Casemates du Bock (Bock Casemates) and the Casemates de la Pétrusse (Pétrusse Casemates), are open to the public in summer. There are spectacular views from openings in the cliffs.

CATHÉDRALE NOTRE-DAME

➕ B3 ⊠ boulevard Franklin-Roosevelt 🕐 Mon.–Fri. 10–5, Sat. 8–6, Sun. 10–6, Easter–Oct. 31; Mon.–Fri. 10–11:30 and 2–5, Sat. 8–11:30 and 2–5, Sun. 10–5, rest of year 🍷 Free

The steeples of the Cathédrale Notre-Dame (Cathedral of Our Lady) are a striking image on the city's skyline. Inside, the lavish high altar is a shrine to Our Lady, "Comforter of the Afflicted." To reach the crypt you must go down stone steps; at the rear, two menacing bronze lions guard the barred entrance to the

The steeples of the Cathedral of Our Lady

burial chamber of the Grand Ducal family. A solitary sarcophagus lies in a dark blue marble setting.

MUSÉE D'HISTOIRE DE LA VILLE DE LUXEMBOURG

➕ B3 ⊠ 14 rue du St. Esprit ☎ 352 47 96 30 61 or 352 22 90 50 🕐 Tue.–Sun. 10–6 (also Thu. 6–8 p.m.) 🍴 Museum café 🍷 $$$

A late 1990s restoration of the Musée d'Histoire de la Ville de Luxembourg (Museum of the History of the City of Luxembourg) has created a superb must-see venue. Take care in some rooms where sunken channels containing hidden lighting run around the edges of the room. The museum is located in several old 17th-, 18th- and 19th-century town houses. This is a sophisticated, interactive museum; visitors are given a card to operate audiovisual displays and touch screens that explain the city's history. Follow the room numbers counter-clockwise and do not miss a trip in the big glass elevator that rises through layers of history and architecture.

MUSÉE NATIONAL D'HISTOIRE NATURELLE

➕ C3 ⊠ rue Munster ☎ 352 462 2331 🕐 Tue.–Sun. 10–6, mid-May to mid-Sep.; Tue.–Fri. 2–6, Sat.–Sun. 10–6, rest of year 🍴 Museum café 🍷 $$

The Musée National d'Histoire Naturelle (National Museum of Natural History) is tucked away in the Grund area, below the

The statue of William II, Grand Duke of Luxembourg, dominates the place de Guillaime II

cliffs. It is housed in the old Hospice of St. John, later a women's prison. The buildings splendid entrance survives. It was refurbished in the late 1990s and features modern interactive activities. There are no English-language programs, but there is enough visual excitement to entertain everyone who visits.

PALAIS GRAND-DUCAL

✚ B3 ✉ rue du Marché aux Herbes
🅘 Information about guided tours at city tourist office (☎ 352 22 28 09) 🖐 $$$

The Palais Grand-Ducal (Ducal Palace), the home of Grand Duke Jean of Luxembourg and his family, is in the narrow rue du Marché aux Herbes. The building is a much-renovated and extended replacement of a medieval town hall, which was destroyed in a fire in 1554. The 16th-century Spanish rulers of Luxembourg rebuilt it after the fire, and you can see the architectural influences of southern Spain in its Renaissance facade. The interiors are exquisite, especially the Main Hall, the King's Room and the Banqueting Hall.

VIEILLE VILLE

✚ C3
Luxembourg's Vieille Ville (Old Town) lies between the rear of the Ducal Palace and the Bock promontory. The area of the Old Town is small, lying within narrow streets and squares such as rue de l'Eau, rue de la Loge, rue de Rost and Marché aux Poissons (Fish Market). The feeling of medieval Luxembourg is palpable here, although today's immaculate streets and elegantly preserved buildings hardly reflect the din and dirt of those days. The market was once the bustling heart of the community outside the castle walls. Down rue Sigefroi from the Marché aux Poissons is St. Michael's Church. It is the oldest church in the city and is located on the site of the 10th-century castle church, but its oldest surviving parts date from the 17th century. The church's baroque altar is superb, and there is a wonderfully vivid carved oak *pietà*.

VILLA VAUBAN

✚ A4 ✉ avenue Emile-Reuter ☎ 352 47 96 30 61
🅘 Tue.–Sun. 10–6 (also Thu. 6–8 p.m.) 🖐 $$

The elegant Villa Vauban (Municipal Art Gallery) stands among flowerbeds and neat lawns in the City Park. The late 19th-century building is on the foundation of the former Vauban Fortress. Today's gallery has a fine collection of the works of Dutch and Flemish masters and of later European painters. There are also temporary exhibitions.

FORTRESS LUXEMBOURG

The history of the city of Luxembourg as a medieval fortress is fascinating. Ringed by impregnable cliffs on every side but the west, it was easy to secure the western approach by building a defensive wall. The narrow and rocky Bock promontory offered the first natural fortification.

It was here on this narrow shelf, 300 feet above the Alzette valley, that prehistoric settlers may have established a camp. The Romans established their own fortifications on the Bock and called it *Castellum Lucilinburhuc*. Then, in AD 963, Count Siegfried of the Ardennes built his castle and linked it to the main plateau by a drawbridge. This *Lützelburg*, the "Little Castle," gave the city and the country its present name.

By 1050 a defensive western wall nearly 30 feet high, with numerous towers and gateways, protected the castle and the community that was growing around it to the west. In 1554 a massive explosion of stored gunpowder destroyed much of the settlement. New fortifications were built during a period of Spanish rule. They included excavation of the Pétrusse Casemates (Casemates de la Pétrusse, see page 331); the Beck Bastion; and the ramparts known today as the Corniche and dubbed the "Balcony of Europe" because of the spectacular views.

In the late 17th century the French military engineer, de Vauban, reshaped and extended the ramparts. In the 18th century the Austrians extended them once more and excavated the Bock Casemates (Casemates du Bock, see page 331). Such was the strategic importance of Luxembourg as a

Medieval tranquility on the Alzette river below the Pétrusse Casemates

fortification that all buildings on the Bourbon Plateau, where Gare (the modern town) now stands, were built of wood so that they could be quickly destroyed before an attack on the fortress, thus robbing the enemy of cover.

On May 11, 1867, Luxembourg became an independent state. As part of the agreement, the city's fortifications were dismantled or destroyed. At that time, the fortress walls enclosed an area to the west that was larger than the city.

What remains today are the Casemates, the retaining walls of the cliffs and numerous ruins concentrated on the cliff edges, all adding drama to the city's already spectacular position. City boulevards and parkland lie where great walls and towers once protected the western approach.

NETHERLANDS

"IN what other country can one find such absolute freedom..."

17th-century French philosopher René Descartes

Opposite: View from the West Church tower, across the rooftops and canals of Amsterdam

NETHERLANDS

Netherlands

The Netherlands is a country where freedom has come with responsibility and hard work. It is a country where the word "land" means something special – a valuable resource won from the sea. For in literal terms, when you walk on dry land in the Netherlands, your head is barely above sea level in some places, and well below it in others. Amsterdam itself is 10 feet below sea level.

Dutch Icons

To the outside world, the enduring image of the Netherlands is of a land unremittingly flat, criss-crossed by canals and dotted with windmills. Popular imagination conjures up pictures of clogs, cheese and swaths of brightly colored tulips. Then there is Amsterdam, its lively, lovely and evocative capital, seen by many as a slightly wicked city.

The Kingdom of the Netherlands is, of course, a far more complex and fascinating entity than popular symbols imply. Although the country is often known as Holland, this name actually only relates to the country's heavily

populated western provinces of Noord (North) and Zuid (South) Holland. These provinces contain the main towns, such as Amsterdam, Rotterdam and The Hague, known collectively as the Randstad, the "Ring Town." Compared with this heavily urbanized area, the Netherlands' other provinces offer the visitor a remarkably diverse landscape and regional cultures that will correct any misconception that the country is homogeneous.

Land from the Sea

The Netherlands is a small country, just under 15,500 square miles in area. Its eastern neighbor, Germany, is nine times larger. To the south lies Belgium, once part of the United Provinces of the Netherlands (see page 50) but an independent nation since 1830. To the north and west of the Netherlands lies the North Sea, and it is with this near neighbor that the Dutch have their most pressing relationship. You will not be too aware of the sea in Amsterdam or The Hague. You need to go north to Noord Holland and Friesland, or south to Zeeland, to fully appreciate the astonishing control over their watery environment that the Dutch have engineered.

For the definitive story of land reclamation, visit the Zuiderzee Museum in Enkhuizen or travel across the Afsluitdijk, a 20-mile dam that seals the great inland lake of IJsselmeer and connects Noord Holland to Friesland. You could go south to Zeeland, a glittering mosaic of water within a vast web of land. There you'll want to visit the Delta Expo Museum to learn about the Delta Plan. This system of huge dams and movable barriers was built after the storm-driven

MORE TOP DESTINATIONS IN THE NETHERLANDS

- Arnhem C2 ● De Hoge Veluwe B2
- Delta Expo A2 ● Edam B3
- Enkhuizen B3 ● Haarlem B3
- Het Loo B2 ● Heusden B2
- Keukenhof B2 ● Maastricht B1
- Orvelte C3 ● Scheveningen A2
- Utrecht B2 ● Zwolle C3

Netherlands

North Sea breached the existing dykes in 1953, killed more than 1,800 people and devastated the countryside.

Exploring Inland

Beyond these water lands – beyond the great dunes and beaches of the North Sea coast, and the red, white and neon-bright lights of Amsterdam – lie the delights of the landlocked Netherlands. In the south, Limburg is known as the Dutch "hill country." In the province of Noord Brabant, the De Kempen region's landscape of sandy heath and woodland is a very different image than that of the "flat" Holland most people envisage. You can explore Gelderland meadows and orchards; the serene villages and waterways of Overijssel; and the moorlands and flower-filled bogs of Drenthe, so beloved by Van Gogh. They all add to the variety of the rural Netherlands. In the north country, in Groningen, lie the quintessential Dutch images of windmills, clogs and flat green landscapes reassert themselves. In neighboring Friesland you will find another country altogether,

Netherlands

a province with its own language and distinctive cultural heritage.

Reaching these fascinating districts of the Netherlands is not difficult. Public transportation in Holland is efficient and generally inexpensive. Virtually every place is within a three-hour train ride from Amsterdam. Excellent bus services run between cities, and there is an extensive bus network linking towns and villages in the provinces. Driving in rural areas is convenient and reasonably straightforward, but in urban areas it can be stressful.

The Dutch

The Dutch people are self-confident, accomplished and tolerant, qualities that have been shaped by their history and surroundings. Although they could easily boast of the way in which they have mastered the environment, they are refreshingly modest and restrained. Once the ice is broken, however, they are enthusiastic and friendly. Above all, the Dutch blend tolerance with a powerful sense of mutuality. Mutual respect is the secret of Dutch maturity and of the success that they have made of their country.

Pancakes and Beer

Modern Dutch cuisine, especially fish dishes, is fast reversing the view that Dutch food is dull. In larger cities – especially in Amsterdam – Holland's colonial past has left a fine tradition of Indonesian cooking. Most hotels have plentiful buffet breakfasts, including smoked meats, pickled herring and a variety of cheeses. For a traditional lunch try *erwtensoep*, a satisfying soup of peas and pork; or *uitsmijter*, an open sandwich of meat or ham with cheese, topped with a fried egg. For dinner have a *hutspot* stew of vegetables, smoked bacon and meat; or *stampotten*,

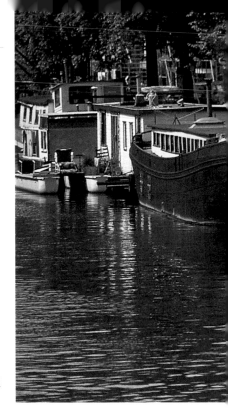

mashed potatoes and vegetables with smoked sausage or bacon. For more exotic experiences, eat Indonesian specialties, especially *rijsttafel* ("rice table"), or any of the several dozen other spiced, sauced, tangy, exquisite dishes. For sweets try *pannekoek*, pancakes with *stroop* (molasses) or *poedersuiker* (powdered sugar). If you're on the move, street stalls also serve a smaller type of pancake, *poffertjes*.

As in Belgium, beer is the most popular drink. Dutch beers tend to be lighter, although you will know that you are drinking something substantial when you sample lager in a Dutch "brown café" – a traditional bar. An excellent light beer is Grolsch, often drunk with meals in preference to wine. Heavier Belgian beers are also available, as is *jenever*, a grain spirit. *Oude jenever* is the sweetest; *jonge* is for the stronger palate. These and vintage gins and liqueurs can be enjoyed in a *proeflokalen*, or "tasting house."

Canal homes – Amsterdammers have traditionally lived on houseboats and barges

Porcelain and Jewelry

Most stores in Holland are closed on Sunday and Monday mornings. Late-night shopping is not yet a universal custom, but stores in the larger cities usually stay open late one night a week. Cities such as Amsterdam and The Hague have a variety of international clothes stores, but the real shopping experience is in the antiques and crafts sector, and in such specialties as jewelry and porcelain. In the provinces, search around and you will find some excellent regional buys.

Take a break in Amsterdam's largest and oldest municipal park, the Vondelpark

Netherlands

TIMELINE

AD 50	Iron Age Frisian and Batavi tribes settle in present-day Netherlands; they build wooden huts above the tide line on artificial mounds of clay and debris called *terpen*.
751	Charlemagne, the Holy Roman Emperor, rules the Low Countries, the lands alongside the North Sea.
12th century	Herring fishermen settle at the mouth of the Amstel river, later site of Amsterdam.
1519	Charles V of Spain is crowned Holy Roman Emperor; the Low Countries come under Spanish rule.
1566–67	Repression by Spain leads to lengthy struggle against Spanish control.
1579	Formation of Republic of the United Provinces of the Netherlands.
1602	Formation of Dutch East India Company; "Golden Age" of Amsterdam as a world trading center lasts for most of the 17th century.
1814	Northern and southern Netherlands become a united kingdom after fall of Napoleon.
1831	Southern Netherlands becomes independent Belgium.
1914–18	The Netherlands remains neutral during World War I.
1940	Germany invades the Netherlands; Amsterdam finally liberated in 1945.
1947	Formation of Benelux Trade Treaty between Belgium, the Netherlands and Luxembourg.
1957	The Netherlands signs up as a founding member of the European Community.
1992	The Netherlands signs the Maastricht Treaty, the key to the European Union.

TULIPS

Tulips are a universal symbol of the country. They are also part of the Dutch flower trade, which accounts for 70 percent of the world market in exported flowers. In the 17th century the importation of tulip bulbs from Turkey led to "tulip mania"; during the 1630s, single bulbs sold for thousands of dollars. The tulip has been a major focus of Dutch flower growing ever since, although carnations, roses and chrysanthemums outsell tulips today. The great floral experience is in late April, when the fields just inland from the east coast are vibrant with color. Also visit the Keukenhof Gardens, near Haarlem, for floral extravaganzas from late March to the end of May.

SURVIVAL GUIDE

- Large cities have regulated routes for pedestrians, cyclists, trams and automobiles. Next to the sidewalk there may be a bicycle lane. Always remember that bicycles approach silently, and always check to your left. Beyond the cycle lane you may find a second sidewalk, then a tram track, then the main thoroughfare for buses and automobiles. This sequence is the same on each side of the road. Remember that trams also approach quietly from the left.

- There are few public restrooms, and those that exist are not known for their cleanliness. Railroad and bus stations, restaurants and the bigger cafés have public bathrooms with attendants. You are expected to pay the equivalent of about 10 cents to use them.

- Eating out in the Netherlands is considered a fashion event as much as an eating experience. The Dutch tend to dress their best when going out for a meal.

- You may tip for good restaurant service. Always tell the waiter or waitress that you're tipping them, and the amount; don't leave a cash tip on the table when you leave.

- You may be tempted to sample raw herring. Follow local custom: Dip the herring in a bowl of diced onions, hold it by its tail, tip your head back, and savor.

- For tasty snacks, try the always-available *patat* (french fries) with mayonnaise or spicy sauce dips;

Great way to get around; there are some half a million bicycles in Amsterdam

kroketten, small rolls of meat filling covered in bread crumbs and fried; and do not forget pickled herring or smoked eel. *Broodjes*, like their Belgian counterparts, are baguettes filled with smoked sausage, spicy meat and cheeses.

- If you buy a present in a shop, especially chocolates, tell the assistant and it will be carefully wrapped in gift paper.

- If you buy Delftware porcelain, make sure the trade name has a D, and buy from reputable outlets.

Not always the traditional blue and white, Delft pottery comes in a variety of styles and colors

Amsterdam

AMSTERDAM

Amsterdam is a city whose dramatic past, generous people, remarkable canals, cobbled streets and decorative buildings have made it into one of the most exciting and seductive capitals in western Europe.

The city, like much of Holland, has triumphed over water. It began life in the 13th century, when fishermen built a dam across the mouth of the Amstel river and settled nearby in rough wooden houses. By the end of the 17th century the city was the leading commercial port of the post-medieval world, its success based on canals and land reclamation.

Amsterdam

For most of the 18th century Amsterdam prospered – until its ships lost command of the seas to England. The city become the capital of the Netherlands in 1813. During World War II, Amsterdam was occupied by the Germans. Its position over the past 50-odd years has been one of consolidation, urban maturity and social liberalism – influences that have produced the vigorous and tolerant city of today.

First Impressions

Most visitors arrive by train at Amsterdam's Centraal Station, a smoothly run modern complex within a handsome 1880s neoclassical building. A helpful tourist information office is on platform (*spoor*) 2; the main tourist office (see page 344) is just outside the railroad station. Immediately in front of the station is the busy Stationsplein, a mix of tram line, bus track, bicycle lane and pedestrian concourse with street entertainers and crowds of people. Straight ahead lies Damrak; watch out for traffic here, and always wait patiently for the green light at pedestrian crossings.

A Cultural and Liberal City

Amsterdam's liberal traditions are apparent in the notorious Red Light District (Prostutiezone), located mainly between Warmoesstraat and Oudezijds Achterburgwal. Be advised – do not take photographs of prostitutes' booths. As in any crowded location, be on the lookout for pickpockets.

Amsterdam is also notorious for its "coffee shops," where hashish and marijuana sold for personal use is tolerated by the authorities. *Eetcafes* and cafés, on the other hand, are conventional places where coffee is served. "Brown cafés" are traditional bars where liquor is sold.

All this alternative culture is a minor aspect of the larger Amsterdam, a sophisticated city and a working community. There are peaceful canals and tree-shaded, cobbled streets lined with narrow gabled houses. It's a flower-filled city of exhilarating art museums, glorious civic buildings, medieval churches, quality stores,

AMSTERDAM

Amsterdam

superb restaurants, and entertaining street life.

Getting to Know Amsterdam

Try a 50-minute round-trip ride on the famous Circle Tram 20, which leaves every 10 minutes from in front of Centraal Station. For a taste of the city's canal culture, take a cruise on one of the sleek, efficient tour boats; you can even enjoy a candlelit wine and cheese cruise. Walking tours show you the city's architecture, history, art and special neighborhoods.

Amsterdam is also a rewarding city to explore by foot on your own. Step away from the city center and discover the serenity of canal-side walks. Enjoy street theater in the Leidseplein Square, or visit the Stoelte Diamond works in

Wagenstraat, near the neon-lit square of Rembrandtplein. The major shopping street of Kalverstraat leads to the busy open space of Spui, or try wandering down to the Bloemen flower market near Singel canal.

Supporting the City

Amsterdam is built on hundreds of thousands of pilings that have been driven through the surface layers of soft peat to rest soundly on hard sand. The 17th-century Royal Palace (Koninklijk Paleis, see page 346) on Dam Square rests on 13,659 wooden pilings. Concrete pilings sunk to 65 feet have replaced the original ones.

ESSENTIAL INFORMATION

TOURIST INFORMATION

Tourist information centers are known as VVV (Vereniging Voor Vreemdelingenverkeer)
• Amsterdam Tourist Office, Box 3901, Amsterdam, NL–1001 AS ☎ 063 403 4066 (for written or telephone queries).
• VVV Stationsplein, Centraal Station, platform 2
• VVV Stationsplein 10, Noord-Zuidhollands Koffiehuis (opposite station entrance)
• VVV Leidseplein 1, corner with Leidsestraat
• VVV Stadionplein, Van Tuyll van Serooskerkenweg 125
• Holland Tourist Information (HTI), Schiphol Airport, Schiphol Plaza shopping center.

URBAN TRANSPORTATION

Trains run from Centraal Station (central railroad station), Stationsplein. For information call ☎ 06 9292. The city transportation authority is Gemeentevervoerbedrijf (GVB). For information and tickets there is a GVB office opposite Centraal Station; open Mon.–Fri. 7–7, Sat.–Sun. 8–7. Amsterdam's subway mainly serves suburban

areas and is not of great use to visitors, except where noted in the text. Subway stations are marked with an "M" on the city map. There is a subway (metro) station and information desk at Centraal Station. Taxis are expensive, but can be picked up at the stands at Schiphol Airport, Centraal Station, Dam Square and Leidseplein. You can also call Taxicentrale (☎ 020 677 7777, 24-hour service).

AIRPORT INFORMATION

Schiphol Airport is one of the most modern facilities in Europe. It is 11 miles southwest from Amsterdam. Fast, efficient trains run from a station just south of the airport complex to Amsterdam's Centraal Station; the journey takes 20 minutes. They depart every 15 minutes daily 6 a.m.–midnight, on the hour midnight–6 a.m. Buses run regularly to Amsterdam and leave from Schiphol Plaza in front of the airport. There are post offices, banks, numerous shops and a Holland Tourist Information Office in Schiphol Plaza, and there is a restaurant and hotel in the airport complex. For airport information call ☎ 063 503 4050.

CLIMATE – average highs and lows for the month

JAN.	FEB.	MAR.	APR.	MAY	JUN.	JUL.	AUG.	SEP.	OCT.	NOV.	DEC.
5°C	5°C	9°C	11°C	15°C	18°C	20°C	21°C	18°C	13°C	9°C	7°C
41°F	41°F	48°F	52°F	59°F	64°F	68°F	70°F	64°F	55°F	48°F	45°F
1°C	0°C	3°C	5°C	8°C	11°C	13°C	13°C	10°C	8°C	4°C	2°C
34°F	32°F	37°F	41°F	46°F	52°F	55°F	55°F	50°F	46°F	39°F	36°F

CITY SIGHTS

Key to symbols

✚ map coordinates refer to the Amsterdam map on page 342–343; sights below are highlighted in yellow on the map.

✉ address or location ☎ telephone number

🕐 opening times 🚌 nearest bus or tram route

🍴 restaurant on site or nearby

💰 admission charge: $$$ more than 10f, $$ 5f–10f, $ less than 5f

AMSTERDAMS HISTORISCH MUSEUM

✚ C3 ✉ Kalverstraat 92 Nieuwezijds Voorburgwal 357 ☎ 020 523 1822 🕐 Mon.–Fri. 10–5, Sat.–Sun. 11–5 🍴 Museum café 🚌 Tram 1, 2, 5 💰 $$

Amsterdam's story is well told in the enjoyable Amsterdams Historisch Museum (Amsterdams Museum of History), in the heart of the city. Once a monastery, and then a city orphanage for four centuries, the museum is now an elegant complex of bright and airy rooms. (Watch for awkward steps in some of them.) Highlights include a superb model of a Dutch East Indiaman sailing ship and the silver drinking horn of the medieval Guild of St. George. To the right of the entrance is the glass doorway into Schuttersgalerij. This was once an open street and is now the Civic Guard Gallery, with splendid group portraits of 17th-century city militiamen.

ANNE FRANKHUIS

✚ B3 ✉ Prinsengracht 263 ☎ 020 556 7100 🕐 Daily 9–7, Apr.–Aug.; 9–5, rest of year. Closed Yom Kippur 🚌 Tram 13, 14, 17 🚢 Museum Boat stop 💰 $$

No matter how often you have heard the Anne Frank story, a visit to Het Achterhuis, "The Secret Annexe," is unforgettable. Here, in the Anne Frankhuis (Anne Frank House), the Frank family and their friends lived secretly in Nazi-occupied Amsterdam until their arrest only months before the Liberation. The only one to survive the concentration camps was Anne's father, Otto. The lively, passionate diary kept by Anne during her years in hiding was later

Visitors pay homage at Anne Frank House, preserved exactly as it was in 1944

published to worldwide acclaim. The museum has absorbing displays and multimedia installations, but the secret annex is the haunting heart of it all. The stark emptiness intensifies the experience, and the atmospheric rooms throng with ghosts. From every corner Anne Frank bears witness on behalf of millions of Nazi victims. After your visit, a quiet walk through the peaceful, reflective Jordaan district, just across the canal, is recommended.

BEGIJNHOF

✚ C2–C3 ✉ Gedempte Begijnsloot 🕐 Daily dawn–dusk 🚌 Tram 1, 2, 5 💰 Free

Amsterdam's secluded Begijnhof (Courtyard of the Beguines) is an outstanding example of a medieval almshouse community. It was built in the 14th century to accommodate Beguines, pious single women of the Catholic faith, who lived a religious and charitable life without the stricture of holy vows. The Beguines were later ostracized because of their faith, and today the discreet facade of the Begijnhof's once clandestine Catholic church masks a

Tomb of Admiral du Ruyter, Holland's most valiant naval hero, honored in the Gothic New Church

haunting little Italianate chapel. Opposite stands the original church that was transferred to the city's Protestant community in the late 16th century. In the south corner of the Begijnhof is the 15th-century Houten Huys, one of Amsterdam's oldest houses, wooden-fronted and steeply gabled. Today's Begijnhof still accommodates single women of modest means.

NIEUWE KERK

✚ C3　✉ Dam　☎ Kerk: 020 626 8168. Paleis: 020 624 8698　🕐 Kerk: hours vary. Paleis: Tue.–Thu. 1–4, Jun.–Aug.; Fri.–Mon. 12:30–5, rest of year. Closed holidays; hours sometimes vary when the Queen is in residence　🚋 Tram 4, 9, 14, 16, 24, 25　✋ Kerk $$$, Paleis $$　ℹ Art exhibitions at various times

The 17th-century Nieuwe Kerk (New Church) was new only in its original form, as compared with the more venerable Oude Kerk (Old Church). The New Church is a fine counterpoint to Dam Square's Koninklijk Paleis (Royal Palace), with its beautifully decorated rooms. Today the church is used for major art exhibitions. There are a dozen or so side chapels and a magnificent vaulted roof. The church's baroque pulpit and its splendid organ are permanent highlights. Dutch monarchs have been crowned here, including the present Queen Beatrix.

OUDE KERK

✚ C3　✉ Oudekerksplein 1　☎ 020 625 8284　🕐 Daily 1–5, Sat. 11–1　🚋 Tram 4, 9, 16, 24, 25　✋ $$　ℹ Art exhibitions and music recitals at various times

The Oude Kerk (Old Church) is the oldest church in Amsterdam. It has been much restored, but it retains an authentic medieval atmosphere. The church stands on the banks of the Oudezijds Voorburgwal canal in the heart of the Red Light District. Its glorious stained-glass windows, featuring Lambert van Noorts' *Annunciation* and *The Visit of Mary to Elizabeth*, look down on prostitutes' booths in the narrow Enge Kerk Straat, much as they might have done in medieval times. A triple nave and high-vaulted roof give added spaciousness to the dramatically bare interior of the Old Church. A poignant feature is the gravestone of Rembrandt's wife Saskia van Uylenburg, set among slabs below the choir organ.

RIJKSMUSEUM

✚ B1　✉ Stadhouderskade 42　☎ 020 673 2121　🕐 Daily 10–5　🍴 Museum café/restaurant　🚋 Tram 2, 5, 6, 7, 10　⛴ Museum Boat stop　✋ $$$　ℹ Audio tour

The Rijksmuseum (National Museum) contains some of the world's greatest works of Flemish art. The building dates from 1885 and was designed by Pierre Cuypers. Its elegant neo-Gothic facade is something of a mirror image to Cuypers' Centraal Station.

Start on the second floor with rooms 201–206, which display Dutch works from the 15th and 16th centuries. There are dozens of superb paintings and numerous highlights, such as Frans Hals' supremely cheerful marriage portrait of *Isaac Abrahamsz Massa and Beatrix Van der Laen* and Johannes Vermeer's *The Kitchen Maid*, a masterpiece of complementary colors. The sequence ends with the Gallery of Honour, displaying Rembrandt's *The Night Watch* or, under its original title, *The Company Of Captain Franz Baning Cocq and Lieutenant Willem van Ruytenburch*. Other sections of the Rijksmuseum have dazzling displays of sculpture, Delftware, Meissen porcelain and historic artifacts.

Entrance to the Rijksmuseum, Amsterdam's national collection

RIJKSMUSEUM VINCENT VAN GOGH

➕ B1 ✉ Paulus Potterstraat ☎ 020 570 5200
🕐 Daily 10–5; closed Jan. 1 🍴 Museum café/restaurant 🚋 Tram 2, 5 ⛴ Museum Boat stop
💷 $$$

To view the finest and largest collection of Vincent Van Gogh's paintings, visit the Rijksmuseum Vincent van Gogh (National Museum of Vincent Van Gogh), where Van Gogh's works chart his intense and ultimately tragic life. The collection takes you through his early period, when he was a missionary in the Dutch coal fields; pieces include such dark social commentary as *The Potato Eaters*. His later Parisian work reflects the influence of the Impressionists, but it is the paintings inspired by his life at Arles, in sunny Provence, that exhilarate with their fiery yellows and oranges. The most famous works are the iconic *Sunflowers* series. Conversely, *The Garden of St. Paul's*

Hospital, painted at St.-Rémy mental asylum the year before Van Gogh's death, is a heartrending evocation of a dejected figure. The trees are as rigid as the bars of a cell. But the sum of the Van Gogh Museum, the painter's legacy of outstanding work, is wholly positive and uplifting. The adjacent Stedelijk Museum is one of the finest and most exuberant collections of modern art in the world.

VONDELPARK

➕ A1 ✉ Stadhouderskade 🕐 Daily dawn–dusk
🍴 Ronde Blauwe Theehuis ("The Round Blue Teahouse," by the lake) 🚋 Tram 1, 2, 3, 5, 6, 12
⛴ Water bus stop ℹ Excellent open-air theater and concerts during summer

The Vondelpark, Amsterdam's principal park, is named after the 17th-century playwright Joost van den Vondel. The park starts modestly enough as a green avenue that leads southwest from a busy corner on Stadhouderskade, a short distance south of Leidseplein. Soon it opens invitingly into a broad green space peppered with trees and interspersed with ornamental lakes and linked waterways. There are children's playgrounds, a sweetly scented rose garden, teahouses and a bandstand. During the summer, music, theater and entertainment in the sun enliven the park even more.

AMSTERDAM'S CANALS

So many northern European capitals claim the title "Venice of the North" that the epithet has become devalued. Some say there is no substitute for the real thing, but perhaps Amsterdam has the strongest claim to the title. The city lacks the romantic splendor of Venice, but there is a cool, restrained beauty about Amsterdam's canals (*gracht*) and their attendant buildings.

The finest canals lie to the west of the city center, beyond the bustling main streets of Damrak and Nieuwezijds Voorburgwal, both of which were canals at one time. A stroll along narrow side streets from Nieuwezijds Voorburgwal and across the busy Spuistraat brings you suddenly to the great waterways of Singel, Herengracht, Keizersgracht and Prinsengracht.

Flower stalls are an essential part of the Amsterdam scene

Herengracht

Herengracht is the finest canal of the *grachtengordel*, the ring or girdle of canals that were built in the early 17th century to defend the city. The name Herengracht translates into English as the "Gentlemen's Canal," a sign of contemporary male ascendancy. This was the district where the wealthiest Amsterdam merchant families built themselves handsome canal-side mansions notable for their superb ornate gables. The houses were designed to be tall and narrow because of limited space.

Take a stroll down Herengracht to appreciate it all. You can start from the canal's northern end at its junction with Brouwersgracht. The Brouwersgracht is the short stretch of canal that links Herengracht to the Singel canal at the Haarlemmer Sluis, one of the 40 or so sluices that are opened each night to flush clean water through the canal system. Haarlemmer Sluis can be reached from Centraal Station by walking northwest along Prins Hendrikkade for about 300 yards and then turning left. Cross the wide sluice bridge. (There is a superb cheese shop on the opposite corner.) Go left, then turn right along Brouwersgracht to reach the tree-shaded bridges at the junction with Herengracht.

Walk south for a mile of scenic history to where the Herengracht meets the Amstel river. You can stroll down either side of the great canal and cross over bridges to get the best views of canal-side houses. Visit the Theater Museum and garden at Herengracht 168, and the exquisite Bartolotti House next door. The latter is a 17th-century Renaissance mansion built by the head of the Bartolotti Bank. Enjoy the *Golden Bocht*, which translates as

House boats and barges line the picturesque Prinsengracht canal in the Jordaan district of Amsterdam

"Golden Bay" or "Bend," between Leidsestraat and Vijzelstraat – note the decorative double-fronted houses along the elegant curve of the canal.

The curve is an engaging motif amid Amsterdam's general flatness – in the decorativeness of house gables, the elegant bridges, the sweep of railings, even in the curved handlebars of the wonderful old upright bicycles still favored by Amsterdammers. There are said to be 550,000 bicycles in the city, and it seems that everybody cycles in Amsterdam. Elderly *dames* and *herens* (ladies and gentlemen) cruise past to the tinkling of bells like songbirds. Stylishly dressed young people skim along with their backs straight and a wary eye on the tourist's uncertain bid to run across the street in front of them.

Connections

Explore the Prinsengracht and the Keizersgracht, as well as the main canals, and don't neglect the connecting waterways. There's the Leidsegracht on the Golden Bend, or the peaceful, leafy Egelantiersgracht near the Anne Frank House (Anne Frankhuis, see page 345) that takes you into the quiet heart of the Jordaan district. Sidestep into enchanting streets between Herengracht and Singel canals, such as Gasthuismolen Steeg or Oude Spiegelstraat, where craft and antique shops and boutiques rub shoulders with delightful little cafés and restaurants. And try a nighttime walk along the great canals, when many of the finest houses are floodlit and the numerous bridges twinkle with lights.

In summer the canals become venues for concerts by the water, rowing regattas, Chinese dragon boat races and various other events. Amsterdam is many things to many people, but the city's fascinating network of canals will always be the enduring motif of this very special city. For the walk route, see the city map on page 342–343.

The Hague

THE HAGUE

The Hague (Den Haag), third-largest city in the Netherlands, is justly proud of its status as the political and royal capital of the country and as a focus of international affairs. It lacks the fast pace and excitement of Amsterdam, yet a sense of well-being and security underpins the rich cultural and political heritage.

The city's name derives from *Gravenhage,* which means "the Count's hedge." In the 13th century the Count of Holland built a hunting lodge among sand dunes – this is where The Hague's historic center, the Binnenhof ("inner court") now stands. The settlement that developed around the lodge was the Count's "hedge" sheltering him against the outside world.

In the 16th century the States General of the United Netherlands met at The Hague, and since then the city has been the seat of Dutch government. The Hague Convention of 1907, which formulated laws governing warfare worldwide, gave this city international status. The 1913 opening of the Peace

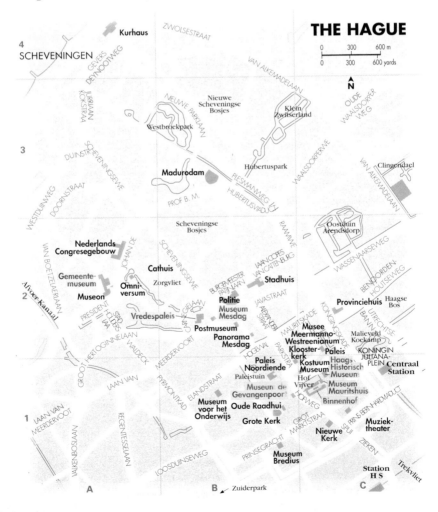

THE HAGUE

Palace (Het Vredespaleis, see page 354) further enhanced The Hague's standing, and it is today considered the center of international diplomacy and business. The Permanent Court of Arbitration and the International Court of Justice are located at the Peace Palace; numerous embassies, ministries and headquarters of international organizations are also based here. In 1980, after the Dutch queen, Juliana, abdicated in favor of her daughter Beatrix, the royal residency was relocated from Utrecht to The Hague, adding even more luster to this small but fascinating city.

Arrival

The Hague's main railroad station, Den Haag Centraal Station, is plain but functional. Local tram and bus stations stand next to it, and the helpful tourist information center is located at the front of the Babylon shopping center, by the railroad station's main entrance. From here you can see the skyline of modern buildings that lies between the station and the city itself. A short walk southwest leads to the sedate, elegant heart of The Hague, where the Binnenhof and several fine museums cluster around the graceful little lake of Hof Vijver.

Guided city tours are offered during the summer. A Royal Tour by bus takes in the main sights, including the seaside resort of Scheveningen and views of three royal palaces, although none of the palaces are open to the public. Tours can be booked through the tourist information center.

On Your Own

Exploring The Hague on your own can be a very rewarding experience. The oldest section centers on the Hof Vijver, the "Court Pond." On its south side the Hof Vijver laps against the walls of the Binnenhof and of the Mauritshuis Museum (see page 354), which houses The Hague's outstanding art collection. Its northern side is lined with trees and is backed by the elegant 18th-century street Lange Vijverberg.

From the Hof Vijver you can stroll north beneath the lime trees on the wide avenue of Lange Voorhout. A colorful antiques market is held here on Thursdays and Sundays. Continue past the grand facade of the Des Indes Intercontinental Hotel to reach Denneweg, a charming street with a Parisian flavor and a host of interesting antique and craft galleries, delicatessens, restaurants, cafés and distinctive fashion boutiques.

Quickening Pace

West of the Hof Vijver and the Binnenhof lies the bustling open area of the Buitenhof, where the pace quickens to that of a busy city. Beyond

Gate at the Binnenhof – the complex where The Hague had its beginnings

the Buitenhof lies The Hague's commercial and shopping district and the pedestrian-only streets that lead to the Kerk Plein (Church Square) and the imposing, hexagonal-towered church, the Grote Kerk.

North of the church is the Hofkwartier, one of the oldest areas of The Hague. There are many specialty shops, small restaurants and cafés here. Best of all, stroll along the Palace Promenade (Hoogstraat) and on into Noordeinde, one of The Hague's most attractive streets. Here you will find a marvelous selection of art galleries, antiques, craft shops and fashion boutiques, restaurants and the Royal Palace (Paleis Noordeinde).

Perhaps the best strategy to enjoying this distinguished city is to keep a relaxed pace. Fill your day with activities involving the arts and history; eat well in any of the excellent restaurants and cafés; and seek out the numerous musical and cultural events that take place in the summer.

A short journey on tram 11 will take you to the coast and the sunny resort of Scheveningen. You can break the journey halfway at the miniature "town" of Madurodam, a favorite with children. Apart from Scheveningen's superb beach and promenade, the numerous attractions include the Holland Casino, the Sea Life Center and a recently refurbished pier. (Proper pronunciation of the name Scheveningen is the sign of a true local. Try "Shravin-eeng-e" and you might get by.)

Hooigracht Canal

Several ring canals were built around The Hague during the 17th century. Although many of them have been filled in, you can walk east from Denneweg to reach the serene little stretch of surviving canal, the Hooigracht, its leafy banks lined with elegant and attractive old buildings.

ESSENTIAL INFORMATION

TOURIST INFORMATION
Tourist Information Centers are known as VVV (Vereniging Voor Vreemdelingenverkeer)
• Tourist information office, Koningin Julianaplein 30, Babylon Shopping Center ☎ 0900 3403505

URBAN TRANSPORTATION
Den Haag Centraal Station (The Hague's central railroad station) is on Koningin Julianaplein. Service to and from Amsterdam arrives at 15-minute intervals; travel time between Amsterdam and The Hague is about 45 minutes. For information and tickets for buses and trams inquire at the tourist information office (☎ 070 384 8666). Taxi stands

are at the central railroad station and at the Buitenhof. To call a taxi, phone ☎ 070 317 8877 or 070 383 0830.

AIRPORT INFORMATION
Schiphol Airport serves The Hague (see page 344). Trains for The Hague leave Schiphol Airport at regular intervals, and travel to Den Haag Centraal Station in about 40 minutes. Another railroad station, Den Haag Hollands Spoor, is located some distance south of Centraal Station and the city center. Trains from Schiphol and Amsterdam stop there first. If you are going to the city center, stay on the train until Centraal Station.

CLIMATE – average highs and lows for the month

	JAN.	FEB.	MAR.	APR.	MAY	JUN.	JUL.	AUG.	SEP.	OCT.	NOV.	DEC.
	5°C	5°C	9°C	11°C	15°C	18°C	20°C	21°C	18°C	14°C	9°C	7°C
	41°F	41°F	48°F	52°F	59°F	64°F	68°F	70°F	64°F	57°F	48°F	45°F
	1°C	0°C	3°C	5°C	8°C	12°C	14°C	13°C	11°C	9°C	4°C	3°C
	34°F	32°F	37°F	41°F	46°F	54°F	57°F	55°F	52°F	48°F	39°F	37°F

The picturesque Hof Vijer, lined with an impressive ensemble of public buildings

CITY SIGHTS

Key to symbols

✚ map coordinates refer to The Hague map on page 350; sights below are highlighted in yellow on the map.

✉ address or location ☎ telephone number

🕐 opening times 🚌 nearest bus or tram route

🍴 restaurant on site or nearby

🎫 admission charge: $$$ more than 10f, $$ 5f–10f, $ less than 5f

BINNENHOF

✚ C1 ✉ 8a Binnenhof ☎ 070 364 6144

🕐 Mon.–Sat. 10–4; closed holidays and Sep. 20–21

🚌 Tram 2, 3, 6, 8, 10 🎫 $ ✚ Last tour at 3:45. Advance bookings are recommended. May be closed to the public on other occasions.

The Binnenhof (Inner Court) of the original lodge of the Counts of Holland is the oldest part of The Hague. The turreted Knight's Hall, where medieval guests were received and entertained, stands at the heart of a central square; behind it is the Parliament building. The complex retains a timeless atmosphere; the main room of the Knight's Hall is the Ridderzaal, an impressive grand hall, restored in 1900 to its medieval glory. It is full of coats of arms, Dutch provincial flags, stained glass and historical artifacts. Important ceremonies, including *Prinsjesdag*, the day of the Queen's speech to the Dutch parliament, are held here. There are guided tours of the Ridderzaal and the first and second chambers of parliament when the chambers are not in use. The entrance to the ticket office is on the right side of the Knight's Hall.

GEMEENTEMUSEUM

✚ A2 ✉ 41 Stadhouderslaan ☎ 070 338 1111

🕐 Tue.–Sun. 11–5 🍴 Museum café 🚌 14; tram 4, 8

🎫 $$

Renovations in 1998 have added to the attractions of the Gemeentemuseum (Municipal Museum), which is located just northwest of the city center. The museum has outstanding collections of musical instruments and ceramics, including Delftware and The Hague silverware. The modern art collection includes works by Vincent Van Gogh and Claude Monet, and there is a large collection of paintings by Piet Mondrian. A recent addition is a fashion gallery featuring temporary exhibitions in Dutch and international fashion.

HAAGS HISTORISCH MUSEUM

✚ C1 ✉ 7 Korte Vijverberg ☎ 070 364 6940

🕐 Tue.–Fri. 11–5, Sat.–Sun. noon–5 🚌 4, 5, 18, 22; tram 1, 7, 8, 9, 12 🎫 $

Haags Historisch Museum (Historical Museum of The Hague) is very much a Dutch institution; there are no English translations to supplement the almost exclusively Dutch labeling of the paintings. A visit is nonetheless rewarding, especially to see such big paintings as Jan van Goyen's *View of The Hague*. In the attic there is a permanent exhibition illustrating the history of The Hague during the 19th and 20th centuries; look for the explanatory panels that are translated in English.

The Peace Palace – seat of the International Court of Justice

private home in the 17th century by Johan Maurits van Nassau-Siegen and was reconstructed after a disastrous fire in 1704. Today it contains an outstanding collection of Dutch art. Highlights include Johannes Vermeer's *Girl with a Pearl Earring* and the crowning glory, Rembrandt's famous *The Anatomy Lesson of Doctor Nicolaes Tulp*. Don't miss Andy Warhol's charming portrait of Queen Beatrix in the cloakroom area.

MUSEUM DE GEVANGENPOORT

✠ B1   ✉ 33 Buitenhof   ☎ 070 346 0861
🕐 Tue.–Fri. 11–5, Sat.–Sun. noon–5   🚋 Tram 7, 8, 16
🎟 $$ ℹ Last tour at 4

A guided tour of the Museum de Gevangenpoort (Prison Gate Museum) is great fun, but is not for the fainthearted. The Prison Gate Museum was The Hague's notorious prison for hundreds of years. Wood-paneled cells, interrogation rooms and a debtors' chamber give a vivid and gruesome picture of medieval justice. The tour commentary is in Dutch only, but information sheets in other languages are available and the guide will answer questions in English. The final visit to the torture room in the basement should finish you off nicely. The Dutch treat the whole thing with a commendable black humor. Be sure to bring yours with you.

MUSEUM MAURITSHUIS

✠ C1   ✉ 8 Korte Vijverberg   ☎ 070 302 3435
🕐 Tue.–Sat. 10–5, Sun. and holidays 11–5   🚋 4, 13; tram 7, 8   🎟 $$

The original Museum Mauritshuis (Mauritshuis Museum) was built as a

MUSEUM MESDAG

✠ B2   ✉ 7f Laan van Meerdervoort   ☎ 070 362 1434   🕐 Tue.–Sun. noon–5   🚋 4, 13; tram 7, 8   🎟 $

Hendrik Willem Mesdag was a leading figure in the art world of The Hague during the 19th century. Famous for his *Panorama Mesdag*, Mesdag was himself a painter and an avid collector of works, especially of the Barbizon school of French painters, including Jean François Millet, Gustave Courbet and Jozef Israels, whose works – along with Mesdag's – grace the salons of the museum. Mesdag built the museum as an annex to his house, and the carpets and artifacts are all original.

VREDESPALEIS

✠ B2   ✉ 2 Carnegielaan   ☎ 070 302 4137
🕐 Mon.–Fri. 10–4, Apr.–Sep.; 10–3, rest of year
🚋 4, 13; tram 7, 8   🎟 $ ℹ Tour times are subject to change. Group tours on Sat.; inquiries and reservations can be made at the tourist information office

The Vredespaleis (Peace Palace) is an awe-inspiring building symbolizing the power of statehood. Scottish philanthropist Andrew Carnegie, who made his fortune in America, paid for its Gothic splendor in the early years of the 20th century. Its exquisite furnishings and artifacts were donated by the nations of the world. A guided tour of the building includes a visit to the International Court of Justice and is conducted in several languages, including English. Due to security control, you must wait in the open at the palace gates for the hourly tour to begin. Peace and justice are worth the wait, but choose a dry day.

DELFT

Fine ceramics and architecture are the main features of Delft. The ceramics have been exported worldwide, but Delft's buildings remain much as they were when immortalized on canvas by Johannes Vermeer, a native of the town.

There are organized coach trips to Delft from The Hague, and seats can be reserved through the tourist information office at the Babylon shopping center. The town is only 20 minutes from The Hague via tram 1, and takes even less time by train. Tram and train both land you on a two-lane highway, but a few steps along cobbled lanes transport you into a delightful medieval world enclosed by Delft's tranquil canals. It's centered on an imposing main square, the Markt, where there is a tourist information office as well as numerous stores, cafés and restaurants.

Delft is a popular tourist destination, and in summer the Markt can be especially crowded. Explore farther afield; follow the canal-side street of Oosteinde from behind the New Church (Nieuwe Kerk) to reach the medieval city gate of Oostport. Visit the Old Church (Oude Kerk) west of the Markt, at the head of the lovely street of Oude Delft. The Old Church is a splendid Gothic building full of interest and charm. View it from the Peperstraat Bridge, three bridges to the south on Oude Delft, to fully appreciate its remarkable leaning tower. Close to the Old Church is the Prinsenhof Museum, with a fine collection of paintings. Stop for coffee and crêpes at Stads Pannekoeckhuys, Oude Delft 113–115.

Many stores on the Markt sell Delft china. The Huis Lambert van Meerten Museum at Oude Delft 199 has a superb collection of Delft earthenware and tiles from around the world. The Koninklijke Porceleyne Fles, a factory involved in producing Delftware since the 17th century, is located a short distance out of town on Rotterdamsweg 196 and offers guided tours.

Take a break from a spring shopping expedition and relax with coffee by one of Delft's canals

NORWAY

*"N OVEMBER always
seemed to me the Norway
of the year. "*

American poet Emily Dickenson, from a letter to friends, 1864

Norway

Opposite: Clean air, clear water and majestic mountains at Sognefjord, in Norway's dramatic fjord region

Norway

NORWAY

Norway is the edge of Europe's most northerly land mass, where sea and mountains have merged to produce one of the world's most breathtaking landscapes. This is a country whose ancient peoples, the Vikings, helped shape the history of northern Europe. The Vikings once controlled half of Britain, and sent mariners as far west as Newfoundland and as far south as the Straits of Gibraltar.

It is this vigorous and resourceful national character, reflected in Viking tradition, that still exemplifies modern Norway. This is a nation that has mastered an inhospitable landscape without despoiling it, even becoming a leading oil producer in the hostile environment of the North Sea.

MORE TOP DESTINATIONS IN NORWAY

- Ålesund A2
- Bergen A1 ● Eidsvoll A1
- Hardangerfjord A1
- Kristiansand A1
- Lillehammer A1
- Lofoten B3 ● Lysefjord A1
- Nordfjord C4 ● Nordkapp C4
- Romsdalen A2 ● Stavanger A1
- Sognefjord A2
- Trondheim A2

Norway

Landscape

Norway's landscape is dominated by intervening seas – the Barents Sea to the north, the Norwegian Sea to the west and the North Sea to the southwest. All three are vast and often stormy. The corrugated coastline measures nearly 13,600 miles, including fjords and the country's 150,000 offshore islands. This scattered mosaic of islands – the "Skerry Guard" – is Norway's natural sea defense. The islands break the onslaught of the ocean, creating the country's sheltered seaways to north and south and protecting the gateways to the fjords.

Norway is shaped like a Viking club, narrowing in the north and with a broad base in the south. The country's mountain system runs from northeast to southwest and reaches its greatest height at Galdhøppigen, at 8,100 feet. The mountains separate the rugged western seaboard, the Vestlandet, from the gentler eastern region, the Øslandet.

The broad southwestern half of the country is known as Sørlandet, the South Country. Here, on the coastal fringe and around Oslo, is lowland Norway, where the sheltered coast is a favorite vacation destination for Norwegian families – a landscape of mellow woods and fields and tranquil blue waters. On the southern tip of Sørlandet is the sunny town of Kristiansand, with its flock of offshore islands. Southwest along the coast is Mandal, where attractive beaches catch the best of the summer sun; nearby is the promontory of Lindesnes, whose lighthouse marks Norway's southernmost point.

Then the coast turns to the northwest, twisting through a rugged landscape of rocky headlands and deeply indented fjords, past the pleasant town of Egersund and finally through rich farming country to Stavanger and the open west.

Fjordland

Norway's famous Fjordland begins at Stavanger. Stretching for more than 375 miles is one of the most spectacular landscapes and seascapes in the world. In the Ryfylke area, northeast of Stavanger, lies the stunning Lysefjord with its flat-topped and sheer-sided Pulpit Rock. Farther north is the mighty Hardangerfjord, with its massive cliffs, and the silver-white waterfalls of Skykkjedalsfoss and Vøringfoss, set off by snowcapped mountains.

Farther north into Hordaland lies fascinating Bergen, against a setting of islands and mountains. Bergen is the starting point for boat journeys to the north along the coastal islands and into the 120-mile-long Sognefjord, the deepest and longest fjord in the world. Its side fjords twist between towering cliffs and penetrate as far as Flåm and Gudvangen, at the head of Nærøyfjord (the narrowest fjord in Europe), and to Fjærland, below the southernmost edge of the great Jostedal glacier.

Along Sognefjord are lovely villages such as Balestrand. Throughout the area, ancient pagoda-like stave churches survive at settlements such as Vik, Kaupanger and Urnes. Inland to the east lies the mighty mountain range of Jotunheimen, known as the "Land of the Giants."

Fjordland

Beyond the Sognefjord lies Nordfjord and then the county, or *fylke*, of Møre og Romsdal. The coastal town of Ålesund is renowned for its art nouveau architecture of turrets, towers and medieval motifs. Inland is the Geirangerfjord and its magnificent waterfalls. From Ålesund, spectacular roads lead over the mountains to the

Traditional embroidered costume, worn at festivals

land, be selective about how and where you explore. Roads are well maintained throughout. Good driving skills are required, however, where roads are narrow and twisting and where they pass through long tunnels. Norway's public transportation system is excellent.

This is a country that copes impressively with some of the most difficult winter conditions in Europe. Only in severe conditions are train services to the northwest likely to be curtailed. Buses serve more remote villages throughout the north and west. Travel by boat is a way of life in Norway, especially on the western seaboard. There is no finer way of touring Fjordland than by boat.

Most of Norway has a mild, wet maritime climate. The west coast and mountains have high rainfalls even in midsummer. But there can be long spells of good weather, when Fjordland is glorious. In eastern and southeastern Norway, summers can be warm and dry. Winter in the higher elevations is cold and extremely snowy, creating excellent skiing conditions at Norway's winter resorts. The Norwegians are philosophical about their weather; to them it is either good or invigorating.

The Norwegians

Norway, as a constitutional monarchy, is extremely well run. The moderate Labor Party has dominated government since the 1930s. The Norwegians are a level-headed, open and generous people. They are unfailingly courteous, and only in busy Oslo does an occasional impatience with visitors emerge.

The people share the Scandinavian tendency toward self-effacement but they are understandably proud of their success at shaping a modern nation out of such a wild landscape.

town of Åndalsnes and the Romsdalsfjord. Along the coast farther north lies the Atlantic Road, a highway linking a chain of islands. Northeast from here lies Trollheimen, the mountainous "Home of the Trolls," and then comes the great expanse of Trondheimsfjorden and Trondheim itself, once called Nidaros, the ancient capital of Norway.

Beyond Trondheim is the narrowing edge of Norway's northwestern seaboard, fertile coastal lands backed by barren mountains that reach into Nordland and to the Arctic Circle. At Narvik, you look out across the waters of Vestfjordan to the spectacular Lofoton Islands before continuing north to Tromso. You then go on through Finnmark, the land of the Sami people and of the midnight sun, to the Arctic island of Honningsvåg and Nordkapp (North Cape), the symbolic northern end of Europe.

Traveling in Norway

Norway is a pleasant country in which to travel but to enjoy this magnificent

Stunning mountain pass at Stalheim

Norway

TIMELINE

2000–1000 BC	Early Neolithic and Bronze Age people leave numerous rock carvings throughout Scandinavia.
AD 787	Viking expansion begins with increased expeditions to Britain and northern Europe.
870	Vikings settle in Iceland.
1000	Christianity is introduced to Norway; Lief Eriksson reaches the coast of Labrador.
circa 1300	Oslo becomes capital of Norway.
1350	The Black Death kills over half of Norway's population.
1397	Union of the Three Crowns of Denmark, Sweden and Norway signed at Kalmar.
1536	Norway is reduced to a "province" of Denmark and remains so for nearly 300 years.
1814	The country is forced into union with Sweden.
1905	Prince Carl of Denmark is invited to become king of an independent Norway.
1914–18	Norway remains neutral during World War I.
1925	City of Christiana reverts to its original name of Oslo.
1940	Invasion of Norway by Germany, in spite of Norway's declaration of neutrality.
1945	German troops surrender in north of country; Norway becomes one of the founders of the United Nations.
1949	Norway becomes a founding member of NATO.
1970s	Oil and gas extraction from Norwegian sector of North Sea boosts Norway's economy.
1994	In a referendum, Norwegians reject membership in the European Union.

THE VIKING SETTLERS

History has painted the Vikings as aggressive, anarchic sea raiders, but this view has changed somewhat in recent times. The restless voyaging that took the Vikings around the coasts of Britain and into the deep estuaries of northern France led to bloody conflict. There seems no question that the Vikings plundered and destroyed. But modern theory argues that a desire for new territory made them settlers in foreign lands more often than just violent raiders. In later, more stable times, the Vikings' commercial success was just as powerful as their military ferocity had been.

SURVIVAL GUIDE

- Mid-June through July is the national vacation period and many Norwegians depart the cities and towns for the fjords, mountains and countryside. Oslo is quieter than normal during this period.

- During the peak summer vacation season, North Cape (Nordkapp) and its approaches are very busy with traffic and visitors.

- If you're driving in Norway between September and March, main headlights must be kept on, even during daylight hours.

- Because of Norway's strict control on the sale of alcohol, you will have difficulty buying your own wines and spirits outside larger towns. Some rural areas are virtually "dry." Special state-controlled *Vinmonopolets* are the only liquor stores, and they are very expensive. Most restaurants are licensed, and you may be able to buy beer in some grocery stores.

- Norwegians are catching up on international fashion, but there is more interest in good outdoor clothing than fancy styles. For something truly Norwegian, such as vividly designed knitwear, try the Oslo sweater stores AS, at the SAS Scandinavian Hotel (✉ Tullins gate 5), or Thv. L. Holm AS (✉ H. Heyerdahls gate 1). Other worthwhile souvenirs include ceramics, pewter, wooden troll figures, enamel jewelry and woven wall hangings.

- You can eat very well in Norway, especially in Oslo and the larger towns. Norwegians are experts at buffet preparation, the ideal lunch experience, often with elaborate fish specialties. Smoked salmon and trout, and lamb dishes such as *fenalår* (smoked leg of lamb) are delicious. You can always try reindeer or elk for a real taste of mountain Norway.

- You will find that, as in Sweden and Finland, some things are about 30 percent more expensive in Norway than in the rest of Europe. Hotel accommodations and restaurants are more expensive. Some consumer items cost the European average, but overall prices are higher than elsewhere in Europe.

A troll statue greets visitors to Lillehammer

Oslo

OSLO

Oslo is a small, modern city of great character, but without the grandeur of many larger European capitals. Its spacious suburbs, forests and parks, all within sight and sound of the sea, give the city great vistas. It has outstanding art galleries and maritime museums, music venues, cafés, restaurants and fashionable boutiques. Yet there is always that inescapable feeling that wide-open spaces are not too far away.

Oslo Through History

Oslo's progress to capital city was checkered. It was significant only as a fjord settlement during the Viking age. In the 11th century, the Norwegian King Harald Hådråda chose to make Oslo a rival to the northern capital of Trondheim. Oslo's fortunes rose and fell thereafter, and in the 17th century, following a devastating fire and while under Danish rule, the settlement was rebuilt to the west of its original site and renamed Christiana, after the Danish King Christian IV.

Christiana became the capital of Norway in 1814. Throughout the 19th century the profitable timber trade and the economic advantages of union with Sweden increased its prosperity. By 1905, when Norway broke with the union, Christiana was a mature city economically and politically, and by 1925 the country was confident enough to reinstate the traditional name of Oslo.

The story of Oslo in the final decades of the 20th century was one of rapid modernization, as much on cultural as on social, political and economic terms. Wealth from the oil industry, the internationalization of Norwegian culture and a growing Norwegian self-confidence transformed the city into the cosmopolitan, vibrant capital of today.

The City's Stage

The most impressive way to arrive in Oslo is by sea. Viewed from the narrow neck of the Oslofjorden, the city's buildings are set against a backdrop of serene peninsulas and wooded hills. The hills are dotted with houses and accented by the great white pylon of the famous Holmenkollen ski jump.

Arrival by train, however, lands you at Jernbanetorget, the big open space in front of Oslo's central railroad station. This is not the most attractive part of the city, but a short walk along Karl Johans gate takes you quickly to Oslo Cathedral (Oslo Domkirke) and the busy open space of Stortorvet, with its colorful flower market.

A few steps farther on is the Parliament (Stortinget). Before it lies the open space of Eidsvollplass, the busy city center, alive with action and

The hub of the city; try Karl Johans gate for shopping, relaxing and eating out entertainment in summer, its pond a skating rink in winter.

To the northwest of Eidsvollplass is the neoclassical National Theater, guarded by statues of Norwegian dramatists Bjørnstjerne Bjørnson and Henrik Ibsen. Farther northwest is tree-lined Slottsparken, which encompasses the unfenced and accessible Royal Park and the Royal Palace within its bounds.

To the south of the National Theater, down busy Olav Vs gate and Roald Amundsen gate, lies the City Hall (Rådhuset) and the open space of Radhusplassen. Adjoining this square is the Rådhus Pier and the local ferryboat dock on Pipervika inlet. Northwest on nearby Vestbaneplassen, located in the old railroad station building, are the Norwegian information center and the main tourist information office in Oslo.

Exploring Oslo

Central Oslo is easily explored on foot, but you should become familiar with the transportation system so you can take one of the many day trips that are within easy reach. Public transportation is very efficient and easily understood; travel on city trams is a relaxing experience in itself. Visit the outlying Bygdøy peninsula, with its clutch of outstanding museums, or Frogner Park and the Vigeland Sculpture Park.

Oslo's main street, Karl Johans gate, is full of stores of all kinds, including David Andersen AS at No. 20, Scandinavia's largest jewelry store. The Paléet shopping mall has its mix of fashion boutiques and restaurants. Stop for coffee and fruit-speckled pastries at the famous Grand Café at No. 31, one of Henrik Ibsen's haunts.

A short distance north of the Royal Palace is the busy shopping street of Hegdehaugsveien and its continuation, Bogstadveien. Down at the harbor, on the western side of Pipervika inlet and beyond the tourist information center, is Aker Brygge, a modern complex with numerous stores, restaurants, cafés and entertainment venues. The area's attractive waterside setting all adds to the character.

Eating out in Oslo offers a remarkable choice of local and international cuisine. Try traditional restaurants such as Restaurant Blom (see page 563) on Karl Johans gate, where you can enjoy seasoned or smoked Norwegian specialties. Feast on excellent music too, in the Konserthus on Munkedamsveien, to the west of Aker Brygge.

The Oslo experience is a relaxed one, because of the compactness of the city center and because of the ease with which you can reach the outlying attractions and surrounding countryside. The openness of the city is reflected in its people, who are brisk but friendly in their attitude. English is a second language, especially to younger Norwegians, and you are

Nobel Peace Prize

The Nobel Prize awards for physics, chemistry, medicine and literature are judged and presented in Stockholm, but the Peace Prize is presented in the Great Hall of Oslo University. The awards were founded at the end of the 19th century by Swedish arms manufacturer Alfred Nobel. Some say that Nobel insisted Norway should have the honor of presenting the Peace Prize, because the union between Norway and Sweden was unraveling and Nobel felt that his gesture would avert conflict between the countries. The union between Norway and Sweden was eventually dissolved peacefully.

never far away from advice and guidance to help you make the most of your stay.

ESSENTIAL INFORMATION

TOURIST INFORMATION
• Norway Information Centre, Vestbaneplassen ☎ 22 83 00 50
• Oslo Sentralstasjon , Jernbanetorget 2 ☎ 81 50 08 88

is at Stortinget Station. Taxis are available by calling Central Taxis (☎ 22 38 80 90). For general information on transportation in the city contact Trafikanten, near Oslo Sentralstasjon (☎ 22 17 70 30).

URBAN TRANSPORTATION
Oslo's main railroad station is Sentralstasjon (Central Station), known as Oslo S; it has modern facilities and is only a few minutes from the city center. For local trains contact Trafikanten (☎ 22 17 70 30). For other services call ☎ 81 50 08 88. Oslo has an efficient bus and tram network. The bus terminal is next to Oslo Sentralstasjon. The city has a subway system, called the T-Bane, with five lines identified by a "T" sign. Its main junction

AIRPORT INFORMATION
Oslo Airport is located at Gardermoen, 31 miles southwest of the city. An airport express train, Gardermobanen, runs between the airport and Oslo S (Central Station) four times an hour; the trip takes 35 minutes. Regular train services also stop at the airport. Airport buses run between the airport and Oslo Bussterminal, located alongside Central Station. Agents for Oslo Airport are Braathens (☎ 67 59 70 00) and SAS (☎ 81 00 33 00).

CLIMATE – average highs and lows for the month

JAN.	FEB.	MAR.	APR.	MAY	JUN.	JUL.	AUG.	SEP.	OCT.	NOV.	DEC.
0°C	0°C	4°C	9°C	16°C	19°C	22°C	20°C	16°C	9°C	4°C	0°C
32°F	32°F	39°F	48°F	61°F	66°F	72°F	68°F	61°F	48°F	39°F	32°F
-7°C	-7°C	-3°C	1°C	7°C	10°C	12°C	12°C	7°C	3°C	-2°C	-5°C
19°F	19°F	27°F	34°F	45°F	50°F	54°F	54°F	45°F	37°F	28°F	23°F

Oslo

CITY SIGHTS

Key to symbols

➕ map coordinates refer to the Oslo map on page 365; sights below are highlighted in yellow on the map.

⊠ address or location ☎ telephone number

⊙ opening times 🚌 nearest bus or tram route

Ⓜ nearest subway 🍴 restaurant on site or nearby

🎟 admission charge: $$$ more than KR50, $$ KR15-50, $ less than KR15

AKERSHUS SLOTT

Slott ➕ B1 ⊠ Oslo Mil./Akershus ☎ 22 41 25 21, ⊙ Variable hours from mid-Apr. through Oct. 🍴 Engebret Café, see page 563 🚌 60; tram 10, 15 🎟 $

Festning ⊠ Oslo Mil./Akershus ☎ 23 09 39 17 ⊙ Outdoor area: daily 6 a.m.–9 p.m. 🍴 Engebret Café, see page 563 🚌 60; tram 10, 15 🎟 Free

Museet ⊠ Oslo Mil./Akershus ☎ 23 09 31 38 ⊙ Mon.–Sat. 10–5, Sun. 11–5, mid–Jun. to Oct. 31; Mon.–Sat. 10–4, Sun. 11–4, mid-Apr. to mid–Jun.; Mon.–Fri. 10–3, Sat.–Sun. 11–4, rest of year. 🍴 Engebret Café, see page 563 🚌 60; tram 10, 15 🎟 $

Akershus Slott (Akershus Castle) stands on a rocky height on the eastern side of the harbor inlet of Pipervika. It was founded in 1299 as a royal residence, but by the end of the 17th century it had been transformed into the powerful Festning (Fortress) by the addition of ramparts. There are guided tours of the fortress and of the castle's halls and subterranean passages. The Hjemme-frontmuseum Norges (Norway's Resistance Museum) at the fortress is a compelling record of Norway's experiences in World War II, when the Nazi occupation headquarters were located at Akershus.

FRAMMUSEET

➕ A1 ⊠ Bygdøynes ☎ 22 43 83 70 ⊙ Mon.–Fri. 11–2:45, Sat.–Sun. 11–3:45, Jan.–Feb; daily 11–3:45, Mar.–Apr.; daily 10–4:45, May 1 to mid-May; daily 9–5:45, mid-May to mid–Jun.; daily 9–6:45, mid-Jun. to Aug. 31; daily 10–4:45, in Sep.; daily 10–3:45, in Oct.; Mon.–Fri. 11–2:45, Sat.–Sun. 11–3:45, Nov.–Dec. 🚌 30 ⛴ Bygdøynes Boat 91, Rådhus Pier (May–Sep.) 🎟 $$

The centerpiece of the Frammuseet (Polar Ship *Fram* Museum) is the preserved Arctic exploration vessel *Fram*, with a bow like a battering ram and a hull as solid as a castle wall. The *Fram* was built in 1892 and was used by Norwegian explorers Fridtjof Nansen, Otto Svedrup and Roald Amundsen in polar expeditions. Go aboard the *Fram* to see its sturdiness and get a sense of the tough, determined life that its crew led.

KON-TIKI MUSEET

➕ A1 ⊠ Bygdøynesveien 36 ☎ 22 43 80 50 ⊙ Daily 9:30–5:45, Jun.–Aug.;10:30–5, Apr.–May and in Sep.; 10:30–4, rest of year 🚌 30 ⛴ Bygdøynes Boat 91, Rådhus Pier (May–Sep.) 🎟 $$

The Kon-Tiki museet (Kon-Tikki Museum) is a colorful celebration of Thor Heyerdahl's voyages. It complements the general maritime themes of the adjacent *Fram* Museum and the Norwegian Maritime Museum. Heyerdahl's ethos of adventure, linked to environmentalism and international cooperation, is vividly expressed. The original *Kon-Tiki* balsa wood raft of his 1947 Pacific crossing and the papyrus vessel *Ra II* of his 1970 Atlantic crossing both express the Norwegian genius for maritime exploration.

MUNCH-MUSEET

➕ C2 ⊠ Tøyengata 53 ☎ 22 67 37 74 ⊙ Daily 10–6, Jun. to mid-Sep.; Tue.–Sat. 10–4 (also Thu. and Sun. 4–6), rest of year 🍴 Museum café Ⓜ T-Bane 1, 2, 3, 4, 5 to Tøyen 🚌 20 🎟 $$$

The Munch-museet (Munch Museum) is a fitting celebration of Norway's most famous artist. Munch's *The Scream*, on display at the National Gallery, is a world-famous cultural icon, but the artist's huge body of work merits even greater attention. The Munch Museum provides an insight into the complex personality of this intense and compelling artist.

NASJONALGALLERIET

➕ B2 ⊠ Universitetsgaten 13 ☎ 22 20 04 04 ⊙ Mon. and Wed.–Fri. 10–6 (also Thu. 6–8), Sat. 10–4, Sun. 11–4 🍴 Grand Café, see page 563

Gustav Vigeland's Monolith at Frogner Park

🚋 Tram 11, 17, 18 to Tullinløkka, tram 12, 13, 19 to Nationaltheatret; buses to Nationaltheatret
🚇 Nationaltheatret ⧉ Free
Oslo's Nasjonalgalleriet (National Gallery) is primarily a Norwegian art experience. The gallery has works by painters such as Georges Braque and Pablo Picasso, but its main collection is of work by Norwegian masters such as Christian Krohg, Johan Christian Dahl, Thomas Fearnley and Edvard Munch. Highlights include Krohg's lively portrait *Oda Krohg, the Painter*, a charming rendition of artist Oda Krohg in vivid red and blue clothes. The romantic Fjordland paintings of Johan Christian Dahl and Thomas Fearnley will encourage you to visit the fjords. Look on the top floor for Ernst Josephson's *The Spanish Blacksmiths*. The room devoted to Munch shows some classic masterpieces, including the iconic *The Scream*, the powerful *Dance of Life*, the sensual *Day After* and the ravishing *Madonna*.

NORSK FOLKEMUSEUM

✚ A1 ✉ Museumsveien 10 ☎ 22 12 36 66
🕐 Daily 10–6, mid–Jun. through Aug. 31 and Sep. 15 through Oct. 31; daily 10–5, mid–May to mid–Jun. and Sep. 1–14; daily 11–3 (also Sun. 3–4), rest of year
🍴 Museum café 🚌 30 ⛴ Bygdøynes Boat 91, Rådhus Pier (May–Sep.) 💲 $$

The Norsk Folkemuseum (Norwegian Folk Museum) gives an excellent view of Norway's folk culture and traditional life. It is located at the heart of the Bygdøy peninsula and includes a large parklike area with more than 150 traditional buildings and reconstructed village streets of the 19th century. The main buildings have displays of traditional crafts, folk costumes and haunting reconstructions of rural interiors. There is a significant exhibition on the culture of the Sami, the indigenous people of northern Scandinavia. Children will be delighted by the toy exhibition.

NORSK SJØFARTSMUSEUM

✚ A1 ✉ Bygdøynes Pier ☎ 22 43 82 40 🕐 Daily 10–7, mid–May through Sep. 30; 10:30–4 (also Tue. and Thu. 4–7), rest of year 🍴 Museum café 🚌 30 ⛴ Bygdøynes Boat 91, Rådhus Pier (May–Sep.) 💲 $$

The Norsk Sjøfartsmuseum (Norwegian Maritime Museum) stands on the tip of the Bygdøy peninsula, overlooking the waters of the Oslofjorden. In the main hall, Christian Krogh's great marine painting, *Leiv Eriksson's Discovery of America*, sets the scene for the numerous exhibits on shipping and the sea. The basement theater shows a video on Norway's maritime history. Look on the main floor for the escape boat secretly made from rough planking by Norwegian sailors while they were imprisoned aboard their ships in West Africa by the Germans during World War II.

VIGELANDSPARKEN

✚ A2 ✉ Kirkeveien ☎ 22 44 11 36 🕐 Open access 🚌 20; tram 12, 15 ⧉ Free
Vigelandsparken (Vigeland's Park) is a memorial to Norwegian sculptor Gustav Vigeland. It is also a celebration of the human body. This is celebratory nudity without a hint of prurience. The centerpiece is the famous Monoliten (Monolith), a tall granite column composed of writhing human figures struggling upward. The park lies within the larger Frogner Park, a green area within easy reach of central Oslo.

FJORD AND MOUNTAIN LINE

Most visitors to Norway go to the western fjords at some time during their stay. Even if your time is limited you can still make the famous "Norway in a Nutshell" journey by train, bus and boat. The trip takes you from Oslo to the Sognefjord via the well-known Flåm mountain railroad. Some people make the roundtrip from Oslo in a day, but it is a very long day indeed. An alternative is to take an early train from Oslo to Bergen, from where you can catch the fast coastal ferry into the Sognefjord.

Try to stay in Bergen, a delightful city amid spectacular surroundings. The ferry from Bergen to the Sognefjord is an experience in itself. The boat races under high bridges, skims past scores of islands and rugged peninsulas, and slows only at narrow channels with mere feet to spare. You travel deeper and deeper into the mighty Sognefjord to Balestrand, a village at a beautiful part of the fjord. Here fruit trees flourish in the fjordland summer, yet glaciers lie only a few miles into the high mountains behind. It is possible to stay overnight here.

From Balestrand, a final boat trip takes you to the very end of Songefjord, the high cliffs crowding ever closer. Flåm (pronounced Flum) is not a traditional fjord village; its purpose is to cater to bus and car parking, and the crowds who arrive by ferry and cruise ship. The famous Flåm to Myrdal railroad is the reason for it all. The stylish train, with its comfortable quarters, takes 50 minutes to travel along the valley floor behind Flåm. It climbs steadily through spectacular scenery to the head of the valley, where the track rises through a series of S-bends, protected in places by snow shelters. Finally, the train reaches the plateau and the Myrdal railroad station, where you connect with the Oslo train for the last leg of one of the world's great round-trips.

You can arrange this tour yourself, or ask at the tourist information center for details regarding organized tours.

Within easy reach of Bergen, the spectacular Hardangerfjord, looking towards the Folgefonn glacier

PORTUGAL

"T HERE is something very extraordinary in the nature of the people of the Peninsula, the most loyal and best-disposed... "

The Duke of Wellington, in an early 19th-century dispatch

Opposite: Spectacular display of color at the fishing village of Sesimbra, south of Lisbon

PORTUGAL

Portugal, lying on the western edge of the Continent and overshadowed by Spain, its powerful neighbor to the east, is sometimes considered the poor relation of southwestern Europe. Political turmoil and poverty have long hindered development, but after joining the European Union in 1986, billions of dollars have poured into the country, helping to modernize its economy.

The Land

For travelers who knew Portugal 20 years ago, some things have changed beyond recognition; others remain stubbornly the same. In many ways Portugal is still old-fashioned and underdeveloped, a real bonus for visitors seeking something a little different from mainstream European travel. The country is small, diverse and beautiful. Stretching 350 miles from north to south, it is packed with mountains, plateaus, river valleys, flat dry plains, rolling forested hills and a truly beautiful coastline. Portugal

MORE TOP DESTINATIONS IN PORTUGAL

- Alcobaça B3 ● Batalha B3
- Braga B4 ● Bragança C4
- Castelo de Vide C3 ● Chaves C4
- Coimbra B3 ● Douro B4
- Évora B2 ● Fátima B3
- Guimarães B4 ● Monsanto C3
- Óbidos B3 ● Parque Nacional da Peneda-Gerês B4 ● Sagres B1
- Serra de Monchique B1
- Silves B1 ● Tomar B3
- Torres Vedras A2

borders the Atlantic, and weather conditions can range from hot and sunny to stormy and wet. In the northern Douro region, winter temperatures drop well below freezing; in summer, it is not uncommon for the thermometer to top 100 degrees.

The Algarve, a popular vacation area on the southern coast that's often visited by northern Europeans, enjoys a Mediterranean climate, and the vegetation is subtropical. On the whole, summers are warm and dry, winters mild and wet, although it can be cold in the mountains. Portugal's highest mountain is Torre, in the Serra da Estrela, which rises above 6,500 feet. The Tagus river (Tejo) roughly divides the country in half. The Tagus and two other important rivers, the Douro and the Guadiana, rise in Spain, and Portugal must share their waters with its bigger neighbor, a factor leading increasingly to difficulties in supply and environmental problems.

Portuguese Empire

It's easy to forget that Portugal was once at the head of a powerful empire. From the early 15th century, Portuguese explorers pushed far into the unknown, challenging the traditional view that the world ended somewhere west of Gibraltar. Madeira and the Azores were the first to be discovered, and these islands remain part of Portugal. Portuguese ships rounded the Cape of Good Hope in 1488, and in 1497 Vasco da Gama reached Calicut, India. By 1560, Portugal had claimed Brazil and had an empire stretching east as far as Japan, with missionary and trading posts in Africa, India, Malaysia, Macao and Timor.

Despite strong rivalry between Portugal and Spain over discoveries in the Americas, the 16th century was a Golden Age, with spices, slaves and gold making Portugal hugely rich. But the voyages and maintenance of an overseas empire were extremely costly, and the home economy was worsening. By 1580, Philip II of Spain had claimed the throne, becoming Philip I of Portugal the following year. Within 100

years, many of the overseas possessions had fallen to the English and Dutch.

The legacy of the empire still exists, however. Portugal extricated itself from Africa in the 1970s, when Angola, Mozambique and Guinea became independent; East Timor in Indonesia

PORTUGAL

N

ATLANTIC

OCEAN

Valença do Minho
Monção
Parque Nacional de Peneda-Gerês
Serra do
Cávado Gerês
Chaves
Bragança
▲1321m

Viana do Castelo
Lima
Barcelos
Braga
Tâmega
Serra da Nogueira
Miranda do Douro
Ofir
Guimarães
Póvoa de Varzim
Douro

Matosinhos
Paredes
Amarante
Vila Real
Sabor
Torre de Moncorvo

PORTO
Douro
Lamego
Espinho

Serra Gralheira

Ria d'Aveiro
Vouga
Trancoso
Côa
Aveiro
Viseu
Pinhel
Vilar Formoso
Agueda
Mondego
Guarda
Mira
Serra da Estrela
▲1993m
Bucaco
Coimbra
Covilhã
Figueira da Foz
Zêzere
Monsanto
Conimbriga
Pampilhosa da Serra
Penela
Segura
Pombal
Serta
Castelo Branco
Marinha Grande
Leiria
Tejo
Batalha
Fátima
Tomar
Nazaré
Abrantes
Caldas da Rainha
Alcobaça
Castelo de Vide
Peniche
Óbidos
Alpahão
Marvão
Cabo Carvoeiro
Tejo
Santarém
Portalegre
SPAIN

Torres Vedras
Montargil
Ericeira
Mafra
Vila Franca de Xira
Monforte
Queluz
Elvas
Sintra
Vimieiro
Cabo da Roca
LISBON
Montemoro-Novo
Estremoz
Cascais
Estoril
Barreiro
Guadiana
Bacalhoa
Setúbal
Évora
Sesimbra
Sado
Monsaraz
Costa da Caparica
Alcácer do Sal
Mourão
Baía de Setúbal
Vidigueira
Grândola
Moura
Santiago do Cacém
Sines
Beja
Serpa
Cabo de Sines
Cercal
Aljustral
Castro Verde
Mértola
Odemira
Mira
Ourique
Almodôvar
Serra de Monchique
Aljezur
Monchique
Barranco do Velho
Guadiana
Alfambras
902m
Silves
Lagos
Portimão
Albufeira
Vila Real de Santo António
Sagres
Vale do Lobo
Tavira
Cabo de San Vicente
Faro
Olhão
Golfo de Cádiz
Cabo de Santa Maria

0 20 40 60 80 100 km
0 20 40 60 miles

Porto Santo
Ilha da Madeira
Machico
Funchal
Ilhas Desertas

ATLANTIC OCEAN

A   B   C

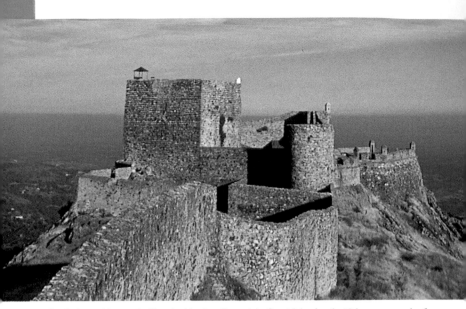

Perched on a ridge overlooking the Altenjo valley and the Spanish border, the 13th-century castle of Marvao dominates the surrounding landscape

was relinquished at the same time. Today there are buildings, churches and monuments wherever the Portuguese held power, but language became the country's most important legacy. Portuguese is the seventh most widely spoken language in the world. Brazil retains strong ties with Portugal and, unlike many other former colonies, there is genuine respect between the two countries.

The People

Geographical isolation from most of Europe has kept Portuguese bloodlines pure, and you'll notice a definite racial type – most people are short, with dark eyes, skin and hair. They are conservative people who are generally courteous and respectful. Northerners, with a harsher climate and historically poorer living conditions, are less easygoing than people in the south, and they tend to be more religious. The Catholic church continues to hold great sway everywhere. Most of the

population still lives in rural areas, although there was a large urban increase in the 1970s, when people came home from former African colonies following independence. In Lisbon in particular, many Afro-Portuguese have integrated into Portuguese life; there's a good level of interracial harmony.

The country still has one of Europe's highest emigration rates, with around 3 million people living and working abroad. With few natural resources, many northerners are forced to seek work overseas; you can see the results of their labors in the new houses and cars found in even the poorest villages.

Society and Language

Being polite and friendly will smooth your path as you travel through Portugal. The Portuguese tend to be welcoming and unhurried, so be prepared for things to take a long time. There are traditional ideas and attitudes toward women, and the farther away from major towns you travel the more obvious this becomes. It's considered disrespectful to wear skimpy clothing, and it is customary to speak formally and politely until you get to know the people you are talking to.

One of the major hurdles in getting to know the Portuguese is the language barrier. Don't try your Spanish in Portugal. Despite – or because of – proximity to Spain, the Portuguese don't appreciate being addressed in Spanish. However, if you can read Spanish you'll have no problem reading Portuguese. It's a romance language with Latin roots, similar to Spanish and Italian. Pronunciation is a different matter altogether however, and spoken Portuguese, with its sibilants, nasal vowels and guttural consonants, reminds some people of Russian and Slavic languages.

The narrow streets of Porto are clusterd majestically on a hillside looking down over the Douro river

The Portuguese are very aware that they speak a difficult language and are excellent linguists; you'll find English spoken in major tourist areas, although rarely in the deep countryside. Do try and tackle one or two words; your efforts will be appreciated and faces will light up when you try to communicate.

Changing Portugal

Since the watershed year of 1986, huge changes have occurred in Portugal. From being one of the poorest nations in Europe, the country now has one of the highest economic growth rates, while unemployment has plummeted. Despite a recession in the early 1990s, things continue to look good for the country as the economy continues to expand. But this has been achieved at the cost of a widening gap between the rich and poor, noticeable wherever you travel. Education levels are low, with an embarrassing percentage of the population having few if any literacy skills. Agriculture still lags far behind the rest of Europe, and a high proportion of national earnings comes from money earned overseas or spent by tourists within Portugal.

For visitors, the blend of old and new is alluring and adds an extra dimension to the travel experience. Recent investment has improved the infrastructure to the visitor's benefit, while the uneven wealth distribution ensures that a rustic way of life is still evident throughout the country.

TIMELINE

1000 BC to AD 400	Occupation by Phoenicians, Carthaginians, Iberians, Celts, Romans and Visigoths.
AD 713	Moors control most of the country and remain in power for 400 years.
1179	Pope recognizes Kingdom of Portugal.
1255	Afonso III makes Lisbon capital of Portugal.
1480–1500s	Age of Discovery.
1488	Bartolomeu Dias rounds Cape of Good Hope.
1580	End of Golden Age with invasion by Philip II of Spain, who declares himself Philip I of Portugal.
1668	Treaty of Lisbon recognizes Portuguese independence.
1755	Lisbon earthquake.
1910	Portuguese monarchy overthrown and replaced by republic.
1916–18	Portugal joins Allies in World War I, an economically disastrous move.
1933	*Estado Novo* (New State) established.
1939–45	Portugal neutral throughout World War II.
1950–70	Rapid industrial growth.
1960s	Goa occupied by India; local nationalist uprisings in Angola, Guinea and Mozambique.
1976	New constitution drawn up after the fall of the *Estado Novo* in 1974.
1986	Portugal admitted to European Union; start of period of huge economic growth and social reform.
1999	Portugal joins European Monetary System.

PRINCE HENRY THE NAVIGATOR

The impetus for the great Portuguese "Age of Discovery" of the late 15th century came from the son of João I, Prince Henry, who was born in 1394. He can be credited with transforming Portugal into a great maritime power whose success was based on a scientific approach to exploration, navigation and cartography. At his base in the Algarve, Henry collected accomplished shipbuilders, sailors, instrument makers and astronomers, encouraging them to prepare for long voyages into the unknown. The highly successful caravel was designed, a speedy ship that made the great voyages possible. Motivated by religion as well as commerce, Henry's ships sailed ever farther south, rounding Cape Bojador in West Africa, then thought to be the end of the world, in 1434. By Henry's death in 1460 the Portuguese had reached Sierra Leone, and the known world had become a bigger place.

SURVIVAL GUIDE

- The Portuguese are committed wine drinkers. Generally, when you order house wine in restaurants you'll get something highly acceptable, even if it appears in an earthenware jug.
- Water everywhere is safe to drink, although sometimes less than delicious. Avoid tap water in the Algarve during the summer and drink bottled water instead, to be on the safe side.
- The modest Portuguese are shocked by scanty clothes worn anywhere except at the beach. If you are wearing a sleeveless top, take along a scarf to wrap around your shoulders as needed.
- Portuguese drivers are among Europe's worst, and the country also has the Continent's highest accident rate.
- Portugal's telephone system is improving, but is still not up to the standards of other European countries. If you call from your hotel room, you'll pay a high surcharge. Use an on-street "Credifone," which accepts plastic phone cards available from street kiosks.
- Be prepared for Portugal to be different in many ways from its neighbors, particularly if you've already visited Spain. Despite their proximity, the two countries are very different.
- Public restrooms are few and far between, but it's acceptable – even if you're not a customer – to ask to use hotel or restaurant facilities. Men's toilets are marked "H" and women's are marked "S."
- Try not to let grime and shabbiness in Portuguese cities affect you; look for the positive qualities, such as daily clean sheets in many hotels.

- Don't be surprised by the sometimes startling amount of garbage in public places. In Portuguese bars and cafés, it's acceptable to throw paper wrappings on the floor.
- You probably won't find luxury accommodations or excellent service if you're away from the major tourist centers. Remember that Portugal is still a poor country.
- Portuguese food can be monotonous, and some dishes are unappealing to foreigners. If you are not feeling adventurous, stick to grilled fish and chicken.
- Leave small change in a bar; otherwise about 10 percent is an adequate tip.
- *Pousadas* are by far the nicest places to stay when traveling in Portugal. These are government-run, deluxe hotels located in historic or beautiful places such as former monasteries, palaces and castles. Advance booking is recommended.

Strong ties with Brazil – a restaurant entrance in Rua Garret, Lisbon

LISBON

Lisbon (Lisboa) is a beguiling city. It has a great past and a promising future. It may easily strike the visitor as old-fashioned and crumbling – but these elements are also an essential part of its charm. Look for the positive: the port city's vigor and life; its great colonial past; the atmospheric old trams; and the evocative sights and scents – laundry flapping in the wind, shoeshine men hawking their trade, the smell of roasting coffee and chestnuts. Most sights of interest are within walking distance of downtown, with the exception of the glorious attractions of suburban Belém, an easy bus or tram ride away.

Lisbon Flavors and *Bacalhau*

Lisbon has a wide range of restaurants at every price level, with the emphasis on traditional Portuguese cooking, although fast-food outlets are easy to find as well. Breakfast consists of small cakes and pastries, but hotels can usually prepare meals tailored to foreign tastes. Lunch is more substantial than in other European cities.

Heavy soups are popular, salads are surprisingly hard to find, and fresh fruit juice virtually non-existent. Lisbon inhabitants eat a lot of fish and seafood, including *bacalhau* (a dried, salted codfish), and the warming winter stews can be good.

You may be surprised at the number of pastry and cake shops; the Portuguese are notoriously sweet-toothed, and Lisbon has many old-fashioned shops selling traditional specialties like the delicious *pastéis de Belém* (pastries filled with custard). Portugal makes good red and white wine, national and foreign beers are everywhere, and all the usual spirits and aperitifs are available.

Souvenirs from Lisbon

Shopping is great fun in Lisbon, and there are many stores selling lovely Portuguese crafts. The area known as the Chiado, in downtown Lisbon, is the

Lisbon

smartest shopping district, with streets lined with numerous classy clothing and jewelry boutiques.

Carpets from the village of Arraiolos are a superb buy, as is the exquisite porcelain manufactured by Vista Alegre. Linen and cotton sheets and tablecloths are another Portuguese specialty. You can even have the lovely glazed tiles, *azulejos,* made to order, or

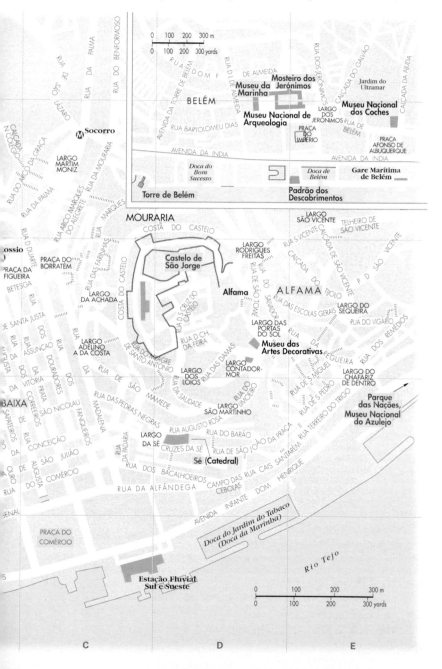

Lisbon

track down something made from cork, one of Portugal's biggest exports.

Film, Music and *Fado*

As befits its capital status, Lisbon offers a variety of music, theater and ballet. Moviegoing is a particular pleasure, as films are all shown in their original language with subtitles, rather than dubbed, so you can catch the latest releases from home.

Fado, a unique style of Portuguese music, is heard at its best in Lisbon and should at least be experienced. This melancholy and passionate music is traditionally sung by a woman, accompanied by guitar. Its origins lie deep in history, a mix of Moorish and African elements, and has been described as a kind of light operetta. The best place to hear it is at one of the *fado* houses in the Upper Town (Bairro Alto, see page 381), or in the Alfama district.

The Lisbon Earthquake

On All Saints Day (November 1) 1755, the Lisbon earthquake struck. Churches were packed for this major feast day, and thousands of lighted candles toppled during the tremors, starting fires that were as destructive as the quake itself. A massive tidal wave followed, swallowing Lisbon's fleet and flooding the already-destroyed lower city.

During the aftermath, corpses were sent to sea on barges and sunk in order to avert the plague. Hospitals opened, prices were fixed and a tax was levied to cover re-building costs, including the renovation of the lower city, today known as the Baixa district. Although Lisbon largely recovered, 1755 marked the end of its role as Europe's leading port city.

ESSENTIAL INFORMATION

TOURIST INFORMATION
• Palacio Foz, Praca dos Restauradores ☎ 01 343 3672
• Portela Airport ☎ 01 849 4323

URBAN TRANSPORTATION
There's a wide choice of transportation in Lisbon; a fairly limited, although useful, subway system, buses, trams, funiculars and even ferries. Subway stations are marked with "M" on the city map. For visitors, the *Passe Turístico* (Tourist Pass) gives three, four or seven days of unlimited travel on all forms of public transportation, except ferries. It's available from the kiosk in the square Praça da Figueira and the Restauradores subway station. Otherwise you can buy bus and tram tickets when boarding, and subway tickets from a machine or office at the subway station. The trams

and funiculars are one of Lisbon's glories, so make a point of traveling on them; the modern tram 15 is a particularly useful line. Ferry tickets are available from offices at the ferry stations; again, a ferry trip is recommended as part of your sightseeing. Taxis are beige, or occasionally green and black, and are inexpensive and efficient. There are taxi stands on the open squares of the Rossio and the Praça da Figueira, or you can call a cab (☎ 01 815 5061 or 01 793 2756). There's an extra charge for luggage carried in the trunk.

AIRPORT INFORMATION
Portela Airport (☎ 01 840 8044, or 01 849 0644 for flight information) is about 4 miles (a 20-minute drive) north of the downtown area. The Aero-Bus shuttle service leaves every 20 minutes daily 7 a.m.–9 p.m. from outside the terminal.

CLIMATE – average highs and lows for the month

JAN.	FEB.	MAR.	APR.	MAY	JUN.	JUL.	AUG.	SEP.	OCT.	NOV.	DEC.
13°C	15°C	17°C	19°C	21°C	25°C	28°C	29°C	27°C	21°C	18°C	14°C
55°F	59°F	63°F	66°F	70°F	77°F	82°F	84°F	81°F	70°F	64°F	57°F
8°C	9°C	10°C	12°C	12°C	15°C	18°C	18°C	17°C	14°C	10°C	9°C
46°F	48°F	50°F	54°F	54°F	59°F	64°F	64°F	63°F	57°F	50°F	48°F

CITY SIGHTS

Key to symbols

✚ map coordinates refer to the Lisbon map on page 378–379; sights below are highlighted in yellow on the map.

⊠ address or location ☎ telephone number

⊙ opening times 🚍 nearest bus or tram route

⛴ nearest ferry 🚇 nearest subway

🍴 restaurant on site or nearby 💲 admission charge: $$$ more than 500Esc, $$ 250Esc to 500Esc, $ less than 250Esc

BAIRRO ALTO

✚ A3 ⊠ Area on slopes to west of Baixa
🚇 Restauradores 🚍 Tram 28

The Bairro Alto (Upper Town) is one of the five areas that constitute Lisbon's historic center. It was virtually untouched by the 1755 earthquake, and the atmospheric jumble of streets and squares tumble down steep slopes to the Baixa (the Lower Town) below. At night it's one of the city's liveliest quarters, where in *fado* houses you can hear melancholy and evocative Portuguese songs. The Elevador de Santa Justa, a wonderfully clanky funicular built in 1902, runs up the hill.

BAIXA AND ROSSIO

✚ B2–B3 ⊠ Praça Dom Pedro IV and streets between it and Praça do Comércio 🚇 Rossio
🚍 All services to Rossio and Praça do Comércio

Rossio Square, properly known as Praça Dom Pedro IV, and the grid of streets forming the Baixa district will repeatedly draw you back. The Teatro Nacional (National Theater) and a soaring column topped by a statue of Dom Pedro IV dominate the spacious Rossio, which is lined with stores and cafés. The square has an ancient history and was the scene of Inquisition burnings in the 16th century. Between Rossio and the waterfront lies Baixa, a perfect example of rational 18th-century planning, erected at the Marquês de Pombal's instigation after the 1755 earthquake. The orderly streets are lined with lovely old stores, gracious buildings and tiled façades.

CASTELO DE SÃO JORGE AND THE ALFAMA

✚ D3–E3 ⊠ Rua Costa do Castelo ⊙ Daily 9–7
🚍 37; tram 2 💲 Free

Visible from many parts of Lisbon, the Castelo de São Jorge (St. George's Castle) stands on the site of the earliest settlement. Fortified by the Romans, Visigoths and Moors, it was besieged in 1147 by Afonso Enriques and his Christian army and finally fell after 17 weeks – a turning point in the struggle to evict the Moors from Portugal. The Moorish battlements still stand, giving superb views over the rooftops to the river. Today, extensive restoration within

Shady cloisters of the 16th-century Jerónimos Monastery enclose formal gardens

the main structure has made a verdant, cool oasis, with terraces, pools and fountains. The Alfama district around the palace is worth exploring.

MOSTEIRO DOS JERÓNIMOS

🔂 See map inset ✉ Praça do Império ☎ 01 362 0034 🕒 Tue.–Sun. 10–5 🍴 São Jerónimo, see page 564 🚍 27, 28, 49, 51; tram 15 💰 $$

The stunning architectural ensemble of the Mosteiro dos Jerónimos (Jeronimos Monastery) stands on the site of an earlier chapel, visited by Portuguese explorers before their great voyages. Building began on the present church in 1502 to celebrate Vasco da Gama's successful voyage to the Indies. It took 50 years to complete, by which time various architectural fashions had come and gone. The church and adjoining cloisters are a glorious mix of Gothic, Renaissance and Manueline styles. Pause first at the great south door. Its intricate carving includes the figure of Henry the Navigator; the west door, equally splendid, features Manuel I, who originally started the construction. The soaring interior contains the simple tomb of Vasco da Gama, a contrast to the surrounding riot of stonework. The two-story cloisters are equally elaborately carved, a wonderful combination of delicacy and weighty strength.

MUSEU NACIONAL DO AZULEJO

🔂 Off the map ✉ Rua de madre de deus 4 ☎ 01 814 7747 🕒 Wed.–Sun. 10–6, Tue. 2–6 🍴 Café in museum 🚍 18, 42, 104, 105 💰 $$

Throughout Lisbon and Portugal, you'll notice the exquisite tiles, or *azulejos*, which adorn the walls of countless buildings. The Museo Nacional do Azulejo (National Tile Museum) traces the history of the painted glazed tile, which has been used in Portugal since the 15th century. You can see how the art developed from simple early tiles to complex, multicolored modern examples. Blue and white has predominated since Chinese porcelain arrived in Europe; the wonderful tiled view of Lisbon, made in 1738, is a fine example.

MUSEU CALOUSTE GULBENKIAN

🔂 Off the map ✉ Avenida de Berna ☎ 01 795 5247 🕒 Tue., Thu.–Fri. and Sun. 10–5, Wed. and Sat. 2–7:30, Jun.–Sep.; daily 10–5, rest of year. Closed holidays 🍴 Café in museum 🚇 S. Sebastião 🚍 16, 26, 31, 56 💰 $$

Portugal's greatest museum, the Museu Calouste Gulbenkian (Calouste Gulbenkian Museum) was financed by a bequest from the Armenian magnate, whose private collection makes up the bulk of the exhibits. It comprises two sections: European art and artifacts, and Oriental and ancient pieces. The museum is not vast, but everything it contains is of the highest quality. Most visitors are particularly enthralled by the Lalique jewelry and glass, distinctive art deco pieces displayed in a darkened room.

MUSEU DA MARINHA

🔂 See map inset ✉ Praça do Império ☎ 01 362 0019 🕒 Tue.–Sat. 10–6, Jul.–Sep.; 10–5, rest of year 🚍 27, 28, 49, 51; tram 15 💰 $

The Museu da Marinha (Maritime Museum), located at Belém, is one of the best of its kind in Europe, as befits this seafaring nation. It's a huge collection, with full-size boats and royal barges, paintings, uniforms and archaic navigational instruments. Most evocative, perhaps, is the polychrome wooden statue of the Archangel Raphael, said to have accompanied Vasco da Gama on his epic voyage to the Indies in 1497.

PADRÃO DOS DESCOBRIMENTOS

🔂 See map inset ✉ Avenida de Brasília ☎ 01 301 6228 🕒 Tue.–Sun. 9:30–5:30; closed holidays 🍴 São Jerónimo, see page 564 🚍 27, 28, 49; tram 15 💰 $

The eye-catching white mass of the Padrão dos Descobrimentos (Monument to the Discoveries) soars up from the water's edge at Belém, serving as a reminder of Portugal's great maritime past. It was erected in 1960 to mark the 500th anniversary of the death of Henry the Navigator, and has an angular front

Topiary gardens in the Italianate grounds of the Fronteira Palace, in north Lisbon

LISBON LIFE

Everyday life in Lisbon, a relatively small city, is far more relaxed than in other capitals. The day starts around 7:30, when commuters are on the move and children make their way to school. Trams, the subway and buses are all crowded. Some people travel to town on the ferries that criss-cross the Tagus. Many grab breakfast in a bar before work. Breakfast is usually tea or coffee, with one of the cloyingly sweet pastries so loved by the Portuguese.

Lunch in Lisbon is taken seriously, and many people eat a full meal rather than a snack, although they eat it fast, often standing at a bar counter. Workers also use the lunch hour to shop for food or browse in stores. At the end of the afternoon, commuters head home but will often re-emerge later to meet friends for a drink or more tea and cakes. Midweek evenings are often spent at home, although in summer the streets will be thronged for a few hours as people stroll and chat outside.

Weekends are a different matter; people head for the Upper Town to eat and drink before going to concerts, movies or the theater, while young Portuguese enjoy the old district's waterfront clubs.

Saturday and Sunday are popular shopping days when crowds flock to huge malls on the outskirts of the city, which stay open until late. Sundays, too, are high points for soccer fans, with the big matches attracting large crowds. Lisbon is blessed by its proximity to a beautiful coastline, and it's easy in summer to drive or catch a train to the coast for a day on the beach and dinner in an excellent fish restaurant. In high summer, an outing to the cool green countryside around Sintra (see page 385), some 15 miles away, is another weekend option.

Statue in the Praça Sao Roque

and curving form that represents a ship's prow and sails. Figures crowd the prow, led by Henry, who holds a ship. An elevator rises more than 435 feet to the top, offering panoramic views. Below, a mosaic map traces the Portuguese voyages of exploration.

PARQUE DAS NAÇÕES

✚ Off the map ⊠ Parque das Nações ⏰ Daily 10–6 🚇 Oriente 🚌 28, 81 💲 $$$

The Parque das Nações (Park of the Nations), the name given to the site occupied by Expo '98, is now used for trade fairs and exhibitions. Impressive buildings, moorings, landscaped gardens, street cafés and restaurants front the Tagus. From the water rises the Pavilhão dos Oceanos (Ocean Pavilion), a state-of-the-art aquarium, which was the focal point of the 1998 fair. Europe's largest aquarium features a vast central tank, surrounded by four others representing the main oceans. Marine mammals and seabirds thrive, as well as fish, underwater creatures and vegetation, making this one of Lisbon's most impressive new attractions.

Belém Tower, rising beside the Tagus, an enduring symbol of Portugal's maritime past

PRAÇA DO COMÉRCIO

✚ C1 ⊠ Praça do Comércio 🚇 Rossio 🚌 All buses to Praça do Comércio; tram 15 ⛴ Terreiro do Paço for ferries to Cacilhas

One side of the spacious Praça do Comércio (Comercio Square) opens on the water, emphasizing its original purpose as an imposing gateway to the city from the sea. To experience its original perspective, take the five-minute ferry trip from nearby Terreiro do Paço across the Tagus to the suburb of Cacilhas. The vista of the square and the triumphal arch leading to the streets of the Baixa opens up to buildings, churches and monuments; an excellent chance to get a feel for the city's past.

SÉ

✚ D2 ⊠ Largo da Sé ☎ 01 886 6752 ⏰ Daily 9–noon and 2–6 🚇 Rossio 🚌 37; tram 12

Construction of the Sé (Cathedral) started in 1150, soon after the expulsion of the Moors. It was the city's first church, a solid and harmonious Romanesque edifice. Its two massive towers are a city landmark. It largely escaped damage in the 1755 earthquake, making it a superb symbol of Lisbon's history. Inside, be sure to see the font where Lisbon-born St. Anthony of Padua was baptized.

TORRE DE BELÉM

✚ See map inset ⊠ Avenida de Brasília ☎ 01 362 0034 ⏰ Tue.–Sun. 10–5; closed holidays 🍴 São Jerónimo, see page 564 🚌 Tram 15 💲 $$

In the nearby suburb of Belém, the Torre de Belém (Belém Tower) rises beside the Tagus. This exquisite honey-colored stone tower, a triumph of Renaissance and Manueline design, is a symbol of Portugal's maritime past. Built between 1515 and 1520, it was designed by Francisco de Arruda, a Portuguese architect whose earlier Moroccan travels influenced his style. His work shows delightful Moorish elements – little domes topping the battlements, corner towers, and arcaded windows and loggias. Built as a bastion against pirate attack, it later served as a prison.

SINTRA

By far the most popular day trip from Lisbon is to beautiful Sintra, a small town packed with delights, set in lush and mountainous country some 15 miles northwest of Lisbon. Once there, the attractions are scattered over a wide area, so unless you have plenty of time, it makes sense to take a tour or rent a car from the city. As a bonus, most tour operators include a detour to Cabo da Roca, the Continent's westernmost point.

Palaces

For more than 500 years Sintra was the summer resort of Portuguese kings – a legacy that is apparent in the town's two astounding palaces. The National Palace (Palácio Nacional) was first built by João I in the 15th century and remained in use until the end of the late 1800s.

Ornate stonework at Sintra's National Palace

Architecturally imposing, it's nevertheless a stylistic muddle. The interior is worth exploring. Note the superb ceramic tiles, as well as the elaborately decorated ceilings: one is painted with gold-collared swans and another with magpies.

The other main palace is the Pena Palace (Palácio da Pena), built in the 1840s by Ferdinand of Saxe-Coburg-Gotha, husband of Queen Maria II. Today, it's a fantastical creation rivaling the best of Disney, complete with towers, turrets and battlements. Inside is a riot of flamboyant furniture, wall hangings and paintings, including a whole room of nudes. Nearby is the eighth-century Castelo dos Mouros, a ruined Moorish stronghold with superb views.

Gardens

The other outstanding attractions in Sintra are its gardens and parks. The warm, damp climate is ideal for a profusion of exotic trees, shrubs and roses, and you'll see everything from rhododendrons and camellias to tree ferns and palms. The Pena Gardens, below the Pena Palace, are lovely, with lakes and mock temples. But the highlight is the Monserrate Gardens, west of Sintra. Two Englishmen laid out the gardens between 1790 and 1860, and they ramble romantically over 74 acres.

Around Sintra lies the Sintra-Cascais National Park (Parque Nacional de Sintra-Cascais), a wonderful area stretching from the tree-clad mountains of Sintra down to the dramatic Atlantic coastline at Guincho.

Tour Operators
Cityrama ✉ Avenida Praia da Vitória 12-B ☎ 01 319 1091 or 01 319 1092
Grayline ☎ 01 352 2594 or 01 356 0668
Portugal Tours ☎ 01 316 0399 or 01 352 2902

Porto

PORTO

Porto, Portugal's second-largest city with about 300,000 residents, stands on the steep and rocky north bank of the Douro river, just a couple of miles from its outlet on the Atlantic. The suburbs sprawl to the coast. Many visitors encounter Porto on their way up the beautiful Douro valley. The city is also known for its long association with port wine, which has been shipped from Vila Nova de Gaia, a suburb of Porto, since the 17th century. It has long been referred to as "Oporto," a name never used by the Portuguese and now declining in use elsewhere.

Development of Porto

Founded in pre-Roman times, the city gave its name to the country, and was the birthplace of Prince Henry the Navigator in 1394. Traditionally liberal, its residents have always had a strong rebellious streak, which goes well with the city's industrious and down-to-earth image.

Porto is a refreshing antidote to the faded elegance of Lisbon – a bustling city lying at the center of Portugal's most important economic area, whose layout is inextricably entwined with the history of the port trade. Grandiose buildings testify to 18th- and 19th-century wealth, but the true spirit of the city lies in the maze of narrow streets below the Cathedral, the old docks and the waterfront houses.

Suggested Itineraries

Two or three days is sufficient to see Porto. Nearly everything of interest is within a short walk or bus ride of the city center. The streets are steep and hilly, so wear comfortable shoes. If you're just passing through on your way up the Douro valley, visit the port lodges in Vila Nova de Gaia, Porto's main tourist attraction. If you've got more time, the city can be neatly divided into cultural itineraries, focusing on medieval, baroque and neoclassic monuments and churches. Pockets throughout the city are endowed with *azulejo* decoration (glazed ceramic tiles). There are good views of the city and tantalizing glimpses of the Douro river from many street corners.

The heart of modern Porto centers around Avenida dos Aliados, a broad avenue with the monumental town hall at one end and the Praça da Liberdade, a transportation hub, at the other. Seething with people, this stretch is a good place to observe locals going about their daily business. The main shopping areas are east and north of this avenue. You can use the river to help you orient yourself to the city.

Porto Flavors

The people of Porto have traditionally been known as *tripeiros*, or "tripe-eaters," allegedly because they sacrificed all their meat except the tripe to their army during a legendary battle – an historic indicator that refined cooking doesn't top the priority list here. Expect hearty, tasty meals, plenty of fish, the much-beloved *bacalhau* (dried, salted cod) and super-sweet desserts on every menu.

On the other hand, a glass of smooth, unctuous and subtle port – drunk on its native soil – may convert even the most inveterate port-hater. An especially atmospheric place to dine is beside the river at Ribeira, in the heart of the oldest part of Porto. Until recently it was run-down and decayed, but most of the area has now been given a face-lift, and it is filled with good, lively restaurants with tremendous tourist appeal.

Porto

Crafts and Shopping

Porto is the place to track down northern handicraft specialties, fine port, locally made shoes and the village of Minho's traditional gold filigree jewelry. The city's wonderfully old-fashioned stores, many of which still retain their turn-of-the-20th-century facades and details, are worth a visit even if you're not buying. Highlights include the Lello and Irmão bookstore on Rua do Carmelitas, with its superb double staircase and somber wooden paneling, and Cardoso Cabeleiro on Rua do Bonjardim, a shop specializing in wigs and toupees. Similar stores cluster together in Porto, so you'll find streets packed with hardware stores, seed merchants, jewelers and linen stores. Marques Soares, a chic department store on Rua do Carmelitas, carries exquisite leather goods.

Excursions and Entertainment

Various operators run cruises on the Douro river, ranging from a weeklong trip up the river in a luxury cruiser to a couple of hours pottering around the lower reaches in a reproduction of a *rabelo*, the glorious old boats once used to carry barrels of port downstream from the vineyards. Sections of the 19th-century narrow-gauge railway still operate in the Douro valley – a fun way to do a little exploring. Tour operators also run bus trips in, around and out of Porto; Diana Tours (☎ 02 377 1230) and Grayline (☎ 02 352 2594) are reliable operators with English-speaking guides. Be sure to visit the port lodges in Vila Nova de Gaia (see page 390), an essential stop on any Porto visit.

For evening entertainment, locals attend theaters, concerts and the movies, although many people prefer to while away the hours at one of the terrace cafés or simply stroll along beside the riverbank.

The Douro river runs through the Riberia docks

ESSENTIAL INFORMATION

TOURIST INFORMATION
• Rua Clube Fenianos 25 ☎ 02 312 740
• Rua do Infante D Henrique 63 ☎ 02 200 9770
• Praça D João I 25 ☎ 02 031 7514

URBAN TRANSPORTATION
Getting around Porto is difficult because there isn't a reliable transportation guide to the city, so it's hard to know where bus stops are located and what routes run where. If you take the bus or the tram, pay as you get on; all buses serving the city center pass through the Praça da Liberdade. You can buy a one-, four- or seven-day travel pass

from kiosks in the city center, a considerable saving on single tickets. Taxis are inexpensive and can be flagged down; there is an additional charge to cross the river to Gaia.

AIRPORT INFORMATION
Francisco Sá Carneiro International Airport (☎ 02 941 3150) is about 12 miles northwest of central Porto. Bus 56 runs daily about every half hour from 6 a.m. until midnight, with a journey time of around 45 minutes, depending on traffic. During the day it terminates at Jardim da Cordoaira, after 9 p.m. at Praça da Liberdade.

CLIMATE – average highs and lows for the month

JAN.	FEB.	MAR.	APR.	MAY	JUN.	JUL.	AUG.	SEP.	OCT.	NOV.	DEC.
13°C	13°C	15°C	17°C	18°C	22°C	23°C	23°C	23°C	19°C	17°C	14°C
55°F	55°F	59°F	63°F	64°F	72°F	73°F	73°F	73°F	66°F	63°F	57°F
6°C	7°C	7°C	9°C	10°C	13°C	14°C	14°C	14°C	12°C	8°C	7°C
43°F	45°F	45°F	48°F	50°F	55°F	57°F	57°F	57°F	54°F	46°F	45°F

CITY SIGHTS

Key to symbols

✚ map coordinates refer to the Porto map on page 387; sights below are highlighted in yellow on the map.

☒ address or location ☎ telephone number

◉ opening times 🚍 nearest bus or tram route

🍴 restaurant on site or nearby

👜 admission charge: $$$ more than 500Esc, $$ 250Esc to 500Esc, $ less than 250Esc

IGREJA E TORRE DOS CLÉRIGOS

✚ B2 ☒ Rua dos Clérigos ☎ 02 200 1729
◉ Church: Mon.–Tue. and Thu.–Sat, 10–noon and 2–5, Sun. 10–1. Tower: Daily 10–noon and 2–5 🚍 88
👜 $

The soaring Igreja e Torre dos Clérigos (Tower of Clérigos), attached to an 18th-century granite church, is a Porto landmark, and most visitors climb it to get their bearings and admire the views. Nicolau Nasoni designed the oval church, with its elaborately festooned facade of swags and garlands, in the 1730s in Italian baroque style.

JARDIM DO PALÁCIO DE CRISTAL

✚ Off the map ☒ Rua de Dom Manuel II ☎ 02 609 3192 ◉ Daily 9–6 🍴 Cafeteria in gardens 🚍 24, 37

The green oasis of the Jardim do Palácio de Cristal (Crstyal Palace Garden), a few minutes' walk from Porto's center, offers one of the best vantage points in the city. A lime tree-lined avenue leads from pools and fountains past rhododendrons, magnolias and camellias to rose gardens and terraces high above the river. Summer concerts are held in the park's pavilion.

MUSEU NACIONAL SOARES DOS REIS

✚ A3 ☒ Rua Dom Manuel II ☎ 02 339 3770
◉ Wed.–Sun. 10–12:30 and 1:30–6, Tue. 1–6.
Frequently closed for restoration or re-arrangement
🚍 3, 20, 52 👜 $

The Museu Nacional Soares dos Reis (Soares dos Reis National Museum), named after the 19th-century sculptor Soares dos Reis, is Porto's most important museum. It's housed in an impressive 1795 neoclassic edifice, occupied in the early 1800s during the Peninsular War by both the French and English. The museum emphasizes pieces by Soares dos Reis, and the exhibits of glass and porcelain are most eye-catching; look for some early pieces from the famous Vista Alegre factory.

MUSEU ROMÂNTICO

✚ Off the map ☒ Rua de Entre-Quintas 220 ☎ 02 609 1131 ◉ Tue.–Sat. 10–12:30 and 2–5, Sun. 2–5:30
🚍 3, 20, 52 👜 $

For insight into how the prosperous bourgeois of Porto lived in the 19th century, visit the Museu Romântico (Romantic Museum), housed in a pretty villa overlooking the river. Wander through the house at will, viewing the furniture and pictures; many of the furnishings have connections with the last king of Piedmont, who lived here in exile. The basement houses the Solar do Vinho do Porto (Port Wine Rooms), where you can sample a wide selection of ports.

PONTE DO DOM LUÍS I

✚ C1 ☒ Ponte do Dom Luís I 🚍 32, 57, 91
Five bridges span the Douro river, all built dramatically high above the water to span the gorge cut by the lower reaches of the river. Perhaps the most impressive is the Ponte do Dom Luís I (Luis I Bridge), a striking bi-level iron construction designed by Téofilo Seyrig (one of Gustave Eiffel's collaborators) and dating from 1886. The bridge effectively links four city areas, so if you can tolerate heights, walk across the upper level for spectacular city views. The lower level will take you directly to the port warehouse area of Gaia.

PRAÇA DA RIBEIRA

Casa do Infante ✚ B1 ☒ Rua de Alfândega, Ribeira ◉ Mon.–Fri. 9–5 🚍 88
Centro Regional de Artes Tradicinais ☒ Rua de Reboleira 37, Ribeira ☎ 02 332 0076 ◉ Tue.–Fri. 10–12:30 and 3–7 🚍 88

The waterfront Praça da Ribeira (Ribeira Square) is the focal point of the Ribeira district, by far the most atmospheric area of Porto and designated a World Heritage Site. Many of the buildings – arcaded neoclassic constructions – were erected between 1776 and 1782. Although you can approach the area by descending the steep rua de Alfândega past Casa do Infante (Prince Henry the Navigator's reputed birthplace), the easiest way is to walk through the warren of canyon-like streets tumbling down to the river from the Cathedral.

There's no better place to experience historic Porto than in this spruced-up district, which has plenty of bars and restaurants. While you're here, visit the Centro Regional de Artes Tradicinais (Regional Center for Arts and Crafts), selling a wonderful range of traditional northern handicrafts.

SÉ

✚ B2　✉ Terreiro da Sé　☎ 02 205 4837
🕐 Mon.–Sat. 10–12:30　🚌 33, 82, 84　💲 $$
Porto's Sé (Cathedral) stands imposingly high above the steep slopes leading to the river, with the clean classical lines of the adjacent Episcopal Palace providing an elegant contrast to its venerable bulk. Built in the 12th century as a fortress church, it was extensively altered in the 1700s in the baroque style, although the vast silver altarpiece in the north transept dates from the mid-16th century. The two-storey cloisters are more appealing than the Cathedral itself; the solid granite lines are enlivened with beautiful tiles and there are good views over the town.

VILA NOVA DE GAIA

✚ C1　✉ Vila Nova de Gaia　🕐 Most lodges open Mon.–Fri. 10–noon and 2–6 (also Sat. in summer)　🍴 Porto Ibérico, see page 565　🚌 57, 91
Officially a separate municipality, Vila Nova de Gaia lies across the Douro river from Porto itself. Its name is synonymous with port, for until 1987 all port had to be matured here in order to merit its name. The riverside slopes are dominated by the solid granite buildings of the port warehouses, or lodges. There are many oportunities for free tours and tastings. This is *the* place to buy port; the white aperitif variety – subtly sweet yet dry – is hard to find overseas. The huge complex high above the river is the old monastery of Serra do Pilar, now a military installation and closed to the public.

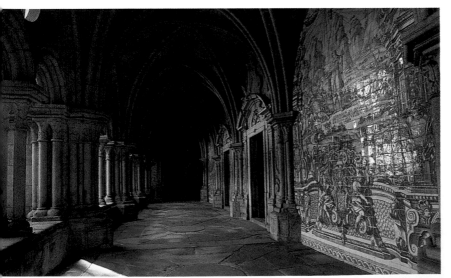

The Cathedral cloisters are beautifully lined with 18th-century *azulejos* (glazed ceramic tiles). This form of tile is arabic in origin but large designs made up of blue-on-white tiles is characteristically Portuguese

PORT WINE

Port is drunk all over the world, as an aperitif and a digestif. In the 18th century, its production area was the world's first demarcated wine zone, helping to make port one of the few wines with a flavor that has remained untouched for centuries. Be sure to try it in Porto, a city more associated with port than any other.

The Wine

Port is a fortified wine, which means that brandy is added to the grapes during the production process. This both "fortifies" the wine, making it stronger, and halts the fermentation process, leaving half the natural grape sugar in the wine. These two factors give port its strength, sweetness and smoothness; its complex flavors come from the soil and climate where the grapes are grown.

To people accustomed to the lush vineyards of other countries, those in the upper Douro valley, which produce port, are a revelation. It's a stony, barren area, a micro-climatic zone where temperatures reach extremes of heat and cold. The soil is a thin top-layer on schist, and the vine roots must force their way through the rock as much as 20 feet to find water. The Portuguese insist, probably rightly, that these conditions are what gives port its unique character.

The vineyards grow on steep terraces, so much of the harvest is done by hand, and until recently the grapes were still trodden by foot. Today more than 90 percent are crushed and fermented at a controlled temperature, sometime between mid-September and mid-October. The new wine is stored

No longer used commercially to transport barrels of port along the Douro valley, *barcos rabelos* (flat-bottomed boats) now decorate the waterside

up-river to clear until the following spring. In March it's ready for transportation. Following strict tradition, until 1987 it could not be called port unless the maturation had taken place in Vila Nova de Gaia, across the Douro from Porto. Now it can mature on site, although much is still stored and bottled down-river.

Drinking Port

Port comes in several varieties: white, a semi-sweet light wine; ruby, a clear, intense red; tawny, which is older and more complex; and late bottled vintage and vintage port. Vintage port is aged in the bottle and comes from grapes from a single year; late bottled is matured for up to four years before further maturing after bottling. White port is delicious chilled before a meal; ruby goes down well with a cup of coffee after lunch or in the early evening. Tawny and vintage port are best after dinner, savored slowly to appreciate the depth of flavor.

SPAIN

"MEN have no idea of time in any country that is or has been connected with Spain."

From *The West Indies and the Spanish Main* by English novelist Anthony Trollope

Opposite: Exploring the enchanting streets of the Barrio de Santa Cruz, Seville

Spain

SPAIN

Spain is a country of diverse landscapes, climates, peoples and cultures, forged over the centuries into a political unity. Physically separated from the rest of Europe by the Pyrenees mountain chain, Spain also found itself isolated internationally, during General Francisco Franco's dictatorship (1939–75). Since Franco's death, however, and with the restoration of its monarchy, Spain has

Spain

regained its place politically, economically and culturally within mainstream Europe. But despite the rate of progress, many aspects of life remain untouched, and Spain still retains much of its traditional character.

Spain Today

Spain's long and checkered history peaked in the Golden Age of the 16th century, when it was one of the most influential nations of the world. It had immense power across Europe and possessed many overseas colonies. The following centuries saw a gradual decline and increasing isolation from the rest of Europe, culminating in the bitter Civil War (1936–39) and Franco's long dictatorship.

In Spain today, political, cultural and artistic life flourishes, along with national confidence. In 1992 Madrid was chosen as the Cultural Capital of Europe, the same year that dynamic Barcelona held the Olympic Games and Seville hosted the World Fair.

From Pyrenees to Portugal

One of Europe's most mountainous countries, Spain occupies most of the Iberian peninsula, stretching southwest from the Pyrenees. Much of the land area is covered by the Meseta, a huge plateau surrounded by long mountain ranges. These stretch from the Sierra Nevada in the south to the Cordillera Cantábrica in the north, and give Spain an average altitude of 2,100 feet. The highest mainland peak is 11,424-foot Mulhacen in the Sierra Nevada, although Mount Teide on the island of Tenerife is nearly 1,000 feet higher.

MORE TOP DESTINATIONS IN SPAIN
● Burgos C4 ● Córdoba B2 ● Costa Brava E4 ● Costa de la Luz A1 ● Costa Verde B4 ● Granada C1 ● León B4 ● Monestir de Poblet E3 ● Pamplona D4 ● Parque Nacional de los Picos de Europa B4 ● Peñíscola D3 ● Ronda B1 ● Salamanca B3 ● Segovia C3 ● Sierra de Montserrat E3 ● Zaragoza D3

Originally from southern Spain, flamenco music is now heard all over the country

The mild, moist Atlantic coast of the Costa Verde in the north contrasts with the sun-baked Mediterranean beaches of the southern Costa del Sol. The grandeur of the Pyrenees is more than rivaled by the dramatic peaks of the Asturian mountains on Spain's northern coast, probably the most beautiful region in Spain. East of Asturia the Ebro valley slashes southeast toward the Mediterranean, where it dissects the coastal plain southwest of Barcelona.

The fertile gardens of Murcia and the agricultural flatlands of the Quadalquivir yield harvests rivaled only by the tourist crop drawn from the golden sands of the Mediterranean beaches. The Mediterranean coast ends on the northern shore of the Straits of Gibraltar, only nine miles

from Africa. Such diversity is echoed in Spain's climate, which varies from the mild, wet weather of the northern Atlantic coast to the typical Mediterranean hot, dry summers and mild wet winters in the south. Winter inland can be very cold. The island groups of the Balearics and the Canaries have their own geographical and climatic characteristics.

Diversities of Spain

Regional differences are reflected in the Spanish people, their looks, their character, their attitudes and above all, their cuisine. The 800 years of Moorish occupation, the eventual unification of a number of small kingdoms, and the power and wealth of 16th-century colonial Spain have all played their part in the evolution of diverse provincial characteristics.

The concept of centralized power is alien to many Spaniards, and regionalism is still strong in Spain. It has its base in the peninsula's linguistic groups: Galician, spoken in the northwest; Basque, another northern language; Castilian, or pure, central Spanish; and Catalan, based in the southeast, with Valencian a variation of this. These different languages are still spoken every day.

In 1977, when the present constitution was established, ethnic groups were provided for in regions such as Catalonia and Galicia, which are both autonomous. Others fared less well, notably the Basques, whose struggle for a separate identity has been marked by decades of conflict.

Spanish Characters

There are physical differences between Spaniards from different parts of the peninsula. With a population of 40 million, there's room for diversity; contrary to popular belief, not all

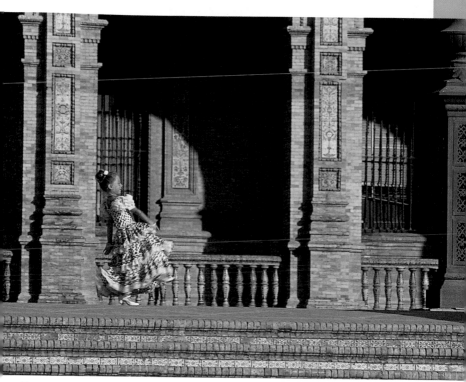

Exuberant, spontaneous and passionate – dancing the flamenco outside the Plaza de España, Seville

Spaniards are dark-eyed and olive-skinned. The Moorish genetic legacy is strongest in Andalucia, where many are delicately-featured and dark, personifying the Spanish stereotype.

Spaniards are sometimes thought of as an exuberant, passionate and light-hearted people, much like the Italians, but nothing could be further from the truth. They are certainly passionate, but there's a strong streak of self-control and melancholy in the national character. History has given them loyalty and tolerance. Kindness to children and respect for the elderly are the norm. You will find a tendency to delay until tomorrow (*mañana*) anything that can wait.

Young Spaniards enjoy a freedom and lifestyle their grandparents could never have imagined, yet society is still in a state of flux, and there are huge contrasts between different regions, towns and rural areas. But wherever you go you'll find the same level of hospitality and friendliness, particularly if you speak a little Spanish. English is widely spoken along the Mediterranean coast and by hotel staff in big cities, but very little elsewhere.

Cities, Towns and Villages

For visitors the three great cities are Madrid, Barcelona and Seville, but in Spanish eyes the industrial centers of Zaragoza and Bilbao are of equal importance, and the inhabitants of each region claim their capital as the most beautiful in Spain. Andalucia, with the architectural treasures of Granada and Córdoba, is rich in Moorish history. The region of Castille has Christian castles built during the struggle to oust the Moors.

Spain

The Mediterranean coast has many remains from the centuries of Roman occupation, while the Atlantic port of Cádiz boasts 2,000 years of maritime history. Rural Spain continues largely unchanged; agriculture is more mechanized, but the way and pace of life are still deeply rooted in the past.

Spanish Lifestyle

Daily life in Spain differs in one major way from other southern European countries; mealtimes are very late. Breakfast in hotels is served from around 7:30 until 9:30 or 10. Most Spaniards rise early and eat very little first thing, so they are ready for a snack around 11. This delays lunch until 2 at the earliest, and therefore dinner is often around 10:30 or later.

An early start means you can take advantage of the cool mornings, vital in a country where air-conditioning is not universal. Virtually everything – stores, offices, churches and museums – closes from 1 until 5, and most people sleep after lunch for a couple of hours, during the fabled siesta.

This bypasses the worst heat and leaves people ready to stay up late and enjoy the comparatively fresh evening air. It's a pleasure to sit at a café or restaurant table until 1 or 2 in the morning, as long as you've had a midday rest.

You'll find that most entertainment begins very late, around 10 p.m., and clubs don't get going until the early hours of the morning. Along the Mediterranean coast things are more geared toward foreigners, and you should be able to have dinner soon after 8:30 p.m.

Spain is a deeply Catholic country. When you visit churches, cover the tops of your arms and shoulders and avoid wearing shorts. The many local fiestas held in every town and village are always in honor of the Virgin or some favorite local saint, and if you get the chance to watch one, you will see how religion plays an integral part in everyday life.

Traveling in Spain

The economic boom of the last two decades has resulted in a sound infrastructure. Spain has an excellent network of well-signed toll roads and highways. Spaniards drive fast but safely, and you should have no problems if you rent a car. Public transport is good, with a choice of internal flights, inexpensive and punctual trains, and long-distance buses going to even the most remote corners.

Hotels are graded and inspected by the government, so you are guaranteed a clean and adequate room no matter how little you pay. Try to spend at least a few nights at one of the *paradores*. These are state-owned hotels housed in historic buildings such as castles and monasteries, often furnished with antiques and offering a high standard of comfort and service.

Spanish Passions

Spaniards throw themselves wholeheartedly into eating out, shopping, going to a soccer match or spending a day on the beach. Their most famous, and often misunderstood, passion is bullfighting (see page 429), but soccer has more supporters. Huge crowds follow the fortunes of teams such as Real Madrid and Barcelona.

Spain has some of Europe's finest golf courses, chiefly along the Mediterranean coast, where you'll also find excellent marinas and water-sports facilities, as well as untouched wilderness areas. Young people travel from all over Europe to experience Spain's club scene, at its most frenetic on the Balearic island of Ibiza.

The Moorish legacy of color and decoration is boldly kept alive in Alicante

Spain

TIMELINE

15,000–12,000 BC Caves at Altamira painted; earliest sign of habitation.

218–210 BC Rome begins conquest of Iberian peninsula.

AD 411 Visigoths invade and establish powerful kingdom at Toledo.

711 Moors defeat Visigoths and begin period of occupation.

1478–79 Spanish Inquisition against Jews, Moors and Protestants.

1492 Columbus discovers New World.

1519 Spanish conquistadores move across America.

1588 Spanish Armada sent against Protestant England; fleet destroyed and maritime pre-eminence lost.

1808–14 Peninsular War (War of Independence) sees expulsion of French and defeat of Napoleon.

1898 Phillippines and Cuba rebel against Spanish rule; the United States occupies Puerto Rico; end of Spanish Empire.

1914–18 Spain remains neutral in World War I.

1936–39 Spanish Civil War; General Franco leads Nationalist troops from Morocco against Republicans.

1939 Franco becomes head of state; Spain enters period of isolation and remains neutral throughout World War II.

1955 Spain joins United Nations.

1975 Death of Franco; Juan Carlos becomes king.

1986 Spain joins the European Union.

1992 Barcelona hosts Olympic Games; Madrid declared Cultural Capital of Europe; Seville is the venue for Expo 92.

THE MOORISH OCCUPATION

In AD 711 a faction of the ruling Visigoth tribe in Spain went to Islamic Africa to seek help with some domestic political problems. They returned with an army of 7,000; after victory at Cadiz, the Moors encountered little resistance in taking over all but a small strip of northern Spain over the next 30 years. Their tactics were a blend of intelligent strategy and diplomacy; they never demanded religious subordination, as long as Christians paid taxes. Beginning in AD 744, however, resistance against the invaders spread south from the small, unoccupied northern territory, fueled by the legend of St. James the Moorslayer. El Cid succeeded in capturing Toledo from the Moors in 1085, and despite some setbacks a coalition of Christian armies were finally victorious at the Battle of Navas de Tolosa in 1212, the last great battle between Moors and Christians. The Moorish occupation left important legacies, however – they brought mathematics, papermaking, oranges, spices and rice to Spain, which were then introduced to the rest of Europe.

SURVIVAL GUIDE

- English is not widely spoken, even in large cities. Keep in mind that the Spanish you may have learned in high school differs in accent, pronounciation and some vocabulary from that spoken in Spain.
- It's best not to discuss politics, since Spaniards are very proud and the subject could be sensitive.
- Beachwear, shorts and revealing necklines are not acceptable away from coastal resorts.
- Public restrooms are few except in museums, but it's acceptable to use the facilities in a bar; leave a small tip on the counter or stop and have a cup of coffee while you're there.
- Inebriation is frowned on in Spain; the Spanish drink alcohol every day, but in moderation.
- The Spanish are formal and polite; it is best to ask, in Spanish, if the person you're addressing speaks English before you start to speak, and shake hands at the end of casual conversations.
- Water is precious in many parts of Spain; you may find that hotel bathrooms have a shower rather than a tub. Shower pressure is generally low.
- You can safely drink the water throughout Spain, although you may prefer to drink bottled mineral water, which is inexpensive and served chilled. Ice is not generally served in drinks unless you ask.
- Throughout Spain, especially along the Mediterranean, bars specialize in *tapas*, delicious selections of hot or cold savory mouthfuls served with drinks. Be sure to try some of

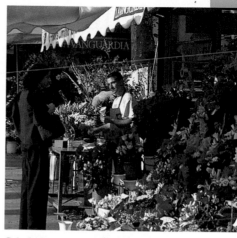

Colorful flower market in La Rambla, Barcelona

the dozens available: fish, smoked ham, stewed peppers, salads, local almonds, olives. Two or three little dishes will make a delicious lunch.
- All large cities have malls, usually away from the town center; downtown department stores; and a range of antique stores, designer boutiques, local craft and souvenir shops, gourmet food stores, and clothing and bric-a-brac markets.
- Prices in Spain are comparable to the rest of the Continent; meals are a little cheaper.
- Try to arrange your trip so that it coincides with a major local festival. Spain has some of the most colorful and exotic celebrations in Europe.

Profile of a bullfighter – the *matador*

MADRID

Unlike most European capital cities, Madrid did not evolve as the nation's capital. It was chosen. In 1561, Philip II settled the court permanently in Madrid, as much for its position in the center of Spain as for political reasons.

Today, Madrid is noisy, vibrant and chaotic – a city of great wealth and grueling poverty, with both a booming economy and high unemployment.

Like so much of Spain, Madrid's spirit is elusive and diffused, and will surprise you repeatedly. Plan to stay in the city center, so you can easily reach your hotel in the middle of the day,

Museo del Pueblo Español   Hospital Clinico
Museo de América
Cuidad Universitaria, Hipodromo de la Zarzuela and El Pardo
Arco de la Victoria
Parque del Oeste
PLAZA CRISTO REY
CALLE DE CEA BERMUDEZ
AV DE FILIPINAS
CALLE DE DONOSO CORTE
GTA DE QUEVEDO
CALLE DE MELENDEZ VALDES
Museo Sorolla
PASEO GEN MARTINEZ
CALLE ELOY GONZALO
PASEC

Parque del Oeste
La Rosaleda
Palácio de Liria
GTA RUIZ JIMENEZ
CALLE CARRANZA
PLAZA ALONSO MARTINEZ
Jardin Arquiteco Ribera
Museo Romántico
Palacio de Justicia

Ermita de San Antonio de la Florida y Panteon de Goya
GTA SAN ANTONIO DE LA FLORIDA
Jardines Cuartel de la Montaña
Templo de Debod
Museo Cerralbo
Información de Tourismo
PL DE ESPANA
Museo Municipal
Ministerio del Ejército

Estación del Norte
Casa de Campo
Museo de Carruajes Reales
Palacio Real
Campo del Moro
Jardines Sabatini
La Encarnación
PLAZA DE ORIENTE
Teatro de la Opera
Palacio del Senado
PLAZA CALLAO
GRAN VIA
Convento de las Descalzas Reales
Real Academia de Bellas Artes de San Fernando
Teatro de la Zarzuela
PLAZA DE LA CIBELES

Catedral Ntra Sra de la Almudena
PUENTE DE SEGOVIA
CALLE DE SEGOVIA
PLAZA DE LA VILLA
MAYOR
PLAZA MAYOR
Casa de la Panadería
Sta Cruz
Ayuntamiento
Información de Tourismo
PLAZA SANTA ANA
Teatro Español
Museo Thyssen-Bornemisza
CARRERA SAN JERÓNIMO
Casa Museo de Lope de Vega
PLAZA CANOVAS DEL CASTILL

Jardines de las Vistillas
PLAZA SAN FRANCISCO
San Francisco el Grande
Catedral San Isidro
El Rasto
Hospital
Museo Nacional Centro de Arte Reina Sofia
PLAZA D EMPERAD(CARLOS

Parque de Caramuel
GTA PUERTO DE TOLEDO
RONDA DE TOLEDO
GTA DE EMBAJADORES
RONDA DE ATOCHA
Palacio de Aranjuez

0   250   500 m
0   250   500 yards
A   Puente de Toledo   B   C

Madrid

when many museums and monuments are closed for the siesta. The best way to tackle sightseeing is to concentrate on one section at a time. There are three historical areas of interest in the vicinity of the city's main plaza, Sun's Gate (Puerta del Sol): Old Madrid (Viejo Madrid), centering on the Plaza Mayor; the Eastern Quarter (Barrio de Oriente), by the Palacio Real; and Bourbon Madrid, the heart of which is the sweeping avenues and sparkling fountains around the Prado museum.

There's a convenient tourist bus, Madrid Vision, which links all three, allowing passengers to get on and off when they want to. Tickets are valid for one or two days, and there's English commentary. The city also has an efficient subway system. Plan your day in advance and also take along a good English-Spanish dictionary, because English is not widely spoken here.

Dining Out

Eating is a real pleasure in Madrid, and there is much to choose from. Local specialties such as offal, blood sausage and pig's ear are usually unpopular with visitors. But there are many regional restaurants featuring traditional dishes from all over Spain. The cuisine of the Basque country and Catalonia is particularly good, or you could try a Latin American restaurant, where even the meat is imported from Argentina. Fast-food outlets are everywhere; take your pick of hamburgers, tortillas or even paella-to-go.

By law, all restaurants have to offer a fixed-price menu, which is usually a good value and includes a choice of first and second courses, a dessert and drink. Madrid has innumerable bars, where you'll find everything from tea and coffee to beer, champagne and exotic cocktails. In summer, bar life moves onto the sidewalks, with hundreds of outdoor venues (*terrazas*) crowded until 4 or 5 in the morning.

Malls and Markets

The central department stores, such as the nationwide chain Corte Ingles, are clustered in the commercial area around the Puerta del Sol. If you're looking for malls, the large Vaguada is in northern

MADRID

Museo de Ciencas Naturales

CALLE DE MARIA DE MOLINA

CALLE SERRANO
CALLE DE VELAZQUEZ
CALLE DE FRANCISCO SILVELA
AV DE AMERICA

PLAZA DOCTOR MARAÑON

GTA DE CAMPOS EMILIO CASTELAR

Museo Lázaro Galdiano

CALLE DIEGO DE LEON

JARDO DATO

CALLE DE JUAN BRAVO

PASEO DE LA CASTELLANA

CALLE DE JOSE ORTEGA Y GASSET

SALAMANCA

CALLE DE PRINCIPE DE VERGARA

AYALA

Plaza de Toros
Monumental de las Ventas

CALLE DE SERRANO
CALLE DE VELAZQUEZ
CALLE DE GOYA

CALLE DE NARVAEZ

PLAZA DE COLON
Museo de Cera

Biblioteca Nacional

CALLE DE ALCALA

CALLE DE O'DONNELL

Museo Arqueológico Nacional

Puerta de Alcalá

PLAZA DE LA INDEPENDENCIA

AVENIDA DE MENENDEZ

CALLE

C DE IBIZA

Museo Naval
Museo Nacional de Artes Decorativas

Estanque

Parque del Retiro

Museo del Ejército

Casón del Buen Retiro

San Jerónimo el Real

C DEL ALCALDE

Palacio de Exposiciones

Hospital del Niño Jesus

Museo del Prado

Palacio de Cristal

Y PELAYO

Jardin Botanico

CALLE DE ALFONSO XII

PASEO DEL DUQUE DE FERNAN NUÑEZ

PASEO DEL URUGUAY

Museo Geológico

Observatorio Astronómico

AV DE MENENDEZ PELAYO

AV DE LA CIUDAD DE BARCELONA

Inst Ramon y Cajal

PASEO REINA CRISTINA

AV DEL MEDITERRANEO

Estación Atocha

Real Fabrica de Tapices

D E

Madrid

Madrid; the Galería del Prado, opposite the museum, is smaller and more upscale. The smartest shopping area is the Salamanca district around the streets of Calle de Serrano and Goya, where you'll find a range of expensive and elegant stores. Madrid is a good place to find Spanish souvenirs from all over the country, and there are many antique stores; the Salamanca district alone has more than 50. Visit the Rastro flea market on a Sunday morning and browse in some of the tiny boutiques.

Evening Entertainment

Classical music, opera and theater thrive in Madrid, and the tourist office publishes a monthly guide, *Qué hacer en Madrid*, with excellent listings. You might enjoy a *zarzuela* performance, a traditional form of musical combining elements of opera, vaudeville and melodrama. Jazz is very popular, with

nightly performances at some of Europe's best venues. If you're looking for flamenco, there are several clubs (*tablaos*) where it is staged. Madrid has an exceptional nightclub scene. A number of movie theaters show movies in their original language.

Late, Late Nights

People eat late and go to bed late all over Spain, especially in the capital. Locals do not eat dinner much before 10 or 11 at night, even in winter; in summer the "night" is still young at 3:30 in the morning. In recent years the siesta has become threatened, as Spanish business practices come in line with the rest of Europe. One result of this is that *Madrileños* are functioning on less and less sleep – a fact beginning to worry Spanish health watchdogs.

ESSENTIAL INFORMATION

TOURIST INFORMATION
• Barajas Airport (international arrivals terminal) ☎ 91 305 8656
• Mercado Puerta de Toledo ☎ 91 364 1875
• Oficina de Informacíon de la Comunidad de Madrid, Calle Duque de Medinaceli 2 ☎ 91 429 4951
• Oficina Municipal de Turismo, Plaza Mayor ☎ 91 366 5477
• Patronato Municipal de Turismo, Calle Mayor 69 ☎ 91 588 2900

URBAN TRANSPORTATION
Getting around Madrid is simple, thanks to the excellent subway (metro) and bus systems. Subway stations are marked on the Madrid city map as the letter "M" in a red circle. The subway has 10 lines and runs daily 6 a.m.–1:30 a.m. Purchase tickets from machines or ticket offices in the stations,

where you can also pick up a map of the system. The Metrobus ticket is a useful combination ticket valid for 10 trips on the subway and bus systems. Buses run daily 6 a.m.–midnight, with a limited all-night service. Pay the driver or stamp your pass in the machine when you board. Taxis are inexpensive and can be hailed on the street; a green light on top means they are free. To call a taxi dial Tele-Taxi (☎ 91 445 9008), Radio Teléfono Taxi (☎ 91 547 8500) or Radio-Taxi Independente (☎ 91 405 1213).

AIRPORT INFORMATION
Madrid's Barajas Airport (☎ 91 393 6000) is 10 miles northeast of the city center, about a 30-minute drive. Buses run every 12 minutes into Madrid, where they terminate beneath the Plaza de Colón, across the square and downstairs from the subway station of the same name.

CLIMATE – average highs and lows for the month

JAN.	FEB.	MAR.	APR.	MAY	JUN.	JUL.	AUG.	SEP.	OCT.	NOV.	DEC.
9°C	12°C	15°C	18°C	21°C	27°C	32°C	31°C	26°C	19°C	13°C	10°C
48°F	54°F	59°F	64°F	70°F	81°F	90°F	88°F	79°F	66°F	55°F	50°F
1°C	2°C	4°C	6°C	9°C	14°C	17°C	17°C	13°C	9°C	4°C	2°C
34°F	36°F	39°F	43°F	48°F	57°F	63°F	63°F	55°F	48°F	39°F	36°F

City Sights

Key to symbols

⊞ map coordinates refer to the Madrid map on page 402–403; sights below are highlighted in yellow on the map.

⊠ address or location ☎ telephone number

🕓 opening times 🚌 nearest bus or tram route

🚇 nearest subway 🍴 restaurant on site or nearby

🎫 admission charge: $$$ more than 900PTA, $$ 600PTA–900PTA, $ less than 600PTA

Convento de las Descalzas Reales

⊞ C2 ⊠ Plaza de las Descalzas Reales 3 ☎ 91 42 0059 🕓 Tue.–Fri. 10:30–12:30 and 4–5:45, Sat. 10:30–12:30, Sun. 11–1:30 🚇 Sol or Opera 🎫 $$

The oddly named Convento de las Descalzas Reales (Convent of the Royal Shoeless Nuns) was founded in 1560 as a convent for aristocratic ladies seeking the religious life. Pious and wealthy, they and their families endowed and decorated 33 chapels, each more opulent than the last and containing treasures by mainly Spanish artists.

Museo de América

⊞ A4 ⊠ Avenida Reyes Católicos 6 ☎ 91 543 9437 🕓 Tue.–Sat. 10–3, Sun. 10–2:30 🚇 Moncloa 🎫 $

The Museo de América (America Museum), an archeological and ethnological museum, is devoted to pre-Columbian and Hispanic artifacts telling the story of European ties with America. The information is in Spanish, but anyone can appreciate the powerful Quimbayas Treasure and the collection's high point, the Cortesiano Codex, which records in Mayan runes the arrival of the Spaniards in the New World.

Museo Nacional Centro de Arte Reina Sofia

⊞ D1 ⊠ Calle Santa Isabel 52 ☎ 91 467 5062 🕓 Mon.–Sat. 10–9, Sun. 10–2:30 🍴 Café and snack bar in museum 🚇 Atocha 🎫 $$

The Museo Nacional Centro de Arte Reina Sofia (Queen Sofia National Art Center), the city's modern art museum, is housed in the former Hospital de San

An allegorical statue outside the America Museum

Carlos. Exterior glass elevators whisk you up to the permanent exhibitions. Most visitors flock to Pablo Picasso's great *Guernica*. When it was commissioned for the 1937 World's Fair, his only instruction was to paint a big picture; this searing black-and-white composition has become the icon of 20th-century antiwar symbolism. Other highlights include paintings by Salvador Dalí, spanning his stylistic development and surreal sexual imagery, and Joan Miró.

Golden altar inside the Descalzas Convent

The Royal Palace viewed from the Campo del Moro

"Olivareo" by Velázquez, in the Prado

MUSEO DEL PRADO

✚ D2 ✉ Paseo del Prado ☎ 91 420 3768
🕐 Tue.–Sat. 9–7, Sun. 10:30–1:30 🍴 Café and snack
bar in museum 🚇 Banco de España or Atocha
👆 $$

Since its opening in 1819 the Museo del
Prado (Prado Museum), with its unrivaled
collection of Spanish paintings, has been
among the world's finest. Once the royal
collection, the Prado represents the
personal taste of the Spanish monarchs,
with a noticeable emphasis on religious
and courtly paintings. Because of space
limitations only about 1,500 of the 7,000
works are on display. Paintings are
frequently moved around or loaned to
other museums, but the most famous are
normally on view; pick up an up-to-date
floor plan as you arrive. Some works,
particularly those by Diego Velázquez and
Francisco Goya, attract huge crowds and
you may have to wait to see them.

Highlights include Velázquez' *Las
Meninas*, often described as "the finest
painting in the world." Goya's work
occupies many rooms; look for his *Majas*,
two paintings thought to be of the
Duchess of Alba, one demure and
clothed, the other sensuously naked. His
pinturas negras, the dark pictures, stand in
stark contrast; disturbing and pessimistic,
they represent the apocalyptic vision of a
man on the edge of madness. The Spanish
monarchs were fascinated by the surreal
work of Hieronymous Bosch; his *Garden
of Earthly Delights*, with its wealth of
weird detail, is one of his finest works.

MUSEO THYSSEN-
BORNEMISZA

✚ D2 ✉ Paseo del Prado 8 ☎ 91 369 0151
🕐 Tue.–Sun. 10–7 🍴 Café and restaurant in
museum 🚇 Banco de España or Atocha 👆 $$

Acquired in 1993 for about $350 million,
the Museo Thyssen-Bornemisza
(Thyssen-Bornemisza Museum) provides
Spain with another world-class museum.
It contains more than 700 works. Western
paintings from the 13th to 20th centuries
are arranged chronologically, so start on
the top floor and work down. Early
portraits and Renaissance works are
grouped together, followed by Dutch
interiors. Nineteenth-century American
paintings include a portrait of George

Madrid's Plaza Mayor, begun in medieval times and still a focus for the social activities of its citizens

Washington's cook by Gilbert Stuart and a fine sea scene by Winslow Homer. The 20th century is well represented by Joan Miró, Salvador Dalí and Mark Rothko.

PALACIO REAL

✚ B2 ✉ Calle Bailén ☎ 91 542 0059
🕐 Palacio/Museo: Mon.–Sat. 9:30–5:30, Sun. 9–2
🚇 Opera 💷 $$$

The vast white bulk of the Palacio Real (Royal Palace) looks particularly striking from the Campo del Moro, a peaceful garden behind the palace where you'll also find the Museo de Carruajes Reales (Royal Carriage Museum). After a fire destroyed the Moorish original, the palace was planned to be three times its existing size. Funds ran out, leaving this structure, which was built between 1737 and 1764. In use until 1931, it is now occasionally used for state receptions. Everything is opulent and awesomely large. Madrid's 1993 Cathedral of the Almudena stands nearby; the Plaza de Oriente, across the road from the palace, is a pleasant square.

PARQUE DEL RETIRO

✚ D2 ✉ Entrances at Calle Alcalá, Avenida de Menendez Pelayo, Paseo de la Riena Cristina
🚇 Retiro or Atocha

The Parque del Retiro (Retreat Park) was laid out in the 1630s as part of the immense French-style pleasure gardens surrounding the Buen Retiro Palace. The building itself was destroyed during the Napoleonic Wars. Today it is Madrid's favorite park, bright with flowers and scattered with statues and fountains. Many people head straight for the lake, dominated by an ornate statue of Alfonso XII, but there are other attractions, including the Palacio de Cristal, a wonderful 19th-century glass palace.

PLAZA MAYOR

✚ B2 ✉ Plaza Mayor 🚇 Sol

One of Europe's most dazzling squares, the present Plaza Mayor stands on the site of the medieval market, the Plaza del Arrabal. When Madrid became Spain's capital, Philip II ordered it to be rebuilt as the focal point, and it was completed in 1619. Harmonious brick facades are punctuated with elegant stonework and arcades. The plaza was used for fiestas, bullfights and royal proclamations, and was the scene of many executions during the dark days of the Inquisition.

PLAZA DE TOROS

✚ Off the map ✉ Avenida de los Toreros ☎ 91 356 2200 🕐 Museo Taurino: Tue.–Fri. 9:30–2:30, Sat.–Sun. 10–1 🚇 Ventas 💷 Museum $; tickets for fights $–$$$

Madrid's Plaza de Toros (Bullring) was opened in 1934, and for aficionados is the most important in the world. The Museo Taurino (Bullfight Museum), devoted to some of bullfighting's famous names, features the "suit of lights" worn by Manolete during his fateful fight in 1947.

The Alcalá gate – Madrid's finest example of neoclassic architecture

PLAZA DE LA VILLA

✚ B2 ✉ Plaza de la Villa ☎ 91 588 2908
🕐 Buildings: Mon. 5–6 🚇 Sol or Opera
Despite their different dates, the three main stone buildings around this little plaza coexist harmoniously. The Gothic Torre de los Lujanes, one of Madrid's few surviving 15th-century structures, is balanced by the Casa de Cisneros, a restored 1537 Plateresque style-house. The Casa del Ayuntamiento was designed as the meeting place for the town council in 1640, a function it still serves today.

PUERTA DE ALCALÁ

✚ D2 ✉ Plaza de la Independencia 🚇 Retiro
Surrounded by roaring traffic, the Puerta de Alcalá (Alcalá Gate) is a symbol of Madrid, along with the equally splendid Plaza de la Cibeles, a street away. Designed in 1778 as the main entrance to the Spanish court, it's a gateway on a monumental scale, with five grandiose arches topped by lion heads, cherubim and coats of arms.

PUERTA DEL SOL

✚ C2 ✉ Puerta del Sol 🚇 Sol
Puerta del Sol (Sun's Gate) has been a plaza since 1570, when the original gate was demolished. This is the heart of Madrid. The headquarters of the regional government are housed on the south side, where a stone in the sidewalk marks Kilometre Zero, from which all distances in Spain are measured.

REAL ACADEMIA DE BELLAS ARTES DE SAN FERNANDO

✚ C2 ✉ Calle Alcalá 13 ☎ 91 522 1491
🕐 Tue.–Fri. 9–7, Sat.–Mon. 9–2 🚇 Sevilla 💲 S
Art lovers will enjoy the peaceful Real Academia de Bellas Artes de San Fernando (Royal Academy of Fine Arts), founded in the 18th century to emulate art venues in Paris and London. The academy has some fine paintings by Francisco Goya and a good Diego Velázquez portrait of Philip IV. The highlight is *Spring* by Italian artist Giuseppe Arcimboldo, a portrait in which the sitter's features are entirely composed of fruit and vegetables.

SAN JERÓNIMO EL REAL

✚ D2 ✉ Calle Moreto 4 ☎ 91 420 3078 🕐 Daily 8–1:30 and 5–8:30 🚇 Atocha
San Jerónimo el Real (St. Jerome the Royal) is the traditional royal church where princes were consecrated and monarchs married. It witnessed the coronation of the present king, Juan Carlos, in 1975. Rebuilt in 1503 by King Ferdinand for his queen, Isabella, this simple Gothic church, with its single nave and side chapels, is in marked contrast to the flamboyance of many other churches in the country.

MONASTERIO DE EL ESCORIAL

Twenty-five miles northwest of Madrid, on the southern slopes of the Sierra da Guadarrama mountain range, stands the massive religious complex known as El Escorial. One of the most impressive monuments in Spain, it's easily accessible from Madrid and gives a true insight into the extraordinary wealth and power of the 16th-century Spanish monarchy.

Harmonious facade of the Monastery of El Escorial

The Story of El Escorial

In 1557 the Spanish forces of Philip II defeated the French at St. Quentin. To give thanks to God, Philip conceived the idea of building a monastery dedicated to St. Lawrence (San Lorenzo), which would also serve as a royal palace and burial place.

The vast complex was principally designed in 1584 by Juan de Herrera, and it required 1,500 laborers to complete the work. It has more than 1,200 doors, 2,600 windows and 16 courtyards, and measures nearly 670 feet long. The granite stone accentuates the severe lines of the building, which is built on a grid plan, and the clear air has kept the stone and tiles pristine. Later Bourbon monarchs also left their stamp on the palace by means of decoration, furnishings and pictures.

El Escorial Today

Philip II's modest private apartments are in marked contrast to his grand throne room. He lived in a suite of relatively small rooms with direct access to the chapel.

Later Bourbon monarchs extended these royal Habsburg apartments near the church to the third floor. You will find sumptuously painted ceilings, frescoes and a wonderful tapestry collection. A frescoed courtyard gives access to the marbled staircase leading down to the Royal Pantheon (Panteón de los Reyes), where many Spanish kings from the time of Charles V onward are buried.

The church itself, in the heart of the monastery, is on a monumental scale. Its 100-foot-high altarpiece with onyx, marble and jasper columns is punctuated by bronze sculptures. Move on to the equally opulent library, with its rare wood shelves, marble tables and ornate ceiling.

One of the highlights is the art museum. Among numerous paintings by Peter Paul Rubens, Titian and Jacopo Tintoretto are Roger van der Weyden's thought-provoking *Calvary* and the acidic angularity of El Greco's *Martyrdom of St. Maurice*.

➕ C3 ✉ El Escorial ☎ 91 890 1554 🕐 Tue.–Sun. 10–6, Apr.–Oct.; 10–5, rest of year 🚃 Trains from Atocha; Autocares Herranz (☎ 91 890 4100); buses leave from outside Moncloa subway station in Madrid 🚌 $$$

BARCELONA

Barcelona, the capital of the autonomous Spanish region of Catalonia (Catalunya), is one of the Mediterranean's most vibrant cities. Catalonia is Spain's leading economic region, the most innovative and prosperous area of the country, with a proud history, an independent spirit and a strong sense of identity.

In 1975 the new king, Juan Carlos, restored Catalonia's status as an autonomous region, which marked the beginning of Barcelona's renaissance. The pride and self-confidence engendered by a thriving economy and urban renewal culminated in the Barcelona Olympic Games of 1992. Since then, the city has continued to forge ahead. With its 2,000-year-old history, exhilarating atmosphere, superb architecture from nearly every age, it can't fail to please.

The City and Its People

Wherever you stay, the excellent public transportation system gives easy access to the entire city. For atmosphere, you might want to be somewhere near the street La Rambla or in the old town, and thus within easy walking distance of many of the main sights and the waterfront. The architecturally interesting Eixample area is more spacious, with excellent shopping and restaurants; other hotels are relatively far out of the city center. Barcelonans are exceptionally helpful and polite, with an ability to combine efficiency with a relaxed Mediterranean attitude.

English is not widely spoken, although most hotel staff speak it adequately. All signs are in both Catalan and Spanish. Both are official languages in Barcelona; like Spanish, Catalan is a romance language with Latin roots.

Barcelonan Themes

Since there's so much to see in Barcelona, concentrate on specific areas and themes. Spend a day on the waterfront taking in the Old Port district, Little Barcelona and the ultra-modern Olympic Port. There's a choice of boat tours around the harbor and up the coast, which is the best way to admire the port.

Head for l'Eixample, the Passeig de Gràcia and the Sagrada Família to enjoy the Modernista architecture for which the city is so well known. Barcelona is blessed with two hills, the Montjuïc and Tibidabo; each offers a refuge from the summer noise and heat and has magnificent views over the city and sea.

Barcelona has more than 50 museums and galleries. The Maritime Museum, the Pedralbes Monastery, the Football Museum, the City History Museum and the Palace of Catalan Music cater to a wide range of interests and are all fascinating. Modern-art lovers shouldn't miss the Contemporary

Gaudí

Antoni Gaudí was born in Barcelona in 1852, and lived and worked in the city throughout his life. His architectural vision was flamboyant and unique, and he designed some of Barcelona's most outstanding Modernist buildings. Curved lines, pinnacles, organically inspired stone and towers are his trademarks, seen at their best in the remarkable Holy Family Temple (Temple Expiatori de la Sagrada Família). He was run over by a tram in 1926 and died, unrecognized, in a hospital. When his body was identified, the people of Barcelona lined the streets for his funeral.

Barcelona

Art Museum and the Modern Art Museum. If time is short, there are plenty of English-language guided tours and excursions that take in the main city sights by day and night, and also offer a chance to explore other parts of Catalonia.

Parks and Pools

Barcelona is rich in parks offering a welcome contrast to the bustle and noise of city streets. The Parc de la Ciutadella, near the old town and waterfront, is particularly nice. It has shady trees, a lake and Spain's best zoo, with more than 7,000 animals. Other parks in the city include the Parc de

Joan Miró, with its flamboyant ceramic sculpture, and the Parc de l'Espanya, laid out in the early 1980s. Good beaches are within easy reach, and Barcelona also has excellent swimming pools.

Where to Shop

Prosperous Barcelona is a great shopping center. You'll find serious shopping along the Passeig de Gràcia and on its surrounding streets, which have all the big fashion names, expensive antique stores and some enticing interior design outlets. The wide avenue of Diagonal is lined with good stores, while the Plaça de

Quirky decoration on a corner of La Rambla

Catalunya has a large branch of the department store Corte Ingles.

For Spanish souvenirs, porcelain, fans and wooden goods, try the stores on Portal de l'Angel and around La Rambla. Els Encants is a second-hand market held on the Plaça de les Glòries on Monday, Wednesday, Friday and Saturday.

Nightlife

Classical music, jazz, rock, dance, theater and movies are popular forms of entertainment, and there are comprehensive listings in the *Guía del Ocio*, available from newsstands. Dancing is very popular, and the club scene is one of the best in Spain, ranging from the elegant to the avant-garde. As everywhere in the country, nightlife doesn't really get going until around 3 a.m. and continues until dawn.

Barcelona has some superb festivals throughout the year, often featuring decorated floats, fireworks and processions of the huge dragon and demon figures, known as *capgrossos*, or "big heads."

ESSENTIAL INFORMATION

TOURIST INFORMATION
- Barcelona airport arrivals hall
  ☎ 93 478 4704
- Plaça de Catalunya 17
☎ 93 238 4000
- Carrer Tarragona 149–157 ☎ 93 423 1800
- Palau de la Virreina ☎ 93 301 7775

URBAN TRANSPORTATION
Getting around is easy, thanks to the excellent subway and bus systems. Subway stations are marked on the Barcelona city map by the letter "M" in a red circle. There are five color-coded lines on the subway. Buy combination tickets valid for one, three or five days, which give unlimited use of the bus and subway; tickets and transportation maps, are available from subway stations. Don't forget to validate tickets by stamping them at the turnstile before boarding trains, or when you get on the bus. Another possibility is the Bus Turístic, which operates daily 9–7:45 from March through December. Its two different routes cover Barcelona's main attractions, taking you closer to the sights than the regular city service. A cable car links La Barceloneta and Montjuïc, and there are two funiculars, serving Montjuïc and Tibidabo; the latter is also served by Barcelona's one surviving tram route. You can pick up a black-and-yellow taxi at a stand, hail one on the street, or call Radio Movil (☎ 93 358 1111), Barnataxi (☎ 93 358 7755) or Radio Taxi (☎ 93 490 2222).

AIRPORT INFORMATION
Barcelona International Airport (☎ 93 298 3838), with connections to most major European cities, is 7 miles southwest of the city center, about a 30-minute drive. It is served by the Aerobus, which runs to and from Plaça de Catalunya every 20 minutes, Mon.–Fri. 5:30 a.m.–10:15 p.m., Sat.–Sun. 6 a.m.–10:15 p.m.

CLIMATE – average highs and lows for the month

	JAN.	FEB.	MAR.	APR.	MAY	JUN.	JUL.	AUG.	SEP.	OCT.	NOV.	DEC.
	13°C	14°C	15°C	17°C	21°C	24°C	28°C	28°C	25°C	21°C	17°C	14°C
	55°F	57°F	59°F	63°F	70°F	75°F	82°F	82°F	77°F	70°F	63°F	57°F
	5°C	6°C	8°C	10°C	12°C	17°C	20°C	20°C	19°C	13°C	9°C	8°C
	41°F	43°F	46°F	50°F	54°F	63°F	68°F	68°F	66°F	55°F	48°F	46°F

Barcelona

CITY SIGHTS

Key to symbols
🕂 map coordinates refer to the Barcelona map on page 411; sights below are highlighted in yellow on the map.
✉ address or location ☎ telephone number
🕐 opening times 🚌 nearest bus or tram route
Ⓜ nearest subway 🍴 restaurant on site or nearby
🎟 admission charge: $$$ more than 900PTA, $$ 600PTA–900PTA, $ less than 600PTA

ANELLA OLÍMPICA

🕂 A1 ✉ Montjuïc ☎ 93 426 0660 🕐 Tue.–Fri. 10–1 and 4–8, Sat.–Sun. 10–2 Ⓜ Espanya 🚌 61
🎟 $
The 1992 Olympic complex, the Anella Olímpica (Olympic Ring), centers around the 1936 Olympic Stadium, which was enlarged to seat 70,000 people. Its basement now houses the Olympic Gallery, recalling the 1992 games with videos and souvenirs. Nearby are Barcelona's sports university; the steel-and-glass Sant Jordi Stadium; and the pools, all dominated by the silhouette of the communications tower, one of Barcelona's modern landmarks.

LA BARCELONETA

🕂 C2 ✉ La Barceloneta Ⓜ Barceloneta 🚌 14, 17, 51, 64
The district of La Barceloneta (Little Barcelona) occupies a triangle of reclaimed land between the harbor and the sea. Developed in the 18th century to house seamen, fishermen and dock workers, the neighborhood still retains its maritime atmosphere. It's a great place to eat; many seafood restaurants (*chiringuitos*) line the seafront, where you'll find the freshest local fish specialties.

CATEDRAL

🕂 C2 ✉ Plaça de la Seu ☎ 93 315 1554 🕐 Daily 8–7:30 🍴 Nou Celler, see page 566 Ⓜ Jaume I 🚌 17, 19, 40, 45
Nothing more strongly represents Barcelona's historic past than the great Catedral (Cathedral). It was built between the 13th and 15th centuries,

Barcelona's fortress-like Cathedral

and the soaring space beneath the Catalan Gothic arches and numerous side chapels houses a wealth of treasures. The tranquil 14th-century cloister, with its fountains, magnolias and palms, is particularly beautiful.

CIUTAT VELLA

🕂 B2 ✉ Bounded by Rambla, Universitat, Laietana and Ferran 🍴 Nou Celler, see page 566 Ⓜ Jaume I 🚌 14, 17, 19
A maze of narrow streets and squares comprises the Ciutat Vella (Old City). It was built within the old Roman walls when Barcelona was one of the richest and most important Mediterranean trading cities. At its heart lies the Barri Gòtic (Gothic Quarter), centered around the Cathedral and Plaça Sant Jaume. This plaza, once the power center of Catalonia's kings, is still the site of city hall and the administrative buildings of the government of Catalonia.

The Plaça del Rei, formerly the medieval marketplace, is said to be where King Ferdinand and Queen Isabella welcomed Christopher Columbus home from America in 1493. Nearby is the Plaça Reial, a fine arcaded square built in 1848. Gothic mansions line the atmospheric streets, and you'll find museums, historic churches, and bars and restaurants.

Gaudí's exuberant Casa Batlló

L'EIXAMPLE

✚ A3 🚇 Diagonal, Catalunya, Girona

Between 1860 and 1920 Barcelona expanded into a grid of uniform streets parallel to the sea, an area known as l'Eixample (the Extension). Today it's a residential, commercial and business district, divided in half by the Diagonal, a grand avenue cutting through the grid at a 45-degree angle. It's an interesting example of innovative town planning, and contains Barcelona's finest Modernist buildings. Some of the best are in the Passeig de Gràcia; look for No. 43, Casa Batlló, with a mosaic facade and wavy roofline that represent St. George's dragon. The block at No. 92 is known as La Perdrera, Gaudí's last secular work. It's without a single straight line or sharp corner.

FUNDACIÓ JOAN MIRÓ

✚ B1 ✉ Plaça Neptú, Parc de Montjuïc ☎ 93 329 1908 🕐 Tue.–Sat. 11–7 (also Thu. 7–9:30 p.m.), Sun. 10:30–2:30 🚇 Espanya 🚌 61 💷 $$$

More than 200 instantly recognizable and vibrantly colored paintings, along with sculptures, tapestries and drawings, are displayed in the white, bright space of the Fundació Joan Miró (Joan Miró

Foundation). Born in Barcelona in 1893, Miró spent most of his life in the city before retiring to Mallorca in 1956. In 1971 he established the foundation to house the world's largest collection of his works and to promote contemporary art.

MERCAT DE LA BOQUERIA

✚ B2 ✉ La Rambla 100 🕐 Mon.–Sat. 7 a.m.–8 p.m. 🚇 Liceu 🚌 14, 38, 59

Make time to visit the glorious Mercat de la Boqueria (Boqueria Market), housed since the 1830s in a covered hall just off the Rambla. If you arrive at lunchtime, take advantage of the snack bars here. The scents and colors of the fish, hams and sausages, succulent fruit and freshly picked vegetables, and the babble of noise from the shoppers and stall vendors, will be one of the most enduring memories of your visit to Barcelona.

MONTJUÏC

✚ A1 🚇 Take the subway to Parallel station, then the funicular to Parc de Montjuïc and *teleféric* cable car to Mirador and Castell 🚌 61

The green hill of Montjuïc, 698 feet high, dominates Barcelona's southern suburbs. Once known as the "Mountain of the Jews," Montjuïc today is a pleasant recreational area, dotted with gardens, museums, galleries and sports facilities. The most impressive approach is through the monumental Plaça de Espanya to the Font Màgica (Magic Fountain). The fountain stands below the pavilions built for the 1929 International Exhibition, many of which now house galleries.

MUSEU D'HISTÒRIA DE CATALUNYA

✚ C2 ✉ Plaça Pau Vila 3 ☎ 93 225 4700 🕐 Tue.–Sat. 10 –7 (also Fri.–Sat. 7–8 p.m.), Sun. 10–2:30 🍴 Café in museum 🚇 Barceloneta 🚌 14, 17, 59 💷 $$$

The Museu d'Història de Catalunya (Catalonian History Museum), Barcelona's newest museum, helps explain Catalonia, a "nation within a nation." It is located in a converted 19th-century warehouse, and exhibits depict the political, historical, cultural and everyday life of this vibrant region. The museum uses state-of-the-art and hands-on displays, interactive screens and special effects to convey its story.

MUSEU NACIONAL D'ART DE CATALUNYA (MNAC)

🔢 A1 ✉ Palau Nacional, Parc de Montjuïc ☎ 93 423 7199 🕐 Tue.–Sat. 10–7 (also Thu. 7–9 p.m.), Sun. 10–2:30 🍴 Café-bar in museum 🚇 Espanya 🚌 13, 38, 55 💲 $$$

Still in the middle of ongoing renovations, the Museu Nacional d'Art de Catalunya (National Museum of Catalonian Art) is among the world's finest medieval art museums. Catalan Romanesque art, with its solid rounded forms and stunning simplicity, is represented by sculpture and carving, gold, enamel and textiles. The outstanding treasures are the 11th- and 12th-century murals, removed from isolated country churches and reassembled in the museum in order to preserve them. The ornate forms of the Gothic sculptures and altarpieces, which form the other major part of the museum, make a perfect contrast.

MUSEU PICASSO

🔢 C2 ✉ Calle Moncada 15–19 ☎ 93 319 6310 🕐 Tue.–Sat. 10–8, Sun. 10–3 🍴 Café-restaurant in museum 🚇 Jaume I 🚌 16, 17, 40, 45 💲 $$$

Pablo Picasso, born in Andalucia in 1881, lived in Barcelona from 1895 until 1904, and he held his first exhibition in the city in 1900. The Museu Picasso (Picasso Museum), Barcelona's top attraction, is the most important collection of his works in Spain. It contains examples from each of his stylistic periods, from the early street scenes to the major cubist works and ceramics he produced in later years.

PARC GÜELL

🔢 Off the map ✉ Calle Olot ☎ 93 424 3809 🕐 Daily 10–9, May–Aug.; 10–8, Apr.and Sep.; 10–7, Mar. and Oct.; 10–6, rest of year 🚇 Vallcarca 🚌 24, 25, 28

With its views and green spaces, Parc Güell (Güell Park) would be worth

Mosaic fountain by Gaudí on Güell Park steps

visiting even without its main attraction, the architectural elements by Antoni Gaudí scattered throughout its 50 acres. Originally planned as a residential landscaped area by Gaudí's main patrons, the Güell family, only the grand entrance, the plaza, paths and steps were completed. These are interspersed with colorful and weirdly shaped sculptures, fountains and columns, many intricately decorated with thousands of pieces of broken ceramics.

POBLE ESPANYOL

🔢 A1 ✉ Avenida de Marqués de Comillas ☎ 93 325 7866 🕐 Tue.–Sat. 9 a.m.–2 a.m. (also Fri.–Sat. 2–4 a.m.), Sun. 9 a.m.–midnight, Mon. 9–8 🚇 Espanya 🚌 61 💲 $$$

The streets and squares of the Poble Espanyol (Spanish Village), built for the 1929 World Exhibition, give a glimpse of the country's many architectural styles. Reproductions range from the gleaming white houses of Andalucia to the flat granite facades of Galicia, all blended to form one "village." The buildings house restaurants, cafés and workshops where you'll find crafts and artifacts from all over Spain, while evening brings dinner, live music and flamenco.

The soaring interior of the Gothic church of Santa Maria del Mar

PORT VELL

✚ C1 ✉ Port Vell 🚇 Drassanes, Barceloneta
🚌 17, 36, 64

The Port Vell (Old Port) district, once decayed and run-down, was transformed for the 1992 Olympics. Once more an integral part of the city, it is a busy recreation area, with a new marina and elegant new bridges and walkways connecting its various attractions. The centerpiece is Maremagnum, a shopping, eating and leisure center, complete with IMAX movie theater and an aquarium.

LA RAMBLA

✚ B2 ✉ La Rambla 🚇 Catalunya, Drassanes, Liceu 🚌 13, 48, 59

La Rambla, Barcelona's most famous street, runs from Plaça de Catalunya to the waterfront. It's an exuberant tree-lined promenade effectively joining the old and new parts of the city, divided into five distinctive sections. Here you will find Liceu, Barcelona's opera house, restored after a fire in 1994. The name Rambla is Arabic, from *ramla*, "a torrent," a reminder that the street follows an old watercourse, although it's tempting to construe it as a place for an enjoyable ramble. From here head to the statue of Christopher Columbus near the waterfront.

TEMPLE DE LA SAGRADA FAMÍLIA

✚ C3 ✉ Plaça de la Sagrada Família ☎ 93 455 0247 🕐 Daily 9–7, Mar.–Oct.; 9–6, rest of year 🚇 Sagrada Família 🚌 10, 19, 51 💷 $$$

Antoni Gaudí, the famous Catalan Modernist architect, worked on the Temple de la Sagrada Família (Church of the Atonement of the Holy Family) for more than 40 years. He envisioned a vast Cathedral, with facades that would show the birth, death and resurrection of Christ, and 18 towers that would represent the Twelve Apostles, the Four Evangelists, the Virgin and Christ. At his death in 1926 only the nativity facade, the crypt and one of the towers was complete, and it seems unlikely the project will ever be completed.

SANTA MARIA DEL MAR

✚ C2 ✉ Plaça de Santa Maria ☎ 93 310 2390 🕐 Daily 9–12:30 and 4:30–8 🚇 Jaume I 🚌 14, 17, 51

Built between 1329 and 1384 at the height of Barcelona's medieval prestige, the beautiful Gothic church of Santa Maria del Mar (Our Lady of the Sea) is tucked away in the narrow Gothic streets of the waterfront Ribera district. Its stark and serene interior allows the elegant architecture to speak for itself.

CATALAN FARE

You can eat as well in Barcelona as anywhere in Spain, sampling local Catalan dishes, fresh fish and seafood, and specialties from other parts of Spain and abroad. Since restaurants here cater to foreigners, dinner is served much earlier than elsewhere in Spain.

Fish and Seafood

Be sure to eat fish during your visit, preferably in one of Little Barcelona's restaurants where it is a specialty. Appetizers often include a selection of shellfish, tiny grilled sardines or giant prawns. Local main fish dishes are often a type of *sarsuela,* fish stew, or *suquet de peix,* a soupy fish and potato casserole. Although not the home of paella (that's Valencia), there are wonderful *arròs* dishes, where rice, subtly flavored with vegetables and spices, is combined with fish and its stock. Try *fideuà,* cooked like paella but using fine pasta in place of rice.

Above: Spain's national dish – paella
Below: Catalan mussels served in a marine sauce

Mar i Muntanya

Mar i muntanya (sea and mountain), or surf 'n' turf, has inspired some of Catalonia's best recipes. Using local ingredients, cooks have created combination dishes featuring rabbit, shrimp, prawns, chicken and meat. Look for *mar i cel* (sea and sky) on local menus, or try some of the excellent pork products. Main dishes are usually accompanied by intensely flavored vegetables, a saffron sauce, a garlic mayonnaise or a crisp salad. The local

bread, baked several times a day, is crisp and light, a reminder of Barcelona's proximity to the French border. Cured ham, spicy sausages and garlic snails are often part of a *tapas* lunch, a good time to try a variety of tastes.

Thirst-quenchers

Bars serve tea, coffee, soda and fruit juice as well as every conceivable form of alcohol. You'll find many familiar drinks, and a range of Spanish beers and wines.

Beer comes in bottles or on tap, and you can buy wine by the glass. Local red, white and rosé wines come from the Penedès area; Torres and Masia Bach are reliable labels. Cava makes a great aperitif; a light sparkling dry wine, it's made the same way as champagne.

Santiago

SANTIAGO

Tucked away in the green fringes of Galicia, in northwest Spain, is Santiago de Compostela – one of the great shrines of medieval Christendom. Millions of pilgrims braved hazardous travel to worship at the shrine of St. James, the patron saint of Spain. People still come here on pilgrimages today, especially during holy years, which occur when St. James' Day falls on a Sunday.

Santiago is one of Europe's most perfect medieval cities – a mix of religious and secular buildings, with an ancient and thriving university and a unique spiritual atmosphere. It is also home to the parliament of Galicia, which is an autonomous region, and there is a lively and prosperous modern town surrounding the central core.

Old Santiago

The historic heart is pedestrian-only and can be traversed on foot in less than a half-hour; everything you'll want to see lies within this small area. Santiago offers quality, not quantity, so most visitors find a stay of a few days ample.

The two main streets, Rúa do Franco and Rúa do Vilar, lead south from the cathedral square and are lined with stores, bars and restaurants. Pick up a map at the tourist office; it's easy to lose your bearings in the maze of streets and squares behind the Cathedral.

Santiago Flavors

Galician cooking is delicious, robust and tasty, and relies on the excellent quality of local ingredients. Seafood and shellfish are extensively farmed in the *rias*, deeply indented coastal inlets, and are of superb quality. Regional specialties include *pulpo*, octopus, cooked in various ways; blood puddings and sausages; and *empanadas*, a flat pie with a meat or fish filling.

This is one of the few Spanish regions where lamb is eaten, and local beef also is particularly good. Santiago

Stone carvings adorn the medieval buildings in the old quarter of the city

has many pastry shops, where you'll find wonderful cakes and cookies. Local wine varieties include Ribeiro and Valdeorra, straightforward whites, and the excellent red Amandi and Condado. If the weather's cold try a cup of hot chocolate; thick enough to eat, it's some of the best in Spain.

Souvenirs and Entertainment

Santiago's streets are lined with stores selling pilgrim souvenirs – medals, rosaries, key rings, holy pictures and statues, all decorated with the image of St. James and his scallop shell emblem. The traditional material for pilgrimage souvenirs is jet, polished and cut, or fashioned into the *figa,* a clenched-fist amulet. The guild of silversmiths, hugely important in the past, is still active and makes some fine pieces.

This is a university town with a thriving cultural life, and there are year-round classical concerts, as well as clubs frequented by students. You'll

Santiago's Main Festivals

Santiago's biggest festival is July 25th, the feast of St. James, when the city is packed with pilgrims, tourists and local people. The night before sees the Apostle's Fire (Fuego del Apóstol), a spectacular fireworks display in front of the Cathedral. The feast itself represents a solemn Mass, with music, choirs and Galician bagpipes, and the huge incense burner, the *botafumeiro,* is swung in the Cathedral. The feast falls in the middle of Santiago's folklore festival, a two-week celebration of Galician culture, with street music, parades, concerts and markets. An international music festival is held in August and September.

hear bagpipes, Galicia's national instrument, played on the streets; this is a favorite way for students to make extra cash.

ESSENTIAL INFORMATION

TOURIST INFORMATION
• Praza de Galicia s/n ☎ 981 584 400 or 981 573 990
• Rúa do Villar 43 ☎ 981 584 081

old town and then walk. Taxis can be found at stands outside the old city, or you can call them (☎ 981 598 488, 981 582 450 and 981 561 028, or 981 560 101 for night service).

URBAN TRANSPORTATION
Santiago's historic center is pedestrian-only; the only vehicular access is for taxis and delivery vehicles. It takes around 15 to 20 minutes to walk from one end of the center to the other, and everything you'll want to see is within this area, even the farthest hotels. If you are staying outside the historic center, take a taxi to the edge of the

AIRPORT INFORMATION
Santiago-Labacolla International Airport (☎ 981 547 400), with services to many European cities, is 7 miles east of the city, about a 15- to 30-minute drive. Buses into Santiago run hourly from outside the terminal, daily 7:15 a.m.–10 p.m. Taxis also leave from outside the airport terminal.

CLIMATE – average highs and lows for the month

JAN.	FEB.	MAR.	APR.	MAY	JUN.	JUL.	AUG.	SEP.	OCT.	NOV.	DEC.
13°C	14°C	15°C	17°C	19°C	22°C	25°C	25°C	24°C	20°C	17°C	14°C
55°F	57°F	59°F	63°F	66°F	72°F	77°F	77°F	75°F	68°F	63°F	57°F
5°C	6°C	7°C	8°C	10°C	14°C	16°C	16°C	14°C	12°C	9°C	7°C
41°F	43°F	45°F	46°F	50°F	57°F	61°F	61°F	57°F	54°F	48°F	45°F

The baroque facade of the Cathedral

CITY SIGHTS

Key to symbols

➕ map coordinates refer to the Santiago map on page 418; sights below are highlighted in yellow on the map.

✉ address or location ☎ telephone number

🕐 opening times 🚌 nearest bus route

🍴 restaurant on site or nearby

💰 admission charge: $$$ more than 900PTA, $$ 600PTA–900PTA, $ less than 600PTA

BARRIO ANTIGUO

➕ B2 ✉ Barrio Antiguo

The Barrio Antiguo (Old Quarter) of Santiago is packed with beautiful, historic buildings. The main streets are lined with arcaded old granite houses in the traditional Galician style. East of the Cathedral, the spacious Plaza da Quintana is surrounded by notable buildings, including the arcaded Casa de la Canónica (Canon's Residence). This faces a gracious flight of steps leading up to the 17th-century Casa de la Parra (House of the Bunch of Grapes). On the third side is the austere facade of San Paio de Antealtares Monastery, founded in the ninth century. Opposite, the Puerta del Perdón (Door of Pardon) opens onto the

east end of the Cathedral – this is only used during holy years. On the Cathedral's north side stands the huge complex of the Monasterio de San Martín Pinario, with its church and three cloisters. Behind the monastery lies the 17th-century Convento de San Francisco, commemorating a pilgrimage by St. Francis of Assisi in 1213. It is now a museum devoted to the Holy Land and incorporates a hotel.

CATEDRAL

➕ A2 ✉ Plaza do Obradoiro ☎ 981 561 527
🕐 Daily 9–9; opening time sometimes varies

The present Catedral (Cathedral) dates from the 11th to 13th centuries. The simple Romanesque lines of the interior provide a superb contrast to the ornate facade, added in 1750, at the Cathedral's main entrance. Here stands the 12th-century triple doorway known as the Pórtico de la Glória (Doorway of Glory), one of the sculptural glories of Spain. Prophets and Apostles surround Christ the Savior and the Four Evangelists, all carved with exceptional imagination and fluidity. Behind the worn entrance pillar and the figure of St. James is a figure said to be Maestro Mateo, the Cathedral's designer. It's customary to bump your head against his in the hope some of his artistic genius may rub off.

You'll notice a pulley system high above the transept; this operates the *botafumeiro*, a monster incense burner used during major feasts, which requires eight men to swing it through a huge arc above the transept. The silverwork and gilded figures of the High Altar glitter under the lights of the candelabra.

MUSEO DAS PEREGRINACIONS

➕ B2 ✉ Rúa San Miguel ☎ 981 581 558
🕐 Tue.–Fri. 10–8 , Sat. 10:30–1:30 and 5–8, Sun. 10:30–1:30 💰 $

The Museo das Peregrinacions (Pilgrimage Museum) tells the story of pilgrimage in general, and the Santiago pilgrimage in particular. Exhibits show how the Cathedral and town grew

ST. JAMES AND SANTIAGO

To medieval Europeans, a pilgrimage (*peregrinacion*) was a means of earning extra grace and thus attaining heaven faster. Pilgrimages were made to many holy places, but the great goals were Jerusalem, Rome and Santiago de Compostela. The apostle St. James is known as "Sant Iago" in Spanish. The city which bears his name is also the site of his shrine and burial place. According to legend, he had preached in Spain before returning to martyrdom in Judaea in AD 44. His disciples brought his body back to Spain, where it lay hidden until AD 844.

Legend tells that he appeared in a vision to Christian leaders and led them to victory against the Muslim invaders, earning him the title of *Matamoros*, the Moorslayer. His body and relics were rediscovered at Compostela, which soon became the center of devotion for Spain's new patron saint. By the 11th century, pilgrims were traveling from all over Europe to pray at Santiago.

The pilgrims' well-trodden route into Santiago

The *Camino de Santiago*

Pilgrims traveled from France, Britain, Germany, Italy and Scandinavia, as well as Spain and Portugal, many of them taking years to complete their journey. By the mid-12th century, between 500,000 and 2 million people were on the move annually, a vast number in relation to population sizes.

Roads to Spain threaded their way across the Continent, but once across the Pyrenees, converged into a well-organized route across northern Spain. This became known as the *Camino de Santiago*, the Way of St. James. Administered by a religious military order, the *camino* was policed and marked along its length, with hostels, inns and churches offering practical and spiritual sustenance to the travelers. Towns grew up around the stopping points, with their own churches, hospitals and hospices.

Dressed in sandals and heavy capes and armed with stout staffs, pilgrims also wore the scallop shell emblem of the saint in their broad-brimmed hats. On arrival in Santiago, the custom was to enter the cathedral and embrace the golden effigy of the saint placed high above his tomb, while giving alms and thanks in gratitude for the safe completion of the pilgrimage.

The *Camino* Today

The custom of walking the *camino* died out during the 16th century, but was revived around 1880. Today, thousands of people make the journey to Santiago, by car, train, plane, and on foot.

Relax amid the grandeur of Obradoiro Square

MUSEO Y TESORO DE LA CATEDRAL

✚ A2　✉ Plaza do Obradoiro　☎ 981 561 527
🕐 Daily 10–1:30 and 4–7:30　🎫 $$

The Museo y Tesoro de la Catedral (Cathedral Museum and Treasury) is housed around the magnificent 16th-century cloisters adjoining the Cathedral. It also includes the Romanesque Old Cathedral (a crypt beneath the Pórtico de la Glória) and the Chapel of San Fernando, which opens off the interior of the Cathedral. In the latter you can see gem-encrusted gold crucifixes and statues still used for important feasts. The museum includes a fine collection of tapestries from the most prestigious workshops. The cloisters, a lovely blend of Castilian-Gothic and Renaissance architecture, are some of the largest in Spain. Stairs lead up to the gallery, completed in 1590. This offers a good vantage point over the cathedral square. The building adjoining the left of the Cathedral is the old Bishop's Palace.

PLAZA DO OBRADOIRO

✚ A2　✉ Plaza do Obradoiro

The sweeping expanse of Plaza do Obradoiro (Obradoiro Square), in front of the Cathedral, is surrounded on its other sides by three harmonious buildings. These are the Hostal de los Reyes Católicos (Hostel of the Catholic Monarchs), the Colegio de San Jerónimo (College of St. Jerome) and the Pazo de Raxoi, or Ayuntamiento (City Hall). The oldest building is the hostel (now a hotel), originally founded by Ferdinand and Isabella as a pilgrims' lodging house. It has an elegantly plain facade centered by a superb Plateresque doorway. Inside, the building is laid out around four lovely patios.

Opposite, the college, with its charming balcony, dates mainly from the 17th century – although its doorway is 200 years younger. Facing the Cathedral, the classical lines of the City Hall, built in the 18th century, seem to unite the whole ensemble.

around the apostle's tomb; how the routes west across Europe developed; what the pilgrims wore; and how they traveled. There's a copy of the fascinating *Codex Calixtinus*, a 13th-century guide to the route, full of tips about travel and information about Santiago. Look for the collection of souvenirs 14th-century pilgrims took home.

MUSEO DO POBO GALEGO

✚ Off the map　✉ San Domingos de Bonaval
☎ 981 583 620　🕐 Tue.–Sat. 10–1 and 4–7　🎫 $

Santiago is more than a noted shrine, it's also one of the main towns in Galicia. The Museu do Poble Galego (Museum of the Galician People), located in the old convent of San Domingo, explains Galicia and the many aspects of traditional life in this remote corner of Spain. There are displays of tools, pottery, costumes and exhibits on Galicia's dolmens, stone circles and hill-forts. The museum's galleries encircle the 17th-century cloister; in one corner a superb staircase, with three intertwining flights of steps, rises to different floors of the building.

The Cathedral of St. James dominates the city skyline

A DAY IN SANTIAGO

A Spiritual Morning

Your first stop should be a visit to the excellent Pilgrimage Museum (Museo das Peregrinacons, see page 420), where you can learn about the history of pilgrimage. This will give you a sense of perspective and will pave the way for a visit to the Cathedral, next on the list. As you go in, place your hand on the worn stones of the entrance pillar, the first gesture of arriving pilgrims.

Spend time admiring the architecture and artistic treasures, then join the line and mount the steps behind the altar to embrace the effigy of St. James, as pilgrims have done for over 1,000 years. You could time your visit to coincide with the daily noontime Pilgrims' Mass.

A Secular Afternoon

Head up Rúa do Franco or Rúa do Vilar, the main streets, and choose one of the many restaurants for lunch – shellfish or octopus are both traditional Galician specialties. After lunch, you could head back toward the Cathedral and visit the Cathedral Museum (Museo y Tesoro de la Catedral) before walking back across town to the Museum of the Galician People (Museo do Pobo Galego). At about 6 p.m. the streets begin to fill with shoppers and university students, and the bars become busy.

A Peaceful Evening

There's no problem finding an excellent restaurant for dinner; try some fish, or one of the flavorful Galician meat dishes, often pork-based, with potatoes and turnip tops. Be sure to order some of the local dome-shaped cheese, and finish with a slice of *tarta de Santiago*, a special almond pastry made only here. As you wander through the ancient streets after dinner, you'll probably hear the strains of bagpipes echoing through some hidden courtyard. For the walk route, see the city map on page 418.

Seville

SEVILLE

Some of Spain's quintessential images are of whitewashed streets, Moorish architecture, flamenco dresses, orange trees and proud horsemen. This mental picture actually reflects Andalucia, and its capital Seville (Sevilla). It is the fourth-largest city in Spain, the seat of a university, an important industrial city and the center of a rich agricultural region. Renowned for architectural treasures, great festivals and a relaxed lifestyle, Seville has attracted visitors for many years, and cares for them far better than many other Spanish cities.

Seville on Foot

In Seville, every building, garden and street is designed as an escape from the sun. If you're visiting in summer, take lengthy siestas during the hottest hours. The central old core is relatively small, and you'll be able to walk to many of the main sights. The narrow, twisting streets can be confusing, so always take a city map with you; maps are free and available at the tourist office and many hotels. Blue-and-white signs direct visitors to the main sights. There's plenty of information in English, and helpful multilingual guides – often university students – offer assistance at the main attractions.

There's plenty to see in Seville besides the main attractions. The range of museums, fine churches and civic buildings attracts many visitors: The Casa de Pilatos, an elegant private palace, is a favorite. Also look for the Tabacco Factory (Fabrica de Tabacos), now part of the university, but also where Carmen (of opera fame), worked.

Walking is only one option. Visitors can take an open-carriage drive from outside the Cathedral that takes in many of the sights. Alternatively, half-hourly cruises run from the Torre del Oro on the Guadalquivir river, one of Spain's greatest waterways, and this is a relaxing way to admire Seville.

Festivals in Seville

Seville has two major festivals: the *Semana Santa* (Holy Week), the last week of Lent, and the *Feria* (Spring

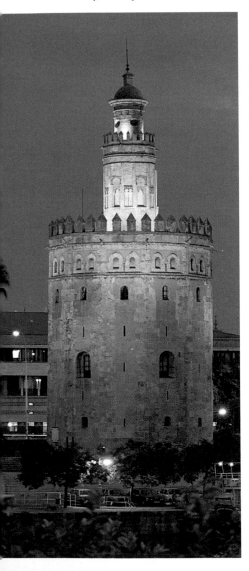

Bathed in light – the Moorish "Tower of Gold"

Festival), held the last week in April. If you plan to visit the city during either of these, reserve a room far in advance. Holy Week is a deeply religious time, celebrated by *pasos* processions held by rival brotherhoods in Seville's different districts. *Pasos* are huge carriers supporting religious statues, sumptuously decorated and carried by up to 60 men. The Spring Festival is completely secular, a weeklong celebration of Andalucia's love affair with horses, music and beautiful women. Carriages filled with laughing girls in flounced dresses, accompanied by horseback riders in traditional dress, parade the streets, and the graceful dance of the *sevillana* is danced all night.

Eating Southern Style

Eating is a pleasure in Seville, with a wide range of restaurants and *tapas*

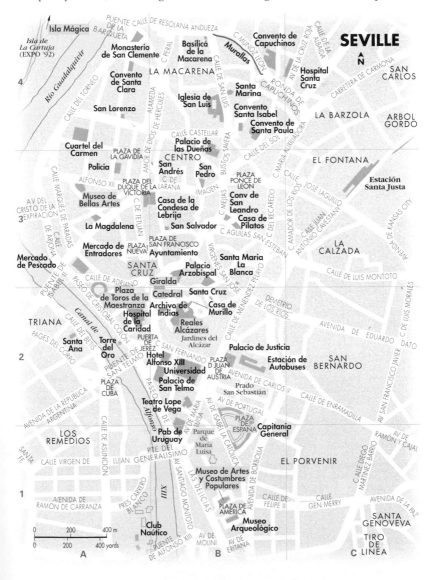

Seville

bars. Almost more than anywhere else in Spain, *tapas* has a special place here, and there's a fabulous choice of dishes. They are traditionally eaten with a *copa*, a glass of sherry, the fortified wine from Jerez – a lovely city south of Seville.

Mealtimes are late, particularly in summer, with lunch often finishing around 4 or 5 and dinner starting at midnight. The more cosmopolitan restaurants are geared to foreigners' dining habits. Andalucian coffee is very strong, so it's best to ask for a *café con agua* (coffee with water) if you like it weaker.

Mantillas and Castanets

Shoppers throng Sierpes – "the Serpent" – the winding pedestrian-only street running north from near the Cathedral. Stroll around and enjoy the traditional storefronts; it's a good place to find Sevillian fans, mantillas, shawls, flamenco dresses, castanets and gourmet candies. You'll find attractive pottery at tiny stores in Santa Cruz or across the river in the Triana district, where they also make fine wrought-iron goods, saddles and guitars.

Flamenco

Flamenco is a synthesis of dance and music, ideally performed spontaneously to express joy and sorrow about everyday life, religion and work. Its heartland lies in Andalucia, but its origins stretch as far afield as Egypt and India. It reaches its zenith in the songs known as *cante jondo* (deep song), expressions of deep feelings. The profound meaning of flamenco is hard for foreigners to grasp, but the music and dance, the distinctive costume, and the click of castanets can be enjoyed by all.

ESSENTIAL INFORMATION

TOURIST INFORMATION
• Avenida de la Constución ☎ 95 422 1404
• Naves del Barranco, Calle Arjona 28 ☎ 95 450 5600
• Paseo de la Delicias 9 ☎ 95 423 4465

URBAN TRANSPORTATION
Seville has an efficient bus system that mainly services the sprawling residential suburbs, with only a few buses going into the heart of the old city. Some city-center routes run past the Cathedral to the Plaza Nueva, and other lines terminate at Plaza de la Incarnación. Maria Luisa Park and the surrounding area also is well served from the center. Buy single tickets when you board, or show your three- or seven-day tourist pass, available at newsstands or from the Tussam bus office. There's also a special tourist bus, run by Sevirama (☎ 95 456 0693). This hop-on-and-off service covers the main sights, with an English commentary, and runs from March through November; tickets are valid all day. Beige-colored taxis can be hailed on the street or at a stand, or you can call Radio Taxi (☎ 95 458 0000 or 95 458 1111), Tele Taxi (☎ 95 462 2222) or Radio Teléfono Giralda (☎ 95 467 5555).

AIRPORT INFORMATION
Seville International Airport, with connections to major European cities, is about 11 miles northeast of the city, a 15- to 30-minute drive. An airport bus runs hourly from the terminal to Puerta Jerez between Mon.–Fri. 6:15 a.m.–9:15 p.m., with a less frequent service at the weekends. Taxis are available outside the airport terminal.

CLIMATE – average highs and lows for the month

JAN.	FEB.	MAR.	APR.	MAY	JUN.	JUL.	AUG.	SEP.	OCT.	NOV.	DEC.
15°C	16°C	18°C	22°C	27°C	32°C	35°C	35°C	32°C	25°C	20°C	16°C
59°F	61°F	64°F	72°F	81°F	90°F	95°F	95°F	90°F	77°F	68°F	61°F
5°C	7°C	8°C	10°C	13°C	17°C	18°C	19°C	18°C	14°C	10°C	4°C
41°F	45°F	46°F	50°F	55°F	63°F	64°F	66°F	64°F	57°F	50°F	40°F

CITY SIGHTS

Key to symbols

map coordinates refer to the Seville map on page 425; sights below are highlighted in yellow on the map.

address or location · telephone number

opening times · nearest bus route

restaurant on site or nearby

admission charge: $$$ more than 900PTA, $$ 600PTA–900PTA, $ less than 600PTA

BARRIO DE SANTA CRUZ

A3 · Santa Cruz · 21, 40, C4

The Barrio de Santa Cruz (Santa Cruz Quarter), with its narrow white streets, ironwork grilles and sun-splashed squares shaded by orange trees, typifies Seville and draws visitors night and day. Originally the Jewish quarter, it was popular with 17th-century nobility, who added mansions along its alleyways.

CATEDRAL

B2 · Plaza Virgen de los Reyes · 95 421 4971

Mon.–Sat. 10:30–5, Sun. 2–6 · El Giraldillo, see page 567 · 21, 30, 41, 42 · $$

Seville's magnificent Catedral (Cathedral), built on the site of the Moorish mosque, is the third largest in Europe; only St. Peter's in Rome and St. Paul's in London are larger. Vast, rich and harmoniously balanced, it was built between 1401 and 1519, a blend of Gothic austerity and Spanish flamboyance. Almost as wide as it is long, the interior is dominated by the chancel, the *Capilla Mayor*, its splendid, richly carved Flemish altarpiece glistening with gold leaf behind immense grilles. Opposite lie the choir stalls. Stand between the two and look up at the transept roof, 184 feet above your head; this riot of stone filigree is supported by massive arches and columns, but its huge size is dwarfed by the scale of the Cathedral. Other highlights include Christopher Columbus' tomb in the south transept; the treasury and sacristy, packed with paintings and precious altar vessels; and the domed Royal Chapel, the burial place of Alfonso X of Castile.

Dine beneath the beautiful 12th-century Giralda

GIRALDA

B3 · Plaza Virgen de los Reyes · 95 421 4971

Mon.–Sat. 10:30–5, Sun. 2–6 · El Giraldillo, see page 567 · 21, 30, 41, 42 · $$

When Christians destroyed the mosque to build the Cathedral, they kept the minaret and transformed it into the new Cathedral's bell tower. Nick-named the *Giralda,* the "weather-vane," the 322-foot-tall tower was built in the 12th century. Instead of stairs, you climb the series of interior ramps; 17 levels lead to the top, from where there are views over Seville. Below the tower lies the lovely Patio de los Naranjos (Courtyard of the Orange Trees), once part of the mosque.

ISLA MÁGICA

Off the map · Pabellón de España, Isla de la Cartuja · 95 446 1616 · Daily 10 a.m.–midnight, Mar.–Nov. · C1, C2 · $$$

Seville hosted Expo '92 on the Isla de la Cartuja, an island between two branches

Seville

of the Quadalquivir river. This is now the site of Isla Mágica, a theme park devoted to the Spanish discovery of the New World in the 15th and 16th centuries. The leisure park has a range of state-of-the-art attractions.

MUSEO DE ARTES COSTUMBRES POPULARES

➕ B1 ✉ Plaza de América, Parque de Maria Luisa ☎ 95 423 2401 🕐 Tue. 3–8, Wed.–Sat. 9–8, Sun. 9–2:30 🚌 34, 35 💲 $

The Museo de Artes Costumbres Populares (Museum of Local Customs), located in one of the 1929 International Exhibition pavilions, is devoted to traditional everyday life in Andalucia. There are reconstructions of workshops where you can see how guitars and castanets are made, old agricultural implements, pottery, furniture and much more. Upstairs there are intricately embroidered costumes, painted fans and delicate lace, and you can learn about the history of Seville's great Spring Festival, the *Fiesta Primaverales*.

MUSEO DE BELLAS ARTES

➕ A3 ✉ Plaza del Museo 9 ☎ 95 422 0790 🕐 Tue. 3–8, Wed.–Sat. 9–8, Sun. 9–3 🚌 13, 43, C1, C2 💲 $

Seville's Museo de Bellas Artes (Fine Arts Museum), housed in a 17th-century convent built around three courtyards, concentrates on the Golden Age of Spanish painting. The former church is devoted to the Spanish religious painter Bartolome Murillo, and pride of place is given to his *Immaculate Conception*. Francisco de Zurbarán, another great master, is also well represented, his masterpeice being the stark, sculptural *Christ on the Cross*.

PLAZA DE ESPAÑA AND PARQUE DE MARÍA LUISA

➕ B1–B2 ✉ Plaza de España 🚌 25, 30, 35

Built as the centerpiece for the 1929 International Exhibition, the Plaza de España overlooks the Parque de María Luisa (María Luisa Park). Traditionally styled and lavishly decorated with thousands of colored tiles, the 650-foot-wide plaza is framed by a semicircular range of buildings and encircled by a canal. The park, laid out in the 19th century, is a tranquil stretch of shady paths, punctuated by pools and fountains. It plays a central part in Seville's Spring Festival, when hundreds of horsemen accompany carriages of smiling girls, dressed in silk, around the park.

PLAZA DE TOROS DE LA MAESTRANZA

➕ A2 ✉ Paseo Colón 12 ☎ 95 422 4577 🕐 Daily 9:30–2 and 3–6 🚌 21, 43, C4 💲 $$

Seville's Plaza de Toros (Bullring) is one of the oldest and most prestigious in Spain. Once built of wood, the present 14,000-seat ring was designed around the Prince's Balcony and is actually oval rather than round. Tours are in Spanish only, and include the museum, stables, chapel and modern operating theater.

REALES ALCÁZARES

➕ B2 ✉ Plaza del Triunfo ☎ 95 450 2323 🕐 Tue.–Sat. 9:30–5, Sun. 9:30–1:30 🍽 El Giraldillo, see page 567 🚌 21, 23, C3, C4 💲 $$

Less swamped with tourists than its cousin in Granada, the unforgettable Reales Alcázares (Royal Palace) epitomizes the elegance and charm of Mudéjar secular architecture. Little remains of the original Moorish Alcazar, and most of the palace you see today was built by Pedro the Cruel in 1362, long after the Moors left Spain. But the builders were christianized Moors, the inventors of Mudéjar style, and this "Arabian Nights" complex is one of the purest examples of their art remaining today. It's a labyrinth of courtyards, delicate stucco and tile rooms, terraces and coffered chambers, fountains and arched patios. From here you pass into the 16th-century Palace of Charles V, with its tapestries and lavish rooms. Outside lie gardens with pools, and shady magnolia and orange trees. Labeling and information are poor, so your best bet is to rent the English-language audio guide.

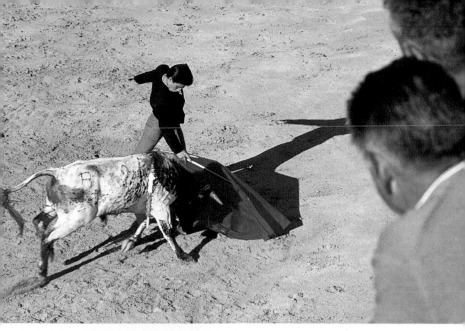
Bullfighter at work: the first stage, assessing the ability of the animal

BULLFIGHTING

Bullfighting is the least understood of all Spanish traditions. Performed on horseback until the 18th century, bullfighting had attained its present form by the 19th century, with established rules and a strict pattern to the *corrida*, or fight. Not all Spaniards enjoy bullfighting, but they are tolerant of it. True aficionados spend years studying the careers of the fighters and the bloodlines of the fighting bulls.

The *Corrida*

Six four-year-old bulls are killed during a *corrida*, which starts at 5 p.m. Bred on huge estates on the rolling grasslands of Andalucia and Castille, the 1,000-pound bulls have never seen an unmounted man until the moment they enter the ring. The afternoon starts with a parade, the *paseo*, by three *matadors*, glittering figures in their "suits of light" who will each kill two bulls. The *matadors* are accompanied by their teams, known as *cuadrillas*.

Each fight falls into three parts, marked by a trumpet call. First the *matador* must appraise the bull, using a cape to make the animal turn so he can judge its speed and dexterity. Bred for aggression, it will charge at the two mounted team members, the *picadores*, who attack its flanks with pikes.

The next act allows the bull to regain its wind while it is further enraged by the *banderillas*, who pierce the neck muscles with ribboned darts. The pikes and darts gradually weaken the bull's immensely strong neck and cause its head to drop, allowing the matador access to the heart.

The final stage of the drama belongs to the matador alone. Working with the *muleta*, a small red cloth, he draws the bull in a series of passes across his body, which can be as elegant as they are fearless. Finally, the bull will stand still, tired but still mesmerized by the *muleta*. This is the moment for the matador to take his sword and, reaching over the horns and shoulder blades, strike the bull cleanly through the heart.

Bullfighting can be seen throughout Spain at all the major summer festivals, although those bothered by a bullfight's inherent cruelty should avoid attending.

SWEDEN

*"THE further I came north, the
more like New England
everything grew to look..."*

American historian Henry Adams

Opposite: Houses on stilts at the waterfront town of Orust

SWEDEN

Sweden is the largest of the Scandinavian countries, and it is famed for the perceived efficiency of its people and the pragmatism of its government. This is a land of wide-open spaces, where even a large city like Stockholm seems to merge urban and rural elements in a way that benefits the people.

Swedish Landscapes

Southern Sweden is an area of forests and farmland punctuated by a vast number of lakes, of which two – Vänern and Vättern – dominate the landscape. The south is also the center of Sweden's industrial powerhouse. The main towns are Gothenburg (Göteborg) and Malmö on the southwest coast.

The most southerly province, Skåne, is a rich farming area where you will find a hint of Danish features, both in the people and in the landscape. This is Sweden's vacation land. Off the east coast, the islands of Gotland and Öland have superb beaches that benefit from calm waters and warm summer sunshine.

Stockholm lies on the east coast of Sweden, within a beautiful mosaic of inland lakes and offshore islands. In the surrounding provinces there is a richly varied countryside centered on mighty Lake Mälaren. North of Stockholm is

MORE TOP DESTINATIONS IN SWEDEN

- Göteborg A2 ● Gotland B2
- Kalmar A1 ● Lund A1 ● Malmö A1
- Siljan A3 ● Skokloster B2
- Uppsala B2

Sweden's ancient capital, the lively university town of Uppsala. This entire area is accessible by ferries and cruise boats that ply a network of waterways and lakes.

Northern Sweden is known as Norrland, with similarities to northern Finland, and it enjoys the same "Land of the Midnight Sun" tag. It is a country of vast forests and tumbling rivers that are fed by icy, crystal waters from the mountains. Lapland, or Sápme (see page 434) is a vast and magnificent wilderness of mountains, moor land, birch forest and tundra.

Travel and Climate

Sweden has an extensive road network, but public transportation throughout the country is also a very efficient and convenient way to get around. Trains are modern and comfortable, and buses serve even the most remote northern parts of the country.

Sweden's climate is similar to that of its neighbors, but the country is generally much drier than Norway's western regions. Summers can be as warm and sunny as anywhere else in northern Europe, and along the southern coast you may even find yourself enjoying a Scandinavian heat wave. Conversely, visitors need to be prepared for wet weather in Sweden's maritime climate.

A remarkable number of Swedes are fluent in English, and most people in the cities have at least some command of English. The people are generally very helpful, and have a great awareness of the world in general; they are politely curious about visitors and are lively conversationalists, once their initial reserve is overcome.

Swedes are conservative by nature, and on first impression may seem overly serious about life. They are very aware that their society operates on the basis

Sweden

of co-operation and willingness to accept the norm. You may mistake Swedish directness for impatience, especially in Stockholm, but this simply reflects a national confidence about how things work.

Sweden's Geography

Like its neighbors Norway and Finland, Sweden is a long, narrow country, but uniform in breadth. It shares its longest border with Norway and the Scandinavian mountain chain runs along this frontier, for over 1,000 miles. In the north, Sweden borders Finland and the Arctic circle sweeps across the furthest reaches of the land, part of an area known as the "Nordic Cap."

East of Sweden lies the Gulf of Bothnia, which eventually gives way to the Baltic Sea in the southeast. To the southwest, a shorter coastline borders the North Sea within the protective shadow of neighboring Norway and Northern Denmark.

Sweden

TIMELINE

8000 BC	Hunter-gatherers move throughout Scandinavia in the wake of retreating ice sheets; the Sami (Lapp) people are thought to descend from these early settlers.
1500 BC	Germanic tribes in southern Sweden develop trading links with the European lands to the south, from which they came.
AD 750	Battle of Brävalla; the Svear emerge as the dominant tribe and give their name to the country (Sverige).
800–1000	Swedish "Vikings" travel east via the great rivers of eastern Europe, as far as Constantinople.
1397	Union of Kalmar unites Denmark, Sweden and Norway under Queen Margaret of Denmark.
1523	Gustav Vasa establishes Sweden's independence and becomes King Gustav I; Lutheran Protestantism becomes the country's main religion.
1658	Treaty of Roskilde secures all of southern Swedish mainland from Danish control.
1814	Sweden wins control of Norway from Denmark.
1905	Norway achieves independence from Sweden.
1914–18	Sweden remains neutral during World War I.
1939–45	Sweden again remains neutral during World War II.
1946	Sweden maintains neutrality but joins the United Nations.
1989	The Sami people are granted their own parliament, known as the Sametinget.
1995	Sweden joins European Union.

THE SAMI

The Sami are the indigenous people of Sápme, the area popularly called Lapland. They are known historically as Lapps, but this is not a native name and is one that the Sami themselves feel is derogatory. The ancient name Sábme, a form of Sami which is said to mean "the people of the interior," is now considered accepted usage. Sápme covers the Scandinavian Arctic region from the Russian Kola peninsula to the northwest coast of Norway, and extends down either side of the Norwegian-Swedish border to the central area of both countries. There are about 60,000 Sami people today, of which about 17,000 live in Sweden. A minority of Sami are reindeer herders, but the Sami are also developing alternative lifestyles while strengthening their self-awareness and political position within Scandinavia. Tourism is increasing in Scandinavian Lapland, but some Sami people are concerned about what they believe is too much intrusion on their fragile environment and culture.

SURVIVAL GUIDE

- For lunch you must experience a smorgasbord, a Scandinavian institution. The name translates as *smörgås* for "bread," *bord* for "table." The reality of a true smorgasbord means much more than this simple image implies. There may be more than 100 different dishes in a true smorgasbord, with items ranging from *gravad lax* (salmon slices in herbs) to *köttbullar* (tasty meatballs), *sillbullar* (herring rissoles) or *kåldolmar* (stuffed cabbage rolls).

- Sweden has the same tight control over alcohol sales as does Norway and Finland, and alcohol is expensive. The government-controlled liquor monopoly, *Systembolaget,* has branches throughout the country, which are open on weekdays. Emphasis is on the sale of good wines. Try some *aquavit* with your food if you want a taste of Sweden. The beverage is distilled from grain or potatoes and is then given added taste with spices or herbs. Drink it in small quantities, consumed in one gulp.

- July is a popular month for vacations in Sweden. You will find the countryside and coast very busy, and especially populated with Swedes.

- Swedish design is world famous, especially in silver, ceramics, glassware and stainless steel. The Småland area in southeast Sweden is particularly noted for its fine glassware. Stores such as NK in Stockholm's Hamngatan have good selections of glassware, as does Nordiska Kristall, a store in Österlånggatan.

- Home furnishings are a Swedish specialty. Visit the big IKEA store at Kungens Kurva outside Stockholm. A free bus leaves every hour between 11 and 5 (except Sundays) from Regeringsgatan, the street leading north from Hamngatan, a short distance east of the NK department store. Or try the very stylish Nordiska Galleriet, in Nybrogatan.

- In mid-August, don't miss the lively Stockholm Water Festival, a 10-day extravaganza of events focusing on the city's waterways and islands. There are concerts from classical music to rock, circus acts, open-air theater, water activities, and food and drink galore.

- In big cities you'll find public restrooms along some main streets, as well as in main subway stations and some department stores. Signs are *Damer* for ladies and *Herrar* for men. If there is an attendant the charge is normally 5SKr.

Replica of the Hand of God by Swedish-American sculptor Carl Milles

Stockholm

STOCKHOLM

Stockholm is probably the only city in
the world where you can catch a salmon
at a busy road intersection under the
walls of a royal palace, and where the
city's subway stations double as eye-
catching art galleries. The salmon
thrive in Stockholm's clean waters at
the very heart of the city, and local
anglers fish from the Strömbron bridge.
And the artwork that enlivens the
subway stations is just one expression of
the vigorous cultural life that makes
Stockholm one of the world's most
civilized cities.

City of Islands

Modern Stockholm is a large,
exhilarating city. The scale of its public
buildings is monumental, the bustle of
its streets all-embracing; yet the city is
given a uniquely open character by the
thousands of islands in its archipelago
and by the mirror images of lakes that
pepper its hinterland. Stockholm stands
on 14 interlocking islands; the city is a
mosaic of land, lake and waterway
stitched together by more than 40
bridges, an exhilarating urban
environment that also seems to ensure
that people are not overwhelmed.

Gamla Stan is the heart of old
Stockholm, a dramatic and fascinating
expression of heritage and tradition. It
stands on an island in the middle of the
narrow bottleneck channel between the
salty Baltic Sea and the inland
freshwater lake of Mälaren. To the
south is the hilly island of Södermalm,
a suburban area with generous expanses
of grass and trees. North of Gamla Stan
and the buildings of state (the Royal
Palace and the Parliament House) is
Norrmalm, the business and
commercial district. This is the heart of
the modern city – glass, steel, concrete

Subway Art

Subway art in Stockholm is not
freelance graffiti but spectacular
and eclectic art. When the Stockolm
Tunnelbana was built in the late
1940s an inspired decision was made
to decorate each station with
individual artworks. T-Centralen,
the hub of the system, has the most,
with examples ranging from terazzo
sofas to line 11's platform where the
natural rock has been left in
decorated, cave-like form. Visit line
10's amazing Kungsträgården
station; not only is it enormously
deep, but it has outstanding
sculptures. Stockholm's subway art
evolves year by year, a stunning
reflection of this sophisticated city.

and good Swedish design – a cityscape
of towering buildings, stylish shopping
malls, busy streets and traffic-free
concourses that satisfy the demands of
both vehicles and pedestrians. East of
Norrmalm is the residential district of
Östermalm and the city's great island
park, Djurgården. To the west, the
island mosaic spreads across the waters
of Lake Mälaren, Stockholm's
magnificent "inland" sea.

Compass Bearings

Most visitors arrive at the city's big,
bustling central railroad station in
Norrmalm, and the experience can be
disorientating at first. Just east of the
railroad station along Klarabergsgatan is
the big sunken square of Sergels Torg,
with its landmark *Kristall* tower of glass
and steel and a huge glass facade on the
south side. This is Stockholm's
contemporary hub. You can orient
yourself here and, within the pedestrian
concourse, even relax in spite of the
surrounding traffic and the bustle.

Running north and south of Sergels Torg are busy shopping streets, such as the pedestrian-only Drottninggatan. Here you will find Åhléns, a huge department store from where the northern section of Drottninggatan runs past many more stores.

Continuing east from Sergels Torg into the street of Hamngatan takes you past the elegant NK, the best name in Swedish shopping, a massive department store with floor after floor of fine shops and such fashionable restaurants as Bobergs Matsal, where Greta Garbo is said to have whiled away the time. Also in Hamngatan is

Gallerian, a big shopping mall. Farther along you reach the offices of the Stockholm tourist center and the great open swath of the Old Royal Gardens (Kungsträdgården) that sweep south to the waters of Strömmen, to the magnificent Royal Palace, and to enchanting Gamla Stan.

Seeing Stockholm

For all its size Stockholm is a city that can be enjoyed on a human scale. You can see it by tour bus, or you can book a knowledgeable personal guide or a taxi tour, although the latter is expensive. Try a boat trip for the wider view of

View over Stockholm's Old Town, with Riddarholm in the foreground

Stockholm's islands and visit some attractions, such as Djurgården and Drottningholm Palace, by ferry boat.

Ask at the tourist center about the Stockholm Card, with special discounts on museum and attraction admissions, among other benefits.

One of the most appealing aspects of Stockholm is that the city is neatly packaged into separate entities because of its island nature; you can plan your days one piece at a time. At night the city becomes even more majestic when it is lit up and vibrant with music and lively entertainment.

Stockholmers

Stockholm's confidence is infectious. Listen closely to advice and don't be afraid to ask for clarification or guidance. Then let the magic of the city take over; relax. The people have created one of the most endearing and enchanting cities in the world, and know how to enjoy it.

ESSENTIAL INFORMATION

TOURIST INFORMATION
• Sweden House, Hamngatan 27
☎ 08 789 24 95
• Hotellcentrallen, Central Station
☎ 08 789 24 25
• Kaknäs Tower, Ladugårdsgärdet ☎ 08 789 24 35
• Gamla Stan, Västerlånggatan 66/Kornhamnstorg
49 ☎ 08 789 24 95

URBAN TRANSPORTATION
Stockholm Central Station
(✉ Klarabergsviadukten ☎ 08 762 25
80) is the main train station. A very
large and comprehensive bus system serves
Stockholm and its environs. The subway
(*Tunnelbana*) is known as T-Bana and radiates out
from Central Station. Subway stations are
indicated by a blue "T" sign on the street. On the
Stockholm city map the subway stations are
marked with the letter "T" in a red circle. Public
transportation in Stockholm has a unified ticket

system, allowing you to transfer between systems.
There is a Transit Authority information center in
the T-Centralen subway station, accessible from
the railroad station. Several taxi companies also
operate in and around the city. For information on
rates, call ☎ 08 30 00 00 or 08 15 00 00.

AIRPORT INFORMATION
Stockholm-Arlanda Airport is 28 miles
north of the city center and is
Stockholm's main air terminal. Airport
buses (Flygbussarna) run at 5- to 10-minute
intervals and take 35 minutes to reach Stockholm
Central Station.
Taxis also depart from the airport. For more
information call ☎ 08 797 60 00. Bromma Airport is
5 miles west of Stockholm and handles domestic
flights only. Flygbussarna buses take 20 minutes to
reach Stockholm Central Station from here. For
information call ☎ 08 797 68 00.

CLIMATE – average highs and lows for the month

JAN.	FEB.	MAR.	APR.	MAY	JUN.	JUL.	AUG.	SEP.	OCT.	NOV.	DEC.
-1°C	-1°C	3°C	8°C	15°C	19°C	21°C	20°C	15°C	9°C	4°C	0°C
30°F	30°F	37°F	46°F	59°F	66°F	70°F	68°F	59°F	48°F	39°F	32°F
-5°C	-6°C	-3°C	0°C	5°C	11°C	13°C	13°C	9°C	4°C	1°C	-2°C
23°F	21°F	27°F	32°F	41°F	52°F	55°F	55°F	48°F	39°F	34°F	28°F

Stockholm

CITY SIGHTS

Key to symbols

➕ map coordinates refer to the Stockholm map on page 437; sights below are highlighted in yellow on the map.

⊠ address or location ☎ telephone number ⓘ opening times 🚌 nearest bus or tram route 🚇 nearest subway ⛴ nearest ferry stop 🍴 restaurant on site or nearby 💶 admission charge: $$$ more than 35SKr, $$ 15SKr–35SKr, $ less than 15SKr

DROTTNINGHOLMS SLOTT

Drottningholms Slott ➕ Off the map ⊠ Drottningholm ☎ 08 402 62 80, Kina Slott 08 402 62 70, Court Theatre 08 59 04 06 ⓘ Daily 10–4, Jun.–Aug.; 11–4, in May; noon–3, in Sep. 🍴 Café 🚇 Brommaplan ⛴ Stadshuskajen 💶 $$

Kina Slott ⊠ Drottningholm ☎ 08 402 62 70 ⓘ Daily 11–4, May–Aug.; noon–3, in Sep.; 1–3, Apr. and Oct. 🍴 Café 🚇 Brommaplan ⛴ Stadshuskajen 💶 $$

Court Theater ⊠ Drottningholm ☎ 08 59 04 06 ⓘ Guided tours daily, May–Sep. 🍴 Café 🚇 Brommaplan ⛴ Stadshuskajen 💶 $$

Drottningholms Slott (Drottningholm Palace) is located on Lovön island, west of the city center. The palace, home of Sweden's royal family, is a superb 17th-century baroque building in the style of Versailles. It overlooks Lake Mälaren amid wooded countryside and its own gardens, a mix of French and English styles. French details enhance the palace's interiors. On the grounds is the 18th-century Kina Slott (Chinese Pavilion), where Asian meets rococo in a delightful piece of extravagance. Nearby is the Court Theater, a venue for classical concerts and ballet in summer.

KUNGLIGA SLOTTET

Festvåning and Stattkammaren ➕ B2 ⊠ Kungliga Slottet ☎ 08 402 61 30 ⓘ Daily 10–4, Jun.–Aug.; Tue.–Sun. noon–3, rest of year 🚇 Kungsträgården 🚌 46, 53, 55 💶 $$$ **Livrustkammaren** ⊠ Slottsbaken 3

☎ 08 519 55 544 ⓘ Daily 11–4, May–Aug.; Tue.–Sun. 11–4, rest of year 🚇 Kungsträgården 🚌 46, 53, 55 💶 $$

The northern corner of Old Town is dominated by the monumental Kungliga Slottet (Royal Palace), a stunning mix of classical styles developed throughout the 17th and 18th centuries on the site of the original Castle of the Three Crowns. There are several museums within the palace. Among them is the Livrustkammaren (Royal Armory), where Sweden's military history is depicted in a colorful way. Visit the basement *Vagnhall* (Wagon Hall), where there is a collection of royal coaches, including a Viennese rococo sleigh that is impossibly romantic. Also visit the Stattkammaren (Royal Treasury), where the state regalia are on display. The palace's Festvåning (State Apartments) are a dazzling expression of French baroque, rococo and imperial styles. Time your visit to observe the changing of the guard in the palace's courtyard (12:10 p.m. on summer weekdays, 1:10 p.m. on weekends).

MEDELTIDSMUSEUM

➕ B2 ⊠ Strömparterren ☎ 08 508 31 790 ⓘ Daily 11–4 (also Tue. and Thu. 4–6), Jul.–Aug.; Tue.–Sun. 11–4 (also Wed. 4–6), rest of year 🚇 Kungsträgården 🚌 43, 62 💶 $$$

The Medeltidsmuseum (Medieval Museum) is one of Stockholm's most fascinating attractions, not least because of its underground location below the Riksdagshuset (Parliament House) on the tiny island of Helgeandsholmen, between Gamla Stan and the main city. Here, in the late 1970s, layers of medieval remains, including sections of old city wall, were uncovered during excavations for an underground parking lot below the terrace of Parliament House. Admirably, the parking plan was

Thespian pose – statue outside Drottningholm Court Theater

Colorful sulptures in the snow outside the Museum of Modern Art

abandoned in favor of preservation. The museum is entered via steps leading down from Norrbro, the bridge between Gustav Adolfs Torg and Gamla Stan. Inside is a treasure house of ancient remains that have been incorporated into displays of artifacts discovered during excavations.

MODERNA MUSEET

✚ C2 ✉ Skeppsholmen ☎ 08 519 55 200
🕐 Tue.–Thu. 11–10, Fri.–Sun. 11–6, mid-Feb. to Dec. 31 🍴 Museum restaurant 🚇 Kungsträgården
🚌 65 ✋ $$$

Visit Stockholm's Moderna Museet (Museum of Modern Art), on the little island of Skeppsholmen, as much for its excellent restaurant as for the art. The collection of contemporary art includes works by Roy Lichtenstein, Willem de Kooning, Rene Magritte and Pablo Picasso. Don't miss Salvador Dalí's startling *The Enigma of William Tell* and Marcel Duchamp's *Fountain*. There are compelling works by such Swedish luminaries as Viking Eggeling and Isaac Grünewald. Within the complex is the Arkitekturmuseet (Swedish Museum of Architecture), which displays splendid models of Swedish buildings in an imaginative way, with English labeling.

NATIONALMUSEUM

✚ C3 ✉ Blasieholmskajen ☎ 08 519 54 300 or 08 519 544 10 🕐 Tue.–Sun. 10–5 (also Tue. and Thu. 5–8), Jun.–Aug.; Tue.–Sun. 11–5 (also Tue. 5–8), rest of year 🍴 Restaurant 🚇 Kungsträgården 🚌 46, 62, 65, 76 ✋ $$$

The Nationalmuseum (National Museum of Fine Arts) is a dignified Italianate building on little Blasieholmen peninsula, across the water east of Gamla Stan and facing the Royal Palace. The museum has a superb collection of Swedish and international art and applied art exhibited in a series of elegant rooms. Among the paintings are works by Rembrandt, Paul Cézanne and Paul Gauguin. Swedish art is well represented and includes superb watercolors by Carl Larsson and fine works by Anders Zorn. The applied art section is a feast of furnishings and artifacts, and there are additional displays of sculpture and Russian icons. The museum restaurant is located in a lovely, glass-roofed atrium.

NORDISKA MUSEET

✚ C3 ✉ Djurgårdsvägen 6–16 ☎ 08 519 56 000
🕐 Tue.–Sun. 11–5 (also Thu. 5–8) 🍴 Restaurant and café 🚌 44, 47, 69 ✋ $$$

The building housing the Nordiska Museet (Northern Museum) is a splendid work in its own right. It stands at the entrance to Djurgården and its gabled facade of brick and stone has elegant turrets and a handsome central steeple. The exhibits are a comprehensive and absorbing collection illustrating Swedish and general Nordic cultural life from the medieval period onward. There is an excellent section depicting the life of the Sami (Lapp) people and delightful exhibits of Swedish traditional dress. Pay your respects as you enter, to the powerful oak statue of Gustav Vasa, the 16th-century warrior who established the Swedish state.

SKANSEN

🚻 Off the map 🖂 Djurgården ☎ 08 442 80 00
🕐 Park and zoo: Daily 10–10, Jan.–Aug.; 10–8, in May; 10–4, rest of year 🍴 Restaurant and café
🚌 44, 47 🚢 Djurgårdsfäjan from Slussen/Gamla Stan 🎫 SS

The Skansen open-air museum is located on Djurgården, Stockholm's island park. This area was the old hunting domain of Swedish royalty and is now preserved as an urban escape zone for Stockholmers and visitors. Individual attractions on Djurgården include the Vasamuseet (Vasa Museum) and the Nordiska Museet (Northern Museum), but the island offers numerous other diversions. Make a day of it, enjoying delightful woodland walks or a stroll alongside the quiet waters of the Djurgärdsbrunnsviken. At the heart of Djurgården, Skansen features more than 150 traditional buildings and a lively working environment in summer for artisans. You can sample traditional Swedish delicacies here, such as herring sandwiches and waffles with cream and cloudberries. Skansen's other attraction is its zoo and animal park, which boasts elk, bear and lynx. There are several smaller museums and art galleries scattered around Djurgården, and fun for everyone at Gröna Lunds Tivoli amusement park.

STADSHUSET

🚻 B2 🖂 Hantverkrag 1 ☎ 08 508 29 059
🕐 Guided tours daily at 10, 11, noon and 2, Jun.–Aug.; at 10, noon and 2, in Sep.; at 10 and noon, rest of year 🚇 T-Centralen, Rådhuset 🚌 48, 62
🎫 SSS

Stockholm's Stadshuset (City Hall) is perhaps the city's finest example of the early 19th-century Scandinavian Romantic Nationalist style. This was the same style that produced the *Jugend* buildings of Helsinki. Built of red brick and with a magnificent Italianate tower, it stands on

The steeple and facade of the Northern Museum

the shores of Lake Mälaren, a striking focus for inland Stockholm. The tower tapers gently to an upper platform and lantern that supports the gleaming *Tre Kroner*, the three crowns symbol of the city. Interiors are no less striking, the highlight being the Golden Hall with its mosaic walls and gleaming marble floor. Guided tours are available, and you can climb the 450-foot tower – or take the elevator.

VASAMUSEET

🚻 C2 🖂 Djurgården-Galärvarvet ☎ 08 519 54 800
🕐 Daily 9:30–7, Jun. 10–Aug. 20; 10–5 (also Wed. 5–8), rest of year 🍴 Restaurant and café 🚌 44, 47, 69 🎫 SSS

The unmistakable Vasamuseet (Vasa Museum) is truly exceptional, a great celebration of a unique historical event. The focus of the museum is the restored sailing ship *Vasa*, which sank spectacularly in Stockholm harbor within minutes of starting its maiden voyage in 1628. The sheer drama of the event is enough to grip you, but the reality of the *Vasa*, 230 feet long and fully restored and rigged, is just as breathtaking. No ordinary ship, the *Vasa* was ornamental as well as functional, and the vessel's finest features were preserved in the muddy waters of the Baltic for more than 330 years. The museum also tells the story of the people who salvaged the *Vasa*, and there are exhibits showing some of the 12,000 artifacts that were recovered and that bring the ship and its story to vivid life.

A STROLL AROUND GAMLA STAN

Stockholm's Gamla Stan (Old Town) – or *staden mellan broarna,* "the city among the bridges," as it is more lyrically known to Swedes – is not a perfectly preserved medieval townscape by any means. Disastrous fires in 1407 and 1640 destroyed the original wooden buildings of medieval Gamla Stan. But the island nature of the settlement, its small area and its crowded layout have spared Gamla Stan from too much modernization. What remains today is a superb enclave of old stone buildings dating from the 15th–18th centuries.

You can wander at will through the Old Town without getting lost. On this tiny island you are never far from the waterside or a bridge to re-orient yourself. Pick up an enlarged Gamla Stan map, widely available in stores, restaurants and tourist venues, to help you find specific places.

There are many easily missed treasures hidden away from the busy main streets of Västerlånggatan and Österlånggatan. Pay a visit to the Great Church (Storkyrkan), Stockholm's 13th-century cathedral, which lies just south of the courtyard of the Royal Palace. The church's finest artifact is the oak- and elkhorn-gilded sculpture of *St. George and the Dragon,* a 15th-century Gothic masterpiece of thorny carving. You may be lucky and catch a lunchtime organ recital or other musical performance in the church.

From the church, go into the narrow street of Trångsund and then turn left past a charming old phone booth to reach Great Square (Stortorget). This was the scene in 1520 of the notorious Stockholm "Blood Bath," when Christian II of Denmark slaughtered 82 Swedish nobles and citizens in a bid to seal with blood his overlordship of Sweden. This brutal act inspired Gustav Vasa, son of a murdered nobleman, to rebel successfully against Denmark and to secure Sweden's independence. On Stortorget's west side are a row of splendid gabled houses with little cafés and restaurants on their ground floors. The 18th-century Bourse, or Stock Exchange, commands the north side of the square. The Swedish Academy, the body that selects Nobel prize winners, meets at the Bourse.

Leave the square via the east side and walk down Köpmangatan, "Street of the Merchants," the oldest street in the Old Town and home to several fine antique shops with attractively painted ceilings. At the end of Köpmangatan, in the little square of Köpmantorget, is a dramatic reprise of the Great Church's statue of *St. George and the Dragon,* this time in bronze but just as powerful. Farther east is Österlånggatan, a long, winding street that was once the Old Town's shoreline.

Go to your right, down the short slope of Köpmanbrinken street, and then keep right along Österlånggatan, past stylish restaurants, antique and craft stores, and fashion salons. There are lots of gift possibilities here, especially for children, in shops such as Textilarna, Kalikå and Tomtar & Troll. The narrow streets running east to the sea, such as Drakens Gränd, Ferkens Gränd and Packhusgränd, mark the old piers of the early medieval era. Near the end of Österlånggatan is the well-known restaurant Den Gyldene Freden (see page 568).

Soon you reach Iron Square (Järntorget), a name probably derived from the days when the Old Town's fortunes were built on its status as the

A rest from sightseeing – sample the delights of Swedish food in the Old Town

main outlet for the Swedish iron and copper trade. Here, against the wall of the old Central Bank, is the remarkably lifelike statue of Stockholm poet Evart Taube, a popular performer who died in 1976. Check out the nearby Sundbergs Konditori, a long-established institution selling coffee and delicious pastries.

From Järntorget, turn right onto Västerlånggatan, the busiest street in the Old Town, crammed with stores and tempting restaurants and cafés. On the right, just past the attractive Mårten Trotzig restaurant (see page 568), you'll pass the narrow entrance to Mårten Trotzigs Gränd, reputed to be the narrowest alleyway in Stockholm and

named after a German medieval copper trader who had a business here.

All the way along Västerlånggatan you will be tempted by souvenir stores such as Thorndahl, at No. 17; the exotic Indiska at No. 50, with Indian clothes and artifacts; the Swedish craft stores Imagolit and Gallery S; and a host of specialty shops. Note the glass-paneled ceilings of many of the stores. Wandering along the delightful side streets is equally rewarding.

To end your Old Town excursion, stroll to where the bridge over the canal Stallkanalen leads through the arched passage to the gate at Riksgatan and back into modern Stockholm, at the shopping street of Drottninggatan.

SWITZERLAND

" S *WITZERLAND is simply a large, humpy, solid rock, with a thin skin of grass stretched over it.* *"*

From *A Tramp Abroad* by Mark Twain

Opposite: Mountains, green pastures and picture-postcard villages – all ingredients for a Swiss landscape

SWITZERLAND

With stunning Alpine scenery, lush meadows, a medley of beautiful lakes and attractive cities and towns, Switzerland has a wonderful variety of natural and man-made attractions.

Neutral Territory

The Swiss Constitution, modeled on that of the United States, was drawn up in 1848 and revised in 1874; it is still in force today. Modern Switzerland is thus a federation of democracies and neutrality is the cornerstone of state policy: Switzerland interferes in no foreign conflicts and makes no alliances.

Remaining neutral through both world wars, Switzerland emerged in 1945 as a powerful commercial player. Banking has long thrived here due to the political stability of the country and because of Swiss financial acumen. The superb infrastructure of railroads, tunnels and roads has overcome the mountainous terrain and allows the country to exploit a trading position at the center of Europe.

The Swiss Landscape

Europe's continental watershed runs through Switzerland, a landlocked, oval-shaped nation, with a central lowland sandwiched between the Jura mountains to the north and the mighty Alps. The Swiss Alps occupy 60 percent of the country (mostly in the south) with their high mountain glaciers and dramatic peaks. Forests cover another quarter of the land. The rest is a delightful mix of lakes and meadow pasture, beautiful throughout the year. Much of Switzerland's weather is typical of central Europe; Ticino canton, south of the Alps, has a Mediterranean climate. You may encounter days of the *föhn* – a warm, dry wind blowing from the northern slopes of the Alps.

MORE TOP DESTINATIONS IN SWITZERLAND

- Ascona D1 ● Baden C3
- Basel B3 ● Bern B2 ● Brienz C2
- Château de Chillon B2
- Engelberg C2 ● Fribourg B2
- Grindelwald C2 ● Gstaad B2
- Interlaken C2 ● Lausanne A2
- Montreux B2 ● St.-Moritz E2
- Schaffhausen C3 ● Wilderswil C2
- Villars B1 ● Zermatt C1

SWITZERLAND

| 0 | 20 | 40 | 60 | 80 km |
| 0 | 10 | 20 | 30 | 40 | 50 miles |

FRANCE

Porrentruy • Delémont
St-Ursanne • Moutier
1607m Biel-
Chasseral Bienne
La Chaux- Twann
de-Fonds • Erlach

Neuchâtel

Lac de Nenchâtel
Murten   BER
Grandson Avenches
Yverdon- Fribourg
les-Bains

Bulle
1679m Gruyères
Mt Tendre Châteaux-
d'Oex
St-Cergue Morges • Lausanne
Montreux Gstaad
Nyon Chateau Leysin
de Chillon Aigle B e r n
Lac Léman Villars Montan
Monthey Sion
St-Maurice
GENEVA Champéry Les
Collons
Martigny Verbi

La Fouly

Grand St Bern
Pass & Tunn
A   B

Language and Manners

Reflecting Switzerland's location in central Europe, the Swiss speak four different languages: Schwyzerdütsch, a Swiss-German dialect (although German is used for reading and writing); French; Italian; and Romansch, an ancient Latin tongue. This linguistic diversity results in very different types of people, and you'll notice this as you travel.

On the whole, the Swiss are extremely law-abiding, and consider punctuality very important. Manners are extremely formal, with hand-shaking and serious toasts in all social circumstances. Efficient, civic-minded and polite, they make Switzerland one of Europe's best-run countries.

Vacationing in Switzerland

The fabled Swiss efficiency has positive benefits for visitors: Trains run punctually, hotels are clean and comfortable, opening times for attractions are reliable, and everyone connected with tourism speaks English. You'll also discover that Switzerland is expensive, so if you're watching your budget, don't plan on staying too long. There's something to enjoy throughout the year – skiing in the mountains during the winter; walking, sailing and other outdoor pursuits all summer. Late spring sees the countryside at its best, with carpets of mountain and meadow wildflowers; autumn, when the leaves turn and the first snow whitens the lower peaks, also is magnificent.

Switzerland

TIMELINE

3,000 BC	Evidence of earliest neolithic settlers by Lake Neuchâtel.
circa 100 BC	Romans invade from the south, incorporating Helvetic tribes.
circa AD 400	Romans expelled southward; Burgundians occupy western areas (modern French-speaking Switzerland) and Alemans the north and east (German-speaking Switzerland).
1032	Existing country incorporated into Holy Roman Empire, followed by gradual emergence of powerful independent nobles.
1515	Defeat at Battle of Marignano inaugurates neutrality.
1526	Zwingli's Reformation takes hold in Zurich, continued by John Calvin in Geneva beginning in 1532.
1648	Treaty of Westphalia recognizes Swiss neutrality and independence of 13 cantons.
1798	French invasion and rule under Napoleon, who establishes Helvetic Republic.
1815	Congress of Vienna guarantees Swiss independence.
1848	Adoption of Swiss Constitution, which defines political organization of the country.
1864	First Convention of Geneva is accepted and signed by 16 nations; the Red Cross is founded.
1914–18	Switzerland remains neutral during World War I.
1919	President Woodrow Wilson chooses Geneva as headquarters of League of Nations.
1939–45	Switzerland remains neutral during World War II, but image is tarnished by pro-Nazi activities.
1946	United Nations takes over role of League of Nations; Geneva retained as European headquarters.
1986	Swiss vote in a referendum against joining the United Nations.
1990	Population votes to freeze nuclear power development.

THE SWISS ARMY PENKNIFE

The oxymoronic Swiss army penknife was first manufactured more than 100 years ago to equip the Swiss army. Over 200 models of this versatile penknife now exist, each with a distinctive white cross in a shield on a red background. Its blades and attachments, ranging from tweezers, corkscrews and magnifying glasses to tiny hacksaws and nail files, can perform a wide range of tasks; it has justifiably been called the "smallest toolbox in the world."

SURVIVAL GUIDE

- Keep more money available than you think you will need; cash seems to be spent alarmingly fast throughout Switzerland. Credit cards are widely accepted.
- Although most Swiss are excellent linguists, it's polite to ask if they speak English before starting a conversation or asking a question.
- Be polite to everyone – *bitte, prego* or *je vous en prie* is the equivalent of "you're welcome," and it's important to use one of these expressions when you're thanked. When you use public transportation, it's customary to give up your seat for elderly people, pregnant women and people with disabilities.
- Be punctual; if you're likely to be arriving later than planned at your hotel, let them know you've been held up.
- It is considered rude to eat or drink on the street. If you purchase food to go, find somewhere to sit down and eat it.
- Don't drop litter; it is a finable offense. When getting rid of trash, make sure you put it in the compartment designated for that particular type of waste.
- In Protestant Switzerland, decorous behavior is expected on Sunday.
- Dress conservatively in cities: avoid shorts, halter tops and beachwear.
- There is no state medical health service in Switzerland; treatment must be paid for on the spot. Therefore, it is very important to carry medical

- travel insurance valid in Switzerland. Many drugs can be bought over the counter. If you need a prescription drug, the prescription must be written by a Swiss doctor.
- In large towns and cities, stores are often closed on Monday mornings. Museums are usually closed on Mondays.
- Always cross the street at designated crossings, and wait for the green man symbol.
- Each canton and community is responsible for its own laws and law enforcement. The police uniform differs widely from place to place, as do local bylaws. Respect authority at all times, even if you see no point in what you are being requested to do.
- Use the superbly efficient public transportation system rather than the inordinately expensive taxis.
- You'll save money by eating and drinking in smaller establishments away from the more upscale areas.
- There is no need to tip in Switzerland; a service charge is automatically added to all bills.

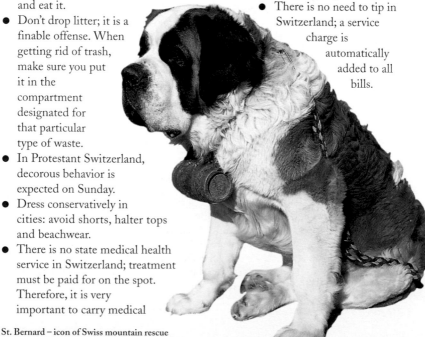

St. Bernard – icon of Swiss mountain rescue

GENEVA

Sparkling Geneva (Genève), beautifully situated by the shores of Lake Geneva (Lac Léman) and backed by the Jura mountains and Alps, is indeed an elegant city. With its key role as an important international meeting place, many visitors are here on business, but others come to enjoy the scenic location, excellent museums, stores, restaurants and lively cultural life.

The Modern City

Strategically positioned at the head of the Rhône river, Geneva joined the Swiss Confederation in 1815, after Napoleon's downfall. Since then the city has grown, prospered and become increasingly cosmopolitan.

Today Geneva hosts meetings, exhibitions, conventions and many organizations involved with humanitarian and social causes. It plays a major part in Swiss industry, finance and commerce, but has succeeded in retaining much of its French style and attitude, resulting in a pleasing blend of charm and efficiency.

An important university and scientific center, Geneva also is home to CERN, the European Center of Nuclear Research. The city is ringed with attractive countryside – the ski slopes of the French Alps are less than an hour away, and Lake Geneva offers superb water sports facilities.

Old Town and Beyond

Geneva is used to foreign visitors, and it's an easy city with which to become familiar. Getting around by public transportation is simple, and the center of the city is small enough to cover on foot, with much of the Old Town pedestrian-only. It's worth spending a couple of hours getting your bearings by walking around the town center, which lies on either side of the Rhône river.

Much of what you'll want to see is in or around the Old Town and is well signed, although with more than 30 museums to choose from, you are likely to take a bus at some point. Tourist trams run through the Old Town, leaving from the place Neuve every half-hour; they're a relaxing way to enjoy the city, although guided walking tours are available.

Tour buses travel to Lausanne and Château de Chillon, and into the Alps to Mont Blanc, Zermatt and Gstaad. Many lake cruises are offered, most lasting from one to three hours and many with an English commentary.

The steeple of St. Peter's Cathedral

Gourmet Geneva

Like all Swiss cities, Geneva has a large range of restaurants offering cuisine from around the world. It also has its own specialties, many of which have more in common with France than the rest of Switzerland. Eating out can be expensive, although away from the city center you'll find friendly and atmospheric neighborhood restaurants where prices are considerably lower.

Many places serve Swiss specialties such as fondue and *rösti*, but you can choose between French, Italian, Thai, Japanese, Korean, Chinese, Russian, Spanish, Australian, Moroccan and many more. You'll find all the usual fast-food outlets in the center, and it's fun to shop for a picnic to eat in one of the lakeside parks. There's a plethora of bars throughout the city; the nicest are in the Old Town and along the lakeside.

Festivals and Fun

Geneva's biggest traditional festival is the *Escalade*, a December commemoration of a 1602 battle. A wonderful costumed parade marches through the Old Town, and the whole city is out in the streets. Summer is festival time, with many celebrations centering around the lake and featuring some of Europe's most spectacular fireworks displays. On July 4th, Geneva stages the largest Independence Day celebration outside the United States.

The globe of unity outside the Palace of Nations

Designer Style and Souvenirs

Geneva stores do not close at lunchtime and are open until 8 p.m. on Thursdays. There are vast malls on the city outskirts, but it's likely you'll be shopping in the downtown area, where the most attractive and elegant stores are located. Many of them are along the rue du Rhône, the rue du Mont Blanc and neighboring streets.

Don't miss the Grand Passage, a large department store that's a Geneva institution. You'll find watches, jewelry, high fashion and superb leather goods from outlets such as Boucheron and Piaget, Christian Dior, Giorgio Armani, Gucci, Hermes and Chanel.

If you're looking for souvenirs to take home, try the tourist boutique in Grand Passage, Swiss Corner on the rue des Alpes, or l'Ours de Berne on the place du Port.

ESSENTIAL INFORMATION

TOURIST INFORMATION
- rue du Mont Blanc 3 ☎ 022 909 7000
- Port de la Machine ☎ 022 311 9827
- Gare Cornavin ☎ 022 909 7050
- Aéroport arrivals ☎ 022 717 8083

URBAN TRANSPORTATION
Geneva is efficiently served by swift and punctual trolley buses and buses that cover the city's various areas; it's likely you'll be traveling mainly inside Zone 10, which covers the city center. You buy and validate your ticket from the machines at each bus stop, which also have route maps and clear instructions about using the system. The best ticket for visitors to buy is the daily or multifare ticket, which provides either unlimited travel for 1 day, or 6 or 12 trips spread over several days. To board or leave the bus, press the red button near the door; the doors will open and close automatically. You can get more information from the Transports Publics Genevois (TPG) head office, route de la Chapelle 1, or at the information and ticket sales office on the square, Rond-Point-de-Rive. Taxis can be found at stands in the city center and can also be hailed on the street or called from your hotel. Try AA New Cab SA (☎ 022 320 2020) or Taxi-Phone SA Genève (☎ 022 331 4133).

AIRPORT INFORMATION
The Aéroport Internationale de Genève-Cointrin (Geneva International Airport, ☎ 022 717 7111) is 3 miles north of the city center. It is linked to the central railroad station by trains departing every 10 minutes, daily 6:30 a.m.–12:30 a.m., with a 6-minute journey time. Bus No. 10 runs approximately every 20 minutes between the airport and the city center; the trip takes around 20–25 minutes. Taxis are available outside the airport terminal.

CLIMATE – average highs and lows for the month

JAN.	FEB.	MAR.	APR.	MAY	JUN.	JUL.	AUG.	SEP.	OCT.	NOV.	DEC.
4°C	5°C	10°C	13°C	18°C	22°C	25°C	25°C	20°C	13°C	8°C	4°C
39°F	41°F	50°F	55°F	64°F	72°F	77°F	77°F	68°F	55°F	46°F	39°F
-2°C	0°C	2°C	3°C	7°C	12°C	14°C	14°C	11°C	6°C	2°C	0°C
28°F	32°F	36°F	37°F	45°F	54°F	57°F	57°F	52°F	43°F	36°F	32°F

CITY SIGHTS

Key to symbols

➕ map coordinates refer to the Geneva map on page 451; sights below are highlighted in yellow on the map.

✉ address or location ☎ telephone number

🕐 opening times 🚌 nearest bus or tram route

🍴 restaurant on site or nearby

💰 admission charge: $$$ more than SF10, $$ SF7–SF10, $ less than SF7

CATHÉDRALE ST-PIERRE

➕ B2 ✉ cour St.-Pierre ☎ 022 310 2929 or 022 311 7575 🕐 Cathédrale: Mon.–Sat. 9–7, Sun. 11–7, Jun.–Sep.; Mon.–Sat. 10–noon and 2–5, Sun. 11–12:30 and 1:30–5, rest of year. Site archéologique: Tue.–Sat. 11–5, Sun. 10–5, Jun.–Sep.; Tue.–Sat. 2–5, Sun. 10–noon and 2–5, rest of year 🚌 7, 12, 16 💰 $

Begin your visit to the Cathédrale St-Pierre (St. Peter's Cathedral) at the *site archéologique* (archeological site), a huge complex beneath the cathedral that has been undergoing excavations since 1976. Here you'll see the remains of the earliest church, built in the fourth century, and learn the history of the site via an audiovisual show. Move on to the vast and austere Cathedral, a Protestant church since 1536. It was built in the 12th and 13th centuries; its facade was added in the 18th century. This is where John Calvin preached; his seat is still in the north aisle. Visitors can climb the 158 steps up the tower to enjoy the fine views over Geneva and the lake.

COLLECTIONS BAUR

➕ C1 ✉ rue Munier-Romilly 8 ☎ 022 346 1729 🕐 Tue.–Sun. 2–6 🚌 1, 8 💰 $

A solidly elegant 19th-century mansion houses the Collections Baur, connoisseur Alfred Baur's collection of Asian art. Here you'll find exquisite Chinese ceramics and jade, snuff bottles, prints and *netsuke* (Japanese carved toggles), and some stunning Japanese and Chinese lacquerwork covering the 1,000 years between the 8th and 18th centuries. It's worth lingering over the porcelain and marveling at the depth and translucency of the yellow and celadon-green glazes.

JARDIN ANGLAIS

➕ B2–C2 ✉ promenade du Lac 🕐 Daily dawn–dusk 🍴 Cafés and restaurants 🚌 6, 8, 10

Statues, trees and colorful flowers help make the lakeside Jardin Anglais (English Garden), with its mountain views, the perfect place to escape the city's bustle. Admire the 1862 fountain, complete with numerous reclining nymphs, before spending a few minutes at the Floral Clock. This huge timepiece, made entirely of 6,500 flowers and plants, was installed in 1955 as a symbol of the Geneva watch industry. A short walk along the lake will bring you to Parc de la Grange, a lovely rose garden seen at its best in mid-June.

MUSÉE D'ART ET D'HISTOIRE

➕ B1 ✉ rue Charles-Galland 2 ☎ 022 418 2600 🕐 Tue.–Sun. 10–5 🍴 Restaurant 🚌 3, 12, 17

Behind the grandiose facade of Geneva's Musée d'Art et d'Histoire (Museum of Art and History) lies a dauntingly large collection of paintings, archeological finds and objets d'art. Ancient history fans will enjoy the Egyptian, Greek, Roman and Etruscan rooms. The galleries cover the full range of European painting, but concentrate on Swiss specialties, such as Ferdinand Hodler's powerful work *The Drinkers* or Konrad Witz's 1444 altarpiece; its background is one of Europe's first accurate landscape representations. Other rooms contain the applied arts collections, fine furniture, silver and porcelain.

MUSÉE D'HISTOIRE NATURELLE

➕ C1 ✉ route de Malagnou 1 ☎ 022 418 6300 🕐 Tue.–Sun. 9:30–5 🍴 Café and snack bar 🚌 1, 6, 8, 12

The splendid modern Musée d'Histoire Naturelle (Natural History Museum) is immensely popular, so get there early. The exhibits cover everything from the history of the Earth through the dinosaur age to comprehensive displays of animals, birds, reptiles and fish from all over the world. It's all excellently displayed, with some very realistic sound effects to help your

Place de Bourg-de-Four – the heart of old Geneva

imagination. Don't miss the relief map of
Switzerland on the fifth floor.

MUSÉE INTERNATIONAL DE L'AUTOMOBILE

➕ Off the map ✉ Voie-des-Traz 40, Grand
Sacconex ☎ 022 788 8484 🕐 Tue.–Sun. 10–7
🍴 Cafeteria 🚌 5, 10, 18

It's worth the trip out of town to Palexpo,
Geneva's impressive exhibition complex,
which houses the Musée International de
l'Automobile (International Automobile
Museum), a must for automobile fans.
Four hundred vehicles are grouped in
chronological order, from early speedsters
to General George Patton's jeep and Elvis
Presley's Cadillac. Space is devoted to cars
of the future, rally and Formula 1 models,
and there are numerous movie clips,
posters, models and hands-on games.

MUSÉE INTERNATIONAL DE LA CROIX ROUGE ET DU CROISSANT ROUGE

➕ Off the map ✉ avenue de la Paix 17 ☎ 022 734
5248 🕐 Wed.–Mon. 10–5 🍴 Restaurant 🚌 8, 12,
V, Z ♿ $$

It's well worth visiting the state-of-the-art
Musée International de la Croix Rouge et
du Croissant Rouge (International Red
Cross and Red Crescent Museum), which
explains the principles and history of the
Red Cross and the Red Crescent during
some of the most serious crises of the
20th century.

PALAIS DES NATIONS

➕ Off the map ✉ avenue de la Paix (Porte 39)
☎ 022 907 4896 or 022 907 4539 🕐 Daily 9–6,
Jul.–Aug.; daily 10–noon and 2–4, Apr.–Jun. and
Sep.–Oct.; Mon.–Fri. 10–noon and 2–4, rest of year
🍴 Cafeteria 🚌 5, 8, 11, 14, V, Z ♿ $$

Built between 1929 and 1936 to house
the League of Nations, the Palais des
Nations (Palace of Nations) is now the
European seat of the United Nations. The
vast marble and travertine-stone complex
is beautifully situated on the slopes above
the lake, with views of Mont Blanc. You
can tour some of the interior and see the
Salle des Pas-Perdus, a room decorated
with marble donated by United Nations
member countries, and the 2,000-seat
Salle des Assemblées, one of the world's
most active conference centers. After the
tour, learn more through the multilingual
interactive games.

PETIT PALAIS

➕ C1 ✉ terrasse St.-Victor 2 ☎ 022 346 1433
🕐 Mon.–Fri. 10–noon and 2–6, Sat.–Sun.10–1 and
2–5 🚌 1, 3, 8, 17 ♿ $$

This imposing 19th-century mansion
contains the Petit Palais (Little Palace)
museum, Geneva's Impressionist gallery,
which features many paintings from the
private collection of the museum's
founder, industrialist Oscar Ghez de
Castelnuovo. Here you'll see Degas' *Nude
Woman Washing*, some fine pointillist
paintings by Paul Signac, and early works
by Pablo Picasso and Marc Chagall.

PLACE DU BOURG-DE-FOUR

➕ B1 ✉ place du Bourg-de-Four 🍴 Cafés and
restaurants nearby 🚌 8, 17

Bourg-de-Four square is the heart of Old
Geneva, historically the site of the Roman
market, medieval trade fairs, and political
and religious meetings. Today the square
and its surrounding streets are a lovely
place to stroll or enjoy a drink at one of
the bars and cafés. Many of the fine
buildings date from the 16th century;
note their extra floors, added later to
accommodate the flood of Protestant
religious exiles.

Headquarters of the International Red Cross, in Geneva

THE RED CROSS

In 1859 Henri Dunant, son of a prominent Genevan family, set off to appeal to Napoleon III of France on a personal matter. Dunant caught up with Napoleon the day after the Battle of Solferino, where he saw more than 40,000 wounded men desperately in need of care and attention.

Dunant returned to Geneva and wrote a moving book, *Souvenir of Solferino*, in which he proposed the establishment of a body of volunteer male nurses to impartially care for the wounded in wartime. He further suggested that these men be recognized through an international agreement. Three friends added their support, the book was published and the International Committee of Help for the Wounded in Case of War (Comité Internationale de Secours aux Blessées en cas de Guerre) was set up.

In 1864, the First Convention of Geneva was accepted and signed by 16 nations; a revised version of its standards of treatment for prisoners of war is still in effect today. An easily recognizable logo for the new movement was needed, and a reverse version of the Swiss flag was used; a red cross on a white background, rather than a white cross on a red background, and a symbol known the world over.

The Red Cross, present in more than 50 countries throughout the world, works hand in hand with the Red Crescent, an identical body functioning in Muslim and other non-Christian countries. Henri Dunant was awarded the Nobel Peace Prize in 1901.

The Red Cross functions at both international and national levels. The international headquarters are in Geneva, and it is from here that major humanitarian relief work is coordinated. Each participating country has its own national committee that deals with day-to-day work in that particular country. The Red Cross is still manned largely by volunteers, who cover everything from terrorist attacks and natural disasters to organizing collections for war victims and refugees, as well as training the public in emergency aid procedures.

ZURICH

Primarily a business center, with an emphasis on international finance and banking, this prosperous and clean city has plenty for visitors to enjoy. It is dotted with fine buildings, museums, historic churches and green spaces, the perfect background for affluent stores, elegant cafés and well-dressed citizens.

Lakeside City

Zurich surrounds the northern end of Zürichsee (Lake Zurich), from which the Limmat river flows to bisect the city. The oldest part lies on either side of the river, with the 19th-century

Swiss precision watch

Peaceful St. Peter's

ZURICH

0   200   400 m
0   200   400 yards

N

grandeur of the Bahnhofstrasse area on the west. East of the river, gentle hills rise to the impressive university complex, while wide boulevards, parks and gardens run along the lake.

A tram ride is an essential experience; these efficient vehicles ensure that city streets are virtually traffic-free. If you feel in need of exercise, the tourist office will rent you a bike to get around like the locals do.

Evenings Out

There's a wide range of excellent restaurants in Zurich, most of them expensive. It is possible to eat well and relatively cheaply on the east side of the river. You'll find the usual fast-food outlets, excellent cafés and tearooms, and cozy taverns and wine cellars.

Notice boards all over the city list movie theaters (often showing American films in English), concerts, theater and opera. For a relaxed evening

with the locals, you'll find plenty of packed bars, open late, in and around the Limmatquai; on summer nights there is an array of street performers. Zurich also has a number of cabarets and discos.

Chocolates and Watches

Bahnhofstrasse, running from the main railroad station to the lake, is one of Europe's great shopping streets. Lined with expensive stores, it is where you'll find luxury items, including fashion, jewelry, watches, porcelain, furs and accessories. It's also home to Schweizer Heimatwerk, a lovely store specializing in every type of Swiss handicraft.

Don't miss Sprüngli, one of the most mouthwatering chocolate shops you'll ever visit. And the narrow old streets on each side of the river are packed with antiques stores, clock and watch outlets, and fun places for picking up souvenirs.

Zurich

ESSENTIAL INFORMATION

TOURIST INFORMATION
• Bahnhofbrücke 1 ☎ 01 215 4000

URBAN TRANSPORTATION
Zurich's superbly efficient tram and bus system, runs daily, 4:30 a.m.–12:30 a.m. It is easy to use, fast and never, ever late. Tickets must be purchased and validated before boarding; all bus stops have ticket machines with detailed transportation maps and instructions for buying and validating your ticket. If you are going to be in Zurich for a couple of days or more, you can buy 24-hour or multiride tickets; like normal tickets, these are also valid for trams, buses, local trains and some boats. Numbers and stops (which are all named) are displayed on the front of the vehicles as well as

inside. You must press the red button on the door to open the door before getting off; it will close automatically. For further English-language information call ☎ 0848 80 18 80 (only from within Switzerland). Taxis are an expensive option; call Zürotaxi (☎ 01 222 2222), Taxi Jung (☎ 01 271 1188) or Taxi 2000 Zürich (☎ 01 444 4444). Boats run on the lake during the summer; their timetables are listed at departure points.

AIRPORT INFORMATION
Zurich-Kloten Airport (☎ 01 157 1060) is just under 6 miles north of the city center. Trains run approximately every 12 minutes from the Hauptbahnhof, daily 5:30 a.m.–12:30 a.m., with a ride time of around 10 minutes. There are two terminals, A and B, which are interconnected. Taxis are available from outside the terminals.

CLIMATE – average highs and lows for the month											
JAN.	FEB.	MAR.	APR.	MAY	JUN.	JUL.	AUG.	SEP.	OCT.	NOV.	DEC.
2°C	3°C	8°C	12°C	16°C	19°C	22°C	22°C	18°C	12°C	6°C	3°C
36°F	37°F	46°F	54°F	61°F	66°F	72°F	72°F	64°F	54°F	43°F	37°F
-2°C	-2°C	2°C	4°C	8°C	11°C	14°C	14°C	11°C	7°C	2°C	0°C
28°F	28°F	36°F	39°F	46°F	52°F	57°F	57°F	52°F	45°F	36°F	32°F

The twin towers of Grossmunster overlook the Limmat river and the Old Town

CITY SIGHTS

Key to symbols

✚ map coordinates refer to the Zurich map on page 456; sights below are highlighted in yellow on the map.

⊠ address or location   ☎ telephone number

🕑 opening times   🚍 nearest bus or tram route

🍴 restaurant on site or nearby

✋ admission charge: $$$ more than SF10, $$ SF7–SF10, $ less than SF7

ALTSTADT

✚ A3–B3   ⊠ Altstadt   🚍 4, 6, 7, 15

The narrow streets and peaceful squares on either side of the Limmat river make up the Altstadt (Old Town). Beautifully preserved old buildings house antiques and curiosity stores, and there's a lovely riverside walkway and plenty of relaxing cafés and bars. Take in the Lindenhof, a square planted with lime trees on the site of the original Roman settlement, before crossing the river to amble down the east side's lively Niederdorfstrasse and Hirschengasse.

FRAUMÜNSTER

✚ A2   ⊠ Fraumünsterstrasse   🕑 Daily 9–noon and 2–6, May–Sep.; 10–noon and 2–5, Oct.–Feb.; 10–noon and 2–4, rest of year   🚍 7, 8, 11   ✋ Free

The graceful spire of the Fraumünster (Our Lady's Minster Church), founded in the ninth century by two German princesses, rises near the west riverbank in the Old Town. The interior dates from 1250 and earlier; against its gray stone serenity, Marc Chagall's stained-glass choir windows vibrate with green, blue and yellow. Alberto Giacometti designed the transept glass.

GROSSMÜNSTER

✚ B2   ⊠ Grossmünsterplatz   ☎ 01 252 5949

🕑 Mon.–Sat. 9–6, Apr.–Oct.; 10–4, rest of year. Open Sun. for services   🚍 4, 15   ✋ $

Grossmünster church played a major part in Zurich's Reformation (a 16th-century religious movement which aimed at reforming the Roman Catholic Church and resulted in the establishment of Protestant churches). It was here that Zwingli, the father of Swiss Protestantism, preached and taught. He transformed this Catholic foundation into a theological college that became the focal point of the University of Zurich. The church, galleries and three naves were built between 1100 and 1260, a superb Romanesque basilica with some outstanding sculpture on the capitals of its columns. Be sure to visit the tranquil cloister, which has exhibits telling the story of the Reformation, and save

Zurich

energy to climb up the tower, which has lovely views over Zurich and the lake.

KUNSTHAUS

✚ B2 ✉ Heimplatz 1 ☎ 01 251 6755 🕐 Tue.–Thu. 10–9, Fri.–Sun. 10–5 🍴 Café and restaurant 🚊 3, 31 🎫 Free

Zurich's Kunsthaus (Art Gallery), a lively museum that often mounts important temporary exhibitions, is mainly devoted to 19th- and 20th-century paintings and artworks. Earlier times are represented by a clutch of Venetian paintings, as well as some splendid Dutch works. The exhibits of modern art are housed in the newer wing. Here you'll find the largest collection of Edvard Munch outside Scandinavia, paintings by Marc Chagall, and a good cross-section of modern work by Mark Rothko, Francis Bacon and Roy Lichtenstein, whose contribution is a baked potato oozing with butter.

SCHWEIZERISCHES LANDESMUSEUM

✚ A4 ✉ Museumstrasse 2 ☎ 01 218 6565 🕐 Tue.–Sun. 10:30–5 🍴 Café and restaurant 🚊 3, 6, 7, 10, 15 🎫 Free

Housed in a bizarre looking castle complete with towers and turrets, the Schweizerisches Landesmuseum (Swiss National Museum) should top your sightseeing list. This is the place to learn about Switzerland's history and development, and it is one of Europe's best organized museums. From prehistoric times, you can follow the flowering of Swiss civilization through frescoes, religious woodcarvings and exquisite jewelry, wood-paneled interiors, and furniture and costumes from every corner of the land. The 16th-century globes, showing all that had so far been discovered, are fascinating, and most visitors will enjoy the reconstruction of rooms from different eras.

ST. PETERSKIRCHE

✚ A2 ✉ St. Peter Hofstatt 🕐 Mon.–Sat. 8–6 🚊 6, 7 🎫 Free

The oldest church foundation in Zurich stands in a tranquil square at the heart of the Old Town, its delightfully restrained baroque interior perfectly typifying Zurich's God-fearing prosperity. Four churches predated the existing one, which preserves the late Romanesque choir and 13th-century tower. All is harmony and balance, from the richly carved choir stalls to the superb plasterwork. The clock in the tower is Europe's largest clock-face, measuring an impressive $28\frac{1}{2}$ feet across.

STIFTUNG SAMMLUNG E. G. BÜHRLE

✚ Off the map ✉ Zollikerstrasse 172 ☎ 01 422 0086 🕐 Tue. and Wed. 2–5 (also Wed. 5–8) 🚊 77 🎫 $$

A lovely suburban villa houses the Stiftung Sammlung E. G. Bührle (E. G. Bührle Collection), a wonderful range of Impressionist and post-Impressionist works of art collected by a German industrialist between 1934 and 1956. The exhibits are outstanding and the building a delight, so allow plenty of time.

There are delicate Jean Honoré Fragonards and François Bouchers – all flowery pinks and blues – sun-filled Camille Pissarros, the dazzling *Poppies near Véthueil* by Claude Monet and the stunning *Chestnut Tree* by Vincent Van Gogh. Upstairs you'll find Pablo Picasso, Henri Matisse and Georges Braque, among others. Linger in the room devoted to Pierre Renoir, where there's also a lovely painting by Monet of his garden at Giverny. The 22 Degas bronzes of *The Dancer* are another highlight.

ZOOH!

✚ Off the map ✉ Zürichberg ☎ 01 252 7100 🕐 Daily 8–6 🍴 Cafés and restaurant on zoo grounds 🚊 6 🎫 $$

Zurich's zoo enjoys a parkland setting on a hill overlooking Zurich. More than 2,000 animals are exhibited, with emphasis on species from South America, Africa and Asia. If you're traveling with kids, arrange to be here at 10 a.m. when the elephants and monkeys enjoy their daily bath. The zoo has a successful breeding program; a board near the entrance gives information about any new arrivals.

A tasty shared experience – fondue, the Swiss national dish

SWISS FLAVORS

Switzerland has a range of regional dishes – German, French and Italian – rather than a national cuisine. With many foreigners working in the country, there's plenty of choice, and in the cities you'll find everything from Japanese to Tex-Mex. The Swiss call a restaurant menu the *Karte* or *carte*; *menu* means the "dish of the day."

Swiss Cheese Specials

The country's best-known specialty, fondue, is made by melting a selection of Swiss hard cheeses, such as Gruyere, Emmental and Vacherin, in white wine spiked with garlic and then adding spices and kirsch. The bubbling pot sits in the middle of the table on a little brazier, and you help yourself by dipping forkfuls of bread into the unctuous mixture. Be careful not to drop the bread in the pot – traditionally the culprit has to buy the next bottle of wine. Fondues are also made by cooking cubed beef in either hot oil (*fondue bourguignonne*) or beef stock (*fondue chinoise*); these are served with a variety of tasty dips. In French Switzerland you'll find raclette; a whole block of cheese is toasted and melted with slices scraped off and draped over boiled potatoes to be eaten with gherkins, smoked ham and sausage. It's delicious!

Main Dishes

Bündnerfleisch – raw, dried smoked beef – is well worth sampling, as are the many kinds of *wurst*, sausages eaten raw, grilled or boiled. The traditional accompaniment is *rösti*, a mouthwatering, crisp potato cake studded with onions and bacon. Hungry diners might enjoy the *Berner Platte*, a groaning plate of sausage, beef and ham served with potatoes and sauerkraut. The Swiss are also fond of liver, pork and veal. Traditional fish recipes in this landlocked country feature lake trout, carp and perch.

A Little Something Sweet

Chocolate and cream feature heavily in Swiss desserts, and you should certainly try some of the smooth Swiss chocolate during your trip; in addition to the ubiquitous Nestlé and Cailler, Lindt, Sprüngli, Teuscher and Tobler are varieties worth sampling. There are some splendid local cakes; try *leckerli* (spiced bread with honey), meringues, and delicious kirsch-flavored cakes and fruit breads. Start the day with a breakfast bowl of muesli, a delicious mixture of grains, fruit and nuts.

ESSENTIAL INFORMATION

"LET your boat of life be light, packed only with what you need..."

From *Three Men in a Boat*
by English author Jerome K. Jerome

Austria – Essential Information

PRE-TRIP ESSENTIALS...

WHAT YOU NEED

ESSENTIAL FOR TRAVELERS

● Required   ● Recommended   ○ Not required

Passport	●
Visa	○
Travel, medical insurance	●
Round-trip or onward airline ticket	○
Local currency	●
Traveler's checks	●
Credit cards	●
First-aid kit and medicines	●
Inoculations*	○

*see also HEALTH section

ESSENTIAL FOR DRIVERS*

Driver's license	●
International Driving Permit	●
Car insurance (for nonrental cars)	●
Car registration (for nonrental cars)	●

*see also DRIVING section

IMPORTANT ADDRESSES

Austrian National Tourist Office
500 Fifth Avenue
New York, NY 10110
☎ (212) 944-6880
Fax (212) 730-4568

Austrian National Tourist Office
Margaretenstrasse 1
Vienna 1040, Austria
☎ 01 58 86.60
Fax 01 58.86.62-0

American Embassy
Boltzmangasse 16
Vienna 1090, Austria
☎ 01 31.3 39
Fax 01 31.00 68-2
Personal callers should phone for an appointment.

COUNTRY ESSENTIALS...

CUSTOMS

YES
Duty-free limits on goods brought in from non-European Union countries:
200 cigarettes or 50 cigarillos/cigars or 250 g. tobacco; 2 L. wine; 1 L. alcohol over 22% volume; 2 L. alcohol under 22% volume; 60 ml. perfume; 250 ml. toilet water; plus any other duty-free goods (including gifts) to the value of S2,500. Personal allowance from Hungary, Slovenia, Czech or Slovak republics: S1,000 (unless you arrive by air, when it is S2,500, as above). This information applies to visitors aged 17 and over. There are no currency regulations. There is no limit on the importation of tax-paid goods purchased within the European Union, provided they are for your own personal use.

NO
No unlicensed drugs, weapons, ammunition, obscene material, pets or other animals, counterfeit money or copied goods, meat or poultry.
For customs limits for returning U.S. citizens see page 16.

MONEY

Austria's currency is the schilling (S or Sch), which is divided into 100 groschen (g). The denominations of schilling bills are 20, 50, 100, 500, 1,000 and 5,000. There are coins of 10 and 50g and 1, 5, 10 and 20S. You can exchange dollars or traveler's checks *(Reiseschecks)* at a bank *(Bank)*, exchange office *(Wechselbüro)*, post office *(Postamt)* and at hotels. Credit cards are widely accepted. On Jan. 1, 1999, the euro became the official currency of Austria, and Austrian schillings became a denomination of the euro. Austrian schilling bills and coins continue to be legal tender during a transitional period. Euro bills and coins are likely to be introduced by Jan. 2002.
Exchange rate at press time: $1 = S13

TIPS AND GRATUITIES

Tips *(Trinkgeld)* are welcomed and expected in restaurants and cafés.

Restaurants (even when service is included)	10%
Cafés/bars	10%
Taxis	10%
Porters	at your discretion
Chambermaids	at your discretion
Hairdressers	5% (and change to shampooer)

Austria – Essential Information

COMMUNICATIONS

POST OFFICES

Buy stamps *(Briefmarken)* singly at a post office *(Postamt)* or newsstand/tobacconist *(Tabak Trafik)* or from a hotel.

Post offices can be recognized by a golden trumpet symbol and can often be found close to the main square or railroad station. Hours for out-of-town post offices may vary.

TELEPHONES

You can use cash or a prepaid phone card *(Wertkarte)* to make a call in Austria. Telephones have direct dialing for national and international calls. Use S1, S5 and S10 coins. Phone cards can be bought from newsstands, gas stations, post offices and hotels. Some city phone booths take credit cards.

Phoning inside Austria
All Austrian telephone numbers in this book include an area code: dial the number that is listed.

To call the operator dial 1611.

Phoning Austria from abroad
The country code for Austria is 43. Note that Austrian numbers in this book do not include the country code; you will need to prefix this number if you are phoning from another country. To phone Austria from the United States or Canada, omit the first zero from the Austrian number, and add the prefix 011 43. (Note that the number of digits in Austrian area codes varies.)
Example: 01 12 23 34-4 becomes 011 43 1 12 23 34-4.

Phoning from Austria
To phone the United States or Canada from Austria, prefix the area code and number with 001.
Example: (111) 222-3333 becomes 001 111 222-3333.

To call international information dial 1614.

EMERGENCY TELEPHONE NUMBERS
Police *(Polizei)*	133
Fire *(Feuerwehr)*	122
Ambulance *(Krankenwagen)*	144

Emergency calls are free from phone booths.

HOURS OF OPERATION

- Stores Mon.–Sat.
- Offices Mon.–Fri.
- Banks Mon.–Fri.
- Post offices Mon.–Fri.
- Museums/monuments
- Pharmacies

| 7 | 8 | 9 | 10 | 11 | 12 | 1 | 2 | 3 | 4 | 5 | 6 | 7 |

Saturday is early closing day and few shops stay open later than 12:30 in the afternoon. Thursday or Friday is late night shopping (until 7 or 8).

Grocery stores and other food stores may have longer hours of operation.

In cities, some post offices open 24 hours a day.

Pharmacies usually follow store opening hours with a 2-hour lunch break. There is always one pharmacy open late in each city: details are displayed in pharmacy windows.

Facilities at tourist resorts may have special hours of operation.

NATIONAL HOLIDAYS
Banks, businesses and most stores close on these days. Also, some museums may be closed or have restricted hours.

Jan. 1	New Year's Day
Jan. 6	Epiphany
Mar./Apr.	Easter Monday
May 1	Labor Day
May	Ascension Day
May/Jun.	Pentecost Monday
May/Jun.	Corpus Christi
Aug. 15	Assumption of the Virgin
Oct. 26	National Day
Nov. 1	All Saints' Day
Dec. 8	Immaculate Conception
Dec. 25	Christmas Day
Dec. 26	St. Stephen's Day

PHOTOGRAPHY

Magnificent and varied subject matter awaits the photographer in Austria. Make sure you choose a perspective that will do justice to the architectural masterpieces and narrow city lanes. Away from the city, the Alpine peaks give enormous scope for landscape photography, and the light is generally very good.

Austria – Essential Information

HEALTH

MEDICAL INSURANCE
The cost of medical treatment in Austria is high, and private medical insurance is recommended. The American Medical Society can suggest a doctor *(Arzt)* or hospital *(Krankenhaus):* Lazarettgasse 13, Vienna, ☎ 01 4054 5680. The south and east are home to *Zecken* – a kind of tick that can transmit encephalitis. This disease is potentially lethal, and it is essential you seek medical advice if you are bitten. An inoculation is available.

DENTAL SERVICES
Dentists *(Zahnarzt)* will charge for any treatment given. Dental work is expensive, so check that it is covered by your medical insurance. Dentists are listed in the telephone directory, or ask for English-speaking dentists at your embassy, a tourist office or hotel.

SUN ADVICE
Austria has strong sun during the summer months so sun protection is needed. Wear a hat, cover shoulders, drink plenty of fluids and use sunblock.

DRUGS
Pharmacies *(Apotheke)* can dispense prescriptions. Many assistants speak English, and a schedule displayed on the door enables you to find a late-opening or 24-hour pharmacy in every town.

SAFE WATER
Tap water is safe to drink throughout Austria. Mineral water *(Mineralwasser)* is widely available.

RESTROOMS

Public restrooms *(Toiletten/WC)* are generally easy to find and immaculately clean. A small charge is levied.

ELECTRICITY

Austria has a 220-volt power supply. Electrical sockets take plugs with two round pins; American appliances will need a plug adapter and will require a transformer if they do not have a dual-voltage facility.

NATIONAL TRANSPORTATION

TRAIN *(Zug)*
The Austrian Federal Railways (Österreichische Bundesbahnen or ÖBB) runs a comfortable and efficient service, with connections to all European countries. If you like a slower pace try a steam train journey through valleys and along lakesides, or a cable car trip; local tourist offices can give details. For rail information ☎ 01 17 17.

BUS *(Bus)*
Austria has a good network of local, federal and private bus companies. Bus travel is slower but less expensive than the train; for information ☎ 01 71 1 01. The Eurolines international bus service also operates in Austria: ☎ 01 71 20 45-3.

FERRY *(Fähre)*
From Easter to the end of October you can enjoy steamer services on the Danube; some continue into neighboring countries. Steamers ply the larger Austrian lakes from May to September. Wiener Tourismusverband can supply details on steamer companies: ☎ 01 21 1 14.

DRIVING

DRIVE ON THE RIGHT

SPEED LIMITS
Police impose on-the-spot fines (for which receipts are issued) although a foreign motorist may refuse and instead be asked to make a surety payment.

Limited-access highways *(Autobahnen)*
130 k.p.h. (80 m.p.h.)

Main roads
100 k.p.h. (62 m.p.h.)

Urban areas
50 k.p.h. (31 m.p.h.)

SEAT BELTS
Must be worn in front seats at all times and in the rear seats where fitted. Children under 12 are not allowed to use a front seat.

BLOOD ALCOHOL
The legal blood alcohol limit is 0.08%. Random breath tests on drivers are carried out frequently, especially late at night, and the penalties for offenders are severe.

Austria – Essential Information

DRIVING continued

TOLLS
To use toll highways, purchase a windshield sticker *(Vignette)* at a border crossing, gas station, automobile club, post office or tobacconist. Nonpayment of tolls results in a fine.

CAR RENTAL
The leading rental firms have offices at airports and train stations. Hertz offers discounted rates for AAA members (see page 15). For reservations:

	UNITED STATES	AUSTRIA
Alamo	(800) 327-9633	01 273 22 33 30
Avis	(800) 331-2112	01 700 73 27 00
Budget	(800) 527-0700	01 7007 2711
Hertz	(800) 654-3080	02 72 64 95-0

FUEL
Many gas stations *(Tankstelle)* are self-service, and 24-hour facilities are common. Unleaded gas *(Bleifrei)* is available at 95 and 98 octane. Diesel is available and credit cards are accepted in most garages.

AAA AFFILIATED MOTORING CLUB
Österreichischer Automobil, Motorrad und Touring Club (ÖAMTC)
Schubertring 1-3, 1010 Vienna
☎ 01 71 19 90, fax 01 71 31 80-7
If you break down while driving, phone ☎ 120 (ÖAMTC breakdown service). Not all automobile clubs offer full services to AAA members.

BREAKDOWNS AND ACCIDENTS
There are 24-hour emergency phones at regular intervals on highways. All accidents involving personal injury must be reported to the police.
Most car rental firms provide their own free rescue service; if your car is rented, follow the instructions given in the documentation. Use of a car repair service other than those authorized by your rental company may violate your agreement.

OTHER INFORMATION
The minimum age for driving a car is 18 (may be higher for some car rental firms).

An International Driving Permit (IDP) is recommended; some rental firms require them, and they can speed up formalities if you are involved in an accident. A Green Card (international motor insurance certificate) is recommended if you are driving a private car; see page 15 for more information.

Dimmed headlights must be used at all times.

In winter, snow tires or chains are essential, and are legal from Nov. 15 to Easter. Rent chains at automobile clubs and border crossings.

USEFUL WORDS AND PHRASES

The official language in Austria is German, although Austrians are very proud of their brand of the language *(Österreichische)*, and are offended if it is treated as a mere dialect of "standard" German *(Hochdeutsch)*. On paper, the differences between the two varieties are not obvious, but the Austrian accent is distinctive, and especially strong in rural regions.

There are numerous words that are peculiar to Austria and the south of Germany. The Austrian diminutive is *-el* or *-lein* compared with the German *-chen*, so *Mädchen* (girl) in German becomes *Mädel* in Austrian. A small number of Austrian words, such as *Fauteuil* (armchair) and *Plafond* (ceiling), are in fact of French origin.

See page 493 for a pronunciation and basic vocabulary guide to the German language; the following list is an eclectic sample of words peculiar to Austrian German.

Everyday life

a maiden, or a girl's dress	*Dirndl*
masked ball	*Fetzenball*
hello	*Grüss Gott*
policeman	*Gendarm*
friend, guy	*Haberer*
legs	*Haxen*
funny	*Hetzig*
work	*Hockn*
guitar	*Klampfe*
goodbye	*Pfiat di*
slippers	*Schlapfen*

Food and drink

blood sausage	*Blunzn*
potato	*Erdäpfel*
green beans	*Fisole*
green salad	*Häuplsalat*
carrot	*Karotte*
croissant	*Kipferl*
lemonade	*Kracherl*
doughnut	*Krapfen*
corn	*Kukuruz*
milky coffee	*Melange*
mushroom	*Schwammerl*

Common words and phrases

how much?	*wieviel kostet es?*
excuse me	*entschuldigen*
I don't understand	*Ich verstehe nicht*
I'd like	*Ich möchte*
where is…?	*wo ist…?*
no smoking	*nicht rauchen*
closed	*geschlossen*
open	*geöffnet*
please	*bitte*
thank you	*danke*
key	*schlussel*
room	*zimmer*
shower	*dusche*
breakfast	*frühstück*

Belgium – Essential Information

PRE-TRIP ESSENTIALS...

WHAT YOU NEED

ESSENTIAL FOR TRAVELERS

● Required   ● Recommended   ● Not required

Passport	●
Visa	●
Travel, medical insurance	●
Round-trip or onward airline ticket	●
Local currency	●
Traveler's checks	●
Credit cards	●
First-aid kit and medicines	●
Inoculations	●

ESSENTIAL FOR DRIVERS*

Driver's license	●
International Driving Permit	●
Car insurance (for nonrental cars)	●
Car registration (for nonrental cars)	●

*see also DRIVING section

IMPORTANT ADDRESSES

Belgian Tourist Office
780 Third Avenue
Suite 1501
New York, NY 10017
☎ (212) 758-8130
Fax (212) 355-7675

Belgian Tourist Office
Rue du Marché aux Herbes 63
1000 Brussels, Belgium
☎ 02 504 0390
Fax 02 504 0270

American Embassy
Régent Boulevard 27
1000 Brussels, Belgium
☎ 02 508 2111
Fax 02 508 2518
Personal visa inquiries: Mon.–Fri. 9–noon and 2:30–4

COUNTRY ESSENTIALS...

CUSTOMS

YES
Duty-free limits on goods brought in from non-European Union countries:
200 cigarettes or 100 cigarillos or 50 cigars or 250 g. tobacco; 2 L. wine; 1 L. alcohol over 22% volume; 2 L. alcohol under 22% volume; 60 ml. perfume; 250 ml. toilet water; plus any other duty-free goods (including gifts) to the value of 8,100BF. There is no limit on the importation of tax-paid goods purchased within the European Union, provided the goods are for your own personal use. There are no currency regulations.

NO
No unlicensed drugs, weapons, ammunition, obscene material, pets or other animals, counterfeit money or copied goods, meat or poultry.

For customs limits for returning U.S. citizens see page 16.

MONEY

Belgium's currency is the Belgian franc (BF), which is divided into 100 centimes. The denominations of franc bills are 100, 200, 500, 1,000, 2,000 and 10,000. There are coins of 50 centimes and 1, 5, 20 and 50BF. Be sure to differentiate between 5BF and 20BF coins, as they are very similar in shape and color. Credit cards are widely accepted but can be unwelcome for small amounts. On Jan. 1, 1999, the euro became the official currency of Belgium, and the Belgian franc became a denomination of the euro. Belgian franc bills and coins continue to be legal tender during a transitional period. Euro bills and coins are likely to be introduced by Jan. 2002.
Exchange rate at press time: $1 = 40BF

TIPS AND GRATUITIES

Tips are not obligatory; a service charge is usually included for restaurants, cafés and taxis.

Restaurants (where service is not included)	10%
Cafés/bars	change
Taxis	change
Porters	change
Chambermaids	change
Cloakroom attendants	20BF

TIME ZONES

BRUSSELS	NEW YORK	CHICAGO	DENVER	SAN FRANCISCO
12:00 noon	6 hours behind Belgium	7 hours behind Belgium	8 hours behind Belgium	9 hours behind Belgium

467

COMMUNICATIONS

POST OFFICES

Buy stamps *(timbres/postzegels)* at a post office *(bureau de poste/postkantoor)*, a tobacconist or newsstand *(tabac/tabaksverkoper)*, or from a vending machine.

Allow a week for mail to reach the United States.
Mailboxes are painted red.

Hours for out-of-town post offices may vary.

TELEPHONES

Coin-operated public phones take 5BF and 20BF coins, but phone card booths are more common. Phone cards *(télécartes/kaarttelephoon)* are available from post offices and some newsstands (phone card booths do not take credit cards.) Dialing instructions in English are often displayed in public booths.

Phoning in Belgium
All Belgian telephone numbers in this book include an area code: dial the number that is listed.
To call the operator dial 1307 (French-speaking areas) or 1207 (Flemish-speaking areas).

Phoning Belgium from abroad
The country code for Belgium is 32. Note that Belgian numbers in this book do not include the country code; you will need to prefix this number if you are phoning from another country. To phone Belgium from the United States or Canada, omit the first zero from the Belgian number and add the prefix 011 32. (Note that Belgian area codes are single or double digits.) Example: 01 122 3344 becomes 011 32 1 122 3344.

Phoning from Belgium
To phone the United States or Canada from Belgium, prefix the area code and number with 001. Example: (111) 222-3333 becomes 001 111 222-3333.

To call international information dial 1204 (French-speaking areas) or 1304 (Flemish-speaking areas).

EMERGENCY TELEPHONE NUMBERS
Police *(police)*	101
Fire service *(pompiers)*	100
Ambulance *(ambulance)*	100

Emergency calls are free from phone booths.

HOURS OF OPERATION

- Stores Mon.–Sat.
- Museums/monuments
- Offices Mon.–Fri.
- Pharmacies Mon.–Sat.
- Banks Mon.–Fri.
- Post offices Mon.–Fri.

7 8 9 10 11 12 1 2 3 4 5 6 7

While Sunday is the official closing day, souvenir shops in many towns stay open.

Many bakeries and *patisseries* also open on Sunday morning.

Department and other major stores often stay open until 8 p.m. on weekdays and 9 p.m. on Friday.

Smaller stores and out-of-town post offices and banks may close for lunch.

Some city post offices and banks open on Saturday morning.

It is common for museums to close on Monday and open later one evening a week. Many close for 2 hours at lunch.

NATIONAL HOLIDAYS

Banks, businesses and most stores close on these days. Most cities, towns and villages celebrate their patron saint's day, but most places stay open.

Jan. 1	New Year's Day
Mar./Apr.	Easter Monday
May 1	Labor Day
May	Ascension Day
May/Jun.	Pentecost Monday
Jul. 21	National Day
Aug. 15	Assumption of the Virgin
Nov. 1	All Saints' Day
Nov. 11	Armistice Day
Dec. 25	Christmas Day
Dec. 26	St. Stephen's Day

PHOTOGRAPHY

Belgium is not renowned for bright sunshine, so pack plenty of 200 ASA-speed film. Check that flash photography is permitted before taking pictures in museums. Film and camera batteries are readily available from tourist stores. Rapid-developing services are also widely available.

Belgium – Essential Information

EMERGENCY PHONE NUMBERS

 POLICE 101
(Police)

Belgium – Essential Information

HEALTH

MEDICAL INSURANCE
Private medical insurance is recommended. Visitors from non-European Union countries can receive treatment in a hospital emergency room but are charged if admitted to a hospital *(hôpital/ziekenhuis)*.

DENTAL SERVICES
Dental treatment is not available free of charge; all dentists practice privately. A list of dentists *(dentiste/tandarts)* can be found in the yellow pages *(pages jaunes/beroepenlijst)*. Check that dental treatment is covered by your private medical insurance.

SUN ADVICE
The warmest months are July and August, with average daytime temperatures of 60°F. Belgian weather can be unpredictable and although the sun is not often very fierce, protection is still required.

DRUGS
Prescription and nonprescription medicines are available from a pharmacy *(pharmacie/apotheek)*. If you need a medicine outside regular hours, the addresses of 24-hour facilities are posted on the door of all pharmacies.

SAFE WATER
Tap water is safe to drink and mineral water *(eau minérale/mineraalwater)* is widely available. The origin of the English word "spa" is in fact the Belgian town of Spa, especially popular during the 19th century for its mineral springs.

RESTROOMS

Public restrooms *(toilettes/toilets)* are not always easy to find, but are usually clean. If you need to use the facilities at a restaurant or café purchase a drink first. Restrooms in the larger restaurants and cafés sometimes have attendants; you should tip them 20BF, which goes toward their wages.

ELECTRICITY

Belgium has a 220-volt power supply. Electrical sockets take plugs with two round pins; American appliances will need a plug adapter and will require a transformer if they do not have a dual-voltage facility.

NATIONAL TRANSPORTATION

TRAIN *(le train/trein)*
The national rail network is the SNCB/NMBS (Société Nationale des Chemins de fer Belges in French, and Nationale Maatschappij der Belgische Spoorwegan in Flemish). It runs an efficient system with many special deals on fares. Reservations can only be made for international journeys, ☎ 02 203 3640 for information.

BUS *(bus/bus)*
Details on the good local services are available at tourist offices, but there are few national long-distance buses. Open the door yourself on buses and trams; where there is no handle, press the black strip or button. International Eurolines buses operate in Belgium; ☎ 02 203 0707.

FERRY *(le ferry/veerboot)*
The two major ports in Belgium are Oostende and Zeebrugge. A ferry across the English Channel to Britain takes under 4 hours from Oostende; from Zeebrugge the journey takes a little longer. A hydrofoil takes under 2 hours.

DRIVING

DRIVE ON THE RIGHT

SPEED LIMITS
Police impose on-the-spot fines (for which receipts are issued), although a foreign motorist may refuse and instead be asked to make a surety payment.

Limited-access highways *(autoroutes/autoweg)* **120 k.p.h. (74 m.p.h.)**
Minimum speed **70 k.p.h. (43 m.p.h.)**

Main roads
90 k.p.h. (55 m.p.h.)

Urban areas
50 k.p.h. (31 m.p.h.)

SEAT BELTS
Must be worn in front seats at all times and in back seats where fitted.

BLOOD ALCOHOL
The legal blood alcohol limit is 0.08%. Random breath tests on drivers are carried out frequently, especially late at night, and the penalties for offenders are severe.

DRIVING continued

TOLLS
Limited-access highways are free.

CAR RENTAL
The leading rental firms have offices at airports, train stations and ferry terminals. Hertz offers discounted rates for AAA members (see page 15). For reservations:

	UNITED STATES	BELGIUM
Alamo	(800) 327-9633	02 753 2060
Avis	(800) 331-2112	02 720 0944
Budget	(800) 527-0700	02 721 5097
Hertz	(800) 654-3080	02 726 4950

FUEL
Gasoline *(essence)* and diesel are priced in liters and are expensive. There are two grades of unleaded gas *(sans plomb/loodvrij)*: normal (92 octane) and super (97 octane). Most gas stations are self-service, and 24-hour facilities are common.

AAA AFFILIATED MOTORING CLUB
Touring Club Royal de Belgique (TCB)
44 rue de la Loi, 1040 Brussels
☎ 02 233 2211, fax 02 233 2205
If you break down while driving, phone ☎ 07 034 4777 (TCB breakdown service) or, on a limited-access highway, use one of the emergency telephones located every 1.2 miles. Ask for *"Touring-Secours."*
Not all automobile clubs offer full services to AAA members.

BREAKDOWNS AND ACCIDENTS
Most car rental firms have their own free rescue service; if your car is rented, follow the instructions given in the documentation. Use of a car repair service other than those authorized by your rental company may violate your rental agreement.

If you are involved in an accident phone 101 for police assistance.

OTHER INFORMATION
The minimum age for driving a car is 18 (may be higher for some car rental firms).

An International Driving Permit (IDP) is recommended; some rental firms require them, and they can speed up formalities if you are involved in an accident.

A Green Card (international motor insurance certificate) is recommended if you are driving a private car; see page 15 for more information.

Beware of cobbled roads, in both cities and rural areas, which can be slippery in wet weather.

USEFUL WORDS AND PHRASES

A linguistic battle has existed in Belgium for many centuries; settlers have long entered from neighboring countries, and there are three marked language communities in Belgium: French, Dutch and German.

The two dominant languages are Walloon (a form of French, spoken in the south) and Flemish (a dialect of Dutch, spoken in the north). Passions run deep between the two groups; prosperity has moved back and forth between them over the centuries, and their relationship is still difficult to this day. The Flemish fear their language is being diminished, aware of the strength that French has as a world language.

Both Walloon and Flemish hold equal status as official languages, and although the bilingual signs can be confusing to the visitor, English is widely spoken.

In Brussels, where Flemish and French are both spoken, the street signs also are in both languages. Place names are not usually a problem, since the Flemish and French proper names have similarities, but there can be differences. Following is a selection of locations:

English	Flemish	French
Aalst	*Aalst*	Alost
Antwerp	*Antwerpen*	Anvers
Bruges	*Brugge*	Bruges
Brussels	*Brussel*	Bruxelles
Ghent	*Gent*	Gand
Jodoigne	*Geldenaken*	Jodoigne
Kortrijk	*Kortrijk*	Courtrai
Liège	*Luik*	Liège
Louvain	*Leuven*	Louvain
Mechelen	*Mechelen*	Malines
Mons	*Bergen*	Mons
Mouscron	*Moeskroen*	Mouscron
Nivelles	*Nijvel*	Nivelles
Ostend	*Oostende*	Ostende
Roeselare	*Roeselare*	Roulers
Ronse	*Ronse*	Renaix
Scheldt	*Schede*	Escaut
Tongeren	*Tongeren*	Tongres
Tournai	*Doornik*	Tournai
Veurne	*Veurne*	Furnes
Ypres	*Ieper*	Ypres

For useful phrases in French, see page 489; for phrases in German, see page 493; for phrases in Dutch, see page 517.

Belgium – Essential Information

Britain – Essential Information

PRE-TRIP ESSENTIALS...

WHAT YOU NEED

ESSENTIAL FOR TRAVELERS

● Required   ● Recommended   ○ Not required

Passport	●
Visa	○
Travel, medical insurance	●
Round-trip or onward airline ticket	○
Local currency	●
Traveler's checks	●
Credit cards	●
First-aid kit and medicines	●
Inoculations	○

ESSENTIAL FOR DRIVERS*

Driver's license	●
International Driving Permit	●
Car insurance (for nonrental cars)	●
Car registration (for nonrental cars)	●

*see also DRIVING section

IMPORTANT ADDRESSES

British Tourist Authority
551 Fifth Avenue
Suite 701
New York, NY 10176
☎ (212) 986-2200
Fax (212) 986-1198

British Tourist Authority
Thames Tower
Blacks Road
Hammersmith
London W6 9EL, U.K.
☎ 020 8846 9000
Fax 020 8563 0302

British Travel Centre (walk-in only)
12 Regent Street (Piccadilly Circus)
London W17 4PQ, U.K.

American Embassy
24 Grosvenor Square
London W1A 1AE, U.K.
☎ 020 7499 9000
Fax 020 7495 5012 (consular service)
Personal and telephone inquiries:
Mon.–Fri. 8:30–noon and 2–4

COUNTRY ESSENTIALS...

CUSTOMS

YES

Duty-free limits on goods brought in from non-European Union countries:
200 cigarettes or 100 cigarillos or 50 cigars or 250 g. tobacco ; 2 L. wine; 1 L. alcohol over 22% volume; 2L. alcohol under 22% volume; 60 ml. perfume; 250 ml. toilet water; plus any other duty-free goods (including gifts) to the value of £145. There is no limit on the importation of tax-paid goods purchased within the European Union, provided the goods are for your own personal use. If you are bringing in more than £10,000 worth of U.S. dollars, customs must be notified and proof of ownership will be required.

NO

No unlicensed drugs, weapons, ammunition, obscene material, pets or other animals, counterfeit money and copied goods, meat or poultry.

For customs limits for returning U.S. citizens see page 16.

MONEY

Britain's currency is the pound sterling (£), which is divided into 100 pence (p). The denominations of pound bills are 5, 10, 20 and 50 (Scotland also has a £1 bill). There are coins of 1, 2, 5, 10, 20 and 50p and £1 and £2. You can exchange dollars or traveler's checks at banks, main post offices, exchange offices and some travel agencies. Buy traveler's checks in pounds sterling, so you do not lose money every time you change them. Credit cards are widely accepted throughout Britain, and ATMs are very common in shopping areas. When sightseeing, it is a good idea to carry a mix of large and small denominations.
Exchange rate at press time: $1 = £0.64

TIPS AND GRATUITIES

Restaurants (where service is not included)	10–15%
Cafés/bars	change
Taxis	10%
Porters	50p–75p
Hairdressers	10%
Tour guides	£1–£2
Chambermaids	change
Cloakroom attendants	10p–20p

Britain – Essential Information

COMMUNICATIONS

POST OFFICES

Buy stamps at post offices, gas stations, tobacconists and supermarkets. Out-of-town post offices

often close 1–2 and Wednesday afternoon. Mailboxes ("pillar-boxes") are red, often with a separate slot for overseas mail. Pillar-boxes show who was monarch at the time of their installation (ER II, for instance, stands for Elizabeth *Regina* II).

TELEPHONES

Public telephones are easy to find, although the traditional red booths are now rare in towns and cities. Use cash, a credit card or a prepaid telephone card. Public telephones take 10p, 20p, 50p and £1 coins, but if you put a higher-value coin in and do not use it all up the difference will not be refunded. Booths

that take prepaid cards are identified by a green stripe on the outside. Buy phone cards from tobacconists, post offices, stationery stores and anywhere displaying the phone card sign.

Phoning in Britain

All British numbers in this book include an area code: dial the number listed. To call the operator dial 100.

Phoning Britain from abroad

The country code for Britain is 44. Note that British numbers in this book do not include the country code; you will need to prefix it if you are phoning from another country. To phone Britain from the United States or Canada, omit the first zero from the British number, and add the prefix 011 44. Example: 011 2233 4455 becomes 011 44 11 2233 4455.

Phoning from Britain

To phone the United States or Canada from Britain, prefix the area code and number with 001. Example: (111) 222-3333 becomes 001 111 222-3333.

To call international information dial 153.

EMERGENCY TELEPHONE NUMBERS

Police	999
Fire service	999
Ambulance	999

Emergency calls are free from phone booths.

HOURS OF OPERATION

● Stores Mon.–Sat.   ● Museums/monuments
● Offices Mon.–Fri.   ● Pharmacies
● Banks Mon.–Fri.
● Post offices Mon.–Fri.

7	8	9	10	11	12	1	2	3	4	5	6	7

The times above are traditional hours of operation. Many malls and city center stores open for longer hours and also on Sunday. Convenience grocery stores stay open until late in the evening.

Banks and post offices open on Saturday, but some out-of-town services have short hours.

Museum opening times vary. Some major sights close on Monday and open later one evening a week; more modest sights of interest may close off season, so it is advisable to check with the local tourist office.

Note that restaurants do not open for dinner until around 6 or 7 p.m. Up to this time fast-food outlets are usually the only places serving meals.

NATIONAL HOLIDAYS

Banks, businesses and smaller stores close on these days, although larger stores may remain open.

Jan. 1	New Year's Day
Mar./Apr.	Good Friday
Mar./Apr.	Easter Monday
1st Mon. of May	May Bank Holiday
Last Mon. of May	Spring Bank Holiday
Last Mon. of Aug.	August Bank Holiday
Dec. 25	Christmas Day
Dec. 26	Boxing Day

PHOTOGRAPHY

British skies are unpredictable, so pack a range of film speeds. The countryside is very green, however, so landscape shots work well if the weather is good. Most museums will not allow you to take pictures; check first. Film and camera batteries are available from grocery stores, pharmacies and camera stores. Rapid-developing services are common and reasonably priced.

Britain – Essential Information

HEALTH

MEDICAL INSURANCE
Private insurance is recommended. Visitors can receive treatment in emergency rooms but are charged if admitted to a hospital. You can seek advice from a doctor at a surgery or health center; you must make an appointment, and a charge will be made. Doctors are listed in the yellow pages, or ask at your hotel or a tourist office.

DENTAL SERVICES
Dentists charge for consultations or treatment. Emergency treatment is available out of hours in towns and cities (see the yellow pages). Check if it is covered by your medical insurance.

SUN ADVICE
Although not renowned for warm weather, Britain does have its moments, and it is not unheard of for July and August to be as hot as the Mediterranean. Visiting historic sights can involve being outside for prolonged periods, so cover up, apply sunscreen and drink plenty of water.

DRUGS
Prescription and nonprescription medicines are available from pharmacies (chemists). Pharmacists can advise on medication for common ailments. Notices in all pharmacy windows give details of emergency facilities open outside regular hours.

SAFE WATER
Tap water is safe to drink, even in remote areas. Mineral water is widely available but is usually quite expensive, particularly in restaurants.

RESTROOMS

Public restrooms (toilets, lavatories, WCs, or, in everyday parlance, "loos") are generally easy to find and maintained to a high standard. Most are free, but a charge is made for those at major rail stations (about 20p).

ELECTRICITY

Britain has a 240-volt power supply. Electrical sockets take plugs with three square pins, so an adapter is needed for American appliances. A transformer is also required for appliances operating on 110 or 120 volts.

NATIONAL TRANSPORTATION

TRAIN
Rail services are good in Britain. First class is comfortable but more expensive than standard class. Intercity (high-speed) trains connect cities. If you plan to use trains frequently, rail cards offer discounts: contact BritRail Travel, 1500 Broadway, New York, NY 10036; (212) 382-3737 or (800) 677-8585. Once you are in Britain, Rail Rover passes are a good value for regional rail travel: ☎ 0345 484950.

BUS
Bus travel is half the cost of rail travel. The main operator for local (bus) and long-distance (coach) travel in Britain is National Express. For details phone 0990 808080. Euroline buses operate from Britain to the rest of Europe: phone 0990 143219.

FERRY
The busiest ferries run between southeast England and France (a high-speed train also shuttles cars through the Channel tunnel). Service is very frequent, especially in summer. Ferries serve the smaller British islands and Spain, Belgium, Netherlands,

DRIVING

DRIVE ON THE LEFT

SPEED LIMITS
British speed limits are stringently enforced by police patrols and also by strategically positioned cameras that detect speeding motorists.

Limited-access highways (motorways); divided highways (dual carriageways) **70 m.p.h.**

Main roads **50 or 60 m.p.h.**

Urban areas **30 or 40 m.p.h.**

SEAT BELTS
Must be worn in front seats at all times and in back seats where fitted.

BLOOD ALCOHOL
The legal blood alcohol limit is 0.08%. Random breath tests on drivers are carried out frequently, especially late at night, and the penalties for offenders are severe.

DRIVING continued

TOLLS
Limited-access highways are free. Some bridges levy a toll, usually minimal. The Severn Bridge, joining England and Wales, is expensive on the way into Wales, but there is no charge on the return trip.

CAR RENTAL
The leading rental firms have offices at airports, train stations and ferry terminals. Hertz offers discounted rates for AAA members (see page 15). For reservations:

	UNITED STATES	BRITAIN
Alamo	(800) 327-9633	0990 996000
Avis	(800) 331-2112	0990 900500
Budget	(800) 527-0700	0800 181181
Hertz	(800) 654-3080	0990 996699

FUEL
Gasoline (petrol) and diesel are priced in liters and are expensive. There are two grades of unleaded gas: super (98 octane) and premium (97 octane). Most gas stations are self-service, and 24-hour facilities are common.

AAA AFFILIATED MOTORING CLUB
The Automobile Association (AA),
Norfolk House, Priestley Road Basingstoke, Hampshire RG24 9NY
☎ 0990 500 600, fax 01256 493389 (administration).
If you break down while driving, phone ☎ 0800 887766 (AA breakdown service).
Not all automobile clubs offer full services to AAA members.

BREAKDOWNS AND ACCIDENTS
There are emergency telephones at regular intervals on limited-access and divided highways.
If you are involved in an accident
☎ 999 for police, fire and ambulance assistance.
Most car rental firms provide their own free rescue service; if your car is rented, follow the instructions in the documentation. Use of a car repair service other than those authorized by your rental firm may violate your rental agreement.

OTHER INFORMATION
The minimum age for driving a car is 17 (may be higher for some car rental firms).

An International Driving Permit (IDP) is recommended; some rental firms require them, and they can speed up formalities if you are involved in an accident.

A Green Card (international motor insurance certificate) is recommended if you are driving a private car; see page 15 for more information.

USEFUL WORDS AND PHRASES

Spotting the differences between American and British English is fun, especially as some regional accents are almost incomprehensible to the untrained ear! Britons have become familiar with Americanisms through imported American television shows, but it is still possible to make a blunder. Below are some illustrations of the "Atlantic divide."

American	British
14 lbs	*1 stone*
ATM	*cashpoint*
ball-point pen	*biro*
to call collect	*to reverse the charges*
check	*cheque*
check (in a restaurant)	*bill*
elevator	*lift*
first/second floor (etc.)	*ground/first floor (etc.)*
movie theater	*cinema*
phone booth	*phone box*
reserve (reservation)	*book (reservation)*
restroom	*loo (colloquial)*
Scotch™ tape	*sticky tape/Sellotape™*
trash or garbage can	*dustbin or rubbish bin*

food and drink

(soft hamburger) bun	*bap*
beer	*bitter (dark)/lager (light)*
candy	*sweets*
(potato) chips	*crisps*
cookies	*biscuits*
corn	*maize*
cotton candy	*candyfloss*
eggplant	*aubergine*
french fries	*chips*
grocery store	*supermarket*
Jell-O™	*jelly*
jelly	*jam*
liquor store	*off-licence*
oatmeal	*porridge*
Saranwrap™	*cling film*
zucchini	*courgette*

fashion

bangs	*fringe*
pants	*trousers*
pantyhose	*tights*
suspenders	*braces*
undershirt	*vest*
vest	*waistcoat*

getting around

hood (of a car)	*bonnet*
one-way trip	*single*
parking lot	*car park*
paved shoulder	*lay-by*
rotary/traffic circle	*roundabout*
round trip	*return ticket*
sidewalk	*pavement*
stick shift	*manual*
subway	*tube/underground*
truck	*lorry*
trunk (of a car)	*boot*

Britain – Essential Information

PRE-TRIP ESSENTIALS...

WHAT YOU NEED

ESSENTIAL FOR TRAVELERS

● Required ● Recommended ● Not required

Passport	●
Visa*	●
Travel, medical insurance	●
Round-trip or onward airline ticket	●
Local currency	●
Traveler's checks	●
Credit cards	●
First-aid kit and medicines	●
Inoculations	●

*Canadian citizens may stay up to 180 days without a visa U.S. citizens who wish to stay longer than 30 days must apply for a visitor permit (this can only be done in the Czech Republic; contact your hotel or a tourist office for details).

ESSENTIAL FOR DRIVERS*

Driver's license	●
International Driving Permit	●
Car insurance (for nonrental cars)	●
Car registration (for nonrental cars)	●

*see also DRIVING section

IMPORTANT ADDRESSES

Czech Tourist Authority
1109-1111 Madison Avenue,
New York, NY 10028
☎ (212) 288-0830
Fax (212) 288-0971

Czech Tourist Authority
Prague Information Service
Na Přikiopě 20, Prague 1, Czech Republic
☎ 02 54 44 44/02 26 40 23
Fax 02 26 40 23

American Embassy
Trziste 15, Mala Strana,
11801 Prague 1, Czech Republic
☎ 057 32 06 63
Fax 057 32 09 20
Telephone inquiries Mon.–Fri. 9–4:30
Personal inquiries Mon.–Fri. 9–noon

COUNTRY ESSENTIALS...

CUSTOMS

YES
Duty-free limits on goods brought in:
250 cigarettes or 100 cigars or 250 g. tobacco; 2 L wine; 1 L alcohol over 22% volume; 2 L alcohol under 22% volume; 50 ml. perfume; 250 ml. toilet water; plus any other duty-free goods (including gifts) to the value of 5,000Kčs. There is no limit on the importation of goods purchased within the European Union countries, provided the goods are for your own personal use. You must have a minimum of 500Kčs per day per person for a stay of under 10 days; for stays longer than 10 days, 7,000Kčs. For all persons under 18, the limits are halved. Currency requirements do not apply to visitors on organized trips.

NO
No unlicensed drugs, firearms, ammunition, offensive weapons, obscene material, unlicensed animals, counterfeit or copied goods, meat and poultry.
For customs limits for returning U.S. citizens see page16.

MONEY

The Czech Republic's currency is the Koruna ceska (Kčs) – or Czech crown – which is divided into 100 haleru (h), although you won't find many of the latter around. The denominations of Koruna ceska bills are 20, 50, 100, 500, 1,000 and 5,000. There are coins of 10, 20 and 50 h and 1, 2, 5, 10, 20 and 50Kčs. You can exchange dollars or traveler's checks (cestovni sek) at a bank (banka), exchange office (smenárna), post office (posta) or hotel; you will need ID. It is an offense to change money through black-market money dealers; in any case, they rarely offer an attractive rate. The Czech Republic is not part of the E.U.
Exchange rate at press time: $1 = 34Kčs

TIPS AND GRATUITIES

Tips are welcomed in restaurants and cafés, although service is normally included.

Restaurants (even when service is included)	5–10%
Cafés/bars	5–10%
Taxis	10%
Porters	40Kčs
Hairdressers	10%
Tour guides	20Kčs

COMMUNICATIONS

POST OFFICES

Buy stamps *(známky)* at a post office *(posta)*, a newsstand/kiosk *(trafika/tabák)* or from a hotel.

The postal service is slow and erratic but not expensive. Mailboxes are orange and blue. Hours for out-of-town post offices may vary.

TELEPHONES

The Czech telephone system is generally modern and efficient. City booths take telephone cards *(telefonní karta)* worth 100, 190 and 280Kčs, which can be bought from kiosks and post offices. Coin operated telephones use 1, 2, 5 and 10Kčs. The gray booths have international dialing facilities; the older, orange ones are for national calls only. There are often instructions in English inside the booth. For an English-speaking operator, dial 132.

Phoning inside the Czech Republic
All Czech telephone numbers in this book include an area code: dial the number that is listed.

To call the operator dial 120.

Phoning the Czech Republic from abroad
The country code for the Czech Republic is 420. Note that Czech numbers in this book do not include the country code; you will need to prefix this number if you are phoning from another country. To phone the Czech Republic from the United States or Canada, omit the first zero from the Czech number, and add the prefix 011 420. Example: 01 12 23 34 becomes 011 420 1 12 23 34.

Phoning from the Czech Republic
To phone the United States or Canada from the Czech Republic, prefix the number with 001. Example: (111) 222-3333 becomes 001 111 222-3333.

To call international information dial 0149.

EMERGENCY TELEPHONE NUMBERS

Police *(policie)*	158
Fire *(pozar)*	150
Ambulance *(ambulance)*	155

Emergency calls are free from phone booths.

HOURS OF OPERATION

- Stores Mon.–Fri.
- Offices Mon.–Fri.
- Banks Mon.–Fri.
- Post offices Mon.–Fri.
- Museums/monuments
- Pharmacies Mon.–Fri.

Saturday afternoon is early closing, and few stores stay open later than noon or 1.

Food stores in the large cities open at 6 a.m. and large stores and shopping centers stay open until 8 p.m. (4 p.m. on Saturday). Most stores are closed on Sunday.

Some city banks and post offices open on Saturday morning. Some tourist resorts may have special opening times.

Museums often close on Monday and opening times may be reduced during the winter.

NATIONAL HOLIDAYS

Banks, businesses and most stores close on these days. Also, some museums may be closed or have restricted hours.

Jan. 1	New Year's Day
Mar./Apr.	Good Friday
Mar./Apr.	Easter Monday
May 1	May Day
May 8	Liberation Day
Jul. 5	SS Cyril and Methodius' Day
Jul. 6	Jan Hus Day
Oct. 28	Independence Day
Dec. 24	Christmas Eve
Dec. 25	Christmas Day
Dec. 26	St. Stephen's Day

PHOTOGRAPHY

After years of official photography restrictions, you are now free to photograph almost anywhere. You can buy film in the numerous small shops at Staré Město in the Old Town and Mala Strana in the Lesser Quarter. Avoid Czech brands of color film, as you may not be able to get them processed outside the country. Many stores in tourist areas offer developing services.

HEALTH

MEDICAL INSURANCE
Private medical insurance is recommended. U.S. and Canadian visitors can receive treatment in a hospital emergency and accident unit, but you will be charged if you are admitted to a hospital (*nemocnice*). You may be asked to show your passport when seeking hospital treatment. Clinics especially for visitors who need medical advice have English-speaking doctors; they are usually only found in major cities.

DENTAL SERVICES
A dentist (*zubař*) will charge for any treatment given, so check if it is covered by your medical insurance. For an English-speaking dentist, ask at your hotel or embassy or at a tourist office.

SUN ADVICE
June through August is the hottest period, when adequate sun protection should be applied.

DRUGS
A pharmacy (*lékárna*) is the only place you can buy over-the-counter medicines. Pharmacies also dispense many drugs normally available only on prescription in other Western countries. However, it is advisable to bring supplies of your own medicines with you. If you need a pharmacy outside regular hours, information about the nearest all-night facility is posted at all pharmacies.

SAFE WATER
It is not advisable to drink tap water. Bottled water is available everywhere; still table water (*Stolní pitní voda*) is the most common.

RESTROOMS

Public restrooms (*toaleta*) are not easy to find, and you will be charged for toilet tissue. It may be best to use a café or restaurant facility after buying a drink. Attendants appreciate small change – 2Kčs or thereabouts – as this may be their only wage.

ELECTRICITY

The Czech Republic has a 220-volt power supply. Electrical sockets take plugs with two round pins; American appliances will need a plug adapter, and will require a transformer if they do not have a dual-voltage facility.

NATIONAL TRANSPORTATION

TRAIN (*vlak*)
The Czech national rail company, České Dráhy (CD), is extensive and inexpensive, but often crowded. The fast trains stop at major cities; local trains stop everywhere and usually have only second-class carriages. All long-distance trains have two classes; some have dining carriages and overnight services. Reserve seats on express trains; don't rely on international trains having air conditioning.

BUS (*autobusy*)
Inexpensive and popular with the Czechs. Reserve for weekends, national holidays or early morning. Tickets are purchased from the bus station kiosk or the driver. Large items of luggage will be stowed for a small charge. Trams (*tramvaj*) and trolley buses (*trolejbus*) are the best way to get around town. Euroline buses connect to other countries: ☎ 022 32 38 77.

FERRY (*prévos*)
From April to September cruise boats chug up and down the Vltava river as far as Troja Château to the north of Prague and Slapy Lake to the south.

DRIVING

DRIVE ON THE RIGHT

SPEED LIMITS
Police can give on-the-spot fines of up to 2,000Kčs. If this should happen to you, ask for a receipt.

Limited-access highways (*dalnice*)
130 k.p.h. (80 m.p.h.)

Main roads
90 k.p.h. (55 m.p.h.)

Urban areas
50 k.p.h. (31 m.p.h.)

SEAT BELTS
Must be worn in front seats at all times and in the rear seats where fitted. Children under 12 (or under 4 feet 10 inches) cannot travel in the front seats.

BLOOD ALCOHOL
The legal blood alcohol limit is zero. Random breath tests on drivers are carried out frequently, especially late at night, and the penalties for offenders are severe.

DRIVING continued

TOLLS
A tax is levied for use of highways and express roads. A sticker must be purchased and displayed, and failure to do so will result in a fine. The sticker can be bought at the Czech border, UAMK offices (see below), gas stations or post offices.

CAR RENTAL
The leading rental firms have offices at airports and train stations. Hertz offers discounted rates for AAA members (see page 15). For reservations:

	UNITED STATES	CZECH REPUBLIC
Alamo	(800) 327-9633	020 11 35 34
Avis	(800) 331-2112	023 16 67 39
Budget	(800) 527-0700	023 16 52 14
Hertz	(800) 654-3080	023 12 07 17

FUEL
Gas is sold in liters and comes in three grades: 95 octane unleaded (natural), 90 octane (special) and 96 octane (super). Some out-of-town stations (benzinová pumpa) close at lunchtime and after 6. There are 24-hour gas stations in cities and along highways.

AAA AFFILIATED MOTORING CLUB
Ustredni automotoklub Ceske republiky (UAMK)
Na Strzi 9, 14601 Prague 4
☎ 02 61 10 42 42, fax 02 61 10 42 35
If you break down while driving, phone the English-speaking 24-hour help line 0123 (omit the zero in Prague) for the UAMK breakdown service. Not all automobile clubs offer full services to AAA members.

BREAKDOWNS AND ACCIDENTS
There are 24-hour emergency phones at regular intervals on highways. Most car rental firms provide their own free rescue service; if your car is rented, follow the instructions given in the documentation. Use of a car repair service other than those authorized by your rental company may violate your agreement. ☎ 158 for police assistance.

OTHER INFORMATION
The minimum age for driving a car is 18 (may be higher for some car rental firms).
An International Driving Permit (IDP) is recommended; some rental firms require them, and they can speed up formalities if you are involved in an accident. A Green Card (international motor insurance certificate) is recommended for a private car; see page 15 for more information. Visible damage to a car entering the country must be certified by border authorities. If damage occurs inside the country, a police report must be obtained at the scene of the accident. Damaged vehicles are allowed out of the country only upon presentation of this document.

USEFUL WORDS AND PHRASES

The official language of the Czech Republic is Czech (Česky) – a highly complex Slav tongue. Czech sounds and looks daunting, but apart from a few special letters, each letter and sound is pronounced as it is written – the key is to stress the first syllable of a word. If you have any knowledge of Polish or Russian you will be able to understand much.

Any attempt to speak Czech will be heartily appreciated, although English is spoken by many involved in the tourist trade. Below are a few words that may be helpful.

Do you speak English?	*Mluvíte anglicky?*
What is your name?	*Jak se jmenujete?*
hello	*ahoj*
good morning	*dobré jitro*
goodbye	*na shledanou*
good night	*dobrou noc*
How much?	*Kolik?*
excuse me	*promiňte*
I am American	*Jsem Američan(ka)*
I would like	*Chtěl(a) bych*
I don't understand	*Nerozumím*
no smoking	*kouření zakazano*
okay	*dobrá*
open	*otevřeno*
closed	*zavřeno*
please	*prosím*
thank you	*děkuji*
ticket	*lístek*
(one-way/round trip)	*(jednosměrnou/zpátečni)*
Where is...?	*Kde je...?*
yes/no	*ano/ne*
you're welcome	*není zač*

the hotel	***hotel***
breakfast	*snídaně*
reservation	*mám reservaci*
key	*klíč*
single/double room	*jednolužkovy/ dvoulužkovy pokoj*
room	*pokoj*
Where is the toilet?	*Kde je záchod?*
shower	*sprcha*
bathroom	*koupelna*

the restaurant	***restaurace***
beef	*hovězi*
bread	*chleb*
chicken	*kuře*
the check	*účet*
coffee	*káva*
dish of the day	*nabídka dne*
dessert	*moučnik*
fish	*ryba*
lamb	*jehněci*
pork	*vepřové maso*
seafood	*mořské ryby*
starter	*předkrm*
wine	*víno*

PRE-TRIP ESSENTIALS...

WHAT YOU NEED

ESSENTIAL FOR TRAVELERS

● Required ● Recommended ● Not required

Passport	●
Visa	●
Travel, medical insurance	●
Round-trip or onward airline ticket	●
Local currency	●
Traveler's checks	●
Credit cards	●
First-aid kit and medicines*	●
Inoculations	●

*see also HEALTH section

ESSENTIAL FOR DRIVERS*

Driver's license	●
International Driving Permit	●
Car insurance (for nonrental cars)	●
Car registration (for nonrental cars)	●

*see also DRIVING section

IMPORTANT ADDRESSES

Danish Tourist Board
655 Third Avenue, 18th Floor
New York, NY 10017
☎ (212) 885-9700
Fax (212) 885-9710

Danish Tourist Board
DK 1577
Bernstorffsgade 1
Copenhagen V, Denmark
☎ 33 11 13 25
Fax 33 93 49 69

American Embassy
Dag Hamarskjolds Alle 24
2100 Copenhagen, Denmark
☎ 35 55 31 44
Fax 35 43 02 23
Personal callers should phone for an appointment.

COUNTRY ESSENTIALS...

CUSTOMS

YES
Duty-free limits on goods brought in from non-European Union countries:
200 cigarettes or 100 cigarillos or 50 cigars or 250 g. tobacco; 2 L. wine; 1 L alcohol over 22% volume; 2 L. alcohol under 22% volume; 50 ml. perfume; 250 ml. toilet water; plus any other duty-free goods (including gifts) to the value of DKr1,350. There is no limit on the importation of tax-paid goods purchased within the European Union, provided they are for your own personal use. There are no currency regulations.

NO
No unlicensed drugs, weapons, ammunition, obscene material, pets or other animals, counterfeit money or copied goods, meat or poultry.

For customs limits for returning U.S. citizens see page 16.

MONEY

Denmark's currency is the krone (DKr), which is divided into 100 øre. The denominations of krone bills are 50, 100, 200, 500 and 1,000. There are coins of 25 and 50 øre and 1, 2, 5, 10 and 20DKr. Banks may not exchange foreign bank notes of high denominations. On Jan. 1, 1999, the euro became the official currency of Denmark and the krone became a denomination of the euro. Danish coins and bills continue to be legal tender during a transitional period. Euro bills and coins are likely to be introduced by Jan. 2002. Senior citizens and holders of International Student Identity Cards (ISIC) can often obtain discounts on travel and entrance fees. Exchange rate at press time: $1 = DKr7

TIPS AND GRATUITIES

Tips are welcomed, but not expected.

Restaurants (service is always included)	10%
Cafés/bars	change
Taxis	change
Porters	change
Chambermaids	change
Cloakroom attendants	change

TIME ZONES	COPENHAGEN 12:00 noon	NEW YORK 6 hours behind Denmark	CHICAGO 7 hours behind Denmark	DENVER 8 hours behind Denmark	SAN FRANCISCO 9 hours behind Denmark	479

COMMUNICATIONS

POST OFFICES

Stamps *(frimerker)* can be bought at a post office *(postkontoret)*, newsstand *(aviskiosk)* or stationer *(papirhandel)*.

Mailboxes *(postkasse)* are red with a yellow horn and crown.

Hours for out-of-town post offices may vary.

TELEPHONES

Danish public telephones *(telefon)* work efficiently for national and international calls, but some will not refund your money if the call is not answered. Some phones require coins to be inserted after dialing, when you hear ringing. Use DKr5 and DKr10 coins. Phone card booths are also

available; buy the cards from a post office or newsstand.

Phoning inside Denmark

All Danish telephone numbers in this book include an area code: dial the number listed.

To call the operator dial 110; to call collect dial 115; for the long-distance operator dial 114.

Phoning Denmark from abroad

The country code for Denmark is 45. Note that Danish numbers in this book do not include the country code; you will need to prefix this number if you are phoning from another country. To phone Denmark from the United States or Canada add the prefix 011 45.
Example: 11 22 33 44 becomes 011 45 11 22 33 44.

Phoning from Denmark

To phone the United States or Canada from Denmark, prefix the area code and number with 001.
Example: (111) 222-3333 becomes 001 111 222-3333.

To call international information dial 113.

EMERGENCY TELEPHONE NUMBERS

Police *(politi)*	112
Fire *(brandvæsen)*	112
Ambulance *(sygevogn)*	112

Emergency calls are free from phone booths.

HOURS OF OPERATION

- ● Stores Mon.–Sat.
- ● Offices Mon.–Fri.
- ● Banks Mon.–Fri.
- ● Post offices Mon.–Fri.
- ● Museums/monuments
- ● Pharmacies Mon.–Fri.

| 7 | 8 | 9 | 10 | 11 | 12 | 1 | 2 | 3 | 4 | 5 | 6 | 7 |

Although Sunday is the official closing day, souvenir shops in many towns stay open.

Many bakeries and *patisseries* also open on Sunday morning.

Department stores and supermarkets often stay open later than 5:30 p.m.

Large gas stations sell a range of convenience foods.

NATIONAL HOLIDAYS

Banks, businesses and most stores close on these days.

Jan. 1	New Year's Day
Mar./Apr.	Maundy Thursday
Mar./Apr.	Good Friday
Mar./Apr.	Easter Monday
Apr. 30	Great Prayer Day
May	Ascension Day
May/Jun.	Pentecost Monday
Jun. 5	Constitution Day
Dec. 24	Christmas Eve
Dec. 25	Christmas Day
Dec. 26	St. Stephen's Day

PHOTOGRAPHY

Denmark is not renowned for bright sunshine and the winter months have short daylight hours, so pack plenty of 200 ASA-speed film. Check that photography is permitted before taking pictures in museums. Film and camera batteries are readily available from tourist stores, and rapid-developing services are widely available.

Denmark – Essential Information

Denmark – Essential Information

HEALTH

MEDICAL INSURANCE

Private medical insurance is recommended. In an emergency, visitors from the U.S. and Canada can receive free temporary treatment in a hospital *(hospitalet)*. You will be charged for more extensive treatment. Health offices *(kommunes social og sundhedforvaltning)* have lists of hospitals and doctors, or ask at your hotel.

DENTAL SERVICES

Dentists *(tandlægen)* will charge for any treatment given. They are listed in the telephone directory, and off-hours treatment is available in some clinics. Advice can be sought at tourist and health offices. Check that treatment is covered by your medical insurance.

SUN ADVICE

The warmest months are July and August. The sun in Denmark is not particularly fierce, but sun protection is still advised, especially on boats or near the water.

DRUGS

To obtain a prescription medicine at a pharmacy *(apotek)* it must be prescribed by a Scandinavian doctor, so make sure that your supply of prescribed medicines will last your stay. Additionally, some preparations available over the counter in the U.S. may be obtained in Denmark only with a prescription. Outside regular hours, the nearest - all-night facility is posted at all pharmacies.

SAFE WATER

Tap water is safe to drink, and mineral water *(mineralvand)* is widely available.

RESTROOMS

Public restrooms *(toiletterne)* are easy to find, clean, well equipped and usually free. They are often indicated by a symbol, or marked WC or *Damer* (women) and *Herrer* (men).

ELECTRICITY

Denmark has a 220-volt power supply. Electrical sockets take plugs with two round pins; American appliances will need a plug adapter and will require a transformer if they do not have a dual-voltage facility.

NATIONAL TRANSPORTATION

TRAIN *(tage)*

Copenhagen is an important meeting point for trains between Europe and the rest of Scandinavia. The Danish state railroad, Danske Statsbaner (DSB), runs an efficient service with trains linking to Germany, Norway, Sweden and Britain (via ferries). Most domestic trains have refreshment facilities; seat reservations are recommended. For information ☎ 33 14 17 01.

BUS *(bussen)*

The domestic bus service is good; ask for details at local tourist offices. Eurolines services run between other European countries (☎ 33 25 12 44 or 86 12 36 11). Trams operate in Danish towns and cities.

FERRY *(færgen)*

There are numerous ferry services from Denmark, with year-round connections to many northern European countries. Scandinavian Seaways has an office in Florida; ☎ (954) 491-7909.

DRIVING

DRIVE ON THE RIGHT

SPEED LIMITS

Police can impose on-the-spot fines.

Limited-access highways *(motorvej)*
110 k.p.h. (66 m.p.h.)

Main roads
80 k.p.h. (48 m.p.h.)
Minimum speed **40 k.p.h. (24 m.p.h.)**

Urban areas
50 k.p.h. (31 m.p.h.)

SEAT BELTS

Must be worn in front seats at all times and in the rear seats where fitted.

BLOOD ALCOHOL

The legal blood alcohol limit is 0.05%. Random breath tests on drivers are carried out frequently, especially late at night, and the penalties for offenders are severe.

DRIVING continued

TOLLS
There are no tolls on highways. However, the "Great Belt" *(Store Bælt)* bridge from Korsør to Nyborg levies a toll, and an impressive 10-mile bridge (toll) linking Denmark and Sweden is due to open in June 2000.

CAR RENTAL
The leading car rental companies have offices at airports, principal railroad stations and ferry terminals. Hertz offers discounted rates for AAA members (see page 15). For reservations:

	UNITED STATES	DENMARK
Alamo	(800) 327-9633	39 63 23 75
Avis	(800) 331-2112	33 26 80 80
Budget	(800) 527-0700	33 11 12 34
Hertz	(800) 654-3080	33 32 33 32

FUEL
Gas *(benzin)* is sold in liters; unleaded gas *(blyfri)* comes in 92, 95 and 98 octane ratings. Self-service gas stations *(tank selv* or *selvbetjening)* are common, except on limited-access highways. Most gas stations take credit cards, and some have automatic pumps for DKr100 and DKr50 bills.

AAA AFFILIATED MOTORING CLUB
Forende Danske Motorejere (FDM)
Firskovvej 32, P.O. Box 500, 2800 Lyngby ☎ 45 27 07 07, fax 45 27 09 93
If you break down while driving, phone ☎ 70 10 80 90 (FDM breakdown service).
Not all automobile clubs offer full services to AAA members.

BREAKDOWNS AND ACCIDENTS
Report accidents to the Dansk Forening for International Motorkoretojsforsikring, Amaliegade 10, 1256 Copenhagen (☎ 33 13 75 55).
Most car rental firms provide their own free rescue service; if your car is rented, follow the instructions given in the documentation. Use of a car repair service other than those authorized by your rental company may violate your agreement.

OTHER INFORMATION
The minimum legal age for driving a car is 17 (may be higher for some car rental firms).

An International Driving Permit (IDP) is recommended; some rental firms require them, and they can speed up formalities if you are involved in an accident.

A Green Card (international motor insurance certificate) is recommended if you are driving a private car; see page 15 for more information.

Use dimmed headlights at all times.

USEFUL WORDS AND PHRASES

Danish is a Germanic language, close to Swedish and Norwegian, but it is tricky to pronounce because some letters *(d, g)* are silent in the middle or at the end of words, *h* before a *v* becomes silent, and some specifically Scandinavian vowels *(å, ø,* and *æ)* are awkward to say correctly. But Danes are aware of this, and most of them speak very good English. In addition, menus are often in English or German.

In the Danish alphabet, the following letters come after *z: å, ø,* and *æ.* (Århus, for example, comes at the end of the alphabet.) *Å* is used in place of *aa,* although the city of Aalborg prefers to write the two vowels out in full.

The following words and phrases should help you:

Do you speak English?	*Taler de Engelsk?*
excuse me	*undskyld*
hello/goodbye	*hej/farvel*
how much is…?	*hvor meget koster det?*
I am American	*hvorfra kommer du*
I'd like…	*jeg kan godt lide…*
I don't understand	*jeg forstår det ikke*
open/closed	*aben/lukket*
please/thank you	*vaerså venlig/tak*
ticket (one-way/	*billet (enkeltbillet/*
round trip)	*en tur-retur)*
where is/are…?	*hvor er…?*
yes/no	*ja/net*

the hotel	*hotel*
breakfast	*morgenmad*
key	*nøgle*
for one/two nights	*en nat/to nætter*
for one person/	*enkeltværelse/*
two people	*dobbeltværelse*
room	*værelse*
shower	*brusebad*

the restaurant	*restaurant*
Danish pastry	*Wienerbrød*
beef	*bof*
bread	*brød*
butter	*smør*
cheese	*ost*
chicken	*kylling*
the check	*regningen*
coffee/tea	*kaffe/the*
dessert	*dessert*
fruit salad	*frugtsalat*
fish	*fisk*
shellfish	*skaldyr*
herring	*sild*
trout	*ørred*
cod	*torsk*
shrimps	*rejer*
pork	*flæsk, svine*
potatoes	*kartofler*
starter	*forretter*
vegetables	*grøntsager*
wine	*vin*

Denmark – Essential Information

PRE-TRIP ESSENTIALS...

WHAT YOU NEED

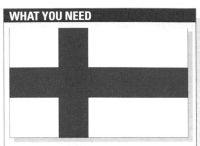

ESSENTIAL FOR TRAVELERS

● Required   ● Recommended   ● Not required

Passport	●
Visa	●
Travel, medical insurance	●
Round-trip or onward airline ticket	●
Local currency	●
Traveler's checks	●
Credit cards	●
First-aid kit and medicines	●
Inoculations	●

ESSENTIAL FOR DRIVERS*

Driver's license	●
International Driving Permit	●
Car insurance (for nonrental cars)	●
Car registration (for nonrental cars)	●

*see also DRIVING section

IMPORTANT ADDRESSES

Finnish Tourist Office
655 Third Avenue
New York, NY 10017
☎ (212) 949-2333
Fax (212) 885-9710

Finnish Tourist Office
Eteläesplanadi 4
00130 Helsinki, Finland
☎ 09 4176 9300
Fax 09 4176 9301

American Embassy
Itainen Puistotie 14B
00140 Helsinki, Finland
☎ 09 171 931
Fax 09 171 546
No personal appointments.
Telephone inquiries Mon.–Fri. 2–4:30

COUNTRY ESSENTIALS...

CUSTOMS

YES
Duty-free limits on goods brought in from non-European Union countries:
200 cigarettes or 100 cigarillos or 50 cigars or 250 g. tobacco; 2 L. wine; 1 L. alcohol over 22% volume; 2 L. alcohol under 22% volume; 15 L. beer; 50 ml. perfume; 250 ml. toilet water; plus any other duty-free goods (including gifts) to the value of Fmk1,100. There is no limit on the importation of tax-paid goods purchased within the European Union, provided they are for your own personal use. There are no currency regulations.

NO
No unlicensed drugs, weapons, ammunition, obscene material, pets or other animals, counterfeit money or copied goods, meat or poultry.

For customs limits for returning U.S. citizens see page 16.

MONEY

Finland's currency is the markka (Fmk, FIM or mk), which is divided into 100 pennia (p). The denominations of markka bills are 20, 50, 100, 500 and 1,000. There are coins of 1, 5 and 10 pennia. Exchange dollars and traveler's checks at a bank *(pankki)* or an exchange office. Avoid exchanging money in city hotels as the exchange rate may be poor, but in rural areas hotels and banks often do not charge for this. On Jan. 1, 1999, the euro became the official currency of Finland and the markka became a denomination of the euro. Finnish coins and bills continue to be legal tender during a transitional period. Euro bills and coins are likely to be introduced by Jan. 2002.
Exchange rate at press time: $1 = Fmk6

TIPS AND GRATUITIES

Tips are welcomed, but not expected.

Restaurants	10%
Cafés/bars	10%
Taxis; hairdressers	none
Porters; restroom attendants	change
Chambermaids	change
Cloakroom attendants; restaurant doormen	Fmk5

TIME ZONES

HELSINKI	NEW YORK	CHICAGO	DENVER	SAN FRANCISCO
12:00 noon	7 hours behind Finland	8 hours behind Finland	9 hours behind Finland	10 hours behind Finland

483

COMMUNICATIONS

POST OFFICES

Most post offices are open Mon.–Fri. 9–5. General delivery can be received from main post offices *(posti)*.

Hours for out-of-town post offices may vary. Stamps *(postimerkki)* can be bought at book stores, newsstands *(R-kiosk)*, railroad stations and some hotels. Mailboxes are usually yellow and set into walls.

TELEPHONES

The Finnish public telephone system is efficient and accepts cash, credit cards and prepaid telephone cards. Public telephones take Fmk1, Fmk5 and Fmk10 coins (some older phones take 50p coins, but these run out quickly). Phone cards worth Fmk30, Fmk50 and Fmk100 are available from R-kiosks, telephone company shops and post offices.

Phoning inside Finland
All Finnish telephone numbers in this book include an area code: dial the number listed.

To call the operator dial 115 .

Phoning Finland from abroad
The country code for Finland is 358; to phone Finland from the United States or Canada, omit the first zero from the Finnish number and prefix with 011 358. (Finnish area codes have one or two digits)
Example: 01 122 3344 becomes 011 358 1 122 3344.

Phoning from Finland
To phone the United States or Canada from Finland, prefix the area code and number with 001. (There are other numbers to dial out of the country depending on what telephone system you are using: 990, 994 or 999.) Example: (111) 222-3333 becomes 001 111 222-3333.
To make a long distance call, phone 02 0222.
For national information, phone 02 0208.

EMERGENCY TELEPHONE NUMBERS

Police *(poliisi)*	112
Fire *(palokunta)*	112
Ambulance *(ambulanssi)*	112

Emergency calls are free from phone booths.

HOURS OF OPERATION

● Stores Mon.–Sat.   ● Pharmacies Mon.–Sat.
● Offices Mon.–Fri.
● Banks Mon.–Fri.
● Post offices Mon.–Fri.

7 8 9 10 11 12 1 2 3 4 5 6 7

Many stores close at 3 on Saturday, but department stores and most shopping malls stay open until 6. During the week, large stores extend their hours to 9, and open on Sunday from June through August.

Grocery stores stay open until 8 or 9.

Some gas stations close on Sunday.

Out-of-town post offices and banks may have shorter hours, and some city post offices and banks stay open into the evening.

Museum and monument opening times vary: they may have shorter hours of operation in the winter, and close on Monday or Tuesday. Check opening times with the local tourist office.

Smaller pharmacies may close earlier on Saturday.

NATIONAL HOLIDAYS

Banks, businesses and most stores close on these days.

Jan. 1	New Year's Day
Jan. 6	Epiphany
Mar./Apr.	Good Friday
Mar./Apr.	Easter Monday
Apr. 30	Great Prayer Day
May 1	May Day
May	Ascension
May/Jun.	Pentecost Monday
Jun. 23	Midsummer's Eve
Jun. 24	Midsummer's Day
Dec. 24	Christmas Eve
Dec. 25	Christmas Day
Dec. 26	St. Stephen's Day

PHOTOGRAPHY

There is a stark contrast in seasonal light conditions: subarctic winter nights are long, while in the north the midnight sun shines throughout the summer. Bring a tripod if you hope to photograph the northern lights *(aurora borealis)*. Check whether photography is permitted in museums. Film and batteries are readily available from tourist stores, and rapid-developing is widely available.

Finland – Essential Information

Finland – Essential Information

HEALTH

MEDICAL INSURANCE
Private medical insurance is recommended. All treatment in a hospital *(sairaala)* has to be paid for. You are likely to receive the best service at a private hospital or health center *(lääkäriasema)* for foreign visitors; for information 09 10023.

DENTAL SERVICES
Dentists *(hammaslääkari)* charge for treatment and can be expensive, so check that treatment is covered by your medical insurance. 24-hour clinics are available in city hospitals.

SUN ADVICE
Southeast Finland has the highest summer temperature in Scandinavia, so precautions are necessary. Use a suitable sunscreen and cover up sensitive skin.

DRUGS
Prescription and nonprescription medicines are available from pharmacies *(apteekki)*. If you need a pharmacy outside regular hours, information about the nearest all-night facility is posted at all pharmacies. Note that drugstores *(kemikaaltkauppa)* sell only cosmetics.

SAFE WATER
Tap water is safe to drink, and mineral water *(kinennäisvesi)* is widely available.

RESTROOMS

Public restrooms are easy to find, immaculately clean and modern, and are designated by *Miehille/Miehet/Herrat* (men) and *Naisille/Naiset/Rouvat* (women). There may be a small charge, but many are free. Attendants welcome loose change as a tip.

ELECTRICITY

Finland has a 220-volt power supply. Electrical sockets take plugs with two round pins; American appliances will need a plug adapter and will require a transformer if they do not have a dual-voltage facility.

NATIONAL TRANSPORTATION

TRAIN *(juna)*
The Finnish state railroad *(Valtion Rautatiet,* or *VR)* runs an efficient, modern service extending north to southern Lapland. Train fares are a good value. For timetable *(suomen kulkuneuvot)* information 01 00121. If you are planning extensive rail travel, buy a Finnrail Pass, which can be bought from a tourist office.

BUS *(bussi)*
Bus lines run to even the most remote corners of Finland. Bus holiday tickets (discount cards) are available for those traveling long distances. For information 09 682 701.

FERRY *(vene)*
There are many excursions exploring Finland's eastern lake system and the country's canal network. Trips into Russia, Estonia, Latvia and Lithuania are possible; check with the tour operator whether a short-term visa is required. These can be obtained through the country's embassy or a travel agent.
Finnjet-Silja Line: 09 8007 4554.
Viking Line: 09 123 577.

DRIVING

 DRIVE ON THE RIGHT

SPEED LIMITS
Minor fines can be imposed on the spot, but not collected. Payment can be made at a post office.

Limited-access highways *(moottoritie)*
120 k.p.h. (74 m.p.h.)
Divided highways
100 k.p.h. (62 m.p.h.)

Main roads
80 k.p.h. (49 m.p.h.)

Urban areas
50 k.p.h. (31 m.p.h.)

SEAT BELTS
Must be worn in front seats at all times and in the rear seats where fitted.

BLOOD ALCOHOL
The legal blood alcohol limit is 0.05%. Random breath tests on drivers are carried out frequently, especially late at night, and the penalties for offenders are severe.

Finland – Essential Information

DRIVING continued

TOLLS
There are no highway tolls in Finland.

CAR RENTAL
The leading rental firms have offices at airports and train stations. Hertz offers discounted rates for AAA members (see page 15). For reservations:

	UNITED STATES	FINLAND
Alamo	(800) 327-9633	09 7515 5700
Avis	(800) 331-2112	09 822 833
Budget	(800) 527-0700	09 6866 5031
Hertz	(800) 654-3080	09 1667 1300

FUEL
There is no leaded gas in Finland. Unleaded 99 octane gas contains some additives, making it suitable for cars not yet converted to unleaded fuel. For cars fitted with a catalytic converter, use 95 octane gas.

AAA AFFILIATED MOTORING CLUB
Autoliitto (AL)
Hameetie 105, 00550 Helsinki
☎ 09 774 761, fax 09 7747 6444
If you break down while driving, phone ☎ 02 008 080 (weekends and holidays) or 09 7747 6400 (Mon.–Fri.) for the AL breakdown service. Not all automobile clubs offer full services to AAA members.

BREAKDOWNS AND ACCIDENTS
There are 24-hour emergency phones at regular intervals on highways. If you are involved in an accident ☎ 112 for police, fire or ambulance. Accidents should be reported without delay to: Finnish Motor Insurer's Center, Bulevardi 28, 00120 Helsinki ☎ 09 680 401, fax 09 6804 0474.
Most car rental firms provide their own free rescue service; if your car is rented, follow the instructions given in the documentation. Use of a car repair service other than those authorized by your rental company may violate your agreement.

OTHER INFORMATION
The minimum age for driving a car is 18 (may be higher for some car rental firms).
An International Driving Permit (IDP) is recommended; some rental firms require them, and they can speed up formalities if you are involved in an accident. A Green Card (international motor insurance certificate) is recommended if you are driving a private car; see page 15 for more information.
Dimmed headlights must be used at all times. In winter, snow tires or chains are essential; you can buy or rent winter driving equipment from Autoliitto. Watch out for signs warning of elk and reindeer crossing roads – these animals are more active at dusk.

USEFUL WORDS AND PHRASES

Finnish is a complex and difficult language to learn, and bears little or no resemblance to neighboring languages. However, Swedish is Finland's second, more accessible, language, and most people speak some English.

Finnish uses compound words, which are pronounced exactly as they are written. The first syllable of a word is always stressed, and each letter is pronounced individually.

Do you speak English?	*Puhutteko englantia?*
excuse me	*anteeksi*
hello	*terve*
goodbye	*näkemiin*
how much?	*kuinka paljon?*
how are you?	*kuinka voitte?*
Is it near?	*Onko se lähellä?*
I'd like…	*Halvaisin…*
I don't understand	*en ymmärrä*
non-smoking	*tupakointi kielletty*
okay	*ja lyh*
open/closed	*avoinna/suljettu*
please/thank you	*olkaa hyvä/kiitos*
ticket (one-way/	*menolippu*
round trip)	*meno-paluulippu*
where is…?	*missä on…?*
yes/no	*kyllä or joo/ei*

the hotel	***hotelli***
breakfast	*aamiainen*
key	*avain*
room	*huone*
shower	*suihku*
it's too expensive	*se on liian kallis*

the restaurant	***ravintola***
beef	*nauta*
bread	*leipa*
chicken	*kana*
steak	*paisti*
coffee	*kahvi*
milk	*maito*
dessert	*jälkiruoka*
main course	*hovedretter*
fish	*kala*
lamb	*karitsa*
pork	*sianliha*
seafood	*ayriaisia*
soup	*keitto*
wine	*viivia*

France – Essential Information

PRE-TRIP ESSENTIALS...

WHAT YOU NEED

ESSENTIAL FOR TRAVELERS

● Required ● Recommended ● Not required

Passport	●
Visa	●
Travel, medical insurance	●
Round-trip or onward airline ticket	●
Local currency	●
Traveler's checks	●
Credit cards	●
First-aid kit and medicines	●
Inoculations	●

ESSENTIAL FOR DRIVERS*

Driver's license	●
International Driving Permit	●
Car insurance (for nonrental cars)	●
Car registration (for nonrental cars)	●

*see also DRIVING section

IMPORTANT ADDRESSES

French Government Tourist Office
444 Madison Avenue
New York, NY 10022
☎ (212) 838-7800
Fax (212) 838-7855

French Government Tourist Office
Maison de la France
20 avenue de l'Opéra
75001 Paris, France
☎ 01 42 96 70 00
Fax 01 42 92 70 71

American Embassy
2 avenue Gabriel
75008 Paris, France
☎ 01 43 12 22 22
Fax 01 42 66 97 83
American Citizens Services: Mon.–Fri. 9–3

COUNTRY ESSENTIALS...

CUSTOMS

YES
Duty-free limits on goods brought in from non-European Union countries:
200 cigarettes or 100 cigarillos or 50 cigars or 250 g. tobacco; 2 L. wine; 1 L. alcohol over 22% volume; 2 L. alcohol under 22%; 60 ml. perfume; 250 ml. toilet water; plus any other duty-free goods (including gifts) to the value of 300Fr. There is no limit on the importation of tax-paid goods purchased within the European Union, provided they are for your own personal use. There are no currency regulations.

NO
No unlicensed drugs, weapons, ammunition, obscene material, pets or other animals, counterfeit money or copied goods, meat or poultry.

For customs limits for returning U.S. citizens see page 16.

MONEY

France's currency is the franc (Fr), which is divided into 100 centimes. The denominations of franc bills are 20, 50, 100, 200 and 500. There are coins of 5, 10, 20 and 50 centimes and 1, 2, 5, 10 and 20Fr. You can exchange dollars or traveler's checks *(cheques de voyage)* at a bank *(banque)* or an exchange office *(bureau de change)*. On Jan. 1, 1999, the euro became the official currency of France and the French franc became a denomination of the euro. Franc bills and coins continue to be legal tender during a transitional period. Euro bills and coins are likely to be introduced by Jan. 2002.
Exchange rate at press time: $1 = 6Fr

TIPS AND GRATUITIES

Tips *(pourboires)* are welcomed, but not expected.

Restaurants (service is almost always included)	change
Cafés/bars (service is almost always included)	change
Taxis	5–10Fr
Porters	5–10Fr
Chambermaids	10–50Fr
Hairdressers	5–10Fr
Cloakroom attendants	2–5Fr

| TIME ZONES | PARIS 12:00 noon | NEW YORK 6 hours behind France | CHICAGO 7 hours behind France | DENVER 8 hours behind France | SAN FRANCISCO 9 hours behind France | 487 |

France – Essential Information

COMMUNICATIONS

POST OFFICES

Buy stamps *(timbres-poste)* at a post office *(poste)*, newsstand *(marchand de journaux)* or tobacconist

(distinguished by its conical red *Tabac* sign). Hours of out-of-town post offices may vary. Mailboxes are yellow and wall mounted.

TELEPHONES

The telephone system in France is very efficient, and phone booths with instructions in English are easy to find. Most phones are operated with a phone card *(télécarte)*, which can be bought from post offices, newsstands and many tobacconists. You can use credit cards in some booths.

Phoning inside France
All telephone numbers are 10 digits, and include the regional code. Dial all digits when making a call.

To call the operator dial 13.

Phoning France from abroad
The country code for France is 33. Note that French numbers in this book do not include the country code; you need to prefix this number if you are phoning from another country. To phone France from the United States or Canada, omit the first zero from the French number, and add the prefix 011 33.
Example: 01 22 33 44 55 becomes 011 33 1 22 33 44 55.

Phoning from France
To phone the United States or Canada from France, prefix the area code and number with 001.
Example: (111) 222-3333 becomes 001 111 222-3333.

To call international information dial 003312 + country prefix.

EMERGENCY TELEPHONE NUMBERS
Police *(police)*	17
Fire *(pompiers)*	18
Ambulance *(ambulance)*	15

Emergency calls are free from phone booths.

HOURS OF OPERATION

- Stores Tue.–Sat.
- Offices Mon.–Fri.
- Banks Mon.–Fri.
- Post offices Mon.–Sat.
- Museums/monuments Tue.–Sun.
- Pharmacies Mon.–Sat.

```
7  8  9  10 11 12  1  2  3  4  5  6  7
```

Many stores close on Sunday and Monday, although opening hours are longer in resort areas and major towns and cities.

Out-of-town banks may stay closed on Monday, while city banks may open on Saturday morning.

Post offices close at noon on Saturday.

Museum times vary considerably, and it is best to check before a visit. Many close on national holidays, and some close on Tuesday instead of Monday. There may be a discount on the entry fee on Sunday.

NATIONAL HOLIDAYS

Banks, businesses and most stores close on these days.

Jan. 1	New Year's Day
Mar./Apr.	Easter Monday
Apr. 30	Great Prayer Day
May 8	VE Day
May	Ascension Day
May/Jun.	Pentecost Monday
Jul. 14	Bastille Day
Aug. 15	Assumption of the Virgin
Nov. 1	All Saints' Day
Nov. 11	Armistice Day
Dec. 25	Christmas Day

PHOTOGRAPHY

The range of subjects to photograph in France is enormous, and the light is usually favorable in the summer months. Film is readily available from stores and photo labs, although development is rather expensive. Some museums and churches will allow you to photograph inside, but permission for flash photography is usually required.

France – Essential Information

HEALTH

MEDICAL INSURANCE
Private medical insurance is recommended. Visitors from non-E.U. countries have to pay for all medical treatment; keep all receipts and medicine labels to claim on your travel insurance. If you wish to see an English-speaking doctor *(médecin)* ask at your consulate or hotel.

DENTAL SERVICES
A dentist *(dentiste)* charges for treatment. Emergency help is available from dentists listed in the yellow pages *(pages jaunes)*. Check that your private medical insurance covers dental treatment.

SUN ADVICE
The yearly average for sunshine is high: 2,500 hours (3,000 hours along the coast). Summers, particularly July and August, can be dry and hot, especially in the south. When outside wear a hat and drink plenty of fluids. On the beach a high factor sunscreen is essential.

DRUGS
Prescription medicines and medical advice can be obtained from a pharmacy *(pharmacie)*, designated by a green cross sign. If you need medicines outside regular hours, information about the nearest 24-hour facility is posted on the door of all pharmacies.

SAFE WATER
It is safe to drink tap water, but never drink from a fountain marked *"eau non potable"* ("not drinking water"). Many French people prefer the taste of bottled mineral water *(eau minérale en bouteille)*, which is widely available. A less expensive alternative is *eau de source*, which is spring water.

RESTROOMS

It is not difficult to find a restroom *(toilettes* or WC, pronounced *vay-say* in French), although you may still find the old-fashioned "squat" variety. Hygiene is usually of a reasonable standard. There is a small fee to use facilities in train stations. If you need to use the restroom in a café or bar, buy a drink first.

ELECTRICITY

France has a 220-volt power supply. Electrical sockets take plugs with two round pins, or sometimes three pins in a vertical row; American appliances will need a plug adapter and will require a transformer if they do not have a dual-voltage facility.

NATIONAL TRANSPORTATION

TRAIN *(train)*
The state rail company is the Société Nationale des Chemins de Fer Français (SNCF): ☎ 08 36 35 35 35.
Trains are fast, reliable and comfortable, with numerous discounts available. A "turn-up-and-go" car-carrying service from Calais (Le Shuttle) and a Paris–London passenger train (Eurostar) both run through the tunnel under the English Channel. For Eurostar details ☎ 01 45 82 50 50.

BUS *(bus)*
Bus services in cities are excellent, but rural areas may be less well served. Long-distance bus stations are usually close to railroad stations, and major train and bus services usually co-ordinate (a long-distance bus is called a *car)*. Bus services shown on train timetables are run by the SNCF, and rail tickets are often valid for them. The Eurolines international bus network operates in France: ☎ 08 36 69 52 52.

FERRY *(ferry)*
There are frequent sailings to Britain from ports along the English Channel. A car-carrying train service also operates – see TRAIN above. Some Mediterranean ferries are summer only and may need reservations in advance.

DRIVING

 DRIVE ON THE RIGHT

SPEED LIMITS
Traffic police can impose severe on-the-spot fines.

Limited-access highways *(autoroutes)*
130 k.p.h. (80 m.p.h.)
Outer lane minimum **80 k.p.h. (49 m.p.h.)**
Divided highways **110 k.p.h. (68 m.p.h.)**

Main roads
110 k.p.h. (68 m.p.h.)

Urban areas
50 k.p.h. (31 m.p.h.)

SEAT BELTS
Must be worn in front seats at all times and in the rear seats where fitted.

BLOOD ALCOHOL
The legal blood alcohol limit is 0.05%. Random breath tests on drivers are carried out frequently, especially late at night, and the penalties for offenders are severe.

DRIVING continued

TOLLS
There are tolls on many limited-access highways *(autoroutes à péage)*. Collect a ticket on entry and keep it in a safe place: you must show the ticket and pay when exiting. Cash and credit cards are accepted.

CAR RENTAL
The leading rental firms have offices at airports and train stations. Hertz offers discounted rates for AAA members (see page 15). For reservations:

	UNITED STATES	FRANCE
Alamo	(800) 327-9633	01 53 20 06 52
Avis	(800) 331-2112	01 53 32 79 10
Budget	(800) 527-0700	01 53 32 79 00
Hertz	(800) 654-3080	01 55 31 93 21

FUEL
Gas stations are generally easy to find, and highway service areas are open 24 hours. Gas *(essence)* is unleaded *(sans plomb)* and sold in liters. Credit cards are widely accepted; many pumps read cards directly, so the customer does not have to pay at the counter. Gas stations are less common in rural areas, and some close on Sunday.

AAA AFFILIATED MOTORING CLUB
Automobile Club Nationale (ACN)
8 place de la Concorde,
75008 Paris, France ☎ 01 53 30 89 30,
fax 01 53 30 89 29
If you break down while driving, phone ☎ 08 00 08 92 22 (ACN breakdown service).
Not all automobile clubs offer full services to AAA members.

BREAKDOWNS AND ACCIDENTS
If you are involved in an accident, ☎ 17 for police assistance. There are orange emergency telephones at regular intervals on highways.
Most car rental firms provide their own free rescue service; if your car is rented, follow the instructions given in the documentation. Use of a car repair service other than those authorized by your rental company may violate your agreement.

OTHER INFORMATION
The minimum age for driving a car is 18 (may be higher for some car rental firms).

An International Driving Permit (IDP) is recommended; some rental firms require them, and they can speed up formalities if you are involved in an accident.

A Green Card (international motor insurance certificate) is recommended if you are driving a private car; see page 15 for more information.

USEFUL WORDS AND PHRASES

You'll be well received if you try to pronounce words correctly. Don't worry too much about rolling your *r*'s, though; the French realize how difficult it can be.

Final consonants are seldom pronounced. For instance, the masculine adjective *ouvert* (open) is pronounced [oo-ver]; the feminine *ouverte* [oo-vert]. The final consonant in a word like *vin, bon* or *grand* alters the last vowel, making it nasal.

h is silent	*hôtel* [o-tel]
th is *t* (but *ch* is *sh*)	*thé* [tay]; *chaud* [show]
ou is full	*tout* [too]
u is tight, as in cupola	*tu* [tu], *menu* [meuh-nu]
c and *g* hard before a, o, u	*car* [car], *guide* [geed]
c and *g* soft before i or e	*cigarette, age* [arzh]
ç is soft (before an a)	*français* [frahn-say]
gn as in union	*agneau* [an-yo]

Do you speak English?	*Parlez-vous anglais?*
excuse me	*excusez-moi*
hello/goodbye	*bonjour/au revoir*
How much is this?	*C'est combien?*
I am American	*Je suis Américain/e*
I'd like…	*je voudrais…*
I don't understand	*Je ne comprends pas*
non-smoking	*non-fumeurs*
okay	*OK (informal)*
open/closed	*ouvert/fermé*
please/thank you	*s'il vous plaît/merci*
ticket	*billet*
(one-way/round trip)	*(simple/aller-retour)*
where is…?	*où est…?*
yes/no	*oui/non*
you're welcome	*de rien*

the hotel	***l'hôtel***
breakfast	*petit déjeuner*
I have a reservation	*j'ai réservé*
key	*clé*
for one/two nights	*pour une/deux nuit(s)*
one/two people	*une/deux personne(s)*
room	*une chambre*
shower	*une douche*
with en-suite bathroom	*avec salle de bains*

the restaurant	***le restaurant***
beef	*boeuf*
bread	*pain*
chicken	*poulet*
the check	*addition*
coffee	*café*
dish of the day	*plat du jour*
dessert	*dessert*
entrée	*plat principal*
fish	*poisson*
lamb	*agneau*
pork	*porc*
seafood	*fruits de mer*
starter	*entrée*
wine	*vin*

France – Essential Information

PRE-TRIP ESSENTIALS...

WHAT YOU NEED

ESSENTIAL FOR TRAVELERS

● Required   ● Recommended   ● Not required

Passport	●
Visa	●
Travel, medical insurance	●
Round-trip or onward airline ticket	●
Local currency	●
Traveler's checks	●
Credit cards	●
First-aid kit and medicines	●
Inoculations	●

ESSENTIAL FOR DRIVERS*

Driver's license	●
International Driving Permit	●
Car insurance (for nonrental cars)	●
Car registration (for nonrental cars)	●

*see also DRIVING section

IMPORTANT ADDRESSES

German National Tourist Office
122 East 42nd Street
New York, NY 10168-0072
☎ (212) 661-7200
Fax (212) 661-7174

German National Tourist Board
Beethovenstrasse 69
60325 Frankfurt am Main, Germany
☎ 069 974 640
Fax 069 751 903

American Embassy
Neustädtische Kirchstrasse 4–5
10117 Berlin, Germany
☎ 030 238 5174
Fax 030 238 6290

COUNTRY ESSENTIALS...

CUSTOMS

YES

Duty-free limits on goods brought in from non-European Union countries:
200 cigarettes or 100 cigarillos or 50 cigars or 250 g. tobacco; 2 L. wine; 1 L. alcohol over 22% volume; 2 L. alcohol under 22%; 60 ml. perfume; 250 ml. toilet water; plus any other duty-free goods (including gifts) to the value of DM115. There is no limit on the importation of tax-paid goods purchased within the European Union, provided they are for your own personal use. There are no currency regulations.

NO

No unlicensed drugs, weapons, ammunition, obscene material, pets or other animals, counterfeit money or copied goods, meat or poultry.

For customs limits for returning U.S. citizens see page 16.

MONEY

Germany's currency is the Deutsche mark (DM), which is divided into 100 pfennigs (Pf). The denominations of Deutsche mark bills are 5, 10, 20, 50, 100, 200, 500 and 1,000. There are coins of 1, 2, 5, 10 and 50 Pf and 1, 2 and 5DM. You can exchange dollars or traveler's checks *(Reiseschecks)* at a bank *(Bank)* or an exchange office *(Wechselbüro)*. On Jan. 1, 1999, the euro became the official currency of Germany and the mark became a denomination of the euro. Mark bills and coins continue to be legal tender during a transitional period. Euro bills and coins are likely to be introduced by Jan. 2002.
Exchange rate at press time: $1 = DM2

TIPS AND GRATUITIES

Restaurants (where service is not included)	10%
Cafés/bars (where service is not included)	10%
Taxis	10%
Porters	change
Chambermaids	change
Hairdressers	change
Restroom attendants	change
Cloakroom attendants	change

COMMUNICATIONS

POST OFFICES

Buy stamps *(Briefmarken)* at a post office *(Postamt)* or newsstand *(Informationsstand)*.

Hours for out-of-town post offices may vary.

TELEPHONES

East and west Germany are supposed to have an integrated telecommunications network, but the eastern system still has room for improvement; if your call is important make it in the west. Black telephones have instructions in English, and most operators are bilingual. Telephone cards *(Kartentelefon)* can be bought at a post office for DM12 or DM50. International calls can be made from most booths except those marked "National."

Phoning inside Germany
German telephone numbers in this book include an area code: dial the number listed.

Operator: dial 01188.

Phoning Germany from abroad
The country code for Germany is 49. Note that German numbers in this book do not include the country code; you will need to prefix this number if you are phoning from another country. To phone Germany from the United States or Canada, omit the first zero from the German number, and add the prefix 011 49. (Note that the number of digits in German area codes varies.)
Example: 011 22 33 44 becomes 011 49 11 22 33 44.

Phoning from Germany
To phone the United States or Canada from Germany, prefix the area code and number with 001.
Example: 111 222-3333 becomes 001 111 222-3333.
To call international information dial 00118.

EMERGENCY TELEPHONE NUMBERS
Police *(Polizei)*	110
Fire *(Feuerwehr)*	112
Ambulance *(Krankenwagen)*	110*

*In some states ambulance is 115
Emergency calls are free from phone booths.

HOURS OF OPERATION

- Stores Mon.–Sat.
- Museums/monuments
- Offices Mon.–Fri.
- Tue.–Sat.
- Banks Mon.–Fri.
- Pharmacies Mon.–Sat.
- Post offices Mon.–Sat.

Store hours of operation vary considerably, so even within cities there is no standard rule. Stores, including pharmacies, tend to close at 2 on Saturday and are open until 10:30 p.m. on Thursday.

Banks stay open until 5:30 on Thursday.

Government offices close promptly at 4, or at 2 on Friday.

Museums often close on Monday and open late on Thursday; some close for lunch.

NATIONAL HOLIDAYS

Banks, businesses and most stores close on these days.

Jan. 1	New Year's Day
Jan. 6	Epiphany (Bavaria and Baden-Württemberg only)
Mar./Apr.	Good Friday
Mar./Apr.	Easter Monday
May 1	Labor Day
May	Ascension Day
May/Jun.	Pentecost Monday
Aug. 15	Assumption of the Virgin (Bavaria and Saarland only)
Oct. 3	Day of German Unity
Nov. 1	All Saints' Day (some areas)
Dec. 25	Christmas Day
Dec. 26	St. Stephen's Day

PHOTOGRAPHY

The light is generally good. In addition to the glorious architecture of the big cities, there are many colorful, quaint street scenes to be snapped in provincial Germany, and the landscapes are equally appealing. Photography is generally forbidden in museums and churches. Quality brand film and batteries are easy to find, and there are many rapid-developing facilities.

Germany – Essential Information

Germany – Essential Information

HEALTH

MEDICAL INSURANCE
U.S. and Canadian visitors must pay for medical treatment from a doctor or at a hospital *(Krankenhaus)*. Keep all receipts to claim on your travel insurance. For details on emergency, weekend or English-speaking doctors, ask your hotel or consulate.

DENTAL SERVICES
A dentist *(Zahnarzt)* always charges for treatment. Emergency help is available from dentists listed in the local telephone directory. Check that your private medical insurance covers dental treatment.

SUN ADVICE
Germany's continental climate brings cold, clear winters and warm summers, when sun protection is needed. Use sunscreen; children and those with fair skin should be vigilant.

DRUGS
Prescription medicines and advice can be obtained from a pharmacy *(Apotheke)*; cosmetics and toiletries at a *Drogerie*. If you need medicine outside regular hours, information about the nearest 24-hour facility is posted on the door of all pharmacies.

SAFE WATER
Water is safe to drink in Germany, but you may prefer to drink bottled mineral water *(Sprudelwasser)*, which is widely available.

RESTROOMS

Finding a restroom *(Toilette)* is not difficult; they are usually identified by symbols, or are designated *Herren* (men) and *Damen* or *Frauen* (women). Most are free, although some are operated by a 10Pf coin. If there is an attendant, small change is appreciated as a tip.

ELECTRICITY

Germany has a 220-volt power supply. Electrical sockets take plugs with two round pins or sometimes three pins in a vertical row; American appliances will need a plug adapter and will require a transformer if they do not have a dual-voltage facility.

NATIONAL TRANSPORTATION

TRAIN *(Zug)*
Germany's fast, efficient rail network is operated by Deutsche Bahn (DB). ICE is a very modern service of long-distance, high-speed trains. Regional trains are modern and comfortable, and connect with long-distance services. Local services are called SE or S-Bahn. There are many fare reductions available; for bookings and information ☎ 01805 996 633.

BUS *(Bus)*
Towns and villages not served by the rail network usually have bus links, with timetables and routes co-ordinating with trains. German towns have their own buses, and one ticket is often transferable to other types of city transport. The Eurolines international bus service operates in Germany: ☎ 089 54 58 70 15.

FERRY *(Fähre)*
Ferries from the ports of Lübeck and Kiel in the north connect to Denmark and Sweden. Boats also offer a service on many German lakes, rivers and canals. Ask for details at your travel agency or a local tourist office, where reservations can often be made.

DRIVING

DRIVE ON THE RIGHT

SPEED LIMITS
Traffic police can impose severe on-the-spot fines.

Limited-access highways *(Autobahn)*
130 k.p.h. (80 m.p.h.)

Main roads
100 k.p.h. (62 m.p.h.)

Urban areas
50 k.p.h. (31 m.p.h.)

SEAT BELTS
Must be worn in front seats at all times and in the rear seats where fitted.

BLOOD ALCOHOL
The legal blood alcohol limit is 0.05%. Random breath tests on drivers are carried out frequently, especially late at night, and the penalties for offenders are severe.

DRIVING continued

TOLLS
There are no highway tolls.

CAR RENTAL
The leading rental firms have offices at airports and train stations. Hertz offers discounted rates for AAA members (see page 15). For reservations:

	UNITED STATES	GERMANY
Alamo	(800) 327-9633	089 97 59 76 80
Avis	(800) 331-2112	089 97 59 76 00
Budget	(800) 527-0700	089 97 59 76 80
Hertz	(800) 654-3080	030 41 01 33 15

FUEL
Gas *(Benzin)* and diesel fuel are sold in liters. Gas stations are easy to find, and most highway services are open 24 hours. Self-service stations are called *Selbstbedienunb* or *SB-Tanken,* and credit cards are widely accepted.

AAA AFFILIATED MOTORING CLUB
Allgemeiner Deutscher Automobil-Club (ADAC)
AM Westpark 8, 81373 Munich
☎ 089 76760, fax 089 76 76 25 00
If you break down while driving, phone ☎ 018 02 22 22 22 (ADAC breakdown service).
Not all automobile clubs offer full services to AAA members.

BREAKDOWNS AND ACCIDENTS
Most car rental firms provide their own free rescue service; if your car is rented, follow the instructions given in the documentation. Use of a car repair service other than those authorized by your rental company may violate your agreement.

If you are involved in an accident ☎ 110 for police assistance.

OTHER INFORMATION
The minimum age for driving a car is 17 (may be higher for some car rental firms).

You must keep an official translation with your driver's license; your embassy or a tourist office can help. An International Driving Permit (IDP) is recommended; some rental firms require them, and they can speed up formalities if you are involved in an accident.

A Green Card (international motor insurance certificate) is recommended if you are driving a private car; see page 15 for more information.

On-the-spot fines can be imposed if you run out of gas on a highway.

USEFUL WORDS AND PHRASES

German has many dialects. Language in the north descended from Old Saxon, and in the south, from Old High German. Their differences were resolved by Standard German (*Schriftdeutsch*), created by Martin Luther when he translated the Bible in the 16th century.

Germans are helpful to visitors who attempt to communicate in German, although English is widely spoken.

ü is like the *u* in cupola	*über* (over)
ie sounds like heat	*Sie* (you)
ei sounds like height	*Eingang* (entrance)
ch is a harsh rasp…	*J. S. Bach*
j is like the English *y*	*ja* (yes)
r is rolled, as in French	*Fräulein* (Miss)
w sounds like English *v*	*wo* (where)
z is like English *ts*	*Zeit* (time)

Do you speak English?	*Sprechen Sie Englisch?*
excuse me	*Verzeihung*
hello/goodbye	*Guten Tag/ Auf Wiedersehen*
How much is…?	*Wieviel kostet…?*
I am American	*Ich bin Amerikanisch*
I'd like…	*Ich hättegerne*
I don't understand	*Ich verstehe nicht*
non-smoking	*Nichtraucher*
okay	*OK*
open/closed	*offen/geschlossen*
please/thank you	*bitte/danke*
one-way ticket	*einfache Fahrkarte*
round trip ticket	*Rückfahrkarte*
where is…?	*wo ist…?*
yes/no	*ja/nein*
You're welcome	*bitte*

the hotel	***das Hotel***
breakfast	*Frühstück*
reservation	*Reservieren*
key	*Schlüssel*
for one/two nights	*für eine Nacht/ zwei Nächte*
one/two people	*für eine Person/ zwei Personen*
room	*Zimmer*
shower	*Dusche*

the restaurant	**das Restaurant**
beefsteak	*Steak*
bread	*Brot*
chicken	*Hähnchen*
the check	*Rechnung*
coffee	*Kaffee*
dish of the day	*Tagesgericht*
dessert	*Desserts*
entree	*Hauptgericht*
fish	*Fisch*
lamb	*Lamm*
pork	*Schweinefleisch*
seafood	*Meeresfrüchte*
first courses	*Vorspeisen*
wine	*Wein*

Germany – Essential Information

Greece – Essential Information

PRE-TRIP ESSENTIALS...

WHAT YOU NEED

ESSENTIAL FOR TRAVELERS

● Required   ● Recommended   ● Not required

Passport	●
Visa	●
Travel, medical insurance	●
Round-trip or onward airline ticket	●
Local currency	●
Traveler's checks	●
Credit cards	●
First-aid kit and medicines*	●
Inoculations	●

*see also HEALTH section

ESSENTIAL FOR DRIVERS*

Driver's license	●
International Driving Permit	●
Car insurance (for nonrental cars)	●
Car registration (for nonrental cars)	●

*see also DRIVING section

IMPORTANT ADDRESSES

Greek National Tourist Office
645 Third Avenue
New York, NY 10022
☎ (212) 421-5777
Fax (212) 826-6940

Greek National Tourist Office
Amerikis 2
10564 Athens, Greece
☎ 01 322 3111
Fax 01 325 2895

American Embassy
Queen Sofias Avenue 91
10160 Athens, Greece
☎ 01 721 2951
Fax 01 725 3025
Personal inquires to the consulate department
Tue. and Thu.–Fri. 8:30–2, Wed. 8:30–1

COUNTRY ESSENTIALS...

CUSTOMS

YES
Duty-free limits on goods brought in from non-European Union countries:
200 cigarettes or 100 cigarillos or 50 cigars or 250 g. tobacco; 2 L. wine; 1 L. alcohol over 22% volume; 2 L. alcohol under 22% volume; 50 ml. perfume; 250 ml. toilet water; plus any other duty-free goods (including gifts) to the value of Dr50,000. There is no importation limit for tax-paid goods purchased within the European Union, provided they are for your own personal use. Visitors may import up to Dr100,000, and there is no limit on foreign currency. Up to Dr20,000, and $1,000 in foreign currency may be exported by visitors.

NO
No unlicensed drugs, weapons, ammunition, obscene material, pets or other animals, counterfeit money or copied goods, meat or poultry.

For customs limits for returning U.S. citizens see page 16.

MONEY

The Greek currency is the drachma (Dr). The denominations of drachma bills are 100, 200, 500, 1,000, 5,000 and 10,000. There are coins of 5, 10, 20, 50 and 100Dr. Traveler's checks are widely accepted, and in some gift stores dollars are accepted as payment for goods. Exchange dollars or traveler's checks *(taxithiotiki epitayi)* at a bank *(trapeza)* or an exchange office *(sarafiko)*. Exchange rates vary considerably. You can get cash at a bank with a credit card, but there is usually a charge. Alternatively, there are a growing number of ATMs at banks.
Exchange rate at press time: $1 = Dr300

TIPS AND GRATUITIES

Tips *(poorbwáar)* are welcomed, but not expected or obligatory.

Restaurants (where service is not included)	10–15%
Cafés/bars	change
Taxis	change
Porters	Dr500
Chambermaids	Dr100 per day
Cloakroom attendants	change

TIME ZONES

ATHENS	NEW YORK	CHICAGO	DENVER	SAN FRANCISCO
12:00 noon	6 hours behind Greece	7 hours behind Greece	8 hours behind Greece	9 hours behind Greece

495

COMMUNICATIONS

POST OFFICES

Buy stamps *(ghramatósima)* at a post office *(takhithromio),* distinguished by a yellow "OTE" sign. City and town post offices often cash traveler's checks. Lines can be long at post office counters; if you simply need stamps, try a corner kiosk *(periptero)* selling postcards.

Hours for out-of-town post offices may vary.

TELEPHONES

Most public telephones take phone cards available from kiosks, local stores and OTE (Organismos Tilepikoinonion Ellados, pronounced O-tay) offices. If your calls are short and local, use a street kiosk *(periptero)* where you pay after the call. For an international call, you can also use a coin-operated telephone in a restaurant, bar or hotel lobby; they take Dr10, Dr20, Dr50 and Dr100 coins. You can be called back on these telephones, and they have instructions in English.

Phoning inside Greece
All Greek telephone numbers in this book include an area code: dial the number that is listed.

To call the operator dial 132 (or 131 in Athens).

Phoning Greece from abroad
The country code for Greece is 30. Note that Greek numbers in this book do not include the country code; you will need to prefix this number if you are phoning from another country. To call a Greek number from the United States or Canada, omit the first zero and add the prefix 011 30. (Note that Greek phone numbers vary in the number of digits.) Example: 01 122 3344 becomes 011 30 1 122 3344.

Phoning from Greece
To phone the United States or Canada from Greece, prefix the area code and number with 001. Example: (111) 222-3333 becomes 001 111 222-3333.

To call international information dial 161.

EMERGENCY TELEPHONE NUMBERS
Police *(astinomia),* general emergencies	100
Tourist police (Athens only)	171
Fire *(fotyá)*	199
Ambulance *(asthenoforo)*	166

Emergency calls are free from phone booths.

HOURS OF OPERATION

- Stores Mon.–Sat.
- Museums/monuments
- Offices Mon.–Fri.
- Architectural sites
- Banks Mon.–Fri.
- Pharmacies Mon.–Fri.
- Post offices Mon.–Sat.

| 7 | 8 | 9 | 10 | 11 | 12 | 1 | 2 | 3 | 4 | 5 | 6 | 7 |

In tourist areas stores open at 8 a.m. and close late; they have shorter hours off-season, and some close completely in winter.

Banks may open for longer hours at peak season in resort areas.

Post offices close at noon on Saturday.

Architectural sites usually close in the afternoon; some reopen in the evening, but all sites vary their hours depending on the time of year. It is best to check locally. Many architectural sites, museums and monuments close on Monday.

Restaurants open all day in resort areas but may close off-season.

NATIONAL HOLIDAYS

Banks, businesses, and most stores and museums close on these days, but restaurants and some stores in tourist areas may stay open.

Jan. 1	New Year's Day
Jan. 6	Epiphany
Feb./Mar.	Carnival season (3 weeks before Lent)
Feb./Mar.	Shrove Monday
Mar. 25	Independence Day
Mar./Apr.	Good Friday
Mar./Apr.	Easter Monday
May/Jun.	Pentecost Monday
Aug. 15	Assumption of the Virgin
Oct. 28	Óchi Day
Dec. 25	Christmas Day
Dec. 26	St. Stephen's Day

PHOTOGRAPHY

The sun in Greece is strong, and slow film is ideal. Photograph the sights early in the morning, before the crowds mass and when the light is at its best. In rural areas deep blue seas and rustic villages make interesting subjects. Beware of taking shots near military bases, and ask first in museums and churches. Brand names of film and camera batteries are widely available.

HEALTH

MEDICAL INSURANCE
Private medical insurance is recommended. Visitors from non-E.U. countries can receive basic treatment at hospital emergency rooms. Admittance to a hospital *(nosokomío)* or consultation with a doctor *(iatrós)* will entail a fee. Ask your hotel, consulate or the tourist police for information on English-speaking doctors.

DENTAL SERVICES
Dentists *(odhondoyatrós)* always charge for treatment, so check that your medical insurance covers it; keep all receipts for insurance purposes. Treatment is available from English-speaking dentists listed in the telephone directory, or ask at your hotel.

SUN ADVICE
Summer, particularly July and August, can be oppressively hot and humid. Seek shelter inside a museum, or cover up, apply a sunscreen and drink plenty of fluids. Be especially careful on boats or near the water.

DRUGS
A pharmacy *(farmakío)*, distinguished by a green cross, has staff qualified to offer medical advice and provide a wide range of prescription medicines. Information about the nearest all-night facility is usually posted at pharmacies. Note that codeine is banned and you can be fined for carrying it.

SAFE WATER
Tap water is safe to drink but because of the high level of minerals it can cause upsets. Bottled water *(metaliko nero)* is available everywhere at a reasonable cost.

RESTROOMS

Finding a clean restroom *(toualéta)* away from tourist areas can be difficult. It is advisable to use facilities in cafés and restaurants after buying a drink. Restrooms are free. The Greek sewage system does not take toilet tissue; use the wastebin provided.

ELECTRICITY

Greece has a 220-volt power supply. Electrical sockets take plugs with two round pins; American appliances will need a plug adapter and will require a transformer if they do not have a dual-voltage facility.

NATIONAL TRANSPORTATION

TRAIN *(tréno)*
Greek trains are run by Organismos Sidirodromon Ellados (OSE), a service predominantly for the mainland. The network is limited, and a reservation is essential on most express trains.

BUS *(leoforío)*
Buses are popular and frequent; few villages or ferry ports are without a bus link. Buy city-to-city tickets from the bus station; in rural areas tickets *(isitirio)* are issued by a conductor on the bus.

FERRY *(féribot)*
Ferries serve all of the Greek islands, and boat excursions run from May to October. You can take a boat from the port of Piraeus to most islands, but check the length of the trip on the timetable – some ferries stop at every island. You can usually buy a ticket on the day of travel unless you are reserving a cabin or taking a car. You may need to reserve in advance in mid-August and over the Easter period; ask at a travel agency or tourist office.

DRIVING

DRIVE ON THE RIGHT

SPEED LIMITS
Police can impose on-the-spot fines but they cannot collect them.

Limited-access highways
120 k.p.h. (74 m.p.h.)
Divided highways
110 k.p.h. (68 m.p.h.)

Main roads
80 k.p.h. (55 m.p.h.)

Urban areas
50 k.p.h. (31 m.p.h.)

SEAT BELTS
Must be worn in front seats at all times and in the rear seats where fitted. Children under 10 are not allowed to travel in the front seat.

BLOOD ALCOHOL
The legal blood alcohol limit is 0.05%. Random breath tests on drivers are carried out frequently, especially late at night, and the penalties for offenders are severe.

☎ FIRE SERVICE 199 *(Fotyá)*   ☎ AMBULANCE 166 *(Asthenoforo)*

497

Greece – Essential Information

DRIVING continued

TOLLS
There are no tolls in Greece.

CAR RENTAL
The leading rental firms have offices at airports, train stations and principal ferry terminals. Hertz offers discounted rates for AAA members (see page 15). For reservations:

	UNITED STATES	GREECE
Alamo	(800) 327-9633	01 994 4257
Avis	(800) 331-2112	01 322 4951
Budget	(800) 527-0700	01 342 8536
Hertz	(800) 654-3080	01 961 3625

FUEL
Gas *(venzini)* is sold in liters and usually comes in five grades: super *(sooper)*, regular *(apli)*, unleaded *(amolyvdhi)*, super unleaded *(sooper amolyvdhi)* and diesel *(petrelaio)*. There are few stations in remote areas; they may not take credit cards.

AAA AFFILIATED MOTORING CLUB
Automobile and Touring Club of Greece (ELPA)
2 Messogion Street, 11527, Athens
☎ 01 748 8800, fax 01 778 6642
If you break down while driving, phone ☎ 104 (ELPA breakdown service).
Not all automobile clubs offer full services to AAA members.

BREAKDOWNS AND ACCIDENTS
There are emergency telephones at regular intervals on highways. If you are involved in an accident ☎ 100 for police assistance.
Most car rental firms provide their own free rescue service; if your car is rented, follow the instructions given in the documentation. Use of a car repair service other than those authorized by your rental company may violate your agreement.

OTHER INFORMATION
The minimum age for driving a car is 17 (may be higher for some car rental firms).

An International Driving Permit (IDP) is recommended; some rental firms require them, and they can speed up formalities if you are involved in an accident. A Green Card (international motor insurance certificate) is recommended if you are driving a private car; see page 15 for more information.

You can be fined for unnecessary use of the horn.

USEFUL WORDS AND PHRASES

The Greek language can be daunting to the visitor; it uses a different alphabet and is spoken with staccato rapidity. The way words and place names are converted into English varies considerably according to which transliteration system a translator happens to prefer.

With patience and a keen ear, you should be able to recognize what sounds these unfamiliar letters stand for. Learning the Greek alphabet may enable you to deduce the meaning of signs and notices. The easiest thing to do, however, is to learn a few basic courtesy phrases.

The Greeks realize how difficult their language appears to foreigners, and they appreciate visitors' attempts to speak it.

Do you speak English?	*milate angliká?*
excuse me	*signomi*
hello/goodbye	*yásou/chérete*
how much?	*póso?*
I'd like	*tha íthela*
I do not understand	*dhen katalaveno*
non-smoking	*khoros ya mi kapnizondes*
okay	*endáysi*
open/closed	*aniktos/klistos*
please/you're welcome	*parakaló*
thank you	*efharistó*
ticket	*isitiro*
one-way/round trip	*apio/isitiro met epistrofis*
where is…?	*poo íne?*
yes/no	*ne/óchi*

the hotel	***xenodochio***
breakfast	*proino*
key	*klithi*
for one/two nights	*ya mía/dhýo vradhiés*
for one/two people	*yiá éna/dhýo átoma*
room	*éna dhomátio*
shower	*doos*

the restaurant	***estiatorio***
food	*fagitó*
starter	*proto piato*
olives	*eliés*
stuffed vine leaves	*dolmadakia*
beans	*fasólia*
bread	*psomi*
water	*neró*
beer	*bira*
wine	*krasí*
coffee	*kafé*
meat balls	*kefthédes*
chicken	*kotópoulo*
lamb	*arnáki*
pork	*hirino*
cod's roe paté	*taramosalata*
lobster	*astakós*
red mullet	*barboúnia*
squid	*kalamarákia*
dessert	*glikisma*
the check	*logariasmos*

Hungary – Essential Information

PRE-TRIP ESSENTIALS...

WHAT YOU NEED

ESSENTIAL FOR TRAVELERS

● Required   ● Recommended   ● Not required

Passport	●
Visa	●
Travel, medical insurance	●
Round-trip or onward airline ticket	●
Local currency	●
Traveler's checks	●
Credit cards	●
First-aid kit and medicines	●
Inoculations	●

ESSENTIAL FOR DRIVERS*

Driver's license	●
International Driving Permit	●
Car insurance (for nonrental cars)	●
Car registration (for nonrental cars)	●

*see also DRIVING section

IMPORTANT ADDRESSES

Hungarian National Tourist Office
150 East 58th Street, 33rd Floor
New York, NY 10155
☎ (212) 355-0240
Fax (212) 207-4103

Hungarian National Tourist Office
1052 Suto utca 2
Budapest, Hungary
☎ 01 317 9800
Fax 01 317 9656

American Embassy
Szabadsag ter 12
1054 Budapest, Hungary
☎ 01 267 4400
Fax 01 269 9326
Personal visa inquiries Tue. 8:30–10:30
Telephone inquiries Mon.–Fri. 1–5

COUNTRY ESSENTIALS...

CUSTOMS

YES

Duty-free limits on goods brought in:
You may bring in personal clothing, articles and other goods which match the purpose and length of your stay. Persons over the age of 16 may also import: 250 cigarettes or 50 cigars or 250 g. tobacco; 2 L. wine; 1 L. alcohol over 22% volume; 2 L. alcohol under 22% volume; 100 ml. perfume; 250 ml. toilet water; plus any other duty-free goods (including gifts) to the value of Ft270,000. Hungary is not yet part of the European Union. The only currency control is the restriction on dollars taken out of Hungary: you may take out the equivalent of Ft100,000.

NO

No unlicensed drugs, weapons, ammunition, obscene material, pets or other animals, counterfeit money or copied goods, meat or poultry.

For customs limits for returning U.S. citizens see page 16.

MONEY

Hungary's currency is the forint (Ft or HUF), which is divided into 100 next-to-valueless fillers. The denominations of forint bills are 100, 200, 500, 1,000 and 5,000. There are coins of 50 fillers and 1, 2, 5, 10, 20, 50 and Ft100. You can exchange dollars or traveler's checks (utazasi csekket) at a bank (bank), exchange office (penzvalto), post office (posta) and some hotels. Do not rely on being able to pay by credit card; although they are increasingly common, they are not accepted everywhere.
Exchange rate at press time: $1 = Ft230

TIPS AND GRATUITIES

Tips (borravaló) are welcomed, but not expected, where service is not included.

Restaurants	10–20%
Cafés/bars	10–20%
Taxis	10%
Porters	to reflect quality of service
Chambermaids	ro reflect quality of service
Hairdressers	10%
Gas station attendants	change
Cloakroom attendants	change

TIME ZONES

BUDAPEST	NEW YORK	CHICAGO	DENVER	SAN FRANCISCO
12:00 noon	6 hours behind Hungary	7 hours behind Hungary	8 hours behind Hungary	9 hours behind Hungary

499

Hungary – Essential Information

COMMUNICATIONS

POST OFFICES

Buy stamps *(bélyeg)* at a post office *(posta),* newsstand/tobacconist *(dohanyaruda)* or from a hotel.

Hours for out-of-town post offices may vary.

TELEPHONES

You can use cash and prepaid phone cards to make a call in Hungary. For direct dialing for national and international calls, use Ft10, Ft20 and Ft50 coins. International calls can be made from red phone booths. Phone cards of Ft50 and Ft100 can be bought from newsstands/tobacconists, gas stations, post offices and hotels.

Phoning inside Hungary

All Hungarian telephone numbers in this book include an area code; dial the number that is listed. Note that numbers in Budapest are seven digits, while others are eight digits including the area code.

To call the operator dial 191.

Phoning Hungary from abroad

The country code for Hungary is 36. Note that Hungarian numbers in this book do not include the Hungarian country code; you will need to prefix this number if you are phoning from another country. To phone Hungary from the United States or Canada, omit the first zero from the Hungarian number, and add the prefix 011 36. (Note that Hungarian area codes are either 1 or 2 digits.) Example: 01 122 3344 becomes 011 36 1 1 122 3344.

Phoning from Hungary

To phone the United States or Canada from Hungary, prefix the area code and number with 001. Example: (111) 222-3333 becomes 001 111 222-3333. To call international information dial 190.

EMERGENCY TELEPHONE NUMBERS

Police *(rëndorség)*	107
Fire *(tüzoltóság):*	105
Ambulance *(mentök)*	104

HOURS OF OPERATION

- ● Stores Mon.–Fri.
- ● Offices Mon.–Fri.
- ● Banks Mon.–Fri.
- ● Post offices Mon.–Sat.
- ● Museums/monuments
- ● Pharmacies Mon.–Sat.

| 7 | 8 | 9 | 10 | 11 | 12 | 1 | 2 | 3 | 4 | 5 | 6 | 7 |

Saturday afternoon is early closing, and few stores remain open after 1. Thursday is late-night shopping until 7 or 8 p.m. Grocery stores and other food stores have longer hours and also open on Sunday morning. In large cities, some stores stay open 24 hours. In smaller towns, stores close over lunchtime.

Post offices close at 1 on Saturday.

Banks close at 1 on Friday.

Many museums close on Monday.

NATIONAL HOLIDAYS

Banks, businesses and most stores are closed on these days; if a public holiday falls on a Tuesday or a Thursday, the day between it and the weekend also becomes a holiday.

Jan. 1	New Year's Day
Mar. 15	Day of the Nation (anniversary of 1848 revolution)
Mar./Apr.	Easter Monday
May 1	Labor Day
May/Jun.	Pentecost Monday
Aug. 20	Constitution Day
Oct. 23	Day of the Proclamation of the Republic
Dec. 25	Christmas Day
Dec. 26	St. Stephen's Day

PHOTOGRAPHY

Hungary has spectacular landscapes, including the Danube bend north of Budapest, one of the most beautiful stretches of this great river, and romantic Lake Balaton, framed by vineyards. Vendors near historic sights sell overpriced 35mm color film; it is widely available, so buy it elsewhere. Batteries and developing services are available in towns and cities.

EMERGENCY PHONE NUMBERS

POLICE 107
(Rëndorség)

Hungary – Essential Information

HEALTH

MEDICAL INSURANCE
Private medical insurance is recommended. U.S. and Canadian visitors can receive free transportation to a hospital *(kórház)* for emergency treatment. All further treatment and care has to be paid for. Fees for medical care are set by the individual hospital or practice. There is a 24-hour private medical care service with English-speaking doctors in Budapest: Falk SOS Hungary. It also has its own ambulance service: 200 0100.

DENTAL SERVICES
Dentists *(forgovos)* charge for treatment, but quality dental work is relatively inexpensive. Check that it is covered by your medical insurance. Dentists are listed in the yellow pages; ask for English-speaking dentists at your embassy or hotel, or at a tourist office.

SUN ADVICE
Hungary has up to 2,500 hours of sun annually, one of the highest levels in Europe. In summer, 9 or 10 hours a day can be expected, so protection is essential.

DRUGS
A pharmacy *(gyógyszetár* or *patica)* sells both prescription and nonprescription medicines (mostly of east European origin – bring your own medication if you need a specific product). Most are cheaper than similar U.S. products. Information about the nearest 24-hour facility is posted at all pharmacies.

SAFE WATER
Although tap water is safe, you may find it causes mild upsets. Bottled mineral water *(sásvány víz)* and soda water *(szoda víz)* are widely available and advised.

RESTROOMS

Public restrooms *(mosdó)* are fairly easy to find, and are usually indicated by a symbol or marked WC, and designated by *férfi* for men and *nöi* for women. A charge of between Ft20 and Ft50 may be made.

ELECTRICITY

Hungary has a 220-volt power supply. Electrical sockets take plugs with two round pins; American appliances will need a plug adapter and will require a transformer if they do not have a dual-voltage facility.

NATIONAL TRANSPORTATION

TRAIN *(vonat)*
The state railroad, Magyar Államvasutak (MÁV), serves most towns. The best trains are express, linking Budapest with provincial centers; when journeying cross-country it may be quicker to go via the capital. Fares are low, and MÁV offers many discounted fares, including rail cards good for unlimited travel; 01 342 9150.

BUS *(busz)*
Long-distance buses are expensive, but sometimes quicker than trains. The main Budapest terminal is at Erzsebét tér: phone 01 317 2960 (for national buses) or 01 317 2562 (for international buses). The main operator is state-owned Volan, whose yellow buses serve even very small communities. Eurolines operates an international bus service; 01 317 2562.

FERRY *(komp)*
Ferries run on Lake Balaton, the Danube between Budapest and Esztergom, and the Tisza river (serving Tokaj, Szolnok, Csongrád and Szeged). Ferries generally run spring to late autumn. Obtain Budapest information from the Vigadó tér landing stage; 01 318 1704.

DRIVING

DRIVE ON THE RIGHT

SPEED LIMITS
On-the-spot fines of up to Ft2,000 can be imposed by the police. Receipts must be issued.

Limited-access highways *(autópályára)*
120 k.p.h. (74 m.p.h.)
Minimum speed **60 k.p.h. (37 m.p.h.)**
Divided highways **100 k.p.h. (62 m.p.h.)**

Main roads
80 k.p.h. (49 m.p.h.)

Urban areas
30–50 k.p.h. (18–31 m.p.h.)

SEAT BELTS
Must be worn in front seats at all times and in the rear seats where fitted.

BLOOD ALCOHOL
The legal blood alcohol limit is zero. Random breath tests on drivers are carried out frequently, especially at night.

TOLLS
There are tolls on the M5 and sections of the M1.

DRIVING continued

CAR RENTAL
The leading rental firms have offices at airports and railroad stations. Hertz offers discounted rates for AAA members (see page 15). For reservations:

	UNITED STATES	HUNGARY
Dollar	(800) 800 4000	01 296 6680 (EuropCar)
Avis	(800) 331-2112	01 296 6421
Budget	(800) 527-0700	01 296 8197
Hertz	(800) 654-3080	01 296 0986

FUEL
Fuel *(benzin)* is sold in liters: unleaded *(olómmentes benzine)* is graded 91, 95 and 98 octane, and leaded is 98 octane. Diesel can be bought along major routes and in cities. Many gas stations *(benzinkút)* are self-service, although you may not be able use a credit card in smaller stations. A map of rural gas stations is available from MAK (see below).

AAA AFFILIATED MOTORING CLUB
Magyar Autóklub (MAK)
Rómer Flóris u 4/a, 1024 Budapest
☎ 01 212 5236, fax 01 212 3890
If you break down while driving, phone ☎ 088 (MAK breakdown service). English-speaking operators are on call 24 hours; there are emergency phones every 2 km (1.2 miles) on highways. Not all automobile clubs offer full services to AAA members.

BREAKDOWNS AND ACCIDENTS
If you have an accident ☎ 107 for police service, and ask for an interpreter at the scene. You are legally required to report personal injury.
Most car rental firms provide their own free rescue service; if your car is rented, follow the instructions given in the documentation. Use of a car repair service other than those authorized by your rental company may violate your agreement.

Vehicles with damaged bodywork may only leave the country with an official certificate. If you have insurance queries after an accident, call the Hungarian Insurance Company, Hamzsabégi utca 60, 1113 Budapest; ☎ 01 209 0730.

OTHER INFORMATION
The minimum age for driving a car is 18 (may be higher for some car rental firms).

An International Driving Permit (IDP) is recommended; some rental firms require them, and they can speed up formalities if you are involved in an accident. A Green Card (international motor insurance certificate) is recommended if you are driving a private car; see page 15 for more information.

Dimmed headlights must be used at all times outside built-up areas.

USEFUL WORDS AND PHRASES

Hungarian, called Magyar by its speakers, is a difficult language, related only to Finnish and Estonian. German is traditionally the second language, but English is gradually replacing it, especially among the younger generation.

Apart from a few international words *(posta, telefon)*, Hungarian offers few clues as to its meaning. However, pronunciation is regular – letters consistently stand for the same sounds.

By learning basic words, street signs, notices and labels will begin to make sense.

Do you speak English?	*Beszél angolul?*
What is your name?	*Hogy hívnak?*
excuse me	*elnézést*
hello	*jo napot kivanok*
goodbye	*viszontlátásra*
yes/no	*igen/nem*
how much?	*mennyibe kerul?*
I am American	*Amerikai vagyok*
I don't understand	*nem értem*
non-smoking	*nem domanyzo*
open	*nyitva*
closed	*zarva*
please	*kérem*
thank you	*köszönöm*
ticket	*jegy*
(one-way/round trip)	*(egyiranyu/retur)*
where is…?	*hol van…?*

the hotel	*szálloda*
you're welcome	*szívesen*
Where is the restroom?	*Hol a mosdó?*
breakfast	*reggeli*
reservation	*foglalás*
key	*kulcs*
room	*szoba*
shower	*zuhany*

the restaurant	*étterem/vendeglo/etkezde*
beef	*marha*
beer	*sör*
bread	*kenyer*
the check	*szamla*
coffee/tea	*kávé/tea*
dessert	*édesség*
fish	*hal*
fruit	*gyümölcs*
ice cream	*fagylalt*
meat	*hús*
pork	*sertés*
potato	*burgonya*
poultry	*csirke*
starter	*elöételek*
vegetable	*zöldség*
wine	*bor*

Hungary – Essential Information

Ireland – Essential Information

PRE-TRIP ESSENTIALS...

WHAT YOU NEED

ESSENTIAL FOR TRAVELERS

● Required   ● Recommended   ● Not required

Passport	●
Visa	●
Travel, medical insurance	●
Round-trip or onward airline ticket	●
Local currency	●
Traveler's checks	●
Credit cards	●
First-aid kit and medicines	●
Inoculations	●

ESSENTIAL FOR DRIVERS*

Driver's license	●
International Driving Permit	●
Car insurance (for nonrental cars)	●
Car registration (for nonrental cars)	●

*see also DRIVING section

IMPORTANT ADDRESSES

Irish Tourist Board
345 Park Avenue, New York, NY 10154
☎ (212) 418-0800, fax (212) 371-9052

Republic of Ireland Tourist Board
Baggot Street Bridge, Dublin 2, Republic of Ireland
☎ 01 602 4000, fax 01 692 035

American Embassy (Republic of Ireland)
42 Elgin Road, Ballsbridge
Dublin 4, Republic of Ireland
☎ 01 668 8777, fax 01 668 8056
American Citizens Services: Mon.–Fri. 9–3

Northern Ireland Tourist Board
551 Fifth Avenue, Suite 701, New York, NY 10176
☎ (212) 922-0101, fax (212) 922-0099

Northern Ireland Tourist Board
59 North Street, Belfast BT1 1NB, County Antrim
☎ (028) 9024 6609, fax (028) 9024 0960

American Embassy (Northern Ireland)
Queen's House, 14 Queen Street
Belfast BT1 6EQ, Northern Ireland
☎ (028) 9032 8239

COUNTRY ESSENTIALS...

CUSTOMS

YES
Duty-free limits on goods brought in from non-European Union countries:
200 cigarettes or 50 cigarillos/cigars or 250 g. tobacco; 2 L. wine; 1 L. alcohol over 22% volume or 2 L. alcohol under 22% volume; 60 ml. perfume; 250 ml. toilet water; plus any other duty-free goods (including gifts) to the value of £142. There is no limit on the importation of tax-paid goods purchased within the European Union, provided they are for your own personal use. There are no currency regulations.

NO
No unlicensed drugs, weapons, ammunition, obscene material, pets or other animals, counterfeit money or copied goods, meat or poultry.

For customs limits for returning U.S. citizens see page 16.

MONEY

The Republic of Ireland's currency is the Irish pound or punt (£), which is divided into 100 pence (p). The denominations of pound bills are 5, 10, 20 and 50. There are coins of 1, 2, 5, 10, 20 and 50p and £1. Credit cards are accepted in hotels, large stores and upscale restaurants; check first in small or rural establishments. Exchange dollars or traveler's checks at a bank, exchange office, post office or a large hotel. On Jan.1, 1999, the euro became the official currency of Ireland and the pound became a denomination of the euro. Irish currency continues to be legal tender during a transitional period. Euro bills and coins are likely to be introduced by Jan. 2002.
Exchange rate at press time: $1 = £0.80.
For information about currency in Northern Ireland, see page 470.

TIPS AND GRATUITIES

Restaurants (if service is not included)	10–15%
Cafés/bars (if service is not included)	10%
Taxis	10%
Porters	50p per bag
Hairdressers	50p–£1
Tour guides	50p–£1
Cloakroom attendants	50p

COMMUNICATIONS

POST OFFICES

Buy stamps at post offices, newsstands/tobacconists, large grocery stores and hotels.

Hours for out-of-town post offices may vary. Mailboxes are green in the Republic of Ireland and red in Northern Ireland.

TELEPHONES

Public phone booths are blue and cream, and take cash (10p, 20p, 50p or £1 coins) or prepaid phone cards bought from newsstands, post offices and local stores. Some city phones take credit cards.

For calls made to or from Northern Ireland, follow the instructions for Britain on page 471.

Phoning inside Ireland
All Irish phone numbers in this book include the area code; dial the number listed.

To call the operator dial 1190.

Phoning Ireland from abroad
The country code for Ireland is 353. Note that Irish numbers in this book do not include the country code; you will need to prefix this if you are phoning from another country. To phone Ireland from the United States or Canada, omit the first zero from the Irish number, and add the prefix 011 353. (Note that the number of digits in Irish area codes varies.)
Example: 01 122 3344 becomes 011 353 1 122 3344.

Phoning from Ireland
To phone the United States or Canada from Ireland, prefix the area code and number with 001.
Example: (111) 222-3333 becomes 001 111 222-3333.

To call international information dial 1197.

EMERGENCY TELEPHONE NUMBERS
Police *(gardaí)*	999
Fire	999
Ambulance	999
Emergency calls are free from phone booths.

HOURS OF OPERATION

- ● Stores Mon.–Sat.
- ● Offices Mon.–Fri.
- ● Banks Mon.–Fri.
- ● Post offices Mon.–Sat.
- ● Museums/monuments
- ● Pharmacies Mon.–Sat.

| 7 | 8 | 9 | 10 | 11 | 12 | 1 | 2 | 3 | 4 | 5 | 6 | 7 |

In addition to the times shown above, some stores stay open until 8 or 9 for late-night shopping on Thursday or Friday.

In smaller towns and rural areas stores close in the afternoon on one day of the week.

Some banks in small towns close 12:30–1:30. Nearly all banks are closed on Saturday, and post offices close at 1 p.m.

Hours for museums and tourist sights vary and are subject to change; always check with the local tourist office. Many places close from October to March or have very limited opening times, although most major sights are open all year.

Pharmacies may close earlier on Saturday.

NATIONAL HOLIDAYS

Banks, businesses and most stores close on these days. Museums also may have restricted hours.

Jan. 1	**New Year's Day**
Mar. 17	**St. Patrick's Day**
Mar./Apr.	**Good Friday**
Mar./Apr.	**Easter Monday**
1st Mon. of May	**May Day Holiday**
1st Mon. of Jun.	**June Holiday**
1st Mon. of Aug.	**August Holiday**
Last Mon. of Oct.	**October Holiday**
Dec. 25	**Christmas Day**
Dec. 26	**St. Stephen's Day**

PHOTOGRAPHY

Irish skies are unpredictable, and the light frequently poor, so you may need fast film. However, the landscapes are justifiably a photographer's favorite, so you may wish to bring a tripod; the rugged nature of the island also lends itself to black and white work. Film and camera batteries are widely available in many stores and drugstores.

Ireland – Essential Information

Ireland – Essential Information

HEALTH

MEDICAL INSURANCE
Private medical insurance is recommended. U.S. and Canadian visitors can receive treatment in emergency rooms, but are charged if admitted to a hospital bed. A general practitioner also will charge for services.

DENTAL SERVICES
Dentists charge for treatment. Dental work is expensive, so check to see if it is covered by your medical insurance. Dentists are listed in the yellow pages, or ask at your embassy, hotel or at a tourist office.

SUN ADVICE
The sunniest months are May and June, with 5–6½ hours of sun a day (the extreme southwest is the sunniest). July and August are the warmest. During these months you should take sensible precautions against the sun.

DRUGS
Pharmacies (also called chemists) sell a range of prescription and non-prescription medicines. If you need medicine outside regular hours, information about the nearest 24-hour facility should be posted on the door of all pharmacies.

SAFE WATER
Tap water is safe to drink throughout Ireland. If, however, you prefer mineral water you will find it widely available.

RESTROOMS

Identify restrooms by *Fir* (men) and *Mná* (women). A small charge is levied in restrooms at some railroad stations, but most other facilities are free. The standards of hygiene are moderate. You will be welcomed into any local pub if you need to use their facilities, but stop for a drink and a talk while you are there.

ELECTRICITY

Ireland has a 220-volt power supply. Electrical sockets either take plugs with two round pins or three square pins; American appliances will need a plug adapter and will require a transformer if they do not have a dual-voltage facility.

NATIONAL TRANSPORTATION

TRAIN
Ireland's rail company is Iarnród Éireann (IÉ). Trains are the fastest way of covering long distances and are generally reliable and comfortable, but the network is limited and one-way tickets cost almost as much as round-trip tickets. Midweek is less expensive than weekends, and there are many special offers on fares. For more information ☎ 01 703 2358.

BUS
Bus Éireann operates a network of express bus routes serving most of the country (some run summer only). For information ☎ 01 836 6111.

FERRY
A car ferry runs between Ballyhack (County Wexford) and Passage East (County Waterford); ☎ 051 382 480. Another serves Killimer (County Clare) and Tarbert (County Kerry), saving 60 miles on the road trip; phone 065 53124. There also are ferries to several islands; ask for details at a local tourist office. There are regular ferries from Belfast and Dublin to ports on the mainland of Britain.

DRIVING

DRIVE ON THE LEFT

SPEED LIMITS
Traffic police can impose on-the-spot fines.

Limited-access highways *(motorways)*
113 k.p.h. (70 m.p.h.)

Main roads
88 k.p.h. (55 m.p.h.)

Urban areas
48 k.p.h. (30 m.p.h.)

SEAT BELTS
Must be worn in front seats at all times and in the rear seats where fitted.

BLOOD ALCOHOL
The legal blood alcohol limit is 0.08%. Random breath tests on drivers are carried out frequently, especially late at night, and the penalties for offenders are severe.

DRIVING continued

TOLLS
There are no highway tolls.

CAR RENTAL
The leading rental firms have offices at airports, railroad stations and large ferry terminals. Hertz offers discounted rates for AAA members (see page 15). For reservations:

	UNITED STATES	IRELAND
Alamo	(800) 327-9633	01 844 4086
Avis	(800) 331-2112	01 605 7500
Budget	(800) 527-0700	01 844 5150
Hertz	(800) 654-3080	01 844 5466

FUEL
Gas is unleaded and sold in liters; diesel also is easily purchased. Gas stations in villages stay open until 8 or 9 p.m. and usually open after Mass on Sunday.

AAA AFFILIATED MOTORING CLUB
The Automobile Association Ireland
23 Rock Hill, Blackrock, County Dublin
☎ 01 283 3555, fax 01 283 3660
If you break down while driving, phone 0800 66 77 88 (AAI breakdown service).
Not all automobile clubs offer full services to AAA members.
Northern Ireland: see BRITAIN section (page 473).

BREAKDOWNS AND ACCIDENTS
There are 24-hour emergency phones at regular intervals on highways: phone 999.

Most car rental firms provide their own free rescue service; if your car is rented, follow the instructions given in the documentation. Use of a car repair service other than those authorized by your rental company may violate your agreement.

OTHER INFORMATION
The minimum age for driving a car is 17 (may be higher for some car rental firms).

An International Driving Permit (IDP) is recommended; some rental firms require it, and it can speed up formalities if you are involved in an accident.

A Green Card (international motor insurance certificate) is recommended if you are driving a private car; see page 15 for more information.

Road signs are marked in kilometers, but you may still come across old direction signs in miles.

In some urban areas, parking is limited to certain times and periods. Where this is signed you must buy a disk from a newsstand and display it on the dashboard of your car.

USEFUL WORDS AND PHRASES

Although the Republic of Ireland is officially bilingual, and the Irish language (Gaelic or *Gaeilge*) is learned by all schoolchildren, English is more commonly spoken. There are around 80,000 native speakers of Irish, making it Europe's least widespread official language.

Because it often reflects expressions in Gaelic, Irish English is famed for its picturesque turns of phrase, much more poetic than American or British English.

The Gaelic language is enjoying a revival: Radio, television and the Internet all stir up interest in the old language. There are Gaelic-speaking clubs as far away as the U.S. West Coast.

You are not likely to pick up very much Irish on a brief trip to Ireland; it is not related to English, and to an English speaker the spelling does not appear to reflect the pronunciation.

Following are pronunciations of words you may come across:

Bord Fáilte (Irish Tourist Board)	bord fawlty
Ceilidh (traditional dance night)	kaylee
Gaeilge (the Irish language)	gale-geh
Gaeltacht (Irish-speaking country)	gale-tackt
Garda (police)	gawrdah
Fleadh (traditional music evening)	flah
Taoiseach (prime minister)	teeschock

Numbers:
1	a haon	a hay-on
2	a dó	a doe
3	a trí	a tree
4	a ceathair	a ca-hir
5	a cuíg	a koo-ig
6	a sé	a shay
7	a seacht	a shocked
8	a hocht	a huct
9	a naoi	a neigh
10	a deich	a de

Other words:
good day	*lá maith*	law mah
goodbye	*slán*	slawn
goodnight	*oíche mhaith*	ee-ha vah
How are you?	*Conas taio?*	co-nus tee?
please	*más é do thoil é*	maws eh duh hull eh
thanks	*gura maith agat*	gurrah mah a-gut
pub	*tábhairne*	taw-er nay
water	*uisce*	ishkek
whiskey	*fuisci*	fwishgee
yes	*sea*	shah

Ireland – Essential Information

Italy – Essential Information

PRE-TRIP ESSENTIALS...

WHAT YOU NEED

ESSENTIAL FOR TRAVELERS

● Required ● Recommended ● Not required

Passport	●
Visa	●
Travel, medical insurance	●
Round-trip or onward airline ticket	●
Local currency	●
Traveler's checks	●
Credit cards	●
First-aid kit and medicines	●
Health innoculations	●

ESSENTIAL FOR DRIVERS*

Driver's license	●
International Driving Permit	●
Car insurance (for private cars)	●
Car registration (for private cars)	●

*see also DRIVING section

IMPORTANT ADDRESSES

Italian Government Tourist Office
630 Fifth Avenue
Suite 1565
New York, NY 10111
☎ (212) 245-4822
Fax (212) 586-9249

Italian State Tourist Authority
Via Marghera 2
00185 Rome, Italy
☎ 06 49711
Fax 06 446 3379

American Embassy
Via Vittorio Veneto 119a
00187 Rome, Italy
☎ 06 46741
Fax 06 488 2672
Open Mon.– Fri. 8:30–12:30 and 2–4

COUNTRY ESSENTIALS...

CUSTOMS

YES
Goods brought into Italy from non-European Union countries limited to:
200 cigarettes or 100 cigarillos or 50 cigars or 250 g. tobacco; 2 L wine; 1 L. alcohol over 22% volume; 2 L. alcohol under 22% volume; 60 ml. perfume; 250 ml. toilet water; plus any other duty-free goods (including gifts) to the value of L30,000. There is no limit on the importation of tax-paid goods purchased within the European Union, provided they are for your own personal use. There are no currency regulations.

NO
No unlicensed drugs, weapons, ammunition, obscene material, pets or other animals, counterfeit money or copied goods, meat or poultry.

For customs limits for returning U.S. citizens see page 16.

MONEY

Italy's currency is the lira (L or Lit; plural lire). The denominations of lira bills are 1,000, 2,000, 5,000, 10,000, 50,000, 100,000 and 500,000. There are coins of 50, 100, 200, 500 and L1,000. Exchange dollars or traveler's checks *(assegni touristici)* at a bank *(banca)* or exchange office *(ufficio di cambio)*. Hotels may exchange traveler's checks, but stores do not. ATMs *(sportello automatico)* are fairly common and accept major credit cards. On Jan. 1, 1999, the euro became the official currency of Italy and the Italian lira became a denomination of the euro. Lira notes and coins continue to be legal tender during a transitional period. Euro bills and coins are likely to be introduced by Jan. 2002. Exchange rate at press time: $1 = 2,000.

TIPS AND GRATUITIES

Restaurants (where service is not included)	10–15%
Cafés/bars	L200
Taxis	15%
Porters	L2,000
Chambermaids	L3,000 weekly
Restrooms	L100 minimum
Cloakroom attendants	L1,000

TIME ZONES

ROME	NEW YORK	CHICAGO	DENVER	SAN FRANCISCO
12:00 noon	6 hours behind Italy	7 hours behind Italy	8 hours behind Italy	9 hours behind Italy

507

Italy – Essential Information

COMMUNICATIONS

POST OFFICES

Buy stamps *(francobolli)* at a post office *(ufficio postale)* or at a tobacconist *(tabaccaio)*. Mailboxes

often have two slots, one for local mail *(città)*, the other for out-of-town mail *(altre destinazione)*. Mail sent to and from Italy can take up to 3 weeks; to speed delivery send it express *(espresso)* or registered *(raccomandata)*.

TELEPHONES

Pay phones are usually found in bars and other public places. Coin-operated phones take L100, L200 and L500 coins. Prepaid cards *(schede telefoniche)* for card-operated phones are available in values of L5,000, L10,000 and L15,000 from tobacconists, bars, post offices, newsstands, railroad stations and dispensers showing a Telecom Italia (TI) logo.

When making international calls use a prepaid card, tear the corner off before using it. Calls from hotel rooms always incur a surcharge.

Phoning inside Italy
All telephone numbers in Italy include an area code that must always be dialed.

To call the operator dial 10.

Phoning Italy from abroad
The country code for Italy is 39. Note that Italian numbers in this book do not include the country code; you will need to prefix this number if you are phoning from another country. To call Italy from the United States or Canada dial the prefix 011 39. Include the first zero of the regional code. There is no standard number of digits in Italian numbers. Example: 01 122 3344 becomes 011 39 01 122 3344.

Phoning from Italy
To phone the United States or Canada from Italy, prefix the area code and number with 001. Example: (111) 222-3333 becomes 001 111 222-3333.

To call international information dial 170.

EMERGENCY TELEPHONE NUMBERS
Police *(policia)*   113 (local), 112 (national)
Fire service *(pompieri)*   115
Ambulance *(ambulanza)*   113
Emergency calls are free from phone booths.

HOURS OF OPERATION

● Stores Mon.–Sat.   ● Museums/monuments
● Offices Mon.–Fri.   ● Architectural sites
● Banks Mon.–Fri.   ● Churches/pharmacies
● Post offices Mon.–Fri.

| | 7 | 8 | 9 | 10 | 11 | 12 | 1 | 2 | 3 | 4 | 5 | 6 | 7 |

Department stores, some grocery stores and stores in tourist areas may not close at lunchtime, and sometimes stay open until later in the evening. Some stores close on Monday morning and may close on Saturday afternoon in summer; most stores close on Sunday.

Some banks close at 2 and do not reopen later in the afternoon.

Many museums are open in the afternoon (usually 5–7), others are open all day, and a few stay open late into the evening. Many museums close early on Sunday (around 1), and most are closed Monday.

Post office times may vary slightly, and they may be open Saturday 8–11:45.

NATIONAL HOLIDAYS

Banks, businesses, and most stores and museums close on these days. Most cities, towns and villages celebrate their patron saint's day, but generally most establishments remain open.

Jan. 1	New Year's Day
Jan. 6	Epiphany
Mar./Apr.	Easter Monday
Apr. 25	Liberation Day 1945
May 1	Labor Day
Aug. 15	Assumption of the Virgin
Nov. 1	All Saints' Day
Dec. 8	Immaculate Conception
Dec. 25	Christmas Day
Dec. 26	St. Stephen's Day

PHOTOGRAPHY

The light in Italy is usually very good, so you will probably be using film with a low ASA rating. Avoid taking shots around noon, when the shadows are harsh. Photography is banned in most museums and churches, but you may be allowed to shoot without a flash. Film *(pellicola)* and developing *(sviluppo)* are expensive, especially near popular tourist sights.

EMERGENCY PHONE NUMBERS

POLICE *(Polizia)*   113 (local)
                         112 (national)

Italy – Essential Information

HEALTH

MEDICAL INSURANCE
Private medical insurance is strongly recommended. Visitors from non-European Union countries can receive treatment in a hospital accident and emergency room, but you will be charged if you are admitted to a bed. A general practitioner *(medico)* can deal with less urgent cases, but also will charge.

DENTAL SERVICES
Emergency dental treatment is available from English-speaking dentists listed in the yellow pages *(pagine gialle)*. A fee will be charged, so check that you are covered for treatment on your private medical insurance.

SUN ADVICE
In summer, particularly in July and August, it can be oppressively hot and humid in cities. On sunny days cover head and shoulders and use a sunscreen. Cathedrals and other stone buildings can be refreshingly cool. Take frequent breaks in the shade and drink plenty of fluids.

DRUGS
A pharmacy *(farmacia)* displays a green cross symbol and has staff who can provide prescription medicines and offer advice on minor ailments. Information about the address of the nearest 24-hour facility is normally posted at every pharmacy.

SAFE WATER
In isolated rural areas it is not advisable to drink tap water. However, across most of the country tap water is perfectly safe, although most Italians prefer to drink bottled mineral water *(acqua minerale)*, which is inexpensive and widely available.

RESTROOMS

Finding a restroom *(gabinetto/bagno/ toletta)* can be difficult away from airports, rail and bus stations, highway service areas and museums. Leave a small tip (about L100) for the attendant. If using the facilities in a bar you will be expected to buy a drink. Some bars have separate restrooms for men *(signori)* and women *(signore)*.

ELECTRICITY

Italy has a 220-volt power supply (in some areas, 125 volts). Electrical sockets take plugs with two round pins or sometimes three pins in a vertical row. American appliances will need a plug adapter and will require a transformer if they do not have a dual-voltage facility.

NATIONAL TRANSPORTATION

TRAIN *(treno)*
Italian State Railways *(Ferrovie dello Stato*, or *FS)* provide an efficient range of services. Regionale, Diretto and Espresso trains are slow for long journeys; InterCity trains, which do not make stops at each station *(stazione)*, cost more but are faster; the Pendolino is the fastest and most expensive.

BUS *(autobus)*
There is no national bus company, but each major city has its own company for short-, medium- and some long-distance bus travel. International Eurolines buses run from the main Italian cities; ☎ 055 215 5151.

FERRY *(tragheto)*
Genoa and Naples are the main Mediterranean ports, with regular services to Sicily and Sardinia. Naples also has services to Capri and other islands. Many services are reduced off-season, and some are cut altogether. Reserve well in advance for car ferries.

DRIVING

DRIVE ON THE RIGHT

SPEED LIMITS
Police can demand up to a quarter of an imposed fine to be paid on the spot.

Limited-access highways *(autostrada)*
130 k.p.h. (80 m.p.h.)

Main roads
110 k.p.h. (68 m.p.h.)

Urban areas
50 k.p.h (31 m.p.h.)

SEAT BELTS
Must be worn in front seats at all times and in back seats where fitted.

BLOOD ALCOHOL
The legal blood alcohol limit is 0.08%. Random breath tests are carried out frequently, especially late at night.

Italy – Essential Information

DRIVING continued

TOLLS
You will be issued a ticket on entering nearly every limited-access highway *(autostrada)*: pay on leaving. You can buy prepaid cards at tollbooths, service areas, tourist offices and tobacconists.

CAR RENTAL
The leading rental firms have offices at airports, railroad stations and ferry terminals. Hertz offers discounted rates for AAA members. Also see page 15 for general information about renting a car in Europe. For reservations:

	UNITED STATES	ITALY
Avis	(800) 331-2112	02 715 123
Budget	(800) 527-0700	06 2293 5620
Dollar	(800) 252-897	055 318 609
Hertz	(800) 654-3080	055 307 370

FUEL
Gas is unleaded *(senza piombo)* and sold in liters. Outside urban areas, stations open daily 7–12:30 and 3–7:30. Highway services are open 24 hours. Credit cards are not widely accepted away from highways.

AAA AFFILIATED MOTORING CLUB
Automobile Club D'Italia (ACI),
Via Marsala 8, 00185 Rome
☎ 06 49 981, fax 06 445 2702
If you break down while driving, phone 116 (ACI breakdown service).
Not all automobile clubs offer full services to AAA members.

BREAKDOWNS AND ACCIDENTS
There are emergency phones at regular intervals on all highways. If you are involved in an accident,
☎ 118 for emergency medical help, 112 or 113 for police help.
Most car rental firms provide their own free rescue service; if your car is rented, follow the instructions given in the documentation. Use of a car repair service other than those authorized by your rental company may violate your agreement.

OTHER INFORMATION
The minimum age for driving a car is 18 (may be higher for some car rental firms).

An International Driving Permit (IDP) is recommended; some rental firms require it, and it can speed up formalities if you are involved in an accident. A Green Card (international motor insurance certificate) is recommended if you are driving a private car; see page 15 for more information.

Dimmed headlights are required by law when passing through tunnels, even if they are well lit.

USEFUL WORDS AND PHRASES

Italian pronunciation is consistent with spelling, and vowels are always pronounced. The letter *h* is always silent, but can modify the sound of letters *c* and *g*. As a general rule, accentuate the next-to-last syllable.

c is hard before a, o, u, h	*medico; Chianti*
c is soft before i or e	*ciao* [chow]
g is hard before a, o, u, h	*Gucci, Lamborghini*
g is soft before i or e	*gelati* [jel-ah-tee]
gl as in Amelia	*figlia* [fee-lyah]
gn as in union	*gnocchi* [nyee-ok-kee]
sc before i or e is soft	*prosciutto* [pro-shoot-toh]

Where two consonants appear together, each belongs to a different syllable.

Do you speak English?	*Parla inglese?*
excuse me	*mi scusi*
goodbye	*arrivederci*
hello	*buongiorno*
How much is...?	*Quanto costa...?*
I am American	*sono Americano/-a*
I'd like...	*vorrei...*
I don't understand	*non capisco*
non-smoking	*per non fumatori*
okay	*va bene*
open/closed	*aperto/chiuso*
please/thank you	*per favore/grazie*
ticket (one-way/round trip)	*biglietto (andata sola/andata ritorno)*
where is...?	*dov'è...?*
yes/no	*sì/no*
you're welcome	*prego*
the hotel	***l'albergo***
breakfast	*prima colazione*
I have a reservation	*ho prenotato*
key	*una chiave*
for one/two nights	*per una/due notte/-i*
one/two people	*una/due persona/-e*
room	*una camera*
shower	*una doccia*
with en-suite bathroom	*con bagno privato*
the restaurant	***il ristorante***
starter	*l'antipasto*
entrée	*il secondo*
beef	*il manzo*
bread	*il pane*
chicken	*il pollo*
coffee	*il caffè*
dish of the day	*il piatto del giorno*
seafood	*i frutti di mare*
fish	*il pesce*
lamb	*l'agnello*
pork	*il maiale*
wine	*il vino*
dessert	*il dolce*
the check	*il conto*

Luxembourg – Essential Information

PRE-TRIP ESSENTIALS...

WHAT YOU NEED

ESSENTIAL FOR TRAVELERS

● Required   ● Recommended   ● Not required

Passport	●
Visa	●
Travel, medical insurance	●
Round-trip or onward airline ticket	●
Local currency	●
Traveler's checks	●
Credit cards	●
First-aid kit and medicines	●
Inoculations	●

ESSENTIAL FOR DRIVERS*

Driver's license	●
International Driving Permit	●
Car insurance (for nonrental cars)	●
Car registration (for nonrental cars)	●

*see also DRIVING section

IMPORTANT ADDRESSES

Luxembourg National Tourist Office
17 Beekman Place
New York, NY 10022
☎ (212) 935-8888
Fax (212) 935-5896

Luxembourg National Tourist Office
B.P. 1001, 1010 Luxembourg
☎ 42 82 82
Fax 42 82 30

American Embassy
Chancellerie 22, Boulevard Emmanuel Servais
2535 Luxembourg
☎ 46 01 23
Fax 46 14 01
Inquiries: Mon.–Tue. and Thu.–Fri. 8:30–11:30

COUNTRY ESSENTIALS...

CUSTOMS

YES
Duty-free limits on goods brought in from non-European Union countries:
200 cigarettes or 100 cigarillos or 50 cigars or 250 g. tobacco; 15 L. beer; 2L. wine; 1 L. alcohol over 22% volume; 2 L. alcohol under 22% volume; 50 ml. perfume; 250 ml. toilet water; plus any other duty-free goods (including gifts) to the value of 7,300F. There is no limit on the importation of tax-paid goods purchased within the European Union, provided they are for your own personal use. There are no currency regulations for francs, but there is a limit of $10,000 in cash or traveler's checks entering or leaving Luxembourg.

NO
No unlicensed drugs, weapons, ammunition, obscene material, pets or other animals, counterfeit money or copied goods, meat or poultry.

For customs limits for returning U.S. citizens see page 16.

MONEY

Luxembourg's currency is the franc (F or Flux), which is divided into 100 centimes. The denominations of franc bills are 100, 500, 1,000, 5,000 and 10,000. There are coins of 50 centimes (rarely seen) and 1, 5, 20 and 50F. Belgian francs have the same value and can be used in Luxembourg, but the Luxembourg franc cannot be used in Belgium. Exchange dollars and traveler's checks *(cheques de voyage)* at a bank *(banque)* or an exchange office *(bureau de change)*. On Jan. 1, 1999, the euro became the official currency in Luxembourg and the franc became a denomination of the euro. Luxembourg franc bills and coins continue to be legal tender during a transitional period. Euro bills and coins are likely to be introduced by Jan. 2002.
Exchange rate at press time: $1 = 40F

TIPS AND GRATUITIES

Restaurants, cafés and bars (service usually included) round up to nearest 50 or 100F	
Taxis	100–200F
Porters, Chambermaids	50–100F
Hairdressers	100F
Restroom attendants	10F
Cloakroom attendants	20F per coat

TIME ZONES

LUXEMBOURG	NEW YORK	CHICAGO	DENVER	SAN FRANCISCO
12:00 noon	6 hours behind Luxembourg	7 hours behind Luxembourg	8 hours behind Luxembourg	9 hours behind Luxembourg

511

Luxembourg – Essential Information

COMMUNICATIONS

POST OFFICES

Buy stamps *(timbres-poste)* at a post office *(poste)*, newsstand/tobacconist *(tabac-journaux)*, or at a bookstore.

Mailboxes are small, bright and yellow, and are attached to walls and post offices. Hours for out-of-town post offices may vary.

TELEPHONES

Finding a public telephone *(cabine téléphonique)* is easy. Phone booths usually have pictorial instructions, with French and German text. You can use most denominations of coins, or buy a prepaid phone card *(télécarte)* from a post office or railroad station. Public phones in restaurants are more expensive than those in post offices or on the street.

Phoning inside Luxembourg
There are no area codes in Luxembourg; dial the number that is listed.

To call the operator dial 017.

Phoning Luxembourg from abroad
The country code for Luxembourg is 352. Note that Luxembourg numbers in this book do not include the country code; you will need to prefix this number if you are phoning from another country. To phone Luxembourg from the United States or Canada, add the prefix 011 352.
Example: 11 22 33 becomes 011 352 11 22 33.

Phoning from Luxembourg
To phone the United States or Canada from Luxembourg, prefix the area code and number with 001.
Example: (111) 222-3333 becomes 001 111 222-3333.

EMERGENCY TELEPHONE NUMBERS
Police *(police)*	112
Fire *(pompiers)*	112
Ambulance *(ambulance)*	112

Emergency calls are free from phone booths.

HOURS OF OPERATION

- ● Stores Tue.–Sat.
- ● Pharmacies Tue.–Sat.
- ● Offices Mon.–Fri.
- ● Banks Mon.–Fri.
- ● Post offices Mon.–Fri.

7 8 9 10 11 12 1 2 3 4 5 6 7

Many stores and pharmacies do not open until 1 or 2 on Monday afternoon, and most are closed on Sunday. Many establishments have long lunch breaks.

Provincial post offices and banks may have shorter hours, but some city post offices and banks stay open into the evening.

Opening times for museums and monuments vary, and they are frequently closed on Monday or Tuesday – check with the local tourist office.

NATIONAL HOLIDAYS

Banks, businesses and most stores close on these days.

Jan. 1	New Year's Day
Feb./Mar.	Carnival Day
Mar./Apr.	Easter Monday
May 1	Labor Day
May	Ascension Day
May/Jun.	Pentecost Monday
Jun. 23	National Day
Aug. 15	Assumption of the Virgin
Nov. 1	All Saints' Day
Dec. 25	Christmas Day
Dec. 26	St. Stephen's Day

PHOTOGRAPHY

Luxembourg enjoys a temperate climate, and the light is good. Check that photography is permitted before taking pictures in museums. Film and camera batteries are readily available from tourist stores, and rapid-developing services are widely available.

EMERGENCY PHONE NUMBERS

POLICE 112 *(Police)*

Luxembourg – Essential Information

HEALTH

MEDICAL INSURANCE
Private medical insurance is recommended; U.S. and Canadian visitors can be treated in emergency rooms, but are charged if admitted to a hospital *(hôpital)*. ☎ 112 for 24-hour information on hospitals and English-speaking doctors.

DENTAL SERVICES
A dentist *(dentiste)* will charge a fee for treatment, so check whether this is covered by your medical insurance. Emergency clinics are available in city hospitals. To find a dentist look in the yellow pages *(pages jaunes)* or ask at your hotel.

SUN ADVICE
You will not experience extremes of climate in Luxembourg, but the sunshine during summer months can burn, so good sun protection is essential.

DRUGS
Prescription medicines and advice can be obtained from a pharmacy *(pharmacie)*, identified by a green cross. Information about the nearest 24-hour facility is posted at all pharmacies, or ☎ 112 for information.

SAFE WATER
Tap water is safe to drink, and bottled mineral water *(eau minérale)* is widely available.

RESTROOMS

Restrooms *(toilettes)* are usually clean, modern and easy to find. They may also be called *"WC"* (pronounced vay-say). Coin-operated facilities take 5F coins; those with an attendant usually charge 10F.

ELECTRICITY

Luxembourg has a 220-volt power supply. Electrical sockets take plugs with two round pins; American appliances will need a plug adapter and will require a transformer if they do not have a dual-voltage facility.

NATIONAL TRANSPORTATION

TRAIN *(train)*
The national rail company is Chemins de Fer Luxembourgeois (CFL). The network is limited, and because of the small size of the country most services run through the city of Luxembourg. Most CFL trains are comfortable, but standards can vary. Bus and train network cards are a good value and valid until 8 p.m. the following day. For information, call ☎ 49 90 49 90.

BUS *(bus)*
Long-distance, CFL-operated buses complement the rail network (phone 22 03 07 07). The Eurolines international bus network serves Brussels; from there you must catch a train to Luxembourg.

RIVER BOAT *(bateau-mouche)*
There are many excursions exploring Luxembourg's magnificent Moselle river, which stretches the entire eastern length of the country. For details, contact the regional tourist office Entente des Communes et des Syndicats d'Initiative de la Moselle Luxembourgeoise, 32 route de Thionville, 6701 Grevenmacher; ☎ 75 82 75.

DRIVING

DRIVE ON THE RIGHT

SPEED LIMITS
Police impose minor on-the-spot fines, but cannot collect them.

Limited access highways *(autoroutes)*
120 k.p.h. (74 m.p.h.)
minimum speed **40 k.p.h. (24 m.p.h.)**

Main roads
100 k.p.h. (62 m.p.h.)

Urban areas
50 k.p.h. (31 m.p.h.)

SEAT BELTS
Must be worn in front seats at all times and in the rear seats where fitted. Children under 12 are not allowed to use a front seat.

BLOOD ALCOHOL
The legal blood alcohol limit is 0.08%. Random breath tests on drivers are carried out frequently, especially late at night, and the penalties for offenders are severe.

DRIVING continued

 TOLLS
There are no highway tolls in Luxembourg.

 CAR RENTAL
The leading rental firms have offices at airports and train stations. Hertz offers discounted rates for AAA members (see page 15). For reservations:

	UNITED STATES	LUXEMBOURG
Alamo	(800) 327-9633	40 42 28 (Inter-rent)
Avis	(800) 331-2112	43 51 71
Budget	(800) 527-0700	43 75 75
Hertz	(800) 654-3080	48 54 85

 FUEL
Many gas stations *(station de service)* are self-service, and 24-hour facilities are common. Stations on highways often have café facilities. The price of gas is fixed by the government, but self-service stations often offer discounts. Major credit cards are accepted.

 MOTORING CLUB
Automobile Club du Grand-Duché de Luxembourg (ACL)
54 route de Longwy, 8007 Betrange,
☎ 45 00 451, fax 45 04 55
If you break down while driving, phone 45 00 451 (ACL breakdown service).
(Note: This club is not affiliated with AAA.)

 BREAKDOWNS AND ACCIDENTS
There are emegency phones at regular intervals on highways. If you are involved in an accident, phone 112 for emergency assistance.
Most car rental firms provide their own free rescue service; if your car is rented, follow the instructions given in the documentation. Use of a car repair service other than those authorized by your rental company may violate your agreement.

OTHER INFORMATION

The minimum age for driving a car is 17 (may be higher for some car rental firms).

An International Driving Permit (IDP) is recommended; some rental firms require them, and they can speed up formalities if you are involved in an accident.

A Green Card (international motor insurance certificate) is recommended if you are driving a private car; see page 15 for more information.

USEFUL WORDS AND PHRASES

Because the Grand Duchy of Luxembourg is tucked between Belgium, France and Germany, Luxembourgers often slip unconsciously between different languages.

The official language (and, unofficially, the language of the elite) is French, but German is used for many situations. In addition to this, there is a third, everyday language: Lëtzebuergesch, a symbol of both national identity and Luxembourg's ability to assimilate other cultures.

The roots of Luxembourg's own language are Germanic, but it has evolved into a dialect that Germans no longer understand. The use of Lëtzebuergesch is primarily an oral tradition. It was only in 1984 that its spelling was decreed by law; up until then Luxembourgers spelled words more or less as they pleased.

French, German and Lëtzebuergesch are taught in schools, and English is also widely spoken, especially among the young and those working in the tourist trade. Don't expect Luxembourgers in rural areas to have mastered a fourth language, however!

Lëtzebuergesch is resilient enough to exist side-by-side with such widely spoken languages as French and German; but as the patois of a tiny, landlocked duchy it's evidently not very exportable. So if you have the opportunity to speak a word or two of this country's uniting language you'll raise a smile and a welcome.

good morning/hello	*moien*
goodbye	*addi*
thank you (very much)	*merci (villmols)*
sorry	*pardon*
excuse me	*entschellest*
please	*wanneschglift*
I don't understand	*ech verstin*

Food and drink

coffee	*Kaffi*
green bean soup	*Bou'neschlupp*
nettle soup	*Brennesselszopp*
potato soup	*Gromperenzopp*
potato dumplings	*Gromperekniddeln*
trout in Riesling sauce	*F'rell am Rèisleck*
pike in green liquor	*Hiecht mat Kraïderzooss*
crayfish	*Kriibsen*
blood sausage	*Trèipen*
pork in aspic	*Jhelli*
chicken in Riesling sauce	*Hong am Rèisleck*
tripe	*Kuddelfleck*
cheesecake	*Kéiskuch*
apple cake	*Äppelkuch*

For useful phrases in French, see page 489; for phrases in German see page 493.

Luxembourg – Essential Information

Netherlands – Essential Information

PRE-TRIP ESSENTIALS...

WHAT YOU NEED

ESSENTIAL FOR TRAVELERS

● Required   ● Recommended   ● Not required

Passport	●
Visa	●
Travel, medical insurance	●
Round-trip or onward airline ticket	●
Local currency	●
Traveler's checks	●
Credit cards	●
First-aid kit and medicines	●
Inoculations	●

ESSENTIAL FOR DRIVERS*

Driver's license	●
International Driving Permit	●
Car insurance (for nonrental cars)	●
Car registration (for nonrental cars)	●

*see also DRIVING section

IMPORTANT ADDRESSES

Netherlands Board of Tourism
355 Lexington Avenue
New York, NY 10017
☎ (212) 370-7360
Fax (212) 370-9507

Amsterdam Tourist Board
P.O. Box 3901
1001 AS, Amsterdam
Netherlands
☎ 020 551 2512
Fax 020 6252 869

American Embassy
Lange Voorhout 102
2514 EJ, The Hague
Netherlands
☎ 070 310 9209
Fax 070 361 4688
Personal callers should phone for an appointment.

COUNTRY ESSENTIALS...

CUSTOMS

YES
Duty-free limits on goods brought in from non-European Union countries: 200 cigarettes or 100 cigarillos or 50 cigars or 250 g. tobacco; 2 L. wine; 1 L. alcohol over 22% volume; 2 L. alcohol under 22% volume; 50 ml. perfume; 250 ml. toilet water; plus any other duty-free goods (including gifts) to the value of 225f. There is no limit on the importation of tax-paid goods purchased within the European Union, provided they are for your own personal use. There are no currency regulations.

NO
No unlicensed drugs, weapons, ammunition, obscene material, pets or other animals, counterfeit money or copied goods, meat or poultry.

For customs limits for returning U.S. citizens see page 16.

MONEY

The Dutch currency is the guilder, or florin (variously denoted as f, FL or G), which is divided into 100 cents (c). The denominations of guilder bills are 10, 25, 50, 100, 250 and 1,000. There are coins of 5, 10 and 25c and 1, 1.50 and 5f. You can change dollars and traveler's checks *(reischeques)* at a bank, an exchange office or the larger VVV (tourist office) bureaus. On Jan. 1, 1999, the euro became the official currency in the Netherlands and the guilder became a denomination of the euro. Guilder bills and coins continue to be legal tender during a transitional period. Euro bills and coins are likely to be introduced by Jan. 2002.
Exchange rate at press time: $1 = 2f

TIPS AND GRATUITIES

Restaurants (service is always included)	change
Cafés/bars (service is always included)	change
Taxis	change
Porters	change
Hairdressers	change
Chambermaids	change
Restroom attendants	25c
Cloakroom attendants	none

COMMUNICATIONS

POST OFFICES

Buy stamps *(postzegels)* at a post office *(postkantoor* or *PTT)*, newsstand or souvenir shop. There are stamp vending machines in post offices, but if you are buying from a counter make sure you are in a line for stamps. Mailboxes have two slots;

foreign mail should be dropped into the slot marked *Overige*. Hours for out-of-town post offices may vary.

TELEPHONES

You can use cash, credit cards and prepaid phone cards *(kaarttelephoon)* to make a call in the Netherlands. Coin-operated phones take 25c, 1f and 2.50f; cards can be bought from newsstands and tobacconists in units of 20, 40 and 100. Calls also can be made from post offices and *Telehouse* booths, where you make your call and pay afterwards; most have the same hours as post offices, although some stay open later.

Phoning inside the Netherlands
All Dutch telephone numbers in this book include an area code; dial the number listed.

To call the operator dial 118.

Phoning the Netherlands from abroad
The country code for the Netherlands is 31. Note that Dutch numbers in this book do not include the country code; you will need to prefix this number if you are phoning from another country. To phone the Netherlands from the United States or Canada, omit the first zero from the Dutch number and dial the prefix 011 31.
Example: 011 223 3445 becomes 011 31 11 223 3445.

Phoning from the Netherlands
To phone the United States or Canada, prefix the area code and number with 001.
Example: (111) 222-3333 becomes 001 111 222-3333.

To call international information dial 0900 8418.

EMERGENCY TELEPHONE NUMBERS

Police *(politie)*	112
Fire *(brandweer)*	112
Ambulance *(ziegenwagen)*	112

Emergency calls are free from phone booths.

HOURS OF OPERATION

- Stores Mon.–Sat.
- Offices Mon.–Fri.
- Banks Mon.–Fri.
- Post offices Mon.–Sat.
- Museums/monuments Tue.–Sat.
- Pharmacies Mon.–Fri.

7 8 9 10 11 12 1 2 3 4 5 6 7

Stores close at 5 on Saturday and are often closed on Monday morning. By law, all stores have to close for half of one day during the week. Larger city stores stay open until 9 p.m. on Thursday or Friday. In rural areas many stores close for lunch.

Post offices close at noon on Saturday. Out-of-town post offices and banks may have shorter hours. Some city post offices and banks stay open into the evening.

Museums usually are open 1–5 on Sunday; in rural areas they may be closed October through March.

NATIONAL HOLIDAYS

Banks, businesses and most stores close on these days.

Jan. 1	New Year's Day
Mar./Apr.	Good Friday
Mar./Apr.	Easter Monday
Apr. 30	Queen's Birthday
May 5	Liberation Day
May/Jun.	Ascension Day
May/Jun.	Pentecost Monday
Dec. 24	Christmas Eve
Dec. 25	Christmas Day
Dec. 26	St. Stephen's Day

PHOTOGRAPHY

The Dutch climate is essentially maritime; conditions for outdoor photography are gentle but changeable. Some museums do not allow photography; check before taking pictures. Film and camera batteries are readily available from stores catering to tourists; rapid-developing services also are widely available.

Netherlands – Essential Information

HEALTH

MEDICAL INSURANCE
Private medical insurance is recommended. U.S. and Canadian visitors can receive emergency treatment, but are charged if admitted to a hospital *(ziekenhuis)*. Doctors *(dokter)* are listed at the beginning of the telephone directory; English is widely spoken throughout the medical profession.

DENTAL SERVICES
Dentists charge for treatment and can be expensive. Look in the telephone directory, or ask about local dentists at your hotel or embassy, or at a tourist office.

SUN ADVICE
The Netherlands' maritime climate is not one of extremes, but precautions against sunburn should be taken from June through August.

DRUGS
For nonprescription medicines go to a pharmacy *(drogisterij)*. If you need prescription medicines you will have to go to an *apotheek*, where staff also are trained to treat minor ailments. If you need medicine outside regular hours, information about the nearest all-night facility is posted at all pharmacies.

SAFE WATER
Tap water is safe to drink throughout the Netherlands. Mineral water is widely available.

RESTROOMS

There are not many public restrooms, although you will usually find adequate and clean facilities in museums, department stores and roadside service areas. Cafés provide restrooms for the use of customers; buy a drink if you need to use them.

ELECTRICITY

The Netherlands has a 220-volt power supply. Electrical sockets take plugs with two round pins; American appliances will need a plug adapter and will require a transformer if they do not have a dual-voltage facility.

NATIONAL TRANSPORTATION

TRAIN *(trein)*
The Nederlandse Spoorwegen (NS) network is comprehensive, fast, clean, modern, punctual and reasonably inexpensive. Information is widely available from stations, usually in English.

BUS *(bus)*
Bus travel is well-organized, with many connections to trains (bus and railroad stations are usually next to each other). If you're planning several trips ask for the Nationale Buswijer, which provides maps and full route details. The Eurolines international bus network operates in the Netherlands; ☎ 020 560 8787.

FERRY *(veerboot)*
A number of ports on the English Channel connect the Netherlands with other European countries. Shop around; many ferry companies arrange one-way fares, so it is possible to leave from one port and return at another (ask a travel agent for details). Canal excursions also are a good way to explore Dutch cities and the countryside; ask at the nearest VVV tourist information office for details.

DRIVING

DRIVE ON THE RIGHT

SPEED LIMITS
Police can impose on-the-spot fines.

Limited-access highways *(autoweg)*
120 k.p.h. (74 m.p.h.)

Main roads
80 k.p.h. (49 m.p.h.)

Urban areas
50 k.p.h. (31 m.p.h.)

SEAT BELTS
Must be worn in front seats at all times and in the rear seats where fitted.

BLOOD ALCOHOL
The legal blood alcohol limit is 0.05%. Random breath tests on drivers are carried out frequently, especially late at night, and the penalties for offenders are severe.

DRIVING continued

TOLLS
There are no highway tolls in the Netherlands.

CAR RENTAL
The leading rental firms have offices at airports and train stations. Hertz offers discounted rates for AAA members (see page 15). For reservations:

	UNITED STATES	NETHERLANDS
Alamo	(800) 327-9633	020 316 4081
Avis	(800) 331-2112	020 655 6050
Budget	(800) 527-0700	020 604 1349
Hertz	(800) 654-3080	020 601 5416

FUEL
Many gas stations are self-service and 24-hour facilities are common.
Unleaded gas and diesel are available, and credit cards are accepted at most garages.

AAA AFFILIATED MOTORING CLUB
Koninklijke Nederlandse Toeristenbond (ANWB)
Wassenaarseweg 220, 2596 EC, The Hague ☎ 070 314 7147, fax 070 314 6969
If you break down while, phone 0800 0888 (ANWB breakdown service).
Not all automobile clubs offer full services to AAA members.

BREAKDOWNS AND ACCIDENTS
There are yellow 24-hour emergency phones at regular intervals on highways. All accidents involving personal injury must be reported to the police; ☎ 112.
Most car rental firms provide their own free rescue service; if your car is rented, follow the instructions given in the documentation. Use of a car repair service other than those authorized by your rental company may violate your agreement.

OTHER INFORMATION
The minimum age for driving a car is 18 (may be higher for some car rental firms).

An International Driving Permit (IDP) is recommended; some rental firms require them, and they can speed up formalities if you are involved in an accident.

A Green Card (international motor insurance certificate) is recommended if you are driving a private car; see page 15 for more information.

In built-up areas, trams and buses have the right of way when leaving bus stops. Also beware of cyclists and skaters.

USEFUL WORDS AND PHRASES

It is not easy to reproduce the guttural sounds that make up the Dutch language. There are many similarities between German and Dutch, although the Dutch go to great lengths to point out the differences.

English is spoken fluently by a large proportion of the population, who learn foreign languages from an early age.

Dutch pronunciation is similar to English, with some variations:

> *j* as in *y*ellow
> *v* like an *f* as in *f*ar
> *w* like a *v* as in *v*at
> *ng* as in bri*ng*
> *nj* as in o*ni*on

Double consonants keep their separate sounds: for instance, *k* and *n* together are never pronounced as in the English "know."

Some letters and diphthongs are tricky. If the letter is doubled, the vowel sound is lengthened. For example:

> a as in sap, aa as in art
> e as in let, ee as in fate
> o as in mop, oo as in mope
> oe as in food
> au, ou and ui as in how
> ei and ij as in line
> ch as in Bach
> tje as in church
> tie as in tee

Do you speak English?	*Spreekt u Engels?*
excuse me	*pardon*
hello	*hallo* or *dag*
goodbye	*tot ziens*
yes/no	*ja/nee*
how much is?	*wat kost?*
I want...	*ik wil...*
I don't understand	*Ik begrijp het niet*
open/closed	*open/gesloten*
please	*alstublieft*
thank you	*bedankt*
ticket (one-way/ round trip)	*enkele reis retour*
where's the...?	*waar is het...?*
airport	*vliegveld*
room	*kamer*
breakfast	*ontbijt*
dinner	*diner*
May I order?	*Mag ik even bestellen?*
steak	*biefstuk*
bread	*brood*
chicken	*kip*
coffee/tea	*koffie/thee*
sandwich	*broodje*
dish of the day	*daschotel*
lamb	*lamsvlees*
pork	*fricandeau*
wine	*wijn*

Netherlands – Essential Information

Norway – Essential Information

PRE-TRIP ESSENTIALS...

WHAT YOU NEED

ESSENTIAL FOR TRAVELERS

● Required ● Recommended ● Not required

Passport	●
Visa	●
Travel, medical insurance	●
Round-trip or onward airline ticket	●
Local currency	●
Traveler's checks	●
Credit cards	●
First-aid kit and medicines	●
Inoculations	●

ESSENTIAL FOR DRIVERS*

Driver's license	●
International Driving Permit	●
Car insurance (for nonrental cars)	●
Car registration (for nonrental cars)	●

*see also DRIVING section

IMPORTANT ADDRESSES

Norwegian Tourist Board
655 Third Avenue, New York, NY 10017
☎ (212) 885-9700
Fax (212) 885-9710

Norwegian Tourist Board
10250 Oslo, Norway
☎ 22 83 00 50
Fax 22 83 81 50

Norway Information Center
Drammensveien 40
P.O. Box 2893 Solli
0230 Oslo, Norway
☎ 22 92 52 00
Fax 22 56 05 05

American Embassy
Drammensveien 18
0244 Oslo, Norway
☎ 22 44 85 50
Fax 22 56 27 51
Personal visits: Mon.–Fri. 9–noon
Telephone inquiries: Mon.–Fri. 8:30–5

COUNTRY ESSENTIALS...

CUSTOMS

YES
Duty-free limits on goods brought in:
400 cigarettes or 50 cigars and cigarillos
or 500 g. tobacco; 2 L. wine or alcohol
under 22% volume; 1 L. alcohol over 22% volume; plus
any other duty-free goods (including gifts) to the value
of KR5,000.

Notify customs if you leave Norway with more than
KR25,000 (in bills and coins of any currency).

NO
No unlicensed drugs, weapons,
ammunition, obscene material, pets or
other animals, counterfeit money or
copied goods, meat or poultry.

For customs limits for returning U.S. citizens
see page 16.

MONEY

Norway's currency is the krone (KR), which is
divided into 100 øre. The denominations of krone
bills are 50, 100, 500 and 1,000. There are coins of
10 and 50 øre and 1, 5 and 10KR. You can
exchange dollars or traveler's checks
(reisesjekk) at a bank *(bank)*, exchange office
(vekslekontor), post office *(postkontor)* or hotel;
you will need ID. Credit cards *(kredittkort)* are
widely accepted in hotels, main stores and more
expensive restaurants.
Exchange rate at press time: $1 = KR8

TIPS AND GRATUITIES

Restaurants (service is usually included)	5–10%
Cafés/bars (service is usually included)	5–10%
Taxis	10% (optional)
Porters	KR5 per bag
Hairdressers	change
Chambermaids	KR5
Restroom attendants	KR3
Cloakroom attendants	change

TIME ZONES

OSLO	NEW YORK	CHICAGO	DENVER	SAN FRANCISCO
12:00 noon	6 hours behind Norway	7 hours behind Norway	8 hours behind Norway	9 hours behind Norway

519

COMMUNICATIONS

POST OFFICES

Buy stamps *(frimerker)* at a post office *(postkontor)*, a newsstand/tobacconist *(narvesen)* or from a hotel.

Hours for out-of-town post offices may vary. Mailboxes are red.

TELEPHONES

You can use cash or a telephone card to make a call in Norway. Most phone booths have direct dialing for international calls. Use KR1, KR5 and KR10 coins (there is commonly a minimum charge of KR2). In cities and large towns, phone company offices are open late into the evening and offer many services. English-speaking operators are normally available to assist with queries.

Phoning inside Norway
There are no area codes in Norway; all numbers are eight digits: Dial the number that is listed.

To call the operator dial 117.

Phoning Norway from abroad
The country code for Norway is 47. Note that Norwegian numbers in this book do not include the country code; you will need to prefix this number if you are phoning from another country. To phone Norway from the United States or Canada, omit the first zero from the Norwegian number and add the prefix 011 47.
Example: 011 22 33 44 becomes 011 47 11 22 33 44.

Phoning from Norway
To phone the United States or Canada from Norway, prefix the area code and number with 001.
Example: (111) 222-3333 becomes 001 111 222-3333.

To call international information dial 181 or 115.

EMERGENCY TELEPHONE NUMBERS

Police *(politi)*	112
Fire *(brannvesen)*	110
Ambulance *(ambulanse)*	113

Emergency calls are free from phone booths.

HOURS OF OPERATION

- ● Stores Mon.–Fri.
- ● Offices Mon.–Fri.
- ● Banks Mon.–Fri.
- ● Post offices Mon.–Fri.
- ● Museums/monuments
- ● Pharmacies Mon.–Fri.

7 8 9 10 11 12 1 2 3 4 5 6 7

Few stores stay open later than 2 or 3 on Saturday. City grocery stores may stay open longer. Most stores are closed on Sunday.

Banks generally stay open an hour later on Thursday, but close an hour earlier in July and August.

Post offices are open 9–1 on Saturday.

Stores around tourist attractions may have special hours.

Museums often close on Monday, and hours of operation may be reduced during the winter.

NATIONAL HOLIDAYS

Banks, businesses and most stores close on these days.

Jan. 1	New Year's Day
Mar./Apr.	Maundy Thursday
Mar./Apr.	Good Friday
Mar./Apr.	Easter Monday
May 1	Labor Day
May 17	Constitution Day
May	Ascension Day
May/Jun.	Pentecost Monday
Dec. 25	Christmas Day
Dec. 26	St. Stephen's Day

PHOTOGRAPHY

Spectacular shots are possible in fjord country if the weather is right (bear in mind that Norway is susceptible to poor light, especially during the winter). Photography is not permitted in some museums and places of historic interest – check before taking pictures. Film and camera batteries are readily available in towns.

Norway – Essential Information

Norway – Essential Information

HEALTH

MEDICAL INSURANCE
U.S. and Canadian visitors will be charged for medical assistance, including treatment in a hospital *(sykehus)* emergency room. Many general practitioners speak English; your hotel can find one for you, or look under *Leger* in the telephone directory.

DENTAL SERVICES
A dentist *(tannlege)* will charge you for treatment, so check your medical insurance for this coverage. Many dentists speak English; ask a tourist office or your hotel to find one for you. Emergency treatment can be sought after hours in city clinics and practices.

SUN ADVICE
Despite its northerly location, Norway is affected by the Gulf Stream, which means warm weather during the summer months. Use an appropriate sunscreen.

DRUGS
A pharmacy *(apotek)* sells prescription medicines, and many pharmacists speak English. Information about the nearest late-night or 24-hour facility is posted at all pharmacies. If you need perfume or cosmetics, go to a *parfymeri*.

SAFE WATER
Tap water is safe to drink throughout Norway. Mineral water *(mineralvann)* is widely available.

RESTROOMS

Public restrooms *(toaletter)* are easy to find. Facilities are separate for men *(herrer)* and women *(damer)*, and are identified by symbols or a "WC" sign. They are invariably clean and modern, and a small charge (usually KR3) may be made.

ELECTRICITY

Norway has a 220-volt power supply. Electrical sockets take plugs with two round pins; American appliances will need a plug adapter and will require a transformer if they do not have a dual-voltage facility.

NATIONAL TRANSPORTATION

TRAIN *(tog)*
The Norges Statsbaner (NSB) network operates south of the Arctic Circle. Travel is comfortable and efficient but not cheap (when you see the mountainous terrain you will understand why). Many express and all overnight trains require reservations. Inquire about discounts when reserving your seat.

BUS *(buss)*
Buses are an excellent, inexpensive way to explore regions that are less well-served by train. Buy your ticket on board (for popular routes it may be best to reserve through a travel agent). Eurolines international buses operate in Norway: ☎ 81 54 44 44.

FERRY *(ferje)*
Norway relies heavily on ferries, especially in the fjords. They often connect with trains and buses. Car ferries operate on a first-come, first-served system; payment is made on board. Some waterways, such as Lake Mjosa and the Telemark Canal, have ferry services. *Hertigrute*, a grand coastal steamer, links Bergen with Kirkenes, in far northern Norway.

DRIVING

DRIVE ON THE RIGHT

SPEED LIMITS
Police can impose on-the-spot fines.

Limited-access highways *(motorvei)*
90 k.p.h. (55 m.p.h.)

Main roads
80 k.p.h. (49 m.p.h.)

Urban areas
50 k.p.h. (31 m.p.h.)

SEAT BELTS
Must be worn in front seats at all times and in rear seats where fitted. Children under four may not travel in the front (unless in a rear-facing child seat in a vehicle not equipped with an air bag).

BLOOD ALCOHOL
The legal blood alcohol limit is 0.05%. Random breath tests on drivers are carried out frequently, especially late at night, and the penalties for offenders are severe.

DRIVING continued

TOLLS
There are tolls to enter Bergen, Oslo and Trondheim. There are also tolls for some highways, bridges and tunnels.

CAR RENTAL
The leading rental firms have offices at airports and train stations. Hertz offers discounted rates for AAA members (see page 15). For reservations:

	UNITED STATES	NORWAY
Dollar	(800) 800-4000	22 60 20 22 (Europcar)
Avis	(800) 331-2112	66 77 10 75
Budget	(800) 527-0700	64 81 06 80
Hertz	(800) 654-3080	64 81 05 50

FUEL *(olje)*
Gas and diesel are sold in liters, and many stations *(bensinstasjon)* are self-service. Gas stations are not as common in the more remote northern areas, and credit cards are not always accepted.

AAA AFFILIATED MOTORING CLUB
Norges Automobil-Forbund (NAF)
Storgaten 2, 0155 Oslo 1,
P.O.Box 494, Sentrum, 0105 Oslo
22 34 14 00, fax 22 33 13 72
If you break down while driving, phone 810 00 505 (NAF breakdown service).
Not all automobile clubs offer full services to AAA members.

BREAKDOWNS AND ACCIDENTS
There are 24-hour emergency phones at regular intervals on highways. All accidents involving personal injury must be reported to the police (112).
Most car rental firms provide their own free rescue service; if your car is rented, follow the instructions given in the documentation. Use of a car repair service other than those authorized by your rental company may violate your agreement.

OTHER INFORMATION
The minimum age for driving a car is 17 (may be higher for some car rental firms).

An International Driving Permit (IDP) is recommended; some rental firms require them, and they can speed up formalities if you are involved in an accident. A Green Card (international motor insurance certificate) is recommended if you are driving a private car; see page 15 for more information.

You are required by law to use dimmed headlights at all times when driving. Snow tires and chains are advised from Nov. 15 until Easter; rent tires and chains from NAF or at border crossings.

USEFUL WORDS AND PHRASES

There are two official, and similar forms of Norwegian. Riksmal, or Bokmal ("book language"), is an old form of Norwegian. Although many bureaucrats speak in Bokmal, it is mostly used in its written form. Landsmal, or Nynorsk, has its roots in Old Norse dialects but developed out of the wave of Norwegian nationalism in the 19th century. You will encounter both during your stay; it is not uncommon for speakers to use a combination of both, but writing rarely mixes styles.

Most people, especially the young, speak some English; alternatively, a knowledge of German will help. The phrases below are translated into Bokmal.

Do you speak English?	*Snakker de engelsk?*
excuse me	*unnskyld*
hello	*goddag*
goodbye	*adjø*
how much?	*hvor mye?*
I would like	*Eg vil gjerne*
I don't understand	*Jeg forstår ikkje*
non-smoking	*røyking forbudt*
open/closed	*åpen/stengt*
please	*vaer så god*
thank you	*takk*
ticket (one-way/	*enkeltbillett/*
round trip)	*tur-returbillett*
Where is...?	*Hvor er...?*
yes/no	*ja/nei*
early/late	*tidlig/sent*
hot/cold	*varm/kald*
big/small	*stor/liten*
good/bad	*god/dårlig*
airport	*lufthavn*
you're welcome	*vaer så god*
the restaurant	***restaurant***
beef	*oksekjøtt*
bread	*brød*
breakfast	*frokost*
biscuits	*kjeks*
chicken	*kylling*
coffee/tea	*kaffe/te*
salad	*salat*
dessert	*dessert*
entree	*hovedrett*
fish	*fisk*
lamb	*lammekjøtt*
pork	*svinekjøtt*
sandwich	*smørbrød*
hot-dog	*varm pølse*
seafood	*fiskemat*
lobster	*hummer*
herring	*sild*
starter	*forrett*
waffles	*vafler*
cranberries	*tyttbær*
ice cream	*iskrem*
wine	*vin*
the check	*rekning/regning*

Norway – Essential Information

Portugal – Essential Information

PRE-TRIP ESSENTIALS... COUNTRY ESSENTIALS...

WHAT YOU NEED

ESSENTIAL FOR TRAVELERS

● Required   ● Recommended   ● Not required

Passport	●
Visa	●
Travel, medical insurance	●
Return or onward ticket	●
Local currency	●
Traveler's checks	●
Credit cards	●
First-aid kit and medicines	●
Inoculations	●

ESSENTIAL FOR DRIVERS*

Driver's license	●
International Driving Permit	●
Car insurance (for nonrental cars)	●
Car registration (for nonrental cars)	●

*see also DRIVING section

IMPORTANT ADDRESSES

Portuguese National Tourist Office
590 Fifth Avenue
New York, NY 10036-4704
☎ (212) 354-4403
Fax (212) 764-6137

Comissão Municipal de Turismo de Lisboa
Avenida 5 de Outubro 293
1050 Lisbon, Portugal
☎ 01 793 4702
Fax 01 793 4628

American Embassy
Avenida Foças Armadas
1600 Lisbon, Portugal
☎ 01 727 3300
Fax 01 726 9109
Mon.–Fri. 8–12:30 and 1–4

CUSTOMS

YES
Duty-free limits on goods brought in from non-European Union countries:
200 cigarettes or 100 cigarillos or 50 cigars or 250 g. tobacco; 2 L. wine; 1 L alcohol over 22% volume; 2 L. alcohol under 22% volume; 60 ml. perfume; 250 ml. toilet water; plus any other duty-free goods (including gifts) to the value of 7,500Esc. Local or foreign currency exceeding 1,000,000Esc must be declared on arrival. Any amount of foreign currency may be exported if it was declared on entry, but no more than 10,000,000Esc may be exported. There is no limit on the importation of tax-paid goods purchased within the European Union if they are for personal use.

NO
No unlicensed drugs, weapons, ammunition, obscene material, pets or other animals, counterfeit money or copied goods, meat or poultry.
For customs limits for returning U.S. citizens see page 16.

MONEY

Portugal's currency is the escudo (Esc), which is divided into 100 centavos. The denominations of escudo bills are 500, 1,000, 2,000, 5,000 and 10,000. There are coins of 1, 2.5, 5, 10, 20, 50, 100 and 200Esc. In stores and markets, do not be misled by the dollar sign, which is frequently applied to the escudo: 75$50, for instance, means 75 escudos and 50 centavos. The 10,000Esc bill is common, and officially known as a "conto." You can change dollars or traveler's checks *(traveller cheques)* at a bank *(banco)* or an exchange office *(casa de cambio)*.
Exchange rate at press time: $1 = 200Esc

TIPS AND GRATUITIES

Restaurants (where service is not included)	10%
Cafés/bars (where service is not included)	change
Taxis	10%
Porters	100–200Esc
Hairdressers	200Esc
Chambermaids	500Esc
Restroom attendants	100Esc
Cloakroom attendants	100Esc

TIME ZONES	LISBON 12:00 noon	NEW YORK 6 hours behind Portugal	CHICAGO 7 hours behind Portugal	DENVER 8 hours behind Portugal	SAN FRANCISCO 9 hours behind Portugal	523

COMMUNICATIONS

POST OFFICES

Buy stamps *(selos)* at a post office *(correio)* or anywhere that has the sign of a red horse on a white circle over a green background. You may also see the words "Correio de Portugal." Hours for out-of-town post offices may vary.

TELEPHONES

You can use 10Esc, 20Esc and 50Esc coins in a phone booth *(telefonar)*. Public phones are easily found on the street and in cafés, main post offices, and at some newsstands and tourist offices. You can make an international call direct from a phone booth, but it is more convenient to find a post office where you can use a private booth and pay after the call. Phone cards are available from post offices for 750Esc and 1800Esc.

Phoning inside Portugal
All Portuguese telephone numbers in this book include an area code; dial the number listed.

To call the operator dial 099.

Phoning Portugal from abroad
The country code for Portugal is 351. Note that Portuguese numbers in this book do not include the country code; you will need to prefix this number if you are phoning from another country. To phone Portugal from the United States or Canada, omit the first zero from the number and add the prefix 011 351.
Example: 01 122 3344 becomes 011 351 1 122 3344.

Phoning from Portugal
To phone the United States or Canada from Portugal, prefix area code and number with 001.
Example: (111) 222-3333 becomes 001 111 222-3333.
For international operator outside Europe dial 098.
To call international information dial 118.

EMERGENCY TELEPHONE NUMBERS

Police *(polícia)*	112 or 115
Fire *(serviço do fogo)*	112 or 115
Ambulance *(ambulância)*	112 or 115

Emergency calls are free from phone booths.

HOURS OF OPERATION

- ● Stores Mon.–Sat.
- ● Museums/monuments
- ● Offices Mon.–Fri.
- ● Pharmacies Mon.–Sat.
- ● Banks Mon.–Fri.
- ● Post offices Mon.–Fri.

7 8 9 10 11 12 1 2 3 4 5 6 7

Most stores and pharmacies close at 1 on Saturday and are not open on Sunday. Stores in large towns or tourist areas are open Mon.–Sat. until 11 p.m.; some also open on Sunday. Grocery stores are usually open until 9 p.m.

Post offices and banks in rural areas often close for lunch.

Museums generally close on Monday (some also close on Wednesday), and the smaller sights may have shorter hours of operation off-season.

NATIONAL HOLIDAYS

Banks, businesses and most stores close on these days. Additionally, there are many local festivals when everything comes to a halt and a whole town takes part in events.

Jan. 1	New Year's Day
Feb./Mar.	Shrove Tuesday
Mar./Apr.	Good Friday
Apr. 25	Liberty Day
May 1	Labor Day
May/Jun.	Corpus Christi
Jun. 10	Portugal Day
Aug. 15	Assumption of the Virgin
Oct. 5	Republic Day
Nov. 1	All Saints' Day
Dec. 8	Immaculate Conception
Dec. 25	Christmas Day

PHOTOGRAPHY

Finding adequate light is rarely a problem in Portugal; rise early for atmospheric shots of fishing ports, villages, castles and the mountains. You will not be permitted to photograph at airports or military areas, and ask permission before taking pictures in museums and churches. Popular brands of film and batteries are widely available.

Portugal – Essential Information

Portugal – Essential Information

HEALTH

MEDICAL INSURANCE
U.S. and Canadian visitors will be charged for emergency medical treatment, consultation with a doctor and/or admittance to a hospital *(hospital)*. Ask at a tourist office or your hotel to find an English-speaking doctor.

DENTAL SERVICES
Dental treatment is charged for in Portugal. Ask at a tourist office or your hotel for a list of English-speaking dentists. Check that dental treatment is covered by your medical insurance.

SUN ADVICE
The sun is strong during summer, particularly in the south. Do not be deceived by the cooling breeze off the Atlantic. Avoid prolonged exposure and protect yourself with a sunscreen or cover up.

DRUGS
Prescription medicines are available from a pharmacy *(fármacia)*, distinguished by a large green cross. Pharmacists can prescribe remedies for minor ailments, and many speak English. Information about the nearest late-night or 24-hour facility is posted at all pharmacies.

SAFE WATER
Tap water is generally safe, but does not always taste too pleasant. It is advisable to drink bottled water *(agua mineral)*, especially in rural areas; *sem gas* means noncarbonated, *com gas* means carbonated.

RESTROOMS

Public restrooms *(retretes* or *lavabos)* are easy to find. Ladies' *(senhoras)* restrooms usually have a minimal charge and are generally clean. Men's *(homens)* restrooms are usually free.

ELECTRICITY

Most of Portugal has a 220-volt power supply, but in some rural areas the supply is 125 volts. Electrical sockets take plugs with two round pins; American appliances will need a plug adapter and will require a transformer if they do not have a dual-voltage facility.

NATIONAL TRANSPORTATION

TRAIN *(comboios)*
The Caminhos de Ferre Portugueses (CP) operates three types of service: *Regional* and *Intercidade* (which both stop at most stations) and *Rapido* (express between Lisbon and Porto). Fares are reasonable, with many discount offers: ☎ 01 346 5022.

BUS *(autocarros)*
The state-owned Rodoviária National (RN) covers most of the country, and buses are generally comfortable (phone 01 354 5775). Several private companies also maintain an extensive network. The Eurolines international bus network operates in Portugal: ☎ 01 357 1745.

FERRY *(barcos)*
Ferries cross the Rio Tejo from Lisbon to the suburb of Cacilhas every 10 to 15 minutes (daily 7 a.m.–9 p.m. at the harbor adjacent to Praça do Comércio, or daily 24 hours from Cais de Sodré). From Setúbal there is a daily 24-hour service to the Tróia peninsula (journey time 20 minutes, departing at least hourly).

DRIVING

DRIVE ON THE RIGHT

SPEED LIMITS
Police can impose on-the-spot fines.

Limited-access highways *(autoestrada)*
120 k.p.h. (74 m.p.h.)
Divided highways
100 k.p.h. (62 m.p.h.)

Main roads
80 k.p.h. (49 m.p.h.)

Urban areas
50 k.p.h. (31 m.p.h.)

SEAT BELTS
Must be worn in front seats at all times and in rear seats where fitted.

BLOOD ALCOHOL
The legal blood alcohol limit is 0.05%. Random breath tests on drivers are carried out frequently, especially late at night, and the penalties for offenders are severe.

DRIVING continued

TOLLS
There are no highway tolls in Portugal.

CAR RENTAL
The leading rental firms have offices at airports and train stations. Hertz offers discounted rates for AAA members (see page 15). For reservations:

	UNITED STATES	PORTUGAL
Alamo	(800) 327 9633	01 848 6191
Avis	(800) 331-2112	01 843 5550
Budget	(800) 527-0700	01 849 5523
Hertz	(800) 654-3080	01 849 2722

FUEL *(gasolina)*
Gas and diesel are sold in liters, and many stations *(posto de gasolina)* are self-service. Gas stations are not as common in the more remote northern areas, and credit cards are not always accepted.

AAA AFFILIATED MOTORING CLUB
Automóvel Club de Portugal (ACP)
Rua Rosa Araujo 24, BP 2594, 1114
Lisbon ☎ 01 356 3931, fax 01 357 4732
If you break down while driving in northern Portugal, phone 02 834 0001; in the south phone 01 942 9103 (both for ACP breakdown service). Not all automobile clubs offer full services to AAA members.

BREAKDOWNS AND ACCIDENTS
There are 24-hour emergency phones at regular intervals on highways. If you are involved in an accident ☎ 115 for police assistance.
Most car rental firms provide their own free rescue service; if your car is rented, follow the instructions given in the documentation. Use of a car repair service other than those authorized by your rental company may violate your agreement.

OTHER INFORMATION

The minimum age for driving a car is 18 (may be higher for some car rental firms).

An International Driving Permit (IDP) is recommended; some rental firms require them, and they can speed up formalities if you are involved in an accident.

A Green Card (international motor insurance certificate) is recommended if you are driving a private car; see page 15 for more information.

You are required by law to carry ID at all times.

USEFUL WORDS AND PHRASES

Portuguese is a Latin language, so an acquaintance with French, Spanish or Italian makes written Portuguese quite easy to understand. Understanding spoken Portuguese, however, is more difficult. Although on paper Portuguese words look similar to Spanish, they actually sound very different. Consonants are slurred, and vowels are flat and truncated, nasal or sometimes disregarded completely.

Although English is widely spoken in tourist areas, knowing a few Portuguese words will make your trip more rewarding.

Do you speak English?	*Fala Inglês?*
I'm sorry	*desculpe*
hello/goodbye	*olá/adeus*
yes/no	*sim/não*
how much?	*quanto?*
I am American	*sou Americano*
I would like	*queria um*
I don't understand	*não entendo*
non-smoking	*não funadores*
okay	*está bem*
today/tomorrow	*hoje/amanhã*
open/closed	*aberto/fechado*
right/left	*direita/esquerda*
near/far	*perto/longe*
big/little	*grande/pequeno*
cheap/expensive	*barato/caro*
please	*se faz favor*
thank you	*obrigado (m.)/obrigada (f.)*
ticket	*bilhete*
one way/return	*ida/ida e volta*
where is...?	*onde é...?*
the hotel	***hotel***
breakfast	*pequeno almoço*
lunch	*almoço*
dinner	*jantar*
I have a reservation	*tenho uma marcacao*
key	*chave*
for one night	*para uma noite*
room	*quarto*
shower	*duche*
with bathroom	*com banho*
the restaurant	***restaurante***
beef	*bife*
bread	*pão*
cheese	*queijo*
chicken	*frango*
the check	*a conta*
Is the service included?	*O serviço está incluido?*
coffee/tea	*café/chà*
dish of the day	*prato do dia*
dessert	*sobremesa*
fish	*peixe*
ham	*fiambre*
lamb	*anho*
pork	*porco*
starter	*entrada*
veal	*vitela*
wine	*vinho*

Portugal – Essential Information

Spain – Essential Information

PRE-TRIP ESSENTIALS...

WHAT YOU NEED

ESSENTIAL FOR TRAVELERS

● Required   ● Recommended   ● Not required

Passport	●
Visa	●
Travel, medical insurance	●
Round-trip or onward airline ticket	●
Local currency	●
Traveler's checks	●
Credit cards	●
First-aid kit and medicines	●
Inoculations	●

ESSENTIAL FOR DRIVERS*

Driver's license	●
International Driving Permit	●
Car insurance (for nonrental cars)	●
Car registration (for nonrental cars)	●

*see also DRIVING section

IMPORTANT ADDRESSES

Tourist Office of Spain
665 Fifth Avenue, 35th floor
New York, NY 10103
☎ (212) 265-8822
Fax (212) 265-8864

Tourist Office of Spain
Plaza Mayor 3
28012 Madrid, Spain
☎ 91 588 1636
Fax 91 366 5477

American Embassy
Serrano 75
28006 Madrid, Spain
☎ 91 587 2200
Fax 91 558 2215
Personal inquiries: Mon.–Fri. 9–1

COUNTRY ESSENTIALS...

CUSTOMS

YES
Duty-free limits on goods brought in from non-European Union countries:
200 cigarettes or 100 cigarillos or 50 cigars or 250 g. tobacco; 2 L. wine; 1 L. alcohol over 22% volume; 2 L. alcohol under 22% volume; 60 ml. perfume; 250 ml. toilet water; plus any other duty-free goods (including gifts) to the value of 33,500PTA. There are no currency regulations. There is no limit on the importation of tax-paid goods purchased within the European Union if they are for personal use.

NO
No unlicensed drugs, weapons, ammunition, obscene material, pets or other animals, counterfeit money or copied goods, meat or poultry.

For customs limits for returning U.S. citizens see page 16.

MONEY

Spain's currency is the peseta (PTA). The denominations of peseta bills are 1,000, 2,000, 5,000 and 10,000. There are coins of 5, 10, 25, 50, 100, 200 and 500PTA. A near-valueless one peseta coin exists, but sums are usually rounded down to the nearest five pesetas. Exchange dollars or traveler's checks *(cheques de viaje)* at a bank *(banco)* or exchange office *(oficina de canvi)*. On Jan. 1, 1999, the euro became the official currency of Spain and the peseta became a denomination of the euro. Peseta bills and coins continue to be legal tender during a transitional period. Euro bills and coins are likely to be introduced by Jan. 2002.
Exchange rate at press time: $1 = 160PTA

TIPS AND GRATUITIES

Tips are welcomed as a sign of good service. Most hotel, restaurant and café checks will include a service charge.

Restaurants (service is normally included)	10%
Cafés/bars (service is normally included)	change
Taxis	10%
Porters, chambermaids	100PTA
Cloakroom attendants	change

TIME ZONES

MADRID	NEW YORK	CHICAGO	DENVER	SAN FRANCISCO
12:00 noon	6 hours behind Spain	7 hours behind Spain	8 hours behind Spain	9 hours behind Spain

527

COMMUNICATIONS

POST OFFICES

Buy stamps *(sellos)* at a post office *(correos)* or a tobacconist *(estancos)* denoted by a "T."

Hours for out-of-town post offices may vary.

TELEPHONES

A public telephone *(telefono)* takes 25PTA, 100PTA and 500PTA coins. A phone card *(credifone)* is available from post offices and tobacconists for 1,000PTA or 2,000PTA. Many public phone booths are thoroughly modern, with instructions in English and lists of national and international dialing codes posted inside them. In major cities,

telecommunications stores offer facilities such as faxing and e-mail.

Phoning inside Spain
All Spanish phone numbers in this book include an area code; dial the number that is listed. To call the operator dial 1003.

Phoning Spain from abroad
The country code for Spain is 34. Note that Spanish numbers in this book do not include the Spanish country code; you will need to prefix this number if you are phoning from another country. To phone Spain from the United States or Canada dial the prefix 011 34. (Note that the number of digits in Spanish area codes varies.)
Example: 11 122 3344 becomes 011 34 11 122 3344.

Phoning from Spain
To phone the United States or Canada from Spain, prefix the area code and number with 001.
Example: (111) 222-3333 becomes 001 111 222-3333.
To call international information dial 025.

EMERGENCY TELEPHONE NUMBERS
Police *(policía)*	091
Fire *(bomberos)*	080
Ambulance *(ambulancia)*	061

Emergency calls are free from phone booths.

HOURS OF OPERATION

- ○ Stores Mon.–Sat.
- ● Museums/monuments Tue.–Sat.
- ● Offices Mon.–Fri.
- ● Banks Mon.–Fri.
- ● Pharmacies Mon.–Sat.
- ● Post offices Mon.–Sat.

| 7 | 8 | 9 | 10 | 11 | 12 | 1 | 2 | 3 | 4 | 5 | 6 | 7 |

Department stores and grocery stores may operate outside the hours shown, especially in summer.

Business hours vary depending on season; many companies work *horas intensivas* (shorter, more intensive hours) from 8–3 in summer.

Banks tend to close on Saturday, but some large branches are open 8:30–2.

Most museums and monuments are closed on Monday, but many open 9–2 on Sunday.

NATIONAL HOLIDAYS

Banks, businesses and most stores close on these days. Some *barrios* (districts) also have their own feast days, when shops and offices also close.

Jan. 1	New Year's Day
Jan. 6	Epiphany
Feb. 19	St. Joseph's Day
Mar./Apr.	Good Friday
Mar./Apr.	Easter Monday
May 1	Labor Day
May/Jun.	Pentecost Monday
Jun. 24	St. John's Day
Aug. 15	Assumption of the Virgin
Sep. 11	National Day (Catalonia)
Sep. 24	Our Lady of Mercy Day
Oct. 12	National Day
Nov. 1	All Saints' Day
Dec. 6	Constitution Day
Dec. 8	Immaculate Conception
Dec. 25	Christmas Day
Dec. 26	St. Stephen's Day

PHOTOGRAPHY

The Spanish summer sun can be powerful at noon, making photos appear flat; take your pictures early in the morning or late in the evening. Ask permission before taking pictures in museums and churches. Film and camera batteries are readily available from specialist stores and *drouguerias* (drugstores).

Spain – Essential Information

Spain – Essential Information

HEALTH

MEDICAL INSURANCE
U.S. and Canadian visitors can receive treatment in a hospital emergency room, but are charged if admitted to a bed. There is an Anglo-American clinic in Madrid; ☎ 91 435 1823.

DENTAL SERVICES
You will be charged for dental treatment, so check whether it is covered by your medical insurance. Dentists *(dentista)* are listed in the yellow pages.

SUN ADVICE
The sun is strong during summer, particularly in the south. Dress sensibly, avoid prolonged exposure and protect yourself with a sunscreen.

DRUGS
Prescription medicines are available from pharmacies *(farmàcias)*, designated by a green cross. Information about the nearest late-night or 24-hour facility is posted at all pharmacies.

SAFE WATER
Tap water is generally safe, although it can be heavily chlorinated. Mineral water *(agua mineral)* is inexpensive and is sold *con gaz* (carbonated) and *sin gaz* (noncarbonated). Drink plenty of water during hot weather.

RESTROOMS

Public restrooms *(servicios)* can usually be found in large department stores, museums and other places of interest to visitors. Elsewhere, restrooms may not be easy to find, but there is no charge. If you use the facilities in a bar you will be expected to buy a drink. Spanish words are *señores* for men and *señoras* for women.

ELECTRICITY

Most of Spain has a 220-volt power supply, but in some rural areas the supply is 125 volts. Electrical sockets take plugs with two round pins; American appliances will need a plug adapter, and either a dual voltage facility or a transformer.

NATIONAL TRANSPORTATION

TRAIN *(tren)*
The Red Nacional de los Ferrocarriles Españoles (RENFE) rail network is inexpensive to use. Take advantage of "blue days" *(dias azules)*, when lower fares prevail. There are two express services for long-distance travel: AVE and Largo Recorrido (reservations advisable for both). Information: ☎ 93 490 1122.

BUS *(autobus)*
Spain has a good bus system, and the Spanish Tourist Board publishes a guide to domestic services. Ask at a tourist office for details. The Eurolines international bus service operates in Spain; ☎ 91 530 7600.

FERRY *(transbordador)*
Barcelona is the Mediterranean's biggest port and offers regular ferry service to the Balearic islands. One of the largest ferry operators is Transmediterránea; ☎ 91 423 8727. "Mini-cruises" of two or three days operate from Northern Spain to and from Britain; obtain details from a travel agent.

DRIVING

DRIVE ON THE RIGHT

SPEED LIMITS
Police can impose on-the-spot fines.

Limited-access highways *(autopistas)*
124 k.p.h. (70 m.p.h.)
Divided highways
100 k.p.h. (62 m.p.h.)

Main roads
90 k.p.h. (56 m.p.h.)

Urban areas
50 k.p.h. (31 m.p.h.)

SEAT BELTS
Must be worn in front seats at all times and in rear seats where fitted.

BLOOD ALCOHOL
The legal blood alcohol limit is 0.05%. Random breath tests on drivers are carried out frequently, especially late at night, and the penalties for offenders are severe.

Spain – Essential Information

DRIVING continued

 TOLLS
A toll *(pedaggi autostradalia)* is levied on limited-access highways. Take a ticket when you enter and pay when exiting.

 CAR RENTAL
The leading rental firms have offices at airports and train stations. Hertz offers discounted rates for AAA members (see page 15). For reservations:

	UNITED STATES	SPAIN
Alamo	(800) 327 9633	91 411 1325 (National)
Avis	(800) 331-2112	91 393 7222
Budget	(800) 527-0700	91 639 6820
Hertz	(800) 654-3080	91 348 0348

 FUEL
Gas *(gasolina)* and diesel are sold in liters. Many gas stations *(gasolineras)* in towns and cities and on highways are open 24 hours.

 AAA AFFILIATED MOTORING CLUB
Real Automovil Club de Espaã (RACE)
José Abascal 10, 28003 Madrid
☎ 91 594 7400, fax 91 447 7948
If you break down while driving, phone 91 593 3333 (RACE breakdown service).
Not all automobile clubs offer full services to AAA members.

 BREAKDOWNS AND ACCIDENTS
There are 24-hour emergency phones at regular intervals on highways. If you are involved in an accident ☎ 091 for police assistance.
Most car rental firms provide their own free rescue service; if your car is rented, follow the instructions given in the documentation. Use of a car repair service other than those authorized by your rental company may violate your agreement.

OTHER INFORMATION
The minimum age for driving a car is 18 (may be higher for some car rental firms).
An International Driving Permit (IDP) is recommended; some rental firms require them, and they can speed up formalities if you are involved in an accident.

A Green Card (international motor insurance certificate) is recommended if you are driving a private car. See page 15 for more information. The police may impound your car if you fail to produce a Green Card after an accident.

It is advisable to obtain a bail bond from your automobile insurer. This will facilitate your release if you commit a traffic offense or are involved in an accident. A bail bond is usually included when you rent a car in Spain; if you rent a car in another country and intend to drive to Spain, advise your rental company.

USEFUL WORDS AND PHRASES

Castilian is the main language in Spain, with three important regional languages: Catalan, spoken in Catalonia and Valencia; Basque, the official language of the Basque north; and Galician, spoken in the northwest.

Catalan is closely related to Occitan (or Provençal), and Galician has noticeable links with Portuguese. The Basque tongue is unique, having no connection with any language in Europe.

The following words and phrases are in Castilian:

Do you speak English?	*¿Habla usted inglés?*
excuse me	*perdóne*
hello	*hola*
goodbye	*adiós*
yes/no	*si/no*
how much?	*¿cuánto?*
I would like	*me gustaría*
I don't understand	*no entiendo*
no smoking	*no fumadores*
okay	*vale*
open/closed	*abierto/cerrado*
today/tomorrow	*hoy/mañana*
here/there	*aquí/allí*
more/less	*más/menos*
please	*por favor*
thank you	*gracias*
you're welcome	*de nada*
how/what	*cómo/qué*
left/right	*izquierda/derecha*
What time is it?	*¿Qué hora es?*
travel ticket	*el billete*
one way/return	*senzill-a/anar i tornar*
where is…?	*¿dónde és…?*

the hotel	***el hotel***
breakfast	*berena*
lunch	*la comida*
dinner	*la cena*
I have a reservation	*Tengo una reserva*
key	*clau*
room	*la habitació*
shower	*dutxa*

the restaurant	***el restaoorante***
beef	*la carne de vaca*
bread	*el pan*
cheese	*queso*
chicken	*el pollo*
coffee	*el café*
dish of the day	*el plato del día*
dessert	*el postre*
fish	*el pescado*
pork	*la carne de cerdo*
starter	*primer plat*
wine, red/white	*el vino tinto/blanco*
the check	*la cuenta*

PRE-TRIP ESSENTIALS...   COUNTRY ESSENTIALS...

WHAT YOU NEED

ESSENTIAL FOR TRAVELERS

● Required   ● Recommended   ● Not required

Passport	●
Visa	●
Travel, medical insurance	●
Round-trip or onward airline ticket	●
Local currency	●
Traveler's checks	●
Credit cards	●
First-aid kit and medicines	●
Inoculations	●

ESSENTIAL FOR DRIVERS*

Driver's license	●
International Driving Permit	●
Car insurance (for nonrental cars)	●
Car registration (for nonrental cars)	●

*see also DRIVING section

IMPORTANT ADDRESSES

Swedish Travel and Tourism Council
655 Third Avenue
New York, NY 10017
☎ (212) 885-9700
Fax (212) 885-9764

Swedish Travel and Tourism Council
P.O.Box 3030, Kungsgatan 36
10361 Stockholm, Sweden
☎ 08 725 55 00
Fax 08 725 55 31

American Embassy
Strandvagen 101
Stockholm, Sweden
☎ 08 783 53 00
Fax 08 60 58 79
Personal inquiries: Mon.–Thu. 9–11 (visas only)
Phone inquiries: 087 83 53 75
Mon.–Fri. 12:30–4

CUSTOMS

YES

Duty-free limits on goods brought in from non-European Union countries:
200 cigarettes or 100 cigarillos or 50 cigars or 250 g. tobacco; 2 L. wine; 2 L. alcohol under 22% volume; 1 L. alcohol over 22% volume; 50 ml. perfume; 250 ml. toilet water; plus any other duty-free goods (including gifts) to the value of 700SKr. There are no currency regulations. There is no limit on the importation of tax-paid goods purchased within the European Union if they are for personal use.

NO

No unlicensed drugs, weapons, ammunition, obscene material, pets or other animals, counterfeit money or copied goods, meat or poultry.

For customs limits for returning U.S. citizens see page 16.

MONEY

Sweden's currency is the krona (SKr or KR; plural kronor), which is divided into 100 öre. The denominations of krona bills are 20, 50, 100, 200, 500, 1,000 and 10,000. There are coins of 50 öre, and 1, 5 and 10SKr. Exchange dollars and traveler's checks *(resechecker)* at a bank or an exchange office. "Forex" exchange offices have distinctive yellow signs. On Jan. 1, 1999, the euro became the official currency of Sweden and the krona became a denomination of the euro. Swedish krona bills and coins continue to be legal tender during a transitional period. Euro bills and coins are likely to be introduced by Jan. 2002. Exchange rate at press time: $1 = 8SKr

TIPS AND GRATUITIES

Tips are welcomed but not expected or obligatory. In restaurants it is usual to round off the check to the nearest 10SKr; service is usually included.

Restaurants, cafés/bars (service is included)	change
Taxis (included in charge)	none
Hairdressers, chambermaids	change
Porters, restroom attendants	change
Cloakroom attendants	7SKr

TIME ZONES

STOCKHOLM	NEW YORK	CHICAGO	DENVER	SAN FRANCISCO
12:00 noon	6 hours behind Sweden	7 hours behind Sweden	8 hours behind Sweden	9 hours behind Sweden

531

COMMUNICATIONS

POST OFFICES

Buy stamps *(frimarken)* at a post office *(postkontoret)*, newsstand *(nyhets-byra)* or stationer *(handel)*.

Hours for out-of-town post offices may vary.

TELEPHONES

You can use cash, credit cards and prepaid phone cards to make a phone call in Sweden. A public phone *(telefon)* takes 1SKr or 5SKr coins. Phone cards can be bought from newsstands or magazine kiosks *(pressbyra)*. Credit card phones are indicated by a "CCC" sign. Operators speak English. You can make a half-price call from a Turist Telefon (only found in cities) from mid-June to mid-August; and these phones are clearly marked.

Phoning inside Sweden
All Swedish numbers in this book include an area code; dial the number that is listed. To call the operator dial 07975.

Phoning Sweden from abroad
The country code for Sweden is 46. Note that Swedish numbers in this book do not include the Swedish country code; you will need to prefix this number if you are phoning from another country. To phone Sweden from the United States or Canada, omit the first zero from the Swedish number and add the prefix 011 46.
Example: 01 122 33 44 becomes 011 46 1 122 33 44.

Phoning from Sweden
To phone the United States or Canada from Sweden, prefix the area code and number with 001.
Example: (111) 222-3333 becomes 001 111 222-3333.

To call international information dial 07977.

EMERGENCY TELEPHONE NUMBERS

Police *(polis)*	112
Fire *(brandkår)*	112
Ambulance *(ambulans)*	112

Emergency calls are free from phone booths.

HOURS OF OPERATION

- Stores Mon.–Fri.
- Museums/monuments
- Offices Mon.–Fri.
- Pharmacies Mon.–Fri.
- Banks Mon.–Fri.
- Post offices Mon.–Fri.

7 8 9 10 11 12 1 2 3 4 5 6 7

In large towns, department stores stay open until 8 or 10 p.m., and some also are open Sunday noon–4. Stores often close on Saturday afternoon, and usually close early the day before a public holiday. Some smaller stores may close for lunch.

Post offices may stay open later in main cities. They are open Sat. 10–1.

Banks may stay open on Thursday until 4 or 5:30.

Some museums close on Monday and stay open late one night a week.

NATIONAL HOLIDAYS

Banks, businesses and most stores close on these days.

Jan. 1	New Year's Day
Jan. 6	Epiphany
Mar./Apr.	Good Friday
Mar./Apr.	Easter Monday
May 1	Labor Day
May	Ascension Day
May/Jun.	Pentecost Monday
Jun. 24	Midsummer's Day
Nov. 1	All Saints' Day
Dec. 24	Christmas Eve
Dec. 25	Christmas Day
Dec. 26	St. Stephen's Day

PHOTOGRAPHY

Make sure you pack film for poor light at certain times in the winter. If you have the right equipment, photographs of the northern lights *(aurora borealis)* are possible. Check first before taking photographs in museums; it may be forbidden or you may have to ask permission. Film and camera batteries are readily available from tourist stores. Rapid-developing services also are widely available.

Sweden – Essential Information

EMERGENCY PHONE NUMBERS

POLICE 112
(Polis)

HEALTH

MEDICAL INSURANCE
Private medical insurance is recommended. Visitors can receive treatment at a hospital accident and emergency room, but you will be charged if you are admitted to a hospital bed. There are no general practitioners; go straight to a hospital clinic *(acutmottagning* or *vardcentral)*.

DENTAL SERVICES
Dentists *(tandlakeren)* always charge for treatment. Emergency treatment is available out of hours in major cities. Clinics are indicated by *"Tandlakard"* or *"Folktanvard"* signs.

SUN ADVICE
The Gulf Stream dictates Sweden's temperate climate of warm sunshine during July and August. Although the sun is not fierce, good sun protection is necessary. Take precautions near the water.

DRUGS
Prescription and nonprescription drugs and medicines are available from a pharmacy *(apotek)*. If you need a pharmacy outside regular hours, information about the nearest all-night facility is posted at all pharmacies.

SAFE WATER
Tap water is safe to drink, and mineral water *(mineralvatten)* is widely available.

RESTROOMS

Public restrooms *(toaletten)* are easy to find. Charges of between 1SKr and 5SKr may be made in some restrooms. Separate facilities for men and women are always clean and modern.

ELECTRICITY

Sweden has a 220-volt power supply. Electrical sockets take plugs with two round pins; American appliances will need a plug adapter and will require a transformer if they do not have a dual-voltage facility.

NATIONAL TRANSPORTATION

TRAIN *(tag)*
The Swedish National Railways (Statens Jarnvagar) runs an efficient and extensive system, extending above the Arctic Circle. The trains are fast and modern. On some trains reservations are required; it is usually advisable to make them. For information call ☎ 08 762 25 80. A free timetable is available from any station *(jarnvagsstation)*.

BUS *(buss)*
Swedish bus travel is straightforward and inexpensive. Express services run between cities and into Norway, Finland and Denmark. A good, frequent domestic service runs to northern Sweden. For long-distance bus service information ☎ 08 440 85 70. International Euroline buses operate in Sweden; ☎ 08 440 85 70.

FERRY *(farja)*
Ferry services in Sweden are not as extensive as those in Finland and Denmark, but you can get various island-hopping boat passes or coupons. Most start from Stockholm; passes are available from Waxholmbolaget Office, Stromkajen, Stockholm.

DRIVING

DRIVE ON THE RIGHT

SPEED LIMITS
Police can impose on-the-spot fines, but cannot collect them.

Limited-access highways
110 k.p.h. (68 m.p.h.)
Divided highways
90 k.p.h. (55 m.p.h.)

Main roads
70 k.p.h. (43 m.p.h.)

Urban areas
50 k.p.h. (31 m.p.h.)

SEAT BELTS
Must be worn in front seats at all times and in rear seats where fitted.

BLOOD ALCOHOL
The legal blood alcohol limit is 0.02%. Random breath tests on drivers are carried out frequently, especially late at night, and the penalties for offenders are severe.

Sweden – Essential Information

DRIVING continued

TOLLS
There are no highway tolls in Sweden.

CAR RENTAL
The leading rental firms have offices at airports and train stations. Hertz offers discounted rates for AAA members (see page 15). For reservations:

	UNITED STATES	SWEDEN
Alamo	(800) 327-9633	08 706 00 66 66
Avis	(800) 331-2112	08 797 99 70
Budget	(800) 527-0700	08 797 84 70
Hertz	(800) 654-3080	08 797 99 00

FUEL *(själva)*
Gas is sold in liters. Major credit cards are usually accepted. Self-service *(tanka själv)* stations require 20SKr or 100SKr bills in their automated machines *(sedel automat)*. Many gas stations on highways and in main towns are open 24 hours.

MOTORING CLUB
Sweden does not have a AAA affiliated motoring club. If you need breakdown assistance the following organization can help: Svenska Turistforeningen (STF), Stureplan 4C, Box 25, 10120 Stockholm, Sweden (08 463 21 00, fax 08 678 19 58).

BREAKDOWNS AND ACCIDENTS
There are 24-hour emergency phones at regular intervals on highways. If you are involved in an accident 112 for police assistance.
If you break down while driving, contact STF (see above) or the Larmtjänst service: 02 091 00 40. Most car rental firms provide their own free rescue service; if your car is rented, follow the instructions given in the documentation. Use of a car repair service other than those authorized by your rental company may violate your agreement.

OTHER INFORMATION
The minimum age for driving a car is 18 (may be higher for some car rental firms).

An International Driving Permit (IDP) is recommended; some rental firms require them, and they can speed up formalities if you are involved in an accident.

A Green Card (international motor insurance certificate) is recommended if you are driving a private car; see page 15 for more information.

Dimmed headlights must be used at all times.

USEFUL WORDS & PHRASES

Swedes are not used to foreigners speaking their language, although efforts to speak Swedish are appreciated; most Swedes also speak English. German, Danish and Norwegian are often understood.

In Swedish, a vowel sound is usually long when it is the final syllable, and verbs are the same regardless of person. Definite articles are determined by the ending of the noun: -en and -et for singular nouns and -na or -n for plural. There are an additional three letters in the Swedish alphabet - å, ä and ö - which always appear at the end in alphabetical lists.

There are two words for "you": *du* and *ni*. *Ni* is the polite form, *du* is the familiar form. Unlike some other European countries, it is not necessarily impolite to address a complete stranger with the familiar form. In fact, many Swedes consider the polite form to be old-fashioned.

Do you speak English?	*Talar ni Engelska?*
excuse me	*ursäkta mig*
hello	*hej*
goodbye	*adjö/hej då*
yes/no	*ja/nej*
how much is it?	*hur mycket kostar den?*
I am American	*Jag är från U.S.A.*
I'd like	*Jag skulle vilja ha*
I don't understand	*Jag förstår inte*
non-smoking	*rökning förbjuden*
open	*öppen/öppet*
closed	*stängt*
please	*snäla, vänligen*
thank you	*tack*
ticket (one-way/round trip)	*en enkelbiljett*
What is your name?	*Vad heter du?*

the hotel	***hotell***
breakfast	*frukost*
lunch	*lunch*
dinner	*middag*
key	*nyckel*
room	*rum*
shower	*dusch*

the restaurant	***restaurang***
bread	*bröd*
coffee/tea	*kaffe/te*
beef	*nötkött, oxkött*
chicken	*kyckling*
fish	*fisk*
lamb	*lammkött*
pork	*fläsk*
poultry	*fågel*
beer	*öl*
wine	*vin*
dessert	*efterrätt*
ice cream	*glass*
please bring the check	*notan tack*

Switzerland – Essential Information

PRE-TRIP ESSENTIALS...

WHAT YOU NEED

ESSENTIAL FOR TRAVELERS

● Required ● Recommended ● Not required

Passport	●
Visa	●
Travel, medical insurance	●
Round-trip or onward airline ticket	●
Local currency	●
Traveler's checks	●
Credit cards	●
First-aid kit and medicines	●
Inoculations	●

ESSENTIAL FOR DRIVERS*

Driver's license	●
International Driving Permit	●
Car insurance (for nonrental cars)	●
Car registration (for nonrental cars)	●

*see also DRIVING section

IMPORTANT ADDRESSES

Swiss Tourism
608 Fifth Avenue
New York, NY 10020
☎ (212) 757-5944
Fax (212) 262-6116

Switzerland Tourism
Toedistrasse 7
CH-8027 Zürich, Switzerland
☎ 01 288 1111
Fax 01 288 1205

American Embassy
Jubiläumstrasse 93
CH-3005 Bern, Switzerland
☎ 031 357 7011
Fax 031 357 7344
Open Mon.–Fri. 9–11:30 and 2:30–4

COUNTRY ESSENTIALS...

CUSTOMS

YES
Duty-free limits on goods brought in from non-European countries:
400 cigarettes or 100 cigarillos or cigars or 500 g. tobacco; 2 L. alcohol under 15% volume; 1 L. alcohol over 15% volume; plus any other duty-free goods (including gifts) to the value of SF100. These limits apply to visitors aged 17 and over. There are no currency regulations. There is no limit on the importation of tax-paid goods purchased within the European Union if they are for personal use.

NO
No unlicensed drugs, weapons, ammunition, obscene material, pets or other animals, counterfeit money or copied goods, meat or poultry.

For customs limits for returning U.S. citizens see page 16.

MONEY

Switzerland's currency is the Swiss franc (SF), which is divided into 100 centimes or "Rappen." The denominations of franc bills are 10, 20, 50, 100, 500 and 1,000. There are coins of 5, 10, 20 and 50 centimes and 1, 2 and 5SF. Exchange dollars or traveler's checks *(Reiseschecks)* at a bank *(Bank)*, exchange office *(Wechselbüro)*, post office *(Postamt)* or hotel. Swiss Bankers' traveler's checks (in Swiss francs) can be obtained from various overseas branches of Swiss banks and are accepted in Switzerland at their face value and without a commission fee. Exchange rate at press time: $1 = 1.6SF

TIPS AND GRATUITIES

Tips are welcomed but not expected, as a service charge is always included. A small tip is accepted for exceptional service.

Restaurants, cafés/bars	change
Taxis (usually includes service)	change
Porters, chambermaids	change
Hairdressers	change
Restroom/cloakroom attendants	change

TIME ZONES

ZÜRICH	NEW YORK	CHICAGO	DENVER	SAN FRANCISCO
12:00 noon	6 hours behind Switzerland	7 hours behind Switzerland	8 hours behind Switzerland	9 hours behind Switzerland

535

COMMUNICATIONS

POST OFFICES

Buy stamps *(Briefmarken)* at a post office *(Postamt)*, newsstand *(Informationsstand)* or from a hotel.

Hours for out-of-town post offices may vary.

TELEPHONES

You can use cash or a prepaid phone card *(Kartentelefon)* to make a call in Switzerland. Most telephones have direct dialing for international calls; if you need to go through an operator dial 114. A Taxcard (phone card) can be bought from newsstands, gas stations and post offices for 5, 10 and 20SF. Check that the phone booth is equipped with a Taxcard reader. You can also make a call with 1 and 5SF coins.

Phoning inside Switzerland
All Swiss telephone numbers in this book include an area code; dial the number that is listed. To call the operator dial 111.

Phoning Switzerland from abroad
The country code for Switzerland is 41. Note that Swiss numbers in this book do not include the country code; you will need to prefix this number if you are phoning from another country. To phone Switzerland from the United States or Canada, omit the first zero from the Swiss number and add the prefix 011 41. (Note that Swiss area codes are either one or two digits.) Example: 01 122 33 44 becomes 011 41 1 122 33 44.

Phoning from Switzerland
To phone the United States or Canada from Switzerland, prefix the area code and number with 001.
Example: (111) 222-3333 becomes 001 111 222-3333.
To call international information dial 191.

EMERGENCY PHONE NUMBERS

Police *(Polizei)*	117
Fire *(Feuerwehr)*	118
Ambulance *(Krankenwagen)*	117 or 114

Emergency calls are free from phone booths.

HOURS OF OPERATION

- ● Stores Mon.–Sat.
- ● Offices Mon.–Fri.
- ● Banks Mon.–Fri.
- ● Post offices Mon.–Fri.
- ● Museums/monuments
- ● Pharmacies Mon.–Sat.

```
7  8  9  10 11 12  1  2  3  4  5  6  7
```

Stores close on Saturday afternoon at 4 or 5. In large towns stores may close on Monday morning, while out-of-town stores often close on a Wednesday or Thursday afternoon; some also may close for lunch.

The hours of operation for banks are varied and complicated depending on the town; inquire at your hotel or a tourist office.

Post offices close at 11 on Saturday morning; small offices have briefer hours of operation.

Museums often close on Monday and hours vary, so check locally.

NATIONAL HOLIDAYS

Banks, businesses and most stores close on these days. Various cantons observe other national holidays such as May 1, Corpus Christi and All Saints' Day.

Jan. 1 & 2	New Year
Mar./Apr.	Good Friday
Mar./Apr.	Easter Monday
May	Ascension Day
May/Jun.	Pentecost Monday
Aug. 1	National Day
Dec. 25	Christmas Day
Dec. 26	St. Stephen's Day

PHOTOGRAPHY

The conditions for taking photographs vary, although generally the light is bright. Check first before taking photographs in churches and museums; it may be forbidden or you may have to ask for permission. Film and camera batteries are readily available around tourist areas, but prices may be high. Rapid-developing services also are widely available.

Switzerland – Essential Information

HEALTH

MEDICAL INSURANCE
Private medical insurance is recommended. U.S. and Canadian visitors will have to pay for all medical treatment, including emergency assistance, consultation or admittance to a hospital *(Krankenhaus)*. If you are planning to take part in winter sports, special sports policies are widely available. For information on medical issues dial Anglo-Phone, 157 5014, from anywhere in Switzerland.

DENTAL SERVICES
A dentist *(Zahnarzt)* will charge for any treatment; dental work is expensive, so check whether it is covered by your medical insurance. Dentists are listed in the telephone directory, or ask for English-speaking dentists at your embassy or hotel, or at a tourist office.

SUN ADVICE
Conditions vary considerably; no country in Europe combines within so small an area such marked climate contrasts. The sun can be deceptively strong in the mountains; protection is essential. The warmest part of Switzerland is south of the Alps as it comes under the influence of the Mediterranean. Sun protection is needed; it is advisable to wear a hat and apply a sunscreen.

DRUGS
Pharmacies sell a range of medicines and drugs and dispense prescriptions. Many pharmacists speak English. At least one pharmacy in every town stays open late; information is displayed on store doors.

SAFE WATER
Tap water is safe to drink throughout Switzerland. Mineral water *(Sprudelwasser)* is widely available.

RESTROOMS

Most toilets *(Toiletten)* are clean and well maintained. They are indicated by a variety of signs, such as "WC" or Toiletten. Women's restrooms are designated *Damen, Frauen, Femmes, Dames, Signore* or *Donne;* men's as *Herren, Manner, Hommes, Messieurs, Signori* or *Uomini.*

ELECTRICITY

Switzerland has a 220-volt power supply. Electrical sockets take plugs with two round pins; American appliances will need a plug adapter and will require a transformer if they do not have a dual-voltage facility.

NATIONAL TRANSPORTATION

TRAIN *(Zug)*
Swiss Federal Railways is Chemins de fer Federeaux (CFF) in French, Schweizerische Bundesbahnen (SBB) in German, and Ferrovie Federali Svizzere (FFS) in Italian. It runs a fast, clean and efficient service. Express trains only stop at major cities. Regionalzuge are slow trains usually running the same routes. To reach an English-speaking operator, 157 2222.

BUS *(Bus)*
The bus service takes passengers to mountainous regions where railroads are unable to go. Mail bus routes encounter magnificent scenery joining villages and towns, occasionally even delivering the mail. There are many special offers; passes and cards that combine train, bus and boat travel are available at reduced rates. Eurolines operates in Switzerland: 01 215 7070.

FERRY *(Fähre)*
There are many excursions on Switzerland's lakes. Regional tourist offices in different cantons can offer information, and some take reservations.

DRIVING

DRIVE ON THE RIGHT

SPEED LIMITS
Police can impose on-the-spot fines for which a receipt is issued.

Limited-access highways *(Autobahn)*
120 k.p.h. (74 m.p.h.)
Divided highways
100 k.p.h. (62 m.p.h.)

Main roads
80 k.p.h. (49 m.p.h.)

Urban areas
50 k.p.h. (31 m.p.h.)

SEAT BELTS
Must be worn in front seats at all times and in rear seats where fitted. Children under 12 are not allowed in a front seat.

BLOOD ALCOHOL
The legal blood alcohol limit is 0.08%. Random breath tests on drivers are carried out frequently, especially late at night, and the penalties for offenders are severe.

DRIVING continued

TOLLS
An annual road tax of SF40 is levied on all cars and motorcycles using Swiss highways. Permits *(Vignettes)* are available at border crossings, post offices and service areas in Switzerland and are valid for multiple re-entry into Switzerland within the duration of the license period. To avoid delay at the border it is advisable to buy the permit in advance from a tourist office, or contact your local AAA club or AAA travel agency.

CAR RENTAL
The leading rental firms have offices at airports and train stations. Hertz offes discounted rates for AAA members (see page 15). For reservations:

	UNITED STATES	SWITZERLAND
Alamo	(800) 327-9633	01 816 3290
Avis	(800) 331-2112	022 929 0330
Budget	(800) 527-0700	031 928 2424
Hertz	(800) 654-3080	031 318 2160

FUEL
Gas and diesel are sold in liters. There are 24-hour gas stations on highways and in cities; many have refreshment facilities and stores. Credit cards are accepted.

AAA AFFILIATED MOTORING CLUB
Touring Club Swisse (TCS)
Chemin de Blandonnet 4, Case postale 820, CH-1214 Vernier, Switzerland
☎ 022 417 2727, fax 022 417 2020
If you break down while driving, phone 140 (TCS breakdown service).
Not all clubs offer full services to AAA members.

BREAKDOWNS AND ACCIDENTS
There are 24-hour emergency phones at regular intervals on highways. If you are involved in an accident ☎ 117 for police assistance. Most car rental firms provide their own free rescue service; if your car is rented, follow the instructions given in the documentation. Use of a car repair service other than those authorized by your rental company may violate your agreement.

OTHER INFORMATION
The minimum age for driving a car is 18 (may be higher for some car rental firms).
An International Driving Permit (IDP) is recommended; some rental firms require them, and they can speed up formalities if you are involved in an accident. A Green Card (international motor insurance certificate) is recommended if you are driving a private car; see page 15 for more information.
Dimmed headlights must be used when passing through tunnels. Yellow mail buses have priority at all times, as do vehicles ascending mountain roads. Many mountain pass roads are closed from October to June.

USEFUL WORDS AND PHRASES

There are four official languages spoken in Switzerland: German, French, Italian and Romansch. About 18% of the population in southwest Switzerland speak French. South of the Alps, Italian (12%) is predominant throughout Ticino and parts of the Grisons (also known as the Graubunden). Most Swiss (65%) speak German. A Swiss-German dialect with a variety of local variations is used in everyday conversation; traditional German is used for business purposes.

The fourth language is Romansch, an ancient hybrid of Celtic and Latin tongues spoken by about 40,000 people in the Surselva region of southeastern Switzerland.

This coexistence of distinct languages results in a true "European" nation. The Romansch area is probably the most "Swiss" part of the country. French influence is evident in Lausanne, while Lugano exhibits both Italian and Swiss influences.

Every Swiss child learns two or three languages. English is spoken throughout the country, but an attempt to say a few words in any of Switzerland's languages will always be appreciated.

See page 489 for French words, page 493 for German and page 509 for Italian.

Switzerland – Essential Information

Hotels and Restaurants

The hotels and restaurants in this book were selected by on-site contributing authors and include establishments in several price ranges. Since price is often the best indication of the level of facilities and quality of service guests can expect, a three-tiered price guide appears at the beginning of the listings for each featured city. Keep in mind that prices vary widely depending on the country; dinner in Helsinki, for example, can cost up to three times as much as a similar dinner in Athens or Prague. Because variable rates will affect the amount of foreign currency that can be exchanged for dollars (and thus affect the cost of a room or a meal), price ranges are given in the local currency.

Although price ranges and any given days/times restaurants are closed were accurate at press time, this information is always subject to change without notice. If there is a certain establishment in which you're interested, it is always advisable to call ahead and verify specific amenities or hours of operation. The larger and more expensive hotels, and the better-known restaurants, are more likely to have someone who speaks English on staff; smaller establishments, particularly in southern Europe, may not. In such cases it may be more productive to inquire by fax rather than phone.

Map coordinates given in each listing relate to the city maps and give an idea of the approximate area in which each establishment is located. Although you may be able to find some of the street locations on these maps, pick up a more detailed city map from the local tourist office to help you find places.

Facilities suitable for travelers with disabilities vary greatly, and you are strongly advised to contact an establishment directly to determine whether it will be able to meet your needs. Buildings in the old sections of city centers may not be adequately designed or equipped for visitors with limited or impaired mobility.

Accommodations

Accommodations have been selected with two considerations in mind: a particularly attractive character or sense of local flavor, or a central location that is convenient for sightseeing. Establishments in differnet price ranges are included for each city.

Centrally located hotels fill up quickly, especially during busy summer vacation periods; make reservations well in advance. Many international hotel chains have Internet sites that either

HOTELS AND RESTAURANTS

*"*N*OTHING helps scenery like ham and eggs.*"*

From *A Tramp Abroad*,
by Mark Twain

allow you to make online reservations or provide a central reservation phone number. In-room bathrooms (usually referred to as "en-suite facilities") may not be available in smaller budget hotels.

European hotels normally provide a light breakfast of rolls or croissants and coffee (where this is not the case, the listing description notes that the rate is for "room only"). Breakfast in British and Irish hotels, however, is likely to be a full meal of bacon, sausage, eggs, fried potatoes and toast that should leave you feeling well-fed most of the day.

Some hotels offer a price for overnight accommodations that includes an evening meal (known as "half-board" in Great Britain and Ireland and *demi-pension* in French-speaking countries).

Eating Out

Listed restaurants range from upscale places suitable for an elegant evening out to small cafés where you can stop and take a leisurely break from a busy day of sightseeing. Some are close to attractions; where this is the case, there is a cross-reference under the attraction listing. Other possibilities for getting a bite to eat are the cafeterias and restaurants on the premises of museums and galleries.

For the homesick, many U.S. fast-food chains have found their way to Europe. But be sure to sample the amazing variety of indigenous European fast food: *crêpes* (filled pancakes) in France; tasty hot *Wurst* (sausages) in Germany and Austria; fish and chips (fish filets and french fries) in Britain; the savory *tapas* appetizers served in Spanish bars; and the wonderful pizzas in Italy – served crusty and piping hot from charcoal ovens or *al taglio* (sliced to go) on street corners.

For a more civilized break, many European hotels, especially the larger ones in big cities, are not only options for an overnight stay but also for a meal. Their lounges and bars often are comfortable, quiet places to stop and relax over morning coffee, afternoon tea with cakes and sandwiches, or an evening drink. A stop also provides an opportunity to use the hotel's restroom. Top-flight hotels often serve fairly reasonably priced snacks, but inquire about prices before ordering if you're traveling on a budget.

Alcoholic beverages have a rich European heritage. France, Germany and Spain produce memorable wines; beers in the Czech Republic, Belgium and Britain are justly famed; and Guinness, of course, is an Irish institution. And the nonalcoholic fruit juices (*portokalada freska*) served in Greece – orange, lemon, watermelon, peach – are wonderfully fresh and a perfect antidote to the hot Greek summer sun.

Austria

KEY TO SYMBOLS

- ✚ map page number and coordinates
- ✉ address
- ☎ telephone number
- 🕐 days/times closed
- Ⓜ nearest subway station
- 🚌 nearest bus/trolley bus/tram route
- ⛴ ferry
- $$$ expensive
- $$ moderate
- $ inexpensive
- AE American Express
- CB Carte Blanche
- DI Diners
- MC MasterCard
- VI VISA

VIENNA HOTELS

Price guide: (double room with breakfast for two people)
$ S700–1,000
$$ S1,000–2,000
$$$ over S2,000

Ana Grand Hotel Wien $$$

This is the ultimate in luxury, combining the style and service of a majestic old European hotel with modern comforts. Ask about the Grand Opera package, which includes a champagne buffet breakfast, the best seats at the opera (book 2 weeks in advance) and a two-course meal afterward in the hotel's smart restaurant, Le Ciel.
✚ 26D2   ✉ Kärtner Ring 9   ☎ 01 51 58 00; fax 01 51 51 31-3
🚌 Tram 1, 2, D, J   AE, DI, MC, VI

Kärtnerhof $$

The Kärtnerhof, situated in the city center, is convenient for sightseeing. It occupies a 19th-century building with a roof garden and sits quietly on a cul-de-sac, where a gate leads to the beautiful courtyard of Heiligenkreuzerhof.
✚ 26D3   ✉ Grashofgasse 4
☎ 01 51 21 92-3; fax 01 513 22 28 33   Ⓜ Stephansplatz, Schwedenplatz   AE, DI, MC, VI

König von Ungarn $$$

This 18th-century building has rooms set around a covered central courtyard, which has been converted into an elegant bar/sitting room. The restaurant serves traditional Viennese meals in the vaulted dining rooms. It's very close to St. Stephen's Cathedral and next to the Figarohaus (Figaro House), so named because Mozart composed his opera *The Marriage of Figaro* while living in an apartment there.
✚ 26D2   ✉ Schulerstrasse 10
☎ 01 51 58 40; fax 01 51 58 48   Ⓜ Stephansplatz   🚌 1A   AE, DI, MC, VI

Pension Felicitas $

Hidden away on a quiet side street in Josefstadt, just behind the parliament building, this accommodation is for those who like a personal hotel touch: It feels a little like you're staying in somebody's home, perfect after a day's sightseeing.
✚ 26C3   ✉ Josefsgasse 7
☎ 01 40 57 21-2   Ⓜ Rathaus
No credit cards

Römischer Kaiser $$

Originally a small baroque palace in the Old City, this is now an exotically furnished hotel with crimson fabrics and sparkling chandeliers. The hotel makes special arrangements such as a casino package, called "Rouge et Noir." There's no restaurant on the premises.
✚ 26D2   ✉ Annagasse 16   ☎ 01 5127 7510; fax 01 512 77 51 13
Ⓜ Stephansplatz   🚌 1, 4   AE, DI, MC, VI

VIENNA RESTAURANTS

Price guide: (dinner per person, excluding drinks)
$ S150–200
$$ S200–300
$$$ over S300

Augustinerkeller $$

A range of good Austrian- and Viennese-style dishes are served with locally produced wines. It's popular with foreign visitors.
✚ 26D2   ✉ Augustinerstrasse 1
☎ 01 53 31 02-6   🕐 Closed Sun.   Ⓜ U1, U2, U4 to Oper   AE, DI, VI

Café Dreschler $$

The first café that opens its doors in the mornings has an interesting mix of customers, including people on their way home from a late night out and stall owners on their way to an early start at the market. Expect a quiet, smoky atmosphere and billiard tables. Hot dishes are served throughout the day.
✚ 26C2   ✉ Linke Wien Zeile 22
🕐 Closed Sun.   Ⓜ U1, U2, U4   🚌 4A, 59A, trams 62, 65   No credit cards

Do & Co Im Haas-Haus $$$

Shellfish, Thai and Japanese dishes are specialties at this trendy top-floor restaurant in the glass-fronted Haas-Haus building. You'll get good views of the Cathedral.
✚ 26D3   ✉ 7th floor, Haas-Haus, Stephansplatz 12   ☎ 01 53 53 96-9 or 01 53 53 51-8   Ⓜ U1, U3   AE, DI, MC, VI

Im Palais Schwarzenberg $$$

For excellent views of the Belvedere gardens come to this classy restaurant, which serves wonderful game dishes like stuffed guinea fowl in white port sauce and medallions of delicious venison.

Austria

📍 26D2 ✉ Schwarzenbergerplatz
9 ☎ 01 79 84 51-5 🚋 Trams D,
1, 2 AE, DI, MC, VI

Stadtbeisel $$

Original Viennese dishes are served
in the oldest part of the Old Town.
Typical items include *Wiener
Tafelspitz* (boiled rump of beef with
apple and horseradish sauce) and
delicious sautéed pike or perch
with garlic butter and venison in
brandy sauce.
📍 26D3 ✉ Naglergasse 21
☎ 01 53 33 50-7 🚇 U3 VI

Steirereck $$$

Tables set out in the green conservatory, and in summer on a veranda,
make this a great spot for a special
occasion or a relaxing lunch. The
food is a mix of traditional, new and
regional, and there is an outstanding wine list from the richly stocked,
vaulted cellars.
📍 26E2 ✉ Rasumofskygasse 2
☎ 01 71 33 16-8 🚫 Closed
Sat.–Sun. 🚇 U3 to Rochusgasse
AE, DI, MC, VI

INNSBRUCK HOTELS
Price guide: (double room with
breakfast for two people)
$ S700–1,000
$$ S1,000–2,000
$$$ over S2,000

Central $$$

This centrally located hotel is big
on comfort and service and has a
wide range of facilities, including
a sunning terrace.
📍 35A1 ✉ Gilmstrasse 5 ☎ 05
12 59 20; fax 05 1258 0310 🚌 4, O
AE, DI, MC, VI

Europa Tyrol $$$

Innsbruck's top hotel has a wide
range of rooms at varying prices,
some elegant public areas, and a
friendly and welcoming staff.
📍 35B1 ✉ Südtirolerplatz 2
☎ 05 12 59 31; fax 05 1258 7800
🚌 1, 3, 6 AE, DI, MC, VI

Goldener Adler $$$

A truly charming and historic hotel
in the heart of old Innsbruck, where
modern comfort goes hand-in-hand
with Tyrolean character. There are
also two excellent restaurants.
📍 35A2 ✉ Herzog-Friedrich Strasse
6 ☎ 05 1257 1111; fax 05 1258
4409 🚌 A, tram 1 AE, DI, MC, VI

Maximilian $$

On the edge of Old Town, this
modern hotel combines comfort with
traditional service and atmosphere.
📍 35A2 ✉ Marktgraben 7–9
☎ 05 12 59 96-7; fax 05 1257 7450
🚌 A, O; tram 1 AE, DI, MC, VI

Weisses Kreuz $$

Mozart once stayed at this 15th-
century Old Town hotel, which
combines Tyrolean charm with
modern comfort. Restaurants are
on the premises.
📍 35A2 ✉ Herzog-Friedrich
Strasse 31 ☎ 05 12 59 47-9 or 05
125 94 79 90 🚌 A, O; tram 1 AE,
DI, MC, VI

INNSBRUCK RESTAURANTS
Price guide: (dinner per person,
excluding drinks)
$ S150–200
$$ S200–300
$$$ over 300

Altstadtstüberl $$

Known for its contemporary cooking,
this Old Town restaurant offers good
vegetarian dishes.
📍 35A2 ✉ Riesengasse 13
☎ 05 1258 2347 🚫 Closed Sun.
🚌 A, O; tram 1 CB, DI, VI

Gasthof-Hotel Weisses Kreuz $$

One of Innsbruck's oldest and best
restaurants serves Tyrolean and
Austrian specialties in charming
dining rooms.
📍 35A2 ✉ Herzog-Friedrich
Strasse 31 ☎ 05 12 59 47-9
🚌 A, O; tram 1 AE, DI, MC, VI

Hirschenstuben $$

This Old Town restaurant offers fish
and international dishes, as well as
traditional favorites.
📍 35A2 ✉ Rebachgasse 5
☎ 05 1258 2979 🚫 Closed Sun.
🚌 A, O; tram 1 AE, DI, MC, VI

Ottoburg $

This cozy restaurant, a good value,
serves a wide range of Austrian and
vegetarian dishes.
📍 35A2 ✉ Herzog-Friedrich
Strasse 1 ☎ 05 1257 4652 🚌 A,
O; tram 1 AE, MC, VI

Restaurant Goldener Adler $$

Its decor and friendly staff make this
traditional restaurant popular with
locals and tourists alike.
📍 35A2 ✉ Herzog-Friedrich

Strasse 6 ☎ 05 1258 6354 🚌 A,
O; tram 1 AE, DI, MC, VI

SALZBURG HOTELS
Price guide: (double room with
breakfast for two people)
$ S700–1,000
$$ S1,000–2,000
$$$ over S2,000

Altstadt Radisson $$$

This renovated luxury hotel, in one of
Salzburg's oldest buildings in the
heart of the Old Town, has lovely
rooms and an excellent restaurant.
📍 40C2 ✉ Rudolfskai
28/Judengasse ☎ 06 628 48 57
10; fax 06 628 48 57 16 🚌 5, 55
AE, DI, MC, VI

Altstadt Wolf-Dietrich $$$

This comfortable family-run hotel on
the edge of the city's historic center
has a good restaurant and an indoor
swimming pool.
📍 40C4 ✉ Wolf-Dietrich-Strasse
7 ☎ 06 6287 1275; fax 06 6288
2320 🚌 5, 6, 51 AE, DI, MC, VI

Am Dom $$

Book ahead to ensure a room at this
good, reasonably priced choice in
the heart of the historic center.
📍 40C2 ✉ Goldgasse 17 ☎ 06
6284 2765; fax 06 6284 2755 🚌 5,
6, 51 AE, DI, MC, VI

Goldener Hirsch $$$

This luxurious, baronial-style hotel is
one of Salzburg's oldest and most
famous accommodations, and provides service to match.
📍 40B3 ✉ Getreidegasse 37
☎ 06 62 80 84-0; fax: 06 628 08 42
88 🚌 5, 6, 51, 55 AE, DI, MC, VI

Schloss Mönstein $$$

This first-class hotel is beautifully
situated in wooded grounds high
above the old center of Salzburg.
📍 40A3 ✉ Am Mönschberg 26
☎ 06 628 48 55 50; fax: 06 6284
8555/50 🚌 60, 29 AE, DI, MC, VI

SALZBURG RESTAURANTS
Price guide: (dinner per person,
excluding drinks)
$ S150–200
$$ S200–300
$$$ over S300

Augustiner Bräu $

This huge restaurant and summer
beer-garden serves beer, wurst and

Austria, Belgium

KEY TO SYMBOLS

- ✚ map page number and coordinates
- ✉ address
- ☎ telephone number
- ⏰ days/times closed
- Ⓜ nearest subway station
- 🚌 nearest bus/trolley bus/tram route
- ⛴ ferry
- **$$$** expensive
- **$$** moderate
- **$** inexpensive
- AE American Express
- CB Carte Blanche
- DI Diners
- MC MasterCard
- VI VISA

---

simple Austrian fare in wood-paneled halls and is very popular with tourists.

✚ 40A4 ✉ Augustinergasse 4 ☎ 06 6243 1246 ⏰ 0 No credit cards

Bei Bruno $$$

This smart restaurant features dishes from the Tyrol, along with local specialties and an interesting wine list.

✚ 40B3 ✉ Makartplatz 4 ☎ 06 6287 8417 ⏰ Closed Sun. 🚌 2, 6, 51 AE, DI, MC, VI

Cafe Winkler $$$

This elegant restaurant, situated at the top of Mönschberg hill, is a wonderful place to dine while enjoying superb views.

✚ 40A3 ✉ Am Mönschberg 32 ☎ 06 6284 7338 ⏰ Closed Mon. 🚌 29, 60 AE

Stiftskeller St. Peter $$

Said to be Europe's oldest restaurant, Stiftskeller is a popular beer cellar serving reasonably priced beer, wine and local dishes in atmospheric rooms.

✚ 40B2 ✉ St. Peter-Bezirk 1 ☎ 06 6284 1268 🚌 1, 5, 6 AE, DI, MC, VI

BRUSSELS HOTELS

Price guide: (double room with breakfast for two people)
- **$** up to 3,000BF
- **$$** 3,000–7,000BF
- **$$$** over 7,000BF

Amigo $$

This charming hotel is located near the heart of old Brussels, just behind Grand-Place. It has modern amenities, but with luxurious style and elegance; there's a good chance you may bump into media stars over sumptuous breakfasts.

✚ 56B2 ✉ 1–3 rue de l'Amigo ☎ 02 547 4747; fax 02 513 5277 🚌 34, 48, 94; tram 23, 52, 55, 56 AE, MC, VI

Conrad $$$

Located on avenue Louise, in Brussels' fashionable shopping quarter, this luxurious, modern hotel is close to tram and subway connections to the rest of the city.

✚ 56B1 ✉ 72 avenue Louise ☎ 02 542 4242; fax 02 542 4200 🚌 Tram 93, 94 AE, MC, VI

Le Dixseptième $$$

Seventeenth-century ambience and quality service typify this very stylish central hotel, not far from Grand-Place.

✚ 56B2 ✉ 25 rue de la Madeleine ☎ 02 502 5744; fax 02 502 6424 Ⓜ Gare Centrale AE, MC, VI

Metropole $$$

This expensive but very luxurious hotel has a long pedigree; it opened in the 1890s and still reflects *fin de siècle* elegance. The in-house restaurant, L'Alban Chambon, has top cuisine to match.

✚ 56B3 ✉ 31 place De Brouckère/De Brouckereplein ☎ 02 217 2300; fax 02 218 0220 Ⓜ De Brouckère 🚌 Tram 23, 52, 55, 81 AE, MC, VI

Noga $

Although this small, charming hotel with modern rooms has a cozy "old" Brussels style (and ample breakfasts), it doesn't have good views from bedroom windows; it's situated in the convenient and attractive St. Catherine district, which does have great character.

✚ 56B4 ✉ 38 rue du Beguinage/Begijnhofstraat ☎ 02 218 6763; fax 02 218 1603 Ⓜ St. Catherine 🚌 47 AE, MC, VI

BRUSSELS RESTAURANTS

Price guide: (dinner per person, excluding drinks)
- **$** 400–500BF
- **$$** 500–1,000BF
- **$$$** over 1,000BF

Aux Armes de Bruxelles $$

Good Belgian cuisine, either in a traditional restaurant setting or in the more relaxed bistro, is offered at this art deco-style restaurant in the rue des Bouchers district.

✚ 56B2–B3 ✉ rues de Bouchers 13 ☎ 02 511 5598 ⏰ Closed Mon. mid-Jun. to mid-Jul. Ⓜ Bourse 🚌 Tram 23, 52, 56, 81 MC, VI

La Belle Maraîchère

Fish and lobster are the specialties at this restaurant, considered one of Brussels' best, in what was once the dockside district of St. Catherine.

✚ 56A3 ✉ 11 Place St.-Catherine ☎ 02 512 9759 ⏰ Closed Wed. and Thu. Ⓜ St.-Catherine 🚌 47

Belgium

Comme Chez Soi $$$
Brussels' top gastronomic experience can be savored at this celebrated restaurant that boasts prestigious awards from leading food critics. New Belgian cuisine with traditional specialties is featured; reserve well in advance.
✛ 56A2 ✉ 23 Place Rouppe ☎ 02 512 2921 ⏱ Closed Sun. and Mon. 🚋 Tram 23, 52, 55, 56 MC, VI

La Maison du Cygne $$$
This stylish restaurant in one of the guild house buildings in Grand-Place was originally a medieval tavern, and then head quarters of the Guild of Butchers. Enjoy truffles and braised turbot while contemplating the fact that Karl Marx wrote part of the *Communist Manifesto* here.
✛ 56B2 ✉ 9 Grand-Place ☎ 02 511 8244 ⏱ Closed Aug. 1–24 🚇 Central Station 🚋 Tram 23, 52, 56, 81 MC, VI

La Rose Blanche $$
Belgian cuisine is cooked in beer at this tavern serving 50 traditional and special beers.
✛ 56B2 ✉ 11 Grand-Place ☎ 02 513 6479 🚇 Central Station 🚋 Tram 23, 52, 56, 81 MC, VI

La Truffe Noire $$$
This top award-winning Italian restaurant, whose name underlines its specialty, serves truffles with just about everything, in luxurious surroundings.
✛ 56 Off the map ✉ 12 Boulevard de la Cambre ☎ 02 640 4422 ⏱ Closed Sun. 🚋 Tram 23, 90

BRUGES HOTELS
Price guide: (double room with breakfast for two people)
$ up to 3,000BF
$$ 3,000–7,000BF
$$$ over 7,000BF

Bourgoensche Cruyce $$
This small, comfortable quality hotel sits within a courtyard and overlooks a lovely stretch of canal. The Dijver and the Markt are nearby.
✛ 62B2 ✉ Wollestraat 41–43 ☎ 050 337 926; fax 050 341 968 🚋 1, 6, 11, 16 AE, MC, VI

De Orangerie $$$
One of Bruges' most lauded hotels is within this 17th-century, ivy-clad

building, with a superb canal-side location and views of the Dijver. Guests can have breakfast in the paneled dining room or on the canal-side terrace; they can also use the pool and sauna of the nearby De Tuilerieen Hotel.
✛ 62B2 ✉ Kartuizerinnensstraat 10 ☎ 050 341 649; fax 050 333 016 🚋 1, 6, 11, 16 AE, MC, VI

Die Swaene $$$
This beautifully furnished hotel is in a central but quiet location; its restaurant is noted for good food and service.
✛ 62C2 ✉ Steenhouwersdijk 1 ☎ 050 342 798; fax 050 336 674 🚋 1, 6, 11, 16 AE, MC, VI

De ter Brughe $$
Located a few minutes' walk north of the Markt is this canal-side hotel, housed in a handsome building dating from the 16th century that is one of the oldest buildings in Bruges. Enjoy hearty breakfasts in the attractive vaulted cellar.
✛ 62B3 ✉ Oost-Gistelhof 2 ☎ 050 340 324; fax 050 338 873 🚋 All buses AE, MC, VI

Prinsenhof $$
A few streets east of the Markt is this pleasant, family-run hotel with friendly service and charming touches, including old clocks, chandeliers and antiques. It's known for its large breakfasts.
✛ 62C2 ✉ Ontvangersstraat 9 ☎ 050 342 690; fax 050 342 321 🚋 All buses AE, MC, VI

BRUGES RESTAURANTS
Price guide: (dinner per person, excluding drinks)
$ 400–500BF
$$ 500–1,000BF
$$$ over 1,000BF

Brasserie Erasmus $$
With more than 150 brands to choose from, it's obvious that this genuine Belgian eatery specializes in beers; among its specialties is *waterzooi*, rabbit stewed in beer.
✛ 62B2 ✉ Wollestraat 35 ☎ 050 335 781 ⏱ Closed Mon. and late Jan.–early Feb. 🚋 1, 6, 11, 16 MC, VI

Den Gouden Harynck $$$
This popular and expensive restaurant has a stylish interior and

serves fine Belgian and international cuisine. Fish dishes from caviar to lobster are the specialty; make reservations in advance.
✛ 62B1–B2 ✉ Groeninge 25 ☎ 050 337 637; fax 050 344 270 ⏱ Closed Sun. and Mon.; mid-Jul. through Aug. 🚋 1 MC, VI

Marieke van Brugghe $$$
Belgian cuisine is at its finest in this traditional restaurant with art nouveau style, popular with the Brugeans (book ahead). Try the North Sea bouillabaisse or the *kalfs blanket*, veal ragout.
✛ 62B1–B2 ✉ Mariastraat 17 ☎ 050 343 366 🚋 1 MC, VI

Ristorante le due Venezie $$$
Arrive early at this trattoria in the heart of Belgian Bruges, which has the best Italian cuisine around. Service is friendly.
✛ 62B2 ✉ Kleine Sint Amandsstraat 2 ☎ 050 332 326 ⏱ Closed Tue. 🚋 1 MC, VI

Tom Pouce $$
This popular and conveniently located café-restaurant on the Burg serves traditional Belgian dishes and delicious waffles, pancakes and home-made ice cream.
✛ 62B2 ✉ Burg 17 ☎ 050 330 336 🚋 All buses MC, VI

GHENT HOTELS
Price guide: (double room with breakfast for two people)
$ up to 3,000BF
$$ 3,000–7,000BF
$$$ over 7,000BF

Chamade $$
Located just north of the railroad station but with quick access to trams for the city center, this modern hotel lacks architectural style but offers excellent service and superb views from the top-floor breakfast room.
✛ 70 Off the map ✉ Blankenbergestraat 2 ☎ 09 220 1515; fax 09 220 1515 🚋 14, 15, 65, 69; tram 1, 10, 12, 40 AE, DC, VI

Erasmus $$
This cozy, old-fashioned hotel with personal touches and antique furnishings is located near historic Kornlei; breakfasts are ample and very good.

KEY TO SYMBOLS

- ➕ map page number and coordinates
- ✉ address
- ☎ telephone number
- 🕐 days/times closed
- Ⓜ nearest subway station
- 🚌 nearest bus/trolley bus/tram route
- ⛴ ferry
- $$$ expensive
- $$ moderate
- $ inexpensive
- AE American Express
- CB Carte Blanche
- DI Diners
- MC Mastercard
- VI VISA

Banquets for All

You can go back through history while enjoying a hearty meal in Ghent. Various traditional banquets are staged in such fascinating venues as a 13th-century monastery, a medieval crypt or the hall of a castle. The Medieval Banquet is accompanied by troubadours, dancers and a court jester. The Belle Époque Cabaret Banquet features song and dance, tap dancers, ventriloquist and other acts with themes from the 1870s to the 1930s. The Renaissance Banquet features court dances by dancers in period costume. The Mississipi Jazz evening features Cajun food and an accompaniment of New Orleans, Dixieland and blues music. For information and reservations, phone 09 2338660

➕ 70A3 ✉ Poel 25 ☎ 09 224 2195; fax 09 233 4241 🚌 16, 18, 38 AE, VI

Gravensteen $$

Housed in a 19th-century mansion, this comfortable hotel is conveniently located close to the Castle of the Counts and other Ghent attractions. Try to get a reservation in the tower room, which has one of the best views over Ghent.

➕ 70A4 ✉ Jan Breydalstraat 35 ☎ 09 225 1150; fax 09 225 1850 🚌 Tram 1, 10, 11, 13 AE, MC, VI

Novotel Gent Centrum $$

With an outdoor swimming pool, restaurant and good location, this large, comfortable hotel in the center of Ghent has quiet rooms overlooking a central courtyard.

➕ 70B3 ✉ Goudenleeuwplein 5 ☎ 09 224 2230; fax 09 224 3295 🚌 16, 17, 18, 19, 38; tram 12, 41 AE, MC, VI

Sofitel Gent Belfort $$$

This is a large luxury hotel in the historic heart of the city, opposite the Town Hall. Its many amenities, including a restaurant and fitness room, make it a decent value.

➕ 70B3 ✉ Hoogpoort 63 ☎ 09 233 3331; fax 09 233 1102 🚌 16, 17, 18, 19, 38; tram 12, 41 AE, MC, VI

GHENT RESTAURANTS

Price guide: (dinner per person, excluding drinks)
$ 400–500BF
$$ 500–1,000BF
$$$ over 1,000BF

De Hel $$$

This is a small restaurant in one of the Kraanlei's most delightful buildings, "The Flying Deer." French and Belgian cuisine are at their best in the candlelit dining room with fine music playing in the background. Reservations are advised.

➕ 70A4–B4 ✉ Kraanlei 81 ☎ 09 224 3240 🕐 Closed Mon. and Tue. 🚌 Tram 1, 11, 12, 40, 42 MC, VI

Graaf Van Egmond $$

Long-established city restaurant with elegant furnishings and a view of the "Towers of Ghent," churches and civic buildings. Traditional Flemish and French cuisine.

➕ 70A3 ✉ Sint Michielsplein 21 ☎ 09 225 0727 🚌 16, 17, 18, 19, 38, tram 12, 41 MC, VI

Jan Breydal $$$

This expensive but very chic canal-side restaurant is a good place to come after a visit to the Museum of Decorative Arts and Design, nearby. Fish dishes are a specialty of the French cuisine.

➕ 70A4 ✉ Jan Breydelstraat 10 ☎ 09 225 6287 🕐 Closed Sat. evening and Sun. 🚌 Tram 1, 11, 12 MC, VI

Restaurant La Petite Provence $$$

As the name implies, this cozy restaurant at the heart of Ghent offers good French cuisine as well as traditional local specialties. Reservations are advised.

➕ 70B3 ✉ Donkersteeg 4 ☎ 09 225 6501 🚌 Tram 1, 11, 12 MC, VI

St. Jorishof Cour St. Georges $$$

This long-established and very popular and busy eatery at the heart of Ghent has good fish dishes and Belgian specialties. Reservations are advised.

➕ 70B2–B3 ✉ Botermarkt 2 ☎ 09 224 2424 🚌 Tram 1, 21, 40 MC, VI

LONDON HOTELS

Price guide: (double room with breakfast for two people)
$ £30–60
$$ £60–100
$$$ over £100

Dorchester $$$

This world-class hotel and its Park Lane address says everything about the very best in luxury accommodations. The rooms and facilities are second to none.

➕ 86B2 ✉ Hyde Park Corner ☎ 020 7629 8888; fax 020 7409 0114 Ⓜ Hyde Park Corner AE, DI, MC, VI

Kingsway $$

A homey touch is what you'll get at this small, quiet owner-run hotel. It's close to Hyde Park but away from the rush.

➕ 86A3 ✉ 27 Norfolk Square ☎ 020 7723 5569; fax 020 7723 7317 Ⓜ Paddington AE, DI, MC, VI

Britain

London County Hall Travel Inn $
This budget hotel is very well kept and has big rooms, making it popular with families. It's located on the south bank of the River Thames but is close to the Hungerford Bridge pedestrian walkway, which goes into central London.
🏨 86D2 ✉ Belvedere Road ☎ 020 7902 1600; fax 020 7902 1619 🚇 Waterloo AE, MC, VI

Ritz $$$
Luxurious Louis XVI interiors and all the expense and style that goes with the name are the details you can expect at this hotel.
🏨 86C2 ✉ 150 Piccadilly ☎ 020 7493 8181; fax 020 7493 2687 🚇 Green Park AE, DI, MC, VI

Wigmore Court Hotel $$
This small, extremely clean and well-kept, lower- to moderate-priced hotel is in a good location and offers comfortable rooms.
🏨 86B3 ✉ 23 Gloucester Place ☎ 020 7935 0928; fax 020 7487 4254 🚇 Marble Arch or Baker Street MC, VI

LONDON RESTAURANTS
Price guide: (dinner per person, excluding drinks)
$ £10–15
$$ £15–30
$$$ over £30

Café in the Crypt $
This inexpensive eatery, in the heart of London on Trafalgar Square (located in the crypt of St.-Martin-in-the-Fields Church), is well known and offers first-class soups, sandwiches and light meals.
🏨 86D3 ✉ 2b Duncannon Street ☎ 020 7839 4342 🚇 Charing Cross No credit cards

Chez Nico $$$
Outstanding French cuisine from one of Europe's top chefs is served here.
🏨 86B3 ✉ 90 Park Lane ☎ 020 7409 1290 🕐 Closed Sun. 🚇 Hyde Park Corner AE, DI, MC, VI

Connaught $$$
Old English and top French cuisine are available at this restaurant in the heart of fashionable Mayfair. Reservations are advised.
🏨 86B3 ✉ Carlos Place ☎ 020 7499 7070 🚇 Bond Street AE, MC, VI

Joe Allen $$
Celebrities dine at this excellent California-style restaurant, located on the edge of Covent Garden.
🏨 86D3 ✉ 13 Exeter Street ☎ 020 7836 0651 🚇 Covent Garden AE, MC, VI

Quaglino's $$$
Located in an old ballroom, superbly designed and stylish Quaglino's is one of London's trendiest eateries. Modern Continental cuisine is served; reservations are advised.
🏨 86C3 ✉ 16 Bury Street ☎ 020 7930 6767 🚇 Green Park AE, MC, VI, DI

Rock and Sole Plaice $
This is one of the city's best places to sample fish and chips, the national dish. Take out in traditional style, or have a sit-down meal.
🏨 86D3 ✉ 47 Endell Street ☎ 020 7836 3785 🚇 Covent Garden No credit cards

EDINBURGH HOTELS
Price guide: (double room with breakfast for two people)
$ £30–60
$$ £60–100
$$$ over £100

26 Northumberland Street $$
Considered a "guest house" rather than a hotel, this accommodation achieves high standards and is splendidly located in New Town. Visitors can expect legendary Scottish hospitality.
🏨 98C3 ✉ 26 Northumberland Street ☎ 0131 556 1078; fax 0131 557 9445 🚇 13, 190, 27, 47 AE, MC, VI

Brodies Guest House $
This is a typical Scottish bed-and-breakfast with comfortable rooms and very friendly service.
🏨 98 Off the map ✉ 22 East Claremont Street ☎ 0131 556 4032; fax 0131 556 9739 🚇 7, 8, 9, 19 AE, MC, VI

Caledonian Hotel $$$
This top-flight hotel, located at the west end of Princes Street, has great views of Edinburgh Castle. The handsome red sandstone building dates to 1903; there's a health club and a restaurant, the Pompadour, on the premises.
🏨 98B2 ✉ Princes Street

☎ 0131 459 9988; fax 0131 225 6632 🚇 17, 21, 26 AE, MC, VI

Greenside Hotel $$
Quietly situated on the north side of Calton Hill, this pleasant, small hotel offers good views to the Firth of Forth from the top floors and has an in-house bar.
🏨 98E3 ✉ 9 Royal Terrace ☎ 0131 557 0022; fax 0131 557 0022 🚇 1, 4, 5, 26, 44, 63 AE, MC, VI

Roxburghe Hotel $$$
Traditional Scottish hospitality prevails at this upscale hotel in the heart of Georgian Edinburgh, with details and features to match its status.
🏨 98B2 ✉ 38 Charlotte Square ☎ 0131 225 3921; fax 0131 220 2518 🚇 34, 35 AE, MC, VI

EDINBURGH RESTAURANTS
Price guide: (dinner per person, excluding drinks)
$ £10–15
$$ £15–30
$$$ over £30

Creelers $$
This restaurant and bistro just off the Royal Mile specializes in superb seafood, much of it delivered from the owner's fishing business on Scotland's west coast. Start with oysters and mussels, then go on to a main dish of turbot, cod, hake, monkfish or shellfish. Reservations are advised.
🏨 98C2 ✉ 3 Hunter Square ☎ 0131 220 4447 🕐 Closed Sun. 🚇 1, 6 MC, VI

Deacon's Café $
A life-size figure of the infamous Deacon Brodie (an 18th-century town councilor, socialite and part-time burglar) invites you down Lawnmarket to this popular café-restaurant. Good Scots broth, light snacks, and afternoon tea and scones are among the menu items.
🏨 98C2 ✉ 304 Lawnmarket ☎ 0131 226 1894 🚇 1, 6 No credit cards

Duck's At Le Marche Noir $$$
The unusual name of this restaurant is derived from the proprietor's last name. Expect excellent Scottish-French cuisine – everything from quail's eggs to venison – and some

Britain

KEY TO SYMBOLS

- map page number and coordinates
- address
- telephone number
- days/times closed
- nearest subway station
- nearest bus/trolley bus/tram route
- ferry
- **$$$** expensive
- **$$** moderate
- **$** inexpensive
- AE American Express
- CB Carte Blanche
- DI Diners
- MC MasterCard
- VI VISA

exquisite desserts. There's also a good wine list.
98 Off the map ✉ 2–4 Eyre Place ☎ 0131 558 1608 🚌 7, 8, 9, 19, 35 AE, DI, MC, VI

Stac Polly $$$

The very best in Scottish cuisine is provided in the most stylish of surroundings. Try haggis in filo pastry with plum sauce. You'll be very pleased with any of the beef, game and salmon dishes. Reservations are advised.
98 Off the map ✉ 29–33 Dublin Street ☎ 0131 556 2231 Closed Sun. 🚌 8, 9, 19, 39 AE, MC, VI

Witchery $$

This restaurant is located by Edinburgh Castle Esplanade and made even more atmospheric by hundreds of candles reflected off gothic furnishings, tapestries and hand-painted timber ceilings. The Scottish menu has international influences, with the focus on seafood. Reservations are advised.
98C1 ✉ 353 Castlehill ☎ 0131 225 5613 🚌 1, 6 AE, DI, MC, VI

OXFORD HOTELS

Price guide: (double room with breakfast for two people)
$ £30–60
$$ £60–100
$$$ over £100

Bath Place Hotel $$$

Situated in converted 17th-century buildings, this hotel has four-poster beds and a restaurant offering top-quality cuisine, including fish and vegetarian dishes.
107B2 ✉ 4–5 Bath Place ☎ 01865 791812; fax 01865 791834 🚌 All buses via High Street AE, MC, VI

The Eastgate $$$

A charming mid-size hotel near Magdalen Bridge and a short distance from river walks. All rooms are en-suite, and the Case Boheme restaurant is attached.
107C1 ✉ High Street (entrance on Merton Street) ☎ 01865 248244 🚌 Bus 2, 4, 13, 15, 51 AE, MC, VI, DI

Isis Guesthouse $

This is a very comfortable guesthouse with excellent facilities and

the added cachet of being owned by St. Edmund Hall, the High Street college with library facilities in a converted church.
107C1 ✉ 45–53 Iffley Road ☎ 01865 248894 or 01865 242466; fax 01865 243492 🚌 Bus 4, 4A MC, VI

Old Black Horse $$

This pleasant hotel was formerly a coaching inn. Located near Magdalen College, it's convenient to riverside walks and the city center.
107C1 ✉ 102 St. Clement's Street ☎ 01865 244691; fax 01865 242771 🚌 2, 2A, 7A, 7B, 10, 13 AE, MC, VI

Randolph $$$

Top-of-the-line hotel with elegant interiors, extremely comfortable rooms and luxury service. Located near Baliol College and close to the city center.
107A2 ✉ Beaumont Street ☎ 01865 247481 🚌 All buses to Oxford bus station AE, MC, VI, DI

OXFORD RESTAURANTS

Price guide: (dinner per person, excluding drinks)
$ £10–15
$$ £15–30
$$$ over £30

Brown's $$

If you want to mix in with the student crowd, Brown's is the place to do it, but don't expect peace and quiet. You can count on such excellent British dishes as steak, mushroom and Guinness pie. You may have to stand in line at this very busy restaurant.
107 A3 ✉ 5–9 St. Giles ☎ 01865 311415 or 01865 319600 AE, DI, MC, VI

Cherwell Boat House $$

Eat by the river at this charming and popular restaurant. You can rent a punt from a nearby boat concession if you want a genuine Oxford experience. Reservations are advised.
107 Off the map ✉ Bardwell Road ☎ 01865 552746 🚌 2, 7 AE, DI, MC, VI

Le Petit Blanc $$

This friendly, popular brasserie includes a special childen's menu, featuring Oxford sausage with mashed potatoes.

➕ 107 Off the map ✉ 71–72 Walton Street ☎ 01865 510999 AE, MC, VI, DI

Restaurant Elizabeth $$$
Fine French cuisine is served at this expensive restaurant opposite Christ Church College. There's a good selection of wines.
➕ 107A1 ✉ 82 St. Aldate's ☎ 01865 242230 🕐 Closed Mon. 🚌 2, 4, 13, 22, 51 AE, DI, MC, VI

Turf Tavern $
At this very traditional English restaurant, in the heart of the university area near Radcliffe Square, you can experience British dishes like pork in cider, beef and beer pie or minted lamb, all at reasonable prices.
➕ 107B2 ✉ Bath Place ☎ 01865 243235 🚌 All buses via High Street Credit cards for food only MC, VI

YORK HOTELS
Price guide: (double room with breakfast for two people)
$ £3–60
$$ £60–100
$$$ over £100

Dean Court Hotel $$$
A handsome Victorian building in an unsurpassed location close to York Minster, with views of the Minster from upper front rooms. Very stylish, first-class facilities, including an award-winning restaurant.
➕ 113B3 ✉ Duncombe Place ☎ 01904 625082; fax 01904 620305 AE, DI, MC, VI

Four Seasons Hotel $$
The Four Seasons, a few minutes' walk from central York, is in a 19th-century building located in a quiet, tree-lined area. It offers the very best in service. Excellent breakfasts are a specialty.
➕ 113 Off the map ✉ 7 St. Peter's Grove, Bootham ☎ 01904 622621; fax 01904 620976 MC, VI

Grasmead House Hotel $$
Four-poster beds add period style to this hotel, embellished with antiques and comfortable furnishings. It's only a few minutes' walk to the city center.
➕ 113 Off the map ✉ 1 Scarcroft Hill ☎ 01904 629996; fax 01904 629996 AE, MC, VI

Judges Lodges $$$
Style, history and atmosphere combine to make a stay in this 18th-century Georgian house a rare experience. Built by a prominent physician, it was the residence of local judges from 1806 to 1976. There's an à la carte restaurant and brasserie, and it is conveniently situated close to the city center.
➕ 113B2 ✉ 9 Lendal ☎ 01904 638733; fax 01904 679947 AE, DI, MC, VI

Royal York $$$
This expensive but top-quality hotel near the railroad station offers easy access to the city center and provides excellent service.
➕ 113A2 ✉ Station Road ☎ 01904 653681; fax 01914 653271 AE, DI, MC, VI

YORK RESTAURANTS
Price guide: (dinner per person, excluding drinks)
$ £10–15
$$ £15–30
$$$ over £30

19 Grape Lane $$
This fine restaurant in old York. just off Petergate, offers excellent modern British cuisine with an emphasis on fresh local produce. Lunch and dinner is served, but reservations are advised for the evening.
➕ 113B3 ✉ 19 Grape Lane ☎ 01904 636366 MC, VI

Blue Bicycle $$
Lively and attractive restaurant with distinctive decor, scrubbed wood tables, and walls sporting mirrors and pictures. Good fish dishes and fine wines. Reservations required.
➕ 113C2 ✉ 34 Fossgate ☎ 01904 673990 AE, DI, MC, VI

Ivy Restaurant $$
This award-winning restaurant in the Grange Hotel offers fine British cuisine. The same venue has a less expensive brasserie.
➕ 113 Off the map ✉ 1 Clifton ☎ 01904 644744 AE, DI, MC, VI

Old Orleans $$
This American-style eatery serves very good Cajun and Creole specialties, complemented by live jazz on some evenings.
➕ 113B2 ✉ 9–11 Low Ousegate ☎ 01904 620158 AE, DI, MC, VI

St. William's Restaurant $
The unbeatable setting of St. William's College, in the shadow of York Minster, enhances outdoor dining in the atmospheric cobbled courtyard (in good weather). Live jazz and good British food make this a delightful way to spend an evening. During the day, for a small fee, you can view the college's elegant medieval rooms.
➕ 113C3 ✉ College Street ☎ 01904 634830 AE, DI, MC, VI

PRAGUE HOTELS
Price guide: (double room with breakfast for two people)
$ 1,000–2,500Kčs
$$ 2,500–4,500Kčs
$$$ over 4,500Kčs

Evropa $$
This landmark art nouveau hotel on Wenceslas Square, rebuilt in 1903, is complete with sculptures, wrought-iron balconies and a glass mosaic. The best rooms overlook the square but can be noisy. The restaurant has even more art nouveau embellishments to admire.
➕ 124E2 ✉ Václavské náměstí ☎ 02 24 22 81 17; fax 02 24 22 45 44 🚇 Václavské náměstí AE, DI, MC, VI

Penzion U Medvíků $–$$
The name of this 15th-century former brewery tavern means "The Bears." There are 17 rooms in two categories: all have bathrooms, but those with extra facilities are double the price. There's a breakfast buffet.
➕ 124C3 ✉ Na Perštýně 7 ☎ 02 24 21 19 16; fax 02 24 22 09 30 🚇 Národní trída AE, DI, MC, VI

Savoy $$$
A relaxed atmosphere prevails at this top Prague hotel, located down the hill from the castle. Rooms are well designed and modernized, making a perfect vacation base.
➕ 124 Off the map ✉ Keplerova 6 ☎ 02 24 30 24 30; fax 02 24 30 21 28 🚋 Tram 22 AE, DI, MC, VI

Sax $$
On the steep hill leading to Prague Castle (just off Nerudova, near Charles Bridge), this hotel has an attractive interior and well-equipped, comfortable rooms.
➕ 124A4 ✉ Jánský Vršek 328/3

Czech Republic, Denmark

KEY TO SYMBOLS

- 🔲 map page number and coordinates
- ✉ address
- ☎ telephone number
- 🕐 days/times closed
- Ⓜ nearest subway station
- 🚌 nearest bus/trolley bus/tram route
- ⛴ ferry
- **$$$** expensive
- **$$** moderate
- **$** inexpensive
- AE American Express
- CB Carte Blanche
- DI Diners
- MC MasterCard
- VI VISA

Danish Smørrebrød

Like their fellow Scandinavians, Danes are great believers in hearty lunches – and nothing is more filling or mouthwatering than *smørrebrod*, which translates simply as "buttered bread." If it sounds like "smothering," then that's exactly what happens to the large slice of rye bread that is the basis of *smørrebrod* when it is piled high with a tasty mix of salads and garnishes, shrimps and chunks of fish, beef or pork. You can accompany this mini-banquet with a Danish lager and a small glass of chilled *akvavit* (aquavit). You can also enjoy the Danish *kolt bord*, or cold table, a fantastic array of meat and fish dishes, salads and savory dips, hot dishes, and a selection of bread and rolls.

☎ 02 53 84 22; fax 02 53 84 98
Ⓜ Malostranská   🚌 Tram 12, 22 AE, MC, VI

U Tří Pštrosů $$$

"The Three Ostriches" was built in 1606 by a feather trader: He sold ostrich feathers to nobles, who wore them in their hats. The painted wooden Renaissance ceilings survive, and the hotel is just a step from Charles Bridge.
🔲 124B3   ✉ Dražického náměstí 12   ☎ 02 57 32 05 65; fax 02 57 32 06 11   🚌 Tram 12, 22   AE, DI, MC, VI

PRAGUE RESTAURANTS

Price guide: (dinner per person, excluding drinks)
$ 100–200Kčs
$$ 200–600Kčs
$$$ over 600Kčs

David $$$

This small, family-run wine bar near the U.S. Embassy specializes in German-imported food, including duck, boar and rabbit. There's also a small vegetarian menu and good salads. Since it's very popular it's important you make reservations well in advance.
🔲 124B3   ✉ Tržistě 21   ☎ 02 53 93 25   🚌 Tram 12, 22   AE, MC, VI

Kosher Restaurace Shalom $$

Kosher lunches are served in the high-ceilinged hall that was formerly the setting for meetings in the Jewish Town Hall, in the heart of the Jewish Quarter. The menu is simple but ample; advance reservations are essential.
🔲 124C4   ✉ Maislova 18, Staré Město   ☎ 02 24 81 09 29   🕐 Closed Sat.   Ⓜ Staroměstská No credit cards

Reykavík $$

Located between Prague's historic Old Town Square and Charles Bridge, Reykavík serves Icelandic specialties and excellent fish dishes. Ingredients, flown in from the North Atlantic, include salmon, cod and haddock; try the delicious fish soup.
🔲 124C3   ✉ Karlova 20, Staré Město   ☎ 02 24 22 92 51   Ⓜ Staroměstská   AE, DI, MC, VI

U Ševce Matouše $$

The name means "Matthew the Cobbler," and this is indeed a former

---

cobbler's workshop, under the arcades in Loreta Square. Generous portions of steak, ham, duck and beef *stroganoff* are served.
🔲 124 Off the map   ✉ Loretánskè náměstí 4   ☎ 02 20 51 45 36   🚌 Tram 22   MC, VI

U Zlaté Hrušky $$$

Excellent Czech specialties, including pâté, duck and venison, and good wines are served in an attractive house with carved, rustic furniture. The name means "The Golden Pear."
🔲 124 Off the map   ✉ Nový svět 3, Hradcany   ☎ 02 53 11 33   🚌 Tram 22   AE, DI, VI

COPENHAGEN HOTELS

Price guide: (double room with breakfast for two people)
$ DKr400–700
$$ DKr700–1,200
$$$ over DKr1,200

Admiral Hotel $$$

This big waterfront hotel, in a superbly renovated, 18th-century redbrick granary warehouse, is located close to Amalienborg Plads square. Regular rooms and family suites are available; a restaurant (breakfast is extra) and sauna are on the premises.
🔲 140D3   ✉ Toldbodgade 24–28   ☎ 33 74 14 14; fax 33 32 55 42   🚌 28   AE, MC, VI

Hotel d'Angleterre $$$

Famous, and famously expensive, this luxury hotel is on Kongens Nytorv Square. An 18th-century building reconstructed from the 1630 original features sumptuous furnishings, making it a favorite with visiting celebrities.
🔲 140C2–C3   ✉ Kongens Nytorv 34   ☎ 33 12 00 95; fax 33 12 11 18   🚌 10, 28   AE, MC, VI

City $$

This attractive, comfortable, modernized hotel is near the center of things, but in a quiet location. Only breakfast is served.
🔲 140D2   ✉ Peder Skramsgade 24   ☎ 33 13 06 66; fax 33 13 06 67   🚌 27   AE, MC, VI

Plaza $$$

Located in the heart of the city across from Tivoli, the luxurious,

Denmark

modern Plaza has superbly furnished rooms. The Library Bar encourages literary browsing over drinks, and there's a good restaurant.

🏠 140B1 ✉ Bernstorffsgade 4
☎ 33 14 92 62; fax 33 93 93 62
🚇 8, 250S AE, MC, VI

Top Hebron $$

This is a friendly, family hotel close to the railroad station and Tivoli. Comfortable rooms have many amenities, and breakfast is available.

🏠 140A1 ✉ Helgolandsgade 4
☎ 33 31 69 06; fax 33 31 90 67
🚇 6, 10, 16, 27, 28 AE, MC, VI

COPENHAGEN RESTAURANTS

Price guide: (dinner per person, excluding drinks)
$ DKr100–250
$$ DKr250–300
$$$ over DKr300

Nyhavns Færgekro $

One of the best restaurants on canalside Nyhaven is this one, with a nautical theme that includes model boats hanging from the ceiling. Superb lunchtime buffets featuring a variety of herring dishes are a great deal; the Danish and French cuisine offered in the evenings is more expensive.

🏠 140D2 ✉ Nyhavn 5 ☎ 33 15 15 88 MC, VI

Peder Oxe $$

Built on the foundation of an old monastery, this noted restaurant/cellar bar is on Grey Brothers Square. Traditional Danish cuisine emphasizes hearty helpings of meat; the lunchtime *smørrebrød* is very good.

🏠 140C2 ✉ Gråbrødre Torv 11
☎ 33 11 00 77 MC, VI

Restaurant Els $$$

Original painted wall panels from the 1850s add style to this popular Nyhavn restaurant, situated on a street leading off Kongens Nytorv Square. Excellent fish specialties and fine wines are served. Reservations are advised.

🏠 140D2–D3 ✉ Store Strandstræde 3 ☎ 33 14 13 41 MC, VI

Riz Raz $

This popular buffet restaurant serves Mediterranean-style hot and cold vegetarian dishes and salads,

as well as Greek lamb and fish dishes. In good weather the garden is open.

🏠 140C2 ✉ Kompagnistræde 20
☎ 33 15 05 75 MC, VI

St. Gertrude's Kloster $$$

Housed in an old monastery building, this smart, candlelit restaurant has a vaulted cellar and atmospheric dining rooms. Fish dishes are the specialty, with everything from mussels to lobster, and there's a big selection of wines. Reservations are advised.

🏠 140C3 ✉ Hauser Plads 32
☎ 33 14 66 30 MC, VI

ODENSE HOTELS

Price guide: (double room with breakfast for two people)
$ DKr400–700
$$ DKr700–1,200
$$$ over DKr1,200

City Hotel $$

This is a comfortable, modern hotel near the Hans Christian Andersen House and about 10 minutes from the city center.

🏠 146C2 ✉ Hans Mulesgade 5
☎ 66 12 12 58; fax 66 12 93 64
AE, MC, VI

Domir $

This friendly, medium-size hotel with comfortable rooms and plenty of amenities is located outside the city center but within minutes of the railroad station and within an easy walking distance of the Town Hall.

🏠 146 Off the map ✉ Hans Tausens Gade 19 ☎ 66 12 14 27; fax 66 12 17 82 AE, MC, VI

First Hotel Grand Odense $$$

Odense's most expensive hotel is situated in a handsome old building in a pleasant location across from the Fyns Kunstmuseum (Art Museum of Funen), close to the city center.

🏠 146B2–B3 ✉ Jernbanegade 18
☎ 66 11 71 71; fax 66 14 11 71
AE, MC, VI

Pjentehus $

Just outside the city center, Pjentehus is a small, reasonably priced and comfortable hotel in a pleasant villa near the Hans Christian Andersen House.

🏠 146C2 ✉ Pjentedamsgade 14

☎ 66 12 15 55; fax 66 17 82 08 No credit cards

Radisson SAS Hans Christian Andersen Hotel $$$

A very luxurious, modern hotel located close to Hans Christian Andersen House and next door to the Concert Hall and the Carl Nielsen Museum, the Radisson has its own restaurant, sauna, solarium, billiards room and casino.

🏠 146C2 ✉ Claus Bergs Gade 7
☎ 66 14 78 00; fax 66 14 78 90
AE, MC, VI

ODENSE RESTAURANTS

Price guide: (dinner per person, excluding drinks)
$ DKr100–250
$$ DKr250–300
$$$ over DKr300

Den Gamle Kro $$$

This Odense restaurant in a magnificent old building dates from 1683. Meals are served in several rooms, including the brick-vaulted cellar. Expect excellent Danish cuisine and other dishes.

🏠 146B2–C2 ✉ Overgade 23
☎ 66 12 14 33 AE, MC, VI

Den Grimme Ælling $$

This charming little restaurant on a cobbled lane just across the main road from the Hans Christian Andersen House is noted for its lavish buffets.

🏠 146B2 ✉ Vesterbro 39 ☎ 65 91 70 30 AE, MC, VI

Jensens Grillbøffer $

This popular lunchtime grill and evening favorite serves steaks with lavish salads.

🏠 146A2 ✉ Kongensgade 10
☎ 66 14 59 59 AE, MC, VI

Marie Louise $$$

This very stylish French restaurant is in a charming courtyard complex surrounded by old houses.

🏠 146B2 ✉ Lottrups Gård 9
☎ 66 17 92 95 No credit cards

Restaurant Air Pub $

This pub and restaurant offers a good atmosphere to go along with hearty Danish cooking and a decent selection of beers.

🏠 146A2 ✉ Kongensgade 41
☎ 66 14 66 08 🕐 Closed Sun. AE, MC, VI

Finland, France

KEY TO SYMBOLS

- ⊞ map page number and coordinates
- ✉ address
- ☎ telephone number
- 🕐 days/times closed
- Ⓜ nearest subway station
- 🚌 nearest bus/trolley bus/tram route
- ⛴ ferry
- $$$ expensive
- $$ moderate
- $ inexpensive
- AE American Express
- CB Carte Blanche
- DI Diners
- MC MasterCard
- VI VISA

Russian Restaurants

You can sample authentic Russian cuisine in Helsinki at one of the city's several Russian restaurants. Russian food is not noted for its lightness of touch, but it can be adventurous and is extremely filling. You can even start with caviar and ice cream if you want, before plunging into hearty meat dishes – lamb is a specialty, with cakes, fruit pies and more ice cream for dessert. Two notable choices to try are Kasakka at Meritullinkatu 13, (☎ 09 135 6288), and Galleria Hariton at Kasarmikatu 44, (☎ 09 622 1717).

HELSINKI HOTELS

Price guide: (double room with breakfast for two people)
$ Fmk400–600
$$ Fmk600–800
$$$ over Fmk800

Grand Marina $$$

Step from ferry to foyer, if you travel by Viking Line, and stay in this large hotel on the western side of the harbor. Rooms are elegant and comfortable; also here are bars, a bistro and the Grand Café.
⊞ 158D4 ✉ Katajanokanlaituri 7 ☎ 09 16661; fax 09 166 6857 🚌 52; tram 4 AE, MC, VI

Helka $

Located in the heart of the city, this recently renovated hotel offers good service, good value and a sauna.
⊞ 158B4 ✉ Pohjoinen Rautatiekatu 23 ☎ 09 613 580; fax 09 441 087 🚌 14, 14B, 32, 39, 45, 47 AE, MC, VI

Lord Hotel $$

This well-appointed hotel in a handsome art nouveau building provides a good restaurant, bars and a relaxing terrace.
⊞ 158C4 ✉ Lonnrotinkatu 29 ☎ 09 615 815; fax 09 680 1315 🚌 20, 20N, tram 10 AE, MC, VI

Scandic Hotel Kalastajatorppa $$

This long-established and popular hotel by the sea and outside the city center has three restaurants and facilities including saunas, swimming pool and jacuzzi, as well as gardens and a private beach.
⊞ 158 Off the map ✉ Kalastajatorppantie 1 ☎ 09 45811; fax 09 458 1668 🚌 502, 503; tram 4 AE, MC, VI

Scandic Hotel Marski $$$

This large hotel, right at the heart of things on Mannerheimintie street, was recently enlarged and renovated.
⊞ 158C4 ✉ Mannerheimintie 10 ☎ 09 68061; fax 09 642 377 🚌 20N, 24, 42; tram 10 AE, MC, VI

HELSINKI RESTAURANTS

Price guide: (dinner per person, excluding drinks)
$ Fmk50–150
$$ Fmk150–200
$$$ over Fmk200

Alexander Nevski $$$

The mix of French and Russian design goes well with Russian cuisine in this long-established restaurant. There are lots of appetizers, including ice cream with caviar.
⊞ 158C4 ✉ Pohjoisesplanadi 17 ☎ 09 639 610 🚌 13, 64S, 77S; tram 1, 1A AE, MC, VI

Amadeus $$$

This top-quality restaurant in the "Street Museum" serves Finnish cuisine enjoyed in comfortable surroundings. Game specialties are offered when in season.
⊞ 158C4 ✉ Sofiankatu 4 ☎ 09 626 676 🕐 Closed Sun. 🚌 Tram 3B, 3T, 1, 2, 4, 7 AE, MC, VI

George $$

Try pigeon stuffed with spinach in herb sauce in this small restaurant, where Finnish cuisine is tempered with French and Italian flair.
⊞ 158C4 ✉ Kalevankatu 17 ☎ 09 647 662 🕐 Closed Sun. 🚌 20N, 24, 42 AE, MC, VI

Kappeli $$

This is a stylish restaurant and café, with outside terraces on the Esplanade, in a pavilion of cast iron and glass dating from 1867. Good Finnish and Scandinavian dishes are offered, and the fish soup is recommended. The restaurant has its own brewery, and in summer there are concerts at the nearby bandstand.
⊞ 158C4 ✉ Eteläesplanadi 10 ☎ 09 179 242 🚌 13, 64S, 77S; tram 1, 1A AE, MC, VI

Lyon $$

Good-quality French cuisine is presented in this unassuming and friendly restaurant, opposite the Helsinki opera house. The roasted breast of goose is a favorite.
⊞ 158C5 ✉ Mannerheimintie 56 ☎ 09 408 131 🕐 Closed Sun. 🚌 16, 13, 21v; tram 4, 10 AE, MC, VI

PARIS HOTELS

Price guide: (double room with breakfast for two people)
$ 400–600Fr
$$ 600–1,000Fr
$$$ over 1,000Fr

Bristol $$$

The Louis XV-style rooms affirm the elegance at this hotel, which has a rooftop pool and superb restaurant.

France

✚ 174B3 ✉ 112 rue du Faubourg-
St.-Honoré ☎ 01 53 43 43 00; fax
01 53 43 43 01 🚇 Miromesnil AE,
DI, MC, VI

Hôtel des Deux-Îles $$
This peaceful hotel, beautifully
housed in a 17th-century house, has
understated charm and elegance.
✚ 174D2 ✉ 59 rue St.-Louis-en-
Île ☎ 01 43 26 13 35; fax 01 43 29
60 25 🚇 Pont-Marie AE, MC, VI

Hôtel des Grandes Écoles $
This typically French hotel has pretty
bedrooms and is set in a garden on a
narrow street in the Latin Quarter.
It's an excellent value.
✚ 174D2 ✉ 75 rue Cardinal-
Lemoine ☎ 01 48 04 77 76; fax 01
42 71 23 50 🚇 Cardinal-Lemoine
MC, VI

Istria $$
This small and comfortable hotel in
the heart of Montparnasse once
hosted Ernest Hemingway.
✚ 174C1 ✉ 29 rue Campagne-
Première ☎ 01 43 20 91 82; fax 01
43 22 48 45 🚇 Raspail AE, DI,
MC, VI

Pavillon de la Reine $$$
This romantic and luxurious hotel,
complete with four-poster beds, is
set in a garden on the beautiful
place des Vosges.
✚ 174E2 ✉ 28 place des Vosges
☎ 01 40 29 19 19; fax 01 40 29 19
20 🚇 Bastille AE, DI, MC, VI

PARIS RESTAURANTS
Price guide: (dinner per person,
excluding drinks)
$ 150–200Fr
$$ 200–300Fr
$$$ over 300Fr

La Coupole $$
This sprawling art deco brasserie,
renowned in the 1920s, serves
seafood, fish and steaks.
✚ 174C1 ✉ 102 boulevard du
Montparnasse ☎ 01 43 20 14 20
🚇 Vavin AE, MC, VI

Le Dôme $$$
The specialties at this famous
Montparnasse brasserie are seafood
and fish. Service is efficient.
✚ 174C1 ✉ 108 boulevard du
Montparnasse ☎ 01 43 35 25 81
🕐 Closed Mon. 🚇 Vavin AE,
MC, VII

Le Grizzli $$
Situated in the heart of Marais, this
old-fashioned bistro serves dishes
from central and southwest France.
✚ 174D3 ✉ 7 rue St.-Martin
☎ 01 48 87 77 56 🕐 Closed Sun.
🚇 Hôtel-de-Ville AE, MC, VI

L'Îlot Vache $$
Named after the cattle that once
grazed nearby, this friendly bistro
specializes in fish.
✚ 174D2 ✉ 35 rue St.-Louis en-
Île ☎ 01 46 33 55 16 🚇 Pont-
Marie AE, MC, VI

Le Rendezvous des Chauffeurs $
For good food at excellent prices,
stop by this neighborhood restaurant
in Montmartre.
✚ 174C4 ✉ 11 rue des Portes-
Blanches ☎ 01 42 64 04 17
🚇 Marcadet-Poissoniers MC, VI

Saint Amarante $
Hearty country cooking is the
specialty at this friendly and relaxed
bistro near the Bastille.
✚ 174E2 ✉ 4 rue Biscornet
☎ 01 43 43 00 08 ☎ Closed
Sat.–Sun. and mid-Jul. to mid-Aug.
🚇 Bastille MC, VI

LYON HOTELS
Price guide: (double room with
breakfast for two people)
$ 400–600Fr
$$ 600–1,000Fr
$$$ over 1,000Fr

Beaux-Arts $$
A renovated turn-of-the-20th-century
building houses this comfortable
hotel in the center of the Presqu'Île.
✚ 186B3 ✉ 75 rue President
Edouard-Herriot ☎ 04 78 38 09 50;
fax 04 78 42 19 19 🚇 Cordeliers
AE, CB, DI, MC, VI

Grand Hôtel des Terreaux $$
This comfortable, medium-size hotel
is convenient for sightseeing and
beautifully situated just behind a
lovely central square.
✚ 186B3 ✉ 16 rue Lanterne
☎ 04 78 27 04 10; fax 04 78 27 97
75 🚇 Hôtel de Ville AE, CB, DI,
MC, VI

Sofitel Lyon Bellecour $$$
If you're looking for good service and
every comfort available, this deluxe
hotel centrally located on the Rhône
river is a good choice.

✚ 186B2 ✉ 20 quai Gailleton
☎ 04 72 41 20 20; fax 04 72 40 05
50 🚇 Bellecourt AE, CB, DI, MC, VI

Terminus St.-Paul $
Consider staying at this excellent
budget choice, in the middle of the
Old Town, with clean, simple and
airy rooms.
✚ 186A3 ✉ 6 rue Lainerie ☎ 04
78 28 13 29; fax 04 72 00 97 27 AE,
CB, DI, MC, VI

La Villa Florentine $$$
This deluxe hotel, with many
amenities – including a pretty
garden – stands above the Old
Town, on the slopes of Fourvières.
✚ 186A2 ✉ 25–27 montée St.-
Barthélémy ☎ 04 72 56 56 56; fax
04 72 40 90 56 🚇 Vieux Lyon AE,
CB, DI, MC, VI

LYON RESTAURANTS
Price guide: (dinner per person,
excluding drinks)
$ 150–200Fr
$$ 200–300Fr
$$$ over 300Fr

Le Café du Soleil $$
One of the oldest *bouchons* in Lyon
serves huge portions of French fare
in a friendly atmosphere.
✚ 186A2 ✉ 2 rue St.-George,
place de la Trinité ☎ 04 78 37 60 02
🕐 Closed Sun. 🚇 Vieux Lyon AE,
CB, DI, MC, VI

Chabert et Fils $$
Sophisticated Lyonnais specialties
served here include a chicken-liver
gâteau and delicate soups.
✚ 186B2 ✉ 11 rue des
Marroniers ☎ 04 78 37 01 94
🚇 Bellecour AE, DI, MC, VI

Christian Têtedoie $$$
Rich but light specialties are on the
menu at this elegant and
professionally staffed restaurant.
✚ 186A3 ✉ 54 quai Pierre-Scize
☎ 04 78 29 40 10 🕐 Closed Sun.
and first 3 weeks in Aug. 🚇 Vieux
Lyon AE, DI, CB, MC, VI

Comptoir du Bœuf $$
You can try a wide range of
Lyonnais specialties in this cozy,
late-night restaurant right next to
the Cathedral.
✚ 186A2 ✉ 3 place Neuve St.-
Jean ☎ 04 78 92 82 35 🚇 Vieux
Lyon AE, CB, DI, MC, VI

France

KEY TO SYMBOLS

➕ map page number and coordinates
✉ address
☎ telephone number
🕐 days/times closed
Ⓜ nearest subway station
🚌 nearest bus/trolley bus/tram route
⛴ ferry
$$$ expensive
$$ moderate
$ inexpensive
AE American Express
CB Carte Blanche
DI Diners
MC MasterCard
VI VISA

The *Belle Époque* in Nice

The *belle époque*, or "beautiful era," was the name the French gave to the early 20th century. During this period Nice's fame soared with the influx of up to 150,000 wealthy English and Russians who came here to while away northern winters in elegance. They expected luxury, and it was for them that sumptuous and grandiose hotels and villas were built. Some buildings survive today along the promenade des Anglais. The Hotel Negresco is the most famous; enjoy a drink there in Edwardian style.

Les Eaux Vives $$$

This wonderful restaurant, in one of Lyon's smartest hotels, uses fine ingredients such as lobster and foie gras in balanced dishes. This is popular choice and reservations are advised.
➕ 186 Off the map ✉ Hotel Metropole, 85 quai Joseph-Gillet ☎ 04 72 10 44 30 🕐 Closed Thu. and first 3 weeks of Aug. 🚌 40, 43, 90E AE, CB, DI, MC, VI

NICE HOTELS

Price guide: (double room with breakfast for two people)
$ 400–600Fr
$$ 600–1,000Fr
$$$ over 1,000Fr

Elysée Palace $$$

There are excellent facilities, including a rooftop pool, at this modern luxury hotel.
➕ 194B1 ✉ 59 promenade des Anglais ☎ 04 93 86 06 06; fax 04 93 44 50 40 🚌 6, 9, 10, 12 AE, CB, DI, MC, VI

Gounod $$

Just a 10-minute walk from the sea is this decent, moderately priced *belle époque* choice, with a quiet, central location.
➕ 194C2 ✉ 18 rue Berlioz ☎ 04 93 88 26 20; fax 04 93 88 23 84 🚌 9, 10, 12 AE, CB, DI, MC, VI

Negresco $$$

One of the world's great hotels in the flamboyant *belle époque* style, with a superlative level of comfort, service and facilities.
➕ 194B1 ✉ 37 promenade des Anglais ☎ 04 93 16 64 00; fax 04 93 88 35 68 🚌 6, 9, 10, 12 AE, CB, DI, MC, VI

Vendome $$

This hotel has pretty rooms, air-conditioning, a peaceful garden and an Old Town location.
➕ 194D1 ✉ rue Pastorelli ☎ 04 93 62 00 77; fax 04 93 13 40 78 🚌 6, 9, 12 AE, CB, DI, MC, VI

Windsor $$

This famous hotel is centrally located and has a garden pool and beautifully frescoed rooms.
➕ 194B1 ✉ 11 rue Dalpozzo Royale ☎ 04 93 88 59 35; fax 04 93 88 94 57 🚌 6, 9, 10, 12 AE, CB, DI, MC, VI

NICE RESTAURANTS

Price guide: (dinner per person, excluding drinks)
$ 150–200Fr
$$ 200–300Fr
$$$ over 300Fr

Barale $$

The set menu is the recommended choice at this huge restaurant, which features local specials. Reservations are advised.
➕ 194E2 ✉ 36 rue Beaumont ☎ 04 93 89 17 94 🚌 9, 10, 12 AE, CB, VI

Chantecler $$$

Nice's finest restaurant, and one of the best in France, is housed in the opulent Hôtel Negresco and serves high-quality traditional French food. Reservations are advised.
➕ 194B1 ✉ Hôtel Negresco, 37 promenade des Anglais ☎ 04 93 88 39 51 🚌 6, 12 AE, CB, DI, MC, VI

Flo $$

The food in this lively open-kitchen brasserie, housed in an old theater, is fine, but the decor and ambience are what make it worth a visit. It's also open late.
➕ 194D1 ✉ 4 rue Sacha-Guitry ☎ 04 93 13 38 38 🚌 1, 4, 10, 22 AE, DI, CB, VI

Nissa Socca $

Locals flock to this Old Town restaurant, which serves a good range of Niçoise specialties, including *socca*, the chickpea pancake.
➕ 194D1 ✉ 5 rue St.-Réparate ☎ 04 93 80 18 35 🕐 Closed Sun.–Mon. and the last 3 weeks in Aug. 🚌 6, 9 10 AE, CB, DI, MC, VI

La Petite Maison $$

Join the regulars who enjoy good home cooking from a menu that features seasonal specialties and a fantastic range of hors d'oeuvres. Reservations are advised.
➕ 194D1 ✉ 11 rue St.-François-de-Paule ☎ 04 93 92 59 59 🕐 Closed Sun. 🚌 9, 10, 12, 22 AE, DI, MC, VI

STRASBOURG HOTELS

Price guide: (double room with breakfast for two people)
$ 400–600Fr
$$ 600–1,000Fr
$$$ over 1,000Fr

Baumann $$

Stunningly situated opposite the Cathedral, this comfortable, traditional hotel has a lovely terrace and good restaurant; an excellent vacation choice.

➕ 200B1–B2 ✉ 16 place de la Cathédrale ☎ 03 88 32 42 14; fax 03 88 23 03 92 🚗 A, D AE, CB, DI, MC, VI

Cathédrale $$

This excellent cathedral square hotel is within easy walking distance of Strasbourg's main sights and some of the city's best restaurants.

➕ 200B1–B2 ✉ 12–13 place de la Cathédrale ☎ 03 88 22 12 12; fax 03 88 23 28 00 🚗 A, D AE, CB, DI, MC, VI

Hôtel des Rohan $$

This pretty hotel on one of Strasbourg's most picturesque historic streets is an easy stroll from the main sights.

➕ 200B1 ✉ 17–19 rue du Maroquin ☎ 03 88 32 85 11; fax 03 88 75 65 37 🚗 A, D AE, DI, VI

Mercure Centre $$

This convenient and comfortable hotel is conveniently located in the historic center, and has large soundproof rooms and offers very good facilities.

➕ 200B2 ✉ 25 rue Thomann ☎ 03 88 75 77 88; fax 03 88 32 08 66 🚗 A, D AE, CB, DI, MC, VI

Moderne $

This good-value budget hotel overlooks the water on the northern side of the old city center.

➕ 200A2 ✉ 1 quai de Paris ☎ 03 88 32 07 33; fax 03 88 23 50 45 AE, VI

STRASBOURG RESTAURANTS

Price guide: (dinner per person, excluding drinks)
$ 150–200Fr
$$ 200–300Fr
$$$ over 300Fr

Aux Armes de Strasbourg $$

Interesting local dishes and a huge variety of beers are served at this wonderfully atmospheric, wood-paneled restaurant.

➕ 200B1 ✉ 9 place Gutenberg ☎ 03 88 32 85 62 🚗 A, D AE, CB, DI, MC, VI

Au Bon Vivant $$

One of the few remaining traditional family-run restaurants in the city center is this winner, serving local specialties in a relaxed atmosphere.

➕ 200B1 ✉ 7 rue du Maroquin ☎ 03 88 32 77 81 🚗 A, D AE, MC, VI

Au Petit Tonnelier $$

This family-run restaurant, on one of the old town's prettiest streets, serves seasonal and regional dishes.

➕ 200B1 ✉ 16 rue des Tonneliers ☎ 03 88 32 53 54 🕐 Closed Sun. lunch 🚗 A, D AE, MC, VI

La Taverne de Maître Kanter $$

This big, busy brasserie serves generous portions of Strasbourg specialties such as *choucroute* (sauerkraut) and *tarte flambée* (onion tart), as well as seafood.

➕ 200B2 ✉ place Kleber ☎ 03 88 32 15 93 🚗 A, D AE, DI, MC, VI

Winstub le Wuerthel $$

An old timbered building in the loveliest part of the old town is the setting for this traditional, family-run restaurant.

➕ 200A1 ✉ 20 rue des Moulins ☎ 03 88 22 44 44 🕐 Closed Mon. and Sun. evening 🚗 A, D AE, MC, VI

BERLIN HOTELS

Price guide: (double room with breakfast for two people)
$ up to DM150
$$ DM150–300
$$$ over DM300

Alsterhof $$$

This is a small 1960s hotel located behind the KaDeWe department store. Despite the plain exterior, it is stylish inside, with 144 rooms, a smart restaurant and an annex conservatory.

➕ 216B2 ✉ Augsburger Strasse 5 ☎ 030 212 420; fax 030 218 3949 🚇 Augsburger Strasse AE, DI, MC, VI

Bristol Kempinski $$$

This hotel, once on Unter den Linden but now in the Ku'damm, has a famous name and a traditional style, with formal furnishings, chandeliers and deep-pile carpets. There are 315 rooms and 44 suites, and an elaborate menu in the restaurant.

➕ 216B2 ✉ Kurfürstendamm 27 ☎ 030 884 340; fax 030 883 6075 🚇 Adenauerplatz AE, DI, MC, VI

Hotel-Pension Wittelsbach $$

The Wittelsbach caters to children, with a family floor including fully equipped playhouses, strollers and high chairs.

➕ 216B1 ✉ Wittelsbacher Strasse 22 ☎ 030 862 1345; fax 030 862 1532 🚇 109, 101 AE, DI, MC, VI

Kronprinz $$

This elegant, privately owned and managed hotel, in a 53-room turn-of-the-20th-century house, is only a few steps from the Ku'damm and has an attractive terraced beer garden.

➕ 216A2 ✉ Kronprinzendamm 1 ☎ 030 896 030; fax 030 893 1215 🚇 S-Bahn to Halensee AE, DI, MC, VI

Transit $

Once a factory, this hotel has been converted into a pleasant, airy accommodation. It's basic but clean, in an attractive part of the Kreuzberg quarter, and the English-speaking staff are welcoming.

➕ 216D1 ✉ Hagelberger Strasse 53–4 ☎ 030 789 0470; fax 030 78 90 47 47 🚇 Mehringdamm AE, MC, VI

BERLIN RESTAURANTS

Price guide: (dinner per person, excluding drinks)
$ up to DM25
$$ DM25–50
$$$ over DM50

Altes Luxemburg $$$

What you get at one of the city's best restaurants is German food by chef Karl Wannemacher, who adds his inventive touch with herbs.

➕ 216A2 ✉ Windscheidstrasse 31 ☎ 030 323 8730 🕐 Closed Sun.– Mon. 🚇 Sophie-Charlotten-Platz AE, DI, VI

Bamberger Reiter $$$

This well-known restaurant, owned by Austrian-born Franz Raneburger, features Austro-Prussian cooking and other national styles. Try the goose-liver tarts.

➕ 216B1 ✉ Regensburger Strasse 7 ☎ 030 218 4282 🕐 Closed Sun. and Mon. 🚇 Spichernstrasse AE, DI, MC, VI

France, Germany

Germany

KEY TO SYMBOLS

+ map page number and coordinates
✉ address
☎ telephone number
🕐 days/times closed
Ⓜ nearest subway station
🚌 nearest bus/trolley bus/tram route
⛴ ferry
$$$ expensive
$$ moderate
$ inexpensive
AE American Express
CB Carte Blanche
DI Diners
MC MasterCard
VI VISA

Strasbourg Specials

Visualize French flair and imagination combined with high-quality ingredients and German influences, and you'll begin to understand the gastronomic delights that await you in Strasbourg. This is the home of foie gras, fatted goose liver eaten whole or made into pâté; choucroute (sauerkraut), assorted meats and spicy sausages served with mounds of pickled cabbage; and kougelhupf, yeast cake traditionally eaten for breakfast. There are other, less well-known regional dishes; look for baeckeoffe, a slow-cooked casserole featuring three different meats, and tarte flambée, an unctuous hot onion tart. The smooth, pungently aromatic Munster is Strasbourg's local cheese.

Berliner Stube $$

Berliner Leber (liver) is the specialty at this large restaurant near the Ku'damm; international dishes are served, too.
+ 216B2 ✉ Los Angeles Platz 1
☎ 030 212 7750
Ⓜ Kurfürstendamm AE, DI, MC, VI

Borchardt $$$

Trendy Berliners love this attractive, 1920s-style bistro, where international and "new" cuisine is featured. Brunch is served here on Sundays.
+ 216D2 ✉ Französische Strasse 47 ☎ 030 229 3144
Ⓜ Französische Strasse AE, VI

Lutter & Wegner $$$

Austrian and German dishes are served in an historic 19th-century restaurant/wine bar on the Gendarmenmarkt, where the world-famous Berlin Symphony Orchestra has its home.
+ 216D2 ✉ Charlottenstrasse 56
☎ 030 20 29 54 10
Ⓜ Hausvogteiplatz AE

Zum Nussbaum $

The name of this traditional Berlin pub-style restaurant, or Gasthaus, means "The Nut Tree." It's pleasantly located in the renovated old area called Nikolaiviertel.
+ 216E3 ✉ Probsstrasse ☎ 030 242 3095 Ⓜ Alexanderplatz

COLOGNE HOTELS

Price guide: (double room with breakfast for two people)
$ up to DM150
$$ DM150–300
$$$ over DM300

Buchholz $$

This private, family-run hotel with a friendly staff has 27 bedrooms and is in a central, but quiet location. Airport shuttle service is provided on request.
+ 225C4 ✉ Kunibertsgasse 5
☎ 0221 16083; fax 0221 131 665
Ⓜ Dom/Hbf AE, DI, MC, VI

Europa am Dom $$

Conveniently located directly opposite the Cathedral, this elegant hotel is close to most museums. Nonsmoking rooms are available.
+ 225B3 ✉ Am Hof 38–46
☎ 0221 20580; fax 0221 936 344
Ⓜ Dom/Hbf AE, DI, MC, VI

Das Kleine Stapelhäuschen $

Two adjacent town houses, in historically interesting buildings on the Rhine promenade, house a friendly hotel with a comfortable wine bar that's just a short walk from the Cathedral.
+ 225C3 ✉ Fischmarkt 1–3
☎ 0221 257 7862; fax 0221 257 4232 🚌 Tram 1, 7, 9 MC, VI

Mondial am Dom $$$

Despite its dull exterior, this is a comfortable, stylish hotel, situated between the Cathedral and the river – ideal for exploring the Old Town. There's also a restaurant serving international and regional cuisine.
+ 225B3 ✉ Kurt-Hackenberg-Platz 1 ☎ 0221 20630; fax 0221 206 3522 Ⓜ Dom/Hbf AE, DI, MC, VI

Viktoria $$

This turn-of-the-20th-century Jugendstil building by the Rhine offers some rooms with river views and a generous breakfast buffet.
+ 225 Off the map ✉ Worringer Strasse 23 ☎ 0221 973 1720; fax 0221 727 067 Ⓜ Reichensperger Platz AE, DI, MC, VI

COLOGNE RESTAURANTS

Price guide: (dinner per person, excluding drinks)
$ up to DM25
$$ DM25–50
$$$ over DM50

Bosporus $$

Located in the multicultural quarter of Weidengasse, Bosporus has four set menus offering a wide range of Turkish dishes. The nearby Eigelstein quarter is equally lively.
+ 225B4 ✉ Weidengasse 36
☎ 0221 125 265 🚌 Tram 6, 15, 17 AE, DI, MC, VI

Brauhaus Sion $$

This busy side-street brewery-tavern, near the Cathedral, is especially popular for lunch and coffee, and for strong Kölsch beer. Traditionally dressed waiters roll out the barrels.
+ 225B3 ✉ Unter Taschenmacher 5–7 ☎ 0221 257 8540 🚌 Tram 1, 7, 9 No credit cards

Kintaro $$

Japanese dishes are served in this popular sushi restaurant, where

Germany, Greece

particularly good entrees include seaweed *(hijiki)* and octopus, cucumber and seaweed in vinegar *(tako su)*. Reservations are advised.
➕ 225A3 ✉ Friesenstrasse 16
☎ 0221 135 255 🚇 Friesenplatz
No credit cards

Päffgen in der Altstadt $$

This pub-cum-restaurant, belonging to Cologne's smallest brewery, is centrally located and convenient to the city's main attractions. Tasty regional dishes and *Kölsch* beer are served in a congenial atmosphere.
➕ 225B2 ✉ Heumarkt 62
☎ 0221 257 7765 🚫 Closed Mon.
🚋 Tram 1, 7, 9 No credit cards

Paul's Restaurant $$$

Located in a former pub in a typical quarter of Cologne, Paul's serves traditional and modern cuisine. Choose a bottle of wine, and you will only be charged for what you drink.
➕ 225B3 ✉ Bülowstrasse 2
☎ 0221 766 839 🚋 Tram 12, 18
AE, MC

MUNICH HOTELS

Price guide: (double room with breakfast for two people)
$ up to DM150
$$ DM150–300
$$$ over DM300

Englischer Garten $

This hotel, at the edge of the English Garden in Schwabing, is housed in a converted watermill. You'll really feel like you're in the heart of the country, especially when eating the breakfast buffet, served in the garden in summer.
➕ 230 Off the map
✉ Liebergesellstrasse ☎ 089 383 9410; fax 089 38 39 41 33
🚇 Münchener Freiheit No credit cards

Opera $$$

This 50-bed hotel, set in an old mansion with elegant arcades and a Renaissance courtyard, is convenient to upscale shopping.
➕ 230D2 ✉ St. Anna-Strasse 10
☎ 089 22 55 33; fax 089 22 55 38
🚇 Lehel 🚋 Tram 19 AE, DI, MC, VI

Raffael $$$

Celebrity guests including Madonna and Prince Charles have stayed at the city's newest luxury hotel, with

54 rooms and 19 suites.
➕ 230D2 ✉ Neuturmstrasse 1
☎ 089 29 09 80; fax 089 22 25 39
🚇 Marienplatz 🚋 Tram 19 AE, DI, MC, VI

Splendid $$

Rooms at this small bed-and-breakfast in the city center are decorated in a range of styles, from baroque to Bavarian.
➕ 230D2 ✉ Maximilianstrasse 54
☎ 089 29 66 06; fax 089 291 3176
🚇 Lehel AE, DI, MC, VI

Torbräu $$

Munich's oldest hotel has been in the heart of the Old Town for more than five centuries. On the premises are an Italian restaurant, café and 100 quiet, individually styled rooms.
➕ 230C2 ✉ Tal 41 ☎ 089 22 50 16; fax 089 22 50 19
🚇 Marienplatz, Isartor AE, MC, VI

MUNICH RESTAURANTS

Price guide: (dinner per person, excluding drinks)
$ up to DM25
$$ DM25–50
$$$ over DM50

Augustiner Grossgaststätten $$

Munich's oldest surviving brewery was producing its own beer until 1897, and now serves Bavarian dishes in its large hall. There's a beer garden in the courtyard.
➕ 230B2 ✉ Neuhauser Strasse 27 ☎ 089 23 18 32 57
🚇 Marienplatz, Karlsplatz AE, DI, MC, VI

Halali $$$

Unpretentious regional cooking, focusing on game dishes such as venison, is served with special touches such as cranberry or wild mushroom sauce.
➕ 230D3 ✉ Schönfeldstrasse 22
☎ 089 28 59 09 🚫 Closed Sun.
🚇 Odeonsplatz AE, MC, VI

Ratskeller $$

Hearty local dishes are served in the New Town Hall's impressive vaulted cellars.
➕ 230C2 ✉ Marienplatz 8
☎ 089 22 03 13 🚇 Marienplatz
AE, MC, VI

Schlosscafé Palmerhaus $$

This elegant café is set in the palm house of the Nymphenburg Palace.

➕ 230 Off the map ✉ Schloss Nymphenburg ☎ 089 17 53 09
🚋 Tram 12, 17 AE, MC, VI

Spatenhaus $$

The atmosphere is relaxed and the service good at this favored after-theater restaurant, which serves a Bavarian menu on the first floor, and other regional and international dishes on the second.
➕ 230C3 ✉ Residenzstrasse 12
☎ 089 290 7060 🚇 Marienplatz
DI, MC, VI

ATHENS HOTELS

Price guide: (double room with breakfast for two people)
$ Dr14,000–20,000
$$ Dr20,000–40,000
$$$ over Dr40,000

Acropolis House $

This clean and simple family-run hotel on the edge of the Plaka is an excellent budget choice, although not all rooms have baths.
➕ 244B2 ✉ 6–8 Kodrou Plaka
☎ 01 322 2344; fax 01 324 4143
🚋 11, 18 AE, DI, VI

Athenian Inn $$

Quietly situated near Kolonaki's smart shops, this hotel has a lot of Greek charm and atmosphere; make reservations in advance.
➕ 244D3 ✉ 22 Haritos Kolonaki
☎ 01 723 8097; fax 01 724 2268
🚋 3, 13 AE, DI, MC, VI

Grande Bretagne $$$

Athens' most historic, grandest and very traditional hotel, offering the highest level of service and ameni-ties, is located on Sindagma Square.
➕ 244C2 ✉ Syntagmatos ☎ 01 333 0000; fax 01 322 8034 🚋 1, 18, 15 AE, CB, DI, MC, VI

Plaka $$

This conveniently located, updated hotel has air-conditioning and a charming rooftop terrace that over-looks the Acropolis.
➕ 244B2 ✉ Mitropoleos and 7-8 Kapnikareas ☎ 01 322 2096-8; fax 01 322 2412 🚋 12 AE, CB, DI, MC, VI

Saint George Lycabettus $$$

Beautifully situated on the quiet, shady slopes of Lycabettus, this first-class hotel offers lovely views from its rooftop restaurant.

Greece, Hungary

KEY TO SYMBOLS

- ✚ map page number and coordinates
- ✉ address
- ☎ telephone number
- 🕐 days/times closed
- Ⓜ nearest subway station
- 🚌 nearest bus/trolley bus/tram route
- ⛴ ferry
- $$$ expensive
- $$ moderate
- $ inexpensive
- AE American Express
- CB Carte Blanche
- DI Diners
- MC MasterCard
- VI VISA

✚ 244D3 ✉ 2 Kleomenous Dexamini ☎ 01 729 0710; fax 01 724 7610 🚌 3, 8, 13 AE, CB, DI, MC, VI

ATHENS RESTAURANTS
Price guide: (dinner per person, excluding drinks)
$ Dr250–350
$$ Dr350–700
$$$ over Dr700

Achillion $$
This pleasant restaurant, near the Acropolis, serves traditional dishes and has a pretty courtyard; live music is presented in the evenings.
✚ 244B2 ✉ 5 Dionissiou Areopagitou ☎ 01 921 8173 🚌 1, 9, 11, 18 AE, DI, VI

O Platanos $
This friendly Plaka *taverna* serves simple and delicious food at both indoor and outdoor tables.
✚ 244B2 ✉ 4 Diogenous, Plaka ☎ 01 322 0666 🚌 1, 9, 11, 18 No credit cards

Psaras $$
Tucked below the Acropolis on one of Plaka's prettiest streets is this 100-year-old *taverna* serving home-cooked traditional dishes.
✚ 244B2 ✉ 16 Erekteos and Erotokritou Plaka ☎ 01 321 8733 Ⓜ Thission 🚌 1, 9, 11, 18 AE, VI

Saita $
This basement restaurant in the Plaka is usually packed with Greeks and foreigners who come for the good food and friendly service.
✚ 244B2 ✉ 21 Kidathineon ☎ 01 322 6671 🚌 1, 5, 9, 18 No credit cards

Vassilenas $$
Winston Churchill and Aristotle Onassis were among the satisfied customers of this family-run *taverna*, serving 16-course meals as well as many traditional specialties.
✚ 244 Off the map ✉ 72 Etolikou, Ayia Sophia, Piraeus ☎ 01 461 2457 🕐 Closed Sun. and in Aug. Ⓜ Piraeus No credit cards

BUDAPEST HOTELS
Price guide: (double room with breakfast for two people)
$ up to Ft17,500
$$ Ft17,500–44,500
$$$ over Ft44,500

Alba $$
This is a spacious and simple Swiss-run hotel at the foot of Castle Hill. Of the 95 rooms – all with excellent facilities – only those on the upper floor have good views, so be sure to request one.
✚ 258B3 ✉ Apor Péter utca 3 ☎ 01 375 9244; fax 01 375 9899 🚌 16, 19 AE, DI, MC, VI

Astoria $$
Set on a busy intersection in the center of Pest this is a splendid hotel in an old building with a relaxing atmosphere. It was the headquarters of the Soviet army during the 1956 revolution.
✚ 258C2 ✉ Kossuth Lajos utca 19–21 ☎ 01 317 3411; fax 01 318 6798 🚌 Astoria AE, DI, MC, VI

Hilton $$$
This modern building is in a prime position on Castle Hill, incorporating the ruins of a 13th-century Dominican cloister and a 17th-century Jesuit cloister. You'll get spectacular views over the Danube. Facilities include salons, cafés, shops and a courtyard concert area.
✚ 258A3 ✉ Hess András tér 1–3 ☎ 01 214 3000; fax 01 356 0285 Ⓜ Moszkva tér, then Várbusz (Castle Bus) AE, DI, MC, VI

Kempinski Hotel Corvinus $$$
This luxury hotel with unusual post-modern design includes two presidential apartments. It's popular with business travelers.
✚ 258C2 ✉ Erzsébet tér 7–8 ☎ 0142 93777; fax 0142 94777 Ⓜ Deák tér AE, DI, MC, VI

Victoria $$
Marvelous views across to the Pest bank are a feature at this small and comfortable 27-room hotel on the Buda bank, overlooking Chain Bridge and convenient to many major tourist sights.
✚ 258B3 ✉ Bem rakpart 11 ☎ 01 457 8080; fax 01 201 5816 Ⓜ Battyány tér 🚌 16; tram 19 AE, DI, VI

BUDAPEST RESTAURANTS
Price guide: (dinner per person, excluding drinks)
$ up to Ft3,000
$$ Ft3,000–6,000
$$$ over Ft6,000

Water in Greece
It's important not to waste water in arid Greece, especially on the islands, where it often has to be shipped in by tankers. Although Athens' tap water is drinkable, bottled water is cheap and better-tasting. Greeks are water connoisseurs, discussing the flavor and mineral properties of favorite spring varieties. Glasses of water are served alongside every drink you order in cafés: Drink it, or pour it in your ouzo and watch the clear spirit turn milky white. Since it's often hot and most places are not air-conditioned, it's important to drink plenty of water.

Hungary, Ireland, Italy

Alabárdos $$$
This smart, formal restaurant serves Hungarian dishes in ancient vaulted dining rooms. You'll get beautiful presentation and attentive staff but there are few tables, so reserve well in advance.
➕ 258A3 ✉ Országház utca 2
☎ 01 356 0851 🚫 Closed Sun.
🚇 Moszkva tér, then Várbusz (Castle Bus) AE, DI, MC, VI

Astoria Empire $$
The grand restaurant in this impressive turn-of-the-20th-century hotel serves first-class Hungarian and international dishes and good wines in elegant surroundings. Gypsy bands serenade evening diners, and there is also an atmospheric café.
➕ 258C2 ✉ Kossuth Lajos utca
☎ 01 317 3411 🚇 Astoria AE, MC, VI

Duna $$
Located in the art nouveau Gellért Hotel, this well-known restaurant rests over a thermal spring at the foot of Gellért Hill. Expect fine views of the river and specialties including pike, perch and veal.
➕ 258C1 ✉ Gellért tér 1 ☎ 01 385 2200 🚇 Trams 18, 19, 47, 49 AE, DI, MC, VI

Gundel $$$
Hungarian meals are served in a 100-year-old restaurant in City Park. The owner, George Lang, also owns the Café des Artistes in New York.
➕ 258E4 ✉ Állatkerti út 2 ☎ 01 321 3550 🚇 Hösök tere AE, DI, MC, VI

Müvész $
It's worth having refreshments at this coffeehouse, which has retained the ambience of Budapest's golden era of café society.
➕ 258C3 ✉ Andrássy út 29
☎ 01 267 0689 🚇 Opera No credit cards

DUBLIN HOTELS
Price guide: (double room with breakfast for two people)
$ £30–60
$$ £60–100
$$$ over £100

Burlington $$$
This very large top-quality hotel is located southeast of St. Stephen's

Green, on the south side of the Royal Canal and about a 10-minute walk from the center. It's best known for its stylish restaurant and bar.
➕ 274C1 ✉ Leeson Street Upper
☎ 01 660 5222; fax 01 660 8496
🚇 11, 13, 46 AE, MC, VI

Fitzwilliam $$
This small, pleasant family-run hotel on a famous Dublin Georgian street is close to the heart of things.
➕ 274C1–C2 ✉ 41 Fitzwilliam Street Upper ☎ 01 660 0448; fax 01 676 7488 🚇 10, 18 AE, VI

Georgian House Hotel $$
This is a small hotel amid the ambience of Georgian Dublin and close to the heart of south Dublin. You'll get good breakfasts here, and the restaurant specializes in fish.
➕ 274C1–C2 ✉ 20–21 Baggot Street Lower ☎ 01 661 8832; fax 01 661 8834 🚇 10, 18 AE, MC, VI

Shelbourne $$$
This famous central Dublin hotel, opened in 1824 (although the present building dates from 1867), is Dublin's oldest. It was recently refurbished to the highest standards, and has a good restaurant and bar. It's popular for fashionable – and expensive – afternoon tea. It overlooks St. Stephen's Green.
➕ 274B2 ✉ 27 St. Stephen's Green ☎ 01 676 6471; fax 01 661 6006 🚇 11, 13, 44, 46, 48 AE, MC, VI

The Townhouse $
A pleasant hotel in a Georgian house, The Townhouse is located north of the river and close to train and bus stations.
➕ 274C3 ✉ 48 Lower Gardiner Street ☎ 01 878 8808; fax 01 878 8787 🚇 Most city center buses AE, MC, VI

DUBLIN RESTAURANTS
Price guide: (dinner per person, excluding drinks)
$ £10–15
$$ £15–30
$$$ over £30

Bewleys $$
Bewley's main restaurant on Grafton Street is a legendary place, with a great feeling of being at the heart of Dublin. You can have breakfast, lunch and dinner here.

➕ 274B2 ✉ 78 Grafton Street
☎ 01 677 6761 🚇 11, 13, 144 AE, DI, MC, VI

Chapter One $$
This literary-themed restaurant in Writers' Museum on north Dublin's Parnell Square has fine Irish cuisine. Discuss Shaw over salmon or Joyce over venison.
➕ 274B3 ✉ 18–19 Parnell Square
☎ 01 873 2266 or 01 873 2281
🚫 Closed Sun. 🚇 3, 10, 11, 13, 16, 19 AE, DI, MC, VI

Cornucopia $
This good-value restaurant serves imaginative vegetarian food.
➕ 274B3 ✉ 19 Wicklow Street
☎ 01 677 7583 🚫 Closed Sun.
🚇 All city center buses AE, DI, MC, VI

Gallagher's Boxty House $$
Good Irish cooking is found at this restaurant, whose name refers to boxty, a traditional potato pancake. If you want straightforward food with an Irish accent, this is the place.
➕ 274B3 ✉ 20–21 Temple Bar
☎ 01 677 2762 🚇 11, 13, 46 AE, MC, VI

Restaurant Patrick Guilbaud $$$
This Michelin-starred French restaurant has a reputation for outstanding nouvelle cuisine. It's superbly understated, stylish and very expensive. There's a wonderful collection of Irish art.
➕ 274C2 ✉ 46 James Place
☎ 01 676 4192 🚫 Closed Sun.–Mon. 🚇 11, 13, 46 AE, DI, MC, VI

ROME HOTELS
Price guide: (double room with breakfast for two people)
$ up to L200,000
$$ L200,000–400,000
$$$ over L400,000

Campo di' Fiore $$
You'll find comfortable rooms and a roof garden at this pretty, moderately priced hotel near one of Rome's liveliest squares. Good value option.
➕ 292B3 ✉ Via del Biscione 6
☎ 06 6880 6865; fax 06 687 6003
🚇 46, 62, 64 AE, DI, VI

Colombus $$
This historic hotel (a favorite of visiting prelates) is housed in a

Italy

KEY TO SYMBOLS

- ⊞ map page number and coordinates
- ✉ address
- ☎ telephone number
- 🕐 days/times closed
- Ⓜ nearest subway station
- 🚌 nearest bus/trolley bus/tram route
- ⛴ ferry
- **$$$** expensive
- **$$** moderate
- **$** inexpensive
- AE American Express
- CB Carte Blanche
- DI Diners
- MC MasterCard
- VI VISA

former Renaissance palace a stone's throw from St. Peter's, and has many original decorative features.
⊞ 292B3 ✉ Via della Conciliazione 33 ☎ 06 686 5435; fax 06 686 4874 🚌 23, 64 AE, DI, VI

Excelsior $$$

A stay at this world-class luxury hotel, with its opulent decor and high standard of service and elegance, is among Rome's most sybaritic experiences.
⊞ 292C4 ✉ Via Vittorio Veneto 125 ☎ 06 47081; fax 06 482 6205 Ⓜ Barbarini 🚌 52, 53, 95 AE, DI, MC, VI

Hotel d'Inghilterra $$$

Located a few minutes from the Spanish Steps is this historic hotel with antique furniture and discreet and excellent service.
⊞ 292C4 ✉ Via Bocca di Leone 14 ☎ 06 69981; fax 06 679 8601 Ⓜ Spagna 🚌 119, 52, 61 AE, DI, VI

Navona $

This comfortable, simple and friendly hotel is a few minutes' stroll from the lovely piazza Navona. Be sure to make reservations ahead of time.
⊞ 292B3 ✉ Via dei Sediari 8 ☎ 06 686 4203; fax 06 880 3802 🚌 70, 81, 90 AE, VI

ROME RESTAURANTS

Price guide: (dinner per person, excluding drinks)
$ L15,000–30,000
$$ L30,000–50,000
$$$ over L50,000

Alberto Ciarla $$$

One of Rome's finest restaurants, this winner has an elegant atmosphere, an outstanding wine list and good fish specials.
⊞ 292B2 ✉ Piazza San Cosimato 40 ☎ 06 581 8668 🕐 Closed Sun. evening and for 15 days during Jan. and Aug. 🚌 44, 75, 170 AE, MC, DI, VI

Baffetto $

For a quintessential Roman experience and the best pizza in town, stand in line to get a table at this tiny pizzeria.
⊞ 292B3 ✉ Via del Governo Vecchio 114 ☎ 06 686 1617 🕐 Closed Sun. 🚌 46, 62, 64 No credit cards

Checchino dal 1887 $$$

This long-established restaurant specializes in the traditional Roman dishes of tripe, brains and offal.
⊞ 292B1 ✉ Via Monte Testaccio 30 ☎ 06 574 3816 🕐 Closed Sun. evenings and Mon., and throughout Aug. 🚌 13, 23, 57 AE, DI, VI

Da Lucia $

A tiny, typical Trastevere trattoria, Da Lucia has a friendly family atmosphere, traditional Roman dishes and great pasta.
⊞ 292B2 ✉ Via del Mattonato 2b ☎ 06 580 3601 🕐 Closed Mon. 🚌 23, 65, 56 No credit cards

Papà Giovanni $$$

Reservations are advised to enjoy this restaurant's light and innovative cooking and excellent wine list.
⊞ 292B3 ✉ Via dei Sediari 4 ☎ 06 6880 4807 🕐 Closed Sun. and throughout Aug. 🚌 70, 81, 90 VI, MC

Paris $$

You can eat outside in summer at this very popular Trastevere restaurant serving fine pasta and fish dishes.
⊞ 292B2 ✉ Piazza San Calisto 7a ☎ 06 581 5378 🕐 Closed Sun. evenings and Mon., and for 3 weeks during Aug. 🚌 44, 56, 60 AE, DI, VI

FLORENCE HOTELS

Price guide: (double room with breakfast for two people)
$ up tp 200,000
$$ L200,000–400,000
$$$ over L400,000

Brunelleschi $$$

Book ahead to stay in this comfortable hotel filled with character and situated in the heart of Florence, around a medieval tower.
⊞ 302C2 ✉ Piazza Elisabetta 3 ☎ 055 571 105; fax 055 219 653 🚌 In the pedestrian zone AE, MC, DI, VI

Excelsior $$$

This is Florence's smartest hotel, with every comfort, exceptional service and a rooftop terrace.
⊞ 302B3 ✉ Piazza Ognissanti 3 ☎ 055 264 201; fax 055 210 278 🚌 C AE, MC, DI, VI

Firenze $

This good budget choice, located close to the center of Florence, is

Bread, Cakes and Cookies

In Italy, bread comes from a *panificio* or *forno*, cakes and cookies from a *pasticceria*. In Tuscany there is no salt in bread, a legacy of an age when baking was done once a week and saltless bread didn't get moldy. Once you're accustomed to it, it goes well with the strong, salty flavors of prosciutto or salami. Italian cakes are outstanding: luscious creations piled with fruit, filled with cream, oozing chocolate and soaked with liqueur. Italians often buy a large cake or selection of smaller ones to eat for Sunday dessert, or a piece of *panforte*, a traditional spiced fruit confection from Siena. It's acceptable to buy a single pastry or cake and eat it on the spot in the shop.

popular with younger travelers.

➕ 302C2   ✉ Piazza dei Donati 4
☎ 055 214 203; fax 055 212 073
🚌 In the pedestrian zone DI, VI

Monna Lisa $$$
Housed in a 15th-century palace, this hotel has grand public rooms and a tranquil garden; be sure to request a quiet bedroom.
➕ 302E3   ✉ Borgo Pinti 27
☎ 055 247 9751; fax 055 247 9755
🚌 6, 31 AE, MC, DI, VI

Porta Rossa $$
This elegant, moderately priced hotel, housed in a 14th-century building near the Old Bridge, has wonderfully atmospheric public areas and is a good value.
➕ 302C2   ✉ Via Porta Rossa 19
☎ 055 287 551; fax 055 282 179
🚌 In the pedestrian zone AE, DI, VI

FLORENCE RESTAURANTS
Price guide: (dinner per person, excluding drinks)
$ L15,000–30,000
$$ L30,000–50,000
$$$ over L50,000

Cantinetta Antinori $$
Enjoy Tuscan food with superb wine in a restaurant housed within the 15th-century Palazzo Antinori and belonging to this great wine-producing family. Dress up to feel in place.
➕ 302B3   ✉ Piazza Antinori 3r
☎ 055 292 234   🚫 Closed Sat.–Sun. 🚌 In pedestrian zone AE, DI, MC, VI

Il Carmine $
This family-run restaurant serves good traditional Tuscan food in a friendly atmosphere.
➕ 302B2   ✉ Piazza del Carmine 18r ☎ 055 218 601   🚫 Closed Sun. 🚌 B AE, DI, VI

Dino $$
This uncluttered and airy restaurant serves simple and elegant food and is popular with locals and tourists alike.
➕ 302D2   ✉ Via Ghibellina 51r
☎ 055 241 452   🚫 Closed Sun.
🚌 14 AE, DI, VI

Gauguin $$
One of Florence's rare vegetarian restaurants serves imaginative dishes and is very popular with the university crowd.

➕ 302D4   ✉ Via degli Alfani 24a
☎ 055 234 0616   🚌 6 AE, DI, VI

Ponte Vecchio $$
Head to this restaurant in the heart of Florence for some real local cooking; it's popular with tourists, but none the worse because of it.
➕ 302C2   ✉ Lungarno Archibusieri 8r   ☎ 055 292 289   🚫 Closed Mon.   🚌 In pedestrian zone AE, DI, VI

NAPLES HOTELS
Price guide: (double room with breakfast for two people)
$ up to L200,000
$$ L200,000–400,000
$$$ over L400,000

Britannique $$
This quietly situated and comfortable hotel has a secluded garden and lovely views over the Bay of Naples.
➕ 309B2   ✉ Corso Vittorio Emanuele 133   ☎ 081 761 4145; fax 081 660 457   🚌 V1 AE, DI, VI

Canada $$
You'll have to reserve well in advance to get one of the sea-view rooms at this small and friendly hotel near the harbor at Mergellina.
➕ 309 Off the map   ✉ Via Mergellina 43   ☎ 081 680 952; fax 081 680 952   🚌 R3 AE, DI

Excelsior $$$
One of Naples' grandest hotels is the Excelsior, in the elegant Chiaia district; it has period rooms and views of Capri.
➕ 309A1   ✉ Via Partenope 48
☎ 081 764 0111; fax 081 764 9743
🚌 R3 AE, DI, VI

Mediterraneo $$
This large, modern hotel is conveniently located near the waterfront, and has good facilities and a lovely rooftop breakfast terrace.
➕ 309B2   ✉ Via Fonte di Tappia 25 ☎ 081 551 2240; fax 081 552 5868   🚌 R2, R3 AE, DI, VI

Santa Lucia $$
This elegant and prestigious waterfront hotel near the Castel dell'Ovo has spacious and well-furnished rooms.
➕ 309A1   ✉ Via Partenope 46
☎ 081 764 0666; fax 081 764 8580
🚌 R3 AE, DI, VI

NAPLES RESTAURANTS
Price guide: (dinner per person, excluding drinks)
$ L15,000–30,000
$$ L30,000–50,000
$$$ over L50,000

A! 53 $$
Naples' oldest restaurant, complete with 17th-century furnishings and original mosaic pavement, serves great hors d'oeuvres, seafood pasta and Neapolitan desserts.
➕ 309B3   ✉ Piazza Dante 53
☎ 081 549 9372   🚫 Closed Mon.
🚌 R1, 24 No credit cards

Amici Miei $$
This elegant, friendly restaurant serves excellent antipasti, risotto and pasta dishes.
➕ 309B2   ✉ Via Monte di Dio 78
☎ 081 764 6063   🚫 Closed Mon.
🚌 R1, R3 AE, DC, VI

La Cantinella $$$
This seafront restaurant specializes in creative fish cooking, which you can enjoy on the terrace. The wine list is outstanding.
➕ 309B1   ✉ Via Cuma 42   ☎ 081 764 8838   🚫 Closed Wed.   🚌 R3 AE, DI, VI

Trattoria Medina $$
This cheerful restaurant, packed with locals, serves authentic Neapolitan dishes, seafood and pizzas, accompanied by live music.
➕ 309B2   ✉ Via Medina 32
☎ 081 551 5233   🚫 Closed Thu.
🚌 R3 AE, DI, MC, VI

Trianon $
Naples' finest and most popular pizzeria, offering numerous combinations, has been in business for more than 60 years.
➕ 309B3   ✉ Via P Colletta 46
☎ 081 553 9426   🚌 R2, 14, 110 No credit cards

VENICE HOTELS
Price guide: (double room with breakfast for two people)
$ up to L200,000
$$ L200,000–400,000
$$$ over L400,000

Hotel agli Alboretti $$
Book well in advance to stay at this pleasant hotel, ideally situated on a tree-lined street between the Accademia and the Záttere.

Italy, Luxembourg

KEY TO SYMBOLS

- ✚ map page number and coordinates
- ✉ address
- ☎ telephone number
- 🕐 days/times closed
- Ⓜ nearest subway station
- 🚍 nearest bus/trolley bus/tram route
- ⛴ ferry
- $$$ expensive
- $$ moderate
- $ inexpensive
- AE American Express
- CB Carte Blanche
- DI Diners
- MC MasterCard
- VI VISA

✚ 314C1 ✉ Rio Terrà Sant'Agnese, Dorsoduro 884 ☎ 041 523 0058; fax 041 521 0158 ⛴ 1, 82 AE, MC, DI, VI

Canada $

This is one of the best budget bets in Venice, with a good location near the Rialto; reserve in advance.
✚ 314D2 ✉ Campo San Lio, Castello 5659 ☎ 041 522 9912; fax 041 523 5852 ⛴ 1, 82 AE, DI, VI

Cipriani $$$

One of the world's most famous luxury hotels, with every comfort and impeccable service, is located amid beautiful gardens on the Giudecca (a chain of islets a short boat ride from central Venice).
✚ 314 Off the map ✉ Giudecca 10 ☎ 041 520 7744; fax 041 520 3930 ⛴ 82, or use hotel's private launch service AE, CB, DI, MC, VI

Danieli $$$

Considered to be Venice's finest hotel, the Danieli has style, elegance and class. Book a room in the older part, not in the modern annex.
✚ 314D2 ✉ Riva degli Schiavoni, Castello 4196 ☎ 041 522 6480; fax 041 522 0208 ⛴ 1 AE, CB, DI, MC, VI

Pensione Seguso $$

This is a wonderfully atmospheric, old-fashioned *pension* overlooking the Giudecca Canal. Antique furniture and painted ceilings enhance many of the rooms, most of which have water views.
✚ 314B1 ✉ Fondamenta ai Gesuati, Dorsoduro 779 ☎ 041 528 6858; fax 041 522 2340 ⛴ 52, 82 AE, DI, VI

VENICE RESTAURANTS

Price guide: (dinner per person, excluding drinks)
$ L15,000–30,000
$$ L30,000–50,000
$$$ over L50,000

Alla Madonna $$

This big, noisy fish restaurant, one of the most traditional in Venice, is hugely popular with locals, business people and tourists.
✚ 314D2 ✉ Calle della Madonna, San Polo 594 ☎ 041 523 3824 🕐 Closed Wed.and for 2 weeks during Aug. ⛴ 1, 82 AE, MC, DI, VI

Da Franz $$$

Situated near the Giardini Pubblici, this excellent fish and seafood restaurant has a summer terrace.
✚ 314 Off the map ✉ Fondamenta San Giuseppe, Castello 745 ☎ 041 522 0861 🕐 Closed Tue. ⛴ 1, 52 AE, MC, DI, VI

Dona Onesta $

The decor is simple and the Venetian dishes straightforward at this friendly local restaurant; reservations are advised. Good quality food at budget prices.
✚ 314B2 ✉ Calle della Dona Onesta, Dorsoduro ☎ 041 522 9586 🕐 Closed Sun. ⛴ 1 AE, VI

Harry's Dolci $$$

This offshoot of the famous Harry's Bar offers equally good food and service with the bonus of a waterfront terrace for summer dining; reserve in advance.
✚ 314 Off the map ✉ Fondamenta San Biagio, Giudecca 773 ☎ 041 522 4844 🕐 Closed Tue., from Nov. –Mar. ⛴ 82 AE, MC, DI, VI

Taverna San Trovaso $

This lively neighborhood restaurant and pizzeria is always busy serving Venetian families and tourists.
✚ 314B1 ✉ Fondamenta Priuli, Dorsoduro 1016 ☎ 041 520 3703 🕐 Closed Mon. ⛴ 1 AE, MC, DI, VI

LUXEMBOURG HOTELS

Price guide: (double room with breakfast for two people)
$ 2,000–3,000F
$$ 3,000–5,000F
$$$ over 5,000F

Français $$

Ideally located for easy strolls to the Old Town, this small hotel is at the heart of the city.
✚ 329B3 ✉ 14 place d'Armes ☎ 47 45 34; fax 46 42 74 🚍 All buses AE, MC, VI

Grand Hotel Cravat $$$

Place d'Armes is a few steps away from this stylish hotel overlooking the Pétrusse valley. The property is part of the well-known restaurant association Luxembourg à la Carte, and its own restaurant offers the very best French and traditional Luxembourg cuisine.

🚫 329B3 ✉ 29 boulevarde F. D.
Roosevelt ☎ 22 19 75; fax 22 67
11 🚌 All buses AE, MC, VI

Italia $
Located just off the place de Paris
on avenue de la Liberté, this
pleasant, comfortable, small hotel
is just a quick bus ride from the city
center. Its restaurant specializes in
Italian cuisine.
🚫 329B2 ✉ 15–17 rue d'Anvers
☎ 48 66 26; fax 48 08 07 🚌 9 AE,
MC, VI

San Remo $$
This small, well-appointed hotel in
the spacious place Guillaume, near
the Ducal Palace, is within easy
reach of the center and Old Town. It
has its own restaurant focusing on
French and Italian cuisine, with good
fish specialties.
🚫 329B3 ✉ 10 place Guillaume
☎ 46 04 31; fax 22 11 35 🚌 All
buses AE, MC, VI

Sofitel $$$
This hotel is very modern, very
luxurious and very expensive. It is
located on the Kirchberg Plateau,
next to the Centre Européen.
🚫 329 Off the map ✉ 6 rue du
Fort Niedergrunewald ☎ 43 77 61;
fax 42 50 91 🚌 All buses to Centre
Européen AE, MC, VI

LUXEMBOURG RESTAURANTS
Price guide: (dinner per person,
excluding drinks)
$ 400–600F
$$ 600–1,000F
$$$ over 1,000F

Caves Gourmandes $$$
This popular and atmospheric
restaurant in the Ilot
Gastronomique complex is within
part of the Old Town wall. The
superb French cuisine features
breast of duck with figs, and crème
brûlée for dessert.
🚫 329 C3 ✉ rue de L'Eau ☎ 46
11 24 🕐 Closed Sun. 🚌 All
buses MC, VI

La Lorraine $$
Located on place d'Armes, this
bright, attractive restaurant offers
French cuisine with excellent fish
dishes. You can choose your lobster
from a tank by the door.
🚫 329B3 ✉ 7 place d'Armes
☎ 47 14 36 🚌 All buses MC, VI

Maison Des Brasseurs $$
This popular restaurant in Grand Rue
serves classic country cooking and
offers local dishes such as *Judd mat
Gaardebounen* (roast and smoked
pork) and vegetarian dishes.
🚫 329B3 ✉ 48 Grand Rue 🚌 47
13 71 🕐 Closed Sun. 🚌 All
buses MC, VI

Restaurant Speltz $$$
This beautifully appointed
restaurant has a pleasant outdoor
eating area in good weather and an
excellent wine collection to
accompany the top-quality French
and Italian cuisine, such as
turbot or scorpion fish with
tomatoes, olives and basil. There is
a very good cheese selection.
Reservations are advised.
🚫 329B3 ✉ 8 rue Chimay ☎ 47
49 50 🕐 Closed Sun. 🚌 All
buses MC, VI

Via Sud $$
French cuisine is offered at this
popular restaurant, where you can
eat outside on nice evenings. Try the
red mullet in olive oil.
🚫 329B3 ✉ 22–24 rue du Cure
☎ 22 82 50 🕐 Closed Sun.
🚌 All buses MC, VI

AMSTERDAM HOTELS
Price guide: (double room with
breakfast for two people)
$ 200–300f
$$ 300–600f
$$$ over 600f

Ambassade Hotel $$
Located on the splendid
Herengracht, the city's most elegant
canal, this beautifully furnished
hotel offers a good breakfast.
🚫 342B2 ✉ Herengracht 335–353
☎ 020 626 2333; fax 020 624 5321
🚌 Tram 1, 2, 5, AE, MC, VI

Amstel Botel $
For a different experience, and
waterside views from some rooms,
stay in this permanently moored
hotel boat near Centraal Station.
🚫 342D3 ✉ Oosterdokskade 2–4
☎ 020 626 4247; fax 020 639 1952
🚌 22 AE, MC, VI

Hotel de L'Europe $$$
The private boat landing at this
expensive luxury hotel overlooking
the Amstel river says it all. A
Victorian exterior welcomes the

traveler into the renovated interior,
where there is every modern ameni-
ty – including the finest *haute cui-
sine* and wine list at the hotel's
Excelsior Restaurant.
🚫 342C2 ✉ Nieuwe
Doelenstraat 2–8 ☎ 020 531
1777; fax 020 531 1778 🚌 Tram 4,
6, 9, 14 AE, MC, VI

Nova $
This modern hotel has a central
location but is sheltered from street
noise. Spotless en-suite rooms;
friendly, efficient service.
🚫 342C3 ✉ Nieuwezijds
Voorburgwal 276 ☎ 020 623 0066;
fax 020 627 2026 🚌 Tram 1, 2, 5,
13, 17 AE, MC, VI

Pulitzer $$$
This stylish luxury hotel recaptures
some of the spirit of old
Amsterdam within its unified complex of 17th-century canal houses
on the handsome Prinsengracht.
Relax in the art nouveau Garden
Room and the 17th-century
Saxenburg Room.
🚫 342B2 ✉ Prinsengracht
315–331 ☎ 020 523 5235; fax 020
627 6753 🚌 Tram 6, 9, 14, 16, 24
AE, MC, VI

AMSTERDAM RESTAURANTS
Price guide: (dinner per person,
excluding drinks)
$ 15–30f
$$ 30–45f
$$$ over 45f

Claes Claesz $$
This relaxed and friendly restaurant
is situated on the banks of the
Egelantiersgracht, in the attractive
Jordaan district. Good Dutch food is
served, often to the accompaniment
of background music.
🚫 342B3 ✉ Egelantierstraat 24
☎ 020 625 5306 🚌 10; tram 13,
14, 17 MC, VI

Dorrius $$$
For a taste of real Dutch cuisine
with a dash of French flair, this is
the place. Try delicious oysters and
eel or salted cod, cheese soufflé,
and Dutch wines and liqueurs.
Only dinner is served regularly, but
lunch is available by appointment;
reservations are advised.
🚫 342C3 ✉ Nieuwezijds
Voorburgwal 5 ☎ 020 420 2224
🚌 Tram 1, 2, 5,13,17 MC, VI

Luxembourg, The Netherlands

The Netherlands

KEY TO SYMBOLS

- ✚ map page number and coordinates
- ✉ address
- ☎ telephone number
- ✪ days/times closed
- Ⓜ nearest subway station
- 🚌 nearest bus/trolley bus/tram route
- 🚢 ferry
- **$$$** expensive
- **$$** moderate
- **$** inexpensive
- AE American Express
- CB Carte Blanche
- DI Diners
- MC MasterCard
- VI VISA

In de Waag $$

For late-night international cuisine among the light of hundreds of candles, come to this fine, friendly French restaurant. A generous three-course lunch and special early evening menus are good values.
✚ 342C3 ✉ Nieuwmarkt 4
☎ 020 422 7772 Ⓜ Waterlooplein
MC, VI

De Silveren Spiegel $$$

Located in a restored redbrick 1614 building with yellow trimmings and shuttered windows, this restaurant has an exceptional menu ranging from traditional Dutch cuisine to fish specialties. Dinner only.
✚ 342C4 ✉ Kattengatt 4–6
☎ 020 624 6589 ✪ Closed Sun.
🚌 Tram 2, 5, 17 MC, VI

Toscanini $$

This stylish Jordaan district restaurant features excellent Italian food. The homemade *biscotti* is a specialty.
✚ 342B4 ✉ Lindengracht 75
☎ 020 623 2813 🚌 Tram 18 MC, VI

THE HAGUE HOTELS

Price guide: (double room with breakfast for two people)
$ 200–300f
$$ 300–600f
$$$ over 600f

Carlton Ambassador Hotel $$$

This luxury hotel in an elegant neighborhood is within easy walking distance of the city center.
✚ 350B2 ✉ Sophialaan 2
☎ 070 363 0363; fax 070 360 0535
🚌 Tram 7, 8 AE, MC, VI

Cattenburch $

This comfortable small hotel with old-fashioned service is located some way from the city center, but it's near a tram connection. There's a restaurant on the premises.
✚ 350B2 ✉ Laan Copus van Cattenburch 38 ☎ 070 352 2335; fax 070 354 3119 🚌 Tram 1, 9 AE, MC, VI

Delft Museum Hotel and Residence $$

When in Delft, spend at least one night in this luxuriously furnished hotel, attractively loctated on Oude Delft overlooking a tranquil canal.
✚ 350 Off the map ✉ Oude Delft 189 ☎ 015 214 0930; fax 015 214

0935 Ⓜ Delft Railroad station
🚌 Tram 1 AE, MC, VI

Mercure $$

This modern hotel is located near the railroad station and city center. It also has a restaurant.
✚ 350C1 ✉ Spui 180 ☎ 070 363 6700; fax 070 363 9398 🚌 Tram 2, 3, 6, 7, 10, 16 AE, MC, VI

Steigenberger Kurhaus Hotel $$$

If you base yourself at Scheveningen by the sea and want to overlook the beach, consider staying at this Old European-style hotel, built in the 1880s and restored in the 1970s.
✚ 350A4 ✉ Gevers Deynootweg 990, Scheveningen ☎ 070 416 2636; fax 070 416 2646 🚌 Tram 1, 9 AE, MC, VI

THE HAGUE RESTAURANTS

Price guide: (dinner per person, excluding drinks)
$ 15–30f
$$ 30–45f
$$$ over 45f

Bodega De Posthoorn $$

This restaurant is housed in an attractive building in the stylish Lange Voorhout; reservations are strongly advised.
✚ 350C2 ✉ Lange Voorhout 39a
☎ 070 360 4906 🚌 Tram 7, 8 AE, MC, VI

't Goude Hooft $$$

This is a very popular inn that was demolished and rebuilt in the 17th century. The decor is handsome and the food is good.
✚ 350B1 ✉ Dag Groenmarkt 13
☎ 070 346 9713 ✪ Closed Wed.
🚌 Tram 2, 3, 6, 10 AE, DI, MC, VI

It Rains Fishes $$$

High-quality, expensive seafood is served in this intimate restaurant in one of The Hague's finest streets. Reservations are advised.
✚ 350B2 ✉ Noordiende 123
☎ 070 365 2598 ✪ Closed Mon.
🚌 Tram 7, 8 AE, MC, VI

Les Ombrelles $$

Located in the attractive Denneweg area, this restaurant serves excellent fish dishes, including lobster and mussels.
✚ 350C2 ✉ Hooistraat 4a
☎ 070 365 8789 ✪ Closed Tue.
🚌 Tram 2, 6, 8, 16 AE, DI, VI

Ristorante Roma $$

You'll find fine Italian cuisine here at the heart of The Hague's old quarter, north of the Kerkplein.
✚ 350B1   ✉ Papestraat 22   ☎ 070 346 2345   ◷ Closed Tue.   🚊 Tram 2, 6, 8, 16 AE, MC, VI

OSLO HOTELS

Price guide: (double room with breakfast for two people)
$ KR800–1,000
$$ KR1,000–1,400
$$$ over KR1,400

Ambassadeur Best Western $$

This stylish, comfortable hotel offers excellent service and a convenient location. It is located in a peaceful area behind the Royal Palace, but within easy reach of the city center.
✚ 365B2   ✉ Camilla Colletts vei 15   ☎ 22 44 18 35; fax 22 44 18 35   🚊 21 AE, MC, VI

Bristol $$$

This elegant hotel in the heart of Oslo has superb furnishings and decorations, as well as several bars and restaurants on the premises.
✚ 365B1–B2   ✉ Kristian IV's gate 7   ☎ 22 82 60 00; fax 22 82 60 61   🚊 33, 45; tram 3, 17, 18 AE, MC, VI

Continental $$$

This top-quality, very expensive hotel offers a prime location between the Royal Palace and City Hall. A member of "Leading Hotels of the World," it has two restaurants.
✚ 365B1   ✉ Stortingsgata 24–26   ☎ 22 82 40 00; fax 22 42 96 89   🚊 30, 31, 32, 83, 84; tram 12, 13, 19 AE, MC, VI

Grand $$$

One of Oslo's most prestigious and luxurious hotels is this handsome 19th-century accommodation right in the heart of the city. It has well-appointed rooms, good restaurants (including the Grand Café), bars, and an inviting rooftop sauna and swimming pool.
✚ 365B1   ✉ Karl Johans gate 31   ☎ 22 42 93 90; fax 22 42 12 25   🚇 Stortinget, T-Bane 1, 2, 3, 4, 5   🚊 33, 45 AE, MC, VI

Ritz $$

Within easy reach of the city's main attractions, this pleasant hotel is nestled in a quiet area on the outskirts of the center. The service is attentive and rooms are attractive.
✚ 365B2   ✉ Frederik Stangs gate 3   ☎ 22 44 39 60; fax 22 44 67 13   🚊 30, 32, 45, 83; tram 10, 15 AE, MC, VI

OSLO RESTAURANTS

Price guide: (dinner per person, excluding drinks)
$ KR50–80
$$ KR80–200
$$$ over KR200

D/S Louise Restaurant and Bar $$

Located in the Aker Brygge complex, where there are good views across the harbor to Akershus Castle, this restaurant has traditional and international specialties.
✚ 365A1   ✉ Stranden 3   ☎ 22 83 00 60   🚊 Tram 10, 15

Engebret Café $$

Founded in 1857 by Engebret Christoffersen, this restaurant still maintains a strong tradition. Try Norwegian and international cuisine, including traditional fish dishes. There's also an excellent lunch buffet.
✚ 365B1   ✉ Bankplassen 1   ☎ 22 82 25 25   ◷ Closed Sun.   🚊 60

Grand Café $$

Great tradition, including regular visits by Henrik Ibsen in his day, makes this Grand Hotel restaurant a favorite with locals. This is where you can sample Norwegian cuisine from elk stew to *lutefisk* (marinated dried fish).
✚ 365B1   ✉ Karl Johans gate 31   ☎ 22 42 93 90   🚊 Tram 11, 13, 17, 18

Restaurant Blom $$$

Excellent Norwegian food is offered in this well-established restaurant. Try *lefse*, savory pastry wrapped around reindeer meat or other fillings. Reservations are advised.
✚ 365B1   ✉ Karl Johans gate 41   ☎ 22 42 73 00   ◷ Closed Sun.   🚇 Stortinget, T-Bane 1, 2, 3, 4, 5

Restaurant Gamle Raadhus $$

Located in the 17th-century building next to Akershus Castle, this restaurant is billed as Oslo's oldest eating establishment. International cuisine and fish specialties are served in a charming atmosphere. Reservations are strongly advised.
✚ 365B1   ✉ Nedre Slottsgate 1   ☎ 22 42 01 07   🚊 Tram 10, 15

LISBON HOTELS

Price guide: (double room with breakfast for two people)
$ up to 15,000Esc
$$ 15,000–30,000Esc
$$$ over 30,000Esc

As Janelas Verdes $$$

This small hotel, housed in an 18th-century townhouse, has large and luxurious rooms. Its location, well west of the city center, is the only drawback.
✚ 378 Off the map   ✉ Rua das Janelas Verdewe 47   ☎ 01 396 8143; fax 01 396 8144   🚊 40, 49, 60 AE, CB, DI, MC, VI

Britânia $$

Just east of the Avenida da Liberdade, this small, friendly, comfortable, art deco-style hotel was refurbished in the 1990s.
✚ 378A5   ✉ Rua Rodrigues Sampaio 17   ☎ 01 315 5016; fax 01 315 5021   🚇 Avenida   🚊 9, 11, 31 AE, CB, DI, MC, VI

Duas Nações $

Although only some rooms have private bathrooms, this hotel, housed in a 19th-century building, is a superb budget choice, located in the heart of the historic Baixa district.
✚ 378B2–C2   ✉ Rua da Victória 41   ☎ 01 346 0710   🚇 Rossio AE, MC, VI

Metropole $$

The elegant Metropoloe is located on Rossio, Lisbon's busiest square; ask for a room at the back to avoid the noise.
✚ 378B3   ✉ Rossio 30   ☎ 01 346 9164; fax 01 346 9166   🚇 Rossio AE, CB, DI, VI

Ritz $$$

Lisbon's most luxurious hotel opened in the 1950s. Sumptuously decorated, it has large rooms and suites and exceptional service.
✚ 378 Off the map   ✉ Rua Rodrigo da Fonseca 88   ☎ 01 383 2020; fax 01 383 1783   🚇 Rotonda   🚊 1, 9, 11 AE, CB, DI, MC, VI

The Netherlands, Norway, Portugal

KEY TO SYMBOLS

➕ map page number and coordinates
✉ address
☎ telephone number
🚫 days/times closed
Ⓜ nearest subway station
🚌 nearest bus/trolley bus/tram route
⛴ ferry
$$$ expensive
$$ moderate
$ inexpensive
AE American Express
CB Carte Blanche
DI Diners
MC MasterCard
VI VISA

Eating in Portugal

The Portuguese do not eat at the same hours as their Spanish neighbors, so you won't have to wait until 10 p.m. for dinner. Many people eat dinner as early as 7:30, and restaurants remain open until about 10:30; they tend to close all day on Sunday. Breakfast is usually a light meal, and the lunch hour starts around 12:30. The daily menu (*ementa turística*) is an excellent value and normally offers a decent variety. Meals often start with a selection of appetizers, which arrive automatically and are charged on your bill. Portuguese helpings are big, but you can ask for a half portion.

LISBON RESTAURANTS

Price guide: (dinner per person, excluding drinks)
$ 1,500–2,000Esc
$$ 2,000–4,000Esc
$$$ over 4,000Esc

Bota Alta $

For large portions of authentic Portuguese food, go to this very popular and traditional restaurant in the Upper Town, with its attractive, rustic ambience.
➕ 378B2 ✉ Travessa da Queimada 35/37 ☎ 01 342 7959 🚫 Closed Sat. lunch and Sun. 🚌 Restauradores AE, VI

Fidalgo $

This welcoming restaurant in the Upper Town serves fish and seafood. It has a trendy clientele.
➕ 378B2 ✉ Rua da Barroca 27/31 ☎ 01 342 2900 🚫 Closed Sun. 🚌 Rossio ⛴ 1, 11; tram 28 AE, DI, VI

Gambrinus $$$

There's an old-fashioned ambience in this deluxe, formal restaurant, where fish and seafood are the specialties; reservations advised.
➕ 378A4 ✉ Rua das Portas de Santo Antão 23 ☎ 01 342 1466 🚌 Rossio AE, CB, DI, MC, VI

São Jerónimo $$

If you're sightseeing in Belém stop at this modern restaurant, close to the Jerónimo monastery, for fish and seafood.
➕ 378 Map inset ✉ Rua dos Jerónimo 12 ☎ 01 364 8797 🚫 CLosed Sat. lunch and Sun. 🚌 28, 49, 51; tram 15 AE, DI, VI

Tágide $$$

Great views, atmosphere and excellent food are what make this one of Lisbon's classiest restaurants.
➕ 378C3 ✉ Largo da Academia Nacional de Belas Artes 12/20 ☎ 01 342 0720 🚌 Rossio ⛴ 58, 100 AE, CB, DI, MC, VI

Via Graça $$

You'll find traditional Portuguese cooking and great views of the city at this candlelit restaurant.
➕ 378D5 ✉ Rua Damasceno Monteiro 9b ☎ 01 887 0830 🚫 Closed Sat. lunch and Sun. 🚌 Intendente ⛴ Tram 28 AE, DI, MC, VI

PORTO HOTELS

Price guide: (double room with breakfast for two people)
$ up to 15,000Esc
$$ 15,000–30,000Esc
$$$ over 30,000Esc

Boa-Vista $$

This peaceful, quiet hotel in the suburb of Foz is very comfortable and has great ocean views.
➕ 387 Off the map ✉ Esplanade do Castelo 58 ☎ 02 618 3175; fax 02 617 3818 🚌 24; tram 18 AE, CB, DI, MC, VI

Hotel da Bolsa $$

Friendly service and spacious rooms are the prevailing characteristics at this comfortable hotel. Excellent location in the heart of the historic center.
➕ 387B2 ✉ Rua Ferreira Borges 101 ☎ 02 202 6768; fax 02 205 8888 🚌 21, 22 AE, DI, VI

Infanta Sagres $$$

Porto's best and classiest hotel is centrally located and has elegant public rooms filled with antiques, a pretty terrace and lovely bedrooms.
➕ 387B3 ✉ Praça Filipa de Lencastre 62 ☎ 02 200 8101; fax 02 205 4937 🚌 20, 21, 22 AE, CB, DI, MC, VI

Internacional $$

Located just off the Praça de Liberdade, this friendly hotel has been recently refurbished.
➕ 387B3 ✉ Rua do Almada 131 ☎ 02 200 5032; fax 02 200 9063 🚌 20, 21, 22 AE, CB, DI, MC, VI

Meridien Porto $$$

This big, international-style hotel has a restaurant and delivers excellent service.
➕ 387 Off the map ✉ Avenida Boavista 1446 ☎ 02 600 1913; fax 02 600 2031 🚌 22 AE, CB, DI, MC, VI

PORTO RESTAURANTS

Price guide: (dinner per person, excluding drinks)
$ 1,500–2,000Esc
$$ 2,000–4,000Esc
$$$ over 4,000Esc

Dona Filipa $$$

The restaurant at the Hotel Infanta Sagres is one of Porto's best, serving Portuguese and international

dishes in elegant surroundings.
✚ 387B3 ✉ Praça Filipa de
Lencastre 62 ☎ 02 200 8101
🚌 21, 22 AE, CB, DI, MC, VI

Filha da Mãe Preta $$
There are lovely river views from this
restaurant specializing in regional
dishes such as squid, octopus, eel
and bacalhau (dried, salted cod).
✚ 387B1 ✉ Rua da Fonte Taurina
39 ☎ 02 315 515 🔵 Closed Sun.
AE, DI, MC, VI

Mercearia $
This traditional restaurant on the
riverbank in old Porto specializes
in fish, seafood, soup and
bacalhau recipes.
✚ 387B1 ✉ Cais da Ribeira 32
☎ 02 200 4389 AE, VI

Porto Ibérico $$
If you're visiting the port
warehouses across the river, this
restaurant – serving a range of
northern Portuguese and Spanish
dishes – is a good choice.
✚ 387B1 ✉ Rua do Rei Ramiro
697 ☎ 02 370 6674 🔵 Closed
Wed. 🚌 57, 91 AE, DI, MC, VI

Taberna de Bebobos $$
Traditional Porto dishes are served
at this atmospheric, historic tavern
on the waterfront, in the oldest part
of town.
✚ 387B1 ✉ Cais da Ribeira 24
☎ 02 313 565 🔵 Closed Sun. AE,
MC, VI

MADRID HOTELS
Price guide: (double room with
breakfast for two people)
$ 6,000–15,000PTA
$$ 15,000–25,000PTA
$$$ over 25,000PTA

Asturias $
This conveniently located budget
choice has a friendly staff and good,
clean rooms.
✚ 402C2 ✉ Sevilla 2 ☎ 91 429
6676; fax 91 429 4036 🔵 Sevilla
AE, MC, VI

Carlos V $$
To be sure of a room, you'll want to
reserve in advance at this good-
value hotel in an excellent location
near the Puerta del Sol.
✚ 402B2 ✉ Maestro Victoria 5
☎ 91 531 4100; fax 91 531 3761
🔵 Sol AE, MC, VI

Palace $$$
Recently refurbished and now
owned by the Sheraton chain, this
grand hotel is ideally situated within
walking distance of Madrid's main
sights of interest.
✚ 402C2 ✉ Plaza Cortes 7 ☎ 91
360 8000; fax 91 360 8100
🔵 Banco de España AE, MC, VI

Ritz $$$
Madrid's Ritz opened in 1910 and
offers a level of luxury, service and
facilities associated with this
chain's stature.
✚ 402D2 ✉ Plaza de la Lealtad 5
☎ 91 521 2857; fax 91 532 3710
🔵 Banco de España AE, MC, VI

Suecia $$
This quiet hotel is located between
the Prado Museum and Puerta del
Sol square.
✚ 402C2 ✉ Marqués de casa
Riera 4 ☎ 91 531 6900; fax 91 521
7141 🔵 Sevilla AE, MC, VI

MADRID RESTAURANTS
Price guide: (dinner per person,
excluding drinks)
$ 2,000–4,500PTA
$$ 4,500–9,000PTA
$$$ over 9,000PTA

El Bodegon $$$
Many people think this is Madrid's
best restaurant. El Bodegon offers a
set menu at dinner and an à la carte
lunch menu, with superb service.
✚ 402C4 ✉ Pinar 15 ☎ 91 562
3137 🔵 Closed Sun. and in Aug.
🔵 Gregorio Marañón AE, MC, VI

La Bola $$
This long-established restaurant
specializes in Madrid cocido,
different stews cooked slowly in
traditional clay pots, and also offers
friendly service.
✚ 402B2 ✉ Bola 5 ☎ 91 547
6930 🔵 Closed Jul. 🔵 Santo
Domingo AE, MC, VI

Botin $$
Immensely popular with visitors, this
restaurant, founded in 1725, serves
good traditional grills and other
meat dishes.
✚ 402B2 ✉ Cuchilleros 17 ☎ 91
366 4217 🔵 Sol AE, MC, VI

Los Galayos $$$
Located on the Plaza Mayor, this
elegant restaurant, with a terrace

and bar, serves Castilian dishes
cooked in wood-fired ovens.
✚ 402B2 ✉ Botoneras 5 (Plaza
Mayor) ☎ 91 366 3028 🔵 Sol
AE, DI, MC, VI

Hogar Gallego $$
This popular restaurant, just off the
Plaza Mayor, serves Galician
dishes; in summer you can eat on
the terrace.
✚ 402B2 ✉ Comandante Morenas
3 ☎ 91 542 4826 🔵 Closed Aug.
🔵 Sol AE, MC, VI

Hylogui $
This traditional restaurant, popular
with locals, offers straightforward
home cooking and a huge menu.
✚ 402C2 ✉ Ventura de la Vega 3
☎ 91 429 7357 🔵 Closed Aug.
🔵 Sevilla AE, MC, VI

BARCELONA HOTELS
Price guide: (double room with
breakfast for two people)
$ 6,000–15,000PTA
$$ 15,000–25,000PTA
$$$ over 25,000PTA

Arts $$$
This 44-story waterfront hotel, with
superb views across the city,
epitomizes modern Barcelona. It has
a high level of luxury.
✚ 411 Off the map ✉ Carrer de la
Marina 19–22 ☎ 93 221 1000; fax
93 221 1070 🔵 Ciutadella/Vila
Olímpica AE, MC

Colón $$
Situated opposite the Cathedral, this
refurbished hotel combines a friendly and old-fashioned atmosphere
with lots of comfort.
✚ 411C2 ✉ Avenida de la
Catedral 7 ☎ 93 301 1404; fax 93
317 2915 🔵 Jaume I AE, VI

Husa Internacional $
A good budget choice, this hotel is
located on La Rambla and has simple rooms (but not all with bath).
✚ 411B2 ✉ La Rambla 78 ☎ 93
302 2566; fax 93 317 6190
🔵 Liceu AE, MC, VI

Rivoli Ramblas $$$
This popular hotel, with excellent
facilities, is housed in a restored art
deco building on La Rambla.
✚ 411B2 ✉ La Rambla 128
☎ 93 302 6643; fax 93 317 5053
🔵 Catalunya AE, MC, VI

Portugal, Spain

Spain

KEY TO SYMBOLS

➕ map page number and coordinates
✉ address
☎ telephone number
🕐 days/times closed
Ⓜ nearest subway station
🚌 nearest bus/trolley bus/tram route
⛴ ferry
$$$ expensive
$$ moderate
$ inexpensive
AE American Express
CB Carte Blanche
DI Diners
MC MasterCard
VI VISA

Andalucian Cuisine

Simplicity is all in Andalucian cooking, in which the superb quality of the ingredients, combined with a Moorish legacy of spices, almonds and oranges, has created one of Spain's most enjoyable cuisines. *Tapas* originated here, as did *gazpacho*, the cold summer soup, and sherry, a fortified wine that is drunk and used in cooking. There are tasty stews and soups, both thickened with lentils and potatoes, and every dish is redolent with olive oil, garlic and tomatoes. Excellent bread and rich Arab-inspired pastries and desserts complete the picture.

Hotel Suizo $$

This comfortable and old-fashioned hotel is a five-minute walk from the Cathedral and the Gothic Quarter.
➕ 411C2 ✉ Plaza Angel 12
☎ 93 310 6108; fax 93 315 0461
Ⓜ Jaume I ▯ 17, 19, 45 AE, CB, DI, MC, VI

BARCELONA RESTAURANTS
Price guide: (dinner per person, excluding drinks)
$ 2,000–4,500PTA
$$ 4,500–9,000PTA
$$$ over 9,000PTA

Conducta Ejemplar Le Rodizio $$

This very popular restaurant features Brazilian-style meat dishes and also offers a huge self-service buffet at good prices.
➕ 411B3 ✉ Carrer Consell de Cent 403 ☎ 93 265 5112
🕐 Closed Fri.–Sat. and Sun. evening Ⓜ Girona AE, VI

Gambrinus $$

The giant lobster sculpture on this seafood and fish restaurant's roof is a waterside landmark; the cooking lives up to all expectations.
➕ 411C1 ✉ Moll de la Fusta 22
☎ 93 221 9607 🕐 Closed Mon.–Wed. Ⓜ Drassanes AE, MC, VI

Neichel $$$

Locally considered the finest restaurant in Barcelona, Neichel is noted for its daily specials, cheeses and desserts, and high level of service.
➕ 411 Off the map ✉ Beltran i Rózpide 16 ☎ 93 203 8408
🕐 Closed Sat. lunch, Sun. and Aug. 1 to first week in Sep. Ⓜ Palau Reial AE, MC, VI

Nou Celler $

This friendly and unpretentious neighborhood restaurant serves good traditional Catalan dishes at reasonable prices.
➕ 411C2 ✉ Carrer de la Princessa 16 ☎ 93 310 4773
Ⓜ Jaume I AE, VI

Set Portes $$$

One of Barcelona's best and most historic restaurants serves a wide range of excellent Catalan food and fine wines.
➕ 411C2 ✉ Passeig de Isabel II 14 ☎ 93 319 3033
Ⓜ Barceloneta AE, MC, VI

SANTIAGO HOTELS
Price guide: (double room with breakfast for two people)
$ 6,000–15,000PTA
$$ 15,000–25,000PTA
$$$ over 25,000PTA

Hogar San Francisco $

This is a simple and peaceful hotel, housed in the old convent of St. Francis in the historic center, only a five-minute stroll from the Cathedral.
➕ 418A2 ✉ Campillo del Convento de San Francisco ☎ 981 572 463; fax 981 571 916 AE, MC, VI

Hostal El Rapido $

An example of a simple, clean pilgrim hostel, El Rapido is on one of the historic center's main streets.
➕ 418A1 ✉ Rua do Franco 22 ☎ 981 584 983 AE, VI

Compostela $$

This comfortable and spacious hotel outside the historic center offers superb views of the heart of the city.
➕ 418 Off the map ✉ Hórreo 1 ☎ 981 585 800 AE, MC, VI

Reyes Católicos $$$

Considered by many to be the finest deluxe hotel in Spain, this *parador* is magnificently located on the cathedral square and housed in a superb 15th-century cloistered building.
➕ 418A2 ✉ Plaza del Obradoiro 1 ☎ 981 582 200; fax 981 563 094 AE, DI, MC, VI

San Carlos $$

This first-class hotel, facing the Galician parliament buildings, is conveniently located only a few minutes' walk from the town center.
➕ 418 Off the map ✉ Hórreo 106 ☎ 981 560 505; fax 981 560 506 AE, CB, VI

SANTIAGO RESTAURANTS
Price guide: (dinner per person, excluding drinks)
$ 2,000–4,500PTA
$$ 4,500–9,000PTA
$$$ over 9,000PTA

Botafumeiro $

This simple, unpretentious local restaurant just behind the Cathedral serves inexpensive shellfish and other Galician specialties.

Spain, Sweden

➕ 418A2 ✉ Azabachería 16
☎ 981 584 439

Don Gaiferos $$

In the heart of the old center, this smart restaurant has a wonderful range of shellfish and seafood, in addition to other typically Galician dishes.
➕ 418A1 ✉ Rua Nueva 23
☎ 981 583 894 AE, CB, DI, MC, VI

Enxebre $$$

This classy wood-paneled restaurant, housed in the Reyes Católicos *parador*, serves many typical Galician specialties with elegance and flair.
➕ 418A2 ✉ Costa do Cristo s/n
☎ 981 582 200 AE, MC, VI

El Estanco del Hórreo $$

Located just outside the historic center, this spacious restaurant is a good place to try local shellfish and the freshest of fish dishes.
➕ 418 Off the map ✉ Hórreo 26
☎ 981 563 808 ⊘ Closed Sun. evenings AE, VI

Toñi Vicente $$$

Probably Santiago's most famous and elegant restaurant, Toñi Vicente's specializes in the imaginative use of local ingredients.
➕ 418 Off the map ✉ Rosalía de Castro 24 ☎ 981 594 100
AE, VI

SEVILLE HOTELS

Price guide: (double room with breakfast for two people)
$ 6,000–15,000PTA
$$ 15,000–25,000PTA
$$$ over 25,000PTA

Alfonso XIII $$$

Seville's top hotel, set in an attractive palm-shaded garden, has every comfort and an exceptional level of service.
➕ 425B2 ✉ San Fernando 2
☎ 95 422 2850; fax 95 421 6033
🚇 21, 23, C3, C4 AE, CB, DI, MC, VI

Becquer $$

This modernized hotel is conveniently located between the river and the center of town and offers excellent service.
➕ 425A3 ✉ Reyes Católicos 4
☎ 95 422 8900; fax 95 421 4400
🚇 43 AE, MC, VI

Casas de la Judería $$

This atmospheric hotel, located in the heart of Santa Cruz, features peaceful shady courtyards with fountains, antique furniture and comfortable rooms.
➕ 425B3 ✉ Callejón de Dos Hermanas 7 ☎ 95 441 5150; fax 95 442 2170 🚇 5, C3, C4 AE, MC, VI

Melia Sevilla $$

This big and efficient modern hotel, conveniently located near lovely Maria Luisa Park, has many facilities, including a pool.
➕ 425B2 ✉ Dr Pedro de Castro 1
☎ 95 442 1511; fax 95 442 1608
🚇 30, 31, 33 AE, MC, VI

San Gil $$

A lovely old building complete with interior courtyards, fountains and palm trees houses this attractive and spacious hotel.
➕ 425B4 ✉ Parras 28 ☎ 95 490 6811; fax 95 490 6939 🚇 C1, 14
AE, MC, VI

SEVILLE RESTAURANTS

Price guide: (dinner per person, excluding drinks)
$ 2,000–4,500PTA
$$ 4,500–9,000PTA
$$$ over 9,000PTA

Becerrita $$

This long-established restaurant serves traditional Andalucian recipes and prides itself on its homemade desserts.
➕ 425B3 ✉ Recaredo 9 ☎ 95 441 2057 🚇 10, 11, C1, C2 AE, VI

Bodegón Torre del Oro $$

A traditional restaurant serving fish and meat dishes in a lovely 16th-century building near the river.
➕ 425B2 ✉ Santander 15 ☎ 95 421 4241 🚇 C4, 40, 41 AE, MC, VI

Enrique Becerra $$$

This pretty, elegant and friendly restaurant serves carefully prepared Andalucian dishes and has long been a favorite with American visitors.
➕ 425B2 ✉ Gamazo 2 ☎ 95 421 3049 🚇 10, 11, 12 AE, MC, VI

El Giraldillo $$

This pretty, tiled restaurant opposite the Cathedral serves fresh fish and local specialties.

➕ 425B2 ✉ Virgen de los Reyes 2
☎ 95 421 4525 🚇 41, 40, 42
AE, VI

El 3 de Oro $$

This lively and friendly restaurant in Santa Cruz, packed with locals, serves straightforward, traditional Andalucian dishes.
➕ 425B3 ✉ Santa María la Blanca 34 ☎ 95 442 6820 🚇 1, C3, C4 AE, VI

STOCKHOLM HOTELS

Price guide: (double room with breakfast for two people)
$ 800–1,500SKr
$$ 1,500–2,200SKr
$$$ over 2,200SKr

Diplomat $$

This comfortable hotel in a handsome early 20th-century building overlooks the waterfront on the road to Djurgården. The Diplomat Tea House is a delightful place to stop for afternoon tea with tasty treats.
➕ 437C2 ✉ Strandvägen 7C
☎ 08 663 58 00; fax 08 459 68 20
🚇 47, 69 AE, MC, VI

First Hotel Reisen $$$

A popular and well-appointed hotel on the east side of Old Town, within easy walking distance of the city center.
➕ 437B2–C2 ✉ Skeppsbron 12–14 ☎ 08 22 32 60; fax 08 20 15 59 🚇 46, 55 AE, MC, VI

Grand Hotel $$$

The handsome facade of this top-quality hotel faces across the Norrström to the Royal Palace. Facilities are luxurious; restaurants serve international, as well as local cuisine, and the hotel is famous for its *smörgåsbord*.
➕ 437C2 ✉ Blasieholmen 8
☎ 08 679 35 00; fax 08 611 86 86
🚇 65 AE, MC, VI

Mälardrottningen Hotel $

Once owned by Barbara Hutton, this 1920s converted luxury yacht is a hotel with a difference. It's moored on the west side of the Old Town. The restaurant serves excellent international and Swedish cuisine.
➕ 437B2 ✉ Riddarholmen 111
☎ 08 24 36 00; fax 08 24 36 76
Ⓜ Gamla Stan 🚇 53 AE, MC, VI

KEY TO SYMBOLS

➕ map page number and coordinates
✉ address
☎ telephone number
🕐 days/times closed
🚇 nearest subway station
🚌 nearest bus/trolley bus/tram route
⛴ ferry
$$$ expensive
$$ moderate
$ inexpensive
AE American Express
CB Carte Blanche
DI Diners
MC MasterCard
VI VISA

Stockholm Water Festival

Lakes and the sea are so much a part of this city that the staging of the Stockholm Water Festival goes without saying. For 10 days in the middle of August, the heart of Stockholm – where freshwater Lake Mälaren meets the Baltic Sea – is given over to the staging of more than 1,500 events, including jousting tournaments, water-skiing races, plays, music shows, circus acts and spectacular fireworks displays. A vast amount of food and drink is consumed and there are scores of street stalls selling all manner of items. For information contact the Tourist Centre, Sweden House, Hamngatan 27 (☎ 08 789 24 90).

Radisson SAS Strand Hotel $$

This comfortable hotel with modern facilities is in a fine old building, on the southwest side of Nybroviken inlet. Enjoy views across the water from the top-floor restaurant.
➕ 437B2 ✉ Nybrokajen 9 ☎ 08 678 78 00; fax 08 611 24 36 🚇 Kungsträgården 🚌 65 AE, MC, VI

STOCKHOLM RESTAURANTS

Price guide: (dinner per person, excluding drinks)
$ 50–150SKr
$$ 150–250SKr
$$$ 250–300SKr

Den Gyldene Freden $$$

Established in 1722, this famous Old Town restaurant has long attracted the rich and famous, including members of the Nobel Prize selection committee. Even the restroom has 18th-century poetry on the wall. International and Swedish cuisine is outstanding, but you'll need reservations.
➕ 437B2 ✉ Österlånggatan 51 ☎ 08 10 90 46 🕐 Closed throughout Jul. 🚌 46, 55 AE, MC, VI

KB $$

Near the Royal Drama Theater and traditionally the haunt of writers and artists, this excellent restaurant serves Swedish and French cuisine. It can be pricey, but a special menu often lists less expensive dishes. It's very busy and reservations are strongly advised, even for lunch.
➕ 437C2 ✉ Smålandsgatan 7 ☎ 08 679 60 32 🕐 Closed Sun. 🚇 Östermalmstorg 🚌 46, 47, 62, 69 No credit cards

Kungshallens Restauranger $

This big food outlet, arranged on several levels in the heart of modern Stockholm, offers every kind of fast food from kebabs to pizzas, salads, sandwiches and hot dogs.
➕ 437B3 ✉ Kungsgatan 44 ☎ 08 10 35 03 🚇 Hötorget 🚌 41, 53 No credit cards

Mårten Trotzig $$

You'll get Old Town ambience and excellent Swedish cuisine at this fine restaurant in the heart of the Gamla Stan.
➕ 437B2 ✉ Västerlånggatan 79

☎ 08 24 02 31 🚌 46, 53, 55 No credit cards

Pontus in the Green House $$$

Another Old Town institution, Pontus in the Green House is expensive and always busy, but superb fish dishes, specialty sauces and great service make it worth the money. Reservations are advised.
➕ 437B2 ✉ Österlånggatan 17 ☎ 08 23 85 00 🕐 Closed Sun. 🚌 46, 55 No credit cards

GENEVA HOTELS

Price guide: (double room with breakfast for two people)
$ SF150–250
$$ SF250–400
$$$ over SF400

Hotel des Bergues $$$

For a taste of ultimate in Swiss style, stay at Switzerland's oldest grand hotel, with its lovely lake and mountain views.
➕ 451B3 ✉ quai des Bergues 33 ☎ 022 908 7000; fax 022 732 1989 🚌 1, 4, 9, 10 AE, DI, MC, VI

Edelweiss Manotel $$

A popular choice with tourists, this chalet-style hotel near the lakeside has attractive, comfortable rooms and stages frequent folklore evenings.
➕ 451B3 ✉ place de la Navigation 2 ☎ 022 731 3658; fax 022 738 8533 🚌 1 AE, DI, MC, VI

Eden $$

In a quiet area near Mon Repos park and the lake, this comfortable hotel has a good restaurant and a friendly, relaxed atmosphere.
➕ 451 Off the map ✉ rue de Lausanne 135 ☎ 022 716 3700; fax 022 731 5260 🚌 4, 18 AE, DI, MC, VI

Luserna $

If you're looking for quiet surroundings choose this friendly, good-value suburban hotel, which has a large garden and is easily accessible by bus.
➕ 451A3 ✉ avenue Luserna 12 ☎ 022 345 4576; fax 022 949 5636 🚌 10, 11 AE, DI, MC, VI

Rio $

This traditional, centrally located hotel, housed in a turn-of-the-20th-century building, is an excellent budget choice.

Switzerland

🏠 451A3 ✉ place Isaac-Mercier
☎ 022 732 3264; fax 022 732 8264
🚋 7, 27 DI, MC, VI

Tiffany $$$

This newly renovated hotel in the heart of Geneva is furnished in *belle époque* style, with comfortable rooms, a bar and a restaurant.
🏠 451A2 ✉ rue des Marbriers
☎ 022 329 3311; fax 022 320 8991
🚋 13, 16 AE, DI, MC, VI

GENEVA RESTAURANTS

Price guide: (dinner per person, excluding drinks)
$ SF25–45
$$ SF45–60
$$$ over SF60

Auberge de Coutance $$$

This elegant French restaurant with exceptional service offers dishes such as foie gras and duck specialties.
🏠 451A3 ✉ rue Coutance 25
☎ 022 732 7919 🕐 Closed Sun. evening 🚋 13, 16, 27 AE, DI, MC, VI

Auberge de Saviese $$

Enjoy a selection of Swiss specialties in this friendly restaurant, which features different types of fondue.
🏠 451B3 ✉ rue des Pâquis 20
☎ 022 732 8330 🚋 1 AE, DI, MC, VI

Cuccagna $$

A good choice when Swiss cheese begins to pall, this cheery Italian restaurant features pizzas.
🏠 451B1 ✉ rue de St.-Joseph 3
☎ 022 342 0882 🚋 12, 16 AE, CB, DI, MC, VI

Restaurant Hung-Wan $$

Geneva's best Chinese restaurant is conveniently located near the lake and features Szechuan, Cantonese and Hong Kong dishes.
🏠 451B3 ✉ quai de Mont Blanc 7
☎ 022 731 7330 🚋 1 AE, DI, VI

Restaurant des Vieux Grenadiers $$

This typical Genevan restaurant specializes in regional dishes and fondues. It has a pretty summer terrace and occasional live jazz. Pleasant after a day's sightseeing.
🏠 451B3 ✉ rue de Carouge 92
☎ 022 320 1327 🕐 Closed Sun. and Thu. evenings 🚋 12, 13 AE, MC, VI

Swiss Cottage $$

Tourists flock to this chalet-style restaurant serving dishes incorporating Swiss cheese. Open evenings only. An Alpine floor show is featured.
🏠 451 Off the map ✉ rue Barton 6
☎ 022 732 4000 🚋 1 AE, DI, MC, VI

ZURICH HOTELS

Price guide: (double room with breakfast for two people)
$ SF150–250
$$ SF250–400
$$$ over SF400

Dolder Grand Hotel $$$

Situated high above Zurich, with wide views from the terraces, this luxury hotel offers every comfort as well as excellent service.
🏠 456 Off the map
✉ Kurhausstrasse 65 ☎ 01 269 3000; fax 01 269 3001 🚋 3, 8, 15 AE, DI, MC, VI

Bristol $

This is a friendly and comfortable hotel near the railroad station, with modern and functional rooms.
🏠 456B4 ✉ Stampfenbachstrasse 34 ☎ 01 261 8400; fax 01 251 1951 🚋 3, 31, 46 AE, DI, MC, VI

Eden au Lac $$$

Stay at this elegant lakeside hotel, built in 1909, for the ultimate in comfort, luxury and service.
🏠 456B1 ✉ Utoquai 45 ☎ 01 266 2525; fax 01 266 2500 🚋 4 AE, DI, MC, VI

Franziskaner $$

This reasonably priced hotel, overlooking a pretty square, has comfortable rooms and a restaurant.
🏠 456B2 ✉ Niederdorferstrasse 1 ☎ 01 250 5300; fax 01 250 5301 🚋 4, 15 AE, DI, MC, VI

Krone Unterstrasse $$

This well-equipped, comfortable hotel caters to business travelers and is located in a quiet residential area 10 minutes fom the city center.
🏠 456 Off the map
✉ Schaffhauserstrasse 1 ☎ 01 360 5656; fax 01 360 5600 🚋 7, 15 AE, DI, MC, VI

Rössli $$

The inconspicuous exterior of the Rössli hides a comfortable and

imaginatively designed hotel with well-equipped rooms.
🏠 456B2 ✉ Rössligasse 7 ☎ 01 252 2121; fax 01 252 2131 🚋 4, 15 AE, DI, MC, VI

ZURICH RESTAURANTS

Price guide: (dinner per person, excluding drinks)
$ SF25–45
$$ SF45–60
$$$ over SF60

Adlers Swiss Chuchi $

This friendly restaurant is a good bet if you want to sample meat or cheese fondue or local veal specialties.
🏠 456B2 ✉ Rosengasse 10
☎ 01 266 9666 🚋 4, 15 AE, DI, MC, VI

Restaurant Bierhall Kropfe $$

This cheerful and typical restaurant with its sumptuously decorated rooms, has been serving local dishes since 1888.
🏠 456A2 ✉ In Gassen 16 ☎ 01 221 1805 🕐 Closed Sun. 🚋 7, 6, 11, 13 AE, DI, MC , VI

Haus zum Rüden $$$

Overlooking the Limmat river, this historic restaurant serves the best of Swiss specialties in an elegant atmosphere.
🏠 456B2 ✉ Limmatquai 42
☎ 01 261 9566 🕐 Closed Sat.–Sun. 🚋 4, 15 AE, DI, MC, VI

Mère Catherine $

This centrally located garden restaurant serves fish and seafood, with an accent on Mediterranean and Provençal dishes.
🏠 456B2 ✉ Näglihof 3 ☎ 01 250 5940 🚋 4, 15 AE

Münsterhof $$

Historic Münsterhof restaurant serves traditional Swiss specialties at good prices and also has a garden.
🏠 456A2 ✉ Münsterhof 6 ☎ 01 211 4340 🚋 4, 15 AE, DI, MC, VI

Walliser Kanne $$

This friendly restaurant features every imaginable type of fondue – meat, cheese, *chinoise* – as well as *raclette* and Swiss specialties such as *rösti* (a potato pancake).
🏠 456A3 ✉ Linthescherҫasse 21
☎ 01 211 3133 🚋 10, 11, 13 AE, DI, MC, VI

European Distance Chart

EUROPEAN DISTANCE CHART

Road distances, in kilometers (km), are calculated by the shortest or quickest routes (highways, main roads) from center to center and do not take into account seasonal weather conditions.

Miles	Km
1	1.6
10	16
20	32
30	48
40	64
50	80
100	160
200	320
300	480
400	640
500	800
1000	1600

Cities (diagonal labels, in order):
Amsterdam (NL), Athina (Athens) (GR), Barcelona (E), Berlin (D), Brugge/Bruges (B), Brussel/Bruxelles (Brussels) (B), Budapest (H), Den Haag (The Hague) (NL), Dublin (IRL), Edinburgh (GB), Firenze (Florence) (I), Genève (Geneva) (CH), Gent (Ghent) (B), Helsinki (FIN), Innsbruck (A), København (Copenhagen) (DK), Köln (Cologne) (D), Lisboa (Lisbon) (P), London (GB), Luxembourg (L), Lyon (F), Madrid (E), München (Munich) (D), Nápoli (Naples) (I), Nice (F), Odense (DK), Oslo (N)

Distance matrix (triangular, by row):

```
1736
1600 1591
653 1577 1889
269 1680 1372 832
210 1568 1403 773 101
1413 1521 2085 874 1473 1368
64 1755 1574 697 211 180 1432
959 2350 1958 1522 704 791 2163 930
1092 2483 2091 1655 837 924 2296 1063 538
1387 544 1103 1228 1331 1219 1085 1406 2001 2134
1004 973 809 1119 769 724 1276 896 1355 1488 606
221 1635 1367 783 52 56 1423 191 742 875 1286 764
1542 2864 2929 1013 1748 1689 2449 1586 2438 2571 2515 2159 1700
1001 832 1381 750 1061 956 731 1021 1751 1884 483 1011 2037
926 2248 2313 397 1132 1073 1833 970 1822 1955 1899 1543 1084 620 1421
262 1481 1419 569 315 210 1158 282 1005 1138 1132 749 265 1502 747 886
2370 2847 1258 2908 2161 2168 3340 2341 2747 2880 2359 2065 2156 3841 2637 3225 2345
482 1873 1481 1045 227 314 1686 453 463 665 1524 878 265 1961 1274 1345 528 2270
410 1356 1190 759 324 212 1193 384 1014 1147 1007 512 279 1697 677 1081 230 2222 537
932 1069 652 1233 779 734 1429 906 1365 1498 693 153 774 2272 727 1656 751 1908 888 522
1809 2188 630 2347 1600 1607 2681 1779 2186 2319 1700 1406 1595 3279 1978 2663 1784 625 1709 1660 1249
834 990 1396 583 894 789 690 854 1584 1717 641 587 844 1870 163 1254 580 2677 1107 566 740 1993
1859 594 1577 1700 1803 1691 1557 1878 2473 2606 474 1080 1758 2987 955 2371 1604 2833 1996 1479 1167 2174 1113
1396 910 681 1347 1268 1223 1403 1394 1853 1986 421 541 1263 2551 700 1935 1142 1937 1376 1011 472 1278 858 895
765 2086 2151 599 971 911 1671 809 1660 1793 1737 1381 922 781 1260 165 724 3063 1183 1915 1495 2502 1093 2209 1774
1510 2832 2897 981 1716 1657 2417 1554 2406 2539 2483 2127 1668 530 2005 588 1470 3809 1929 1665 2241 3247 1838 2954 2519 749
589 1980 1588 1152 334 421 1793 560 396 598 1631 985 372 2068 1381 1452 635 2377 90 644 995 1816 1214 2103 1483 1290 2036
509 1508 1067 1047 300 307 1494 480 888 1021 1141 542 295 1980 953 1364 484 1856 411 376 466 1295 831 1614 954 1202 1948
2170 2647 1213 2708 1961 1968 3140 2141 2547 2680 2159 1865 1956 3641 2437 3025 2145 318 2070 2022 1708 564 2477 2632 1737 2863 3609
967 1375 1754 343 1027 922 531 987 1717 1850 1026 984 977 1377 549 761 713 2895 1240 747 1098 2333 382 1498 1243 957 1345
1663 521 1381 1504 1607 1495 1362 1683 2277 2410 278 885 1562 2791 759 2175 1409 2637 1800 1283 971 1978 917 219 700 2014 2759
977 1007 1535 726 1037 932 553 997 1727 1860 658 725 987 2013 180 1397 723 2791 1250 722 879 2132 139 1129 875 1236 1981
2078 2555 1166 2616 1869 1876 3048 2049 2454 2587 2067 1773 1864 3549 2345 2933 2053 549 1977 1930 1616 646 2385 2540 1645 2771 3517
2354 2599 1041 2892 2145 2152 3092 2325 2733 2866 2111 1817 2140 3825 2389 3209 2329 408 2256 2206 1660 543 2404 2584 1689 3047 3793
1542 2864 2929 1013 1748 1689 2449 1586 2438 2571 2515 2159 1700 1800 2037 620 1502 3841 1961 1697 2273 3279 1870 2986 2551 781 530
628 1133 1147 753 543 431 1063 602 1213 1346 784 401 498 1793 471 1177 354 2335 736 219 491 1744 360 1256 794 1015 1761
1345 537 1256 1126 1289 1177 847 1364 1959 2092 256 584 1244 2413 381 1797 1090 2512 1482 965 701 1853 539 728 574 1636 2381
1157 1124 1843 637 1217 1112 244 1176 1907 2040 843 1020 1167 2193 475 1577 902 3084 1430 937 1174 2440 434 1315 1161 1415 2161
805 2196 1804 1368 550 637 2009 776 322 311 1847 1201 588 2593 1597 1668 851 2593 339 860 1211 2032 1430 2319 1699 1506 2252
831 940 1095 844 775 663 996 851 1446 1579 591 285 730 1986 284 1370 577 2351 969 451 439 1692 306 1062 600 1209 1954
```

European Distance Chart

Oxford (GB)	Paris (F)	Porto (P)	Praha (Prague) (CZ)	Roma (Rome) (I)	Salzburg (A)	Santiago de Compostela (E)	Sevilla (Seville) (E)	Stockholm (S)	Strasbourg (F)	Venézia (Venice) (I)	Wien (Vienna) (A)	York (GB)	Zürich (CH)
518													
2177	1656												
1347	1049	2695											
1907	1419	2437	1303										
1347	987	2591	377	934									
2084	1564	231	2603	2345	2499								
2363	1840	679	2762	2389	2543	910							
2068	1982	3641	1377	2791	2013	3548	3827						
843	489	2135	618	1060	516	2042	2157	1793					
1589	1119	2312	816	532	436	2219	2266	2413	742				
1537	1238	2884	294	1119	297	2791	2853	2193	807	605			
295	734	2393	1563	2123	1573	2300	2579	2284	1059	1805	1753		
1076	664	2151	712	867	445	2058	2105	1986	229	548	740	1292	

Index

Index

Index

Acknowledgements

Abbreviations for terms appearing below: (t) top; (b) bottom; (l) left; (r) right; (c) centre
The Automobile Assocation wishes to thank the following photographers and libraries for their assistance in the preparation of this book. Mary Evans Picture Library 45(t), 278(t); Ghent Altarpiece, Central Panel, 1432: Lord in Majesty between Virgin Mary and St. John the Baptist; below – Adoration of the Lamb by Jan van Eyck (c.1390–1441) St. Bavo Cathedral, Ghent, Belgium/Bridgeman Art Library 75; Bruce Coleman Collection 193; Corbis/Layne Kennedy 152; Des Hannigan 71, 163(c), 439, 440, 441, 467(t), 479(b), 483(t), 483(b), 511(t), 515(t), 515(b), 519(t), 519(b), 531(t), 531(b); John Heseltine Archive 308, 312, 313; Innsbruck Tourism 39; The J Allan Cash Photolibrary 229, 455; Mri Bankers Guide To Foreign Currency 462, 466, 470, 474, 478, 482, 486, 490, 494, 498, 502, 506, 510, 514, 518, 522, 526, 530, 534; Pictures Colour Library 47(c), 157, 189, 192, 364, 456(t); Rex Features Ltd 121; Spectrum Colour Library 73, 154, 197, 201, 331, 351, 463(t), 491(t); World Pictures 38, 43, 44, 45(b), 47(b), 48, 55, 61, 69, 74, 155, 162, 163(t), 169, 187, 191(t), 199, 202, 203(t), 203(c), 205, 224, 322, 324, 327, 332, 333, 341(b), 353, 354, 355, 356, 360, 361, 368, 369, 375, 391(t), 418, 420, 421, 422, 423, 435, 438, 443, 450, 452, 454, 456(b), 458, 460; Carol Weitz 463(b), 515(t), 535(b)

The remaining photographs are held in the Association's own library (AA Photo Library) and were taken by the following photographers: AA Photo Library 57, 83, 93, 109, 110, 117, 281(b), 363, 390; Adrian Baker 34, 211, 449, 538; Peter Baker 18, 22, 32, 37, 97(t); M Birkitt 471(t); Liam Blake 270; Jamie Blandford 266; Jim Carnie 82; Michelle Chaplow 399, 417(b), 527(t), 527(b); Douglas Corrance 101, 102; Steve Day 401(t); 413, 414, 415, 444; J Edmanson 168; Philip Enticknap 409; Derek Forss 76, 132, 137, 139, 145, 148, 150; Terry Harris 246, 247, 249; A Hemmison 227; Stephen Hill 503(b); Jim Holmes 5, 507(t); JW Jorgensen 135, 144, 151(tl), 151(tr), 479(t); Alex Kouprianoff 52, 53, 58, 59(t), 59(b), 63, 64, 65, 66, 67, 68, 374, 377, 381, 383(t), 383(b), 384, 385, 388, 391(b), 467(b), 511(b), 523(t); Andrew Lawson 106; S&O Mathews 471(b), 495(t), 495(b); Eric Meacher 81, 191(b), 262, 417(t); Dario Miterdiri 294, 299(c), 300; Andrew Molyneux 392, 397, 424, 427; Rob Moore 487(t), 487(b); George Munday 271; Kim Naylor 430; Rich Newton 112, 115; D Noble 23, 25, 30, 33, 181(t); Ken Paterson 98, 104, 170, 176, 178, 179, 185, 238, 257, 261, 263, 264, 265, 287, 334, 338/339, 339, 341(t), 345, 346, 347, 348, 499(t); Bertrand Rieger 181(c); Douglas Robertson 396; Clive Sawyer 29, 126, 130, 164, 212, 215, 219, 220, 222, 234, 235(t), 237(b), 282, 289, 291, 296, 297, 298, 299(t), 301, 305, 307(b), 317, 319, 320, 321(t), 321(b); Michael Short 273, 278; M Siebert 31(t), 31(c); Slide File 277, 280; Barrie Smith 90, 94, 97(b), 507(b); Antony Souter 118, 171(b), 173, 180, 182, 183, 221(t), 221(c), 223, 233, 235(b), 236, 237(t), 491(b); Rick Strange 171(t), 198, 401(b), 405(t), 405(b), 406(t), 407, 408; R Surman 251; JA Tims 2, 96, 429; D Traverso 206; Jonathon Welsh 111; Stephen Whitehorn 276, 279, 281(t), 503(t); Peter Wilson 116/117, 243, 248, 250, 252, 260, 370, 412, 416, 523(b); TimWoodcock 85; Gregory Wrona 499(b); John Wyand 123, 127, 128, 129(t), 129(c), 131(t), 131(b), 475(t), 475(b); Wyn Voysey 95